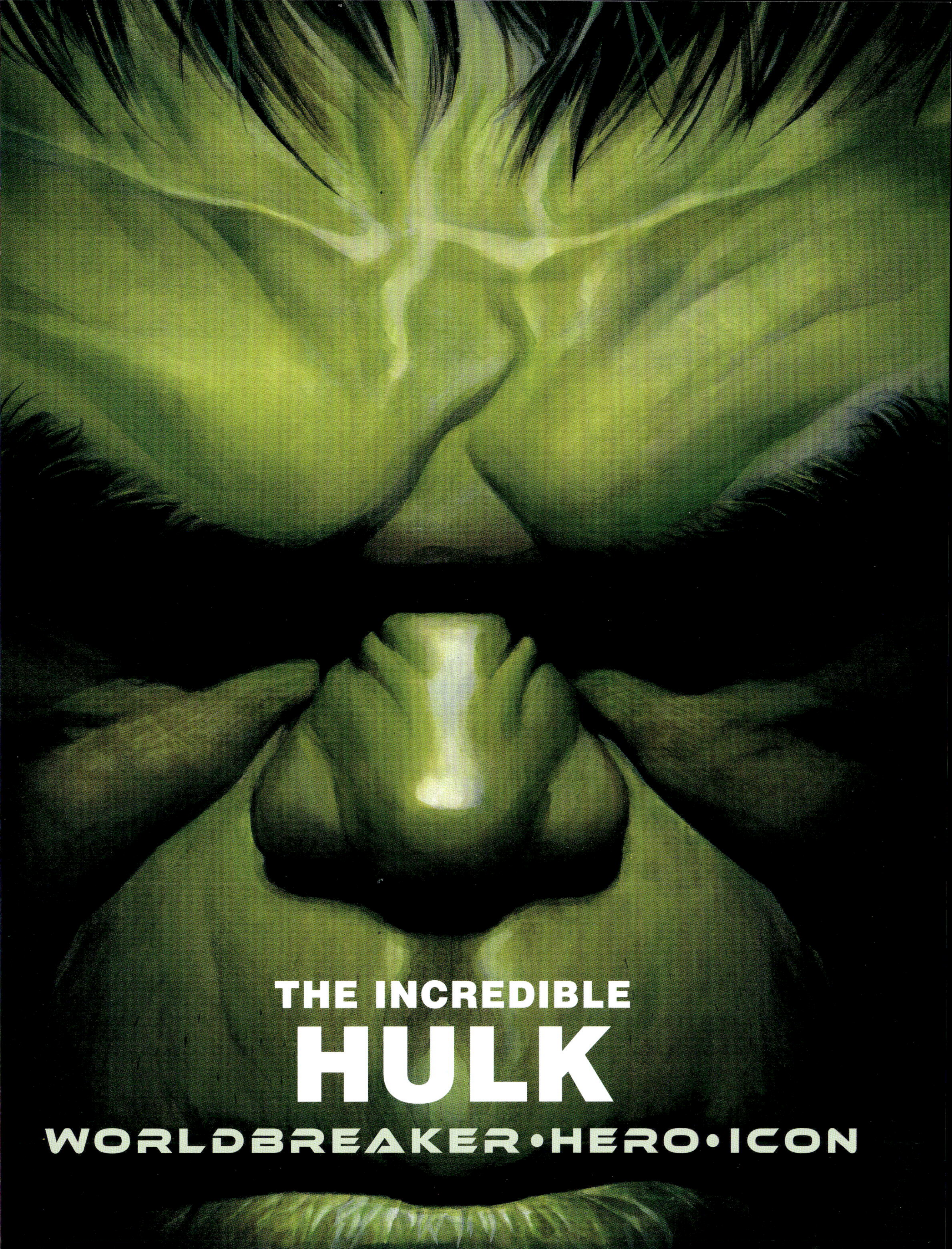
THE INCREDIBLE
HULK
WORLDBREAKER•HERO•ICON

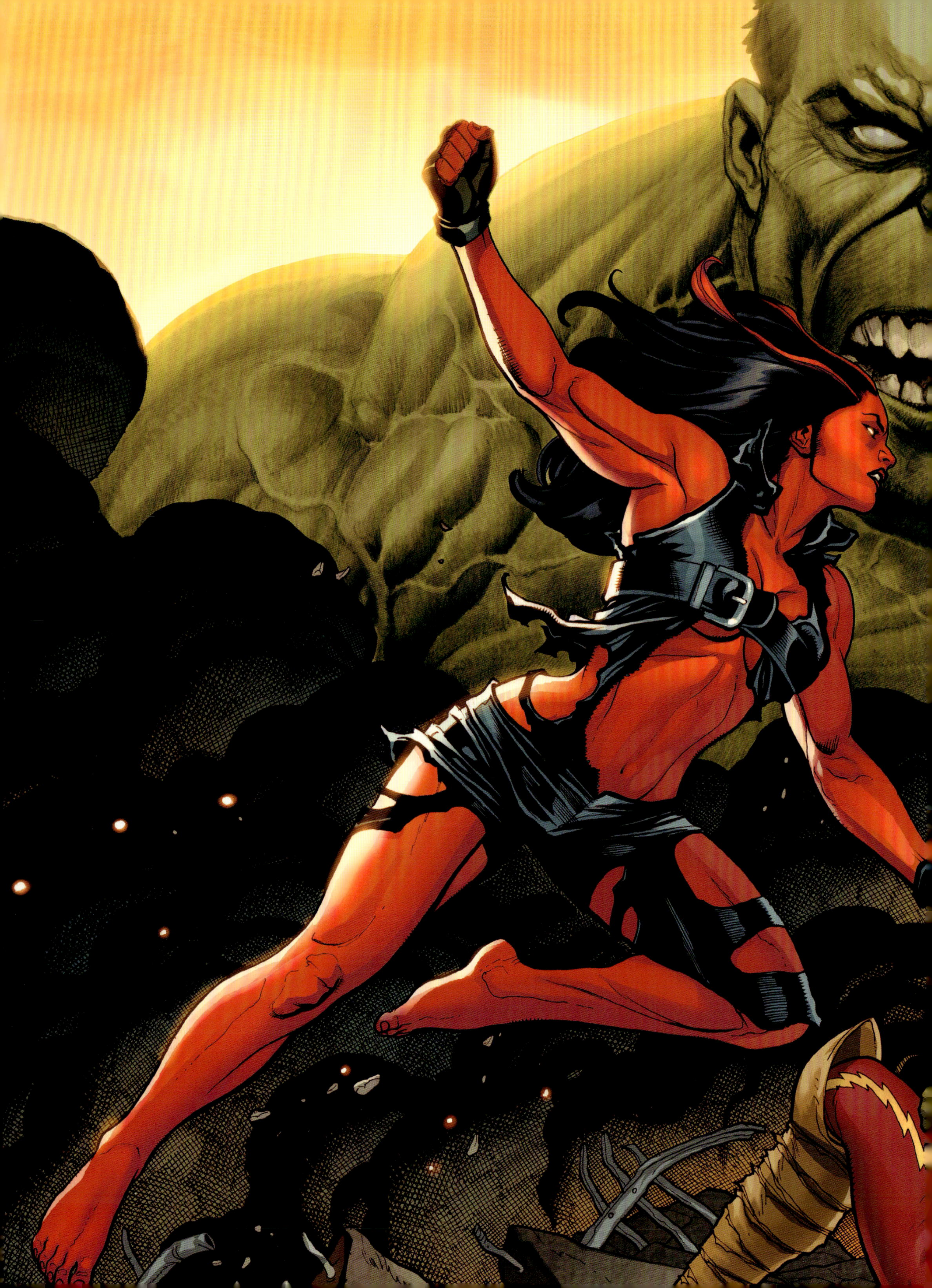

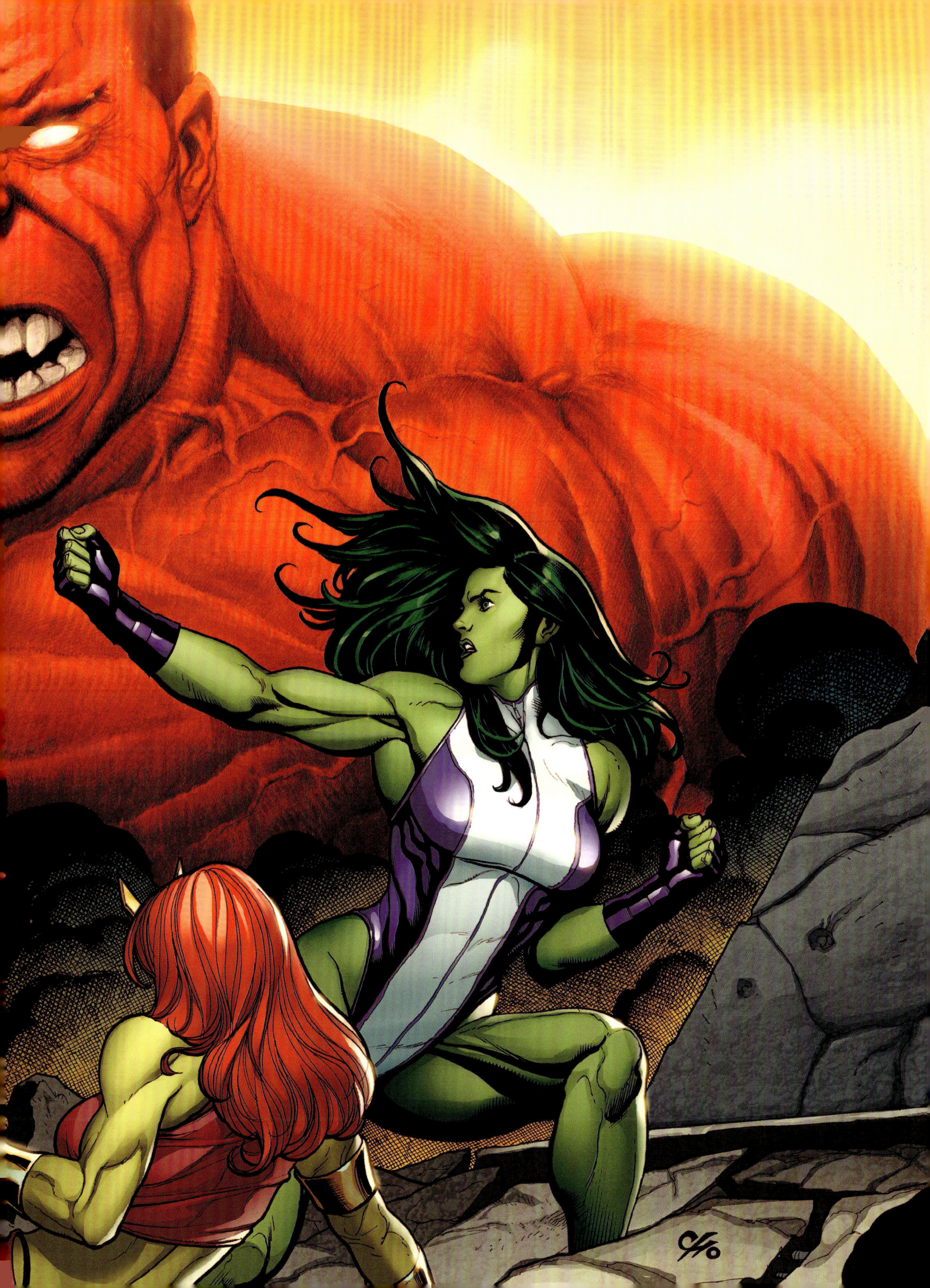

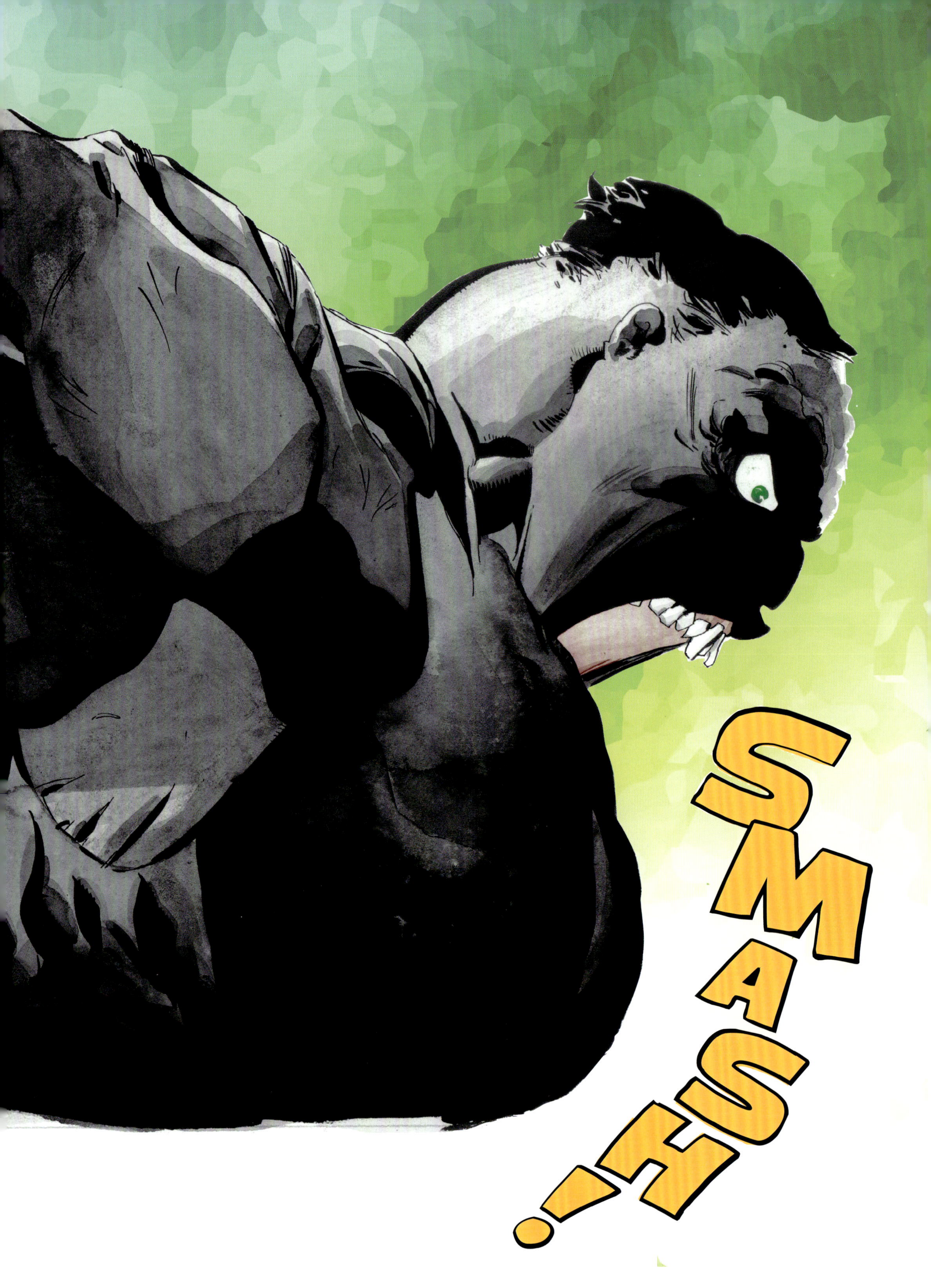
SMASH!

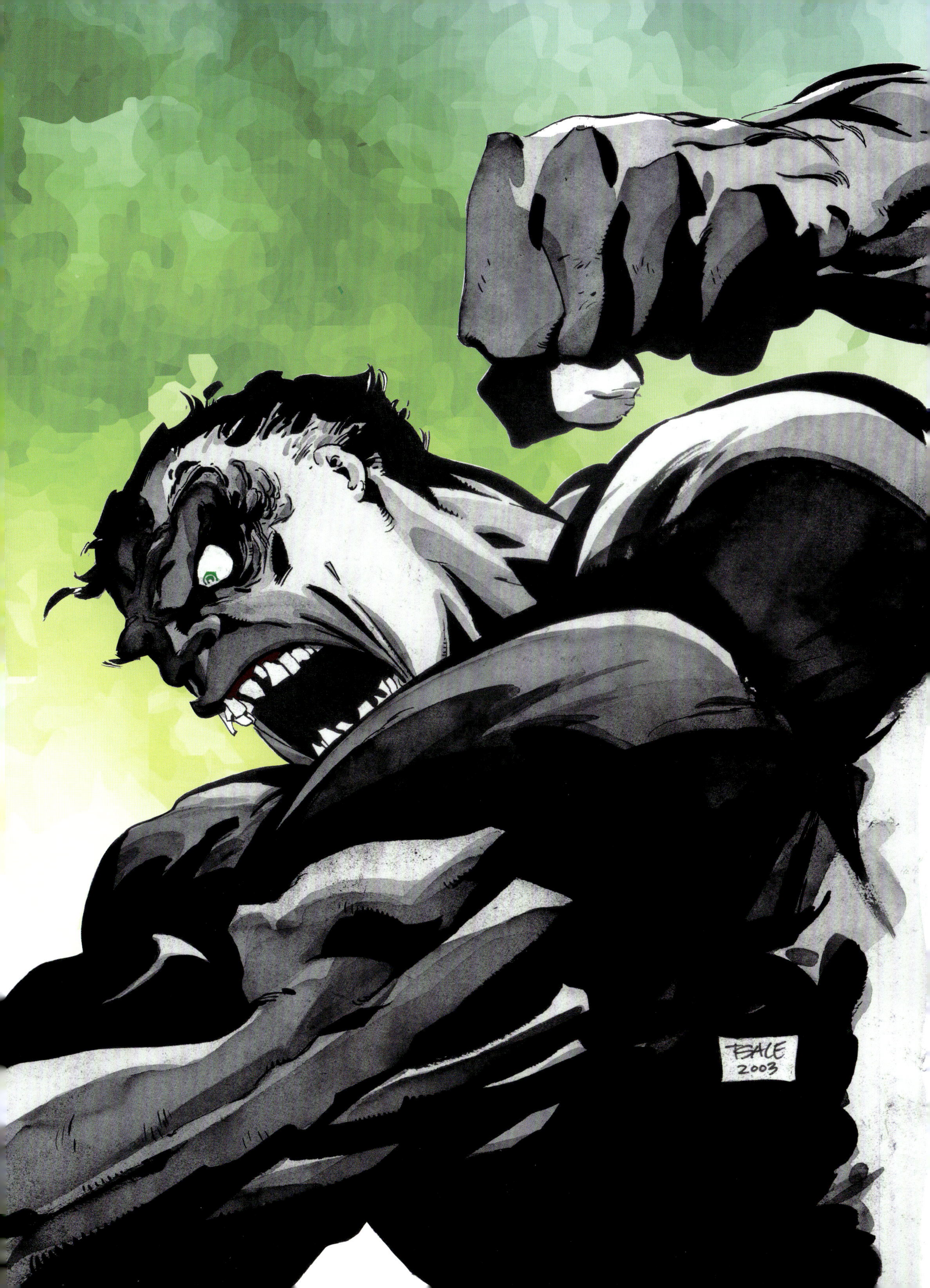

TSALE
2003

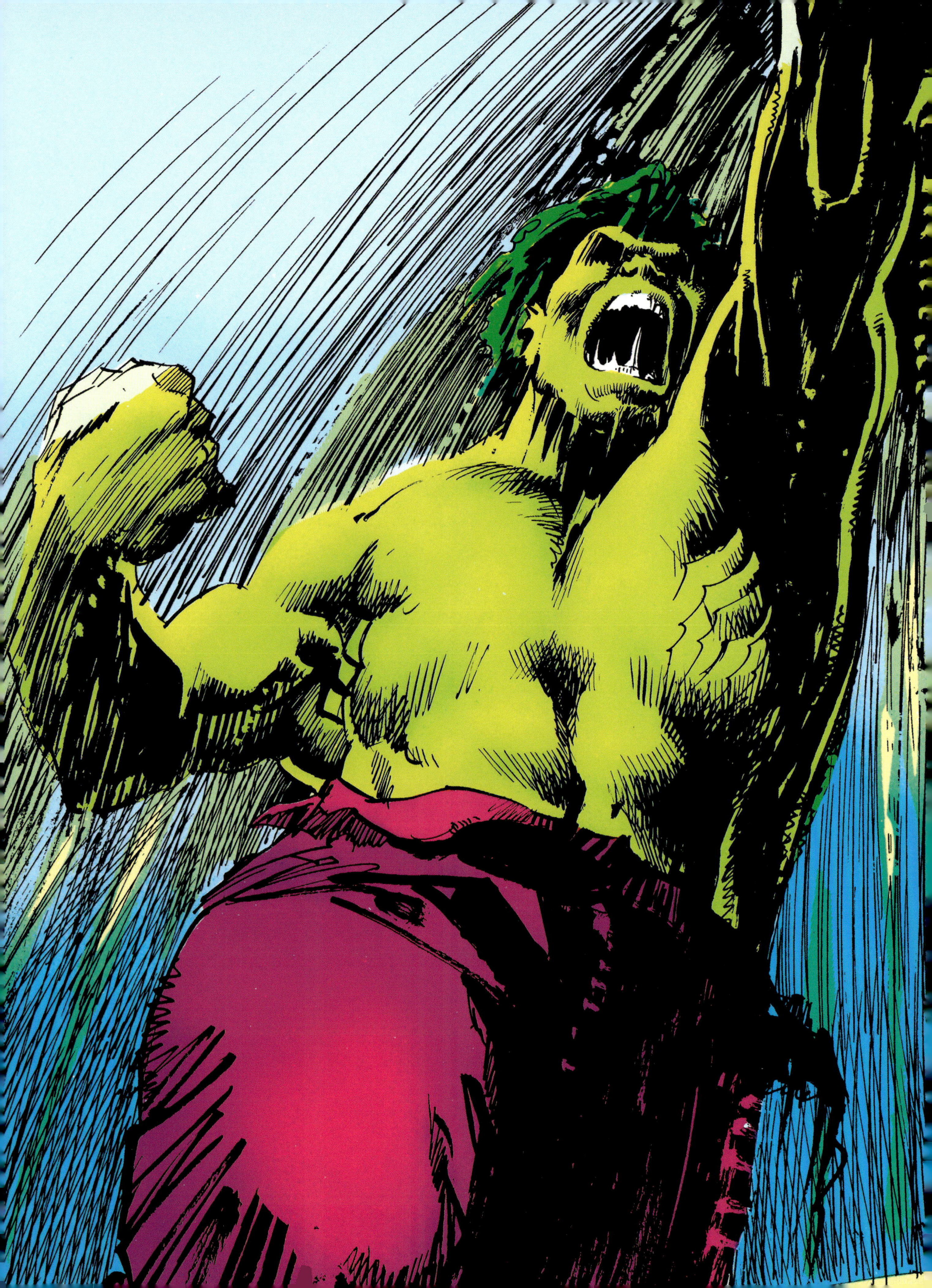

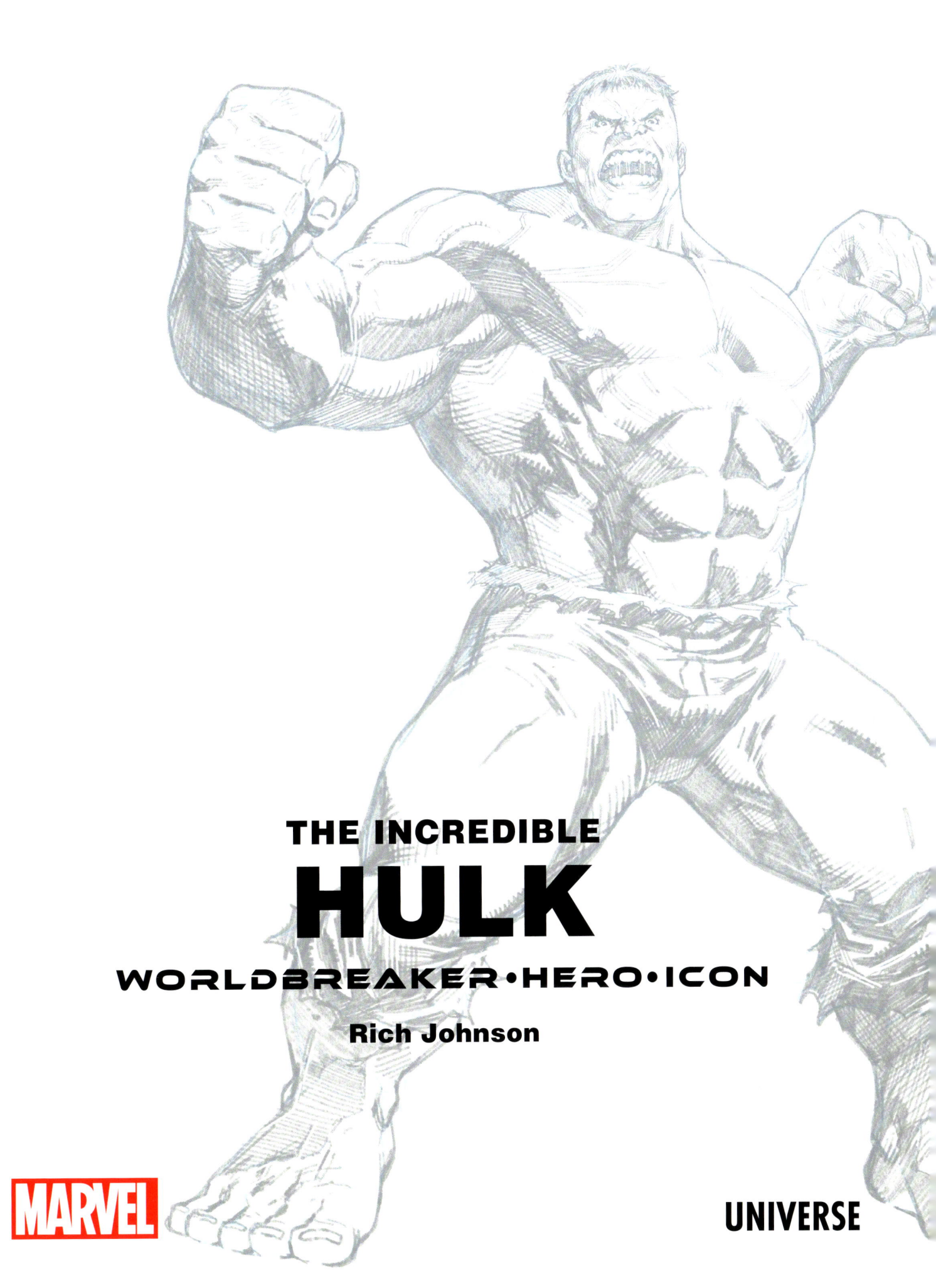

# THE INCREDIBLE
# HULK
## WORLDBREAKER • HERO • ICON

Rich Johnson

**MARVEL**

UNIVERSE

# INTRODUCTION 10

# CHAPTER 1: INCREDIBLE 12

FIRST APPEARANCE 14

HULK: GRAY 20

THE SENSATIONAL SHE-HULK 26

INCREDIBLE HULK & THE THING: HARD KNOCKS 32

THE SAVAGE SHE-HULK 38

# CHAPTER 2: RAMPAGING 44

CROSSROADS 46

PARDONED 52

ULTIMATE WOLVERINE VS. HULK 58

FUTURE IMPERFECT/THE END 68

THE RETURN OF THE MONSTER 74

GOING GRAY 80

TOTALLY AWESOME HULK 86

# GAMMA BASE 92

# CHAPTER 3: SAVAGE 106

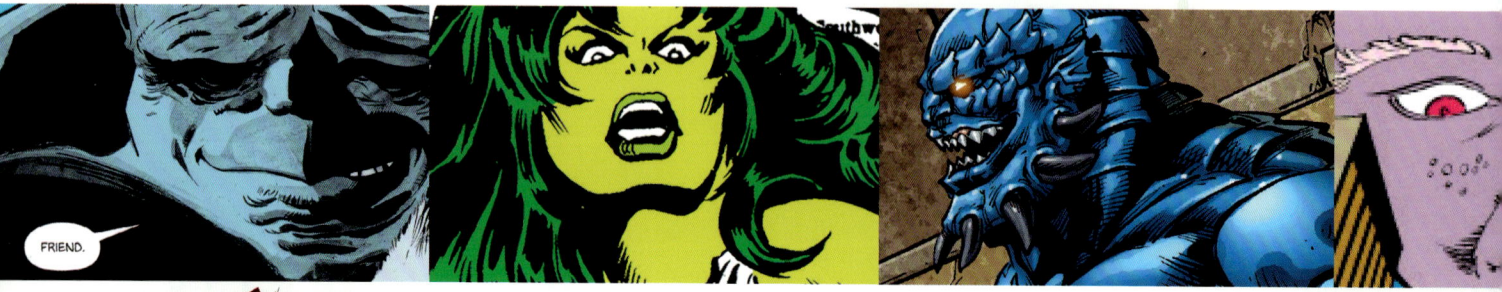

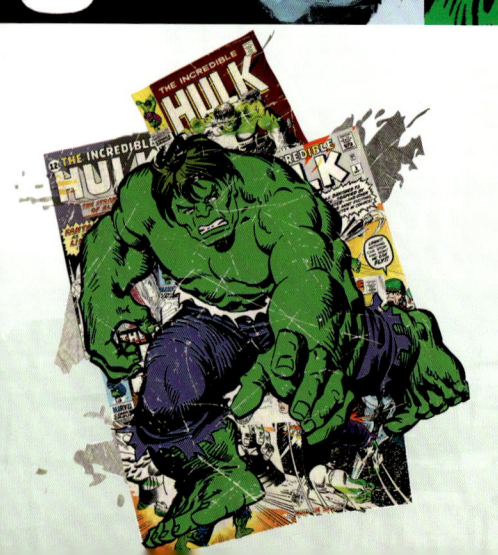

First published in the United States of America in 2022
by Universe Publishing
A Division of Rizzoli International Publications, Inc.
300 Park Avenue South, New York, NY 10010
www.rizzoliusa.com
Printed in Italy

2022 2023 2024 2025 / 10 9 8 7 6 5 4 3 2 1

ISBN 13: 9780789341242
Library of Congress Control Number: 2022940338

*Visit us online*
Facebook.com/RizzoliNewYork Twitter: @Rizzoli_Books
Instagram.com/RizzoliBooks Pinterest.com/RizzoliBooks
Youtube.com/user/RizzoliNY Issuu.com/Rizzoli

OR IS HE BOTH? 108

THE GREEN DOOR 114

HULK IN HELL 120

ABOMINATION 126

BREAKER OF WORLDS 132

RED HULK 138

PLANET RED HULK 144

INDESTRUCTIBLE HULK: AGENT OF S.H.I.E.L.D. 150

HEART OF THE ATOM 156

PAST PERFECT 162

# CHAPTER 4: IMMORTAL 168

LOVE AND DEATH 170

ASUNDER/HULK VS. BANNER 176

CHAOS WAR 184

HEART OF THE MONSTER 190

CODE RED 196

TEMPEST FUGIT 202

PLANET HULK 208

WORLD WAR HULK 214

# CREDITS 221

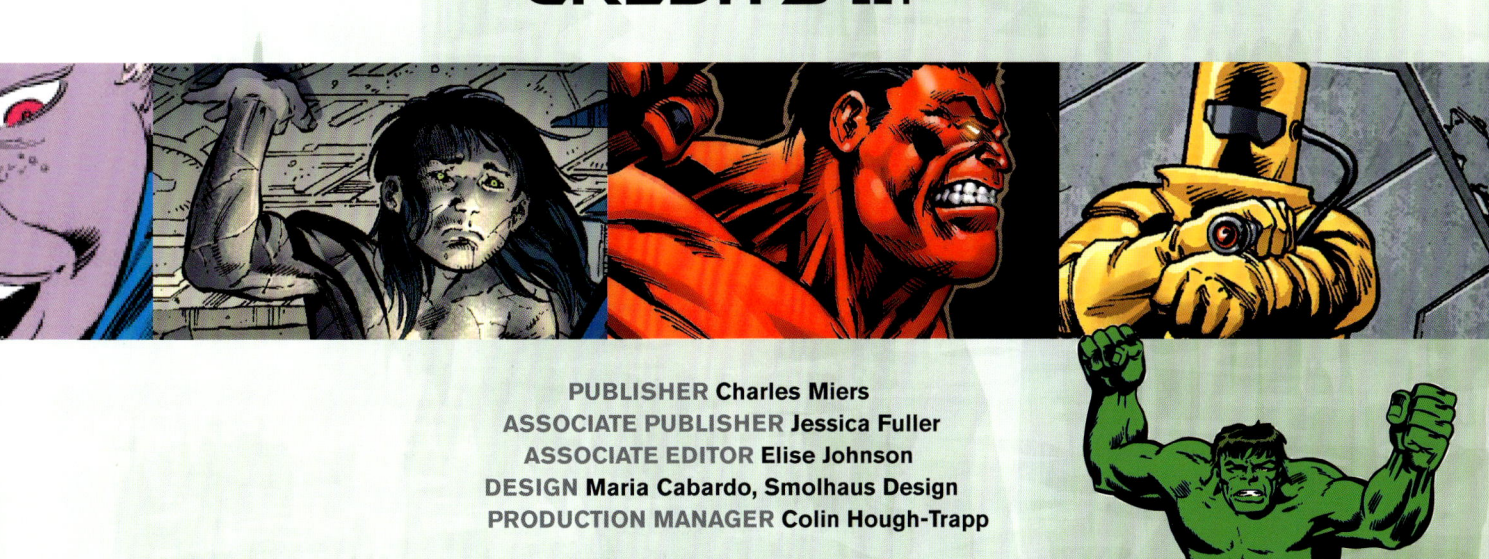

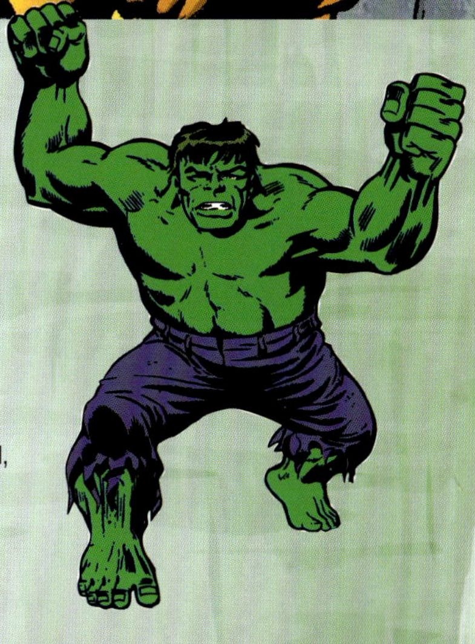

**PUBLISHER** Charles Miers
**ASSOCIATE PUBLISHER** Jessica Fuller
**ASSOCIATE EDITOR** Elise Johnson
**DESIGN** Maria Cabardo, Smolhaus Design
**PRODUCTION MANAGER** Colin Hough-Trapp

**FRONT COVER ART** Adi Granov
**BACK COVER ART** Jim Cheung

All rights reserved. No part of this publication may be reproduced, stored in a retrieval system, or transmitted in any form or by any means, electronic, mechanical, photocopying, recording, or otherwise, without prior consent of the publishers.

© 2022 MARVEL

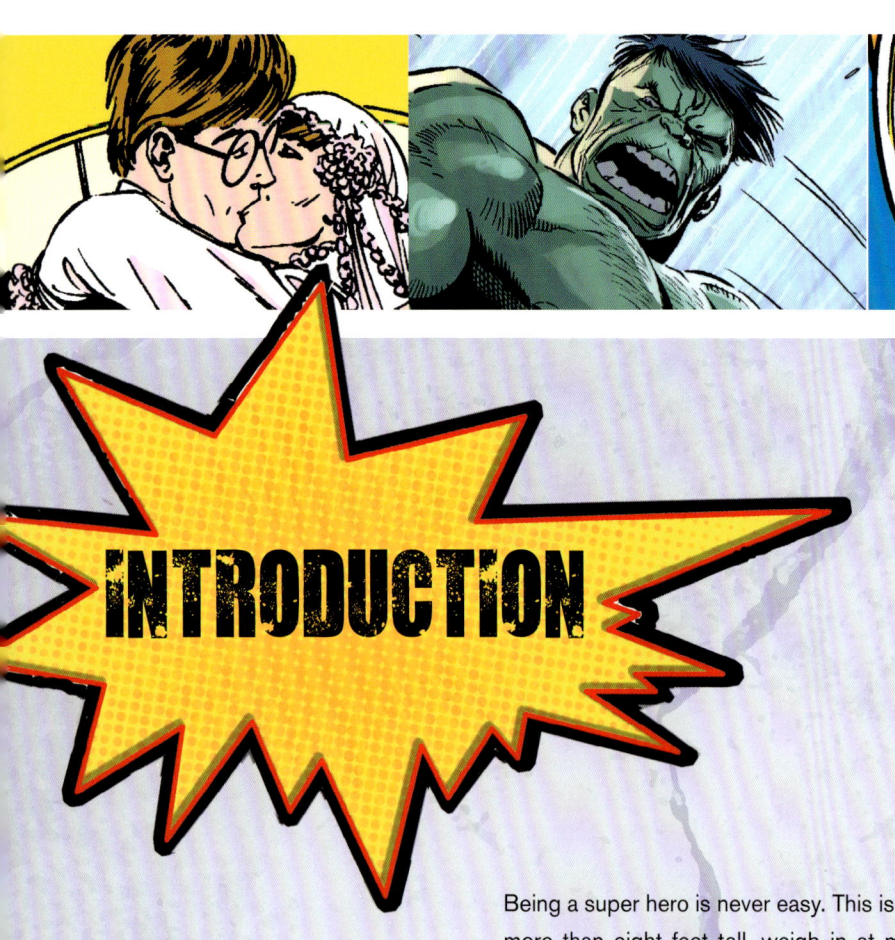

# INTRODUCTION

Being a super hero is never easy. This is particularly true if you're more than eight feet tall, weigh in at more than one thousand pounds, have super-strength, are indestructible, and suffer from severe anger management issues. It's also not easy being a scientist who specializes in gamma bombs or being one of the smartest people on the planet, and the person that has that big green rage monster living inside of him.

It is forever a struggle. The Hulk is the primitive side, all reaction and anger, and Banner is the logical side—the reasoned mind of a scientist. Because they are opposites, they struggle. Well, they do more than struggle; they both hate having to share. Occasionally, they have merged, with the brain living in the beast's body, but it usually doesn't last long. And sometimes they are separated into two. But in the end they realize that they can't live with each other, and they can't live without each other. And so it goes.

That attempt at balance is what makes the Hulk and his stories so popular. Come on: no matter what your age, haven't you, at one time, put on a pair of foam or rubber Hulk fists? When you slipped them on didn't you feel more powerful in some way? That you, too, could "Hulk smash!"? That you could pull up those purple pants and go out and crush a car, toss a boulder?

Maybe the reason the Hulk has been popular for so long is that he reminds us of the strength we all have inside us. And that if needed we, too, could reach down inside and find the power to move a mountain in order to save the day.

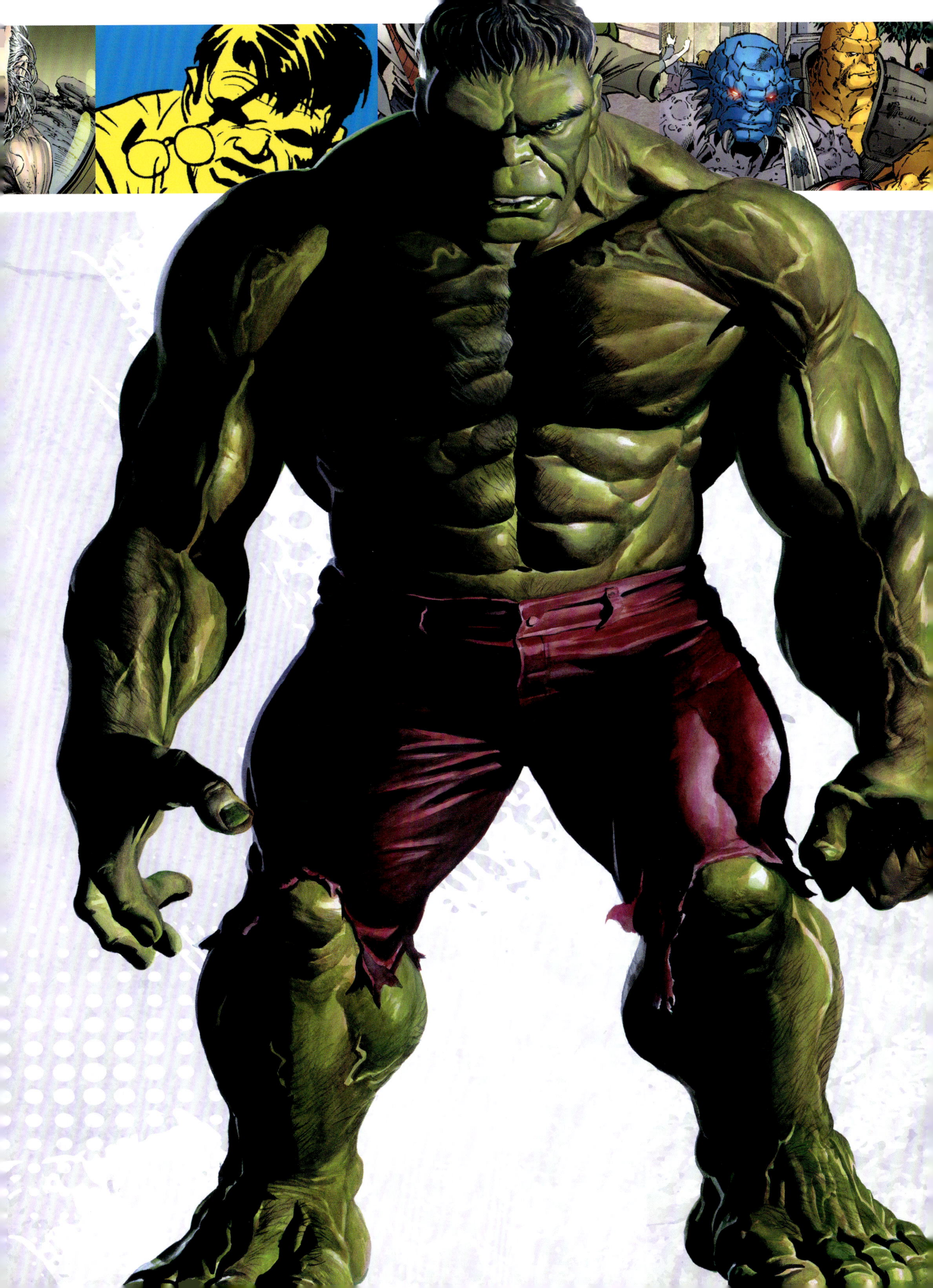

# C1

## CHAPTER ONE:
## INCREDIBLE

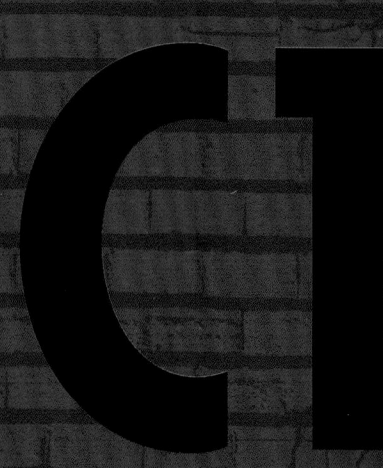

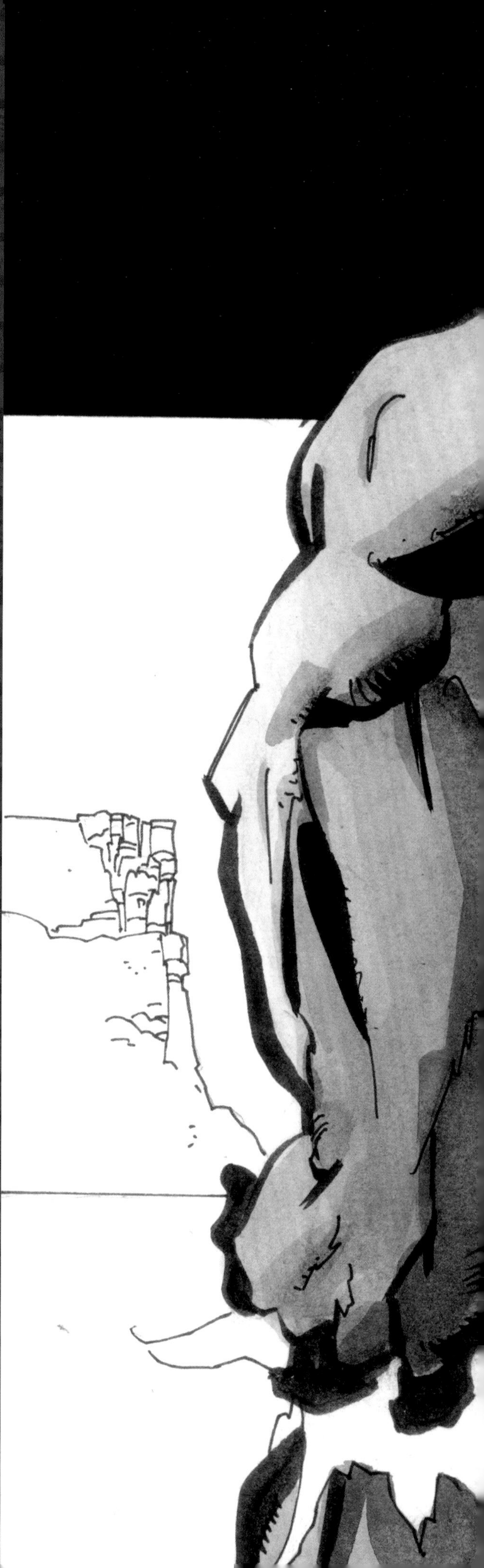

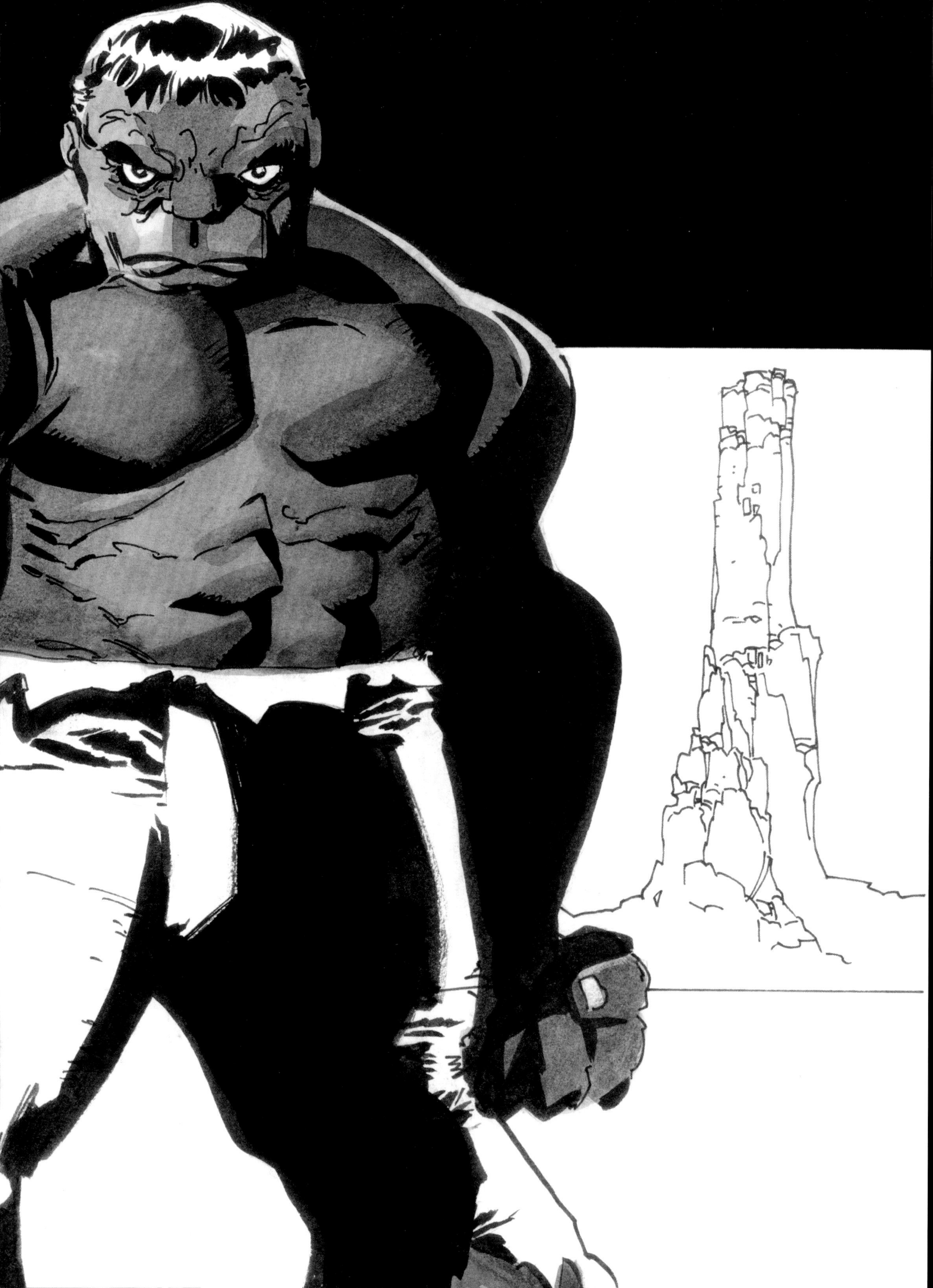

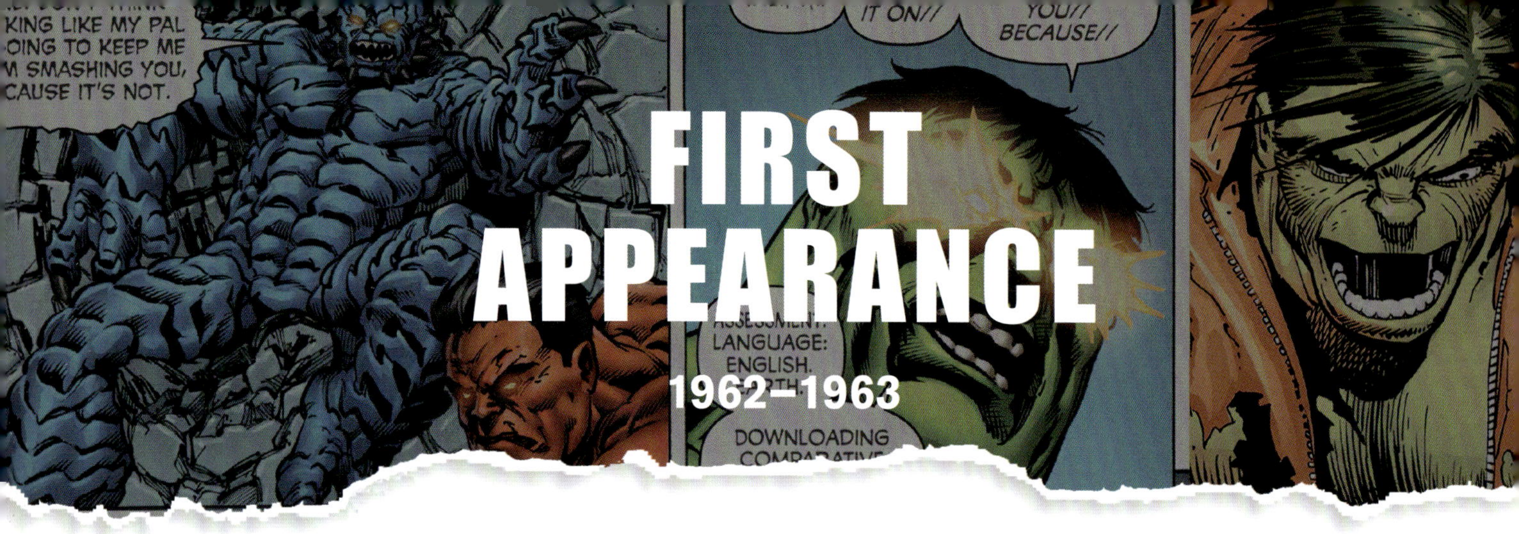
IT ON//
BECAUSE//
LANGUAGE:
ENGLISH.
DOWNLOADING

# FIRST APPEARANCE

## 1962–1963

They say we all have a dark side that we keep at bay; that we merely control it, keep it in check. But for Dr. Bruce Banner, his dark side was revealed for all the world to see when he survived the blast of a gamma bomb. The gamma radiation changed Banner forever—it turned him into a big *gray* rage monster. That's right: in the Hulk's first comic book appearance in *The Incredible Hulk* #1, he was not green, but gray. By *Incredible Hulk* #2 he became the green giant we have come to know and love. Another story change from the early issues was that nightfall, and not his anger, transformed Banner into the Hulk. The Hulk catalyst was also adjusted early, which set the stage for the eternal battle between Bruce Banner and the Hulk.

The Hulk hated Banner for being weak, and Banner hated that he couldn't control the rage inside him that would bring out the monster. Over the years they constantly fought for control. Sometimes, Banner was dominant, and the Hulk was held in check for a time. Other times, the Hulk would dominate, and Banner would recede into the darkness. And then there were the occasions in the stories where the Hulk had Banner's intelligence, where there was a fusion of the two. On rare occasions, they even occupied two bodies. But Banner and the Hulk never were far apart. Their connection inevitably remained, and their struggle continued.

Transforming into the Hulk wasn't only about anger; it was also about strength. The angrier he got, the more powerful the Hulk became. Often, he used his strength in a positive way, but sometimes the rage was uncontrollable, and it grew out of hand. Maybe that's what fans like about the Hulk and Banner—the uncertainty, the danger, and the power that lies beneath it all.

In some way, can't we all relate to the struggle for control? How many times have we been cut off in traffic and we

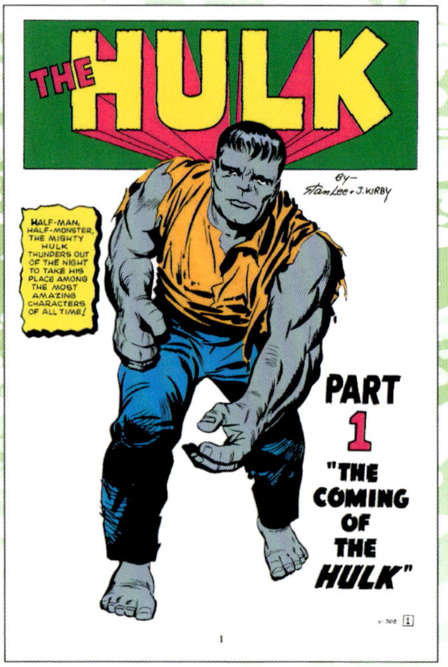
THE HULK
By— Stan Lee • J. Kirby
HALF-MAN, HALF-MONSTER, THE MIGHTY HULK THUNDERS OUT OF THE NIGHT TO TAKE HIS PLACE AMONG THE MOST AMAZING CHARACTERS OF ALL TIME!
PART 1
"THE COMING OF THE HULK"
1

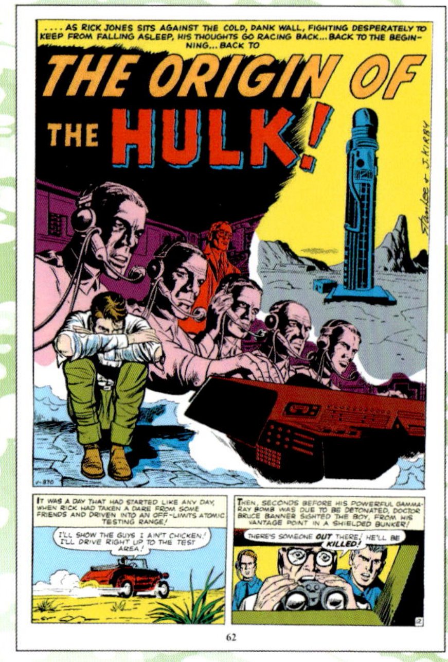
....AS RICK JONES SITS AGAINST THE COLD, DANK WALL, FIGHTING DESPERATELY TO KEEP FROM FALLING ASLEEP, HIS THOUGHTS GO RACING BACK...BACK TO THE BEGINNING...BACK TO
THE ORIGIN OF THE HULK!
J. KIRBY
IT WAS A DAY THAT HAD STARTED LIKE ANY DAY, WHEN RICK HAD TAKEN A DARE FROM SOME FRIENDS AND DRIVEN INTO AN OFF-LIMITS ATOMIC TESTING RANGE!
I'LL SHOW THE GUYS I AIN'T CHICKEN! I'LL DRIVE RIGHT UP TO THE TEST AREA!
THEN, SECONDS BEFORE HIS POWERFUL GAMMA-RAY BOMB WAS DUE TO BE DETONATED, DOCTOR BRUCE BANNER SIGHTED THE BOY, FROM HIS VANTAGE POINT IN A SHIELDED BUNKER!
THERE'S SOMEONE OUT THERE! HE'LL BE KILLED!
12
62

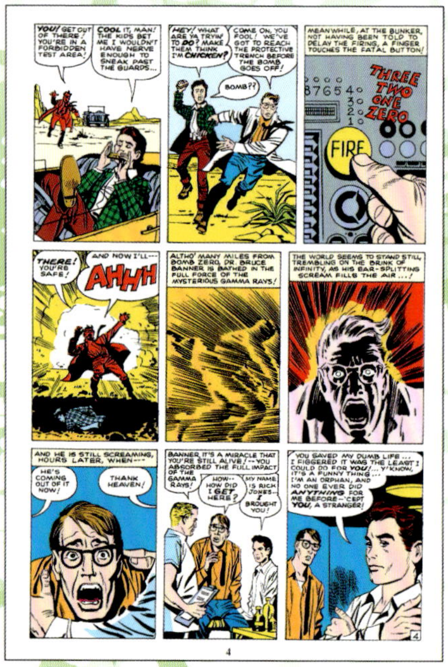
YOU! GET OUT OF THERE! YOU'RE IN A FORBIDDEN TEST AREA!
COOL IT, MAN! THE KIDS BET ME I WOULDN'T HAVE NERVE ENOUGH TO SNEAK PAST THE GUARDS...
HEY! WHAT ARE YA TRYIN' TO DO? MAKE THEM THINK I'M CHICKEN?
COME ON, YOU FOOL! WE'VE GOT TO REACH THE PROTECTIVE TRENCH BEFORE THE BOMB GOES OFF!
BOMB??
MEANWHILE, AT THE BUNKER, NOT HAVING BEEN TOLD TO DELAY THE FIRING, A FINGER TOUCHES THE FATAL BUTTON!
THREE TWO ONE ZERO
FIRE
THERE! YOU'RE SAFE!
AND NOW I'LL---
AHHH
ALTHO' MANY MILES FROM BOMB ZERO, DR. BRUCE BANNER IS BATHED IN THE FULL FORCE OF THE MYSTERIOUS GAMMA RAYS!
THE WORLD SEEMS TO STAND STILL, TREMBLING ON THE BRINK OF INFINITY, AS HIS EAR-SPLITTING SCREAM FILLS THE AIR...!
AND HE IS STILL SCREAMING, HOURS LATER, WHEN---
HE'S COMING OUT OF IT NOW!
THANK HEAVEN!
BANNER, IT'S A MIRACLE THAT YOU'RE STILL ALIVE!--YOU ABSORBED THE FULL IMPACT OF THE GAMMA RAYS!
HOW-- HOW DID I GET HERE?
MY NAME IS RICK JONES-- I BROUGHT YOU!
YOU SAVED MY DUMB LIFE... I FIGGERED IT WAS THE LEAST I COULD DO FOR YOU!... Y'KNOW, IT'S A FUNNY THING... I'M AN ORPHAN, AND NO ONE EVER DID ANYTHING FOR ME BEFORE--'CEPT YOU, A STRANGER!
4
4

MARVEL

THE INCREDIBLE HULK®

MARVEL MASTERWORKS®

# THE INCREDIBLE HULK®

VOLUME 1

IND.
12¢
THE INCREDIBLE
HULK
APPROVED BY THE COMICS CODE AUTHORITY
MC
1 MAY
THE STRANGEST MAN OF ALL TIME!!
IS HE MAN OR MONSTER ?
OR...
IS HE BOTH
FANTASY AS YOU LIKE IT!


**THE INCREDIBLE HULK** NOS. 1-6

STAN LEE & JACK KIRBY

WITH STEVE DITKO

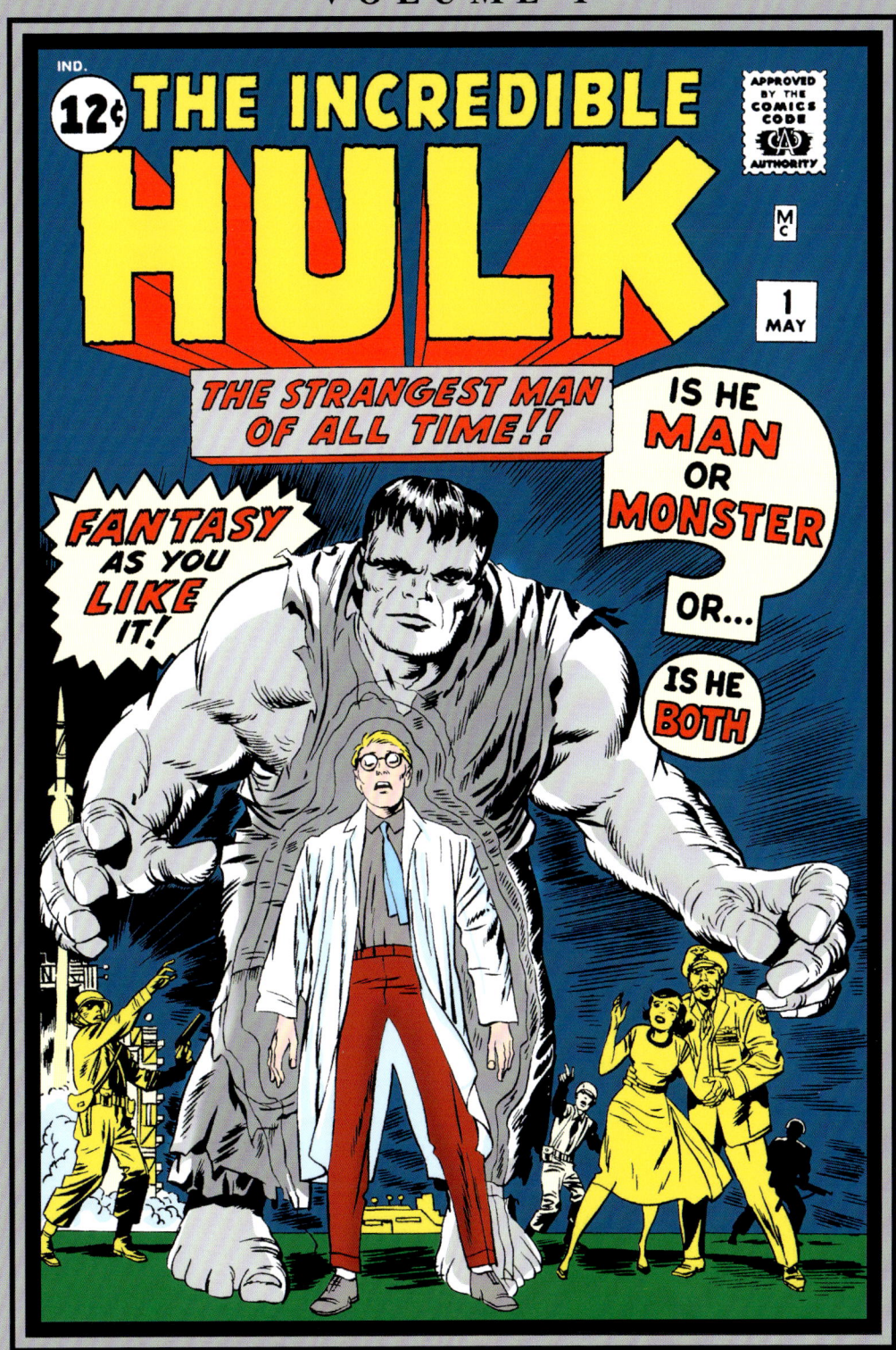

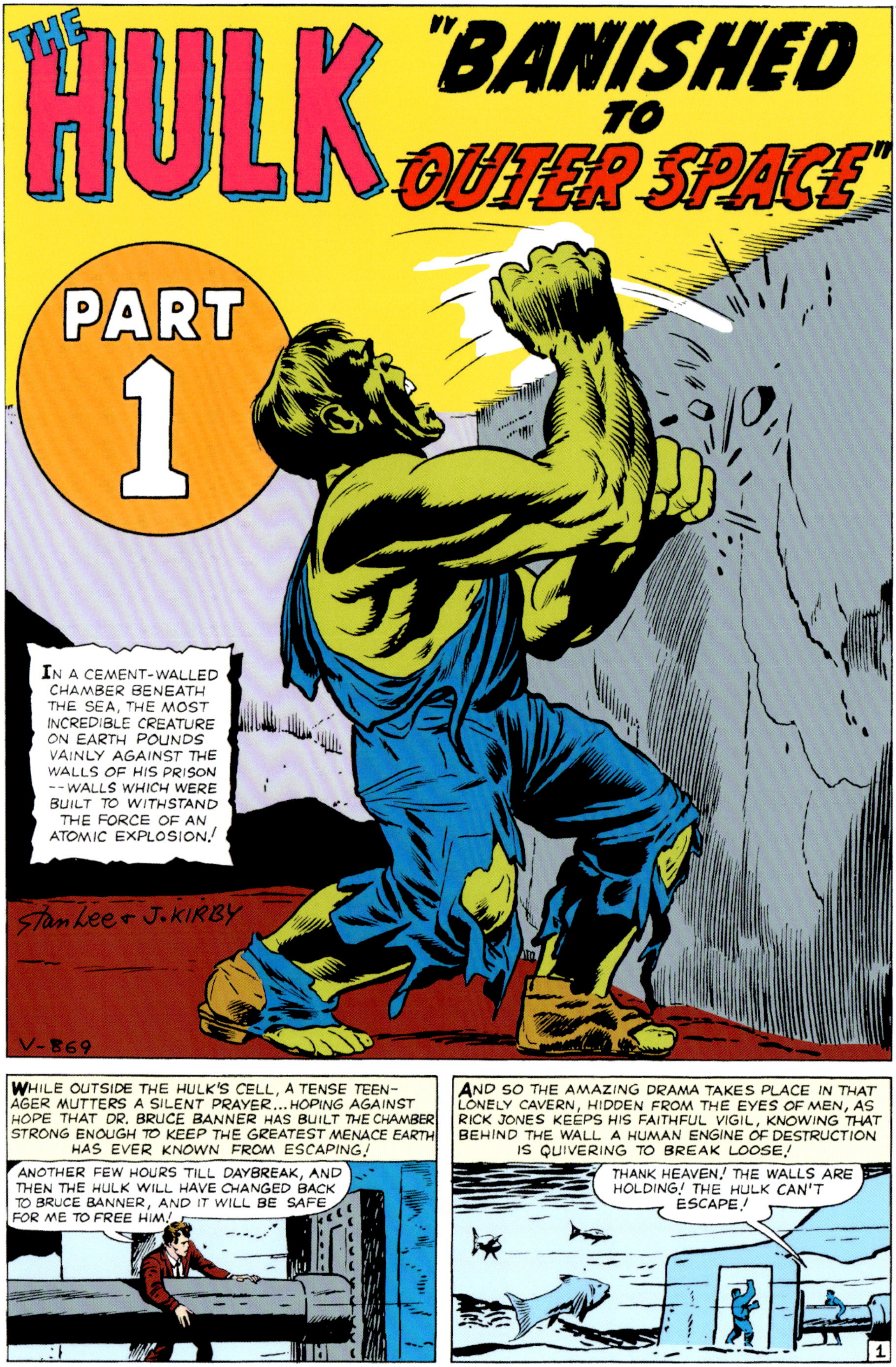
THE HULK
"BANISHED TO OUTER SPACE"
PART 1
IN A CEMENT-WALLED CHAMBER BENEATH THE SEA, THE MOST INCREDIBLE CREATURE ON EARTH POUNDS VAINLY AGAINST THE WALLS OF HIS PRISON --WALLS WHICH WERE BUILT TO WITHSTAND THE FORCE OF AN ATOMIC EXPLOSION!
Stan Lee + J. KIRBY
V-869
WHILE OUTSIDE THE HULK'S CELL, A TENSE TEEN-AGER MUTTERS A SILENT PRAYER... HOPING AGAINST HOPE THAT DR. BRUCE BANNER HAS BUILT THE CHAMBER STRONG ENOUGH TO KEEP THE GREATEST MENACE EARTH HAS EVER KNOWN FROM ESCAPING!
ANOTHER FEW HOURS TILL DAYBREAK, AND THEN THE HULK WILL HAVE CHANGED BACK TO BRUCE BANNER, AND IT WILL BE SAFE FOR ME TO FREE HIM!
AND SO THE AMAZING DRAMA TAKES PLACE IN THAT LONELY CAVERN, HIDDEN FROM THE EYES OF MEN, AS RICK JONES KEEPS HIS FAITHFUL VIGIL, KNOWING THAT BEHIND THE WALL A HUMAN ENGINE OF DESTRUCTION IS QUIVERING TO BREAK LOOSE!
THANK HEAVEN! THE WALLS ARE HOLDING! THE HULK CAN'T ESCAPE!
1

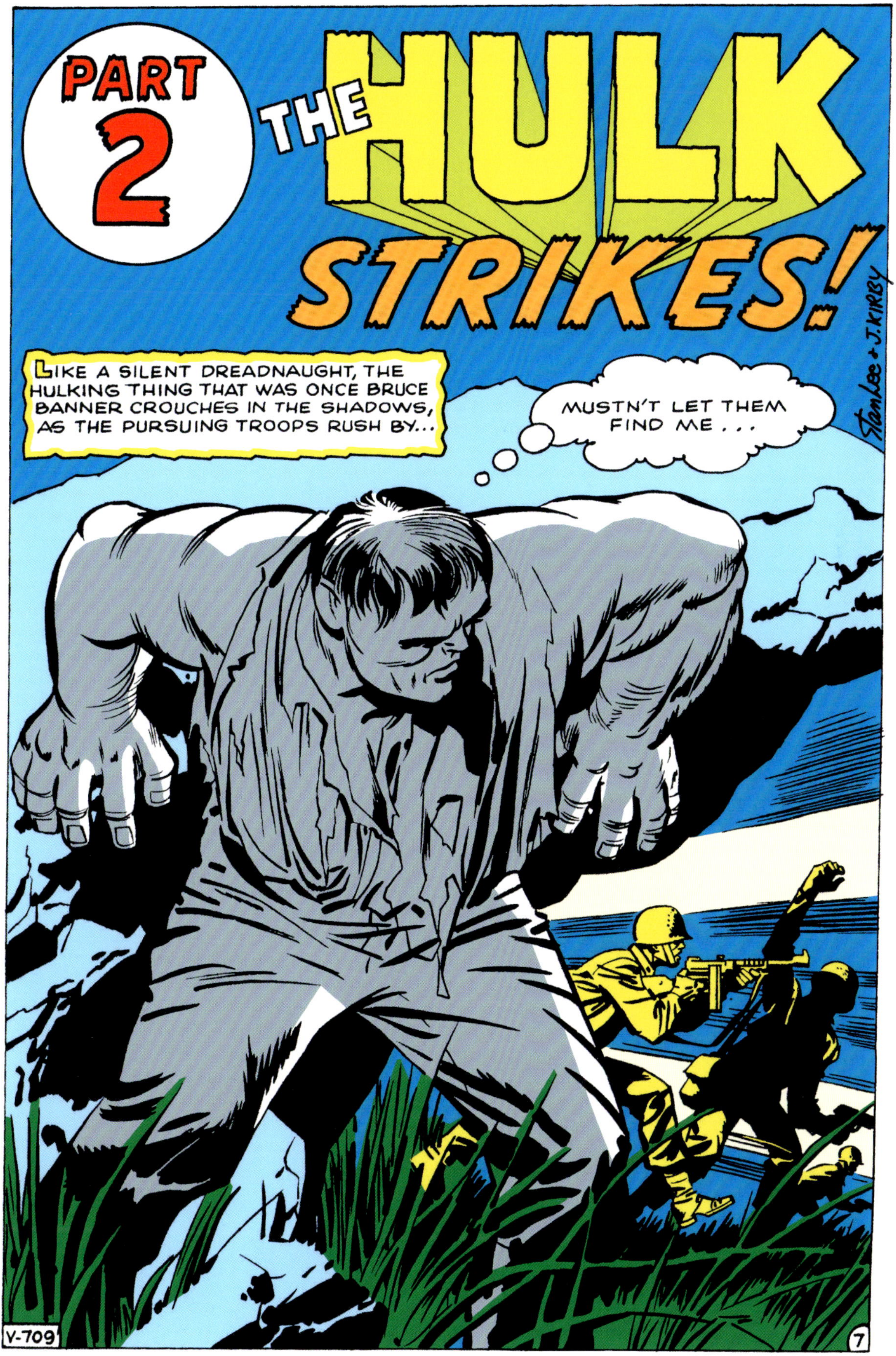

PART 2
THE HULK STRIKES!
Stan Lee + J. Kirby
LIKE A SILENT DREADNAUGHT, THE HULKING THING THAT WAS ONCE BRUCE BANNER CROUCHES IN THE SHADOWS, AS THE PURSUING TROOPS RUSH BY...
MUSTN'T LET THEM FIND ME . . .
V-709
7

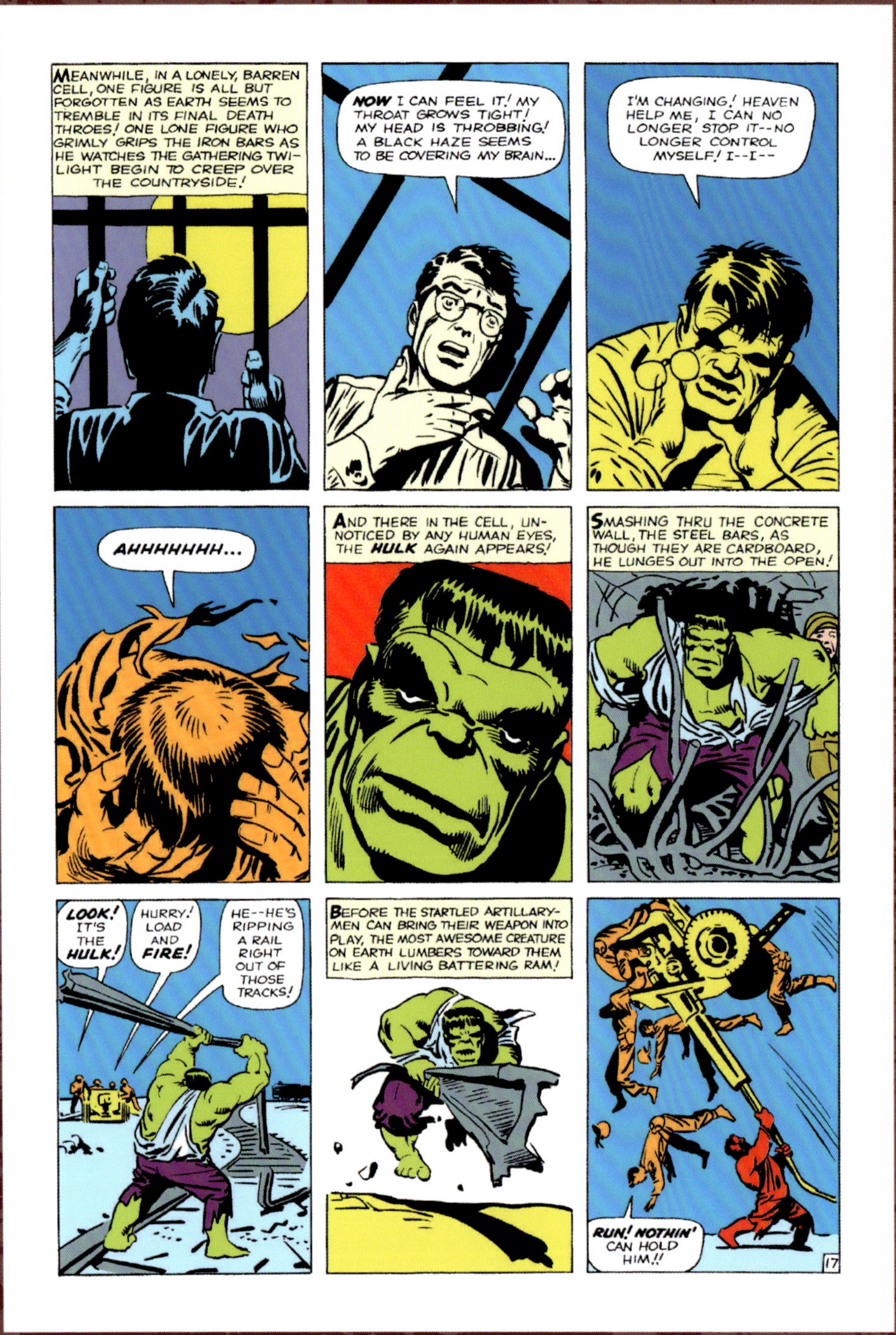
MEANWHILE, IN A LONELY, BARREN CELL, ONE FIGURE IS ALL BUT FORGOTTEN AS EARTH SEEMS TO TREMBLE IN ITS FINAL DEATH THROES! ONE LONE FIGURE WHO GRIMLY GRIPS THE IRON BARS AS HE WATCHES THE GATHERING TWI-LIGHT BEGIN TO CREEP OVER THE COUNTRYSIDE!
NOW I CAN FEEL IT! MY THROAT GROWS TIGHT! MY HEAD IS THROBBING! A BLACK HAZE SEEMS TO BE COVERING MY BRAIN...
I'M CHANGING! HEAVEN HELP ME, I CAN NO LONGER STOP IT--NO LONGER CONTROL MYSELF! I--I--
AHHHHHHH...
AND THERE IN THE CELL, UN-NOTICED BY ANY HUMAN EYES, THE HULK AGAIN APPEARS!
SMASHING THRU THE CONCRETE WALL, THE STEEL BARS, AS THOUGH THEY ARE CARDBOARD, HE LUNGES OUT INTO THE OPEN!
LOOK! IT'S THE HULK!
HURRY! LOAD AND FIRE!
HE--HE'S RIPPING A RAIL RIGHT OUT OF THOSE TRACKS!
BEFORE THE STARTLED ARTILLARY-MEN CAN BRING THEIR WEAPON INTO PLAY, THE MOST AWESOME CREATURE ON EARTH LUMBERS TOWARD THEM LIKE A LIVING BATTERING RAM!
RUN! NOTHIN' CAN HOLD HIM!!
17

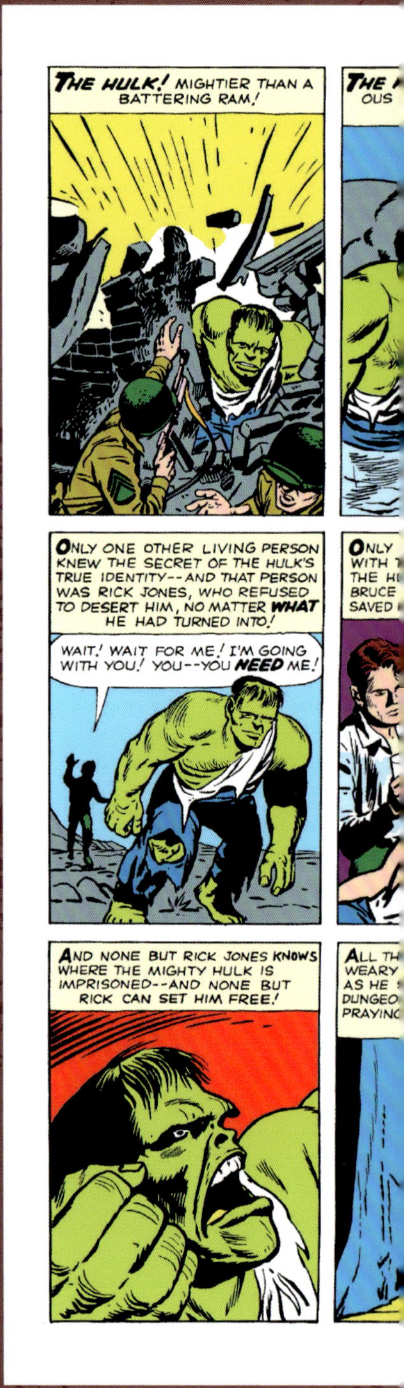
THE HULK! MIGHTIER THAN A BATTERING RAM!
ONLY ONE OTHER LIVING PERSON KNEW THE SECRET OF THE HULK'S TRUE IDENTITY--AND THAT PERSON WAS RICK JONES, WHO REFUSED TO DESERT HIM, NO MATTER WHAT HE HAD TURNED INTO!
WAIT! WAIT FOR ME! I'M GOING WITH YOU! YOU--YOU NEED ME!
AND NONE BUT RICK JONES KNOWS WHERE THE MIGHTY HULK IS IMPRISONED--AND NONE BUT RICK CAN SET HIM FREE!

wished we could morph into an eight-foot-tall green monster? Who doesn't want a more powerful self simmering beneath the surface? The Hulk has a phrase he uses constantly. He's famous for it. Give it try: insert your name where the Hulk's name usually goes—you there—"Brenda smash!" Feels good, doesn't it? May-be we all have a little bit of the Hulk in us. There is another Banner catchphrase: "You wouldn't like me when I'm angry." Actually, as Hulk fans: we do.

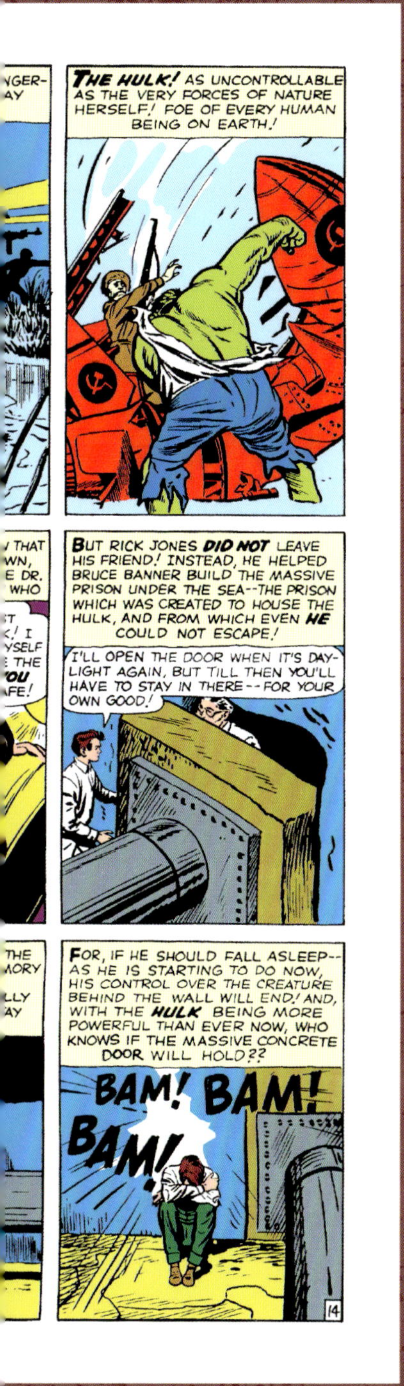
THE HULK! AS UNCONTROLLABLE AS THE VERY FORCES OF NATURE HERSELF! FOE OF EVERY HUMAN BEING ON EARTH!
BUT RICK JONES DID NOT LEAVE HIS FRIEND! INSTEAD, HE HELPED BRUCE BANNER BUILD THE MASSIVE PRISON UNDER THE SEA--THE PRISON WHICH WAS CREATED TO HOUSE THE HULK, AND FROM WHICH EVEN HE COULD NOT ESCAPE!
I'LL OPEN THE DOOR WHEN IT'S DAYLIGHT AGAIN, BUT TILL THEN YOU'LL HAVE TO STAY IN THERE--FOR YOUR OWN GOOD!
FOR, IF HE SHOULD FALL ASLEEP--AS HE IS STARTING TO DO NOW, HIS CONTROL OVER THE CREATURE BEHIND THE WALL WILL END! AND, WITH THE HULK BEING MORE POWERFUL THAN EVER NOW, WHO KNOWS IF THE MASSIVE CONCRETE DOOR WILL HOLD??
BAM! BAM! BAM!
14

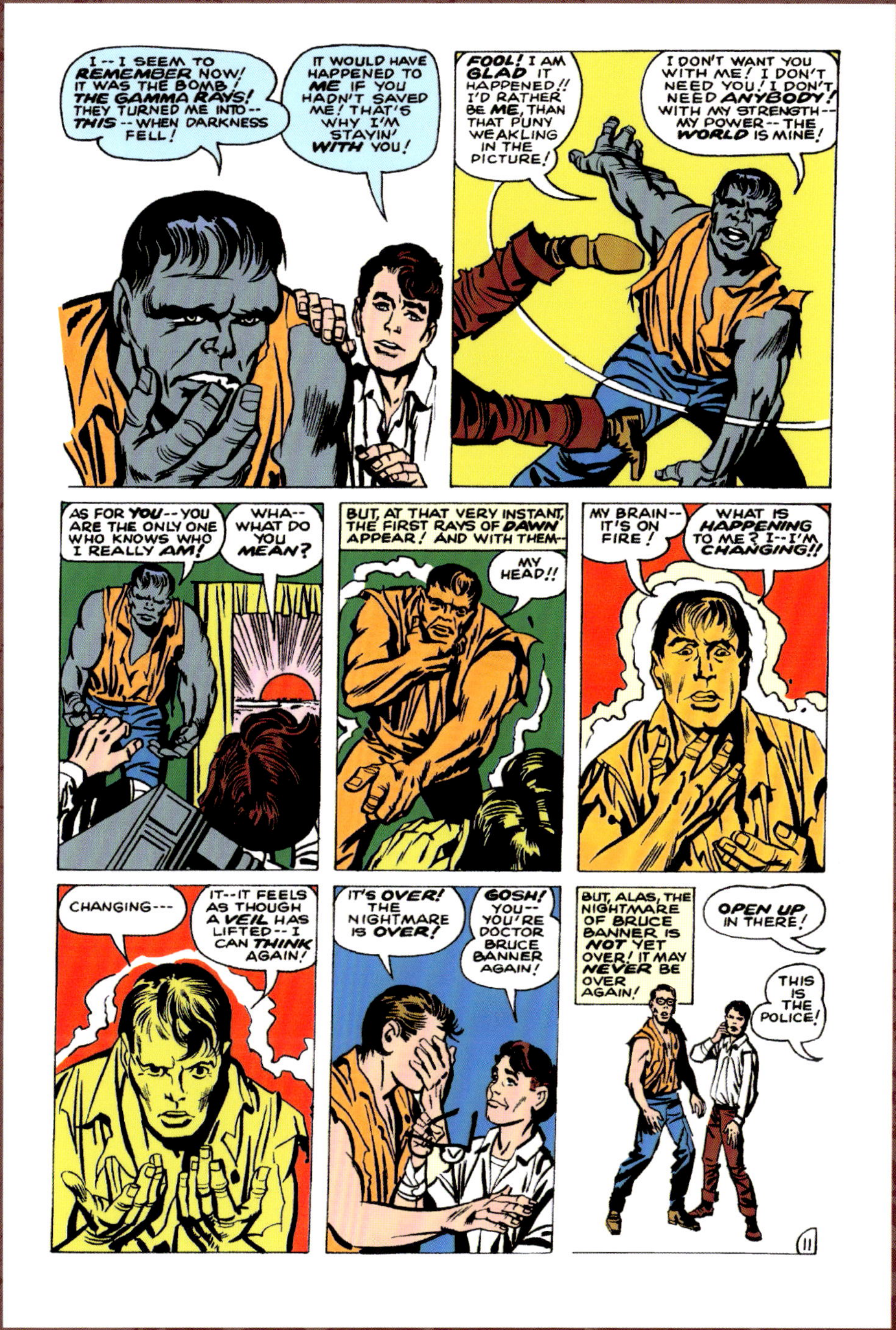
I--I SEEM TO REMEMBER NOW! IT WAS THE BOMB! THE GAMMA RAYS! THEY TURNED ME INTO--THIS--WHEN DARKNESS FELL!
IT WOULD HAVE HAPPENED TO ME IF YOU HADN'T SAVED ME! THAT'S WHY I'M STAYIN' WITH YOU!
FOOL! I AM GLAD IT HAPPENED!! I'D RATHER BE ME, THAN THAT PUNY WEAKLING IN THE PICTURE!
I DON'T WANT YOU WITH ME! I DON'T NEED YOU! I DON'T NEED ANYBODY! WITH MY STRENGTH--MY POWER--THE WORLD IS MINE!
AS FOR YOU--YOU ARE THE ONLY ONE WHO KNOWS WHO I REALLY AM!
WHA--WHAT DO YOU MEAN?
BUT, AT THAT VERY INSTANT, THE FIRST RAYS OF DAWN APPEAR! AND WITH THEM--
MY HEAD!!
MY BRAIN--IT'S ON FIRE!
WHAT IS HAPPENING TO ME? I--I'M CHANGING!!
CHANGING---
IT--IT FEELS AS THOUGH A VEIL HAS LIFTED--I CAN THINK AGAIN!
IT'S OVER! THE NIGHTMARE IS OVER!
GOSH! YOU--YOU'RE DOCTOR BRUCE BANNER AGAIN!
BUT, ALAS, THE NIGHTMARE OF BRUCE BANNER IS NOT YET OVER! IT MAY NEVER BE OVER AGAIN!
OPEN UP IN THERE!
THIS IS THE POLICE!
11

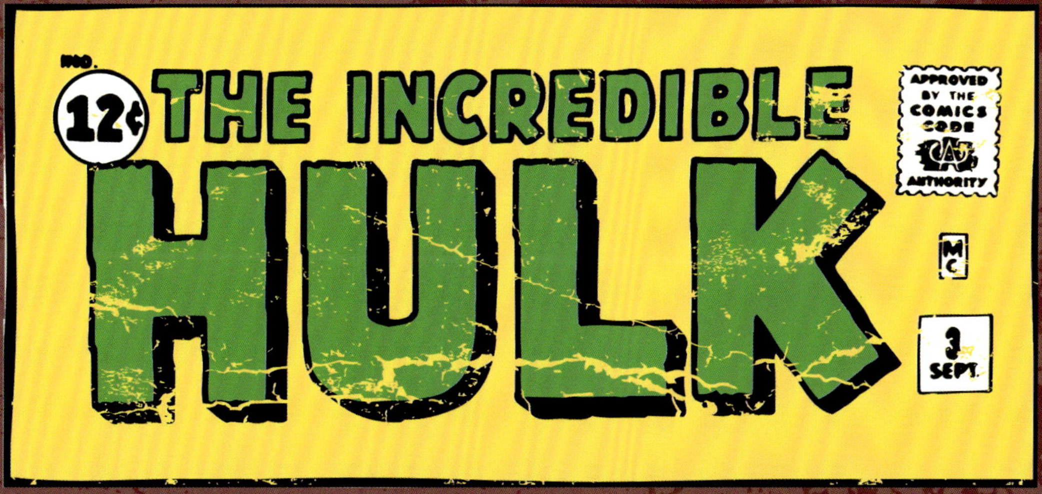
NO. 12¢ THE INCREDIBLE HULK
APPROVED BY THE COMICS CODE AUTHORITY
MC
3 SEPT.

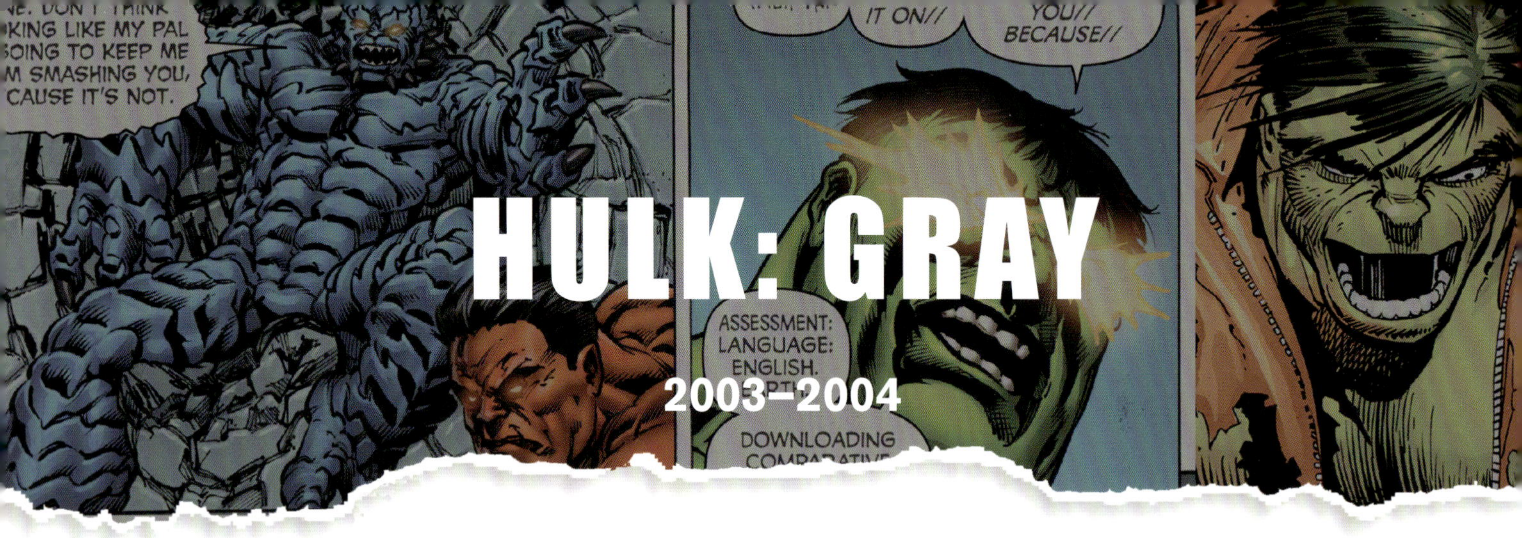
CAUSE IT'S NOT.
IT ON//
BECAUSE//
ASSESSMENT: LANGUAGE: ENGLISH.
DOWNLOADING

# HULK: GRAY

## 2003–2004

*Hulk: Gray* is an origin story told as a flashback. We first meet Bruce Banner at Doctor Leonard Samson's office. Samson is Bruce's friend and his psychiatrist. Something is bothering Bruce; then again, something always seems to be bothering Bruce. He is haunted by the fact that he has no control over when he turns into the Hulk, the green rage monster. Well, initially, he was the gray rage monster.

We see the test for the gamma bomb that Bruce created for the US military. Bruce's young friend Rick Jones had driven out to the blast site on a dare. Bruce goes to the blast site to try and save him. Bruce saves Rick, but absorbs the blast created by the bomb he designed. Rick takes Bruce to a doctor in town. Amazingly, Bruce seems fine—the doctor can't find anything physically wrong with him. But when the doctor steps out of the exam room, Bruce tries to explain to Rick how the blast incident has ruined his life. Bruce is a physicist and understands the dangers of gamma radiation. As Bruce gets angrier, he begins to change physically. His eyes glow green, and his body morphs and grows into a huge muscle-bound monster. He has transformed for the first time.

Instead of being scared, Rick is oddly curious. He seems almost amused at what has just happened to his friend Bruce. Rick refers to him as "hulking," and the gray giant repeats the word hulk. And when the monster smashes his way out of the building and is confronted by soldiers he says, "Hulk smash!" He has just named himself.

He ends up outside a house. Inside that house is Betty Ross, Bruce Banner's girlfriend and the daughter of General "Thunderbolt" Ross, the military man who is in charge of the gamma bomb testing. There are still bits of Bruce's memory in the Hulk. The Hulk knows that he needs to see her, and he gently knocks on the door. But when Betty answers the door and asks where Bruce is, the Hulk tells her that he hates Bruce Banner. Betty fears that the monster has killed Bruce, and she faints. Just then, General Ross and his troops show up and train their guns on the Hulk. The Hulk also recognizes General Ross. The Hulk, who had been holding her, gently puts Betty down and walks away, stating that he wants to be left alone.

The Hulk doesn't want any trouble; he is merely misunderstood. People call him a monster, and yet he doesn't believe that he is a

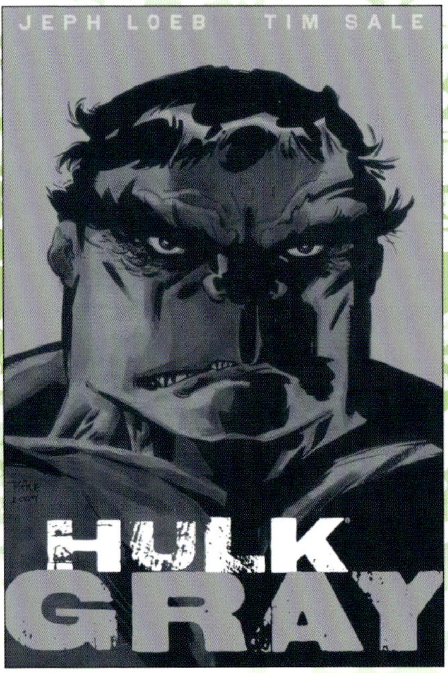
JEPH LOEB TIM SALE
HULK
GRAY

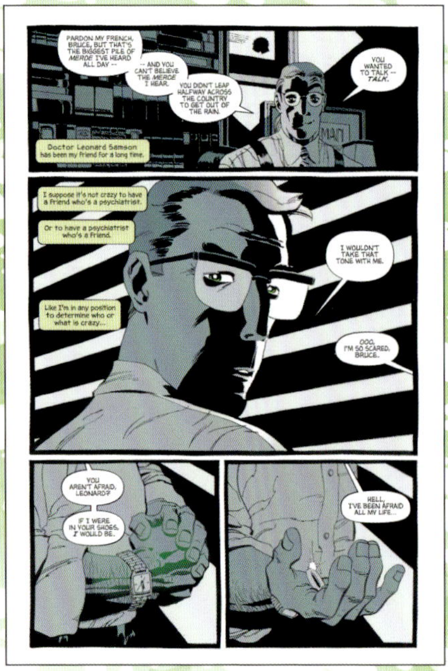
PARDON MY FRENCH, BRUCE, BUT THAT'S THE BIGGEST PILE OF MERDE I'VE HEARD ALL DAY --
-- AND YOU CAN'T BELIEVE THE MERDE I HEAR.
YOU DIDN'T LEAP HALFWAY ACROSS THE COUNTRY TO GET OUT OF THE RAIN.
YOU WANTED TO TALK -- TALK.
Doctor Leonard Samson has been my friend for a long time.
I suppose it's not crazy to have a friend who's a psychiatrist.
Or to have a psychiatrist who's a friend.
I WOULDN'T TAKE THAT TONE WITH ME.
Like I'm in any position to determine who or what is crazy...
OOO, I'M SO SCARED, BRUCE.
YOU AREN'T AFRAID, LEONARD?
IF I WERE IN YOUR SHOES, I WOULD BE.
HELL, I'VE BEEN AFRAID ALL MY LIFE...

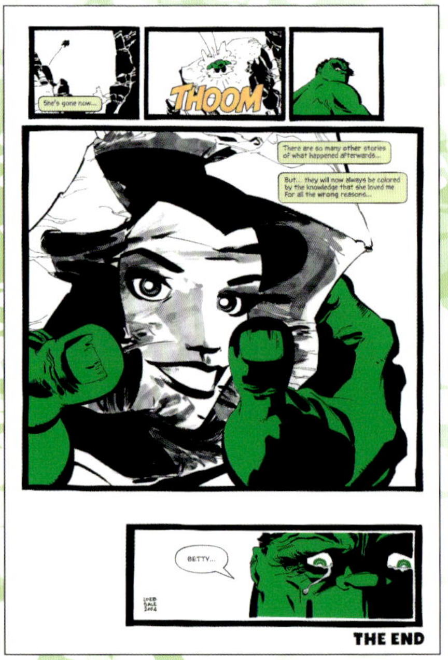
She's gone now...
THOOM
There are so many other stories of what happened afterwards...
But... they will now always be colored by the knowledge that she loved me for all the wrong reasons...
BETTY...
THE END

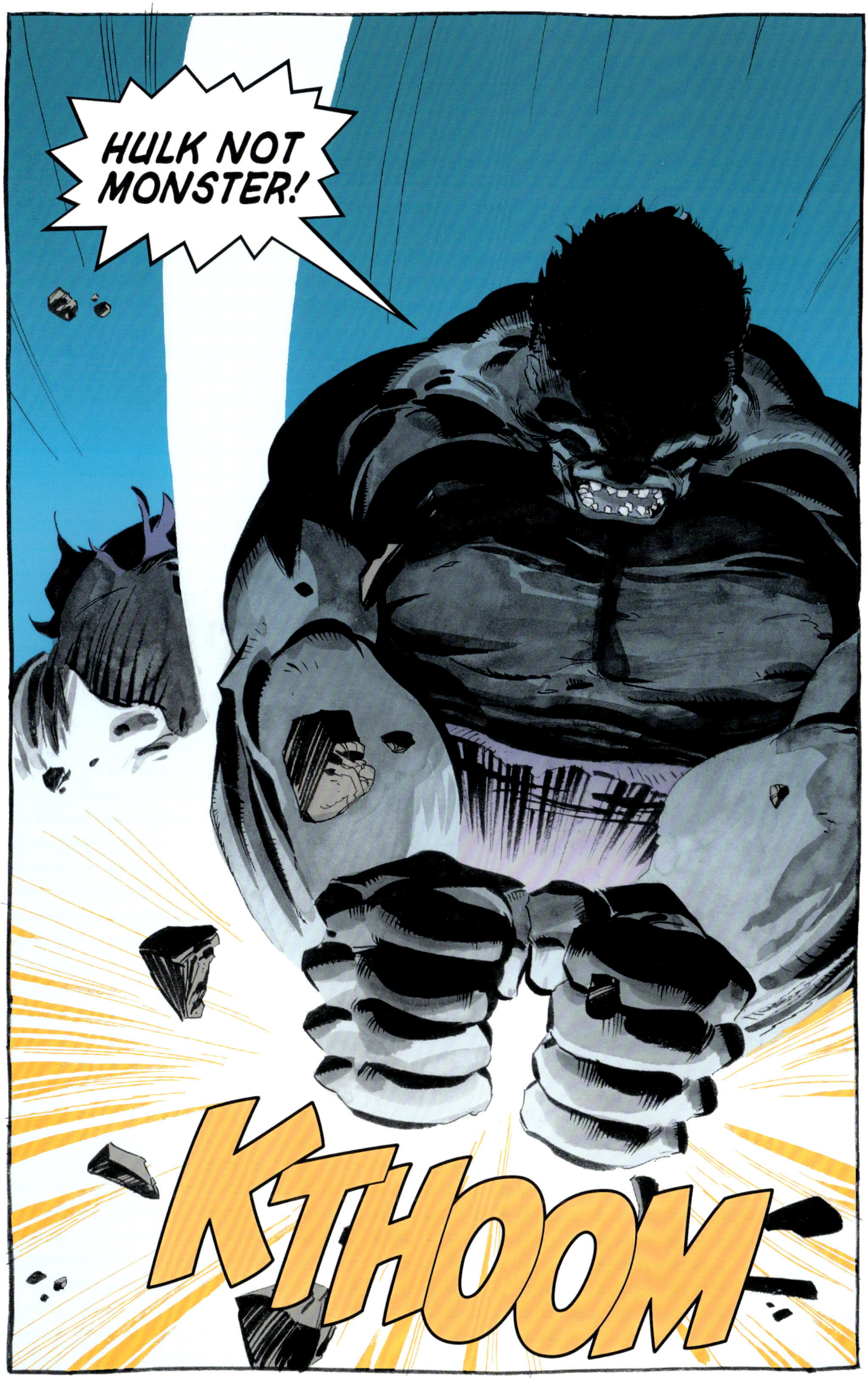
HULK NOT MONSTER!
KTHOOM

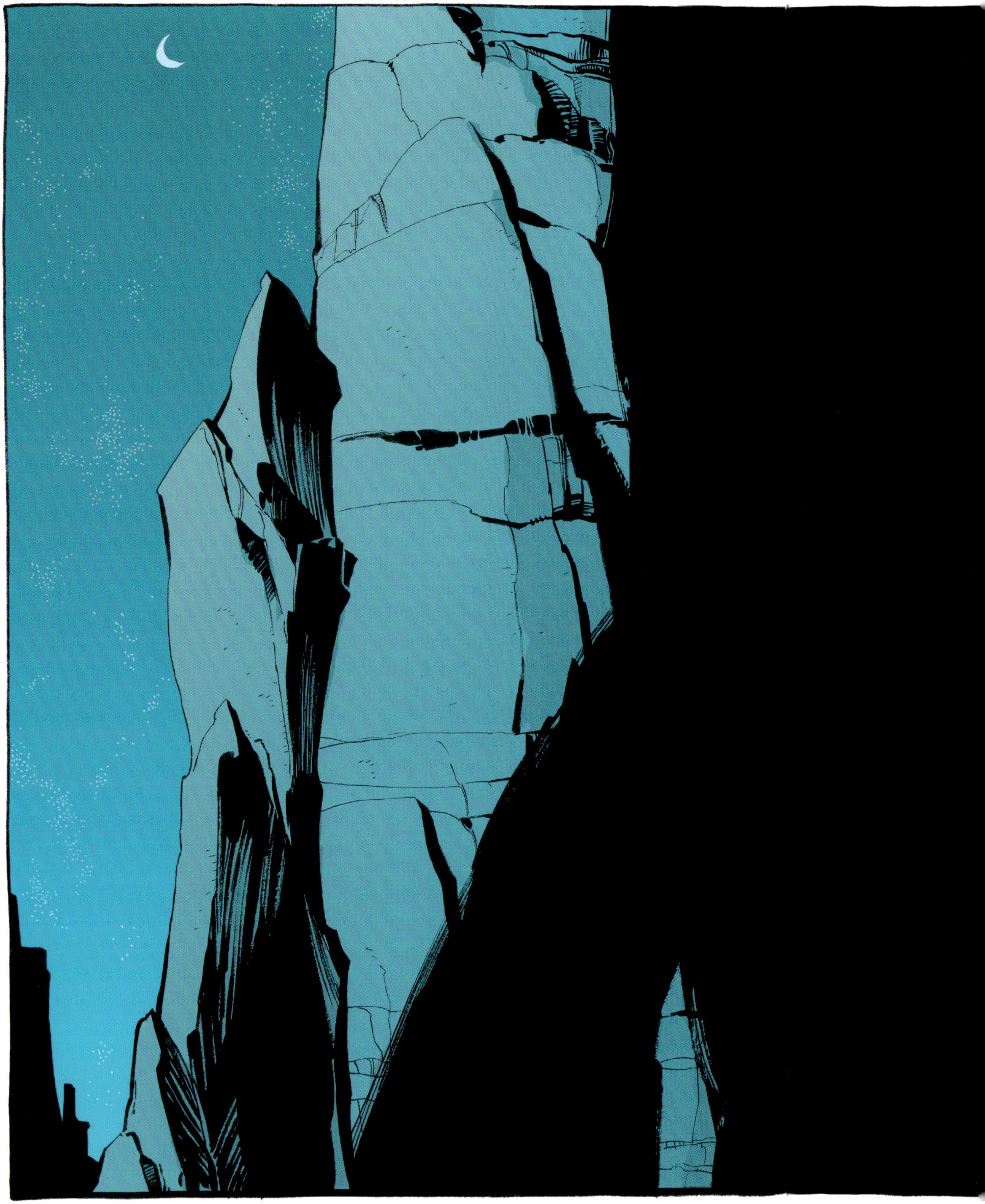

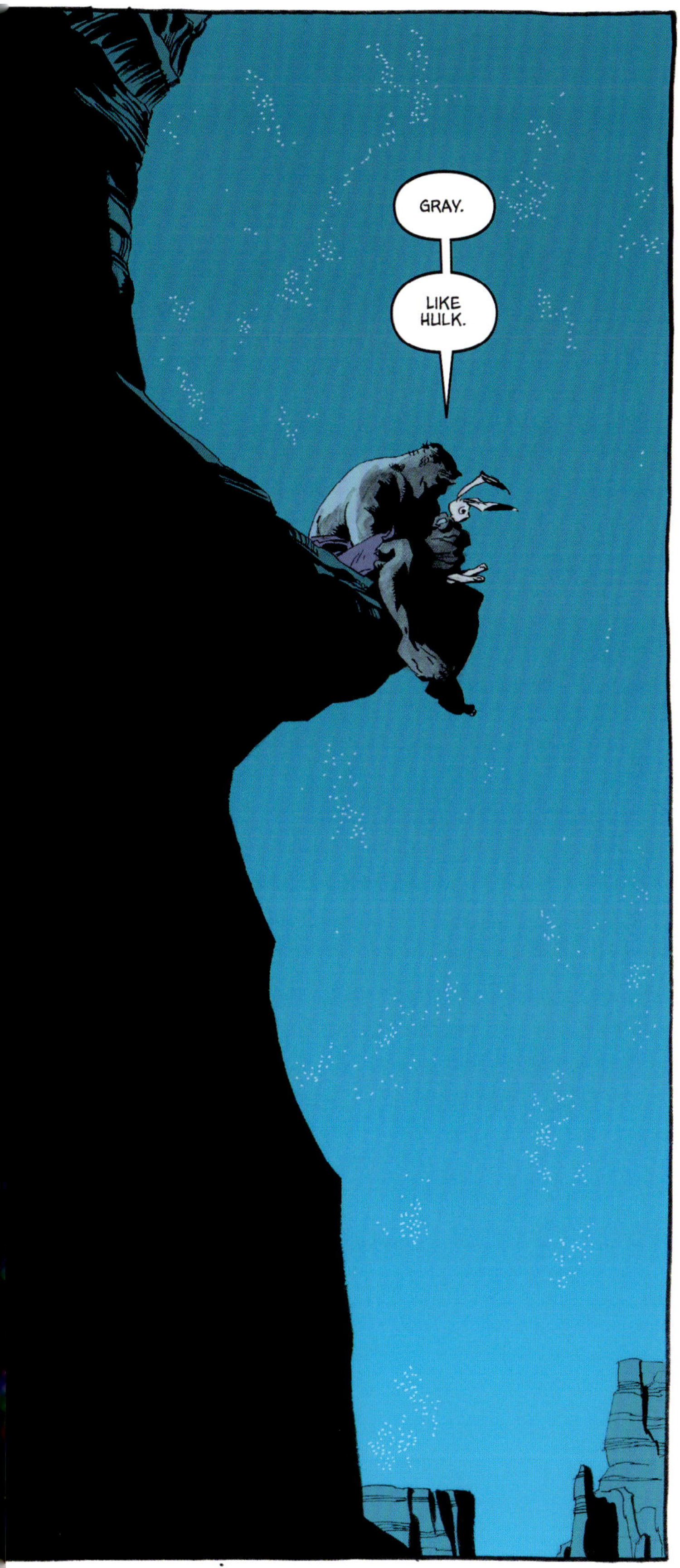
GRAY.
LIKE HULK.

monster, even though his actions can be scary and monstrous. And, like Banner, he has a temper. He is an angry man and an angry monster, each of them struggling for control over who they are.

There have been countless articles written about the psychology of the Hulk. A quick Google search will reveal terms like Hulk Syndrome, intermittent explosive disorder (IED), Bruce Banner dissociative identity disorder, and others. In many ways, the Hulk/Bruce Banner is one of the most complex characters in comics. Bruce Banner is a brilliant man forced to face his primitive instincts, but he is also a man of science. The Hulk is a creature driven by emotion, specifically anger, while Bruce is measured, reasonable. He is a creature of opposites battling for control over which physical form is dominant.

Many super heroes get their powers in some sort of accident: Peter Parker was bitten by a radioactive spider, and the Fantastic Four team was exposed to cosmic rays in space (yes, there were a lot of rays and radiation in the creation of Marvel's heroes—it was the 1960s, after all). But when those people got their powers, they each made the choice to become a super hero. They created costumes and gave themselves cool names. But Bruce Banner doesn't fit that traditional super hero mold. He doesn't get to choose when he can be the Hulk or be Banner. And his costume isn't a brightly colored jumpsuit with a cool logo and maybe a matching helmet. It's a torn pair of pants and no shirt. His powers lay him literally bare.

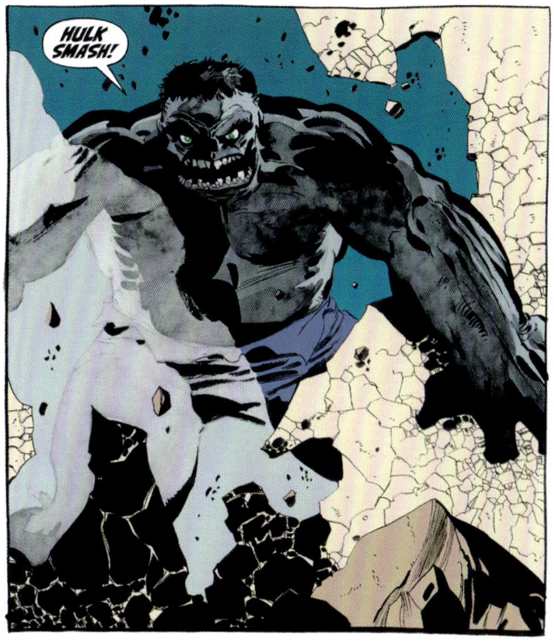
HULK SMASH!

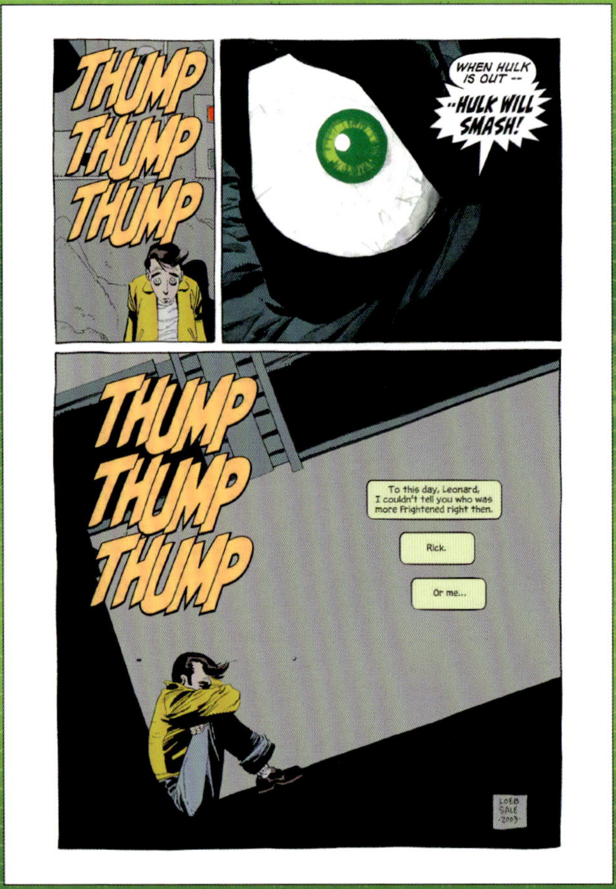
THUMP
THUMP
THUMP
WHEN HULK IS OUT --
--HULK WILL SMASH!
THUMP
THUMP
THUMP
To this day, Leonard, I couldn't tell you who was more frightened right then.
Rick.
Or me...
LOEB SALE 2003

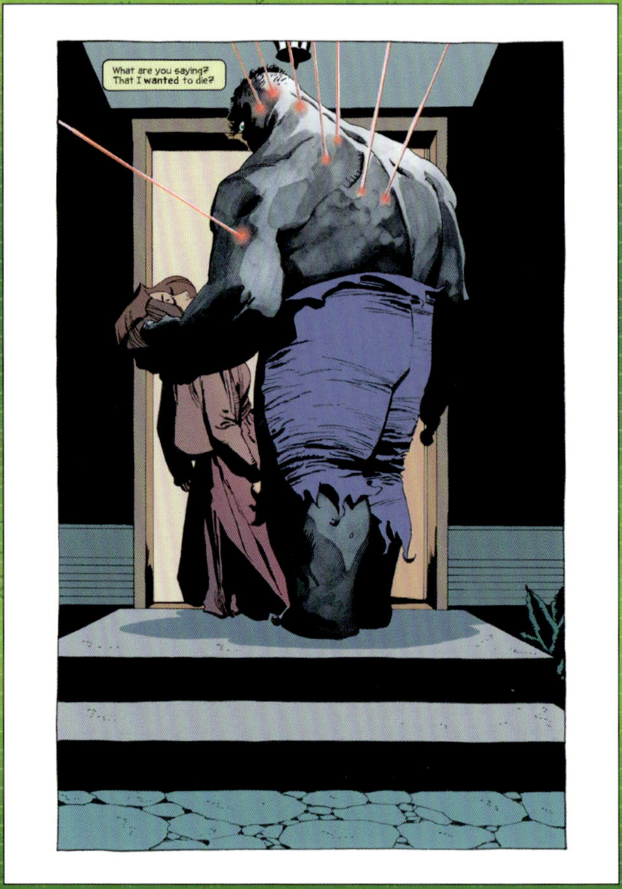
What are you saying? That I wanted to die?

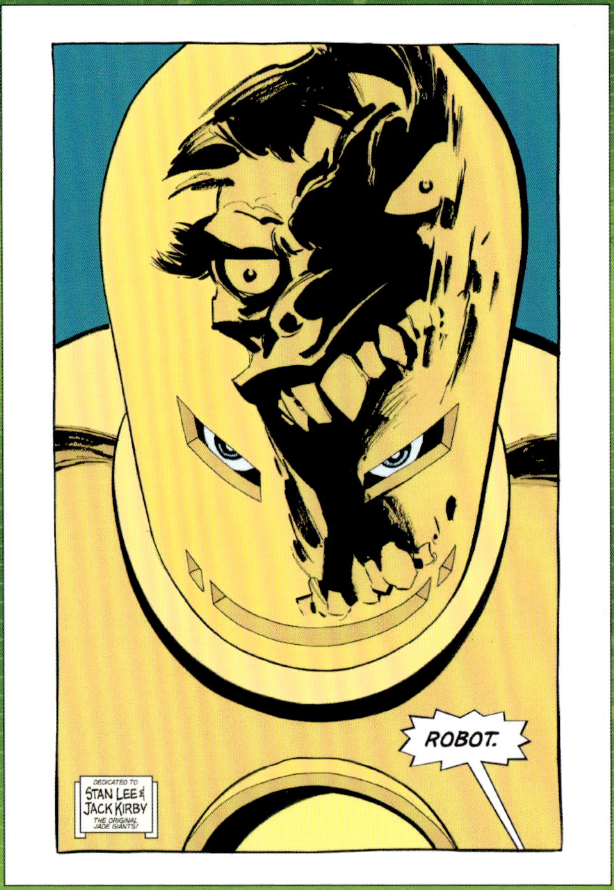
ROBOT.
DEDICATED TO STAN LEE & JACK KIRBY THE ORIGINAL JADE GIANTS!

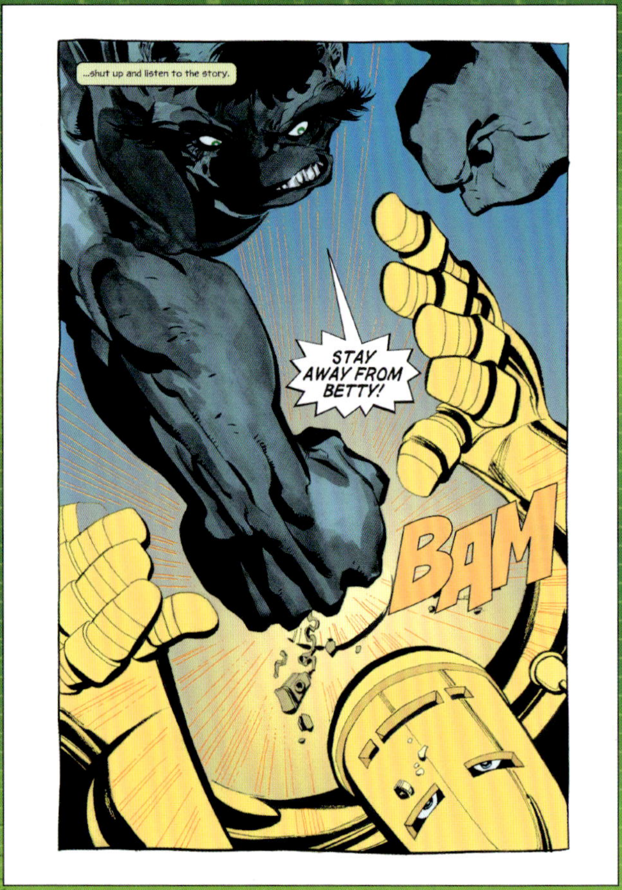
...shut up and listen to the story.
STAY AWAY FROM BETTY!
BAM

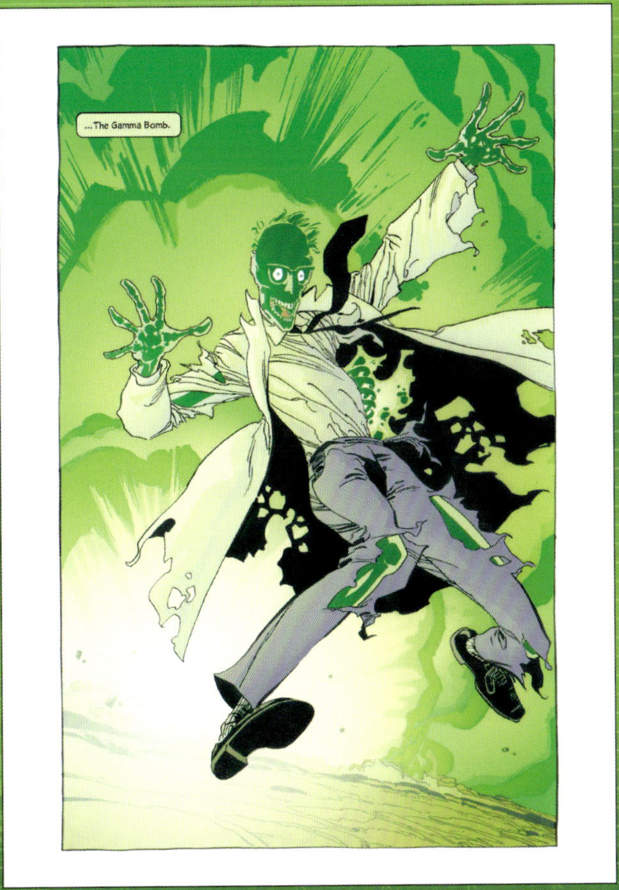
...The Gamma Bomb.

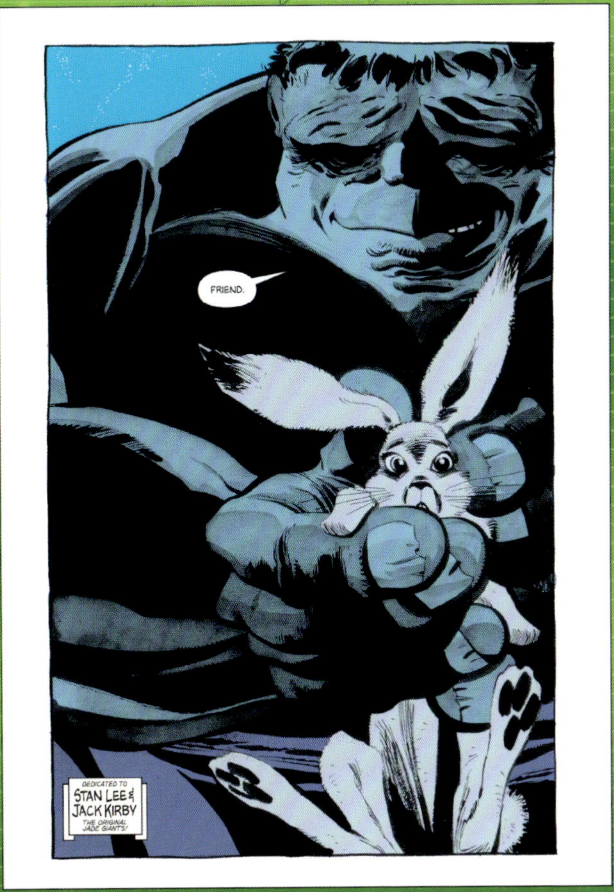
FRIEND.
DEDICATED TO
STAN LEE & JACK KIRBY
THE ORIGINAL JADE GIANTS!

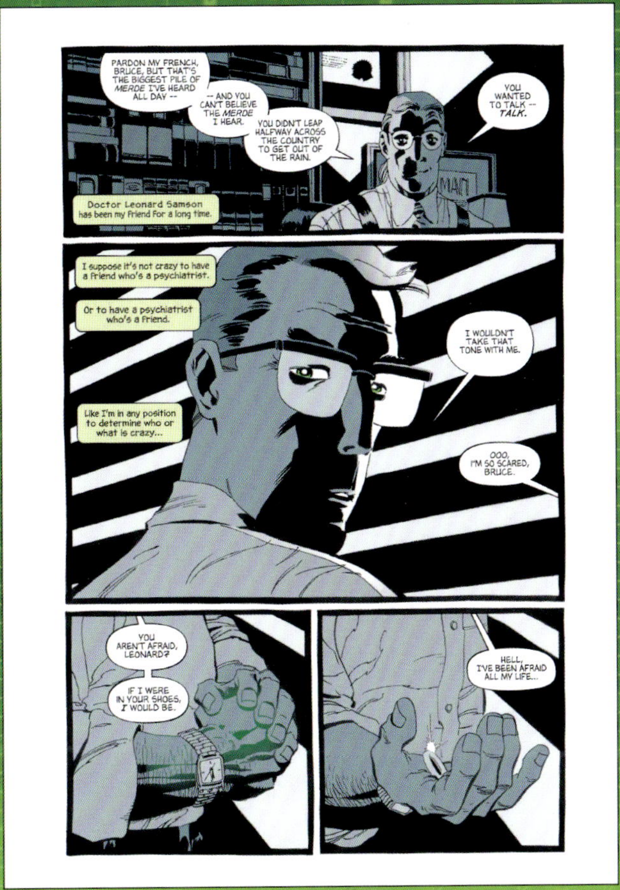
PARDON MY FRENCH, BRUCE, BUT THAT'S THE BIGGEST PILE OF MERDE I'VE HEARD ALL DAY --
-- AND YOU CAN'T BELIEVE THE MERDE I HEAR.
YOU DIDN'T LEAP HALFWAY ACROSS THE COUNTRY TO GET OUT OF THE RAIN.
YOU WANTED TO TALK -- TALK.
Doctor Leonard Samson has been my friend for a long time.
I suppose it's not crazy to have a friend who's a psychiatrist.
Or to have a psychiatrist who's a friend.
I WOULDN'T TAKE THAT TONE WITH ME.
Like I'm in any position to determine who or what is crazy...
OOO, I'M SO SCARED, BRUCE.
YOU AREN'T AFRAID, LEONARD?
IF I WERE IN YOUR SHOES, I WOULD BE.
HELL, I'VE BEEN AFRAID ALL MY LIFE...

The Hulk has often been compared to Frankenstein's monster and Dr. Jekyll and Mr. Hyde. Frankenstein's monster was built using technology Dr. Frankenstein created; Frankenstein invented a way to reanimate dead tissue. Mr. Hyde manifests after Dr. Jekyll took a serum, which he initially developed to subdue his darker impulses. However, the serum did the opposite and turned him into the monster Mr. Hyde. The team of Jeph Loeb and Tim Sale adds to this Hulk story a touch of John Steinbeck's character Lennie Small from his classic novella *Of Mice and Men*. Lennie is physically a huge man, but he is mentally disabled. Lennie has a simple dream; all he wants to do is live on a rabbit farm so he can pet the soft creatures. Unfortunately, Lennie often accidently kills the rabbits because he can't control his own strength. This concept is something the Hulk learns very early on. There is a scene in *Hulk: Gray* where he is holding and petting a rabbit, and just like Lennie, he pulls back a bloody finger. He was too rough with it, because he can't control himself.

The Hulk was the result of a tragic accident that took one man and gave him the ability to split himself in two. One side is the simple-minded strongman; the other, a skinny scientist. Bruce and the Hulk's eternal struggle is to learn how to live with themselves, and with each other.

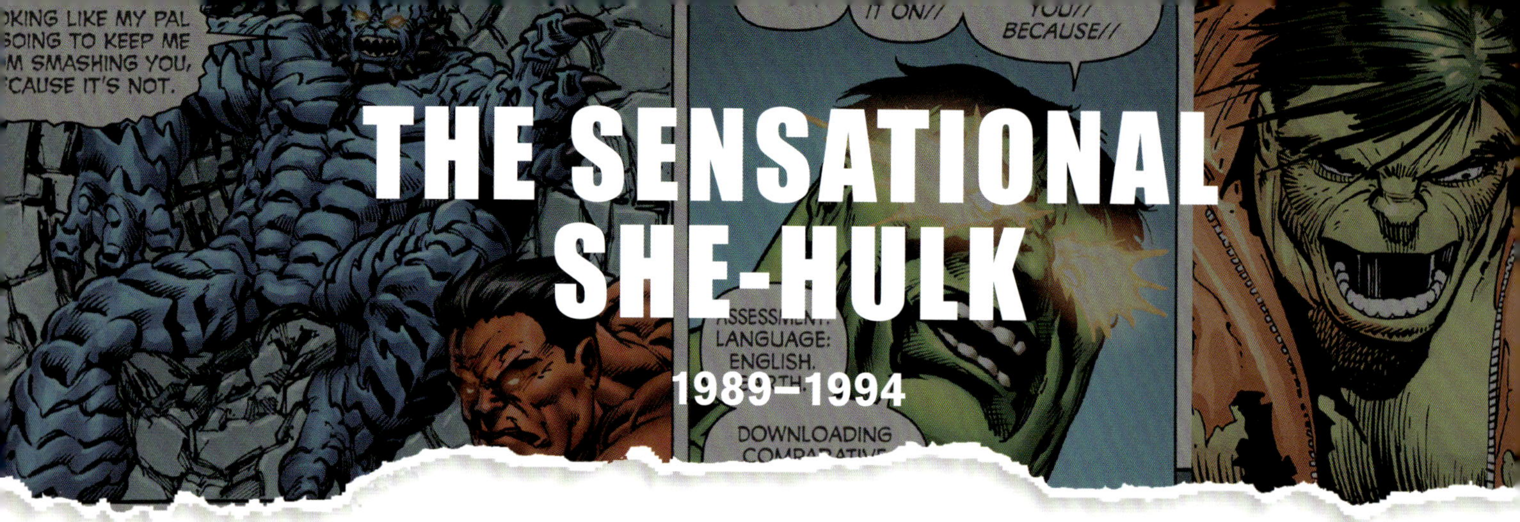
BECAUSE//
LANGUAGE:
ENGLISH.
DOWNLOADING

# THE SENSATIONAL SHE-HULK

## 1989–1994

She-Hulk loves to break the fourth wall. No, she isn't punching through a physical wall. It's an invisible wall. In film, television, and theatre, breaking the fourth wall is when an actor ignores the imaginary wall that exists between them and the audience. Groucho Marx famously did this in many films, where he directly addressed the audience. In comics, breaking the fourth wall happens occasionally. In the Marvel Universe, there are two Marvel characters who do this routinely: Deadpool (who first appeared in 1991) and She-Hulk.

On the cover of the very first issue of *The Sensational She-Hulk*, She-Hulk, a revamped version of the character from an earlier comic series named *The Savage She-Hulk*, sets the tone of the comic book—she stares straight out from the cover and greets the reader with a threat: "Okay, now. This is your second chance. If you don't buy my book this time I'm gonna come to your house and rip up all your *X-Men*." It might be best to listen to her and buy the comics. *The Sensational She-Hulk* was released in 1989 and ran until 1994. Throughout the run she spoke directly to her audience both on the covers and in the pages of the comics.

She-Hulk often commented on the conventions of comics. For example, on one cover she pointed out that the label on her shirt was the seal of the Comics Code Authority. Historically, this symbol assured the reader that the Authority approved the contents of the comic, and that it was safe to sell on newsstands. On another cover she teased that a Golden Age Comics (those comics published 1938–1956) character was appearing in the issue. Often, she made a direct pitch to the reader to buy her comics. She is her own best salesperson.

On the cover of the third issue, she announced, "It's my third issue: time for the obligatory guest star! And here he is now!" That guest was Spider-Man and the issue featured Mysterio and the Headmen, who abduct her and experiment on her. She actually inserts a type of "intermission" in the story to state the comic is getting too "serious," and she tells a couple of jokes. She even refers to events in her past by issue number.

Other characters accept the convention. In one scene, after She-Hulk meets her handsome new boss at a legal firm and

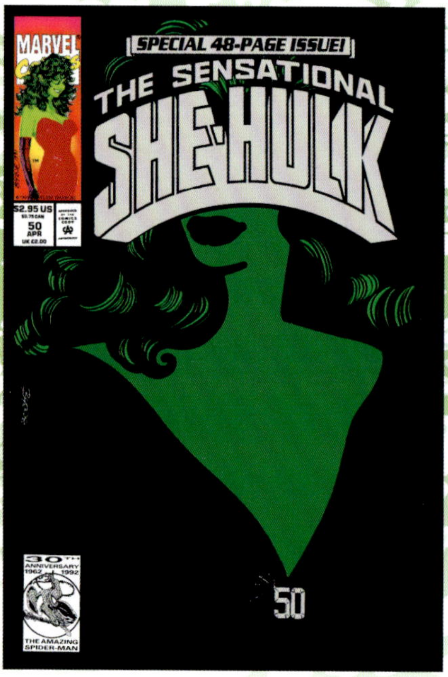
MARVEL
SPECIAL 48-PAGE ISSUE!
THE SENSATIONAL SHE-HULK
50

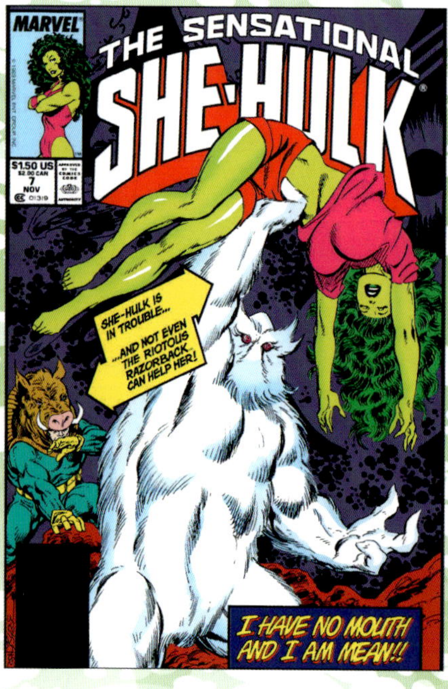
MARVEL
THE SENSATIONAL SHE-HULK
SHE-HULK IS IN TROUBLE...
...AND NOT EVEN THE RIOTOUS RAZORBACK CAN HELP HER!
I HAVE NO MOUTH AND I AM MEAN!!

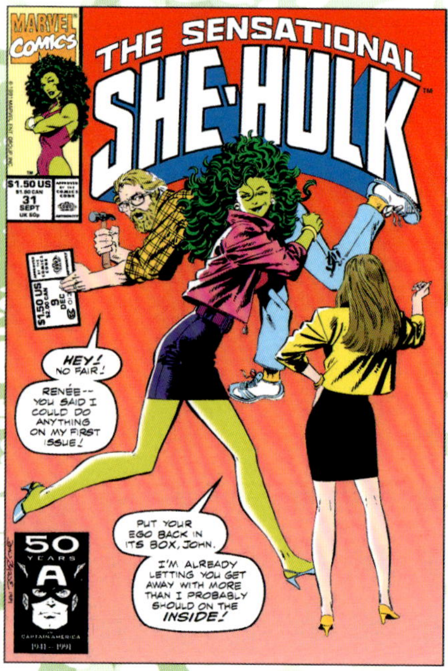
MARVEL COMICS
THE SENSATIONAL SHE-HULK
HEY! NO FAIR!
RENÉE-- YOU SAID I COULD DO ANYTHING ON MY FIRST ISSUE!
PUT YOUR EGO BACK IN ITS BOX, JOHN.
I'M ALREADY LETTING YOU GET AWAY WITH MORE THAN I PROBABLY SHOULD ON THE INSIDE!

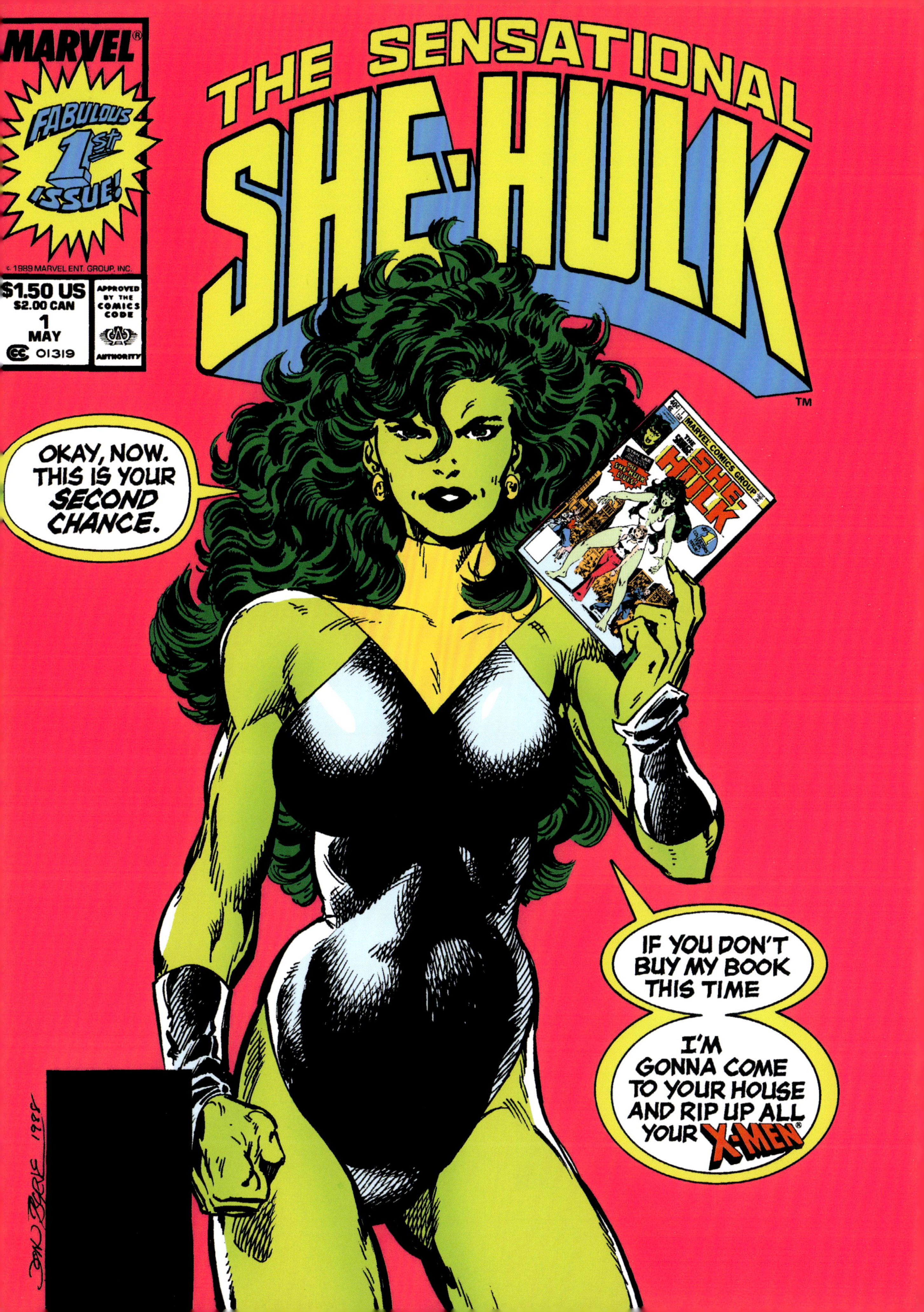
MARVEL®
FABULOUS 1st ISSUE!
THE SENSATIONAL SHE-HULK™
© 1989 MARVEL ENT. GROUP, INC.
$1.50 US $2.00 CAN 1 MAY CC 01319
APPROVED BY THE COMICS CODE AUTHORITY
OKAY, NOW. THIS IS YOUR SECOND CHANCE.
IF YOU DON'T BUY MY BOOK THIS TIME
I'M GONNA COME TO YOUR HOUSE AND RIP UP ALL YOUR X-MEN®

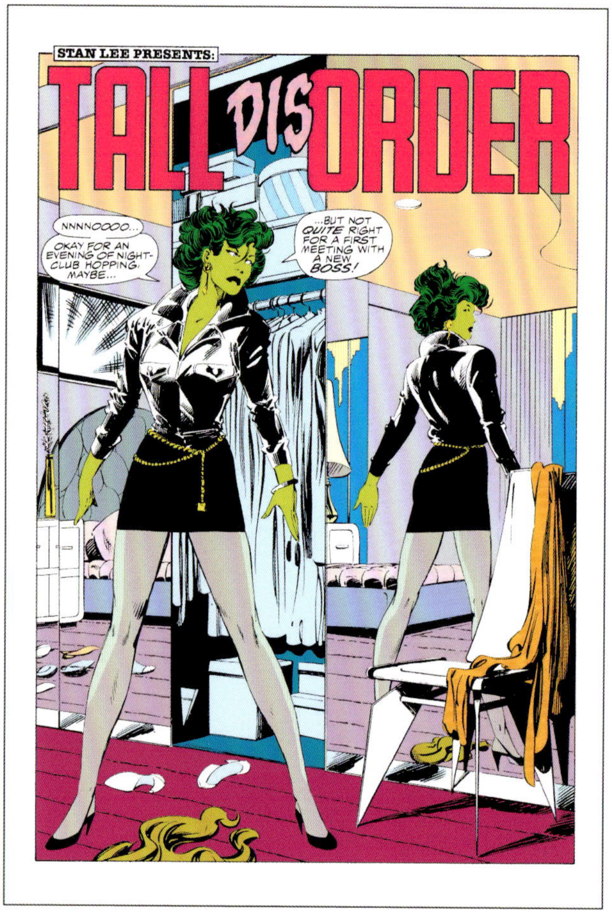
STAN LEE PRESENTS:
TALL DIS ORDER
NNNNOOOO... OKAY FOR AN EVENING OF NIGHT-CLUB HOPPING, MAYBE...
...BUT NOT QUITE RIGHT FOR A FIRST MEETING WITH A NEW BOSS!

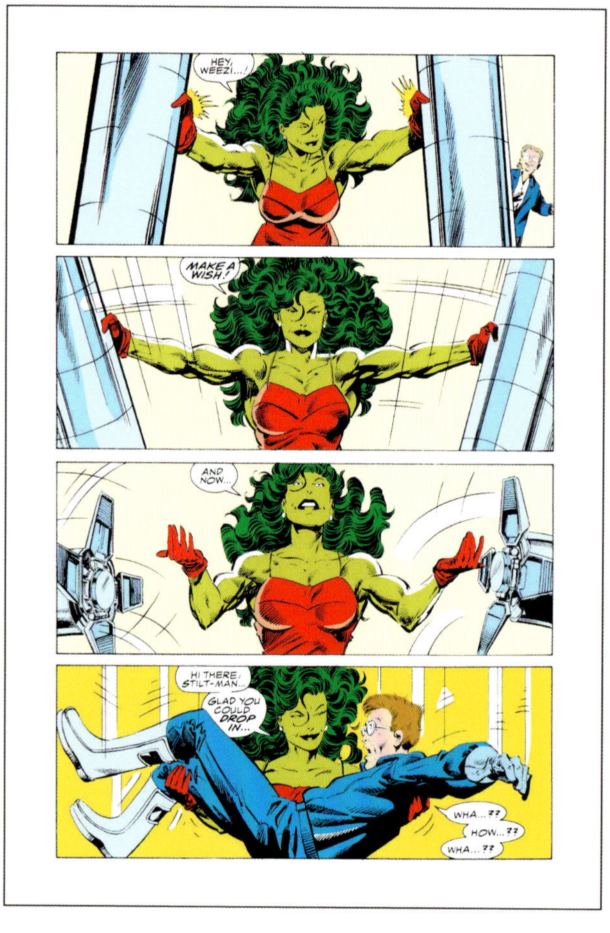
HEY, WEEZI...!
MAKE A WISH!
AND NOW...
HI THERE, STILT-MAN...
GLAD YOU COULD DROP IN...
WHA...??
HOW...??
WHA...??

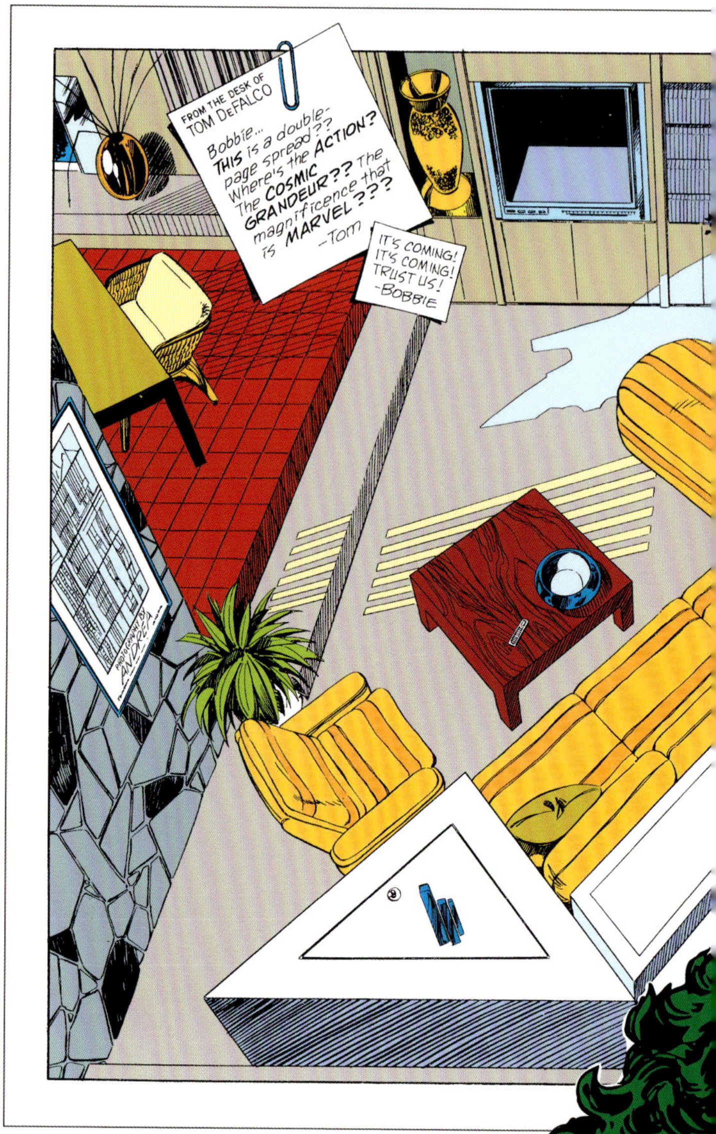
FROM THE DESK OF TOM DeFALCO
Bobbie... THIS is a double-page spread?? Where's the ACTION? The COSMIC GRANDEUR?? The magnificence that is MARVEL???
-Tom
IT'S COMING! IT'S COMING! TRUST US! -BOBBIE

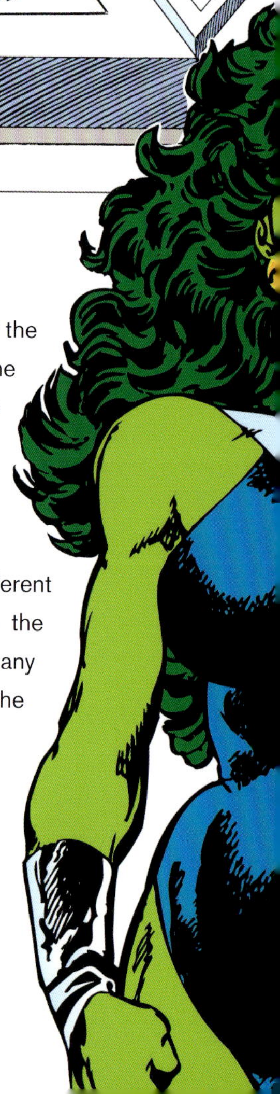

learns that he is married, she climbs out of the panel to yell at the writer. The assistant to the new boss holds her back, and comments that they both have already been "inked, colored, and printed," and that there are readers watching.

The fourth wall convention was a different approach to the character compared to the first run of She-Hulk comics. There were many differences in the characters. For instance, the

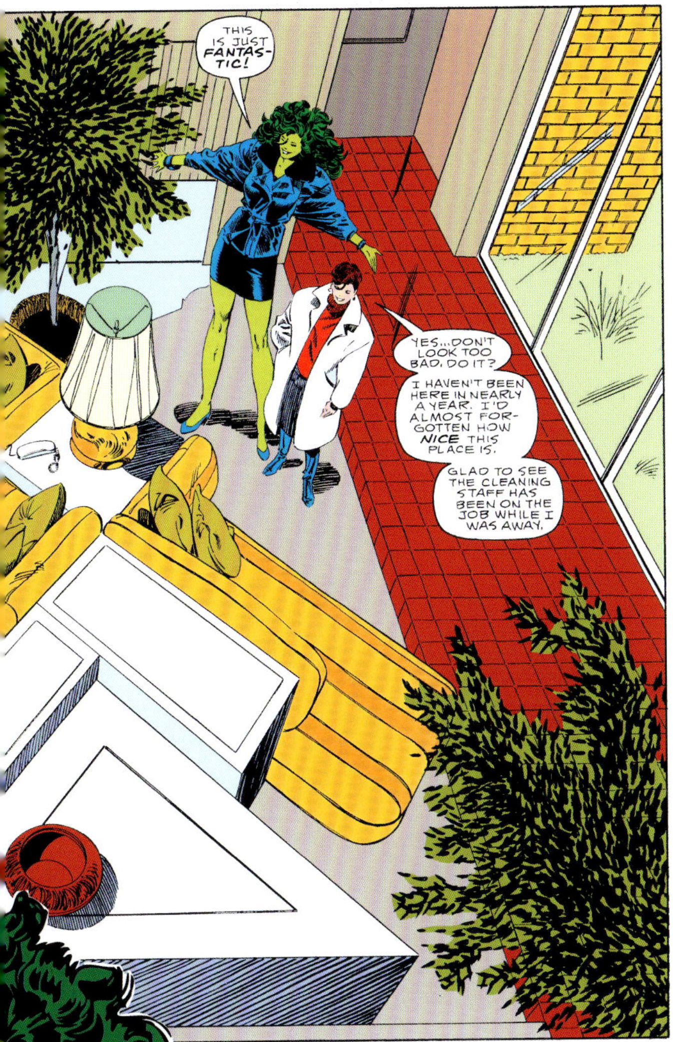

THIS IS JUST FANTASTIC!
YES...DON'T LOOK TOO BAD, DO IT?
I HAVEN'T BEEN HERE IN NEARLY A YEAR. I'D ALMOST FORGOTTEN HOW NICE THIS PLACE IS.
GLAD TO SEE THE CLEANING STAFF HAS BEEN ON THE JOB WHILE I WAS AWAY.


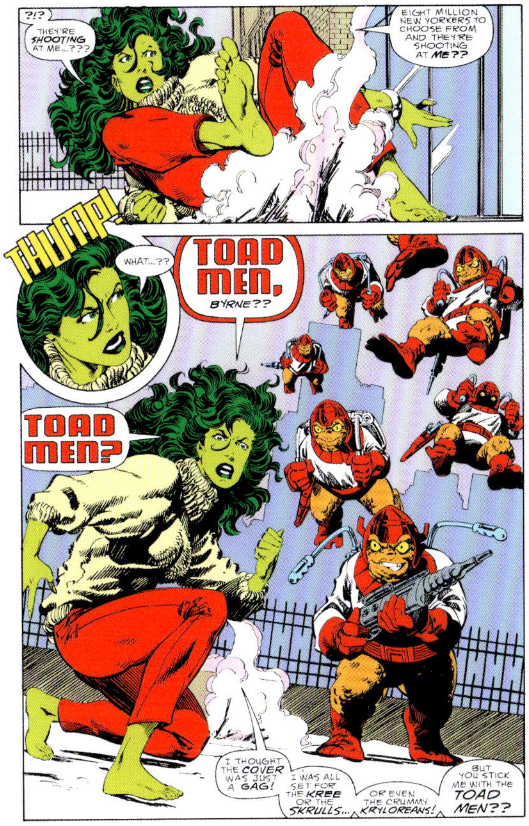

?!?
THEY'RE SHOOTING AT ME...???
EIGHT MILLION NEW YORKERS TO CHOOSE FROM AND THEY'RE SHOOTING AT ME??
THUMP!
WHAT...??
TOAD MEN, BYRNE??
TOAD MEN?
I THOUGHT THE COVER WAS JUST A GAG!
I WAS ALL SET FOR THE KREE OR THE SKRULLS...
OR EVEN THE CRUMMY KRYLOREANS!
BUT YOU STICK ME WITH THE TOAD MEN??


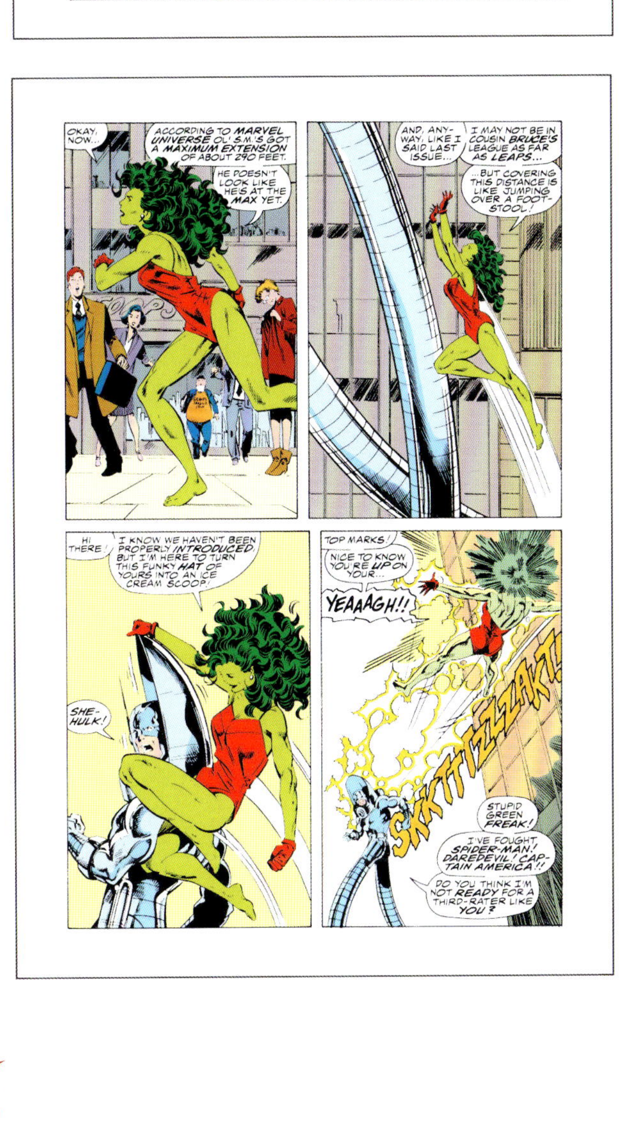

OKAY, NOW...
ACCORDING TO MARVEL UNIVERSE OL' S.M.'S GOT A MAXIMUM EXTENSION OF ABOUT 290 FEET.
HE DOESN'T LOOK LIKE HE'S AT THE MAX YET.
AND, ANYWAY, LIKE I SAID LAST ISSUE...
I MAY NOT BE IN COUSIN BRUCE'S LEAGUE AS FAR AS LEAPS...
...BUT COVERING THIS DISTANCE IS LIKE JUMPING OVER A FOOTSTOOL!
HI THERE!
I KNOW WE HAVEN'T BEEN PROPERLY INTRODUCED BUT I'M HERE TO TURN THIS FUNKY HAT OF YOURS INTO AN ICE CREAM SCOOP!
SHE-HULK!
TOP MARKS!
NICE TO KNOW YOU'RE UP ON YOUR...
YEAAAGH!!
SKKTTTZZZAKT!
STUPID GREEN FREAK!
I'VE FOUGHT SPIDER-MAN! DAREDEVIL! CAPTAIN AMERICA!!
DO YOU THINK I'M NOT READY FOR A THIRD-RATER LIKE YOU?


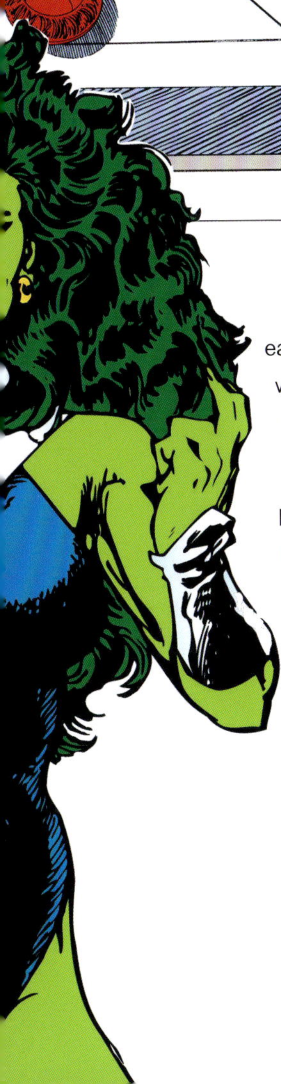

earlier She-Hulk did not break the fourth wall, and the new She-Hulk doesn't revert to her alter-ego Jennifer (although she is occasionally referred to as Jennifer).

In many ways it's refreshing to see a comic book character not take themselves seriously. She-Hulk is smart, strong, beautiful, and funny, and she uses her strength not only to defeat villains, but to shatter longstanding comic book conventions.

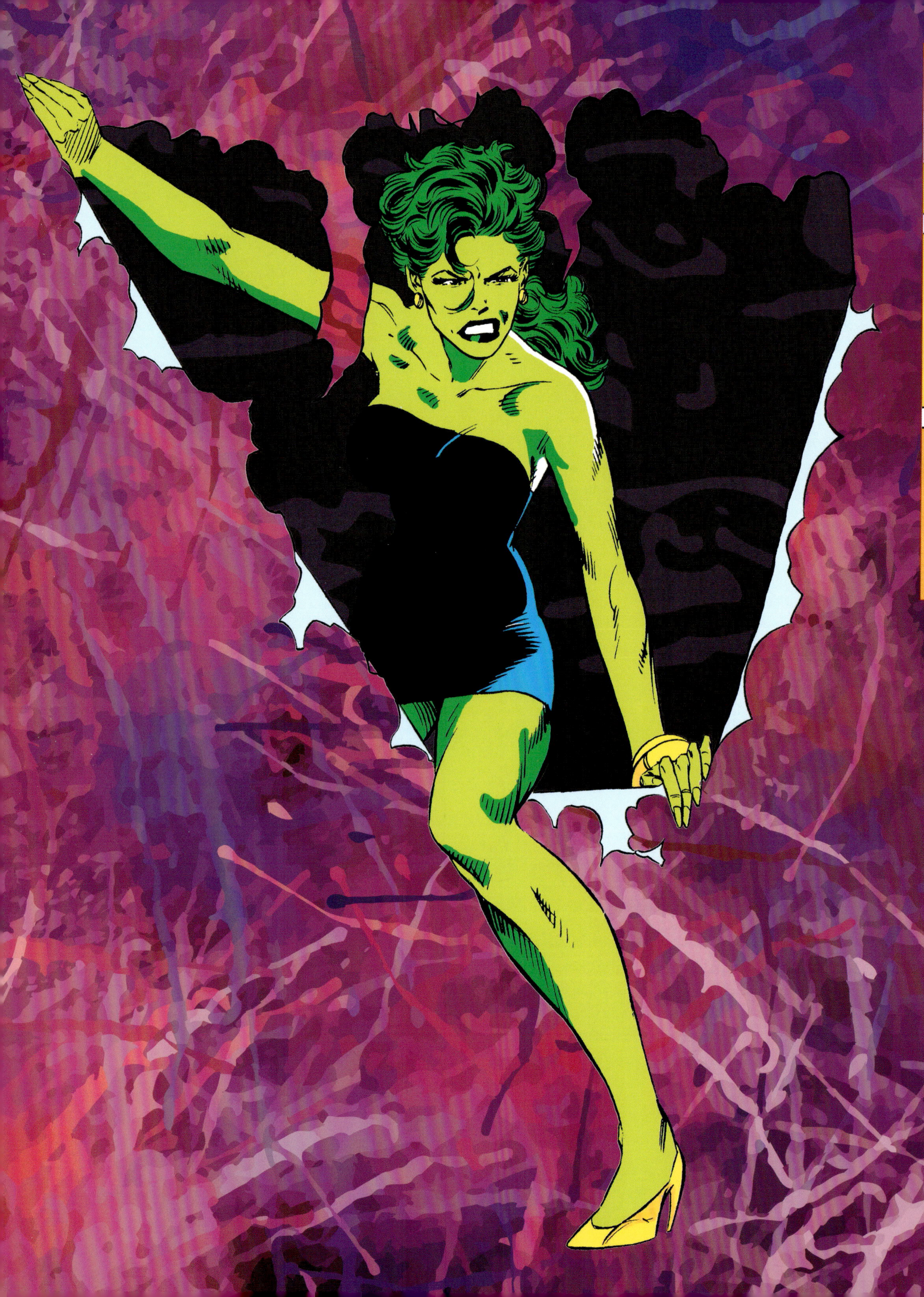

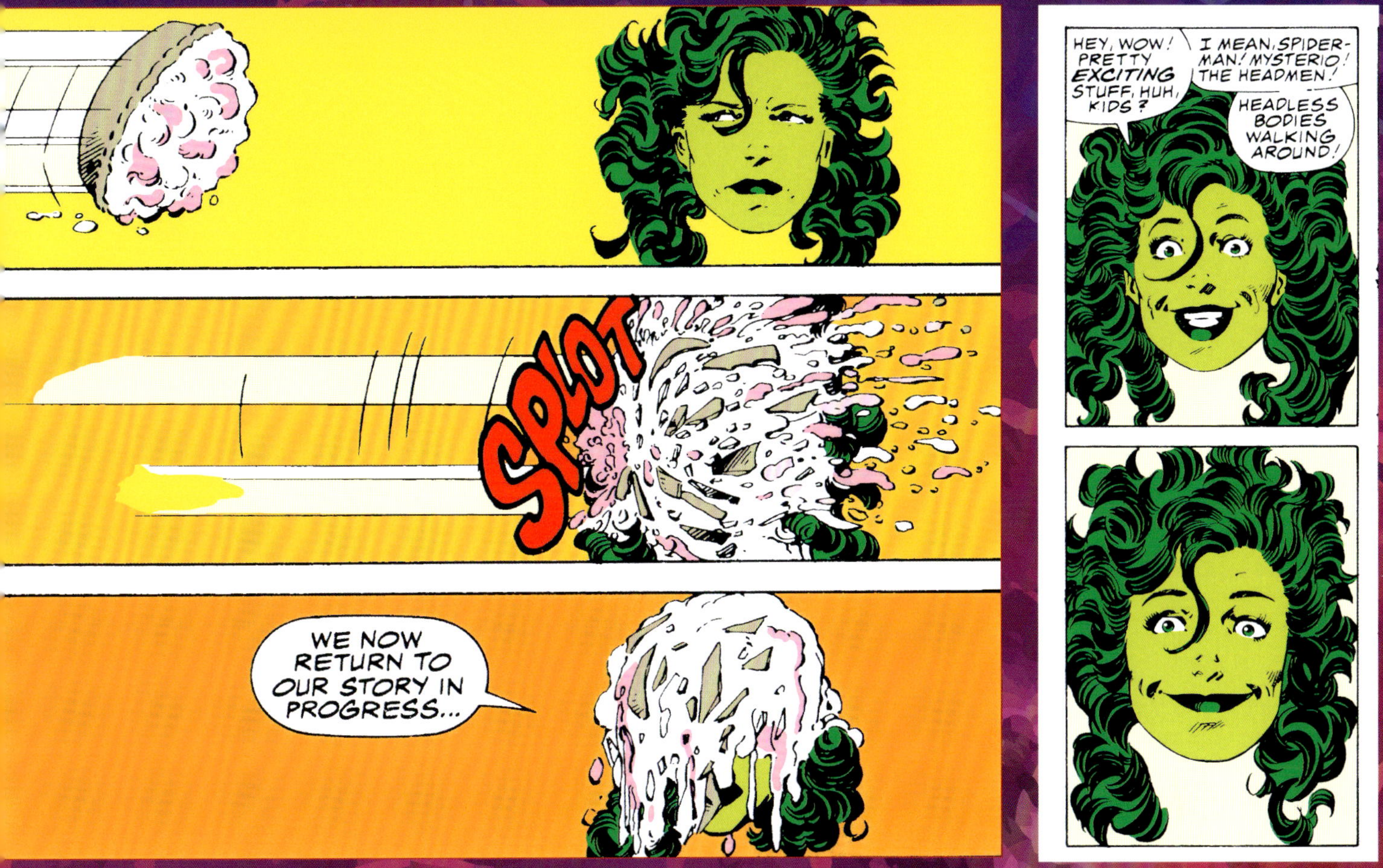
SPLOT
WE NOW RETURN TO OUR STORY IN PROGRESS...
HEY, WOW! PRETTY EXCITING STUFF, HUH, KIDS?
I MEAN, SPIDER-MAN! MYSTERIO! THE HEADMEN!
HEADLESS BODIES WALKING AROUND!

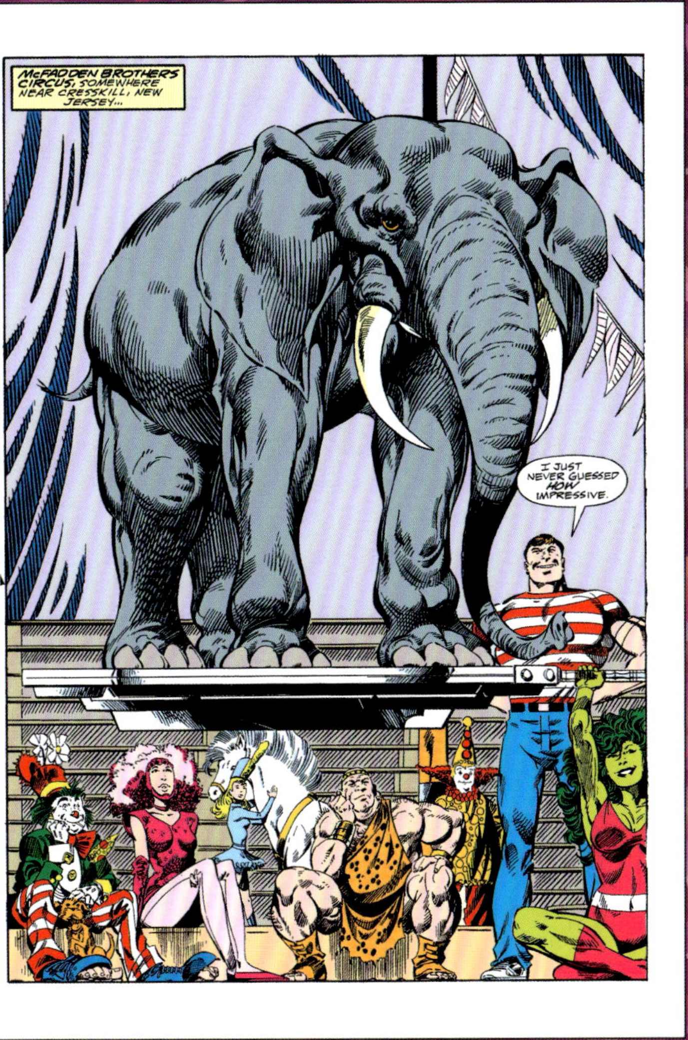
McFADDEN BROTHERS CIRCUS, SOMEWHERE NEAR CRESSKILL, NEW JERSEY...
I JUST NEVER GUESSED HOW IMPRESSIVE.

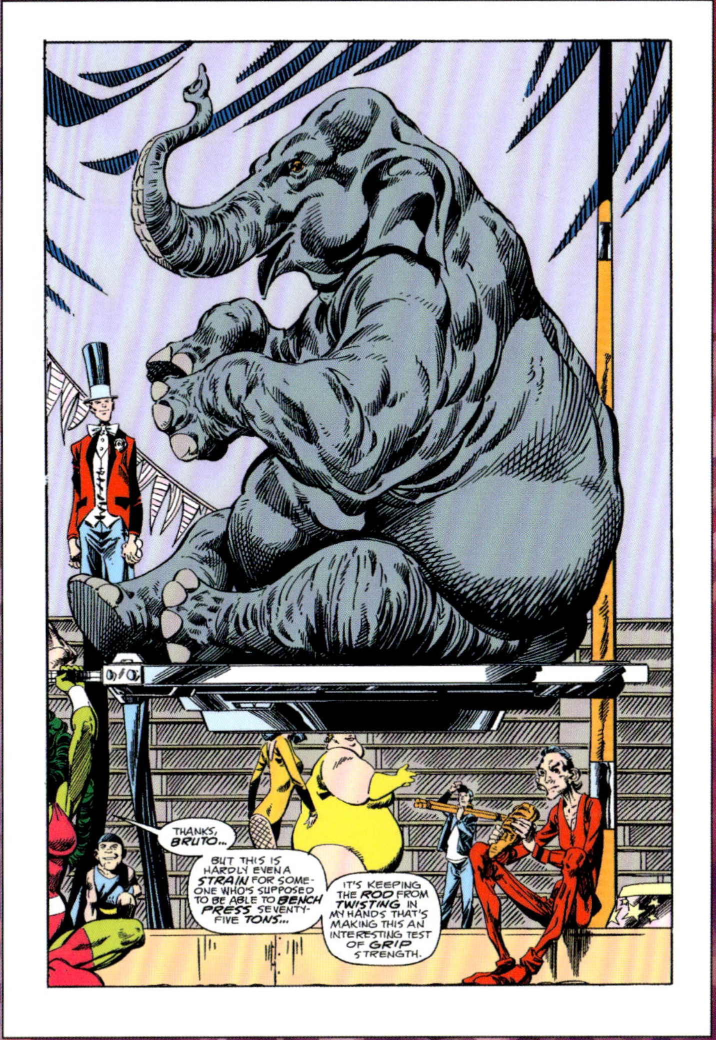
THANKS, BRUTO...
BUT THIS IS HARDLY EVEN A STRAIN FOR SOME-ONE WHO'S SUPPOSED TO BE ABLE TO BENCH PRESS SEVENTY-FIVE TONS...
IT'S KEEPING THE ROD FROM TWISTING IN MY HANDS THAT'S MAKING THIS AN INTERESTING TEST OF GRIP STRENGTH.

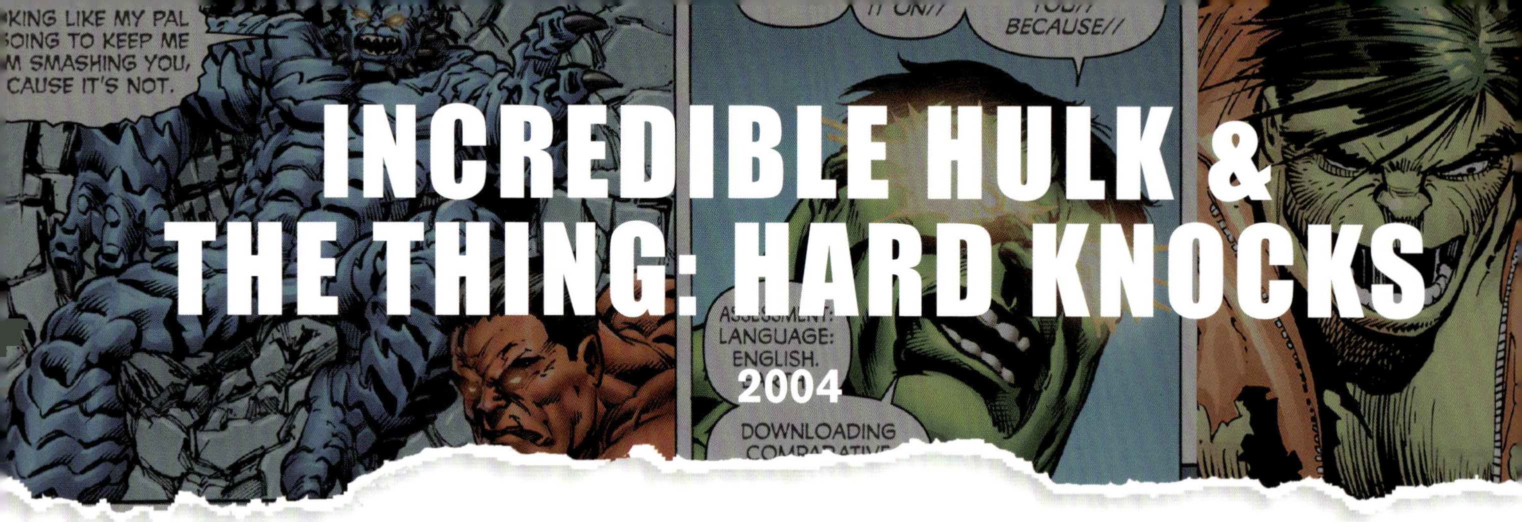
CAUSE IT'S NOT.
BECAUSE//
LANGUAGE:
ENGLISH.
DOWNLOADING

# INCREDIBLE HULK & THE THING: HARD KNOCKS

## 2004

A man sits alone in a diner in the middle of the desert sipping a cup of coffee. He knows that the desert is where it started, and where it all changed for him. He wasn't supposed to have been out there in the desert; he wasn't supposed to have been caught in the blast. But he spotted someone who needed help, someone was in the blast zone. He saved that person who later became a friend—Rick Jones. Bruce Banner saved the young man in the desert, but he paid a price. That day, Bruce Banner became the Hulk.

A large orange figure appears on the stool next to him. The stool groans under the weight. Bruce's new companion is someone he has known a long time. They call him the Thing, aka Ben Grimm. Like Banner, his life, too, was transformed by a dose of radiation. Grimm was exposed to cosmic radiation during his fateful trip into space, which morphed him into the Thing.

While they were both transformed into creatures who have enormous strength, there is one major difference between the two: the Hulk can turn back into Banner. The Thing is unable to change back into Ben Grimm. This former test pilot and astronaut is now trapped within his new rocklike body, and he has never been happy about it.

But Grimm isn't there to talk to Banner—the Thing wants to talk to the Hulk. Something is troubling Grimm, and he wants to share it with the Hulk. In order for the Hulk to manifest, Grimm needs to make Banner angry and Grimm figures that the quickest way to do that is to knock Banner though the diner wall. It works just fine; the Hulk appears and sits down to join the Thing for coffee.

The Thing has a story to tell the Hulk. He relays an incident with Doctor Doom. Doom enlisted the Fantastic Four to help him find Blackbeard's treasure chest, and so he and the team traveled back in time. The Thing and Doom soon battled, but he quickly found out that this Doom was not the real Doom, but a robot. The Fantastic Four found themselves trapped by Doom in the pirate's chamber. Doom drained the air out of the chamber. Mr. Fantastic, the Invisible Girl, and the Human Torch found a way out of the

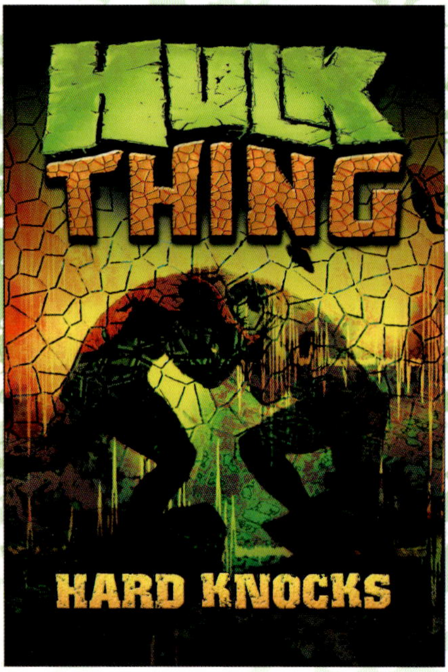
HULK
THING
HARD KNOCKS

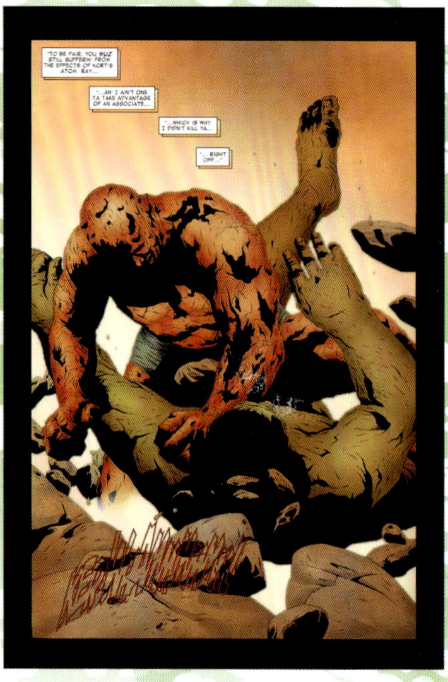

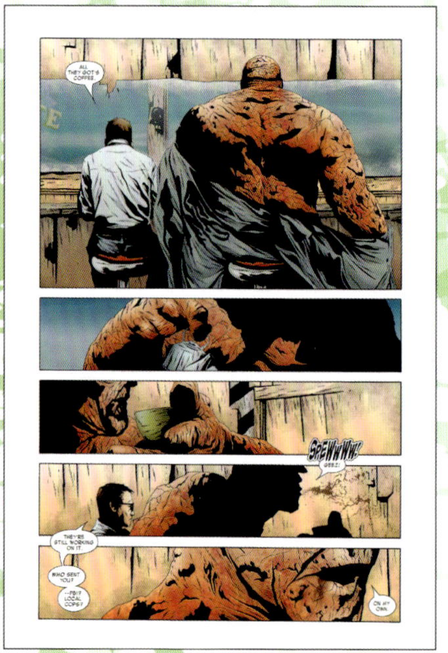

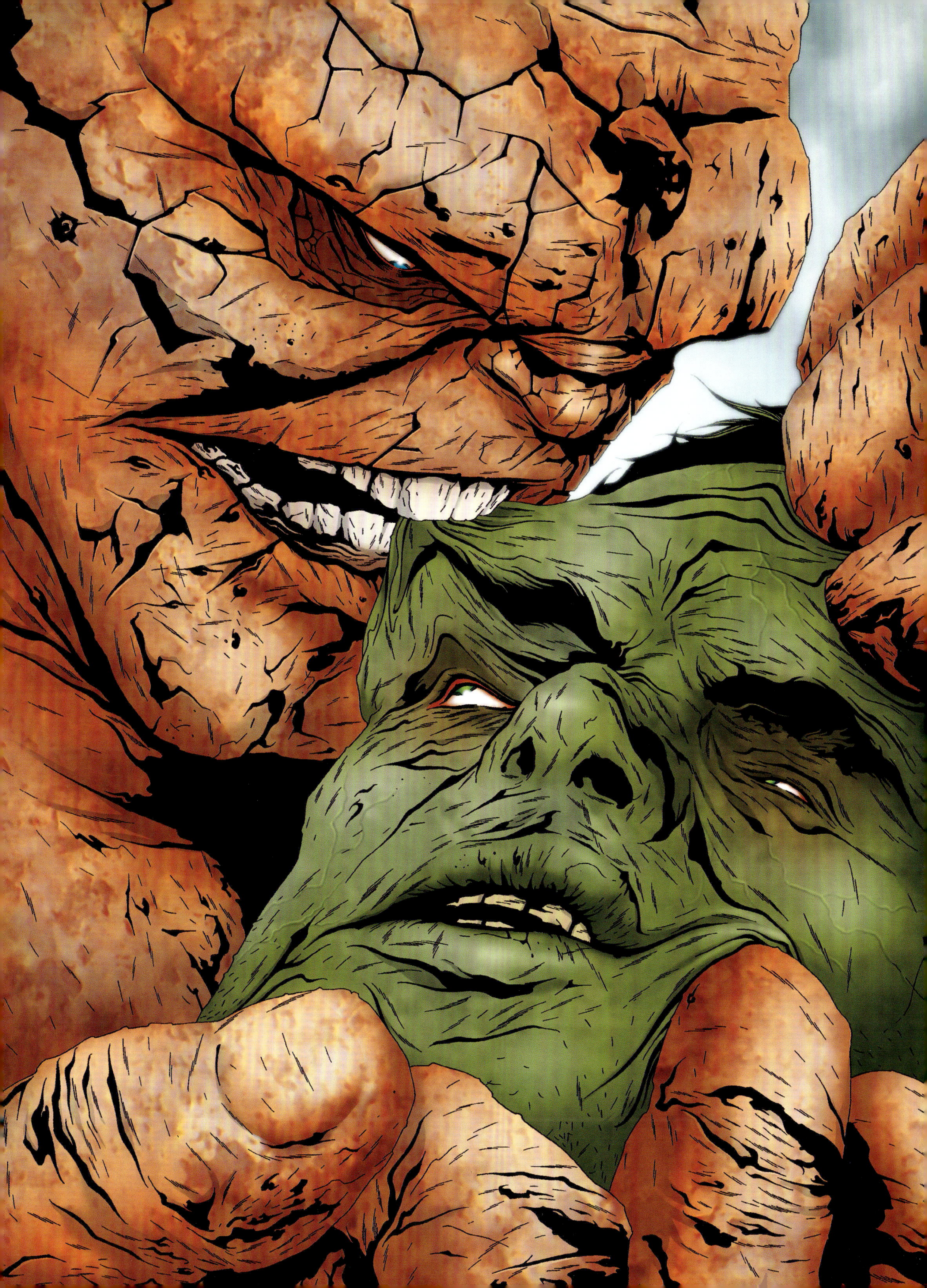

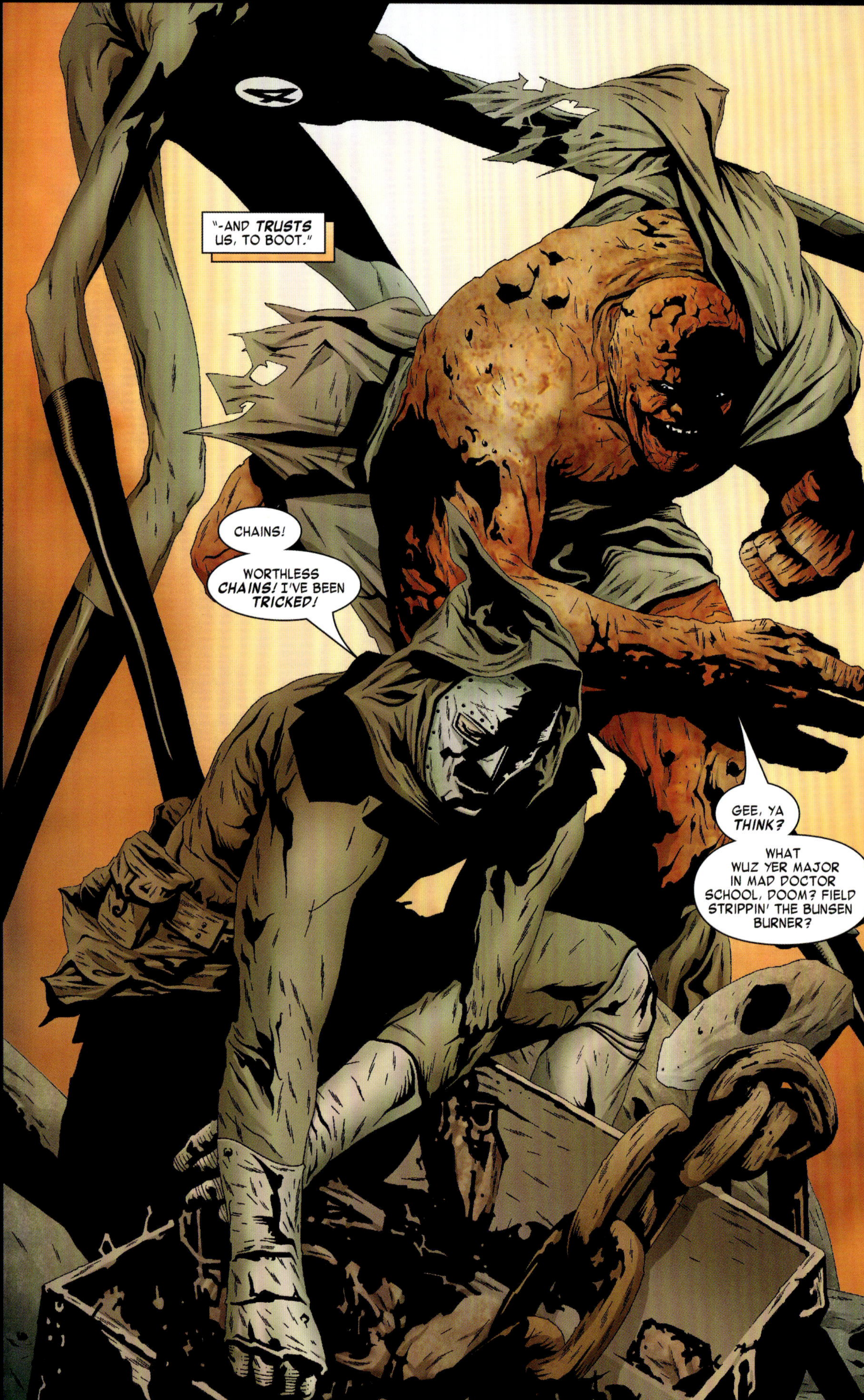
"-AND TRUSTS US, TO BOOT."
CHAINS!
WORTHLESS CHAINS! I'VE BEEN TRICKED!
GEE, YA THINK?
WHAT WUZ YER MAJOR IN MAD DOCTOR SCHOOL, DOOM? FIELD STRIPPIN' THE BUNSEN BURNER?

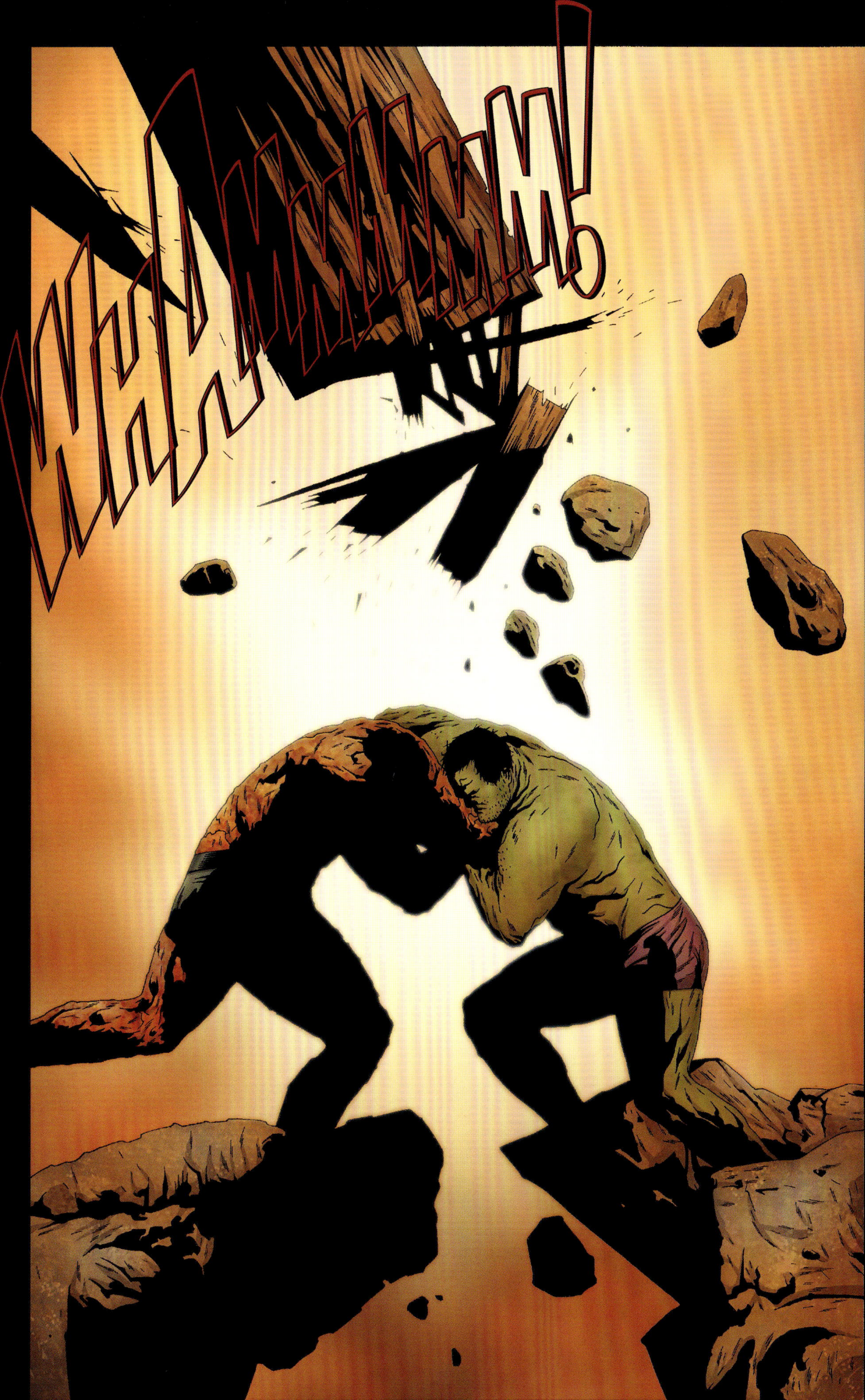

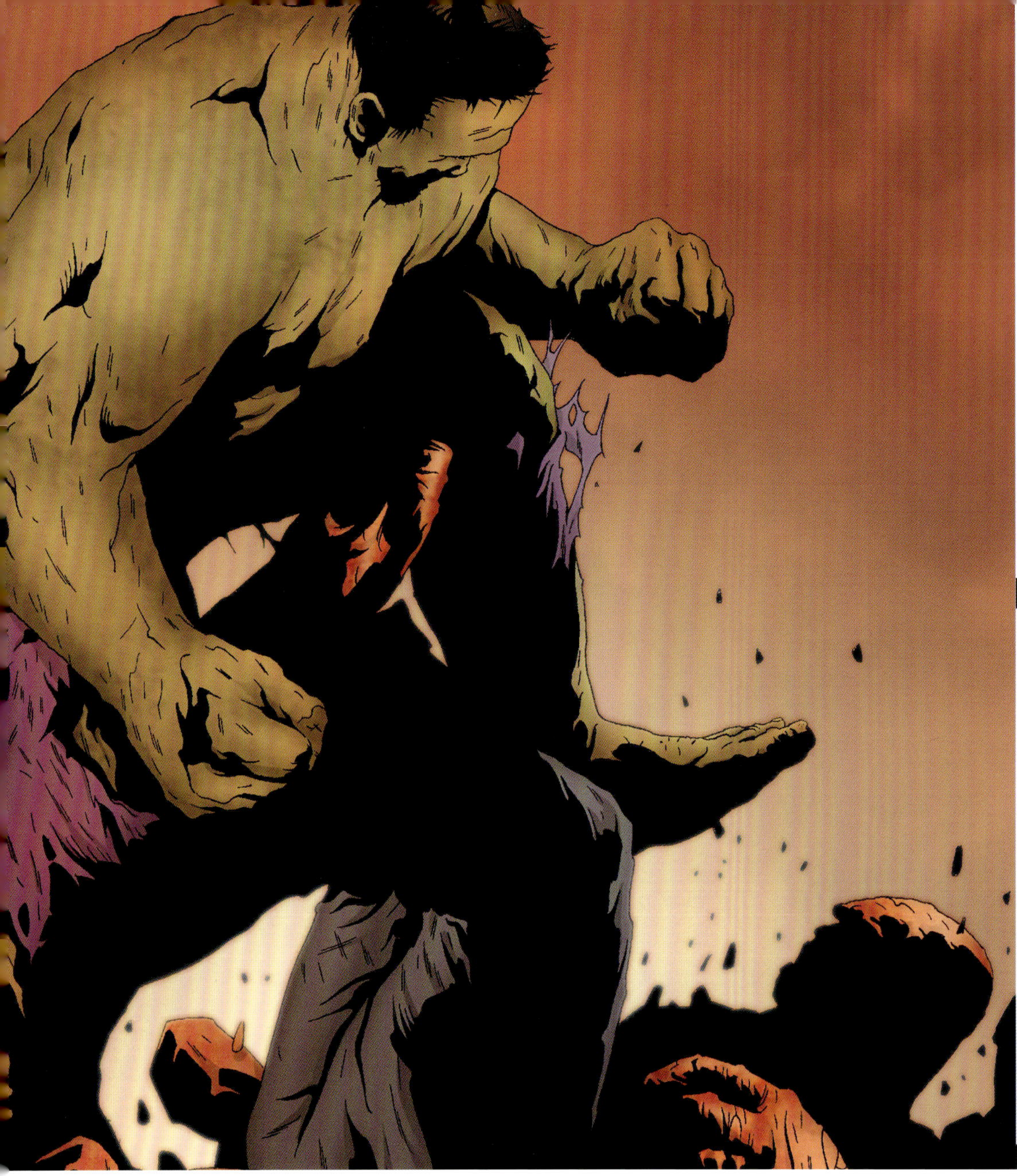

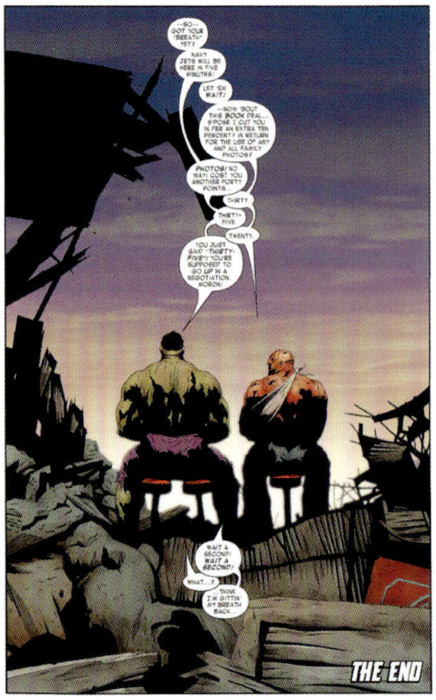
--SO-- GOT YOUR "BREATH" YET?
NAVY JETS WILL BE HERE IN FIVE MINUTES!
LET 'EM WAIT!
--NOW 'BOUT THIS BOOK DEAL... S'POSE I CUT YOU IN FER AN EXTRA TEN PERCENT? IN RETURN FOR THE USE OF ANY AND ALL FAMILY PHOTOS?
PHOTOS! NO WAY! COST YOU ANOTHER FORTY POINTS...
THIRTY.
THIRTY-FIVE.
TWENTY.
YOU JUST SAID "THIRTY-FIVE"! YOU'RE SUPPOSED TO GO UP IN A NEGOTIATION, MORON!
WAIT A SECOND! WAIT A SECOND!
WHAT...?
...THINK I'M GITTIN' MY BREATH BACK...
THE END

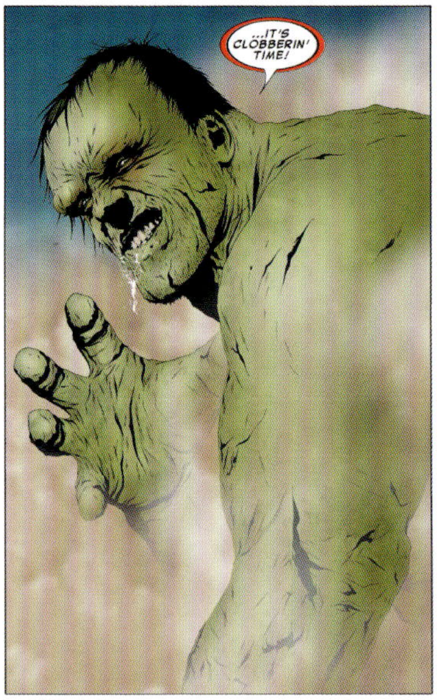
...IT'S CLOBBERIN' TIME!

chamber, and when they returned to their own reality, the real Doom mocked the Thing for having done nothing to save himself and his friends. Doom questioned the Thing's intelligence, asking, "Is this the face of a hero?" Doom calls him the Thing—a freak, a monster. He said that he "will kill the mon—," and the Thing finishes his sentence: the word was monster.

The Thing's exchange with Doom is the reason the Thing has come to see the Hulk. They were both ordinary men who, through freak accidents, were changed forever. Because of their appearances and their strength, the Hulk and the Thing are viewed by many as monsters. Consider even the names of their alter egos. Ben Grimm is called the Thing. A thing is not a person, but an object. He didn't get a cool super hero name. In fact, in the Thing's origin story, Sue Storm, the Invisible Woman, shouts to her husband, Reed Richards, "He's turned into a—a—some sort of thing!" The name the Hulk was coined in first issue of *The Incredible Hulk*. One soldier who was part of a group sent to track down the creature that appeared in the desert after the bomb dropped referred to the creature as a Hulk.

The Thing reminds the Hulk of the first time they fought. In their first battle, after the Thing finally knocked out the Hulk, something unexpected happened. The Hulk turned back into the human Banner. Until that moment, the Thing didn't realize there was a man beneath the monster, and that they were the same: men trapped inside monstrous bodies. Ben wants Bruce to know that he understands him and that he is not alone.

But the bonds Grimm tries to build are tested when suddenly the US Army attacks the Hulk. They were outside with the Thing all this time. After all, can Banner really trust someone who extends an olive branch with military backup? How do you apologize for helicopters in the air and rockets exploding? Will the Thing and the Hulk join forces? And will they finally realize they have more in common than they are willing to acknowledge?

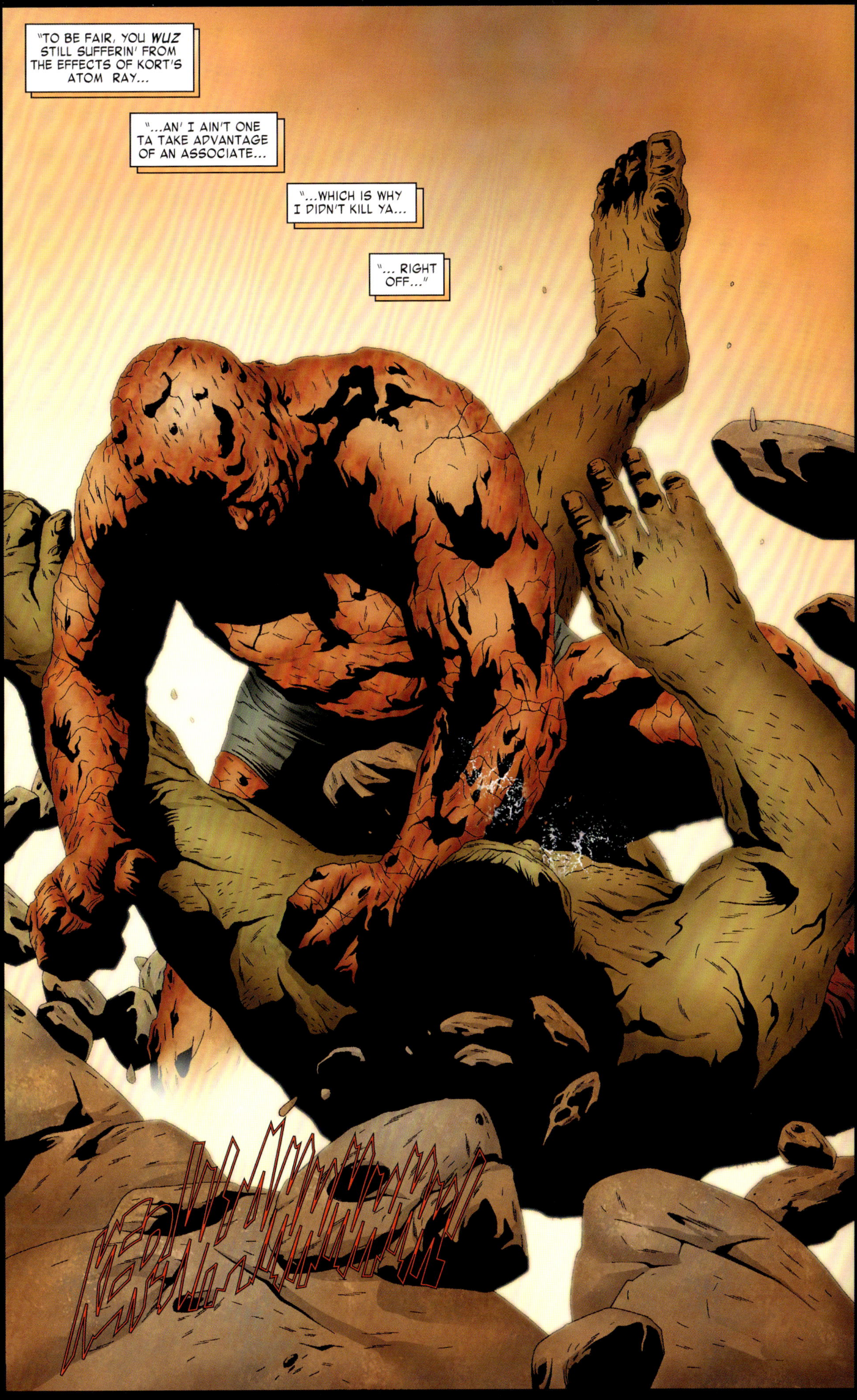
"TO BE FAIR, YOU *WUZ* STILL SUFFERIN' FROM THE EFFECTS OF KORT'S ATOM RAY...
"...AN' I AIN'T ONE TA TAKE ADVANTAGE OF AN ASSOCIATE...
"...WHICH IS WHY I DIDN'T KILL YA...
"... RIGHT OFF..."

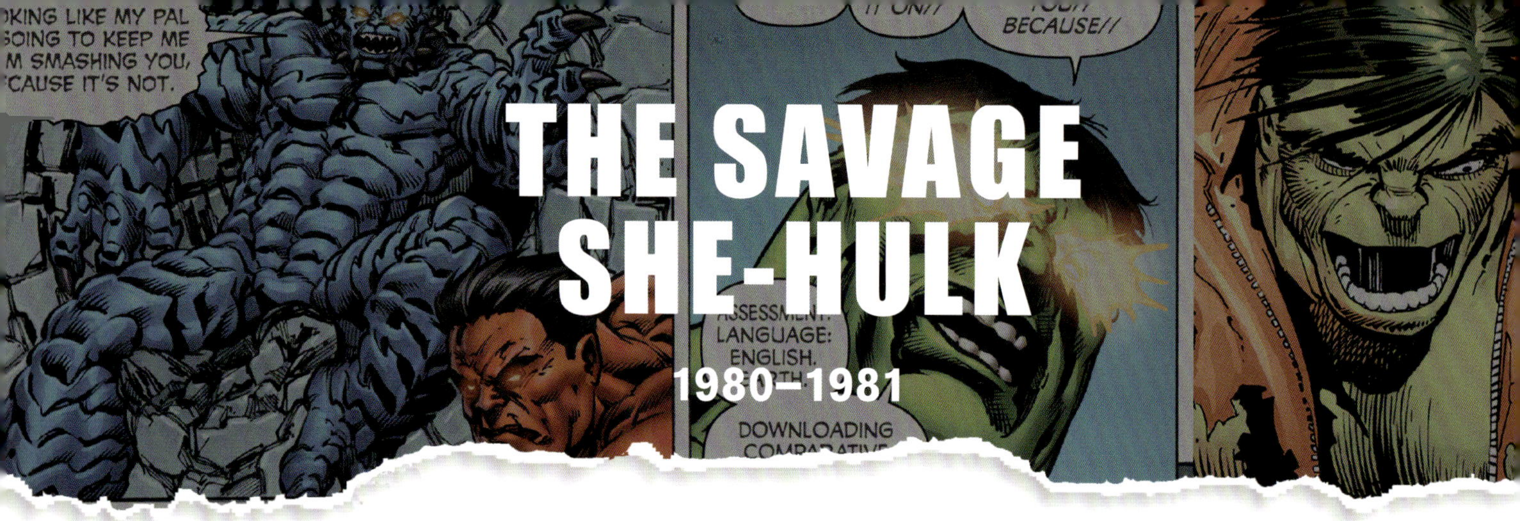
BECAUSE//
LANGUAGE:
ENGLISH.
DOWNLOADING

# THE SAVAGE SHE-HULK

## 1980–1981

Bruce Banner is in Los Angeles to reconnect with Jennifer Walters, his younger cousin who has become a successful criminal lawyer. At one time she was like a younger sister to the scientist. Banner surprises Jennifer at her office, and she is thrilled to see him. But Banner can't hide the burden he carries. He tells Jen that he is a wanted man and he confesses that the police (and also what sometimes feels like the whole human race) are after him. Banner explains to her what happened to him in the desert when the gamma bomb turned him into the Hulk.

Jen offers to help him, but Banner is afraid that her help will put her in danger. However, she finds that, as a criminal lawyer, she, too, is often in danger. For example, she is defending a thug named Monkton, who is accused of killing the bodyguard of crime boss Nick Trask. While Jen has no evidence to prove it, she believes Monkton was framed for the murder. She has devised a plan to lure out the real killer: Jen has planted evidence that would point the finger back to Trask, hoping to spark a reaction from him.

Indeed, it does garner a reaction, a couple of Trask's thugs shadow Bruce and Jennifer. Jennifer picks up Bruce at the airport, and as they are pulling into her driveway the mobsters jump out of a car and take a shot at Jen, hitting her in the back. Banner uses a garden hose to hold back the hit men, knowing that if he turns into the Hulk, he can't help save his cousin's life. The shooter and his companions speed off as Banner manages to get Jen to a doctor's office. He breaks in and tends to her wound. She has lost a lot of blood. Banner happens to know that he and his cousin have the same blood type, so he starts a transfusion using his own blood.

Banner calls the police, and Jen is taken to the hospital. They inform Banner that he is a suspect in Jen's injury, but they leave him alone in a room while they go to phone the DA. Banner's temper rises. The cops return to a giant hole in the wall and Banner gone.

Back at the hospital, Jen is recovering. But walking down the hall are the goons who tried to kill her, and they are there to finish the

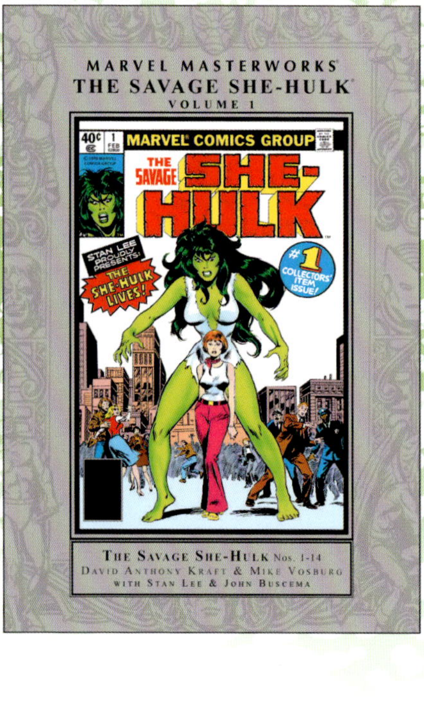
MARVEL MASTERWORKS
THE SAVAGE SHE-HULK
VOLUME 1
MARVEL COMICS GROUP
THE SAVAGE SHE-HULK
STAN LEE PROUDLY PRESENTS!
THE SHE-HULK LIVES!
#1 COLLECTORS' ITEM ISSUE!
THE SAVAGE SHE-HULK Nos. 1-14
DAVID ANTHONY KRAFT & MIKE VOSBURG
WITH STAN LEE & JOHN BUSCEMA

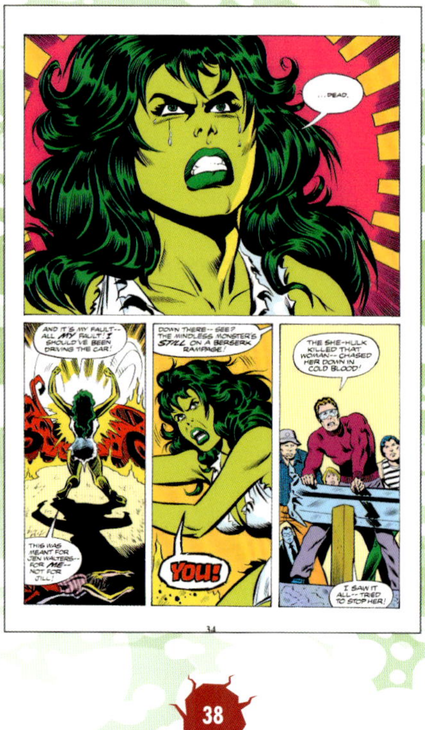
...DEAD.
AND IT'S MY FAULT-- ALL MY FAULT! I SHOULD'VE BEEN DRIVING THE CAR!
THIS WAS MEANT FOR JEN WALTERS-- FOR ME-- NOT FOR JILL!
DOWN THERE-- SEE? THE MINDLESS MONSTER'S STILL ON A BERSERK RAMPAGE!
YOU!
THE SHE-HULK KILLED THAT WOMAN-- CHASED HER DOWN IN COLD BLOOD!
I SAW IT ALL-- TRIED TO STOP HER!

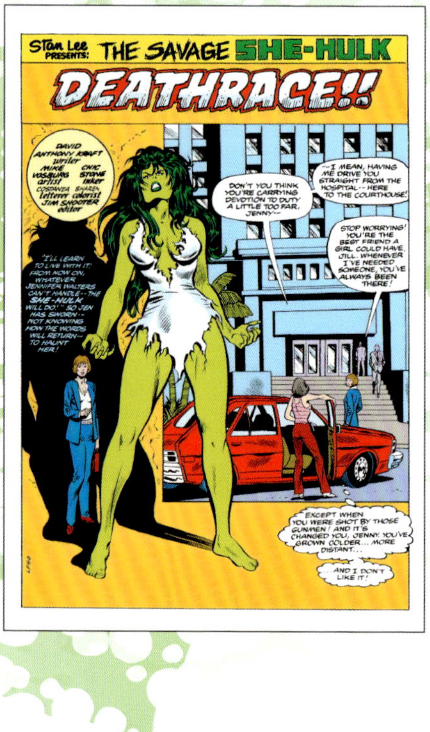
STAN LEE PRESENTS: THE SAVAGE SHE-HULK
DEATHRACE!!
DAVID ANTHONY KRAFT writer
MIKE VOSBURG artist
CHIC STONE inker
COSTANZA letterer
SHAREN colorist
JIM SHOOTER editor
"I'LL LEARN TO LIVE WITH IT! FROM NOW ON, WHATEVER JENNIFER WALTERS CAN'T HANDLE-- THE SHE-HULK WILL DO!" SO JEN HAS SWORN-- NOT KNOWING HOW THE WORDS WILL RETURN-- TO HAUNT HER!
DON'T YOU THINK YOU'RE CARRYING DEVOTION TO DUTY A LITTLE TOO FAR, JENNY--
--I MEAN, HAVING ME DRIVE YOU STRAIGHT FROM THE HOSPITAL-- HERE TO THE COURTHOUSE!
STOP WORRYING! YOU'RE THE BEST FRIEND A GIRL COULD HAVE, JILL. WHENEVER I'VE NEEDED SOMEONE, YOU'VE ALWAYS BEEN THERE!
EXCEPT WHEN YOU WERE SHOT BY THOSE GUNMEN! AND IT'S CHANGED YOU, JENNY. YOU'VE GROWN COLDER... MORE DISTANT...
...AND I DON'T LIKE IT!

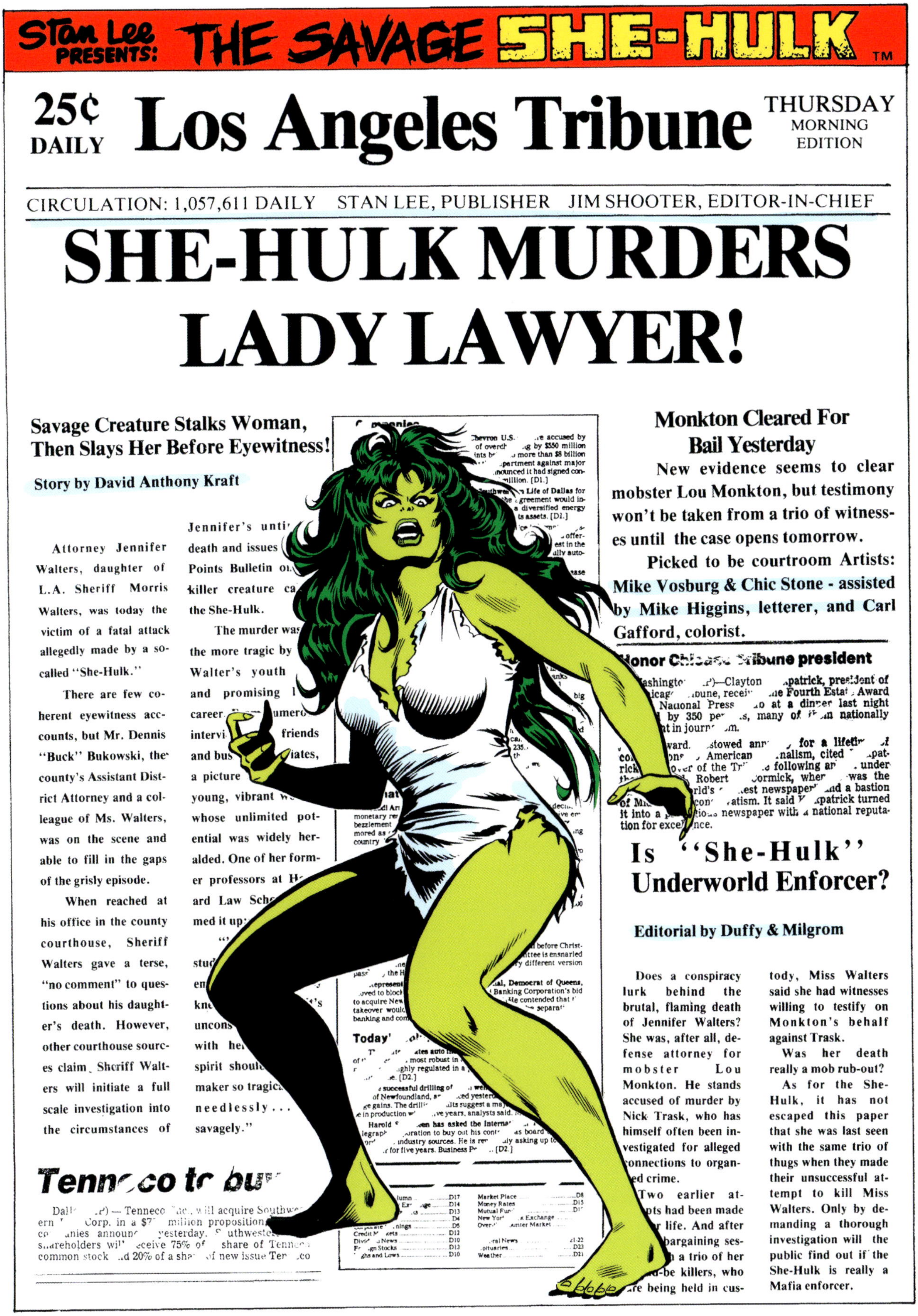

Stan Lee PRESENTS: THE SAVAGE SHE-HULK TM
25¢ DAILY
Los Angeles Tribune
THURSDAY MORNING EDITION
CIRCULATION: 1,057,611 DAILY STAN LEE, PUBLISHER JIM SHOOTER, EDITOR-IN-CHIEF
SHE-HULK MURDERS LADY LAWYER!
Savage Creature Stalks Woman, Then Slays Her Before Eyewitness!
Story by David Anthony Kraft
Attorney Jennifer Walters, daughter of L.A. Sheriff Morris Walters, was today the victim of a fatal attack allegedly made by a so-called "She-Hulk."
There are few coherent eyewitness accounts, but Mr. Dennis "Buck" Bukowski, the county's Assistant District Attorney and a colleague of Ms. Walters, was on the scene and able to fill in the gaps of the grisly episode.
When reached at his office in the county courthouse, Sheriff Walters gave a terse, "no comment" to questions about his daughter's death. However, other courthouse sources claim Sheriff Walters will initiate a full scale investigation into the circumstances of
Jennifer's
death and issues
Points Bulletin
killer creature
the She-Hulk.
The murder was
the more tragic by
Walter's youth
and promising
career.
interv
friends
and bus
iates,
a picture
young, vibrant
whose unlimited potential was widely heralded. One of her former professors at
ard Law
med it up:
stu
en
kn
uncons
with
spirit should
maker so tragic
needlessly...
savagely."
Monkton Cleared For Bail Yesterday
New evidence seems to clear mobster Lou Monkton, but testimony won't be taken from a trio of witnesses until the case opens tomorrow.
Picked to be courtroom Artists: Mike Vosburg & Chic Stone - assisted by Mike Higgins, letterer, and Carl Gafford, colorist.
Is "She-Hulk" Underworld Enforcer?
Editorial by Duffy & Milgrom
Does a conspiracy lurk behind the brutal, flaming death of Jennifer Walters? She was, after all, defense attorney for mobster Lou Monkton. He stands accused of murder by Nick Trask, who has himself often been investigated for alleged connections to organized crime.
Two earlier attempts had been made on her life. And after plea bargaining sessions with a trio of her would-be killers, who are being held in custody, Miss Walters said she had witnesses willing to testify on Monkton's behalf against Trask.
Was her death really a mob rub-out?
As for the She-Hulk, it has not escaped this paper that she was last seen with the same trio of thugs when they made their unsuccessful attempt to kill Miss Walters. Only by demanding a thorough investigation will the public find out if the She-Hulk is really a Mafia enforcer.

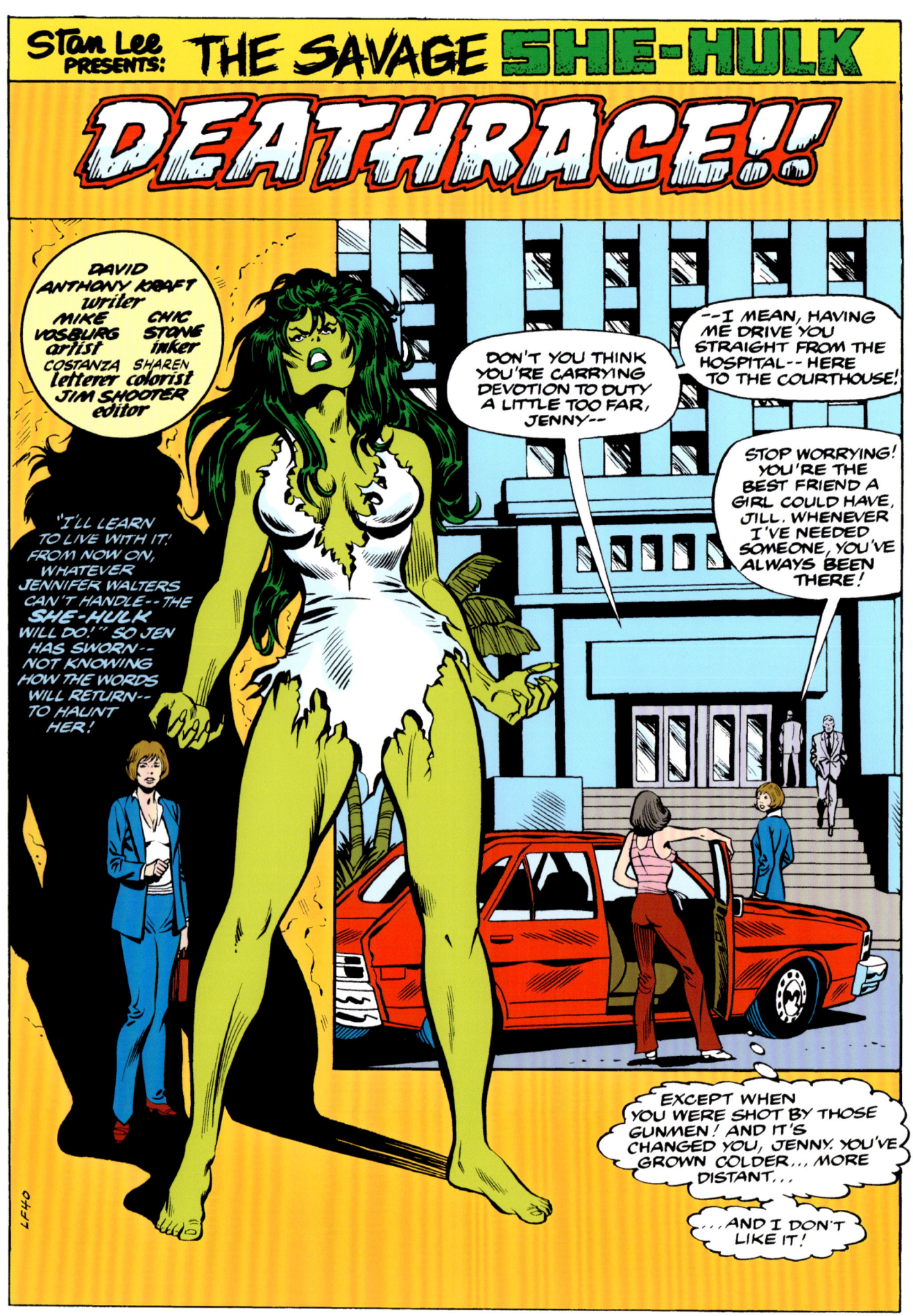

# THE SAVAGE SHE-HULK

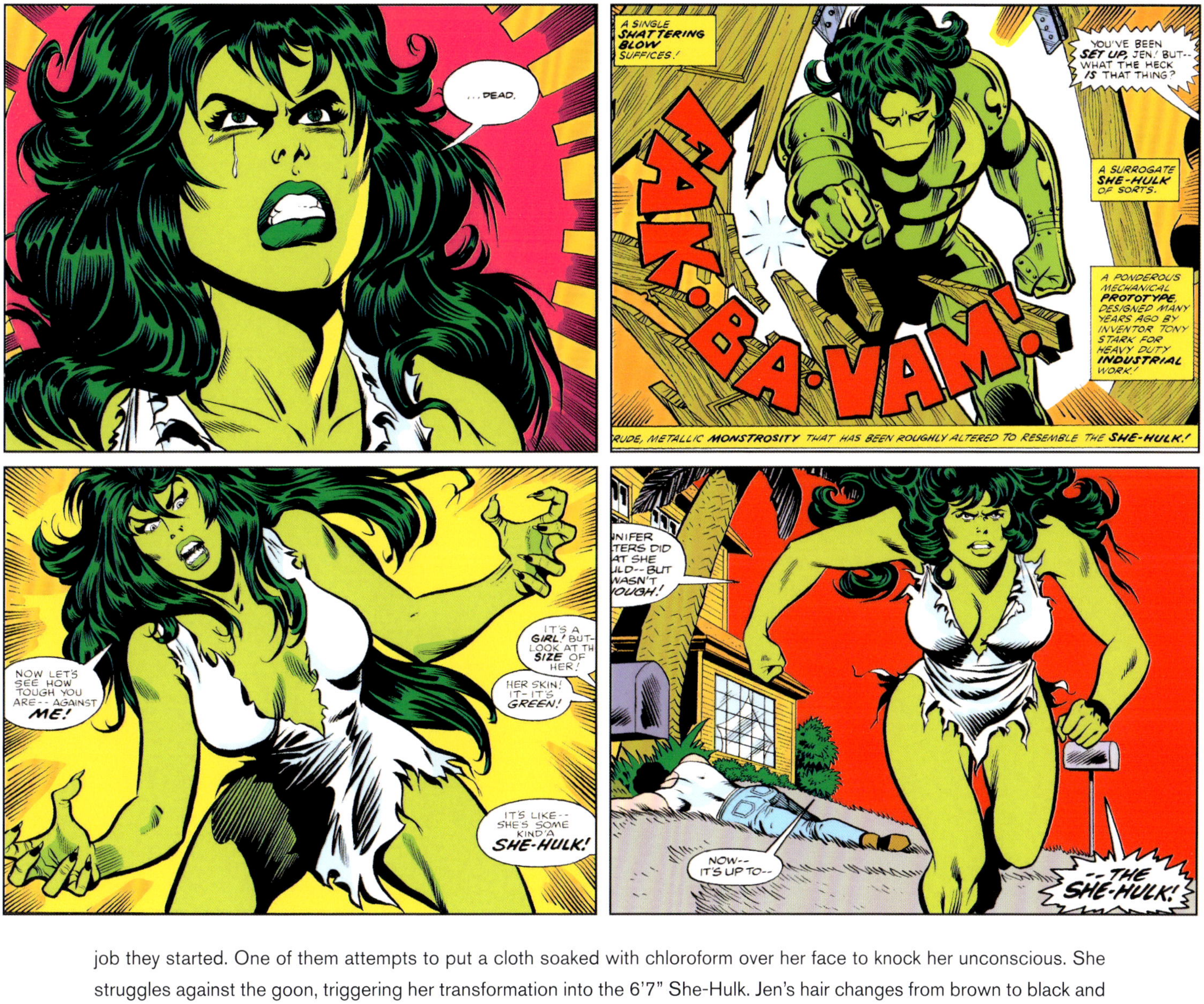
...DEAD.
A SINGLE SHATTERING BLOW SUFFICES!
YOU'VE BEEN SET UP, JEN! BUT-- WHAT THE HECK IS THAT THING?
A SURROGATE SHE-HULK OF SORTS.
FAK-BA-VAM!
A PONDEROUS MECHANICAL PROTOTYPE, DESIGNED MANY YEARS AGO BY INVENTOR TONY STARK FOR HEAVY DUTY INDUSTRIAL WORK!
RUDE, METALLIC MONSTROSITY THAT HAS BEEN ROUGHLY ALTERED TO RESEMBLE THE SHE-HULK!
NOW LET'S SEE HOW TOUGH YOU ARE-- AGAINST ME!
IT'S A GIRL! BUT-- LOOK AT TH SIZE OF HER!
HER SKIN! IT-- IT'S GREEN!
IT'S LIKE-- SHE'S SOME KIND'A SHE-HULK!
NOW-- IT'S UP TO--
--THE SHE-HULK!

job they started. One of them attempts to put a cloth soaked with chloroform over her face to knock her unconscious. She struggles against the goon, triggering her transformation into the 6'7" She-Hulk. Jen's hair changes from brown to black and green, and her skin has also turned green. But, unlike her cousin Bruce, she retains her own mind. As the powerful She-Hulk, she soon learns that she can use the combination of her intelligence and her muscle for good.

Eighteen years after the Hulk made his first appearance, a female counterpart of big green finally appeared in the pages of the comics. Jennifer Walters would fight crime—both as a lawyer and a super hero. The combination of brains, beauty, and brawn proved irresistible to readers, and She-Hulk quickly became a fan favorite.

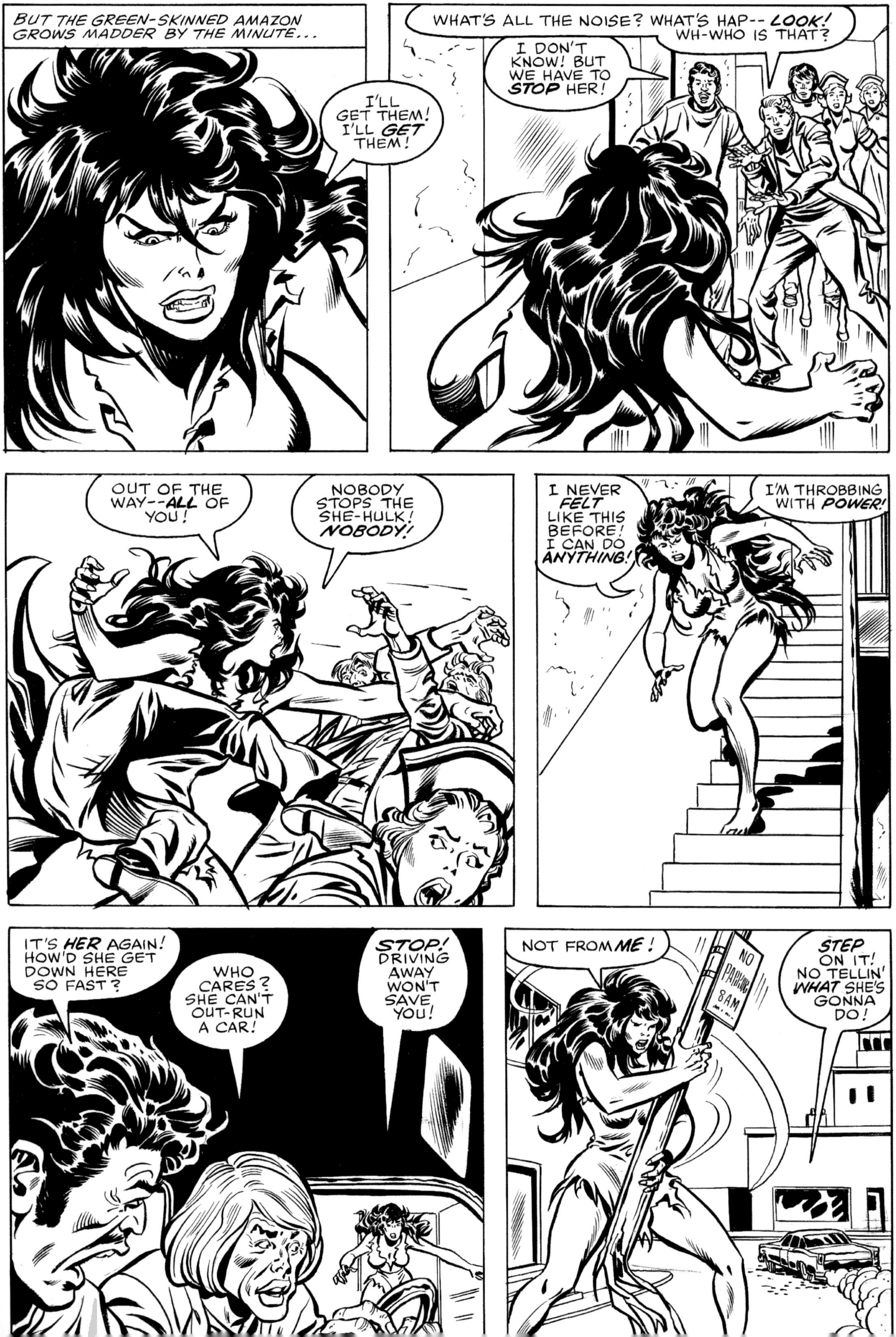
BUT THE GREEN-SKINNED AMAZON GROWS MADDER BY THE MINUTE...
I'LL GET THEM! I'LL GET THEM!
WHAT'S ALL THE NOISE? WHAT'S HAP-- LOOK! WH-WHO IS THAT?
I DON'T KNOW! BUT WE HAVE TO STOP HER!
OUT OF THE WAY--ALL OF YOU!
NOBODY STOPS THE SHE-HULK! NOBODY!
I NEVER FELT LIKE THIS BEFORE! I CAN DO ANYTHING!
I'M THROBBING WITH POWER!
IT'S HER AGAIN! HOW'D SHE GET DOWN HERE SO FAST?
WHO CARES? SHE CAN'T OUT-RUN A CAR!
STOP! DRIVING AWAY WON'T SAVE YOU!
NOT FROM ME!
NO PARKING 8AM
STEP ON IT! NO TELLIN' WHAT SHE'S GONNA DO!

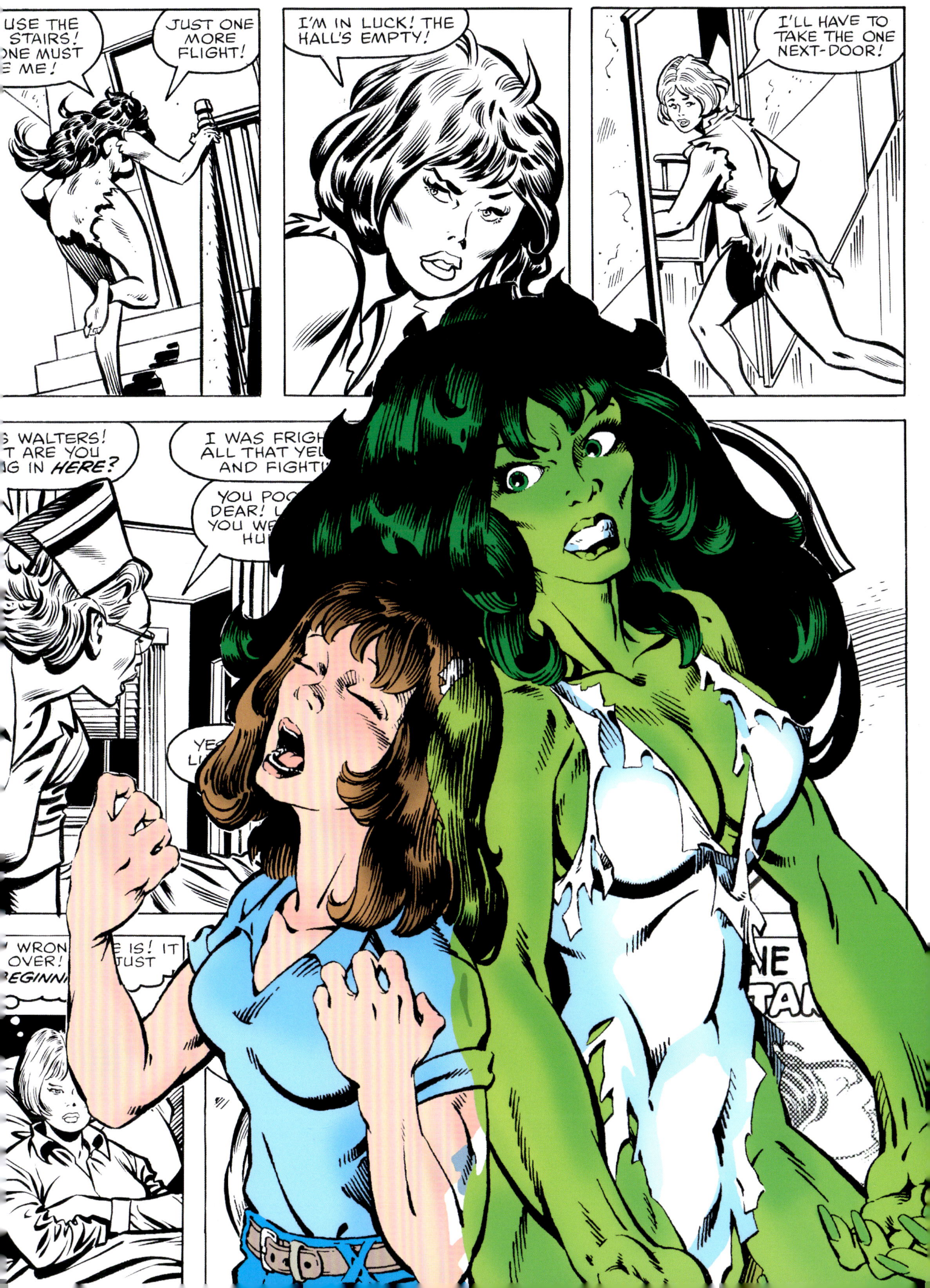
JUST ONE MORE FLIGHT!
I'M IN LUCK! THE HALL'S EMPTY!
I'LL HAVE TO TAKE THE ONE NEXT-DOOR!

# C2

## CHAPTER TWO:

# RAMPAGING

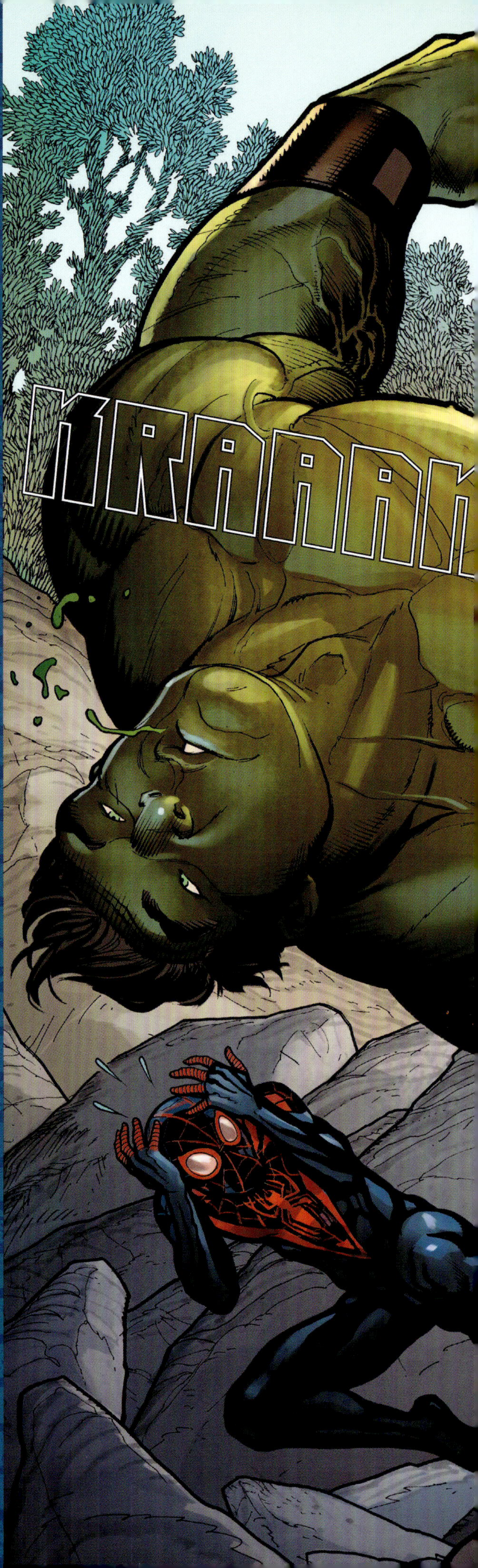
KRAAAK

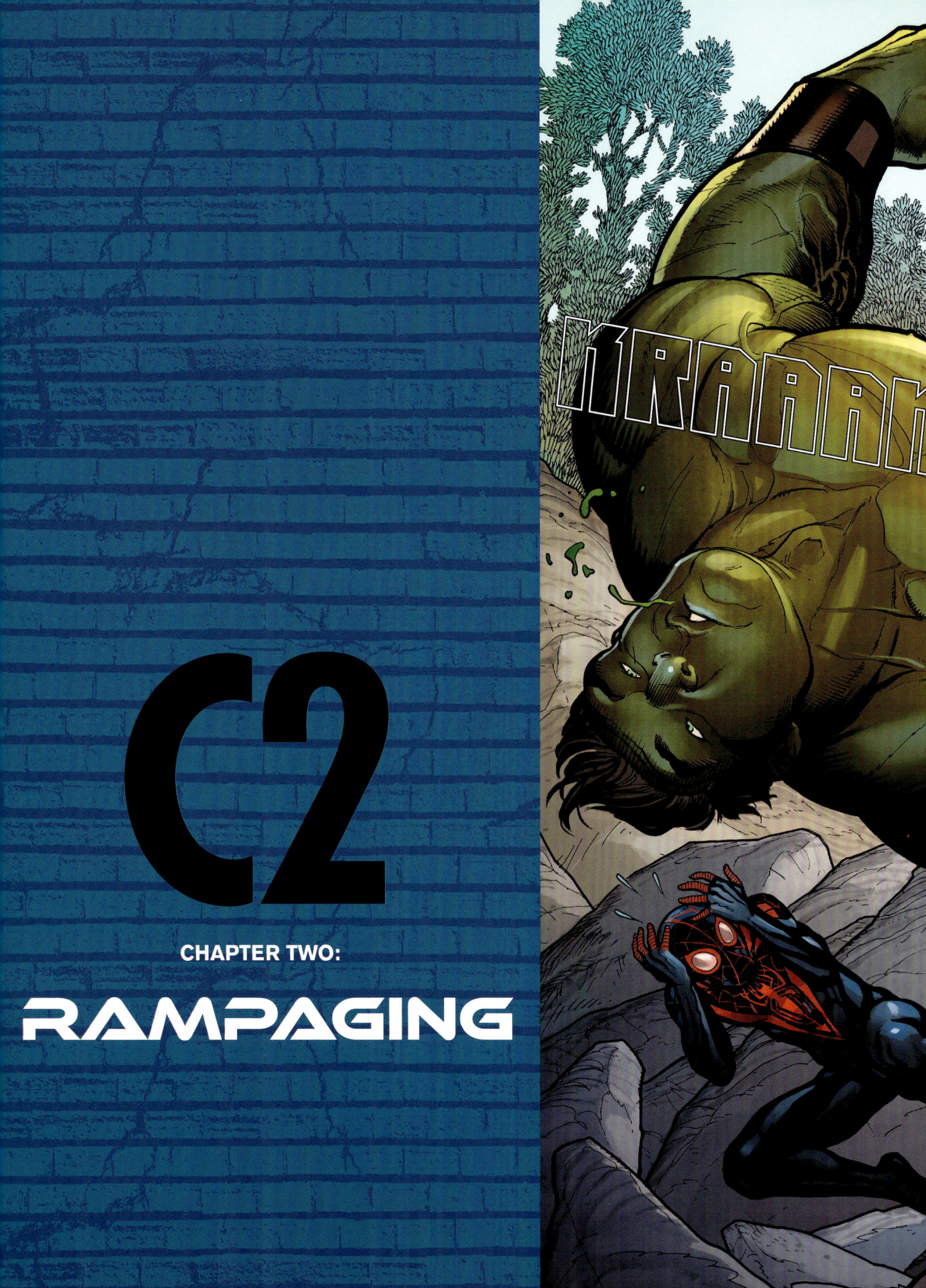

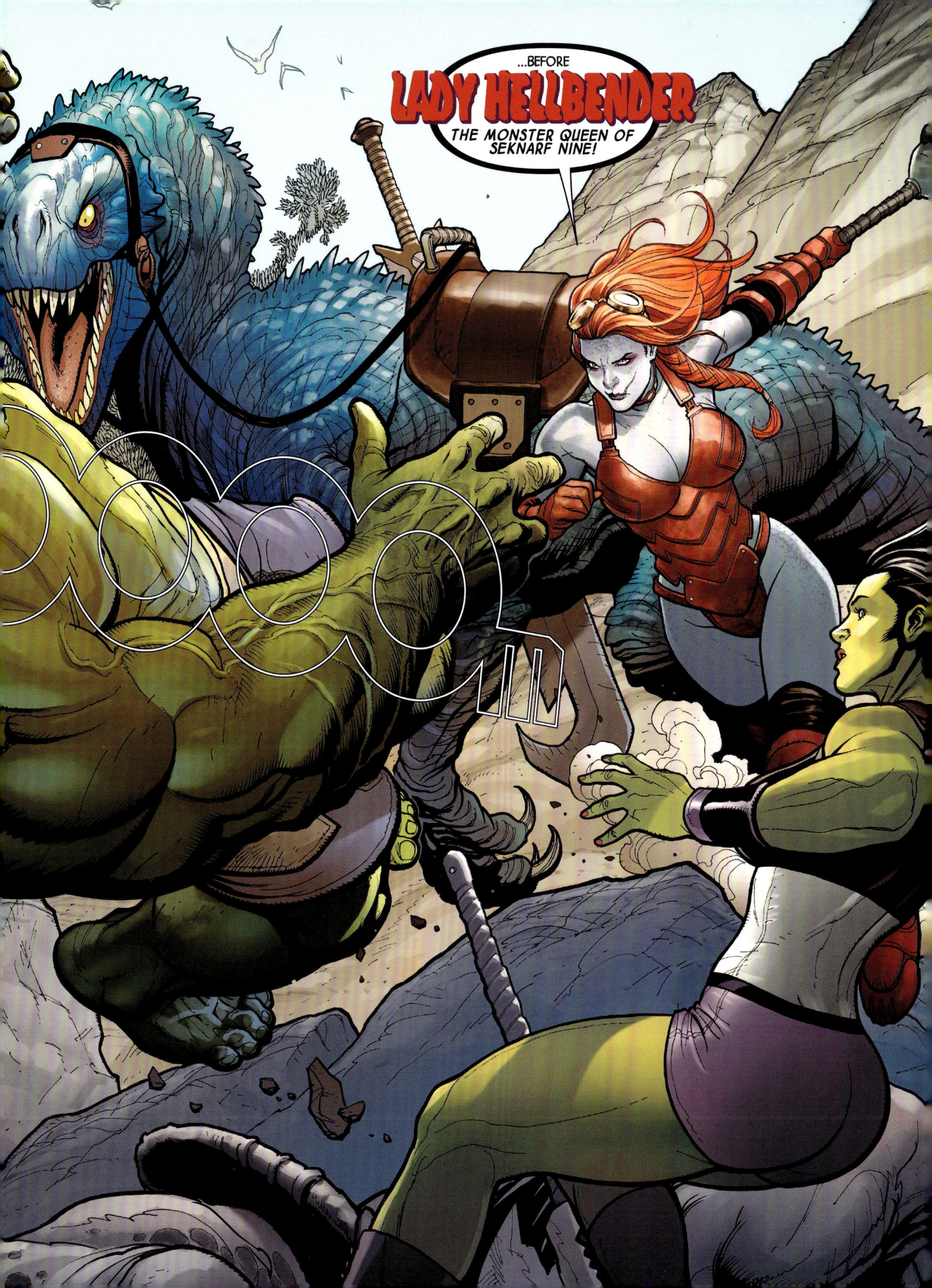
...BEFORE
LADY HELLBENDER
THE MONSTER QUEEN OF SEKNARF NINE!

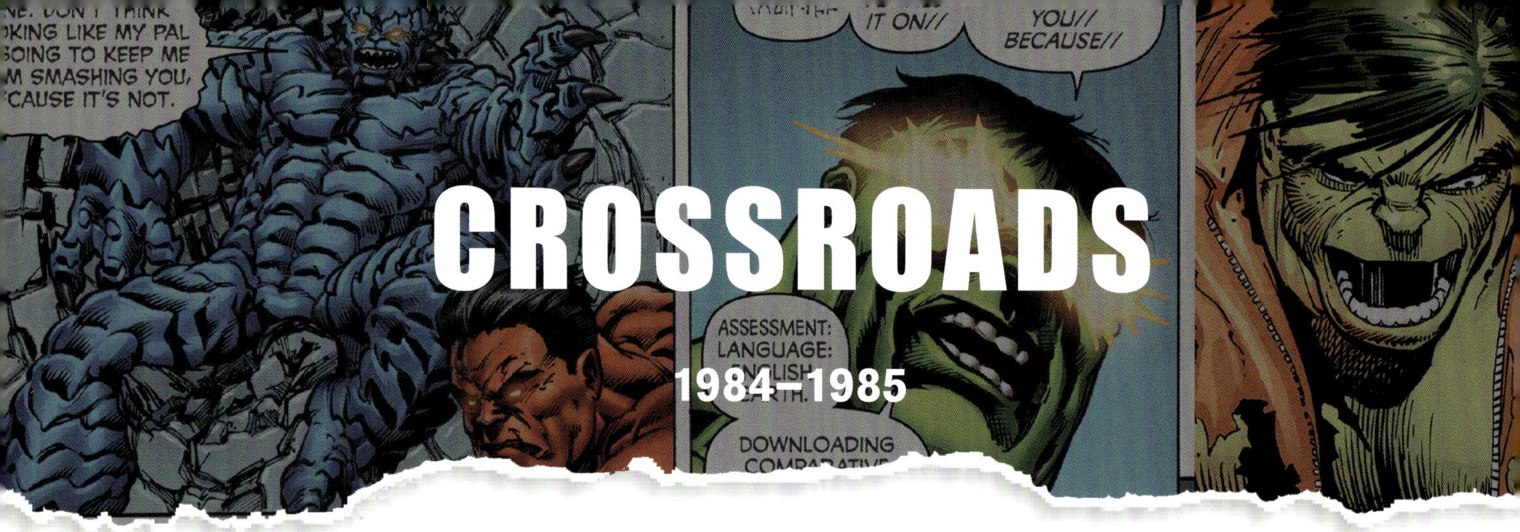

'CAUSE IT'S NOT.
IT ON//
YOU// BECAUSE//
ASSESSMENT:
LANGUAGE:
DOWNLOADING


# CROSSROADS

## 1984–1985

Ever since the Hulk was pardoned by the President of the United States, the distance between Banner and the Hulk has grown. There is less of Banner in the Hulk, and more of Hulk in the Hulk. He is becoming increasingly aggressive. Eventually, when Banner has all but disappeared and what remains is the rage machine, something needs to be done. The Hulk's aggression peaks, and Doctor Strange gets involved. He decides the only thing to be done is to exile the Hulk to another dimension where he can't do anyone any harm.

The Hulk is sent to another dimension, and the first thing he sees is something that looks like a tree. This tree has hands extending outward like branches that point in different directions. The tree is a dimensional guidepost, and these hands direct the Hulk to other dimensions. It is an indication that this may not be the Hulk's last stop.

A glowing blob appears. It can transform into different shapes, including one that looks like the Hulk and another that looks like Banner. We later learn these creatures are the Puffball Collective. But the Hulk isn't long for this dimension; soon he lands in what looks like a bombed-out city. Something is off here; the people who attack him are actually robots. The tanks that roll into town shoot rockets that break apart on impact, doing no damage. And all the buildings are nothing but facades, like a Hollywood movie set.

The Hulk takes down a fighter jet and discovers that it's powered by strings! He grabs the plane and follows the string. To his shock, a giant alien child with purple skin and yellow hair holds the other end of the string. The Hulk has been battling in a child's playset. Suddenly, he is back in front of the guidepost, which immediately sends him to another dimension.

The Hulk bounces between the guidepost, called the Crossroads, and a series of diverse dimensions. One dimension is an alien world that resembles medieval times on Earth, and he is quickly captured, chained, and put into slavery. In the next dimension he roams an alien world and almost starves to death. But then he is sent to an area where he meets a

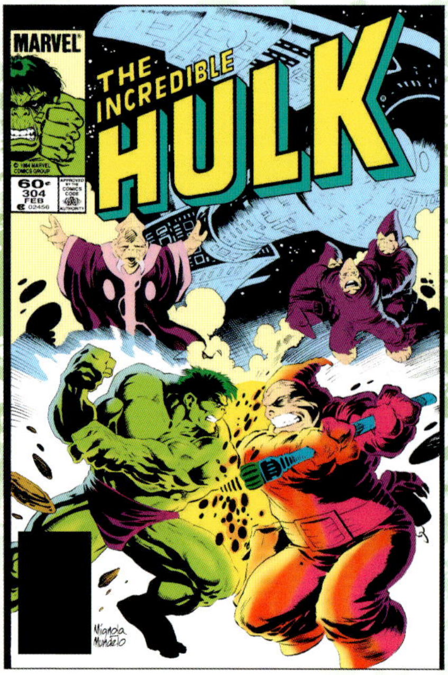

MARVEL
THE INCREDIBLE
HULK
60¢
304
FEB


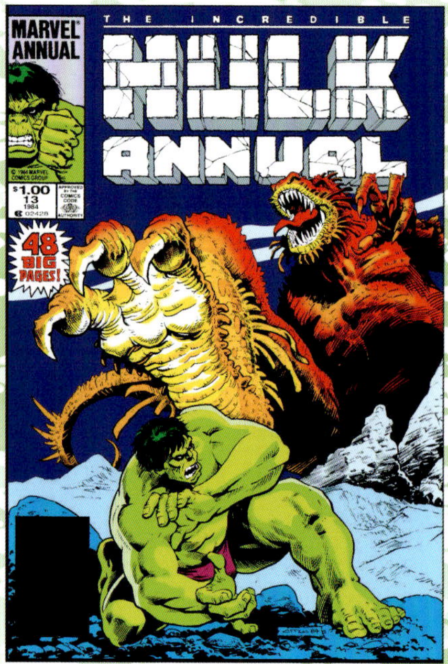

MARVEL ANNUAL
THE INCREDIBLE
HULK
ANNUAL
$1.00
13
1984
48 BIG PAGES!


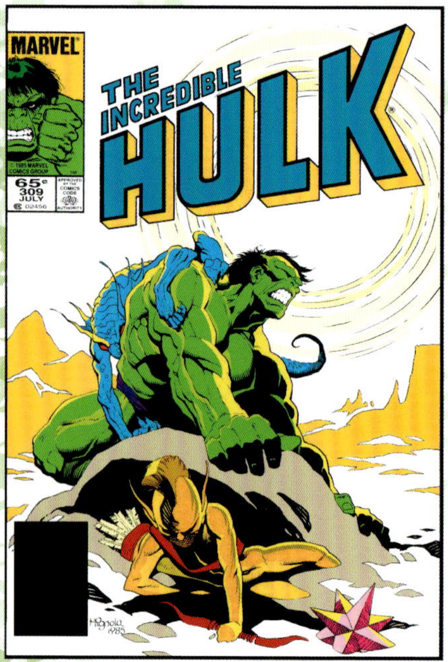

MARVEL
THE INCREDIBLE
HULK
65¢
309
JULY

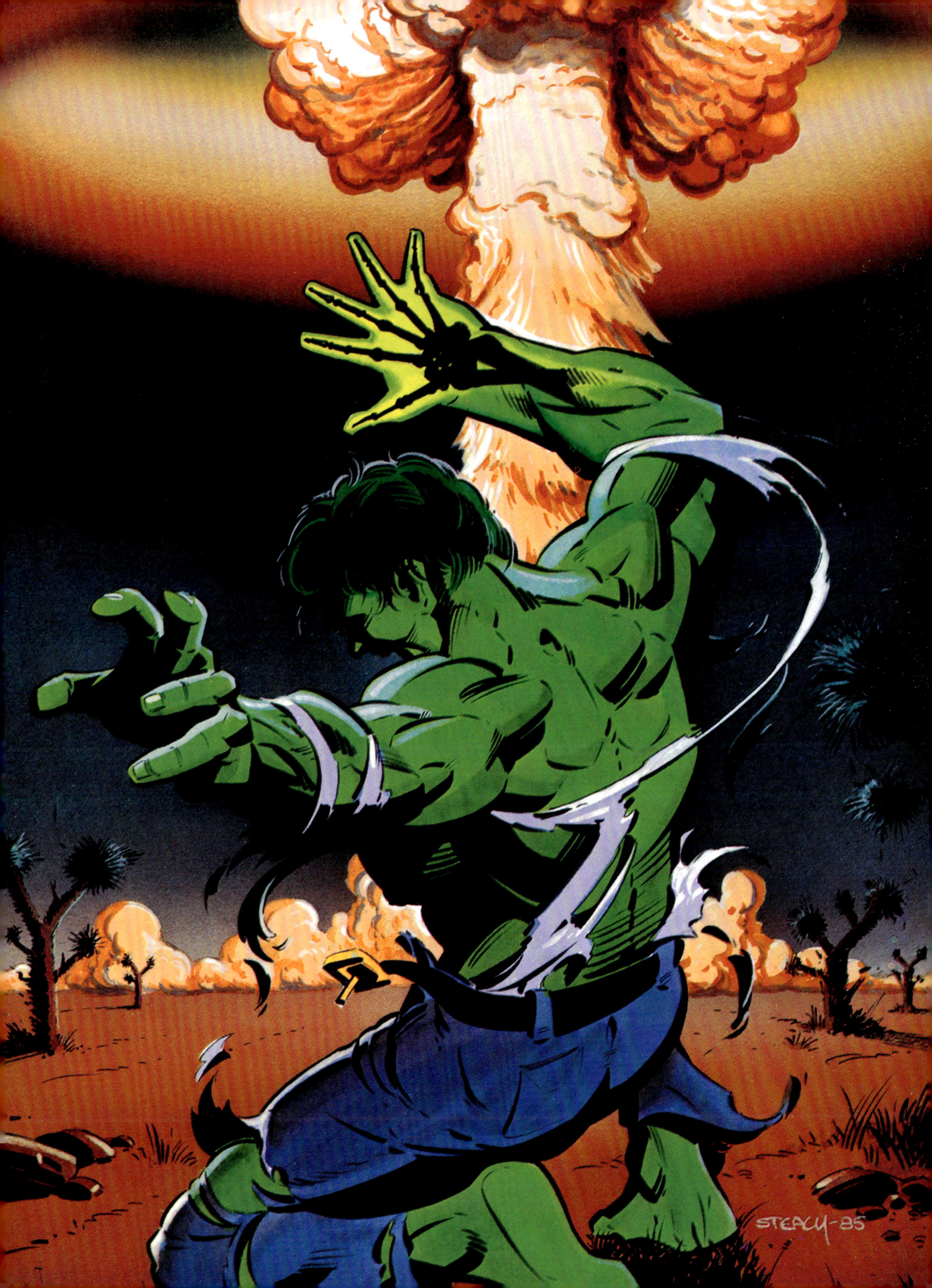
STEACY-85

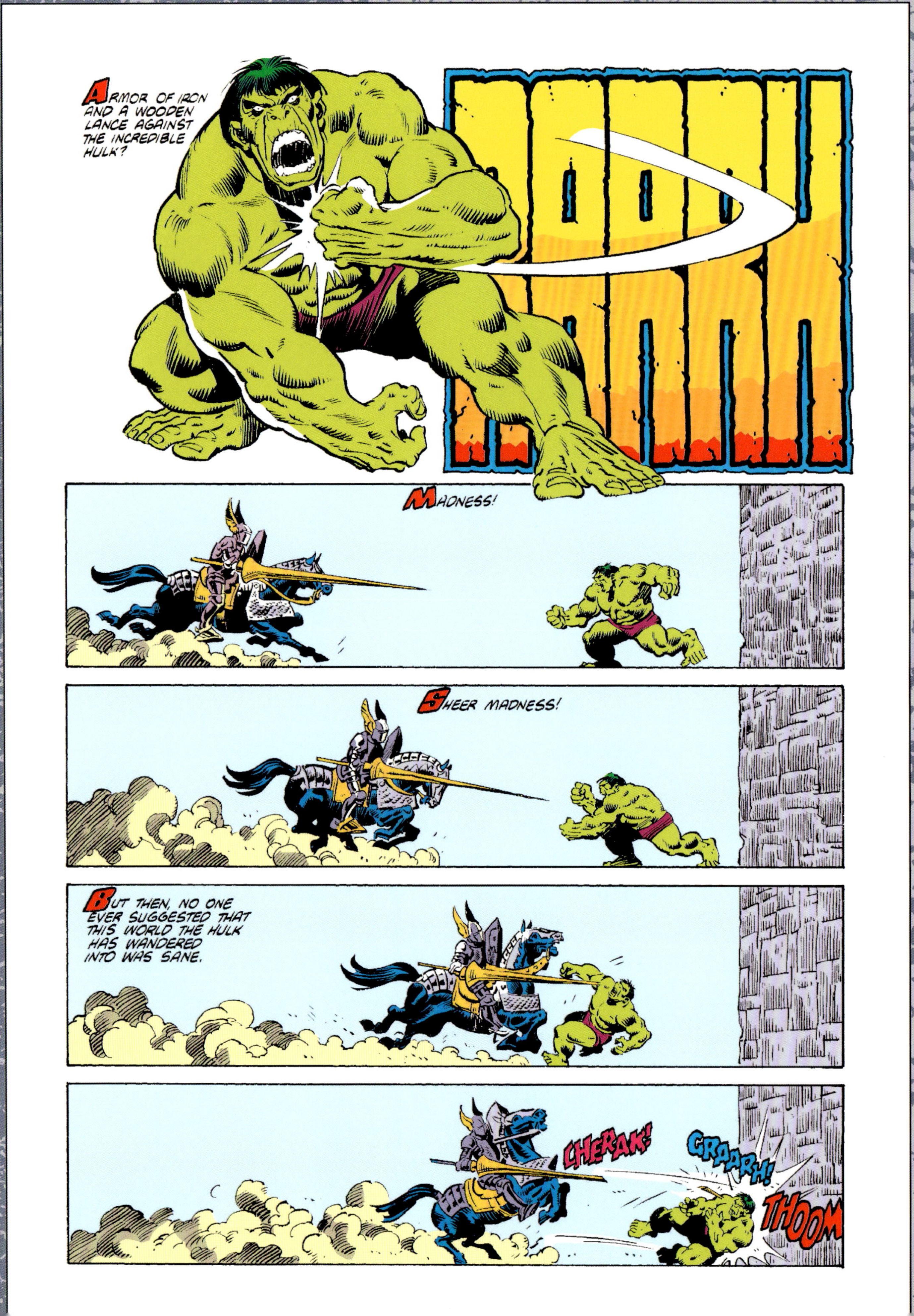

ARMOR OF IRON AND A WOODEN LANCE AGAINST THE INCREDIBLE HULK?
MADNESS!
SHEER MADNESS!
BUT THEN, NO ONE EVER SUGGESTED THAT THIS WORLD THE HULK HAS WANDERED INTO WAS SANE.
CHERAK!
GRAARH!
THOOM

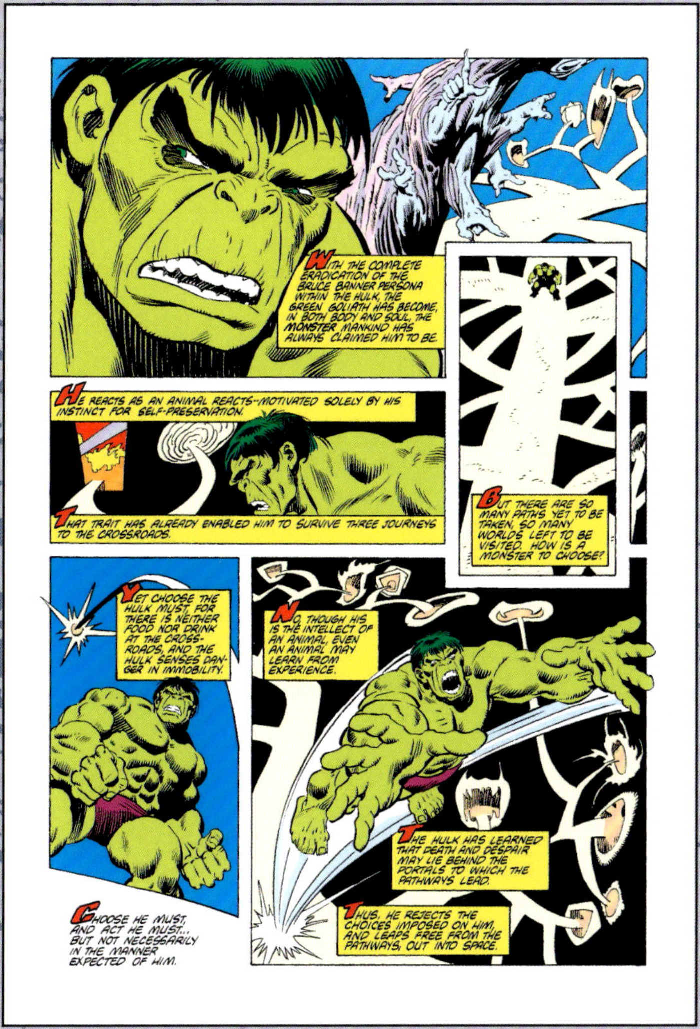
WITH THE COMPLETE ERADICATION OF THE BRUCE BANNER PERSONA WITHIN THE HULK, THE GREEN GOLIATH HAS BECOME, IN BOTH BODY AND SOUL, THE MONSTER MANKIND HAS ALWAYS CLAIMED HIM TO BE.
HE REACTS AS AN ANIMAL REACTS--MOTIVATED SOLELY BY HIS INSTINCT FOR SELF-PRESERVATION.
THAT TRAIT HAS ALREADY ENABLED HIM TO SURVIVE THREE JOURNEYS TO THE CROSSROADS.
BUT THERE ARE SO MANY PATHS YET TO BE TAKEN, SO MANY WORLDS LEFT TO BE VISITED. HOW IS A MONSTER TO CHOOSE?
YET CHOOSE THE HULK MUST, FOR THERE IS NEITHER FOOD NOR DRINK AT THE CROSS-ROADS, AND THE HULK SENSES DAN-GER IN IMMOBILITY.
CHOOSE HE MUST, AND ACT HE MUST... BUT NOT NECESSARILY IN THE MANNER EXPECTED OF HIM.
NO, THOUGH HIS IS THE INTELLECT OF AN ANIMAL, EVEN AN ANIMAL MAY LEARN FROM EXPERIENCE.
THE HULK HAS LEARNED THAT DEATH AND DESPAIR MAY LIE BEHIND THE PORTALS TO WHICH THE PATHWAYS LEAD.
THUS, HE REJECTS THE CHOICES IMPOSED ON HIM, AND LEAPS FREE FROM THE PATHWAYS, OUT INTO SPACE.

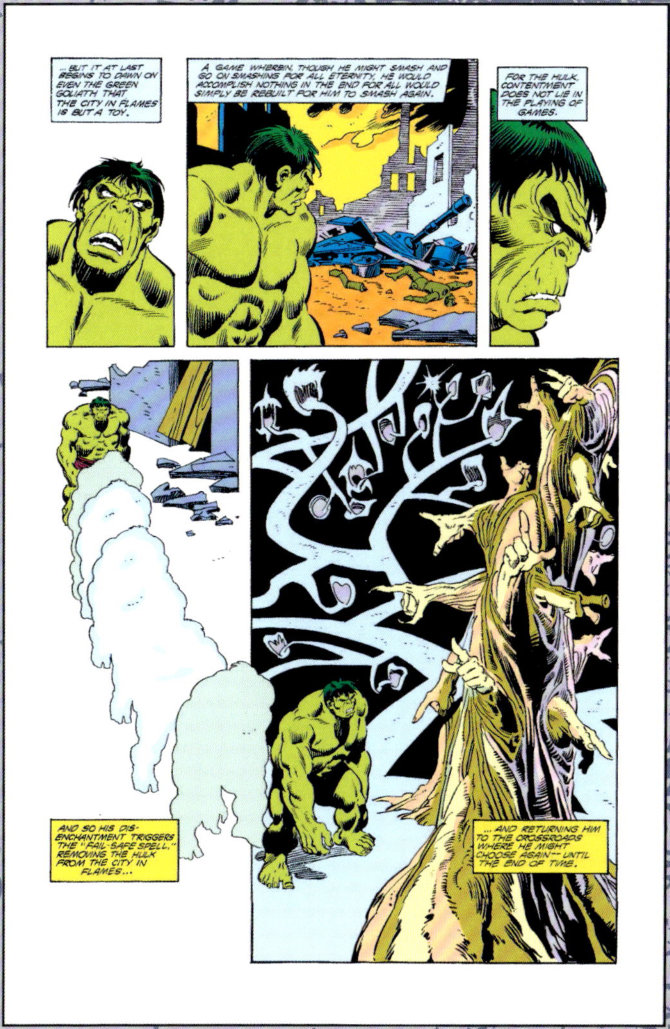
...BUT IT AT LAST BEGINS TO DAWN ON EVEN THE GREEN GOLIATH THAT THE CITY IN FLAMES IS BUT A TOY.
A GAME WHEREIN, THOUGH HE MIGHT SMASH AND GO ON SMASHING FOR ALL ETERNITY, HE WOULD ACCOMPLISH NOTHING IN THE END FOR ALL WOULD SIMPLY BE REBUILT FOR HIM TO SMASH AGAIN.
FOR THE HULK, CONTENTMENT DOES NOT LIE IN THE PLAYING OF GAMES.
AND SO HIS DIS-ENCHANTMENT TRIGGERS THE "FAIL-SAFE SPELL," REMOVING THE HULK FROM THE CITY IN FLAMES...
...AND RETURNING HIM TO THE CROSSROADS WHERE HE MIGHT CHOOSE AGAIN-- UNTIL THE END OF TIME.

creature equal in size, who befriends him and shows him where he can find food. The creature's name is Zgorian, and he, too, was exiled. The Hulk saves Zgorian from a rock avalanche and the two become friends, two creatures in exile taking care of each other. But it can't last; Zgorian is soon tracked down by his fellow aliens, who accuse him of the crime of showing compassion to the enemy. This alien race doesn't tolerate compassion, and they quickly kill Zgorian. The Hulk tries to battle these killers but is quickly subdued, and they take off in their ship. The Hulk cries over the body of his dead friend. And then he is again transported to another dimension.

The Hulk is transported over and over, from dimension to dimension, where he has to fight. He faces foes, including the villainous team U-Foes, Klaatu, and others. In one dimension he meets the Triad, three creatures named Goblin, Guardian, and Glow. Goblin is a blue creature with sharp claws and a tail, Glow is a floating star-shaped entity, and Guardian looks like Cupid, complete with bow and arrow—that is, if Cupid were orange with a mohawk haircut. Together, they try to help the Hulk and guide him to a better place.

The group travels through this dimension, and Guardian shoots the Hulk in the head with an arrow. It triggers memories of his past life on Earth. He remembers Banner, and Betty, and General Ross.

During a battle outside a fort in yet another dimension, another arrow from Guardian hits the Hulk, which transforms him back into Bruce Banner. As he recovers his full memory, and transforms back into the Hulk, he realizes that the one thing he wants is to go home.

The Hulk has a flashback to when he was born in Dayton, Ohio. We meet his mother and his abusive, alcoholic father. His father never wanted kids and blames young Bruce for the difficult delivery his wife had. We also discover that Banner's father worked at Los Alamos during the development of the nuclear bomb and was exposed to radiation. Could this have affected Bruce? Is this the reason he was able to absorb the gamma rays? And will he ever get home? If he does manage to make it back to Earth, he must still face the struggle between the man and the monster—between Bruce Banner and the Hulk. They are both at a crossroads.

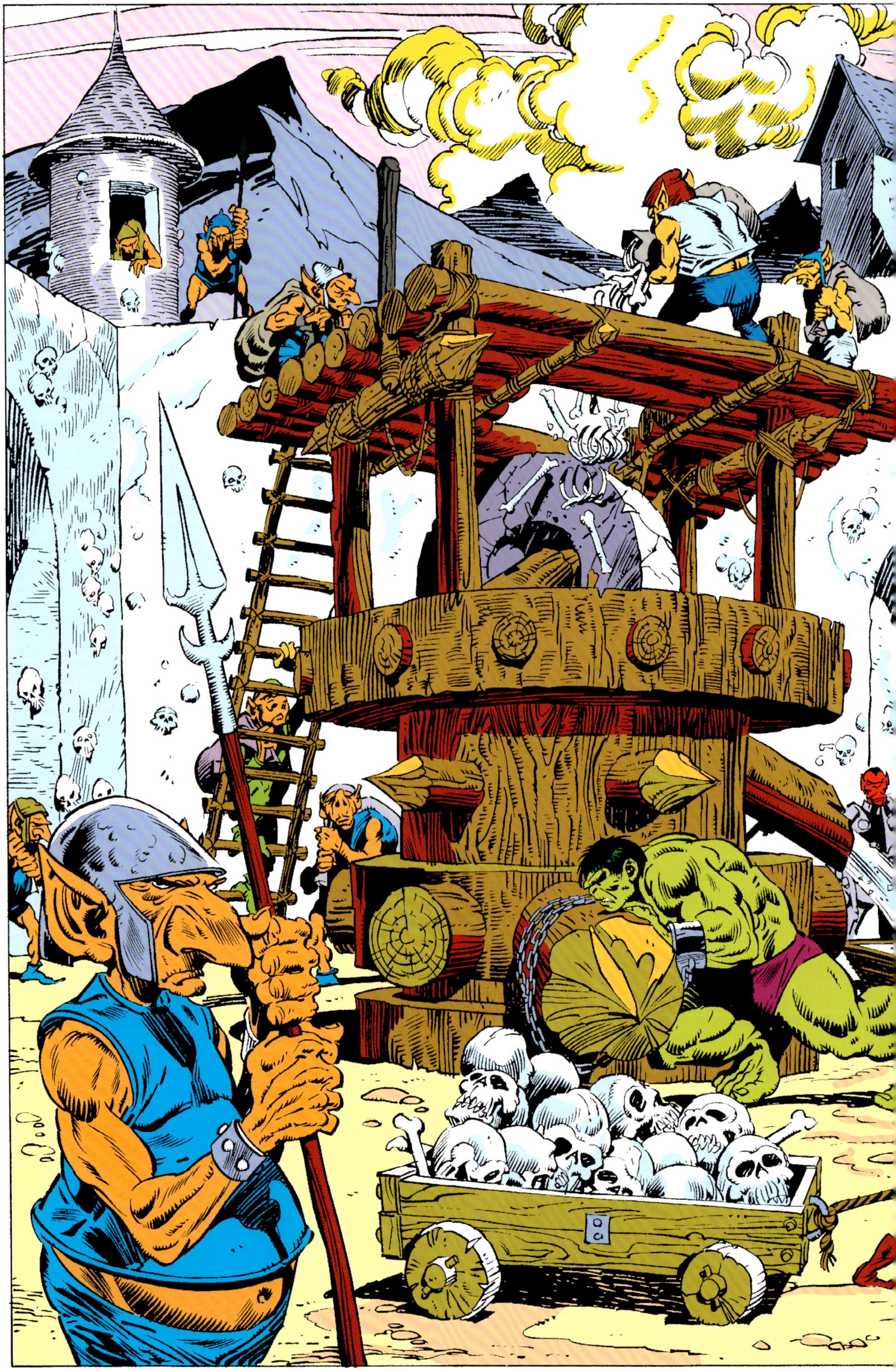

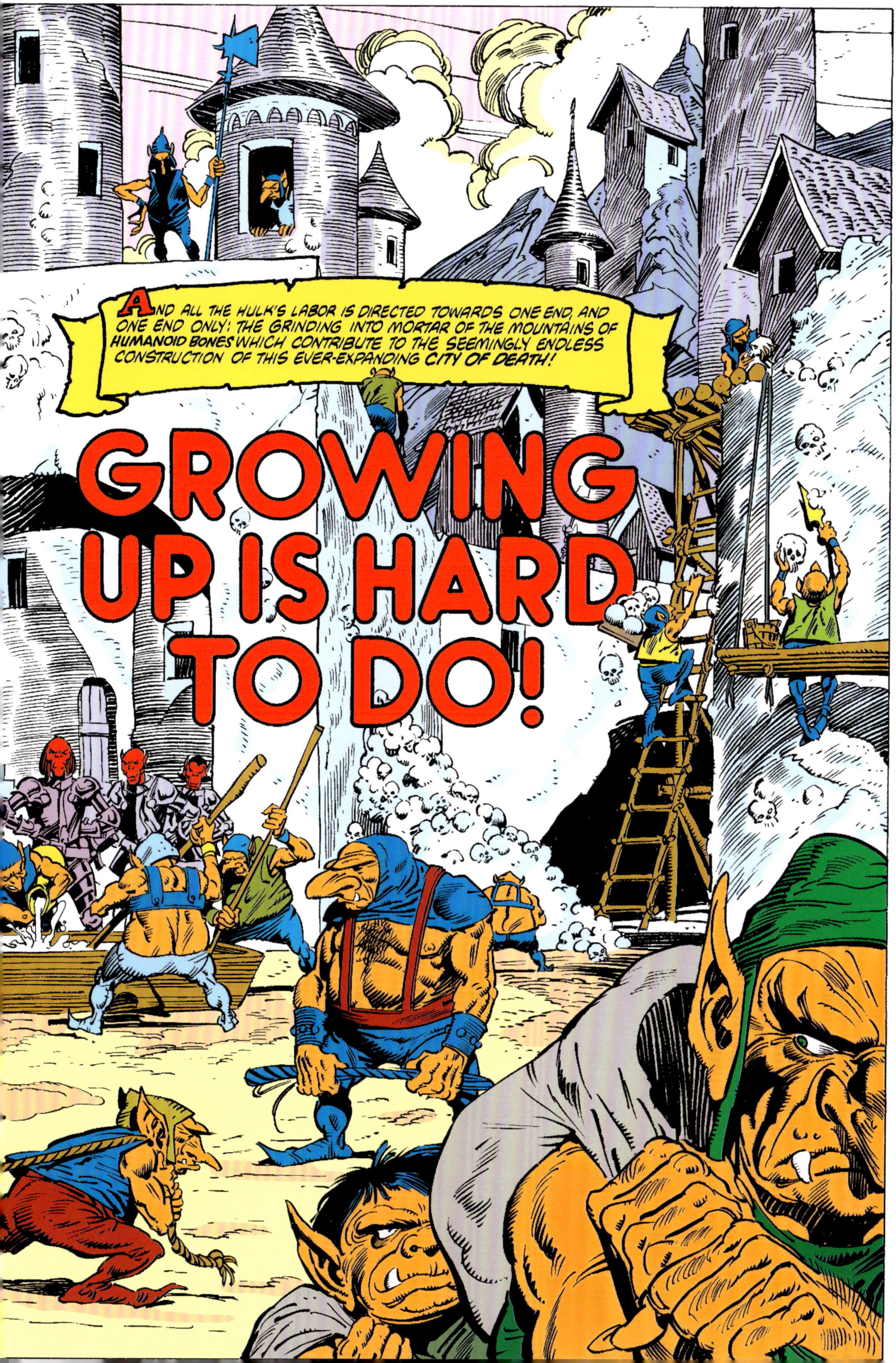
AND ALL THE HULK'S LABOR IS DIRECTED TOWARDS ONE END, AND ONE END ONLY: THE GRINDING INTO MORTAR OF THE MOUNTAINS OF HUMANOID BONES WHICH CONTRIBUTE TO THE SEEMINGLY ENDLESS CONSTRUCTION OF THIS EVER-EXPANDING CITY OF DEATH!
GROWING UP IS HARD TO DO!

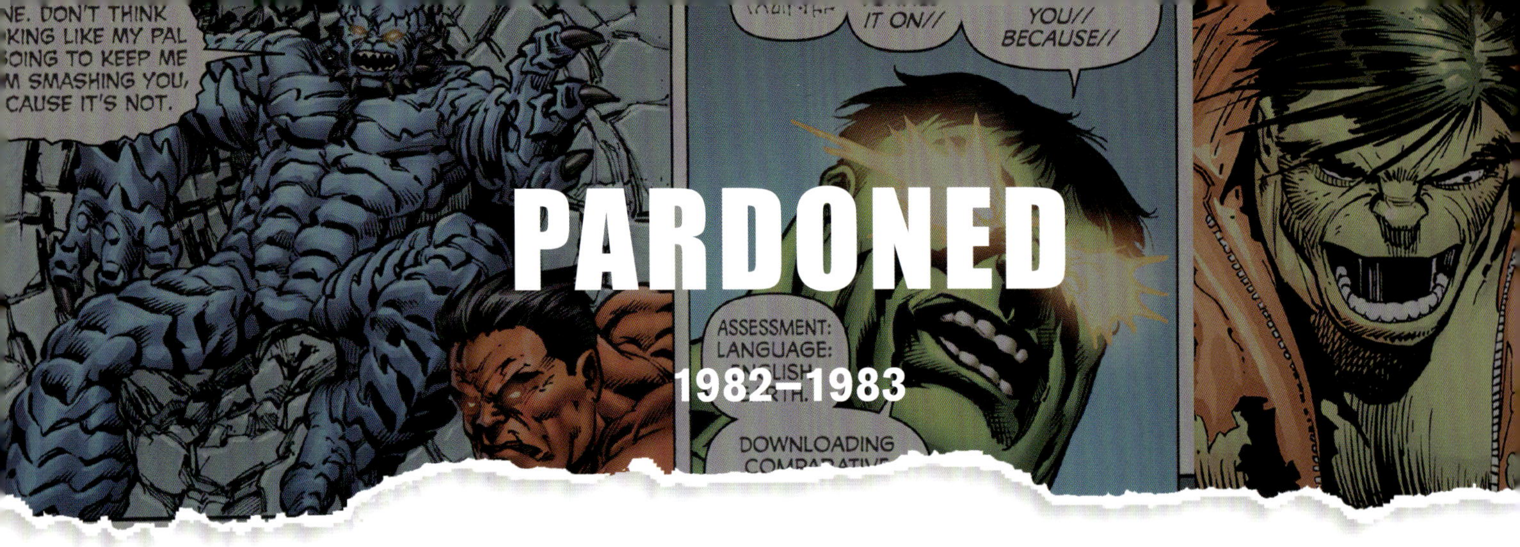
IT ON//
YOU// BECAUSE//
ASSESSMENT: LANGUAGE:
DOWNLOADING

# PARDONED

## 1982–1983

The Hulk has become a movie star on another planet. On the planet Kaylor, humanlike aliens are gathered to watch a movie starring Earth's Hulk with the film's director. The audience cheers the action flashing before them. When the film ends, they cheer and shout for the director to take a bow. But she has already left, leaving the audience wanting more. The director's name is Bereet, and she is looking to film another documentary about the Hulk. But she has never been to Earth; she has only shot the Hulk from afar. Bereet decides that in order to make another Hulk movie, she needs to travel to Earth to film her star in person. She dons a mask, which transforms into a spaceship around her, and it sends her into space toward Earth.

Back on Earth, Bruce Banner is brooding in the desert. The lab where he is researching a way to rid himself of the Hulk is nearby. His devoted girlfriend, Betty Ross, joins him. She tries to help him with his constant struggle of managing both Banner and the Hulk. Banner hates the Hulk, and the Hulk hates Banner. Both are in constant turmoil sharing the same body. Betty tells him that he must destroy the Hulk if she and Banner are to stay together.

Betty and Bruce's desert encounter is suddenly interrupted by three missiles descending from the sky. A beam shoots from the missiles, and three creatures appear: Amphibion of far Xantares; Torgo, robot ruler of Mekka; and Dark-Crawler, sole survivor of the Dark Dimension. They are Hulk Hunters, and, because of them, the Hulk is launched on a journey that sends him all over the galaxy.

The Hulk bounces around the galaxy, where he has adventures with a wide variety of characters: Rocket Raccoon, Black Jack O'Hare (leader of the Black Bunny Brigade), a turtle reading a Gideon's Bible, Sasquatch, a Wendigo, a spaceship full of insectile creatures, Ironclad, Killer Clowns, and the Canadian police. During his galaxy adventures, Banner/Hulk is exposed to several more doses of gamma rays.

Back on Earth, Bereet materializes as the Hulk heads out for other galaxies, but also as the Hulk's old friend Rick Jones

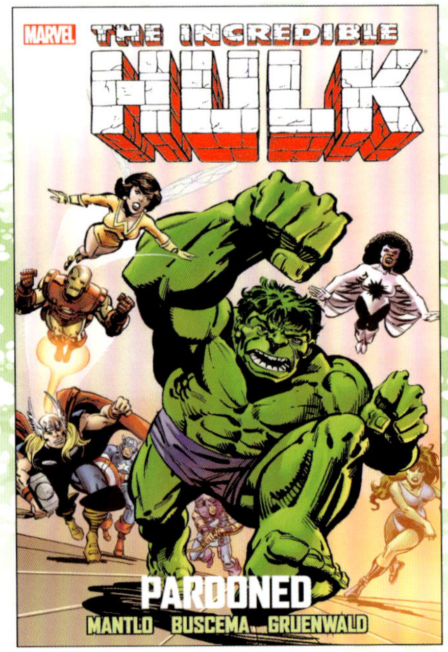
MARVEL
THE INCREDIBLE
HULK
PARDONED
MANTLO BUSCEMA GRUENWALD

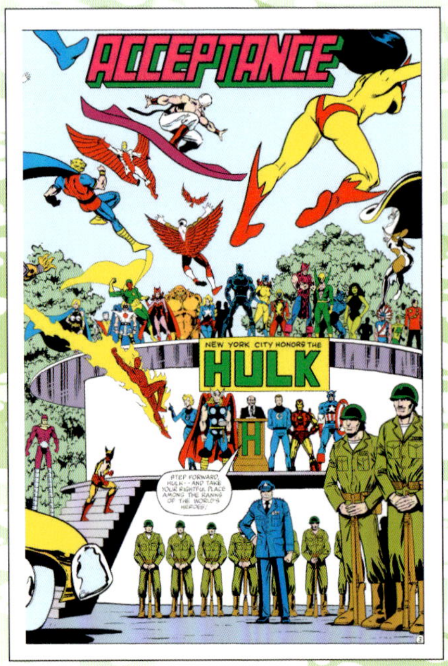
ACCEPTANCE
NEW YORK CITY HONORS THE
HULK

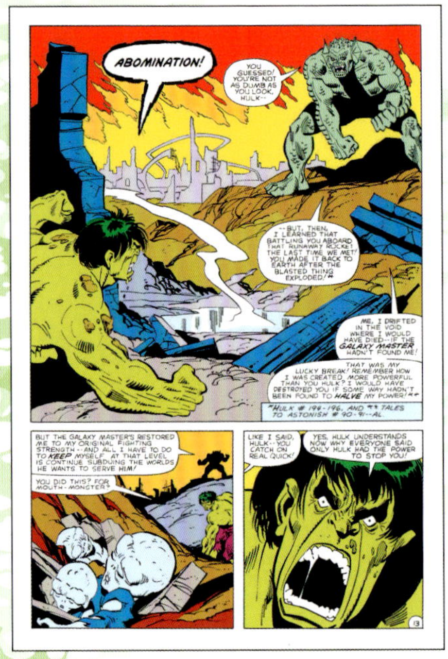
ABOMINATION!

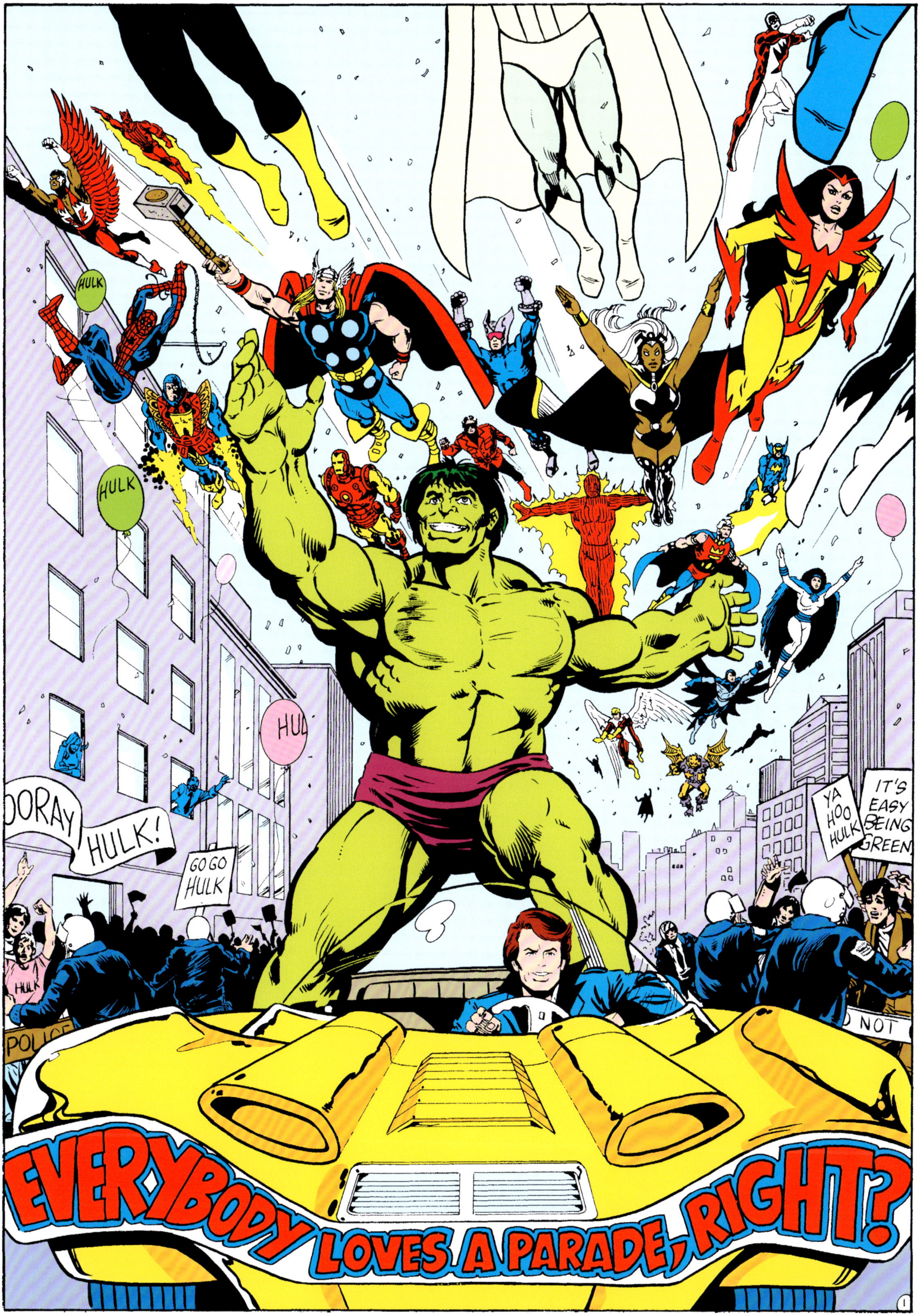
HULK
HULK
HUL
OORAY HULK!
GO GO HULK
HULK
POLICE
YA HOO HULK
IT'S EASY BEING GREEN
NOT
EVERYBODY LOVES A PARADE, RIGHT?

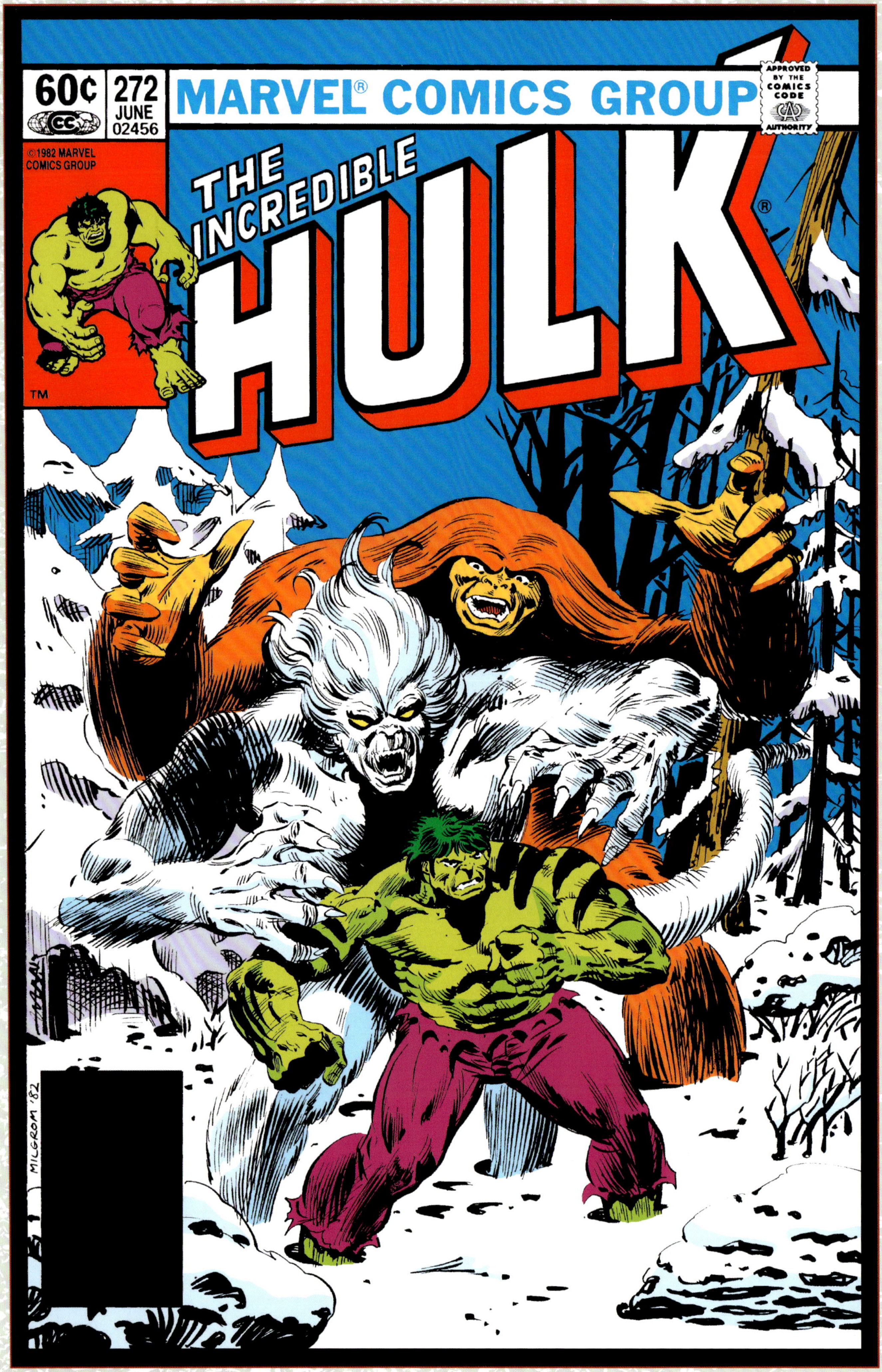
60¢
272
JUNE
02456
MARVEL® COMICS GROUP
APPROVED BY THE COMICS CODE AUTHORITY
©1982 MARVEL COMICS GROUP
THE INCREDIBLE HULK®
TM
MILGROM '82

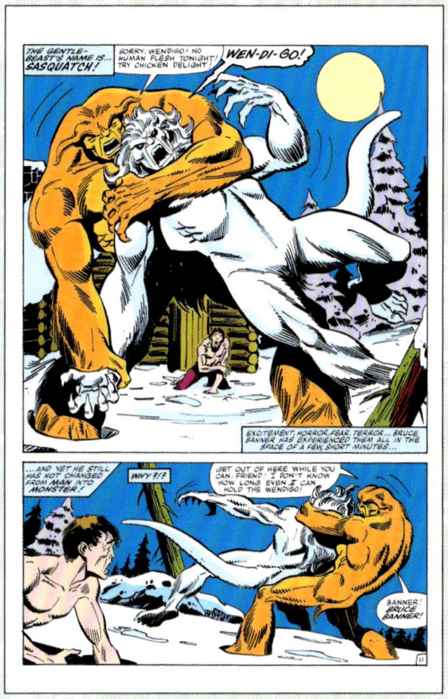
THE GENTLE-BEAST'S NAME IS-- SASQUATCH!
SORRY, WENDIGO! NO HUMAN FLESH TONIGHT! TRY CHICKEN DELIGHT!
WEN-DI-GO!
EXCITEMENT, HORROR, FEAR, TERROR... BRUCE BANNER HAS EXPERIENCED THEM ALL IN THE SPACE OF A FEW SHORT MINUTES...
...AND YET HE STILL HAS NOT CHANGED FROM MAN INTO MONSTER!
WHY?!?
GET OUT OF HERE WHILE YOU CAN, FRIEND! I DON'T KNOW HOW LONG EVEN I CAN HOLD THE WENDIGO!
BANNER, BRUCE BANNER!

is in the lab, exposing himself to gamma rays in an attempt to recreate the accident that transformed Banner into the Hulk. The gamma ray exposure renders Jones unconscious. Bereet sees Betty, who pleads with Bereet to help him. Bereet manages to put Rick on a life support system.

Meanwhile, the additional gamma exposure changes the Hulk; consequently, the Hulk and Banner merge. Suddenly the Hulk is not merely the beast who speaks in short, basic sentences. Instead, he sounds like the brilliant scientist Bruce Banner. With Banner's brain in the Hulk's body, Banner/Hulk's actions become more measured. The Hulk acts not on pure instinct, but instead with reason. He thinks through his situation and acts accordingly. No longer is "Hulk smash" his first and sometimes only reflex.

People are uncertain how to react to this Hulk. People are accustomed to the Hulk acting in a specific way—they expect him to smash things and to rampage. They expect the raging monster, but they hear the intelligent man. But when he returns to Earth, they continue to react like he is the old Hulk; they shoot first and ask no questions. This frustrates and angers both Hulk the beast and Banner the man.

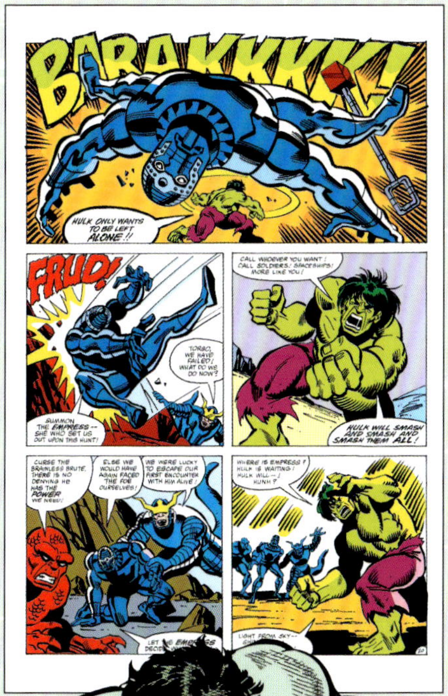
BARAKKKK!
HULK ONLY WANTS TO BE LEFT ALONE!!
FRUD!
HULK WILL SMASH AND SMASH AND SMASH THEM ALL!

However, there are those who see potential in the new Banner-Hulk. The Avengers, the Fantastic Four, Thor, Iron Man, Daredevil, Black Panther, Doctor Strange, Captain Britain, the Canadian super-team Alpha-Flight, and many others support a government pardon for the Hulk for all the destruction he has caused. He even begins receiving fan mail from ordinary citizens.

The President of the United States is hesitant about giving the Green Goliath a free pass for the laws he has broken and destruction he has caused. That is, until there is an alien invasion in Washington, DC. The US looks to super heroes, including the Hulk, to fight the invading aliens. The Hulk is largely responsible for stopping them, which is enough to convince the president to pardon him.

But will the Banner-Hulk symbiosis last? Will the rampaging monster return? What will become of Rick Jones? And how will Betty react to Bereet's developing feelings for the Hulk?

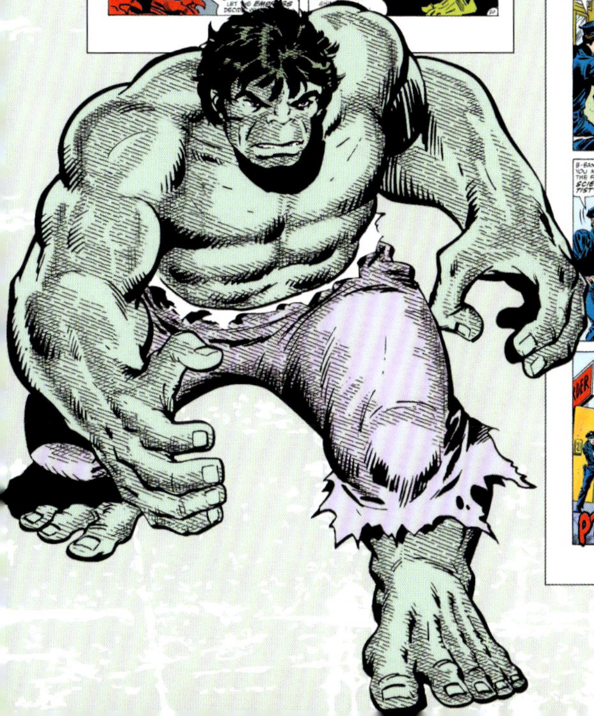

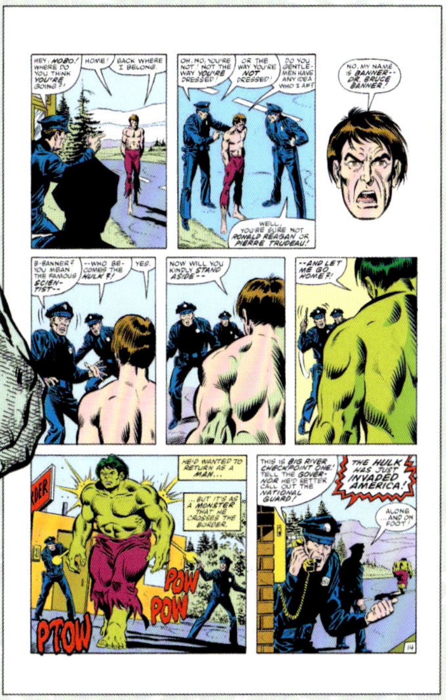
THE HULK HAS JUST INVADED AMERICA!
POW
POW
PTOW

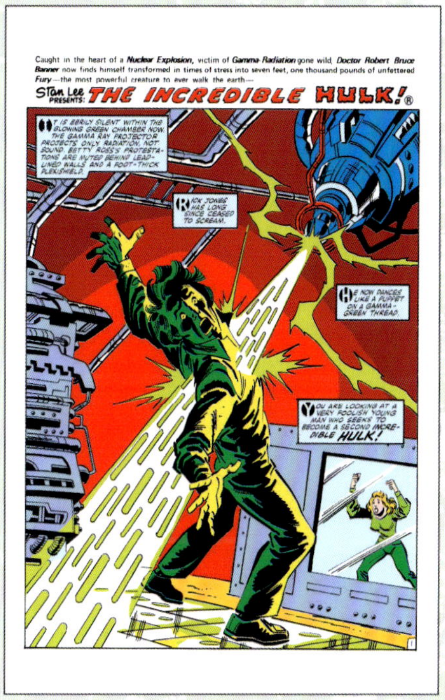
STan Lee PRESENTS: THE INCREDIBLE HULK!
RICK JONES HAS LONG SINCE CEASED TO SCREAM.
YOU ARE LOOKING AT A VERY FOOLISH YOUNG MAN WHO SEEKS TO BECOME A SECOND INCREDIBLE HULK!

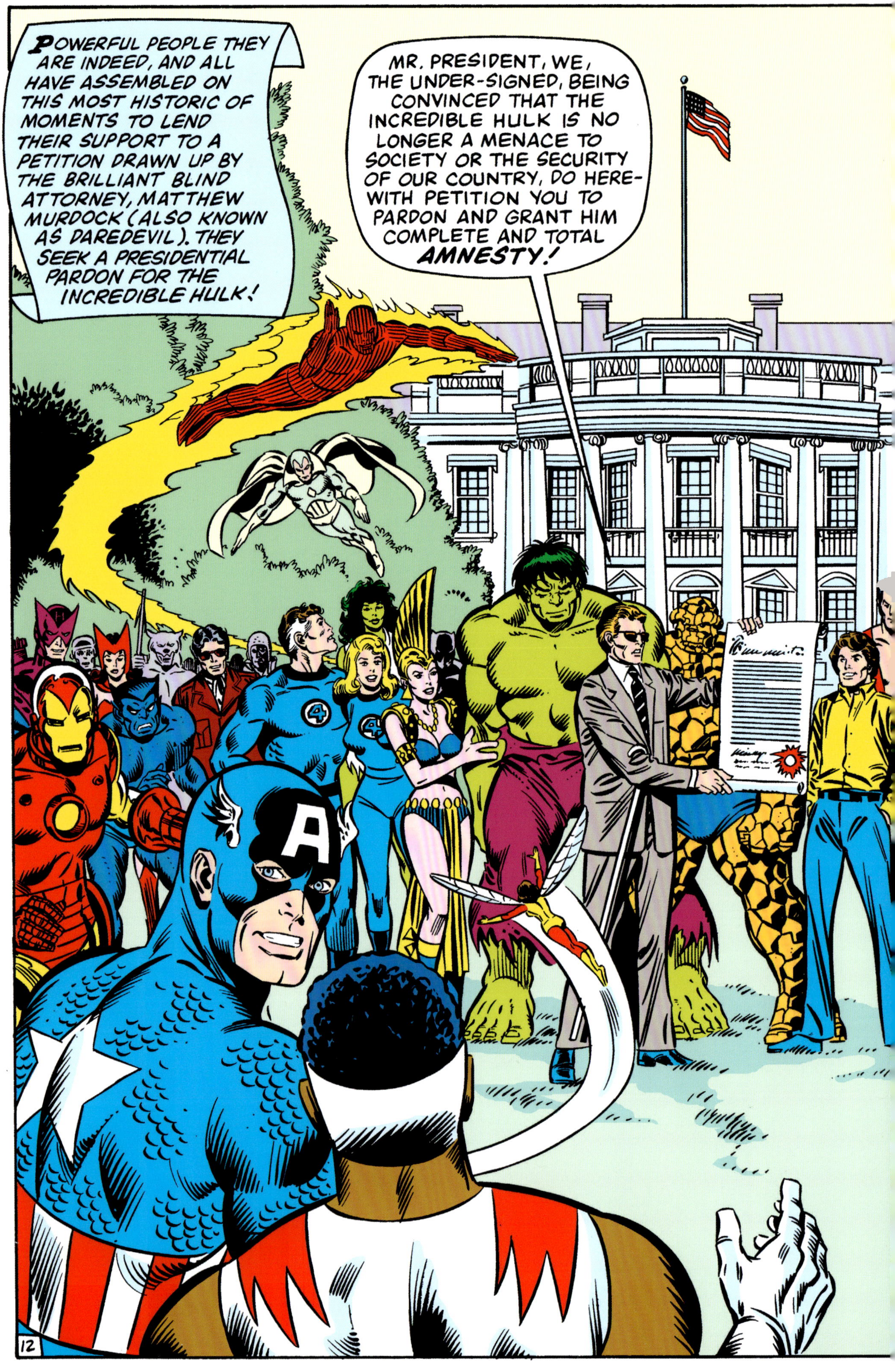
POWERFUL PEOPLE THEY ARE INDEED, AND ALL HAVE ASSEMBLED ON THIS MOST HISTORIC OF MOMENTS TO LEND THEIR SUPPORT TO A PETITION DRAWN UP BY THE BRILLIANT BLIND ATTORNEY, MATTHEW MURDOCK (ALSO KNOWN AS DAREDEVIL). THEY SEEK A PRESIDENTIAL PARDON FOR THE INCREDIBLE HULK!
MR. PRESIDENT, WE, THE UNDER-SIGNED, BEING CONVINCED THAT THE INCREDIBLE HULK IS NO LONGER A MENACE TO SOCIETY OR THE SECURITY OF OUR COUNTRY, DO HERE-WITH PETITION YOU TO PARDON AND GRANT HIM COMPLETE AND TOTAL AMNESTY!

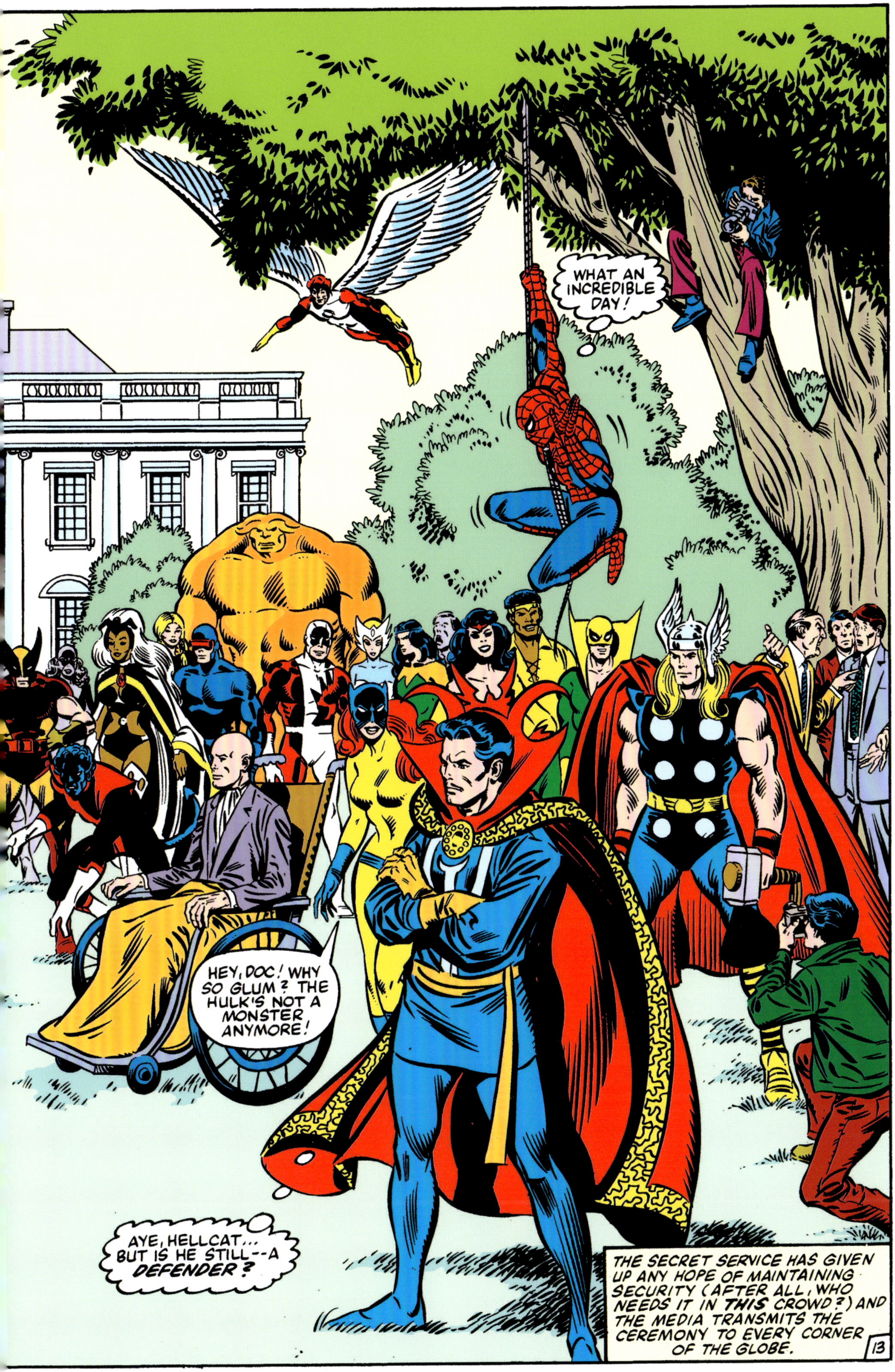

WHAT AN INCREDIBLE DAY!
HEY, DOC! WHY SO GLUM? THE HULK'S NOT A MONSTER ANYMORE!
AYE, HELLCAT... BUT IS HE STILL--A DEFENDER?
THE SECRET SERVICE HAS GIVEN UP ANY HOPE OF MAINTAINING SECURITY (AFTER ALL, WHO NEEDS IT IN THIS CROWD?) AND THE MEDIA TRANSMITS THE CEREMONY TO EVERY CORNER OF THE GLOBE.
13

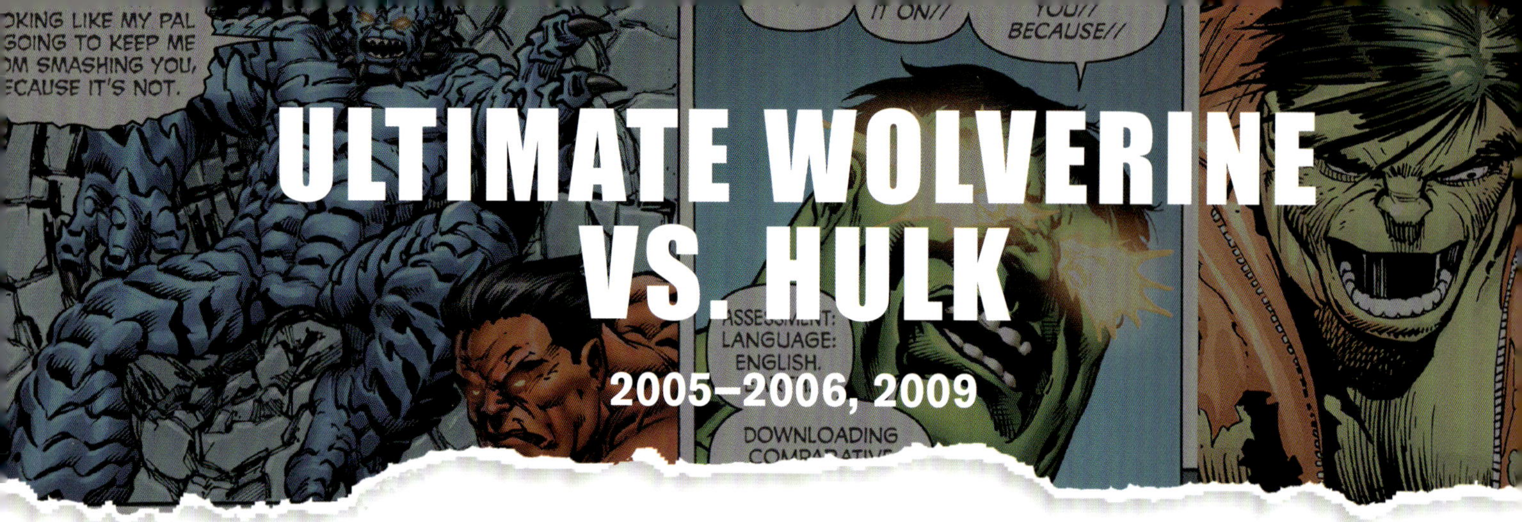

BECAUSE//
LANGUAGE:
ENGLISH.
DOWNLOADING


# ULTIMATE WOLVERINE VS. HULK

## 2005–2006, 2009

Wolverine/Logan is lying face down in the snow in a pool of his own blood. Well, half of him is lying face down in a pool of his own blood. Wolverine has been torn in half by the Hulk, and his legs are four miles up the Tibetan mountains—because that's where the Hulk threw them. Logan has to crawl up the mountain in order to put himself back together.

This limited series was written by award-winning producer, comic book writer, and screenwriter Damon Lindelof. In his hands, the story recasts the Hulk's classic rage monster as a jealous rage monster.

In Marvel's *Ultimate* issues #4 and #5, Wolverine is sent by Nick Fury to find and kill the Hulk. The Hulk had been on another murderous tear, this time in Manhattan. The Hulk went berserk when he learned that Betty Ross, Bruce Banner's on-again, off-again girlfriend, was having dinner with another man.

Bruce calls Betty to tell her that he took Hulk Serum, mixed it with Captain America's blood, and injected it into the cephalic vein of his antecubital fossa (in other words, his arm). This infusion, combined with Bruce finding out that Betty is with another man, sends him into a new type of rage: jealous rage. The Hulk destroys buildings, drinks a truckload of beer, and steals someone's pants on his journey to track down Betty. Unfortunately, 815 innocent people are killed along the way, including children, during his rampage.

Logan goes out to search for big green. He sniffs out the Hulk and finds him behind a huge door in the side of a mountain in Tibet. Inside, the Hulk is surrounded by dozens of scantily clad women. We all seek enlightenment in different ways.

Logan enters into the Hulk's lair, and the Hulk offers him a hot cocoa. Not exactly the reception he expected from a world-breaker. The Hulk asks Logan, "Who sent you? Was it Fury?" Logan replies, "Fury who?" They banter back and forth, Logan trying to light a fire under the Hulk and the Hulk explaining that he's decided to be less angry. But Logan pushes it and tells the Hulk that Betty, the Hulk's old girlfriend, wants him

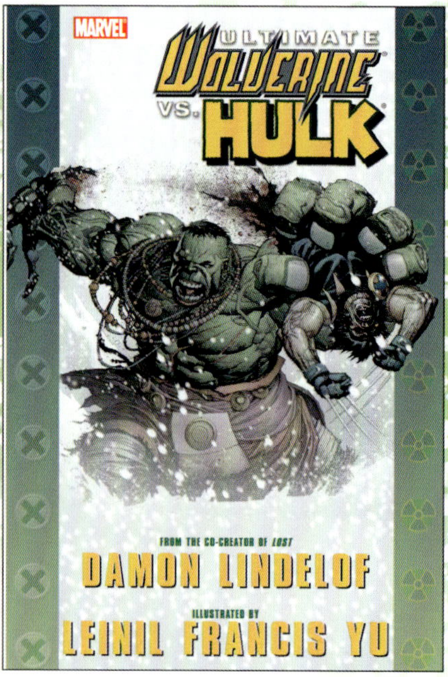

MARVEL
ULTIMATE
WOLVERINE
VS.
HULK
FROM THE CO-CREATOR OF LOST
DAMON LINDELOF
ILLUSTRATED BY
LEINIL FRANCIS YU


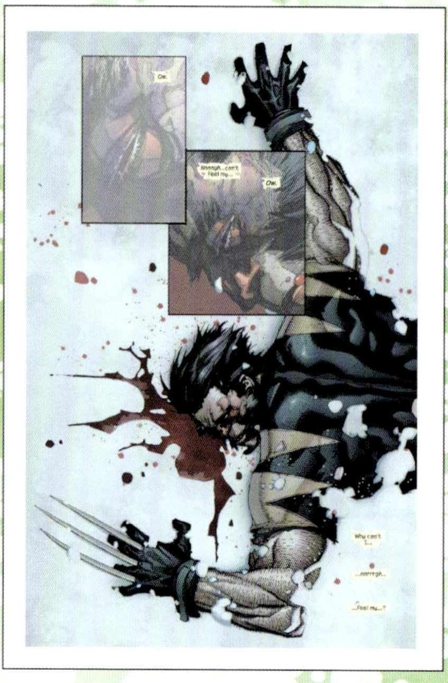

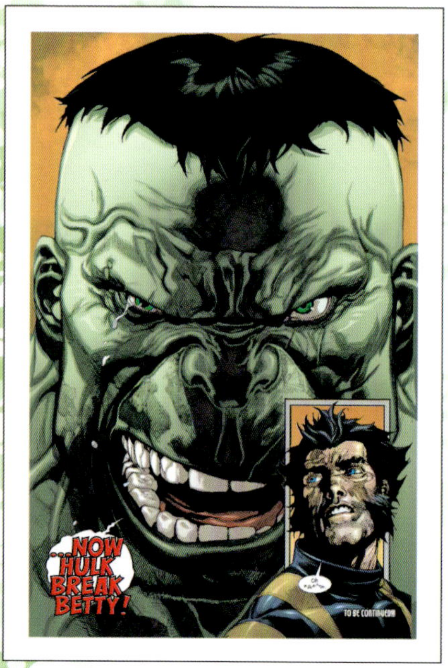

...NOW HULK BREAK BETTY!

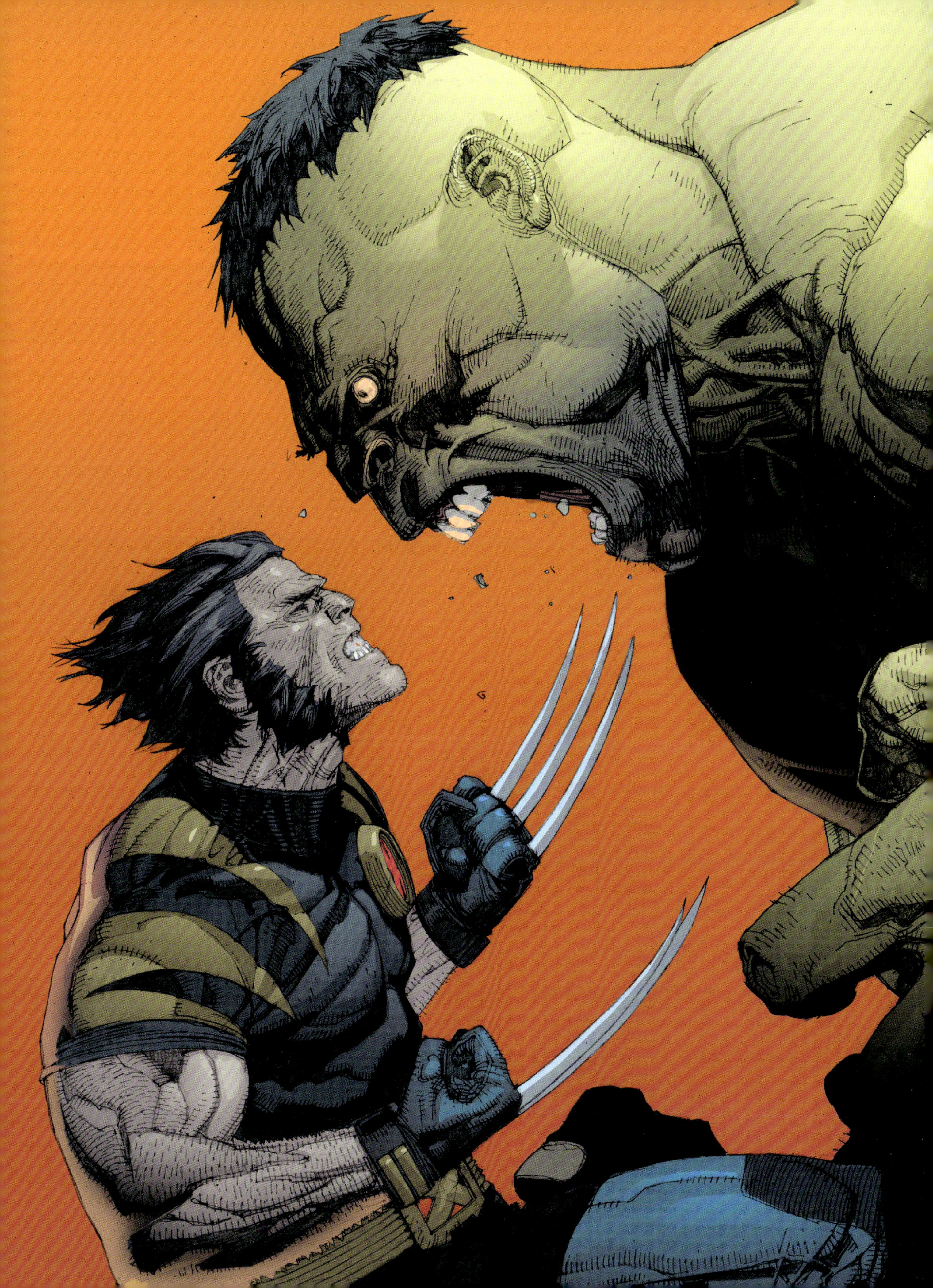

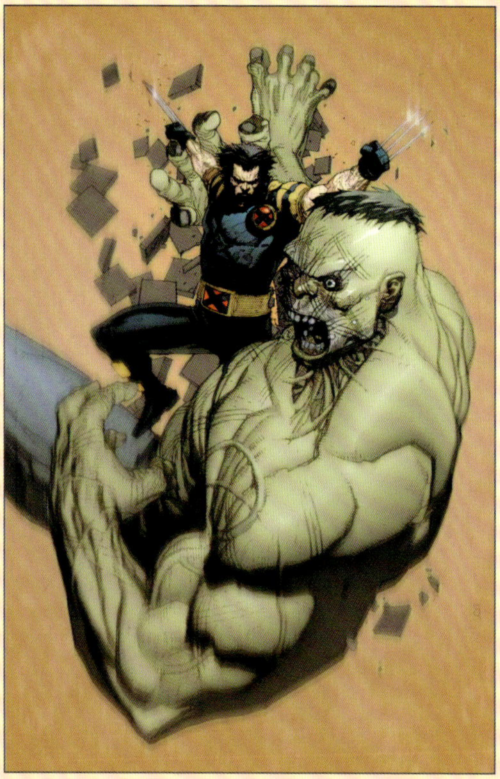

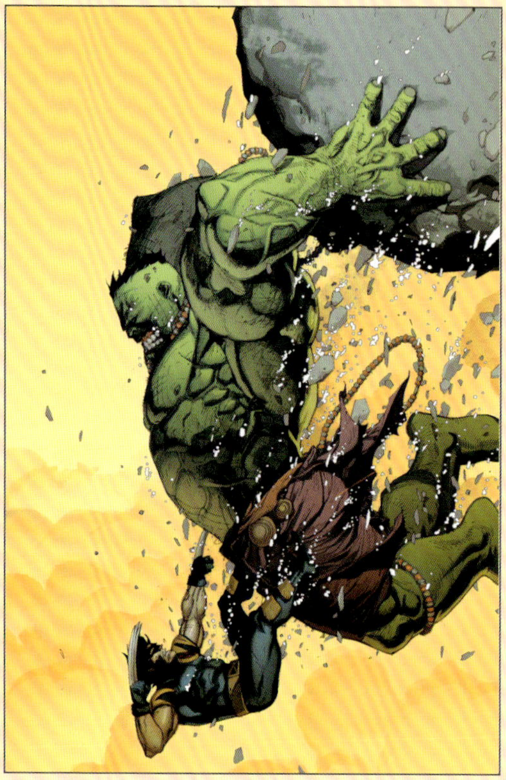

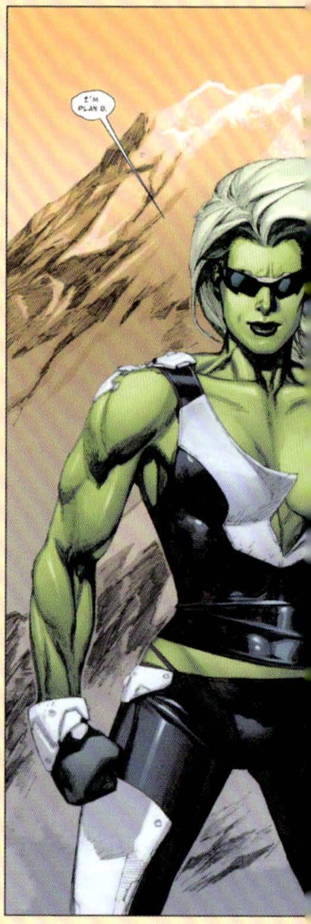
I'M PLAN B.

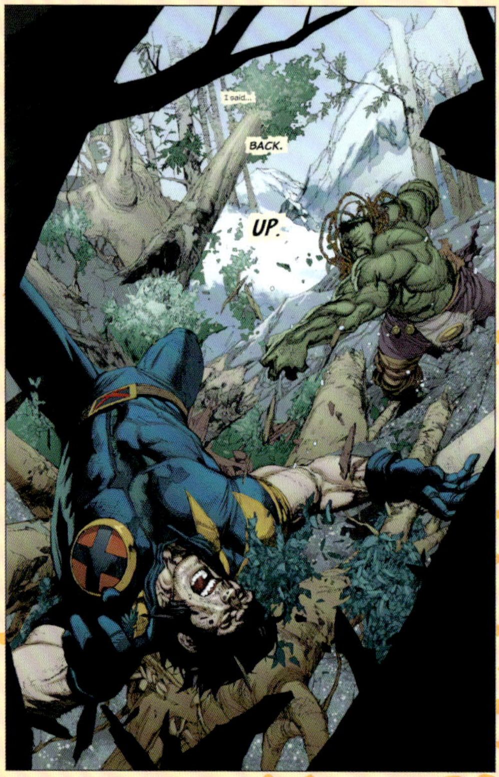
I said...
BACK.
UP.

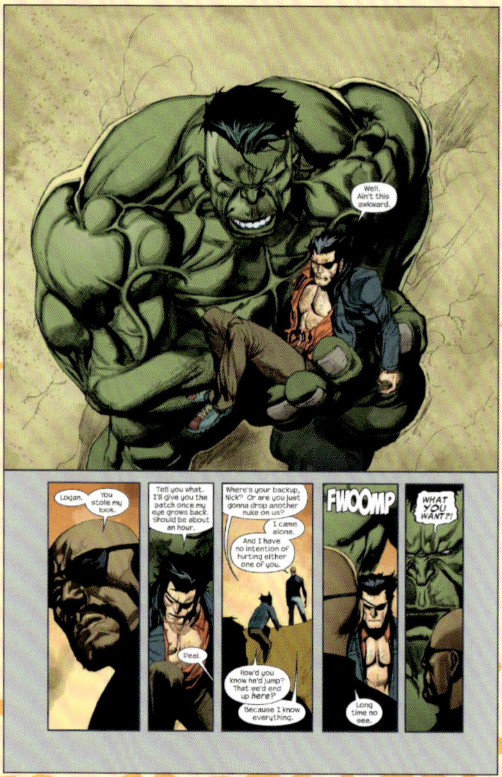
Well. Ain't this awkward.
Logan.
You stole my look.
Tell you what. I'll give you the patch once my eye grows back. Should be about an hour.
Deal.
Where's your backup, Nick? Or are you just gonna drop another nuke on us?
I came alone.
And I have no intention of hurting either one of you.
How'd you know he'd jump? That we'd end up *here*?
Because I know everything.
FWOOMP
Long time no see.
WHAT YOU WANT?!

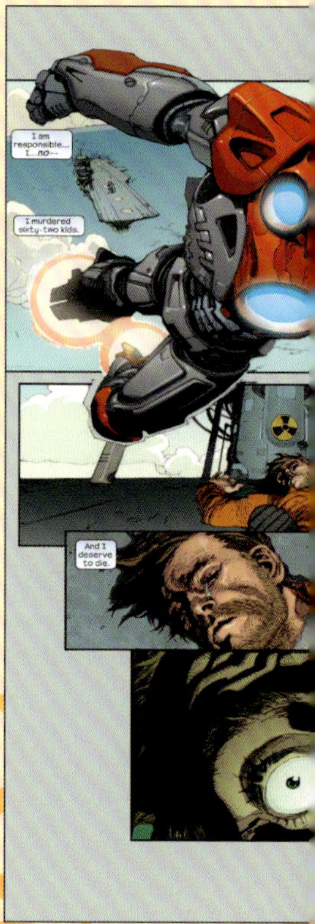
I am responsible... I...*no*--
I murdered sixty-two kids.
And I deserve to die.

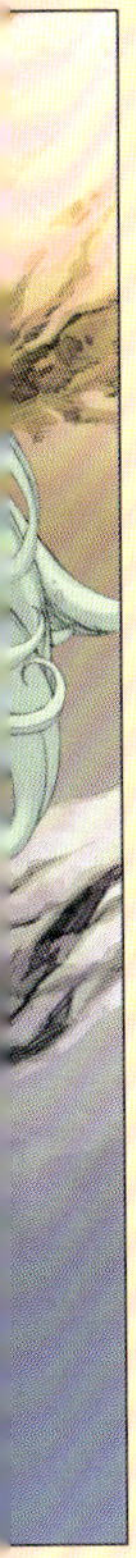

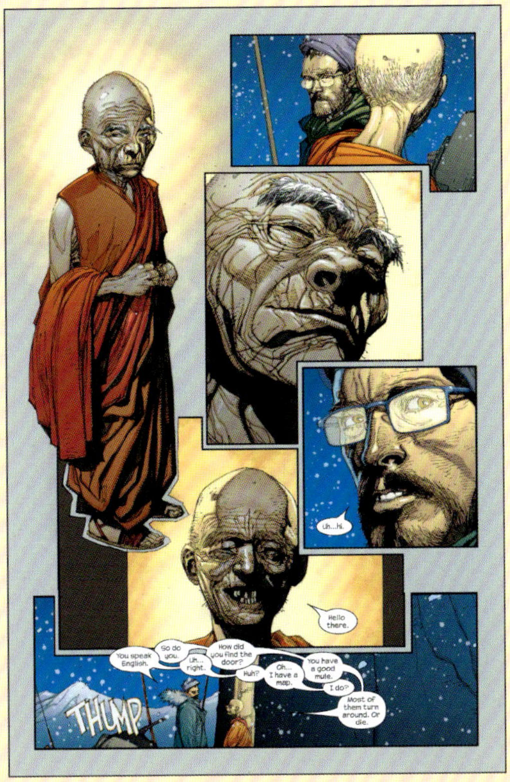
Uh...hi.
Hello there.
You speak English.
So do you.
Uh... right.
How did you find the door?
Huh?
Oh... I have a map.
You have a good mule.
I do?
Most of them turn around. Or die.
THUMP

dead. This annoys the Hulk, but doesn't send him into the rage that Logan is looking for. Logan, as a friend, asks the Hulk if, since he doesn't seem to care about Betty anymore, Logan can ask her out. That does it. All hell breaks loose and the Hulk attacks. The Hulk is now an angry ex-boyfriend.

A plane appears overhead as the two titans try to tear each other apart—literally—and a green figure falls from the sky. It's Betty, who has taken an experimental serum, which turns her into a Hulk! When she approaches the Hulk he says to her, "Betty break Hulk's heart . . . now Hulk break Betty!"

Lindelof portrays the Hulk as an obsessed boyfriend, one who would require the most severe restraining order on record. In turning Betty into a Hulk, Lindelof's solution to deal with the Hulk's jealousy and rage is to fight fire with fire. He attempts to create a level playing field on which Betty can better defend herself.

As the battle escalates, Fury sends a nuke to end it, and just before the bomb strikes, Betty screams at the Hulk "I still love you!" The Hulk begins to reply, but then the bomb hits. They all survive the explosion, and they scatter.

At the end of the story, Fury visits the Hulk and Wolverine in Casablanca, and Fury offers the Hulk a chance to work for S.H.I.E.L.D. again, which he turns down. Fury also informs the Hulk that Betty has been captured and is locked up; they're researching a way to reverse the serum that turned her into a Hulk. Fury also lets the Hulk know that if he ever does come back to S.H.I.E.L.D. he would be in a cell next to Betty while they try to figure out a way to reverse the effects of the gamma rays on him. The Hulk tells Fury that he and Banner are one and the same. One man, split in two, creating someone whole.

Fury realizes that he can't kill the Hulk and he lets him walk away with Wolverine. They are in the middle of the desert and have to walk back to civilization. As they walk, Logan tells the Hulk that he's still angry that he ripped him in two. The Hulk suggests Logan get some help managing his anger.

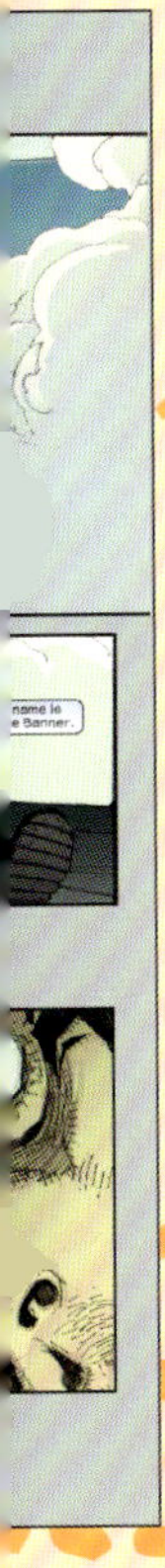

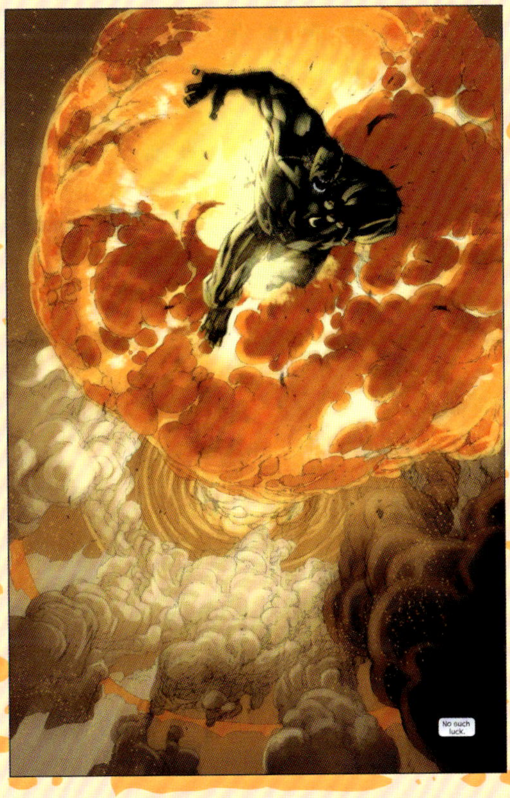
No such luck.

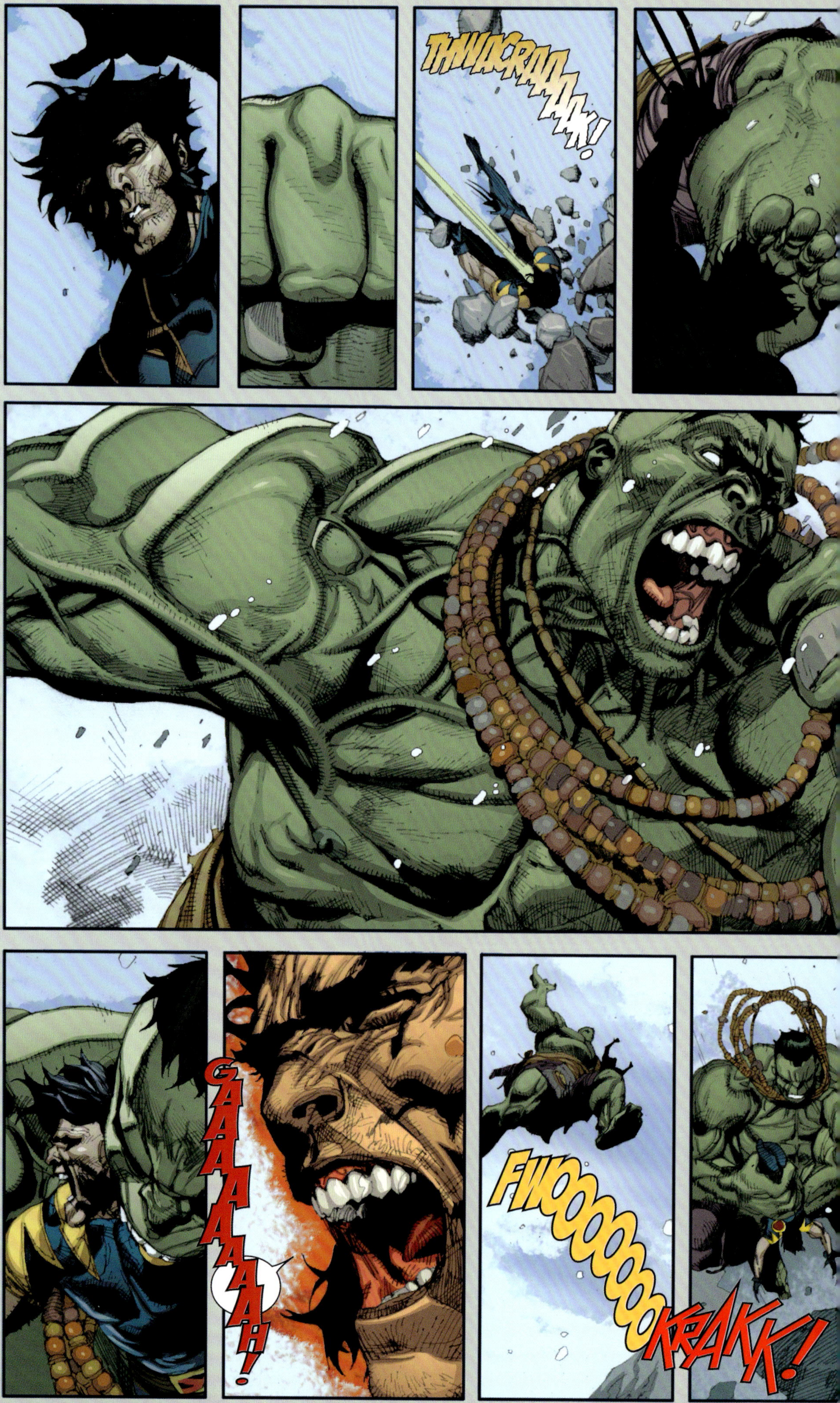
THWACRAAAAK!
GAAAAAAAH!
FWOOOOOOOKRAKK!

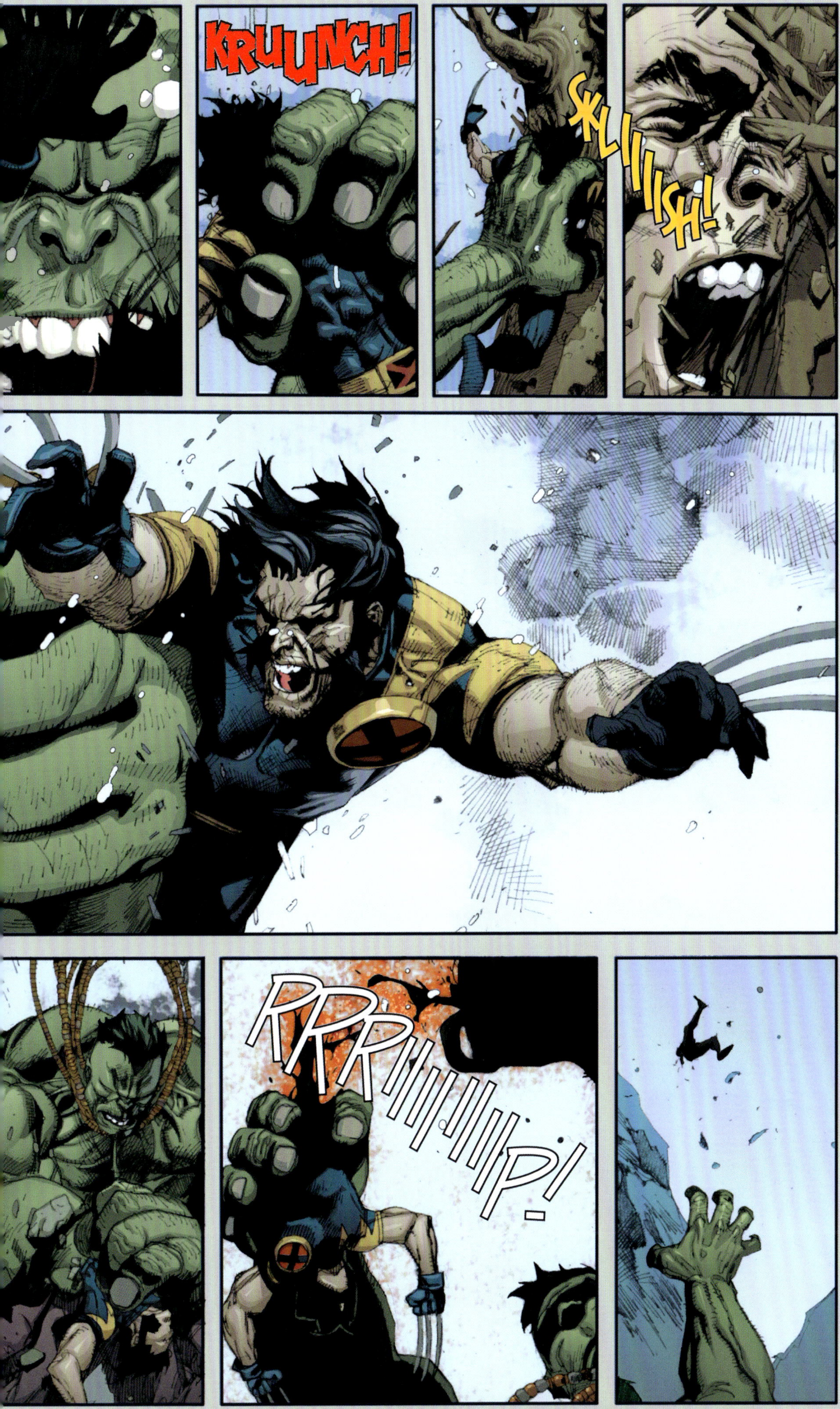

KRUUNCH!
SKLIIIISH!
RRRIIIIIIIIP!

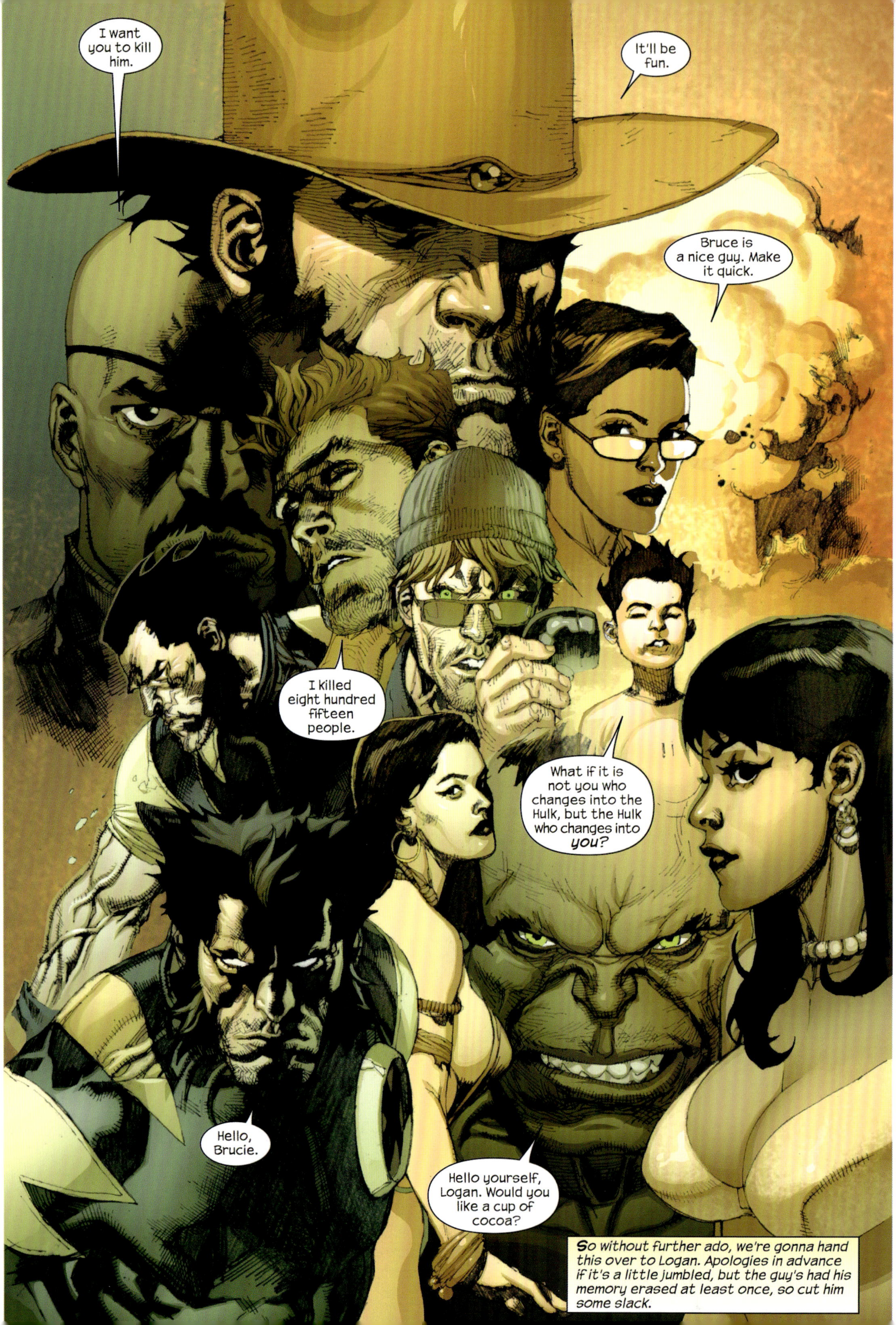
I want you to kill him.
It'll be fun.
Bruce is a nice guy. Make it quick.
I killed eight hundred fifteen people.
What if it is not you who changes into the Hulk, but the Hulk who changes into *you?*
Hello, Brucie.
Hello yourself, Logan. Would you like a cup of cocoa?
*So without further ado, we're gonna hand this over to Logan. Apologies in advance if it's a little jumbled, but the guy's had his memory erased at least once, so cut him some slack.*

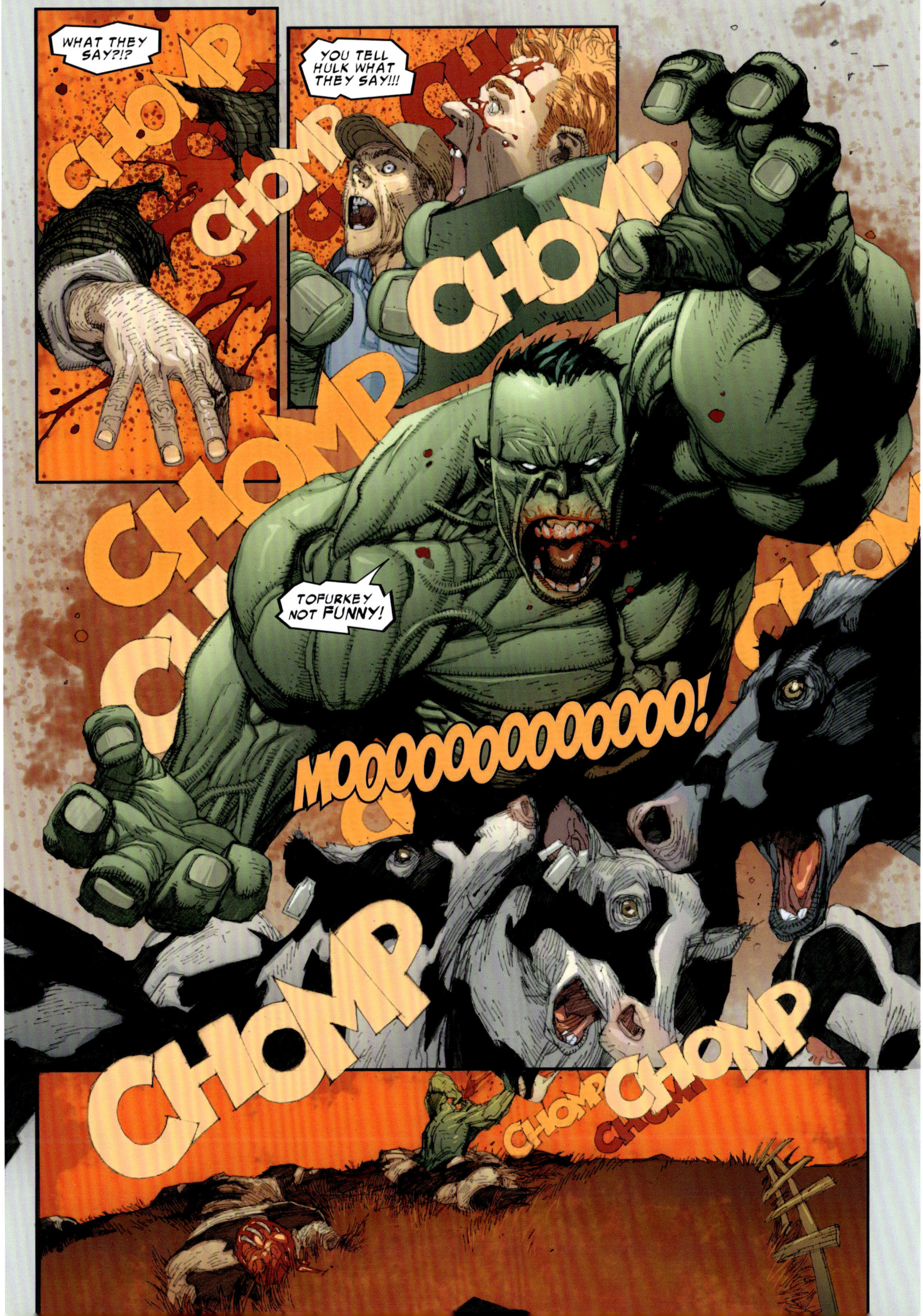
WHAT THEY SAY?!?
CHOMP
CHOMP
YOU TELL HULK WHAT THEY SAY!!!
CHOMP
CHOMP
TOFURKEY NOT FUNNY!
MOOOOOOOOOOOOO!
CHOMP
CHOMP
CHOMP

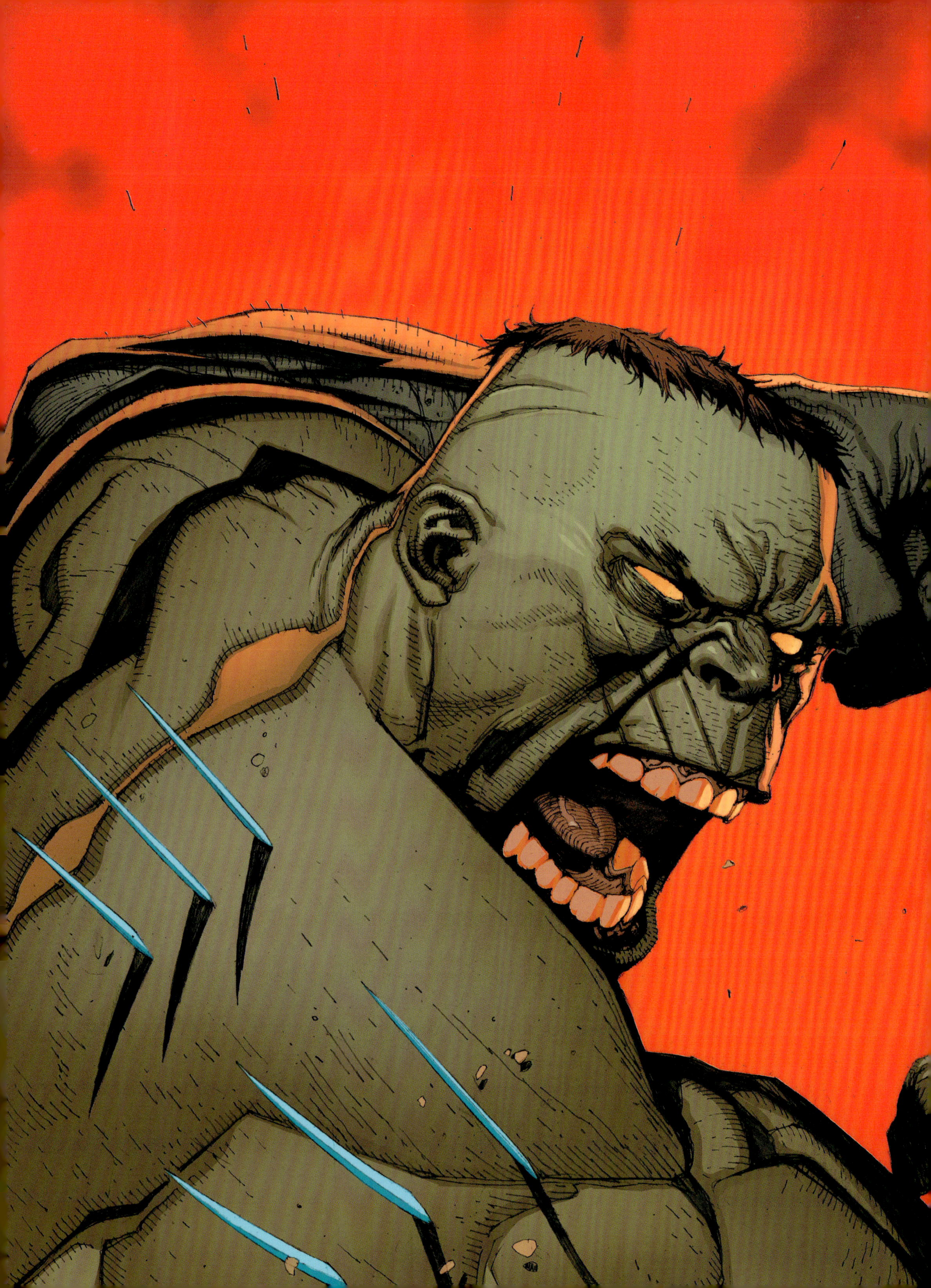

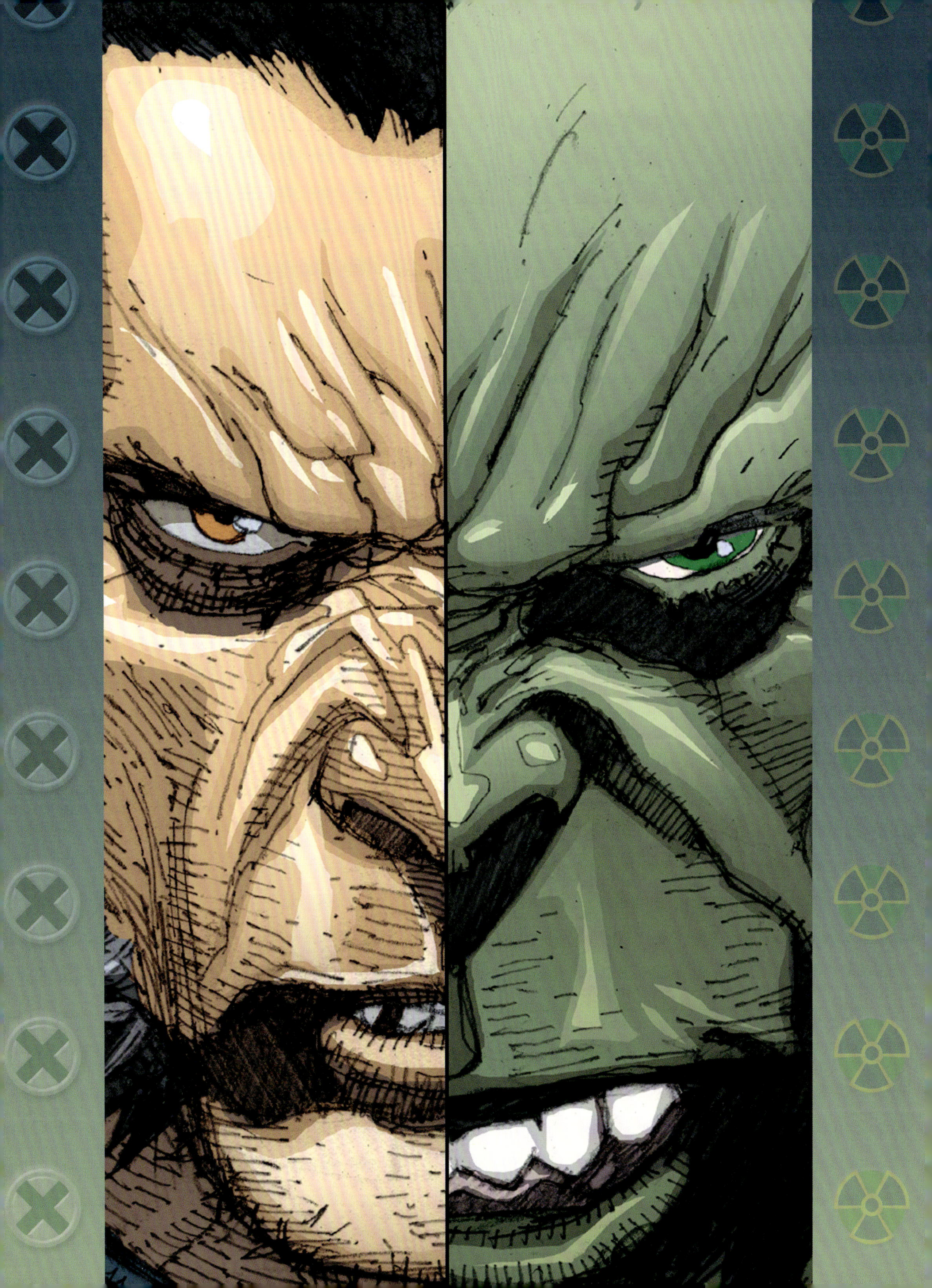

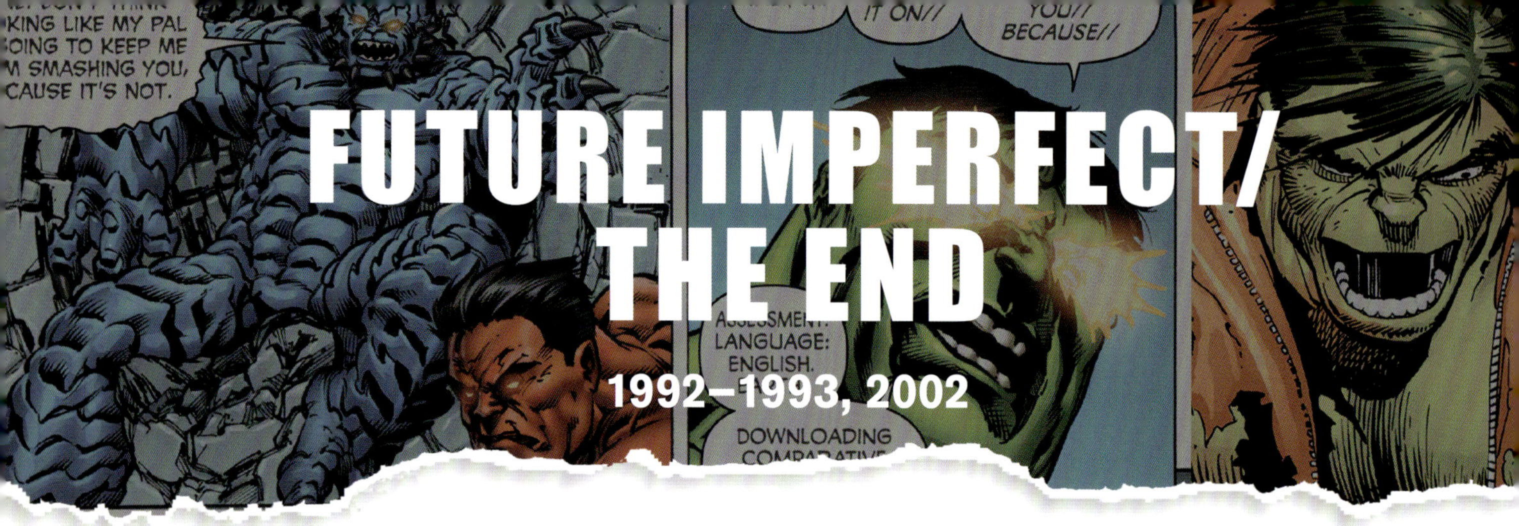
BECAUSE//
LANGUAGE:
ENGLISH.
DOWNLOADING

# FUTURE IMPERFECT/ THE END

## 1992–1993, 2002

The title of this story is a fair description of the events that unfold. *Future Imperfect* and its sequel *The End* (released ten years later) are set in a dystopian future. Earth has had a nuclear war, and most survivors now live in a city called Dystopia. The city is overcrowded and chaotic, and has a central marketplace where people gather. There is a group of radicals in the middle of the marketplace who wants to change the city. A red dot suddenly appears on the forehead of one of the radicals; a shot rings out and he drops, dead. The Gravity Police are on the scene. These cops are tasked with keeping the resistance down, and they are brutal and ruthless.

The police and the insurgents clash, and a building is destroyed. From under the wreckage a large green figure appears. The Hulk has arrived from the past. He chooses to defend the renegades, and a new battle begins in earnest. The Hulk is forced to confront an enormous robotic dog-like machine. The Hulk defeats the machine and the Gravity Police, and he and the renegades retreat to an underground community.

Underground, the Hulk sees the oppression of these people up close. The Hulk is led to a large room where he is shocked to see relics from super heroes' past are hanging from the ceiling, mounted on the walls, and encased in glass: helmets and masks from Thor, Magneto, Iron Man, Spider-Man, and more; Captain America's shield is there; and so is Wolverine's adamantium skeleton. And sitting in an electronic chair is the insurgents' leader. He is an ancient, shriveled old man, and the Hulk is shocked to learn it is his old friend Rick Jones. Rick was the person Bruce Banner rushed out into the desert years ago to save from the gamma ray blast. How could he possibly be alive after all these years?

The ruler who controls the city has been informed about the events that happened in the market and about this mysterious green giant. The leader, Maestro, emerges, and we discover that he is an older version of the Hulk from an alternative future. He possesses the Hulk's strength and Bruce Banner's intelligence. This is the first appearance of this older version of the Hulk. Is the Hulk destined to become this version?

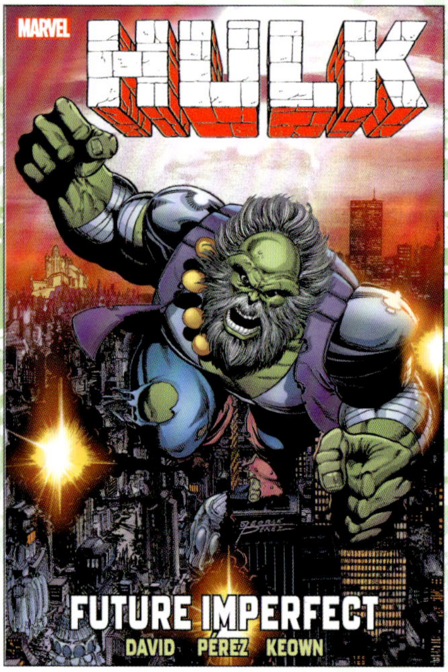
MARVEL
HULK
FUTURE IMPERFECT
DAVID PÉREZ KEOWN

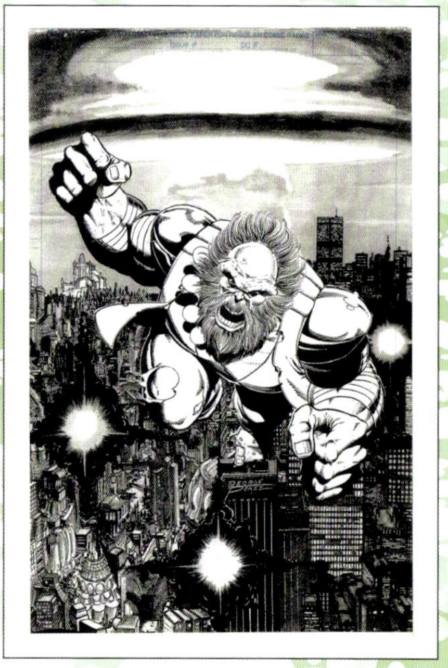

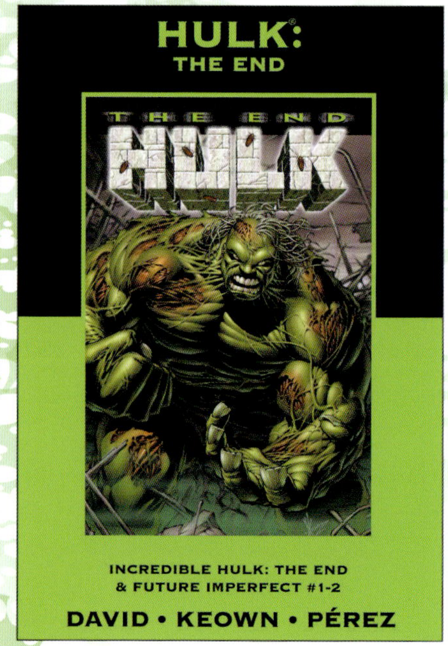
HULK:
THE END
THE END
HULK
INCREDIBLE HULK: THE END
& FUTURE IMPERFECT #1-2
DAVID • KEOWN • PÉREZ

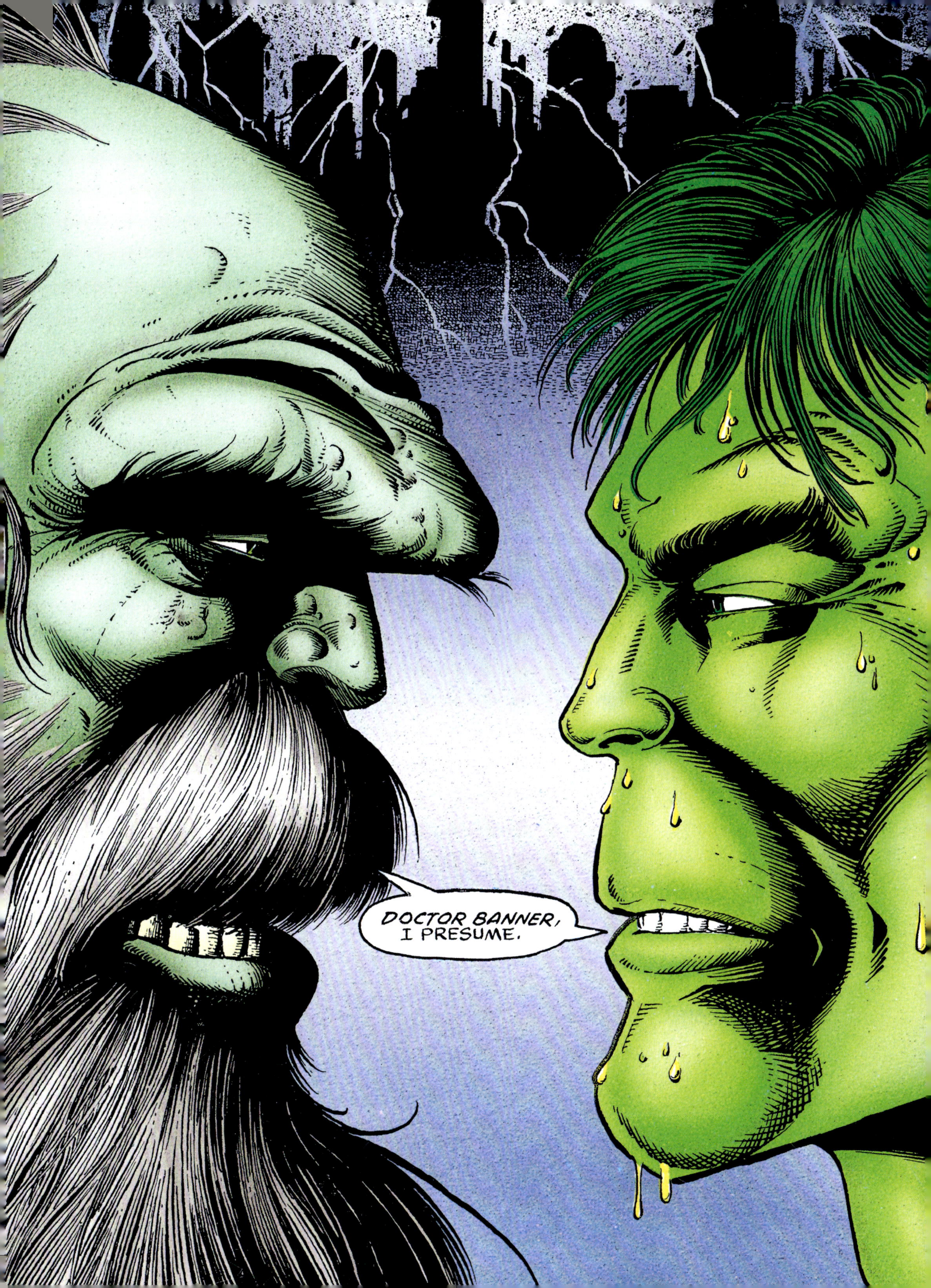
DOCTOR BANNER, I PRESUME.

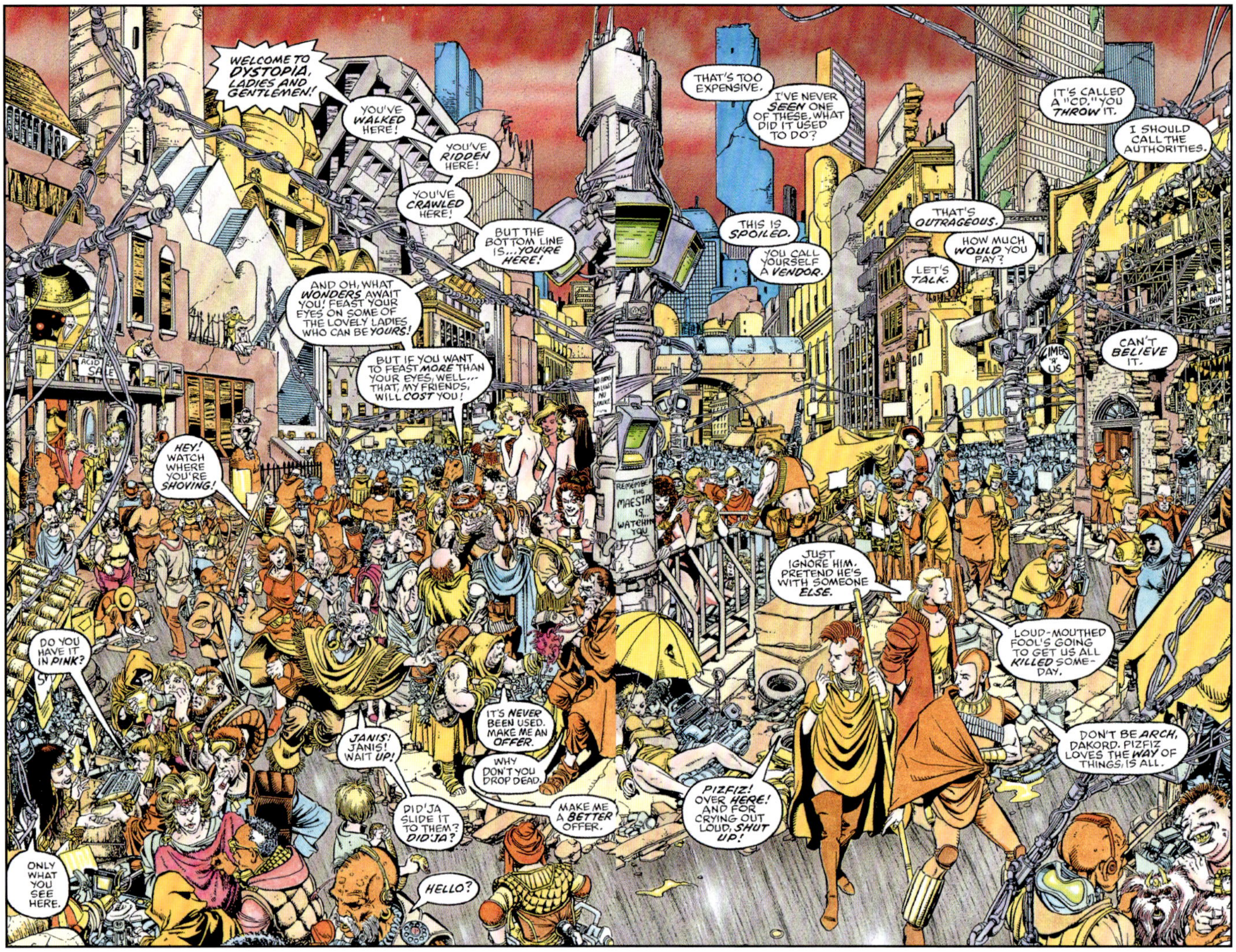
WELCOME TO DYSTOPIA, LADIES AND GENTLEMEN!
YOU'VE WALKED HERE!
YOU'VE RIDDEN HERE!
YOU'VE CRAWLED HERE!
BUT THE BOTTOM LINE IS... YOU'RE HERE!
AND OH, WHAT WONDERS AWAIT YOU! FEAST YOUR EYES ON SOME OF THE LOVELY LADIES WHO CAN BE YOURS!
BUT IF YOU WANT TO FEAST MORE THAN YOUR EYES, WELL... THAT, MY FRIENDS, WILL COST YOU!
HEY! WATCH WHERE YOU'RE SHOVING!
REMEMBER THE MAESTRO IS WATCHING YOU
DO YOU HAVE IT IN PINK?
JANIS! JANIS! WAIT UP!
DID'JA SLIDE IT TO THEM? DID'JA?
IT'S NEVER BEEN USED. MAKE ME AN OFFER.
WHY DON'T YOU DROP DEAD.
MAKE ME A BETTER OFFER.
HELLO?
ONLY WHAT YOU SEE HERE.
THAT'S TOO EXPENSIVE.
I'VE NEVER SEEN ONE OF THESE. WHAT DID IT USED TO DO?
THIS IS SPOILED.
YOU CALL YOURSELF A VENDOR.
THAT'S OUTRAGEOUS.
HOW MUCH WOULD YOU PAY?
LET'S TALK.
IT'S CALLED A "CD." YOU THROW IT.
I SHOULD CALL THE AUTHORITIES.
CAN'T BELIEVE IT.
JUST IGNORE HIM. PRETEND HE'S WITH SOMEONE ELSE.
LOUD-MOUTHED FOOL'S GOING TO GET US ALL KILLED SOME-DAY.
DON'T BE ARCH, DAKORD. PIZFIZ LOVES THE WAY OF THINGS, IS ALL.
PIZFIZ! OVER HERE! AND FOR CRYING OUT LOUD, SHUT UP!

Maestro captures one of the rebels and he uses a device that lets him look into a person's mind and see their memories. Among the prisoner's memories he discovers that the rebels have been working on a time-travel machine. Maestro heads out to hunt down both the Hulk and the time-travel machine.

Maestro is a brutal tyrant. He tries to convince his younger self to side with him against the rebels. But it's not who the younger Hulk is, and a battle ensues between the two versions of the Hulk. The Hulk defeats Maestro, but the question remains—is Maestro the Hulk's destined-to-be future, or is there a different path for him?

The answer arrived years later when author Peter David revisited *Future Imperfect* with a piece called *The End*. *The End* opens with a shriveled old man in shredded purple pants roaming a barren world, his wisps of white hair blowing in the hot desert wind. His body shakes as he walks through the wreckage of Las Vegas. There isn't another human to be seen.

The only visible living things are a swarm of mutant bugs, which attacks him. As he swats the bugs off, he gets angry. The old man transforms into the Hulk. But the insects quickly devour most of his body. He lies in the desert, his body eaten away, but he is not quite killed. Because of the Hulk's healing powers, his body regenerates. This is the Hulk's fate—he can't die. He has traveled all over the globe looking for other human beings, but is unsuccessful. The Hulk is the last living human on Earth. The Hulk has always said he wanted to be alone—and now he finally gets his wish.

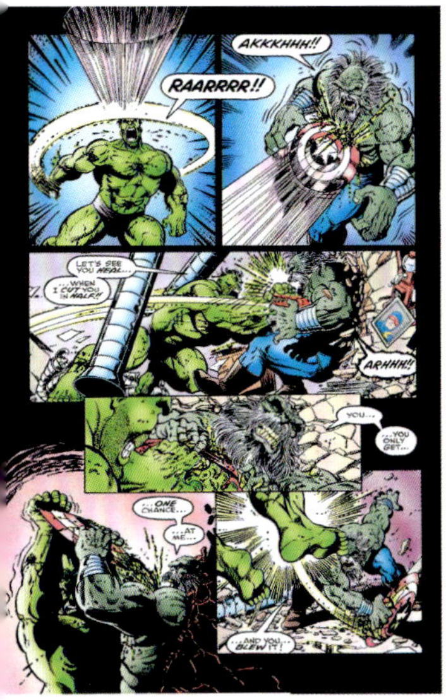
AKKKHHH!!
RAARRRR!!
ARHHH!!

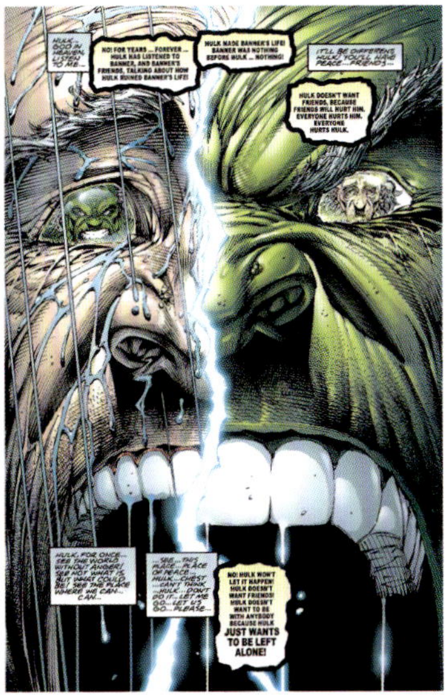
HULK... GOD IN HEAVEN, LISTEN TO ME...
NO! FOR YEARS ... FOREVER ... HULK HAS LISTENED TO BANNER, AND BANNER'S FRIENDS, TALKING ABOUT HOW HULK RUINED BANNER'S LIFE!
HULK MADE BANNER'S LIFE! BANNER WAS NOTHING BEFORE HULK ... NOTHING!
IT'LL BE DIFFERENT, HULK! YOU'LL HAVE PEACE... FRIENDS...
HULK DOESN'T WANT FRIENDS, BECAUSE FRIENDS WILL HURT HIM. EVERYONE HURTS HIM. EVERYONE HURTS HULK.
HULK, FOR ONCE... SEE THE WORLD WITHOUT ANGER! SEE NOT WHAT IS, BUT WHAT COULD BE! SEE THE PLACE WHERE WE CAN... CAN...
...SEE... THIS PLACE... PLACE OF PEACE... HULK... CHEST ...CAN'T THINK ...HULK... DON'T DO IT... LET ME GO... LET US GO... PLEASE...
NO! HULK WON'T LET IT HAPPEN! HULK DOESN'T WANT FRIENDS! HULK DOESN'T WANT TO BE WITH ANYBODY BECAUSE HULK JUST WANTS TO BE LEFT ALONE!

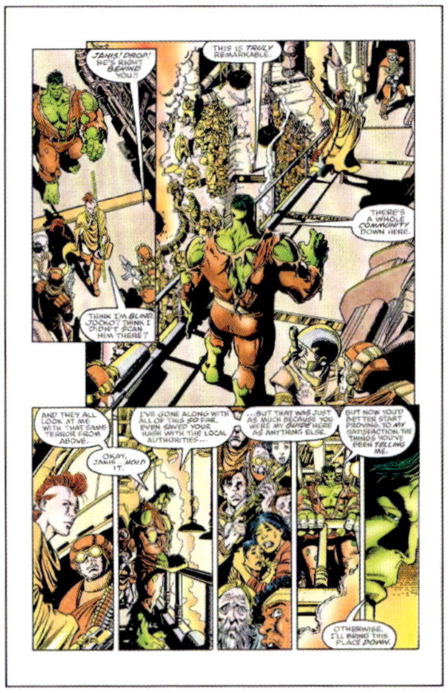

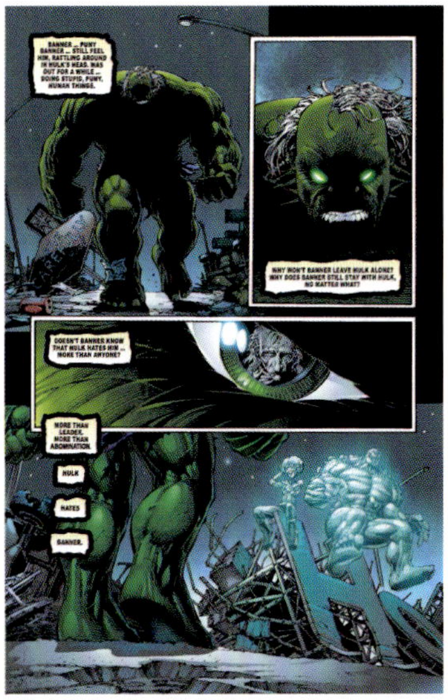
BANNER ... PUNY BANNER ... STILL FEEL HIM, RATTLING AROUND IN HULK'S HEAD. WAS OUT FOR A WHILE ... DOING STUPID, PUNY, HUMAN THINGS.
WHY WON'T BANNER LEAVE HULK ALONE? WHY DOES BANNER STILL STAY WITH HULK, NO MATTER WHAT?
DOESN'T BANNER KNOW THAT HULK HATES HIM ... MORE THAN ANYONE?
MORE THAN LEADER. MORE THAN ABOMINATION.
HULK
HATES
BANNER.

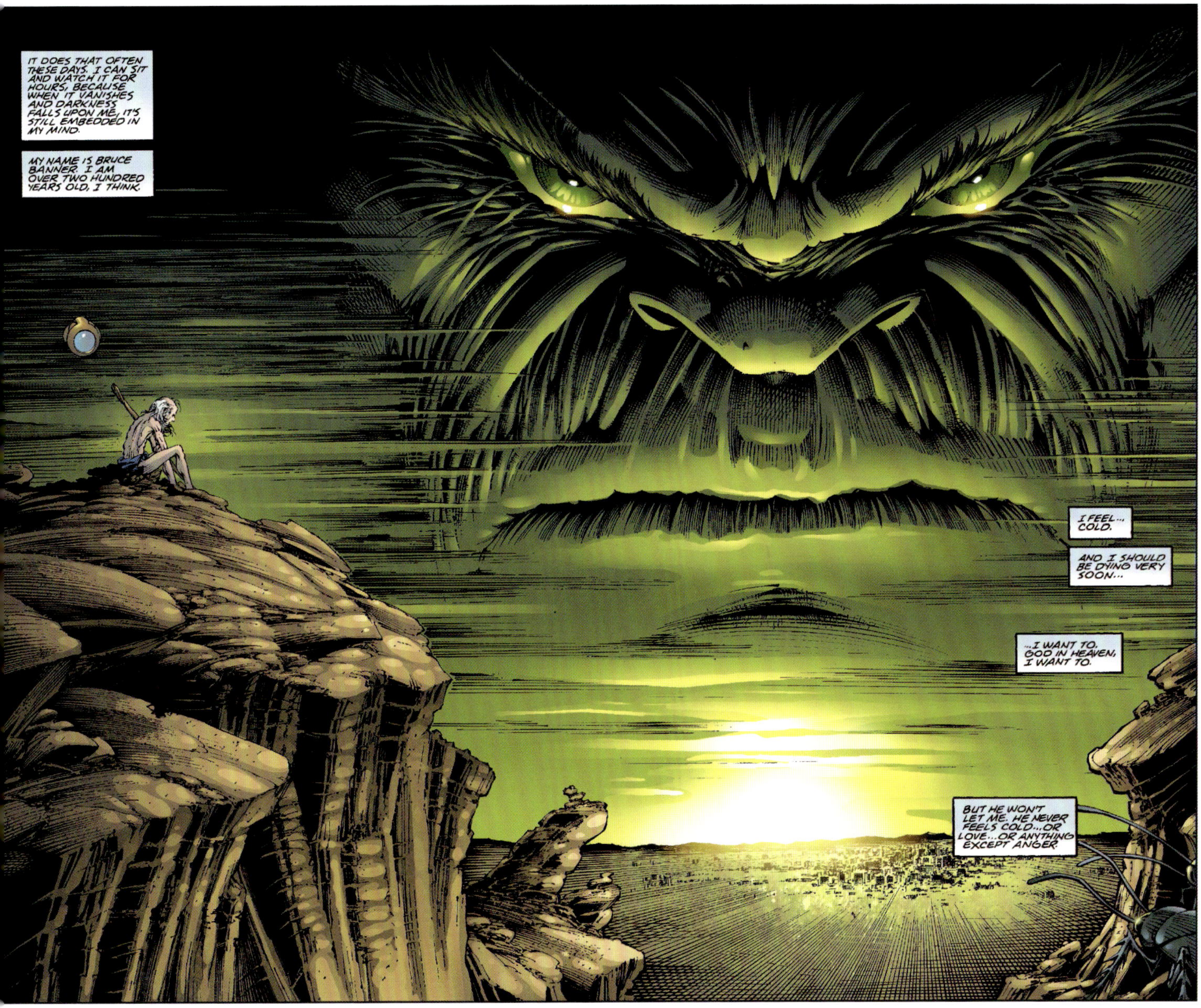
IT DOES THAT OFTEN THESE DAYS. I CAN SIT AND WATCH IT FOR HOURS, BECAUSE WHEN IT VANISHES AND DARKNESS FALLS UPON ME, IT'S STILL EMBEDDED IN MY MIND.
MY NAME IS BRUCE BANNER. I AM OVER TWO HUNDRED YEARS OLD, I THINK.
I FEEL... COLD.
AND I SHOULD BE DYING VERY SOON...
...I WANT TO. GOD IN HEAVEN, I WANT TO.
BUT HE WON'T LET ME. HE NEVER FEELS COLD... OR LOVE... OR ANYTHING EXCEPT ANGER.

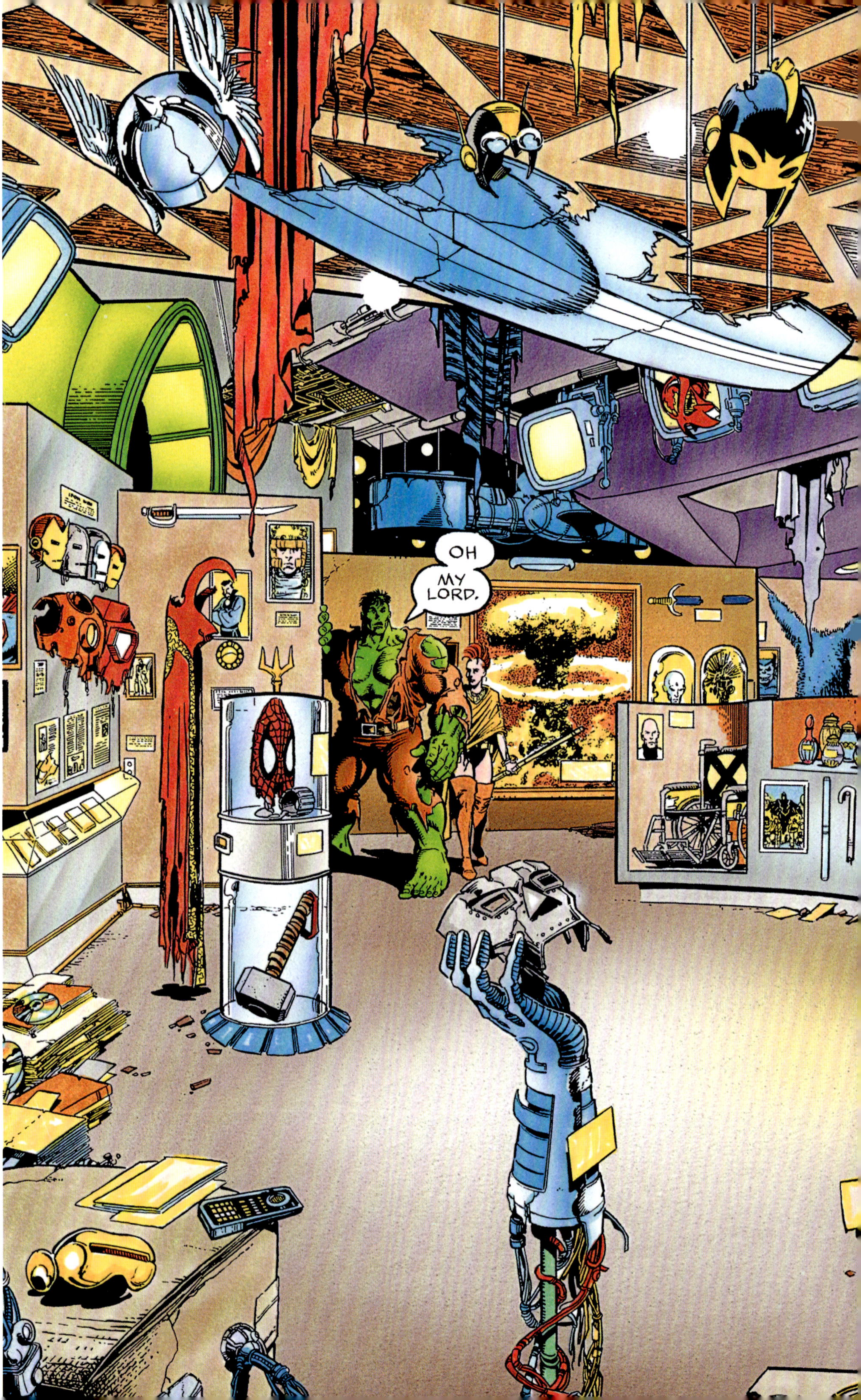
OH MY LORD.

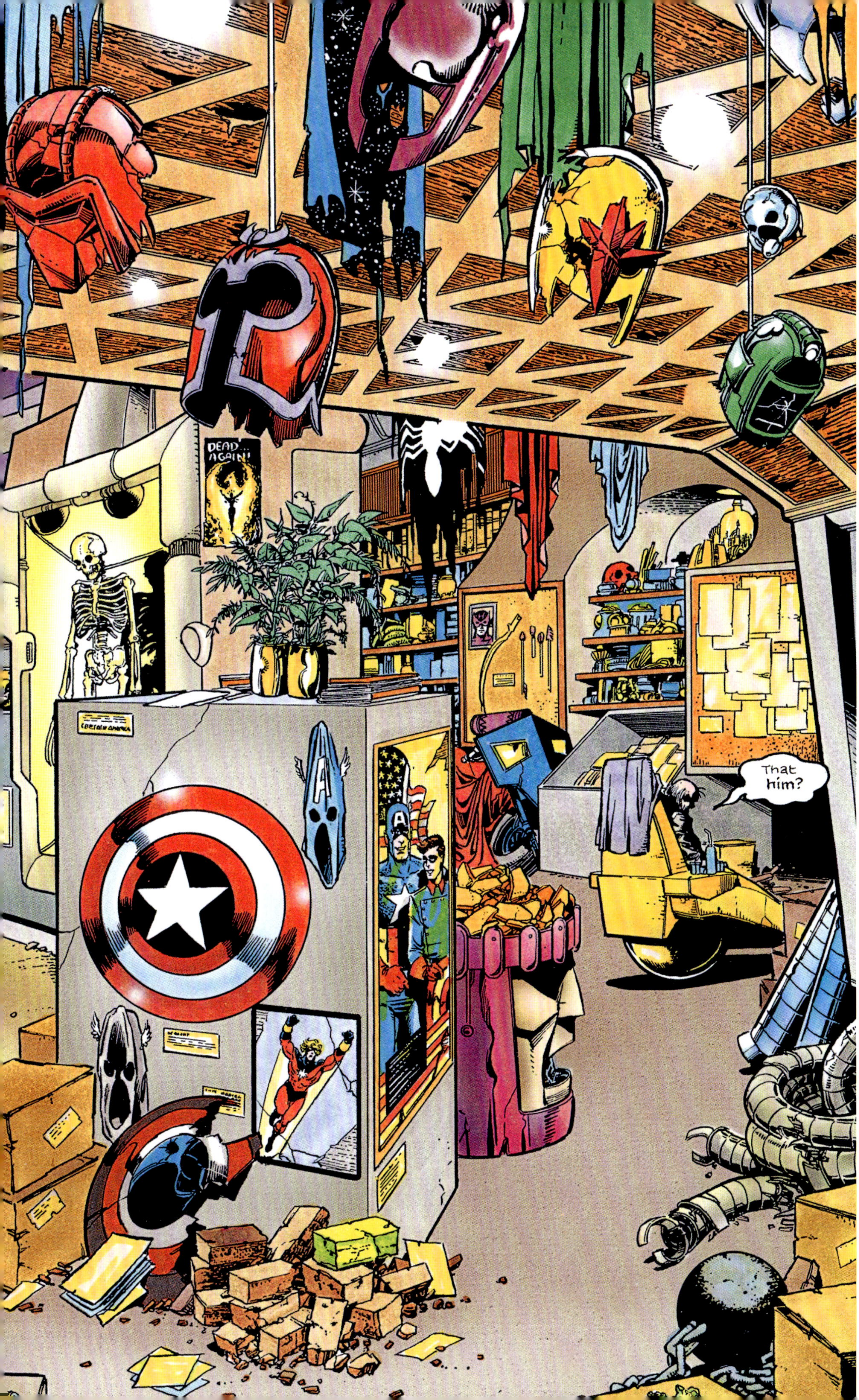
DEAD...
AGAIN!
That him?

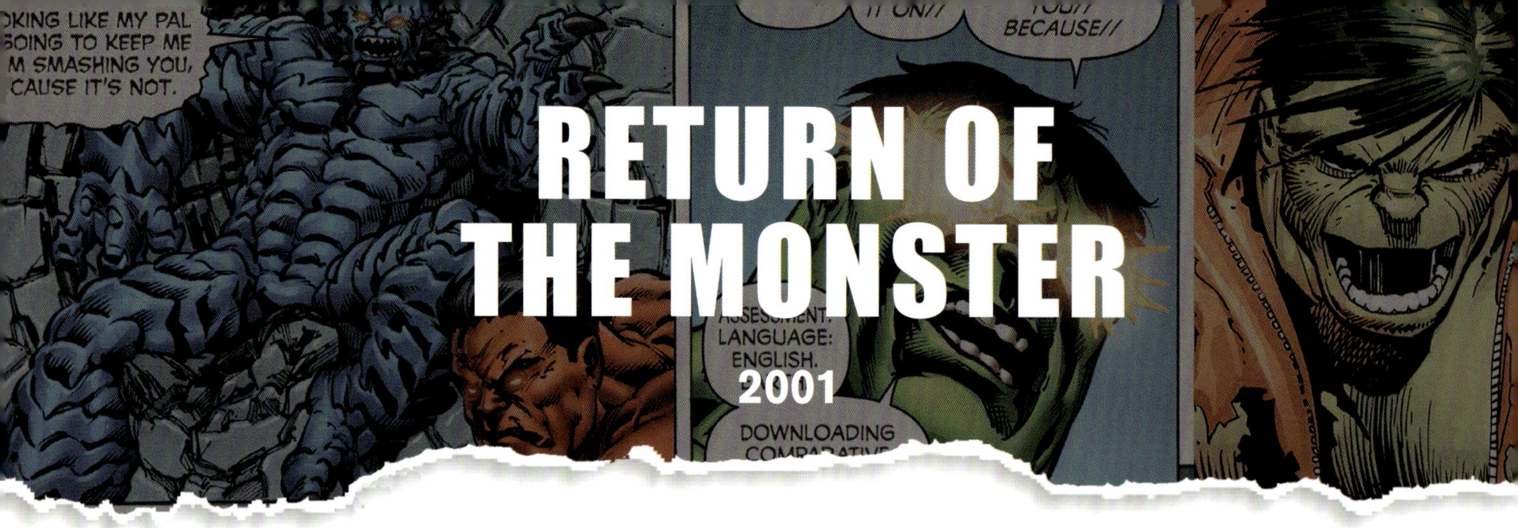
BECAUSE//
LANGUAGE:
ENGLISH.
DOWNLOADING

# RETURN OF THE MONSTER

## 2001

A man wearing a baseball cap, winter coat, and purple pants walks through a run-down neighborhood. He wears glasses and has grown a beard as a disguise. He checks into a seedy motel. He only wants one night. The clerk, who is wolfing down a burger, tells him that he can't break the hundred-dollar bill the man offers. They settle on two nights.

In his room the man unpacks his few belongings that include men's hair dye, a book titled *Exercises in Mind-Controlling Yoga*, a laptop, and a portable television. He opens the laptop and sends a message to a man he calls Mr. Blue. He refers to himself as Mr. Green. Mr. Blue tells Mr. Green that he can't talk right now.

Mr. Green heads out into the hallway for the communal bathroom. Across the hall, a door bursts open and Green sees a woman throw a handful of cash at a young man she calls Jerome, telling him she doesn't want his dirty money. After Jerome leaves, she complains to Mr. Green that her son used to be a kid who was at the top of his class, but "now look at him!"

Mr. Green heads into the bathroom to soak in the bathtub. He watches the news on the portable TV about a Hulk rampage in Chicago. They show a photo of a man they identify as Robert Bruce Banner. The news anchor advises not to approach Banner, who may have a beard. Now out of the tub, Mr. Green looks into the mirror at his bearded face. He leaves the bathroom bald and clean-shaven.

Banner sleeps, and Jerome, the kid from across the hall, sneaks into his room and takes his laptop and wallet. Banner wakes up and confronts the thief. He tells Jerome that he's not going to leave with his belongings. Jerome asks him how he's going to stop him. Banner replies, "By asking." Sure enough Jerome leaves the man's laptop and wallet, but not before he sees Banner react to the sound of a distant police siren by quickly standing to the side of the window and out of sight.

The next day, Banner sees Jerome being threatened by a gang. Banner tries to intervene, but Jerome tells him not to.

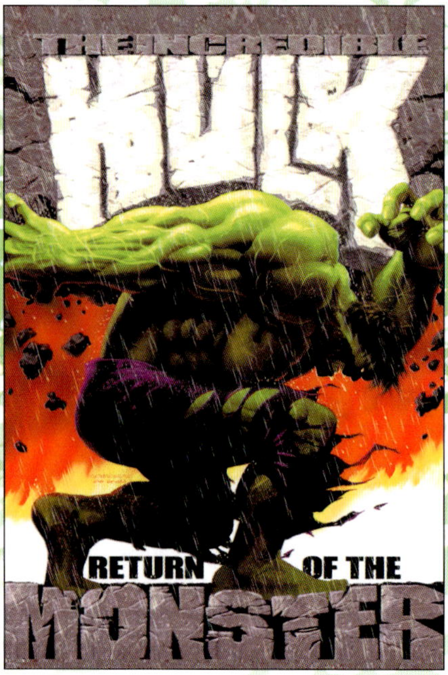
THE INCREDIBLE
HULK
RETURN OF THE
MONSTER

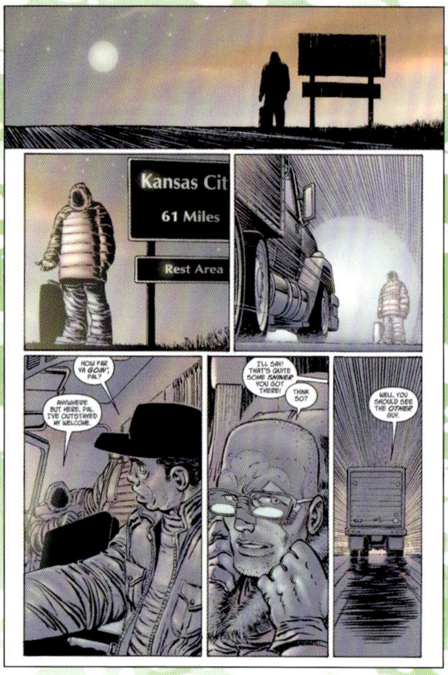
Kansas Cit
61 Miles
Rest Area

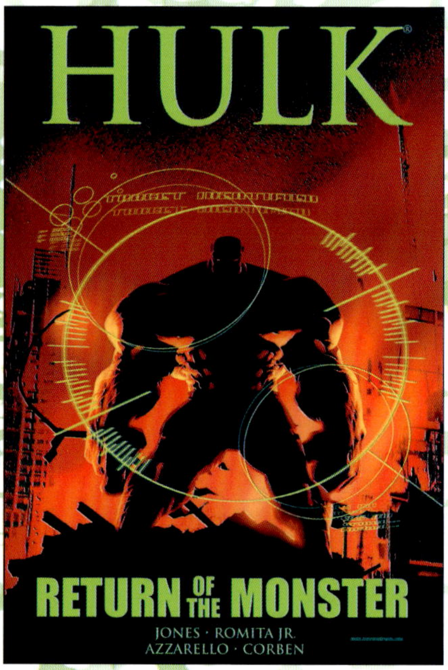
HULK
RETURN OF THE MONSTER
JONES · ROMITA JR.
AZZARELLO · CORBEN

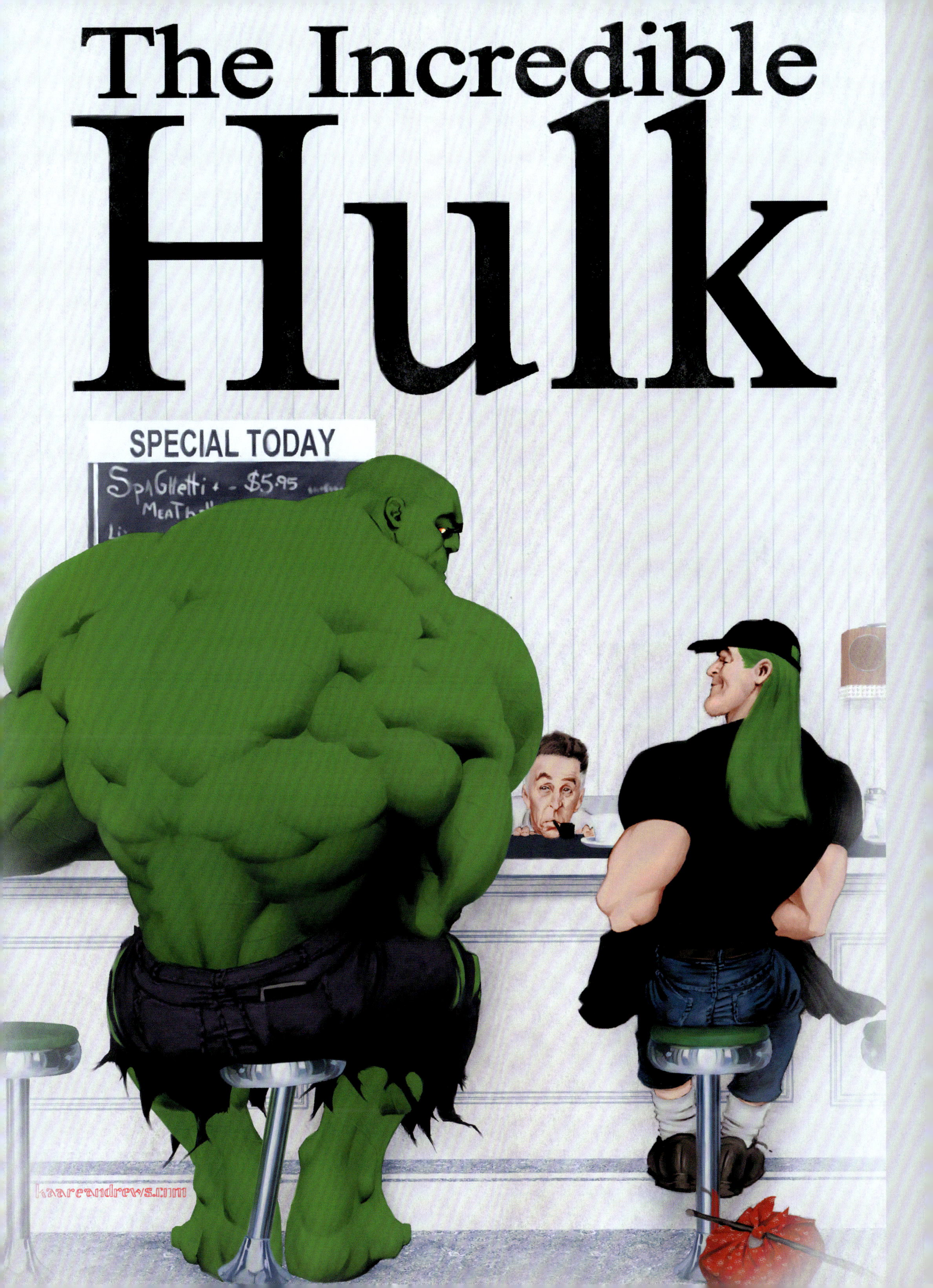

The Incredible Hulk
SPECIAL TODAY
SpaGhetti + - $5.95
kaareandrews.com

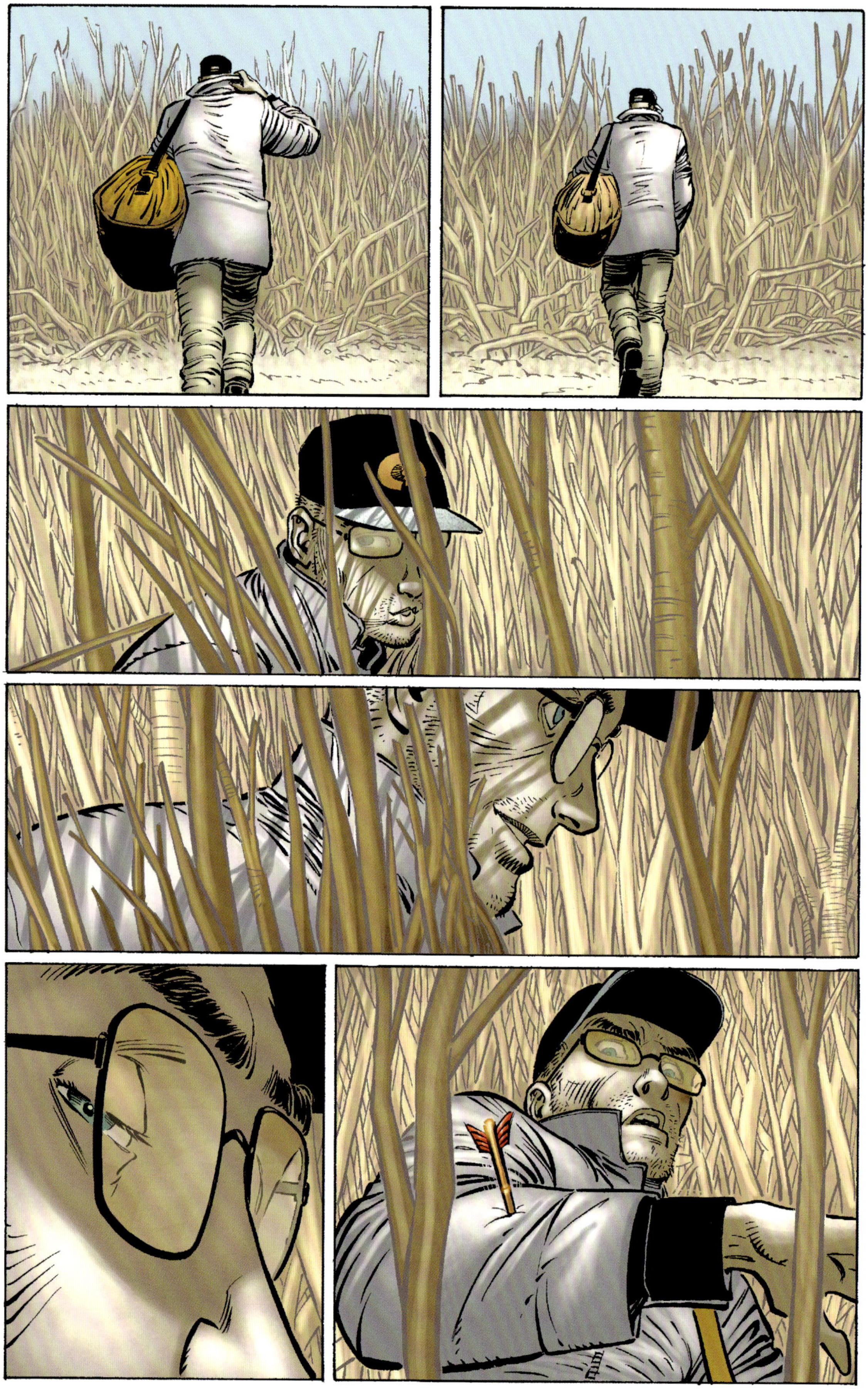

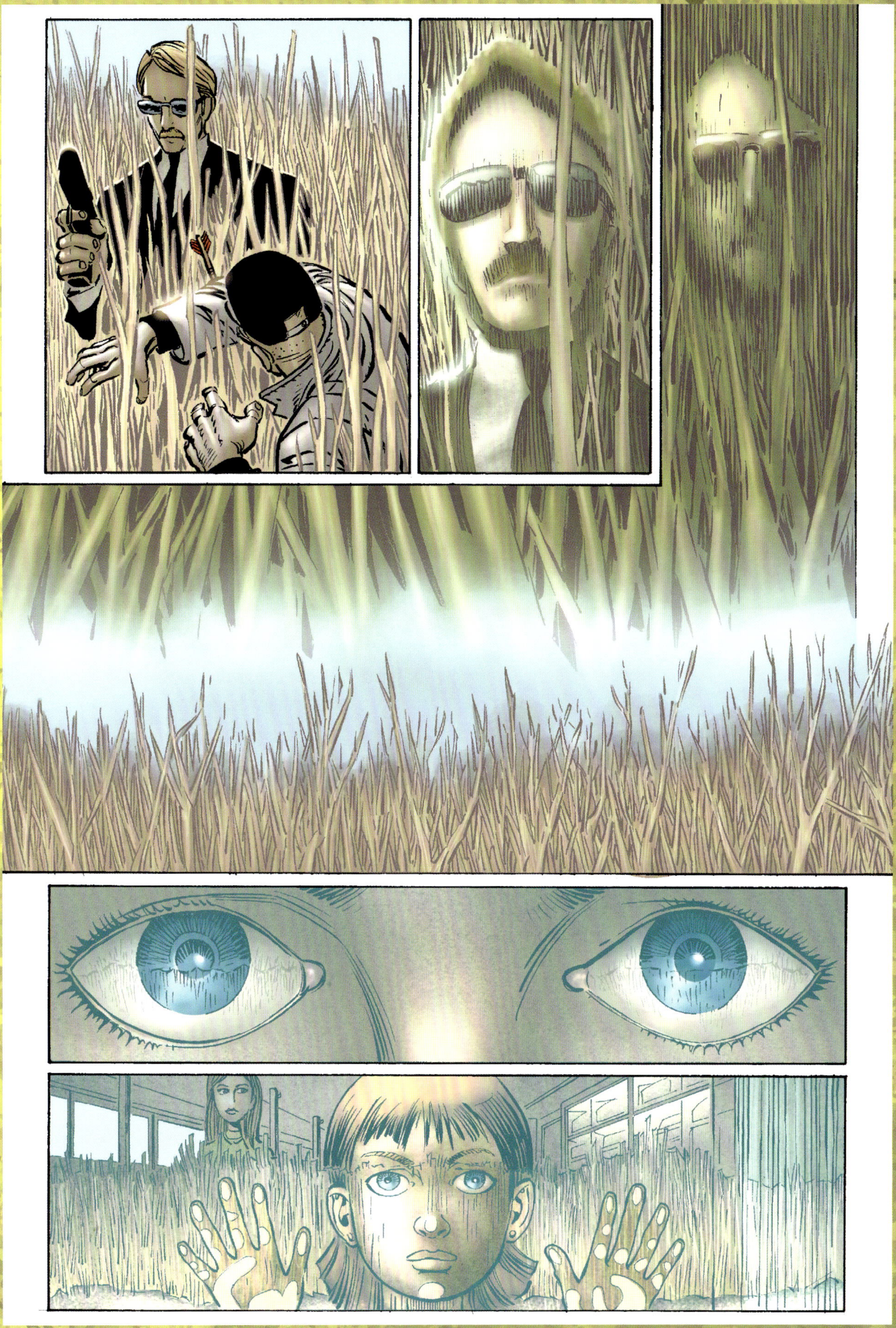

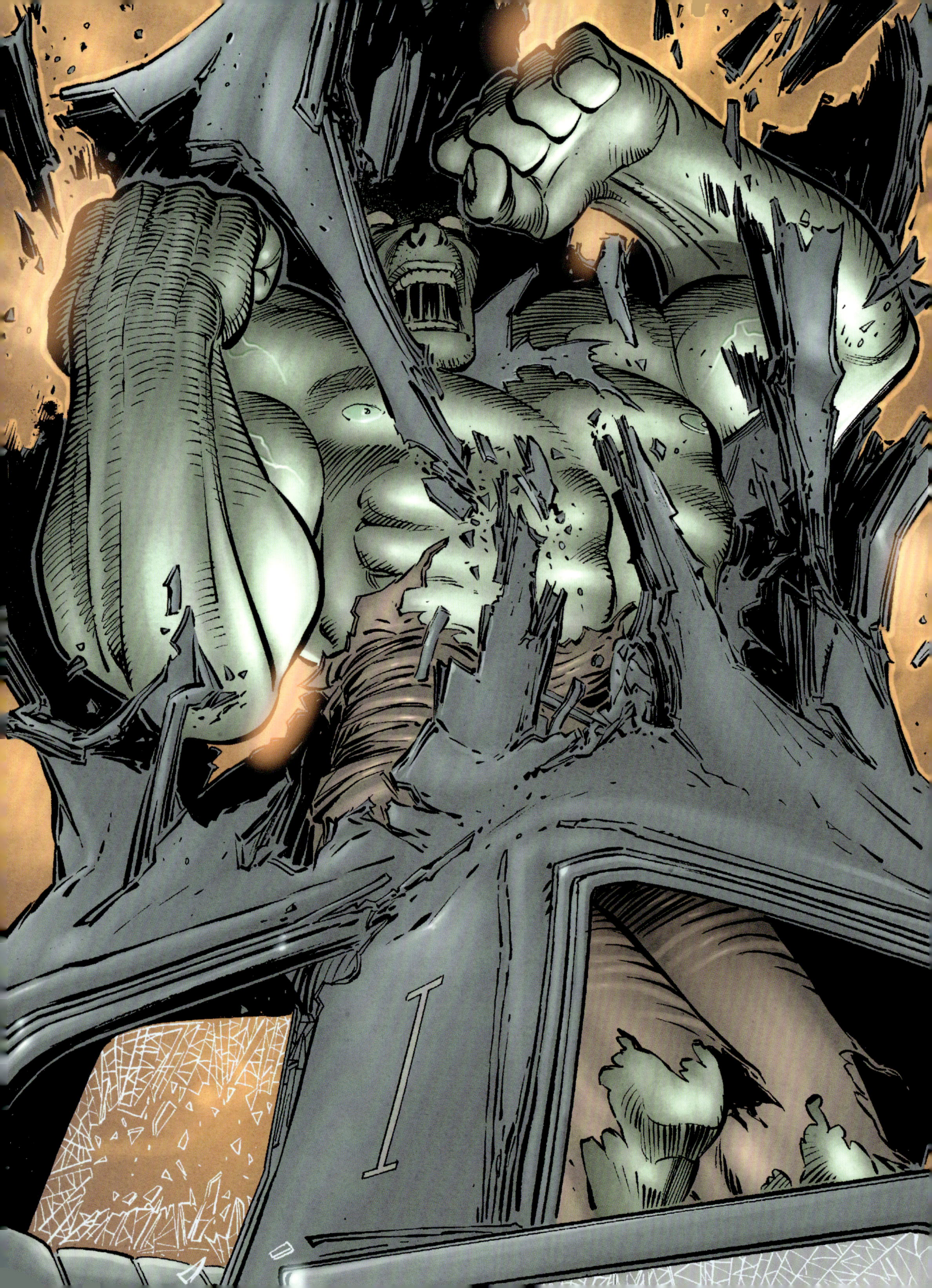

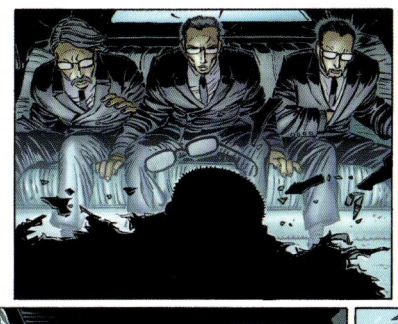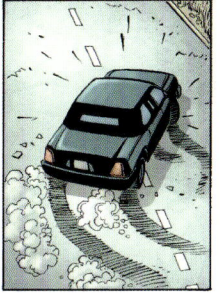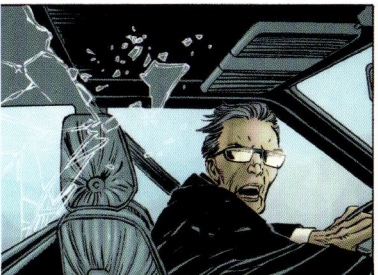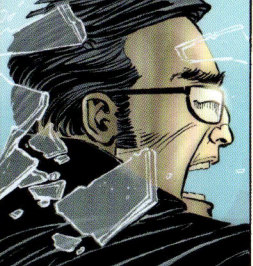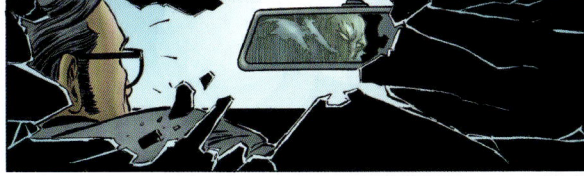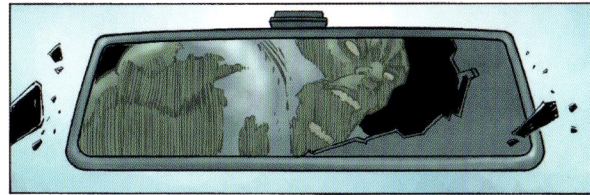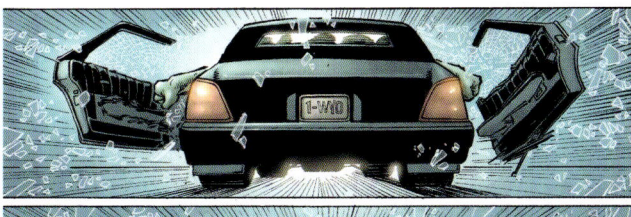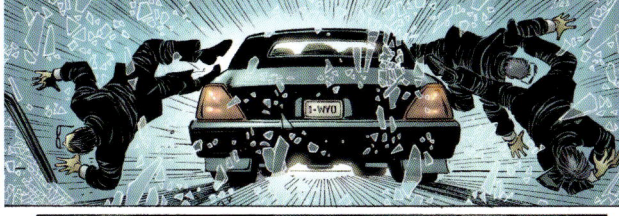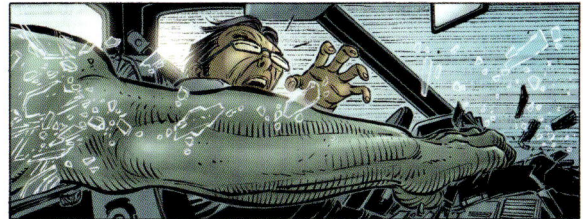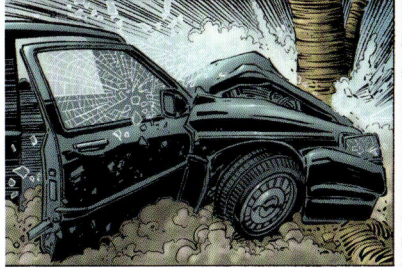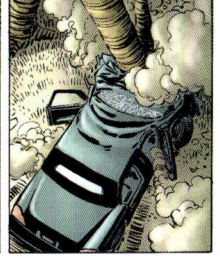

Banner goes back to confront the gang on the street. Later, the gang leader wakes up naked in a pile of rubble and sees the headline of a discarded newspaper that reads "Fugitive Banner Eludes Police." The thug whispers the word "Hulk."

Banner heads out of town wearing the gang leader's parka. Banner ends up at a roadside diner. A woman with her young daughter sits in the booth across from him. The daughter stares at Banner. In her hands she holds the book *Jack and the Friendly Giant*. Banner waves but gets no response.

Banner takes out his laptop and sends a message to Mr. Blue asking for a "weather report." While he waits for the answer, a black car pulls into the parking lot. Mr. Blue replies that a possible storm is headed his way.

Three men in black suits, white shirts, black ties, and sunglasses walk into the diner. Banner slips out the back. He heads into the tall grass in the back, but a dart pierces his parka. Banner's unconscious body is thrown into the back seat of the black car—but it's the Hulk who wakes up.

When he is done raging, the car and the men are all in need of repair. Banner, now wearing the black suit and sunglasses, heads back to the diner. The young mother is just leaving. As mother and daughter get up to leave, they drop a book. Banner bends down to pick it up; the book is titled *The Autistic Child*. Banner and the girl exchange a smile.

Banner finds himself again alone in another cheap motel. The news plays in the background. There is footage of the Hulk ripping into a building, and of young Ricky Myers being buried in the rubble. Banner can't remember, and can't believe he did this.

Why can't Banner remember? Is he destined to be on the run—one cheap motel after the next, another roadside diner? And the battle between the man and the monster—will it ever end?

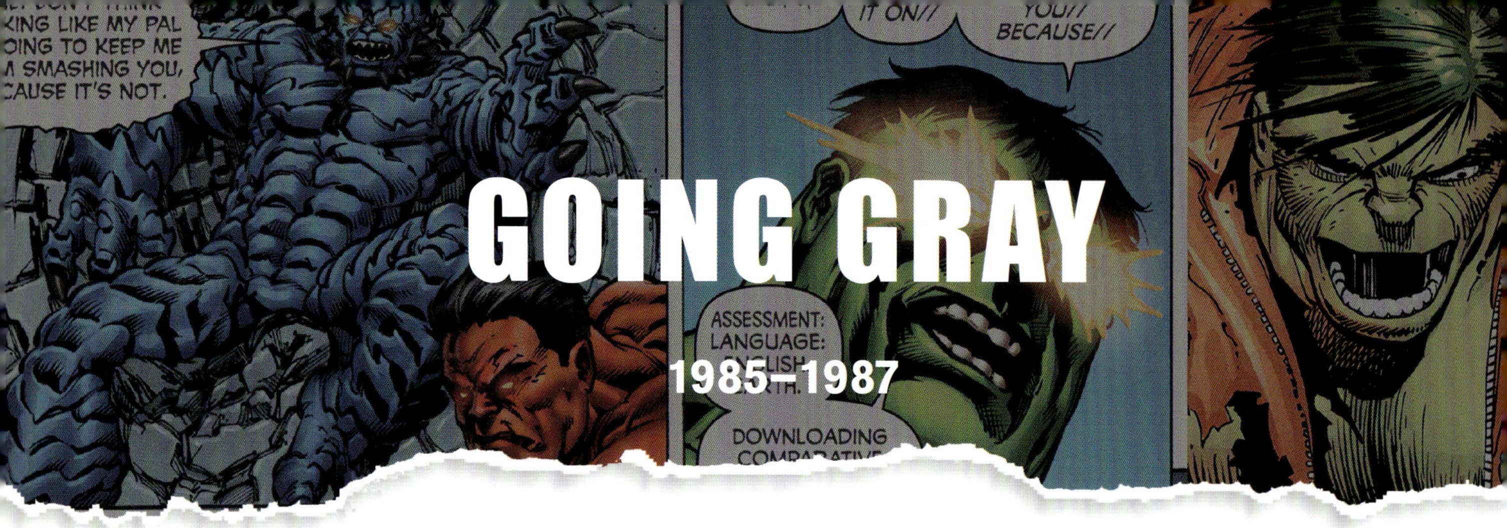
ASSESSMENT:
LANGUAGE:
DOWNLOADING

# GOING GRAY

## 1985–1987

Bruce Banner is constantly at war; this war is being waged in his head. The battle between Banner and the Hulk seems to be never-ending. Neither are willing to stop. What if the simple solution is to separate the two sides, like schoolkids on a playground? But could they survive without each other?

Leonard "Doc" Samson wants to know if it's possible. He leaves the college where he is a professor to head up to Gamma Base, the same lab that helped to create the Hulk. There has been a Hulk sighting, and it looks like he is heading to the lab. Samson plans to find a way to permanently separate the two.

When the Hulk arrives, Samson refers to the Hulk as Banner, which sends him into a rage. They fight, and Samson is knocked out. But that doesn't stop the Hulk from throwing punches. He imagines that some of his foes are there, and they are ready to fight: Juggernaut, M.O.D.O.K., and Rhino. The Hulk swings wildly at the air as he battles his invisible enemies. During the chaos, Samson rallies and takes down the Hulk.

The Hulk is submerged into a nutrient bath, where he continues to hallucinate. Banner has been pulled out of the Hulk, who is now a blank slate. But Samson quickly loses control of the lab when Clay Quartermain, an agent of S.H.I.E.L.D., bursts into the lab and takes over. Quartermain and the other S.H.I.E.L.D agents are there to kill the Hulk. Quartermain loads the Hulk into a transport vehicle. Samson is determined to help him and tries to break him out. The rescue goes sideways, and the Hulk is released into the desert.

Meanwhile, a skinny, weak body is pulled out of the nutrient bath: it's Bruce Banner. He is quicky taken to a medical bay. His body will need time to heal. He even needs to use a wheelchair for a while.

In the desert, the Hulk is on a seemingly endless rampage. Samson believes he has to track down and subdue the Hulk because he was the one who released him. But the Hulk seems unstoppable. Some of the Avengers and West Coast Avengers assemble to lend a hand to bring the Hulk

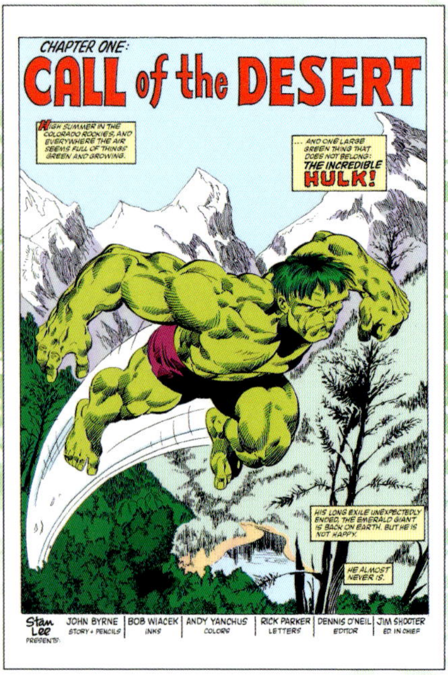
CHAPTER ONE:
CALL of the DESERT
... AND ONE LARGE GREEN THING THAT DOES NOT BELONG: THE INCREDIBLE HULK!

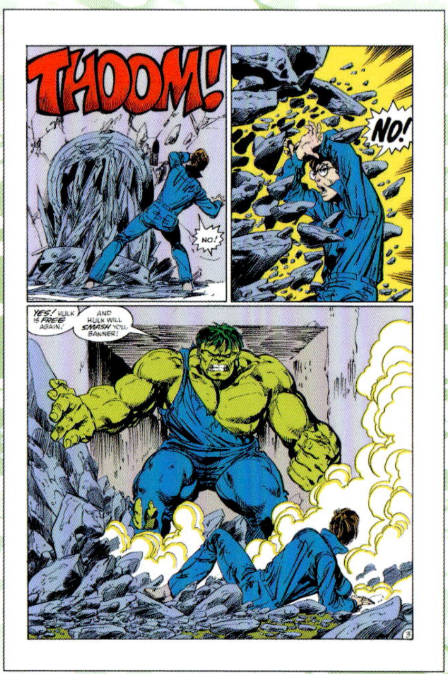
THOOM!
NO!

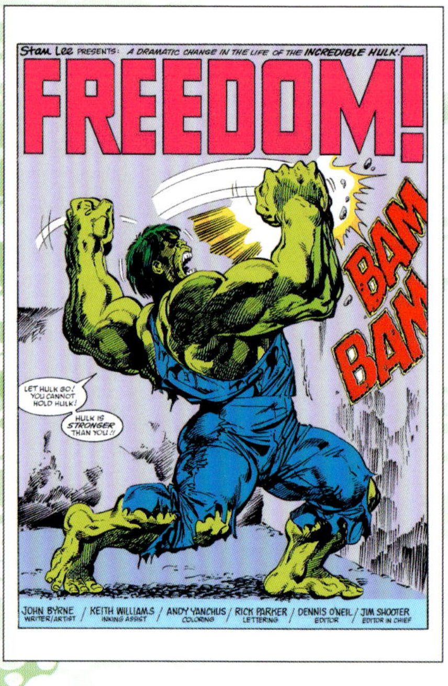
FREEDOM!
BAM
BAM

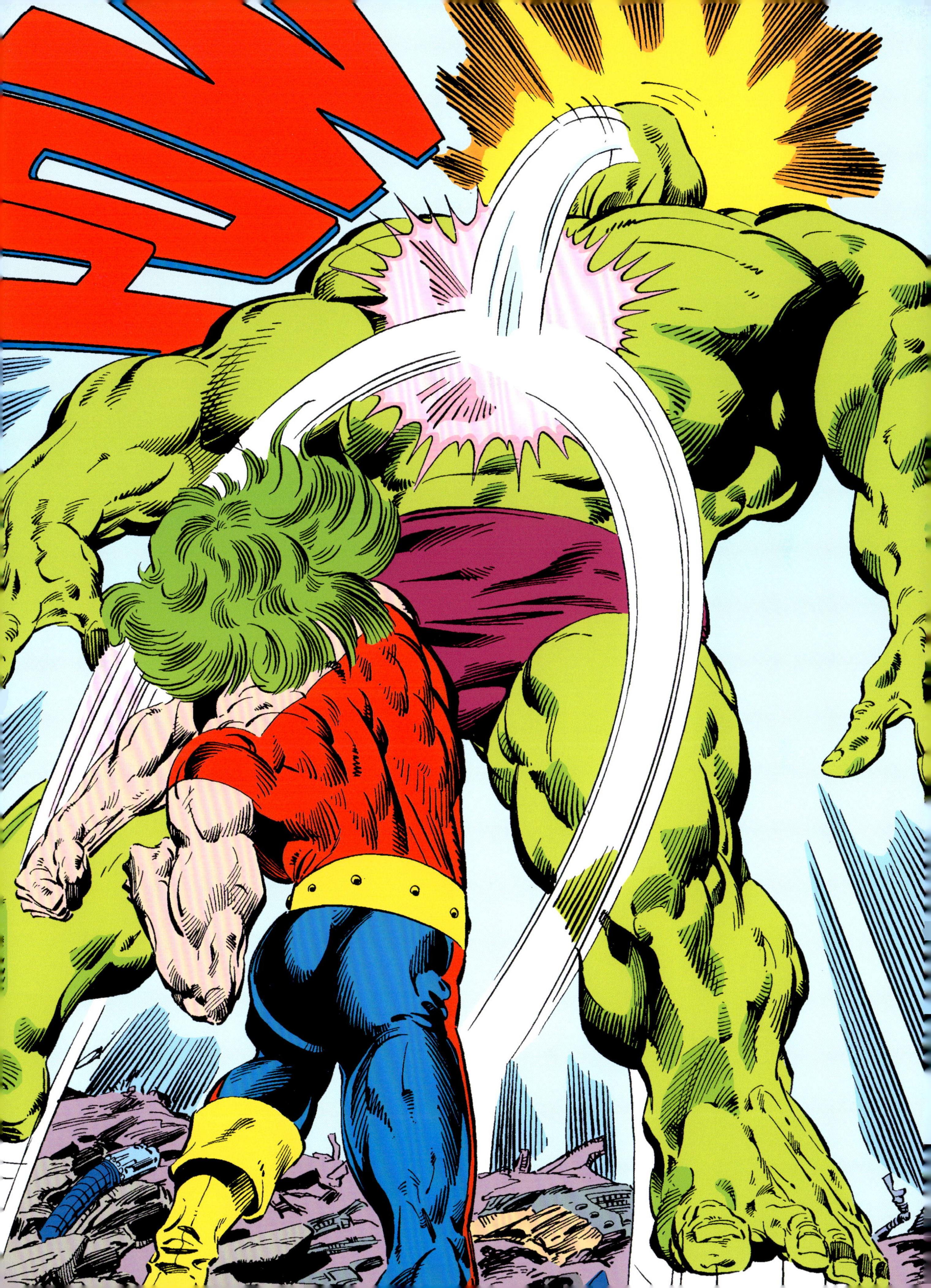

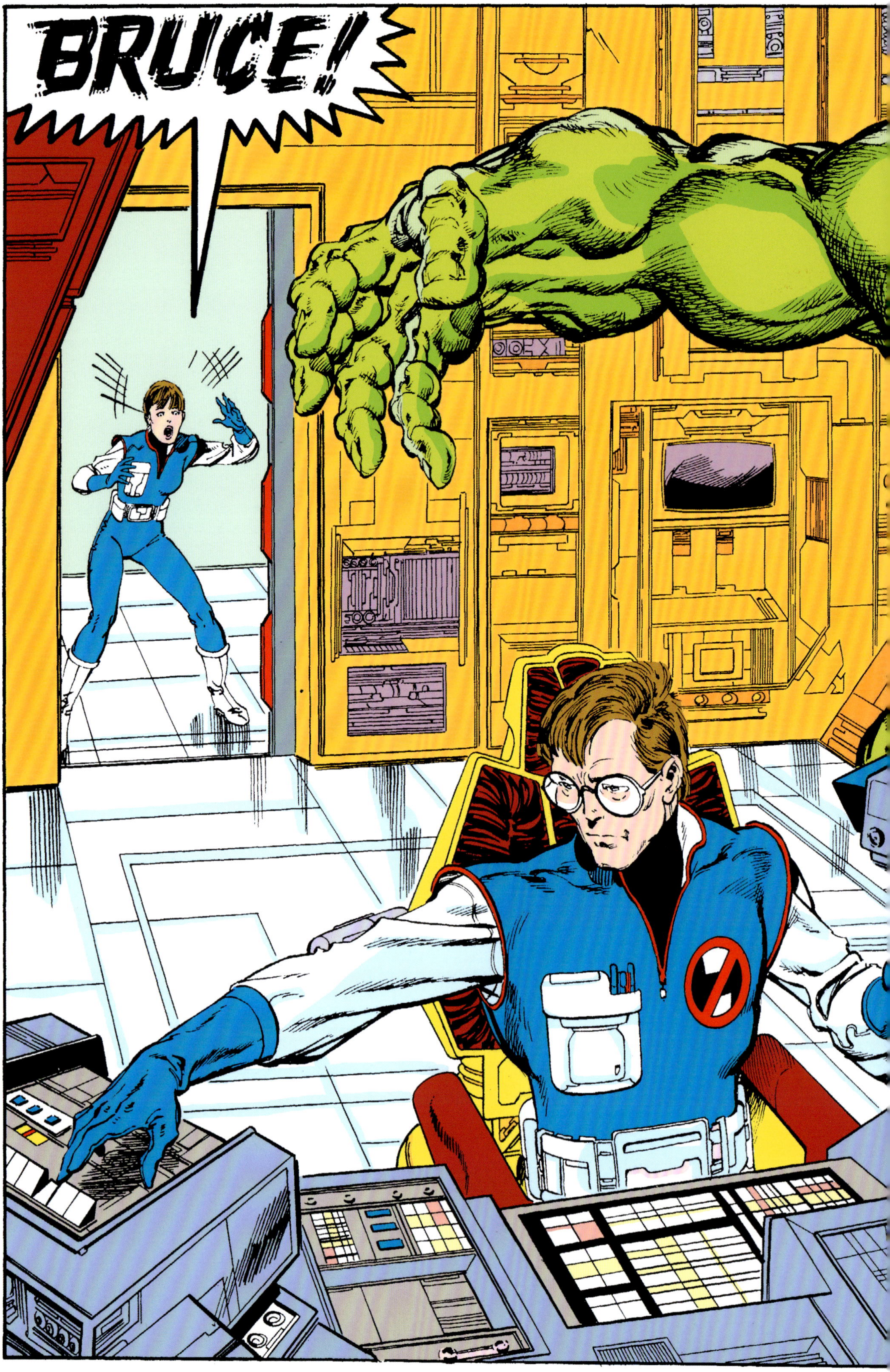
BRUCE!

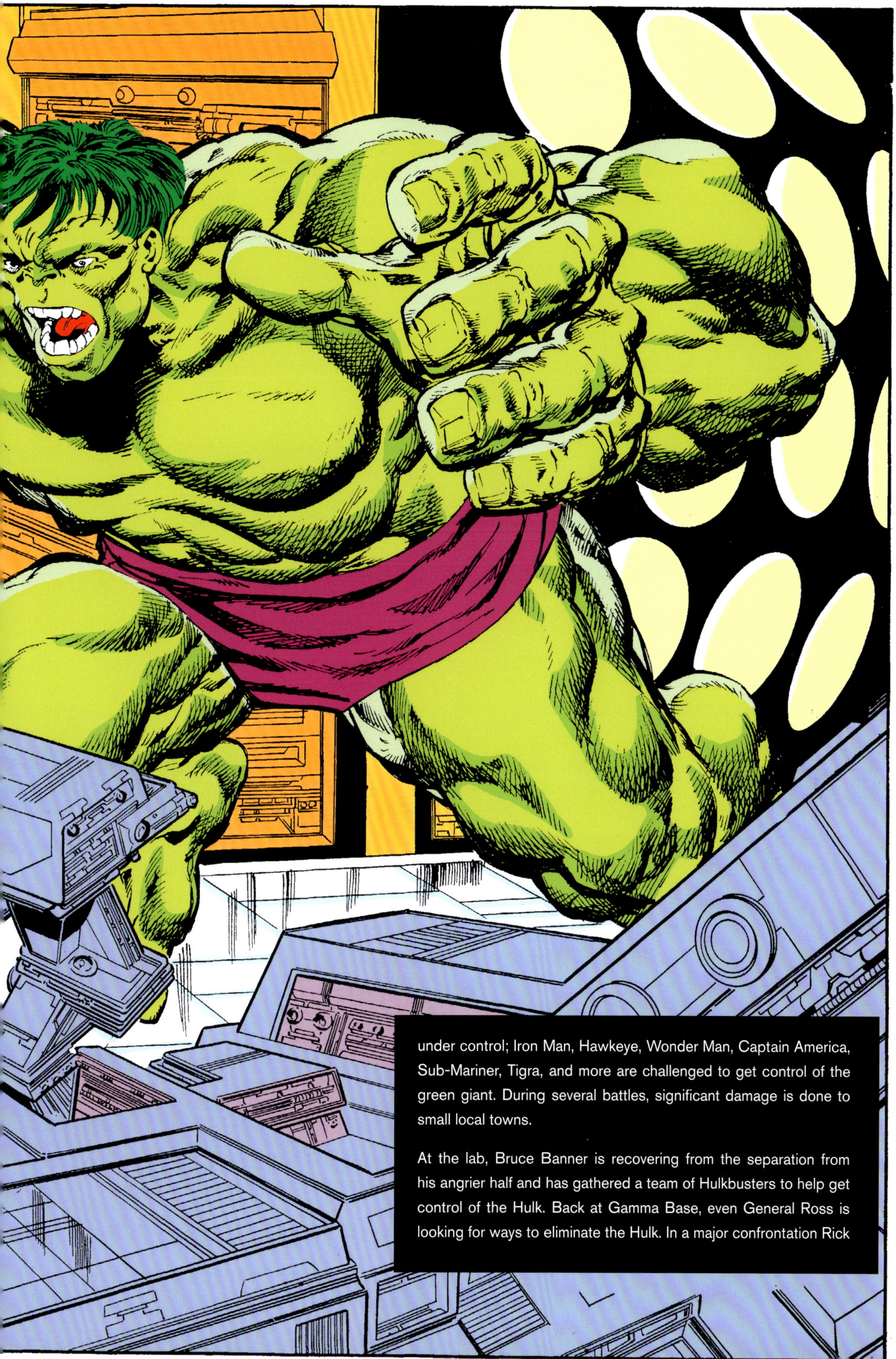

under control; Iron Man, Hawkeye, Wonder Man, Captain America, Sub-Mariner, Tigra, and more are challenged to get control of the green giant. During several battles, significant damage is done to small local towns.

At the lab, Bruce Banner is recovering from the separation from his angrier half and has gathered a team of Hulkbusters to help get control of the Hulk. Back at Gamma Base, even General Ross is looking for ways to eliminate the Hulk. In a major confrontation Rick

Jones is shot by the general and Jones ends up in the nutrient bath. What will become of Rick being in the same solution as the Hulk and Banner?

In spite of all that's going on, Banner and his beloved Betty Ross manage to get back together. Banner even finds it in himself to ask Betty for her hand in marriage. Betty marries Banner with the hope that his separation from the Hulk is permanent.

When the Hulk is finally captured, several events happen: a new Hulk appears, General Ross absorbs the power of an energy creature, and there is an attempt to join the Hulk and Banner together again. In one horrific scene Banner and the Hulk blend together. Bits of Banner appear and disappear. At one point Banner's head surfaces and he begs them to kill the Hulk. But with Banner inside, would he die as well? What happens next is completely unexpected: the Hulk that finally emerges is the original gray Hulk, looking like he did after the gamma bomb blast. There is a silver lining: it seems like Banner might be able to control this retro-Hulk a bit better.

For all the Hulk's strength, is he weaker without Banner? Does having the Hulk as his other half make Bruce Banner a stronger man? In the end, do they need each other to thrive?

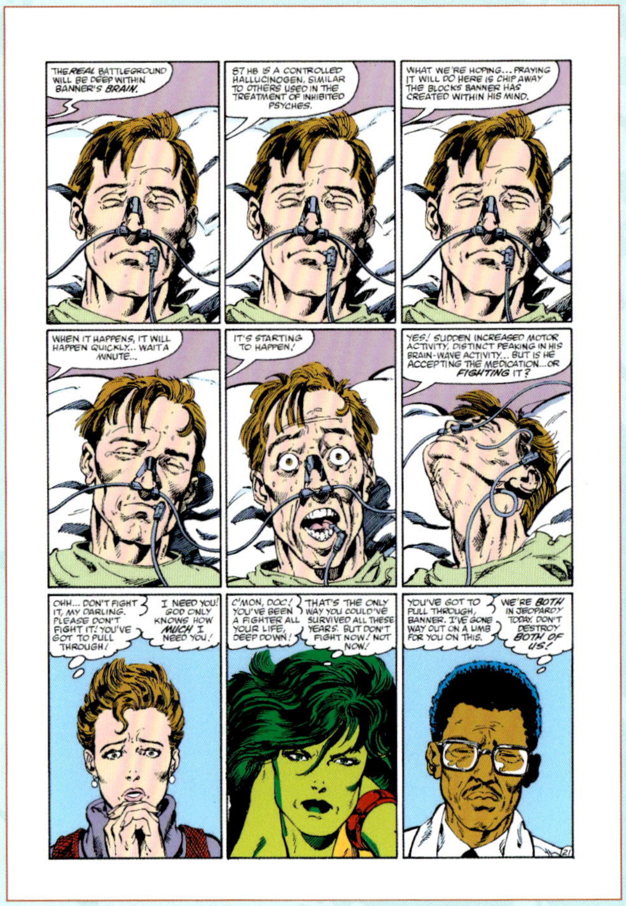
THE REAL BATTLEGROUND WILL BE DEEP WITHIN BANNER'S BRAIN.
87 HB IS A CONTROLLED HALLUCINOGEN, SIMILAR TO OTHERS USED IN THE TREATMENT OF INHIBITED PSYCHES.
WHAT WE'RE HOPING... PRAYING IT WILL DO HERE IS CHIP AWAY THE BLOCKS BANNER HAS CREATED WITHIN HIS MIND.
WHEN IT HAPPENS, IT WILL HAPPEN QUICKLY... WAIT A MINUTE...
IT'S STARTING TO HAPPEN!
YES! SUDDEN INCREASED MOTOR ACTIVITY, DISTINCT PEAKING IN HIS BRAIN-WAVE ACTIVITY... BUT IS HE ACCEPTING THE MEDICATION...OR FIGHTING IT?
OHH... DON'T FIGHT IT, MY DARLING. PLEASE DON'T FIGHT IT! YOU'VE GOT TO PULL THROUGH!
I NEED YOU! GOD ONLY KNOWS HOW MUCH I NEED YOU!
C'MON, DOC! YOU'VE BEEN A FIGHTER ALL YOUR LIFE, DEEP DOWN!
THAT'S THE ONLY WAY YOU COULD'VE SURVIVED ALL THESE YEARS. BUT DON'T FIGHT NOW! NOT NOW!
YOU'VE GOT TO PULL THROUGH, BANNER. I'VE GONE WAY OUT ON A LIMB FOR YOU ON THIS.
WE'RE BOTH IN JEOPARDY TODAY. DON'T DESTROY BOTH OF US!

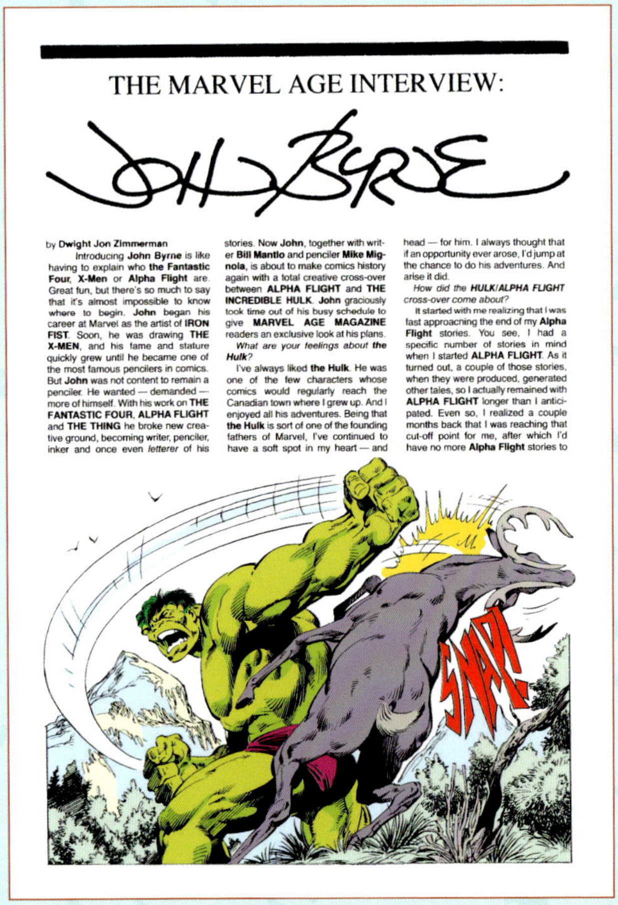

THE MARVEL AGE INTERVIEW:

JOHN BYRNE

by **Dwight Jon Zimmerman**

Introducing **John Byrne** is like having to explain who **the Fantastic Four**, **X-Men** or **Alpha Flight** are. Great fun, but there's so much to say that it's almost impossible to know where to begin. **John** began his career at Marvel as the artist of **IRON FIST**. Soon, he was drawing **THE X-MEN**, and his fame and stature quickly grew until he became one of the most famous pencilers in comics. But **John** was not content to remain a penciler. He wanted — demanded — more of himself. With his work on **THE FANTASTIC FOUR**, **ALPHA FLIGHT** and **THE THING** he broke new creative ground, becoming writer, penciler, inker and once even *letterer* of his stories. Now **John**, together with writer **Bill Mantlo** and penciler **Mike Mignola**, is about to make comics history again with a total creative cross-over between **ALPHA FLIGHT** and **THE INCREDIBLE HULK**. **John** graciously took time out of his busy schedule to give **MARVEL AGE MAGAZINE** readers an exclusive look at his plans.

*What are your feelings about* ***the Hulk****?*

I've always liked **the Hulk**. He was one of the few characters whose comics would regularly reach the Canadian town where I grew up. And I enjoyed all his adventures. Being that **the Hulk** is sort of one of the founding fathers of Marvel, I've continued to have a soft spot in my heart — and head — for him. I always thought that if an opportunity ever arose, I'd jump at the chance to do his adventures. And arise it did.

*How did the* ***HULK/ALPHA FLIGHT*** *cross-over come about?*

It started with me realizing that I was fast approaching the end of my **Alpha Flight** stories. You see, I had a specific number of stories in mind when I started **ALPHA FLIGHT**. As it turned out, a couple of those stories, when they were produced, generated other tales, so I actually remained with **ALPHA FLIGHT** longer than I anticipated. Even so, I realized a couple months back that I was reaching that cut-off point for me, after which I'd have no more **Alpha Flight** stories to

SNAP!

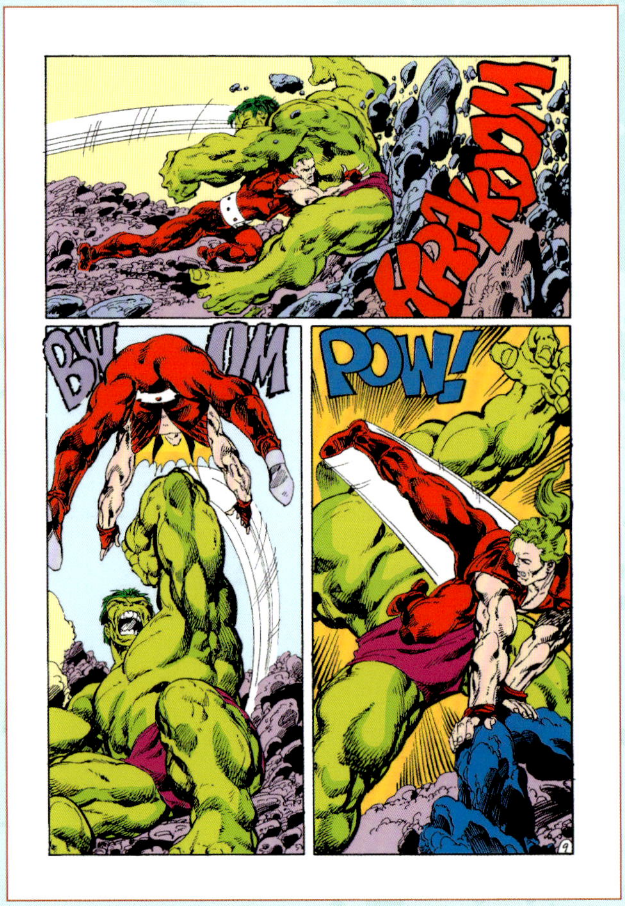
KRAKOOM
POW!

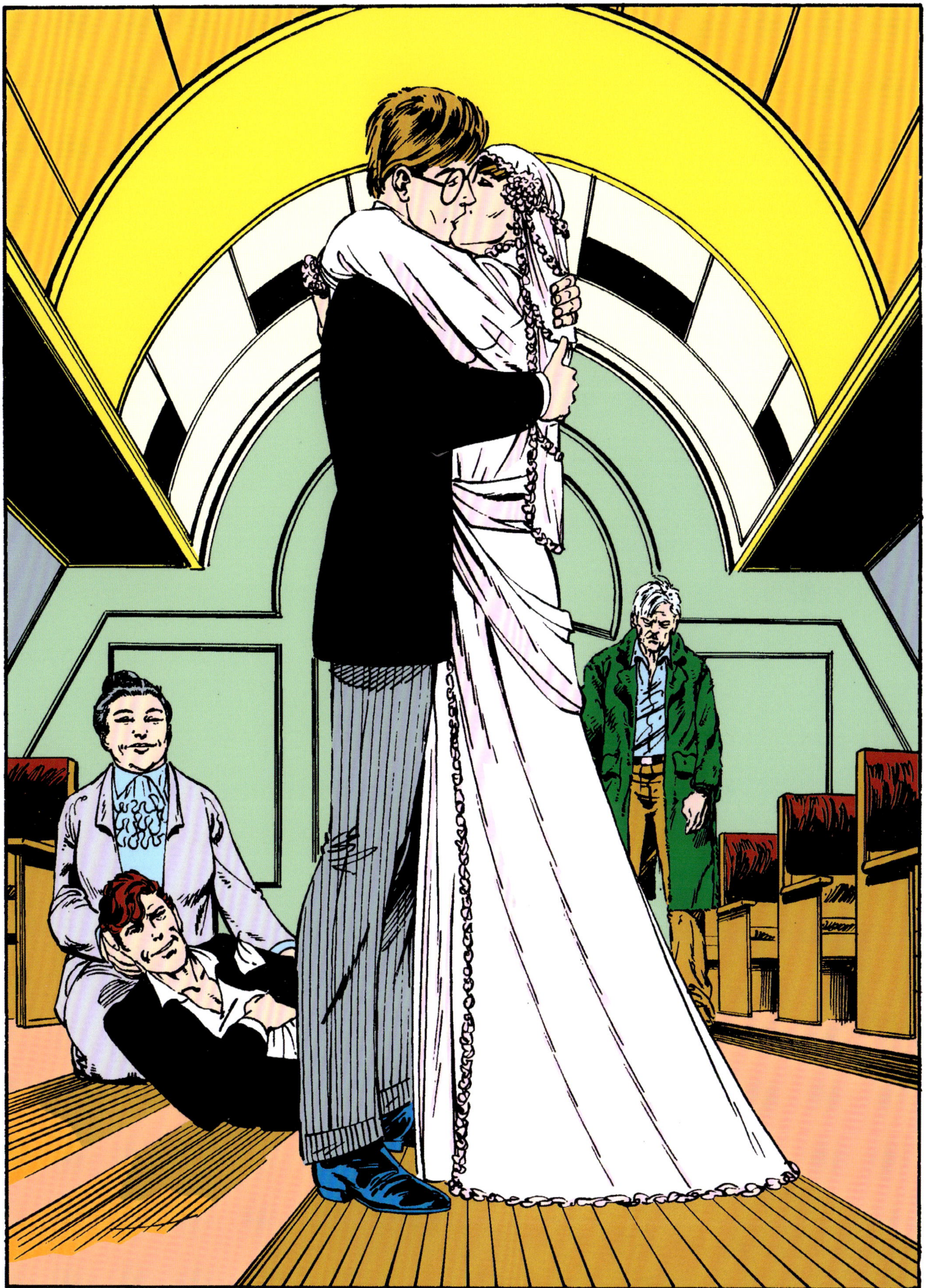

THIS ISSUE WAS A Stan Lee PRESENTATION.
JOHN BYRNE WRITER/ARTIST / KEITH WILLIAMS BACKGROUND INKS / ANDY YANCHUS COLORING / RICK PARKER LETTERING / DENNIS O'NEIL EDITOR & / JIM SHOOTER EDITOR IN CHIEF

NEXT ISSUE: THINK THINGS ARE MOVIN' FAST *NOW*?!?! TUNE IN NEXT ISH FOR "HONEYMOON'S OVER!!!"

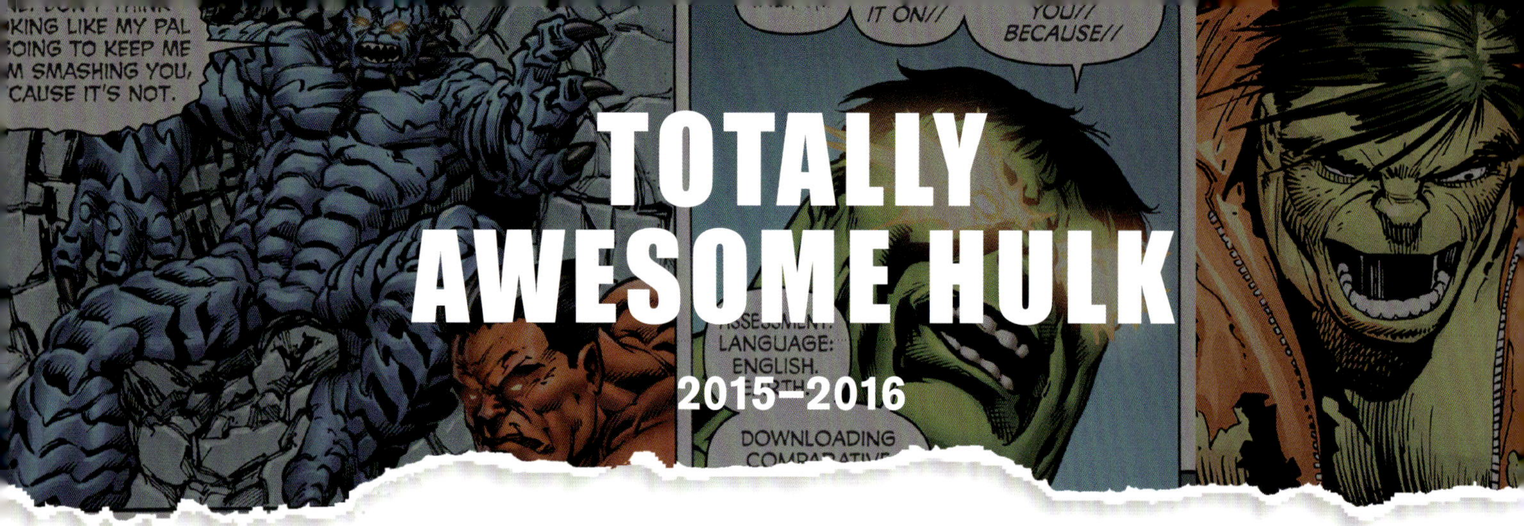
IT ON//
YOU// BECAUSE//
LANGUAGE: ENGLISH.
DOWNLOADING

# TOTALLY AWESOME HULK

## 2015–2016

An Asian teenager sits at a beachside eatery wolfing down a stack of cheeseburgers, a mountain of fries, and a river of soda when a robot taps him on the shoulder and tells him that a kid is in danger. The robot calls the teenager Amadeus. Amadeus puts down his burger, taps a device on his wrist, and suddenly his jacket and tie are replaced by a pair of perfect purple shorts. As he runs down the beach, he grows in size, and turns green. He has transformed into the Hulk!

A creature that looks kind of like a giant two-headed turtle is threatening a boy and his nanny. The Hulk takes a mighty swing at the creature, who strikes back and unleashes a stream of fire at the big green guy. The creature seems to be more dragon than turtle.

The Hulk grabs a propane tank from the restaurant and hurls it into the mouth of the creature. The tank explodes, and it seems to put out the fire in the creature's mouth. The Hulk quickly uses a device to shrink the sea creature down to a manageable size. The Hulk then saunters over to a woman in a bikini and he flirts with her. The Hulk flirting? She tells him that she has a boyfriend and informs the Hulk that he is naked—his shorts were burned off by the turtle-dragon! The Hulk quickly takes off.

He transforms back into a teenager. Who is this kid? And why is he able to transform into the Hulk? Meet Amadeus Cho, a nineteen-year-old Korean American who is considered one of the smartest people on Earth. How, and why, is the seventh smartest person on Earth transforming into the Hulk?

We travel back four months: a fusion reactor on the Kenyan Coast is melting down. Some of the Avengers are there to evacuate the plant and to control the reaction. Only one of these super heroes has been previously exposed to high levels of radiation and can withstand them, and that's the Hulk.

The Hulk heads into the reactor and begins to absorb radiation. But the radiation he is absorbing is not gamma radiation. The Hulk manages to absorb enough radiation to avoid a meltdown, but it has taken its toll on him, and he is left lying on the floor of the reactor screaming.

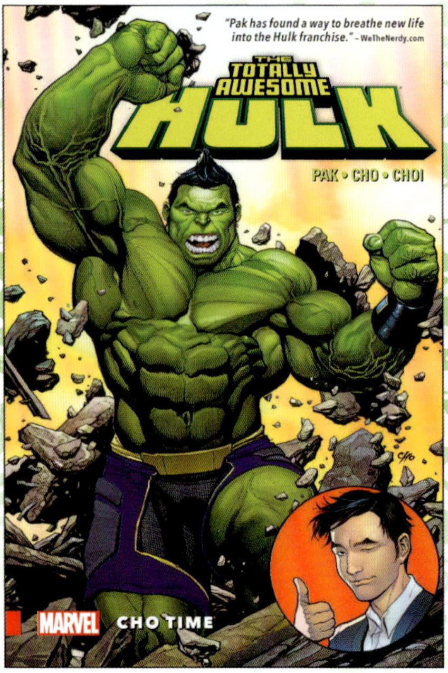
"Pak has found a way to breathe new life into the Hulk franchise." – WeTheNerdy.com
THE TOTALLY AWESOME HULK
PAK • CHO • CHOI
MARVEL
CHO TIME

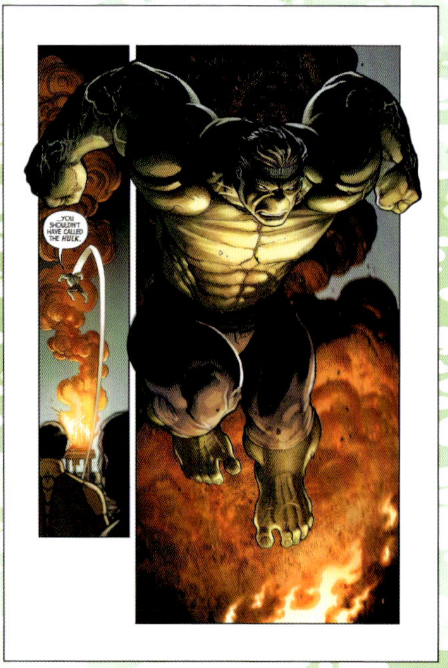

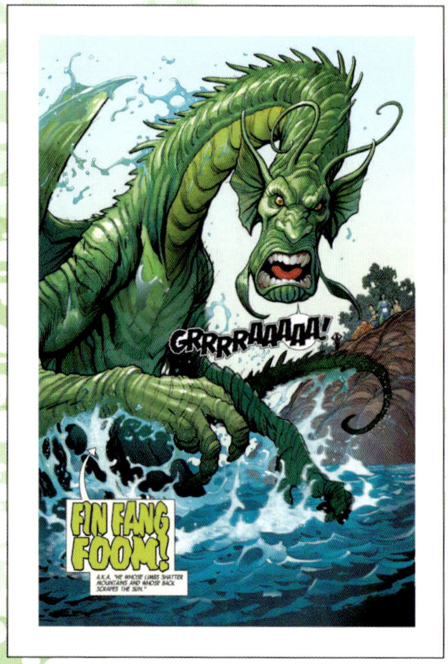
GRRRRAAAAAA!
FIN FANG FOOM!

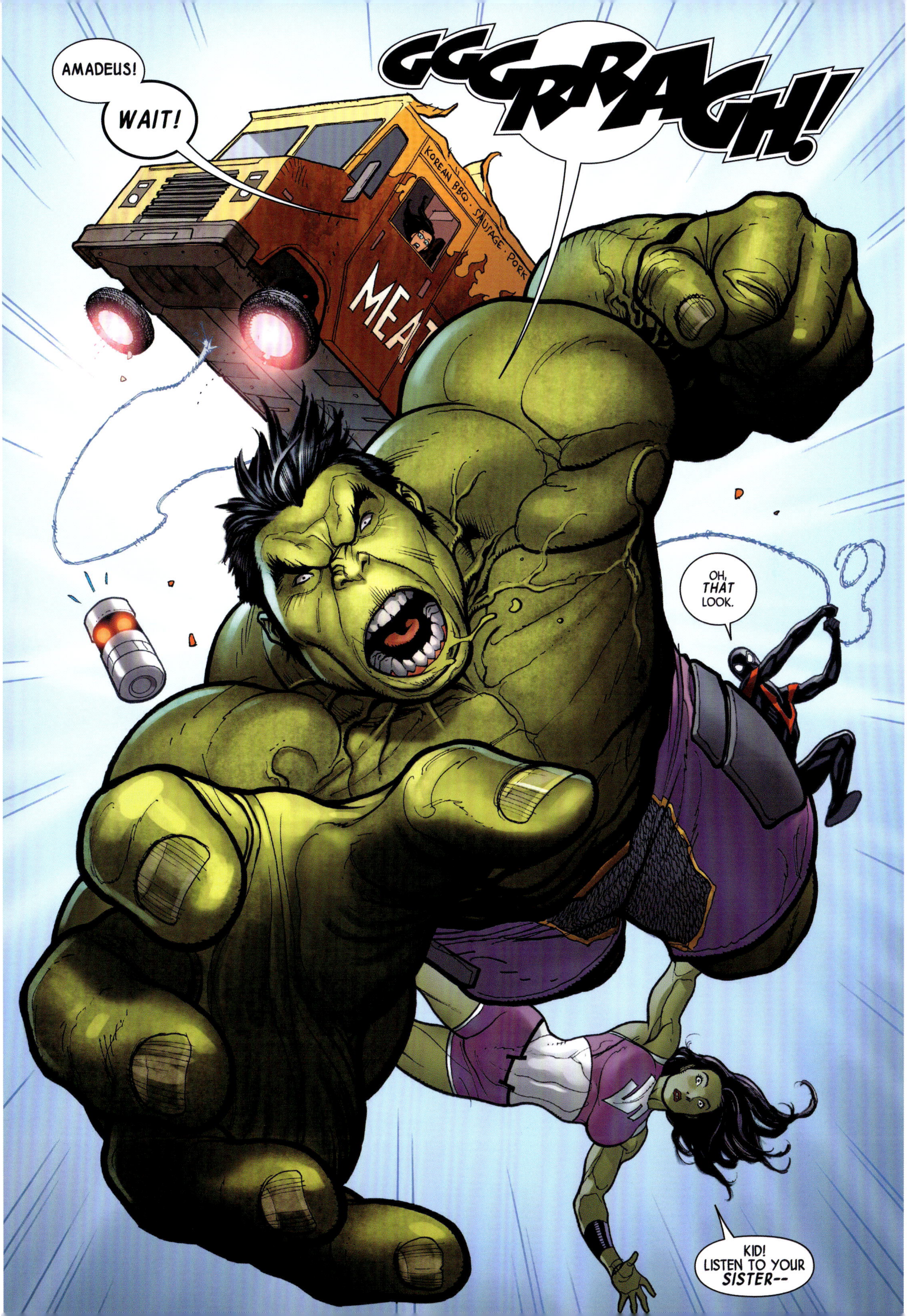
AMADEUS!
WAIT!
GGGRRAGH!
KOREAN BBQ · SAUSAGE · PORK
OH, THAT LOOK.
KID! LISTEN TO YOUR SISTER--

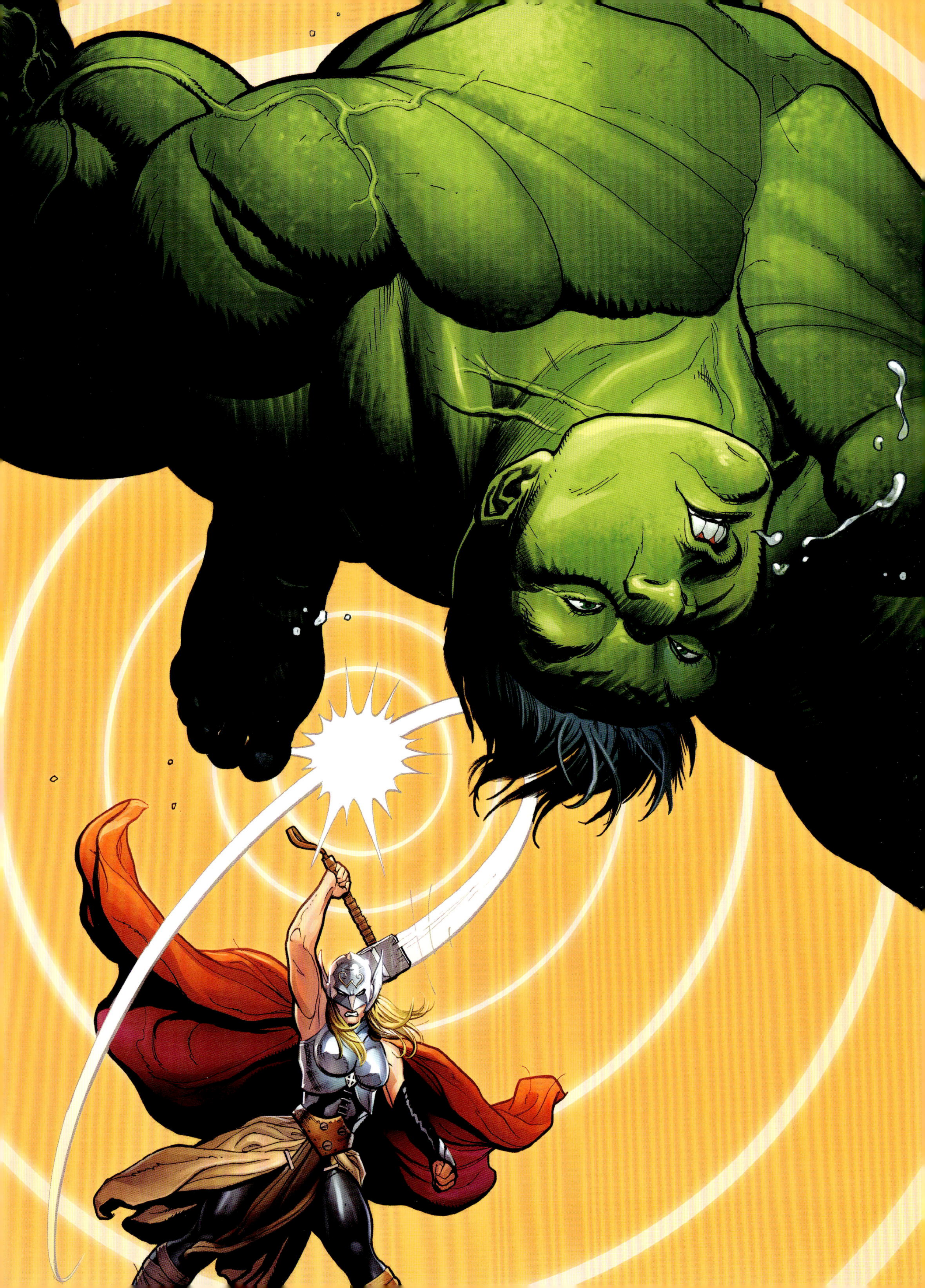

Flash forward to Amadeus Cho. His Hulk is different; this teenager retains his personality when he transforms into the Hulk. He is confident, even arrogant—the license plate on his car reads CHO TIME. He has an outsized metabolism, and becomes massively hungry when he transforms back to Cho from the Hulk. He also cracks jokes. The Hulk cracking jokes? Who does he think he is—Spider-Man? Cho is a flirt. He even flirts with She-Hulk, even though he thinks she's forty years old. One time, he is captured by Lady Hellbender who knocks him unconscious with a tranquilizer and chains him to a chair. When he wakes up, she brings her face close to his to show her dominance over him, and he puckers his lips, ready for a kiss. He is a teenager in a big, green body!

Luckily, Cho has someone who tries to keep him in line: the voice of his companion robot, and the one who tries to keep him focused is his sister, Maddy. She speaks to him from a safe distance when he is the Hulk. Maddy is his voice of reason, the one who will yell at him when he does stupid things. She is also fiercely protective of Amadeus. She will do anything for him.

But back to Banner—the heroes have put the Hulk in a diving suit and placed him in the ocean to keep him cool. Cho shows up both to offer his assistance and to annoy Tony Stark with his arrogance. Cho dons a diving suit and heads to the ocean floor to see the Hulk. Cho grabs the Hulk, who somehow transforms back into Banner. Banner starts to cry. Cho tries to reassure Banner by telling him that he doesn't need to worry anymore, that he's free. Banner tells Cho that he is not crying for himself, he's crying for Cho—whose eyes suddenly turn green. The baton has been passed.

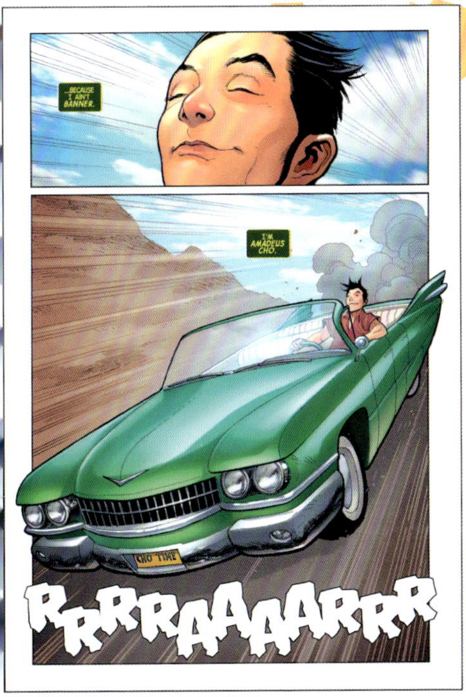
...BECAUSE I AIN'T BANNER.
I'M AMADEUS CHO.
CHO TIME
RRRRAAAAARRRR

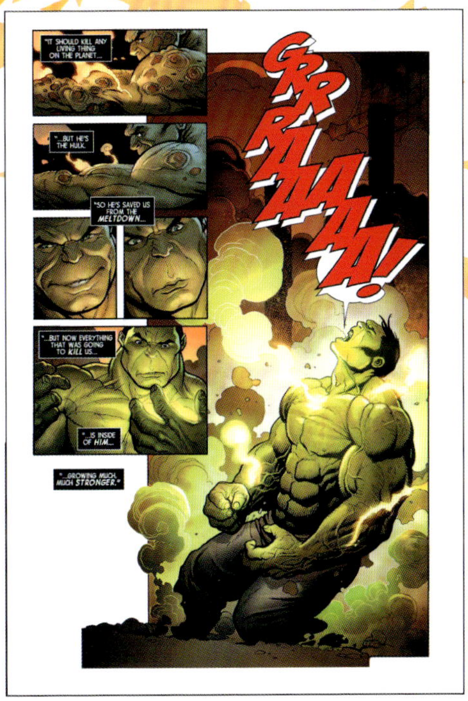
"IT SHOULD KILL ANY LIVING THING ON THE PLANET...
"...BUT HE'S THE HULK.
"SO HE'S SAVED US FROM THE MELTDOWN...
"...BUT NOW EVERYTHING THAT WAS GOING TO KILL US...
"...IS INSIDE OF HIM...
"...GROWING MUCH, MUCH STRONGER."
GRRRAAAAAA!

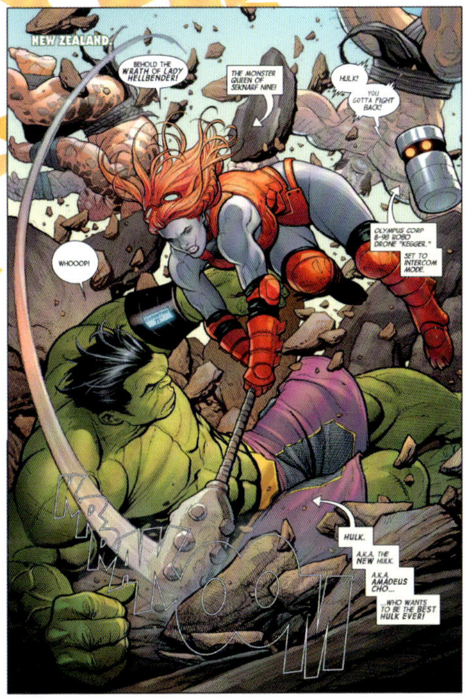
NEW ZEALAND.
BEHOLD THE WRATH OF LADY HELLBENDER!
THE MONSTER QUEEN OF SEKNARF NINE!
HULK!
YOU GOTTA FIGHT BACK!
OLYMPUS CORP B-98 ROBO DRONE "KEGGER."
SET TO INTERCOM MODE.
WHOOOP!
HULK.
A.K.A. THE NEW HULK.
A.K.A. AMADEUS CHO...
...WHO WANTS TO BE THE BEST HULK EVER!

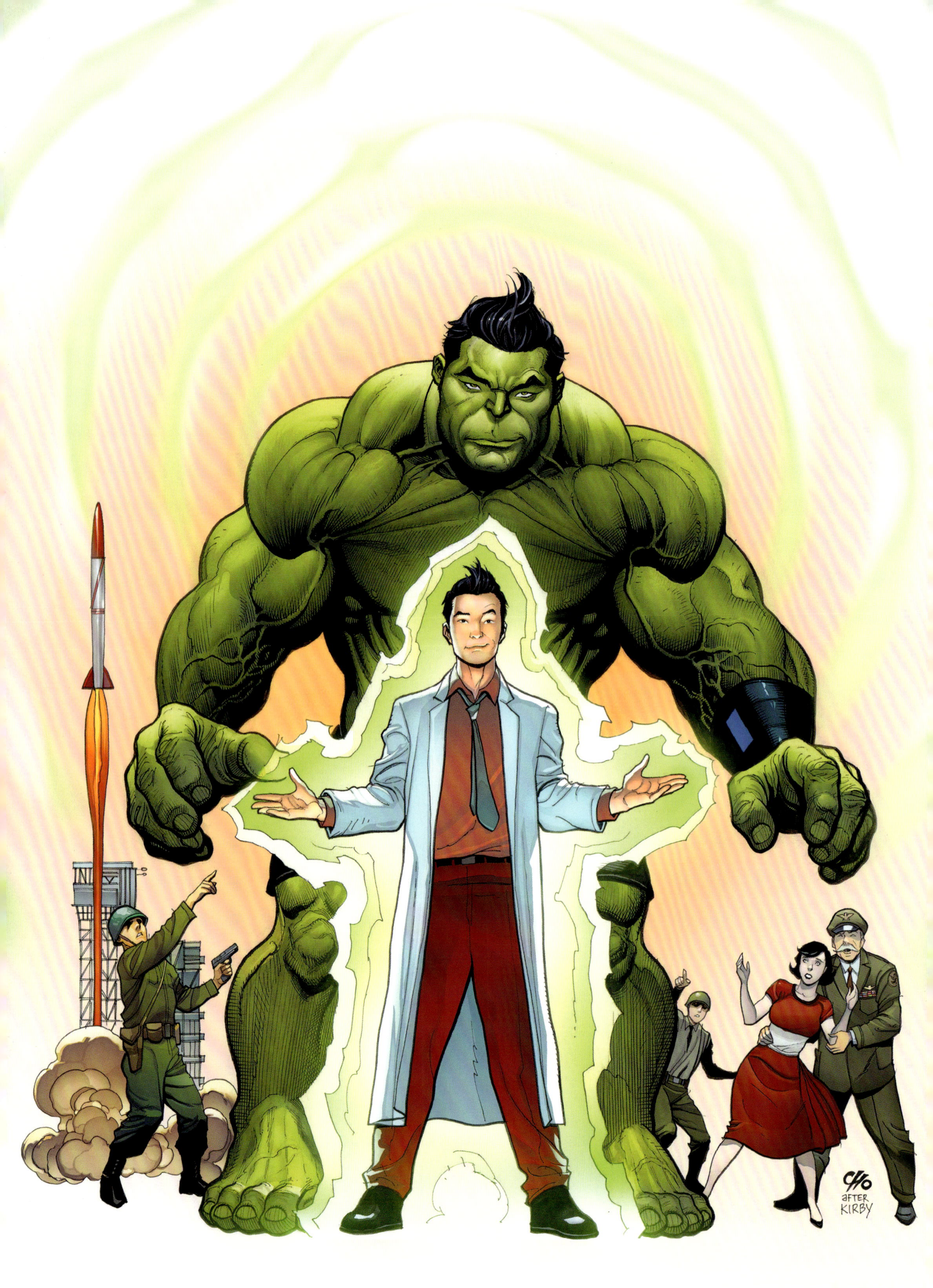
CHO
AFTER
KIRBY

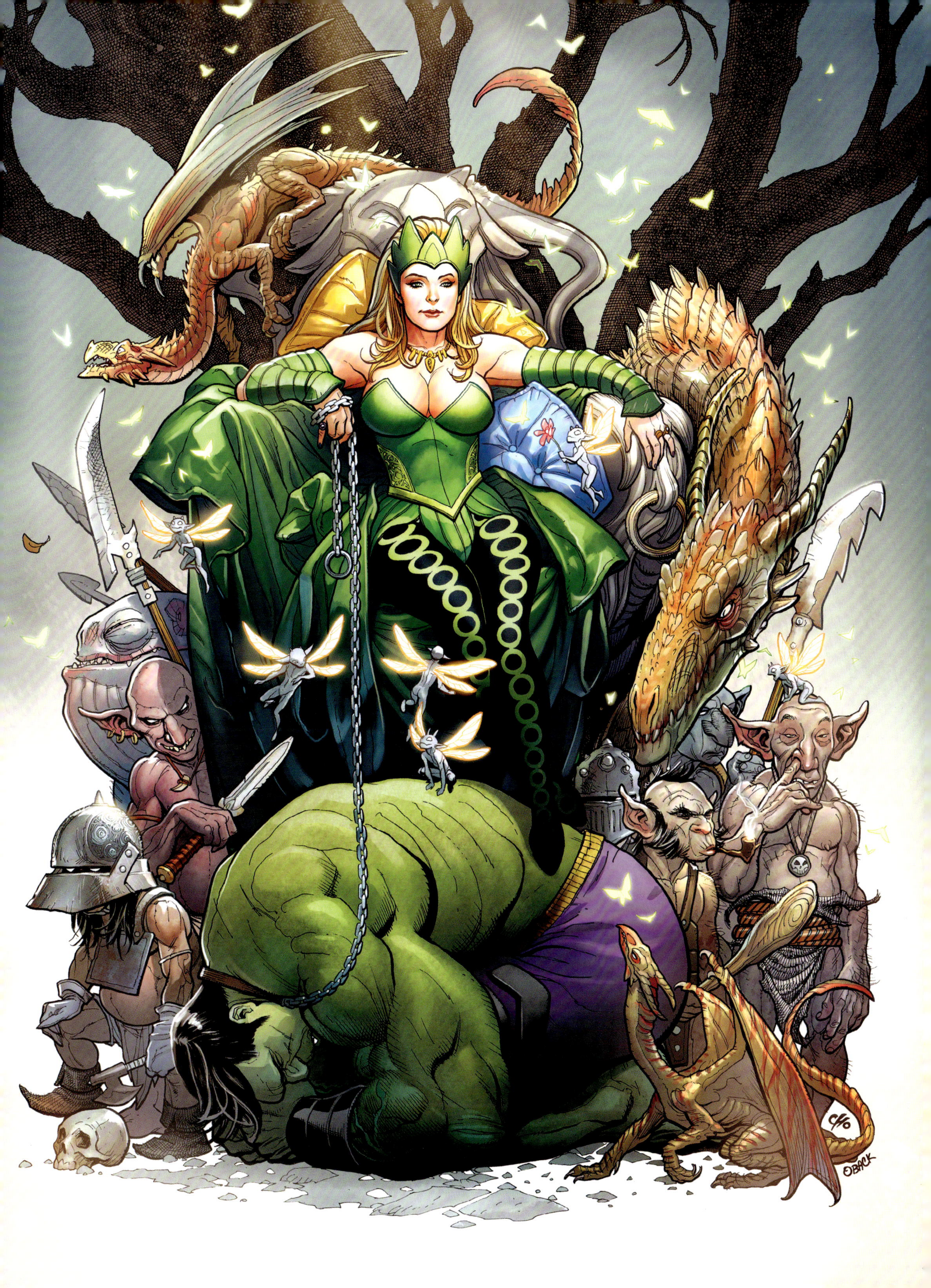

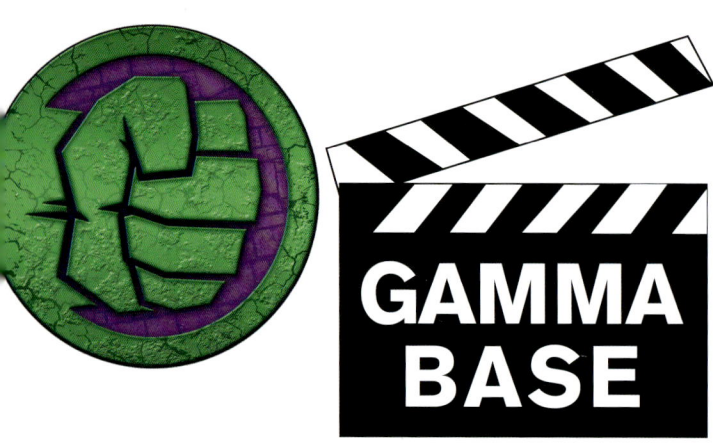

# GAMMA BASE

Marvel Studios' *The Incredible Hulk* debuted June 2008, one month after the release of Marvel Studios' *Iron Man*. It was the second movie in Phase One of the Marvel Cinematic Universe. The Hulk, played by Edward Norton, is hiding out in Brazil, suppressing his alter ego. We see him in his apartment watching television when an image of the actor Bill Bixby appears on the screen, a nod to Bixby's starring role as David Banner (not Bruce) in the television series *The Incredible Hulk* that ran 1978–1982. Bixby starred in eighty episodes alongside the man who embodied Banner's alter ego, bodybuilder and actor Lou Ferrigno. Ferrigno even made a cameo appearance as a security guard in the 2008 film and was also the voice of the Hulk in additional Marvel Cinematic Universe films.

Although we knew Ferrigno was a guy in green makeup and a fright wig, we collectively believe he could lift a car, jump great distances, and swing a steel girder like a baseball bat at a bad guy. Still, when the Hulk came to the big screen in 2008, we watched in awe as he scaled skyscrapers to battle Abomination.

We wouldn't see our green hero again onscreen until 2012's *Marvel's The Avengers*. Mark Ruffalo took over the role of Banner/Hulk who has been hiding out in India working as a doctor and trying to keep his alter ego in check. That is, until Natasha Romanoff arrives to recruit "the big guy."

Over eight films, we watched Banner go from counting the days from his last transformation to defending the world from countless threats. Eventually Banner stopped battling himself, merging man and beast. As he says in Marvel Studios' *Avengers: Endgame*, he had to stop viewing the Hulk as a disease and start thinking of him as the cure. "I put the brains and brawn together," he explains. "The best of both worlds." Indeed. And while we love the new intelligent, well-spoken, big green guy who wears cardigan sweaters, a part of us misses the beast in ripped purple pants.

More Hulk arrived by way of Marvel Studios' original series *She-Hulk: Attorney at Law*, starring Tatiana Maslany as Jennifer Walters/She-Hulk, Bruce Banner's cousin and a lawyer. The Hulk was last seen as one with Banner. Bruce is training Jennifer how to control her powers and live her life as a Hulk. Unlike the Hulk, Jen learns that she can control her powers and doesn't let fear and anger trigger her. She recently joined a new law firm, and her first case is also her worst nightmare: defending her cousin Bruce's archnemesis, Abomination!

She-Hulk is a great addition to the Marvel Cinematic Universe; we love to "Hulk out" with She-Hulk!

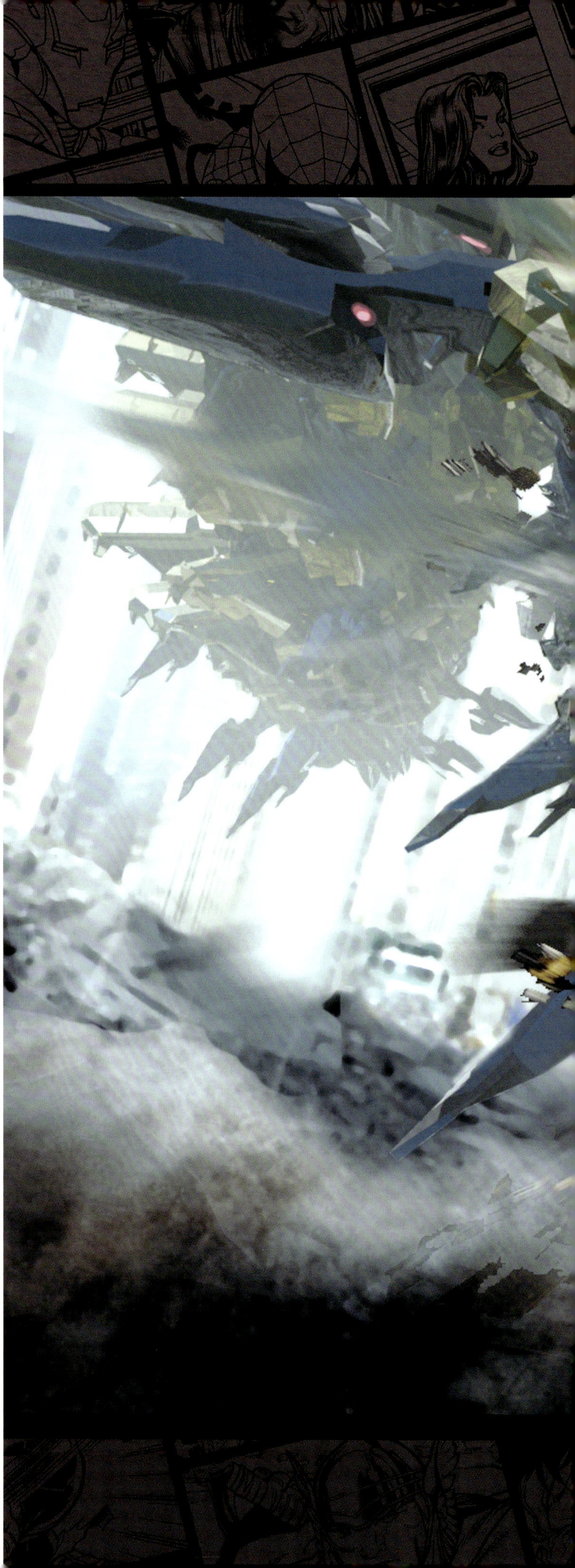

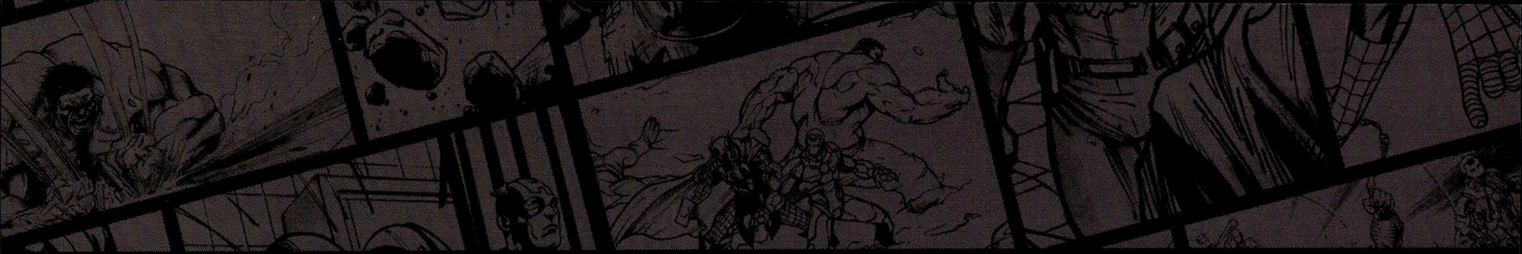

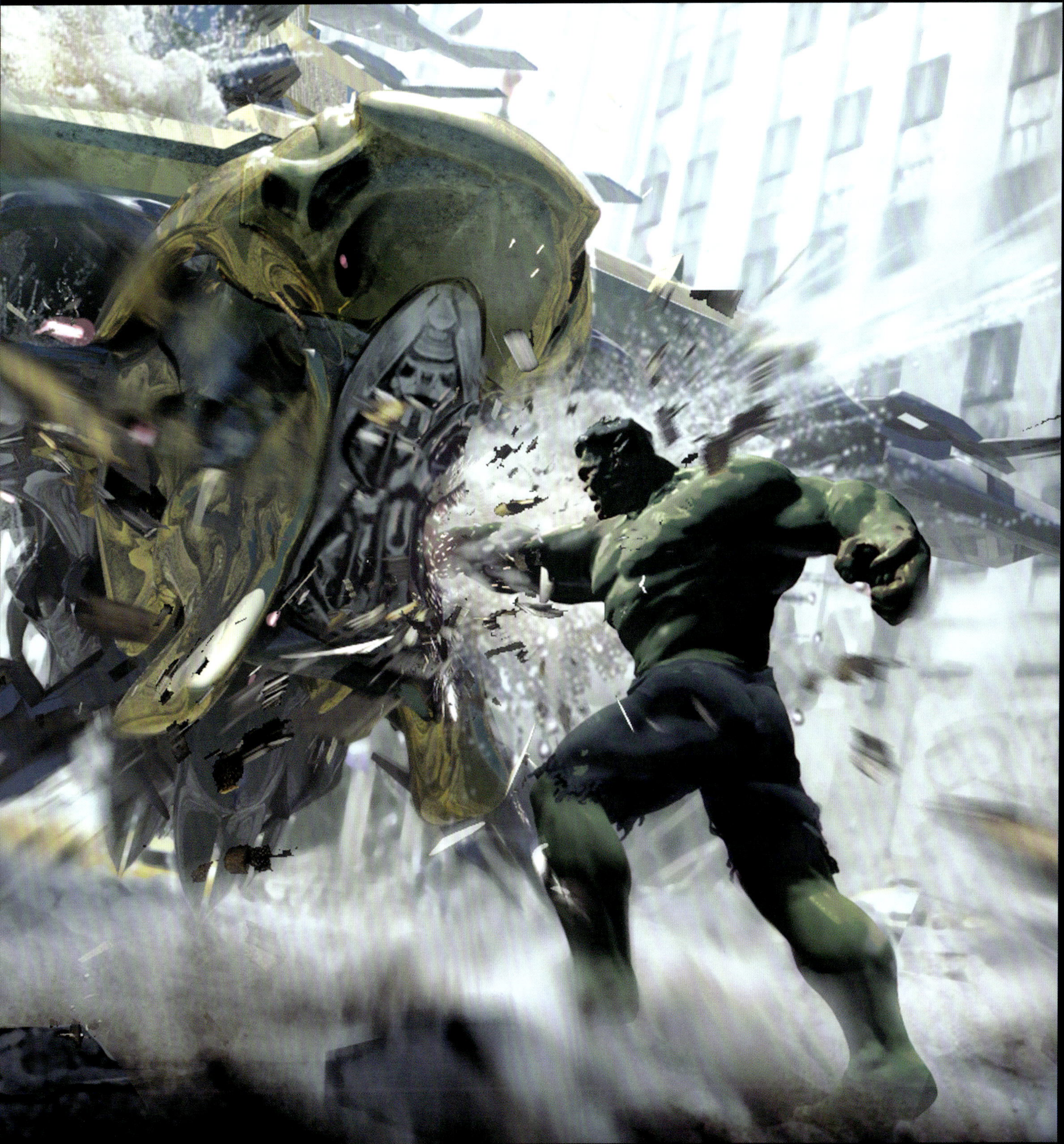

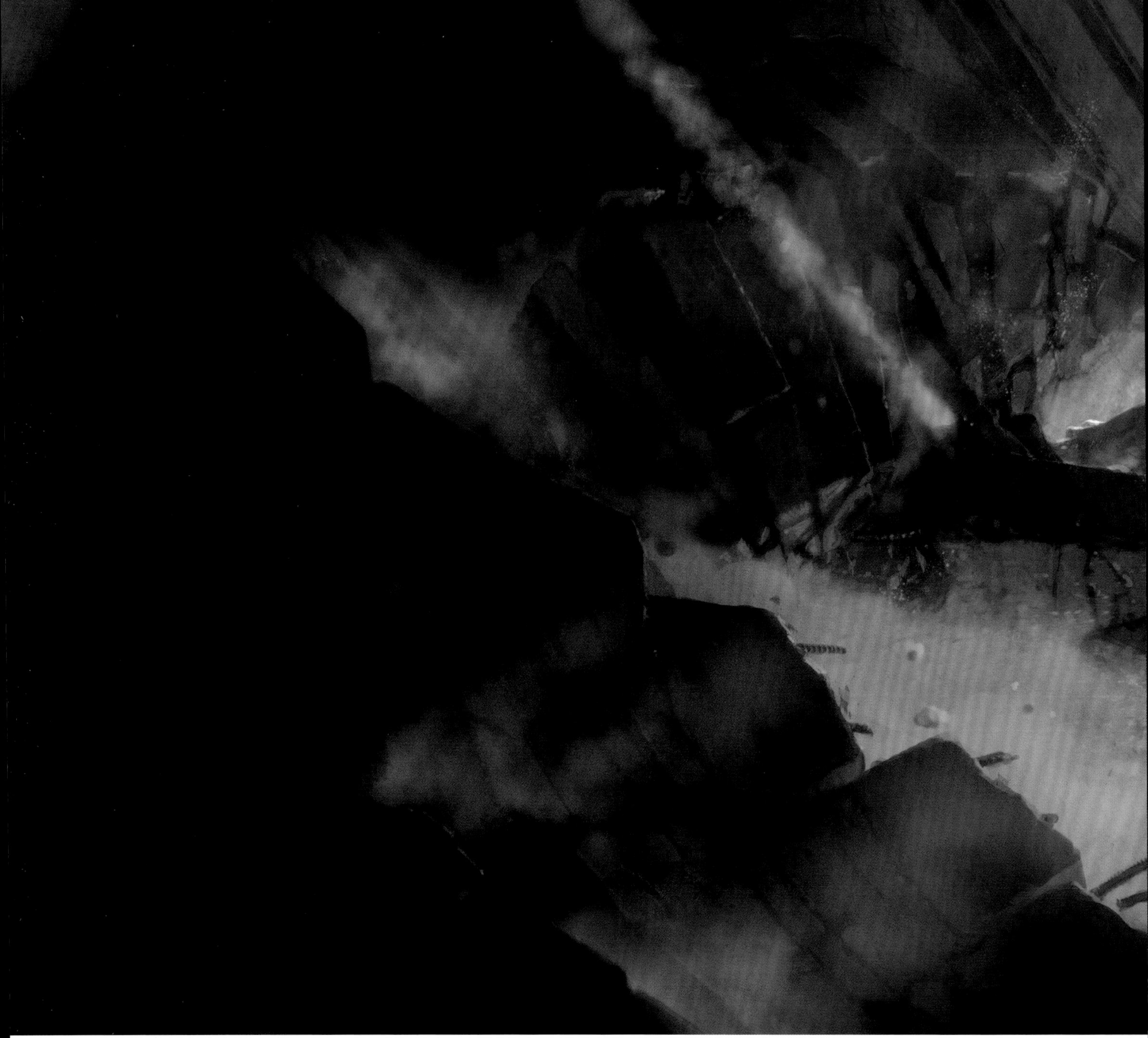

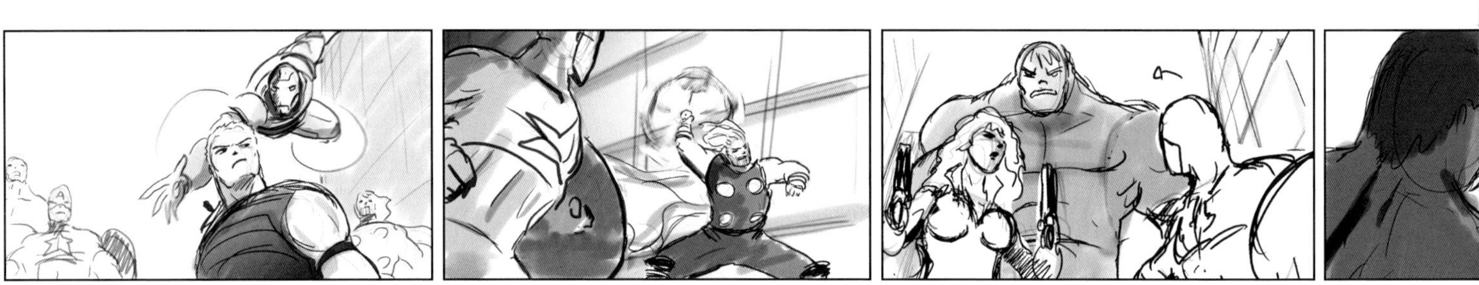

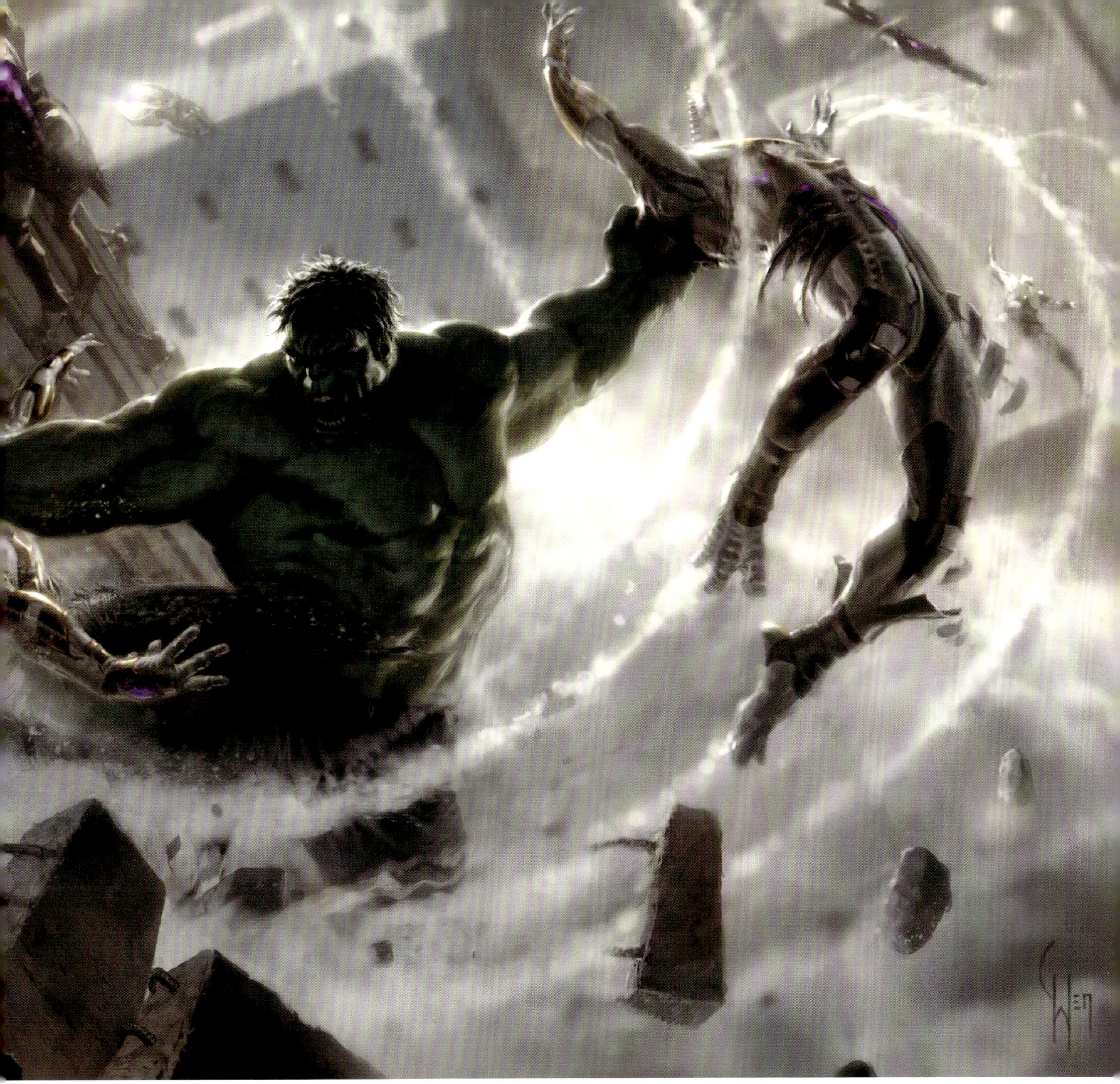

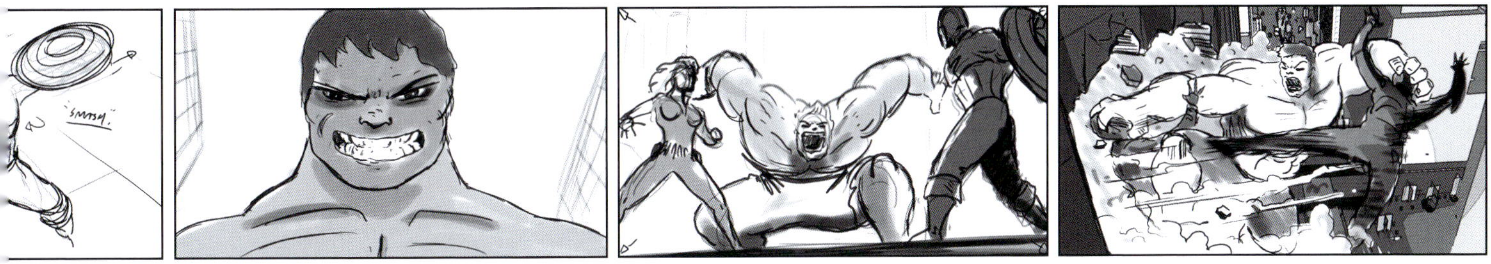
SMASH!

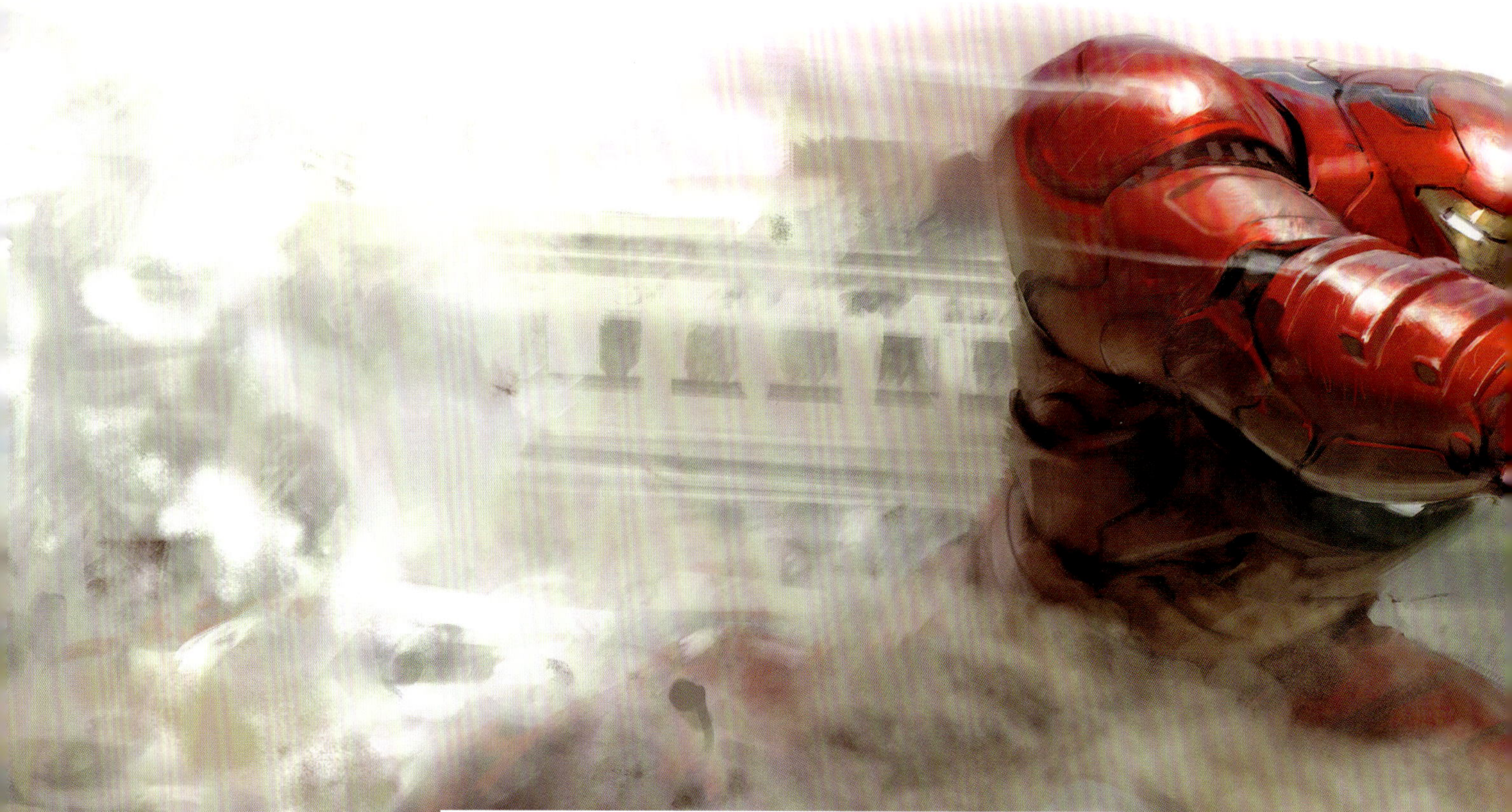

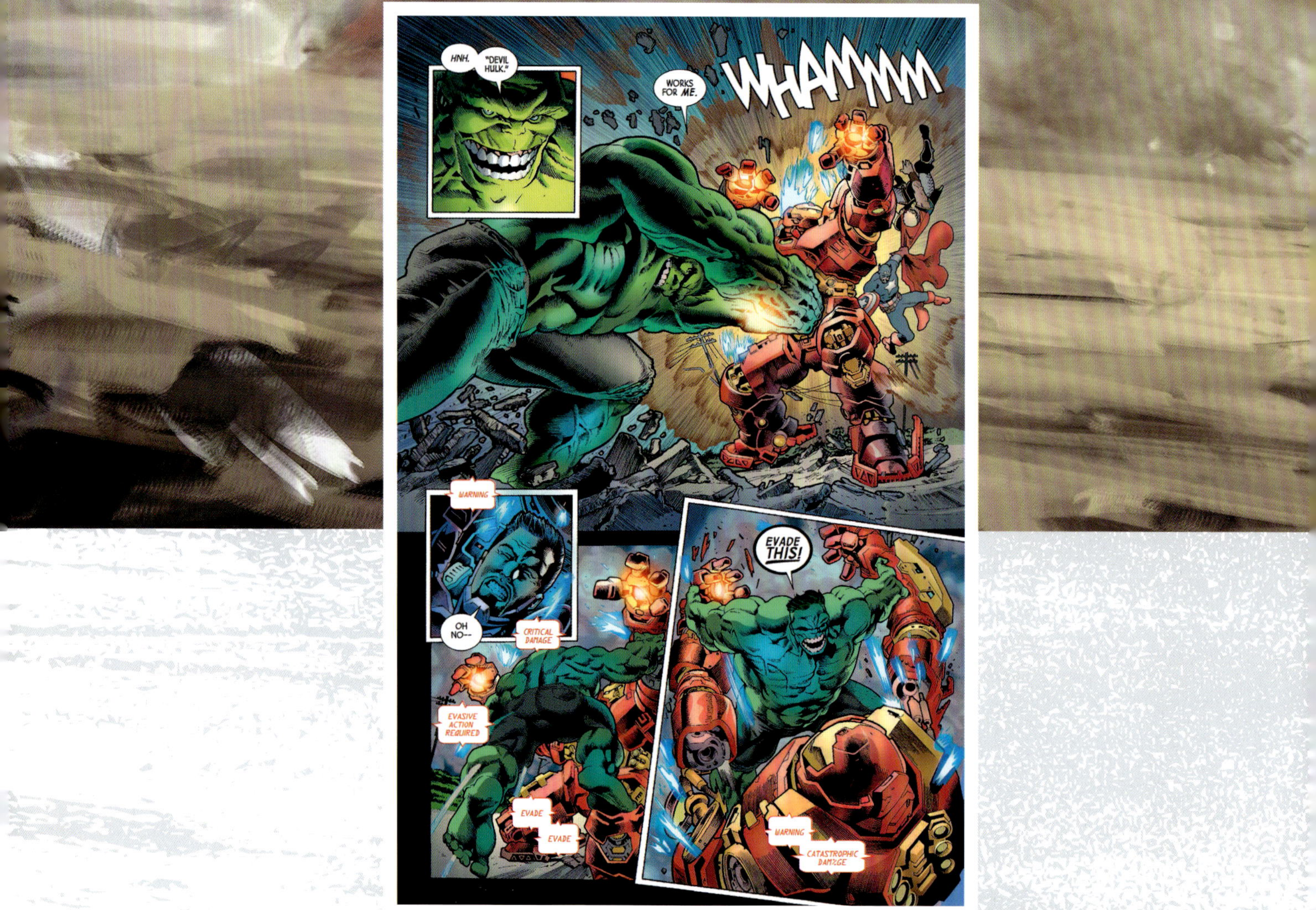
HNH.
"DEVIL HULK."
WORKS FOR ME.
WHAMMM
WARNING
OH NO--
CRITICAL DAMAGE
EVASIVE ACTION REQUIRED
EVADE
EVADE
EVADE THIS!
WARNING
CATASTROPHIC DAMAGE

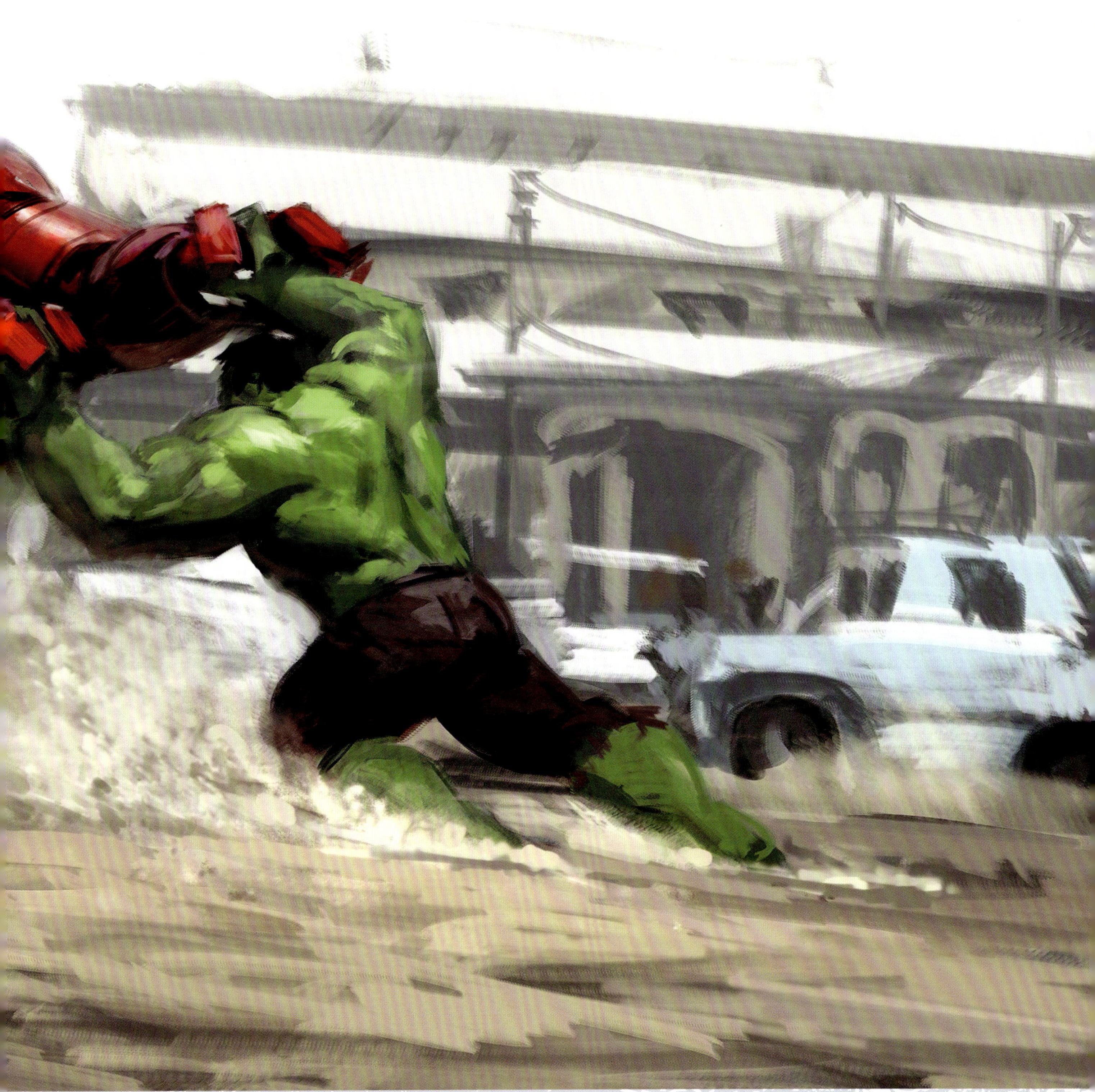

**Above**

The first live-action depiction of the Hulkbuster armor, as the Hulk faces off against Iron Man in Marvel Studios' *Avengers: Age of Ultron.*

**Left**

Featured in several comics throughout the years, the Hulkbuster makes an appearance in *Immortal Hulk* #7.

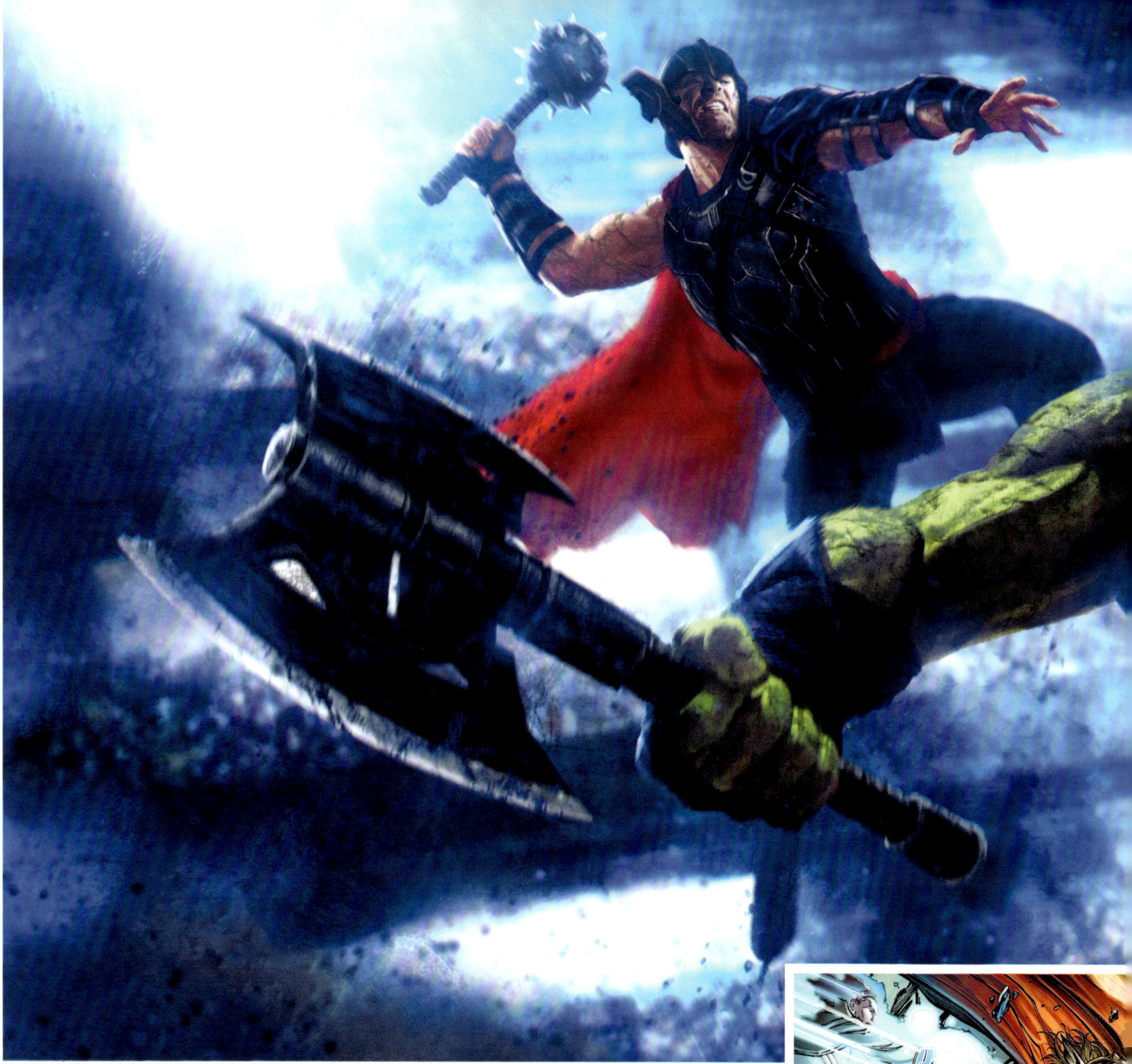

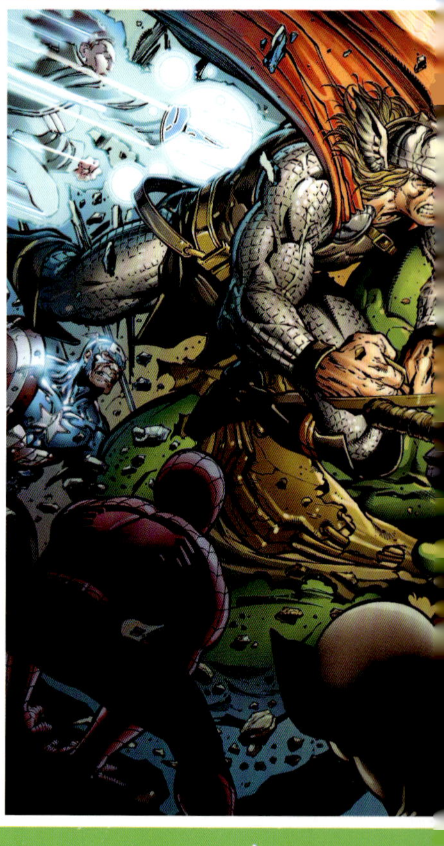

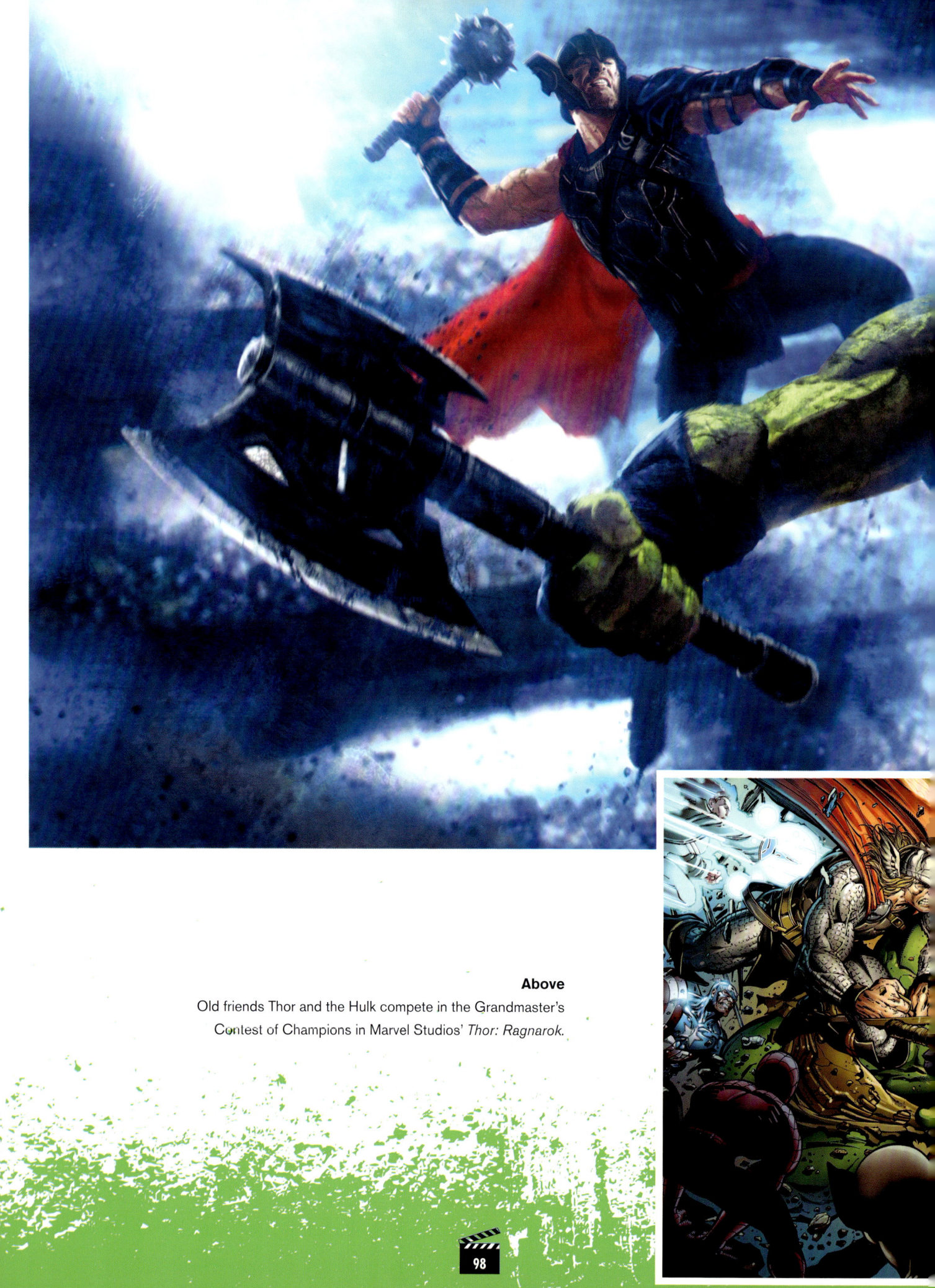

**Above**

Old friends Thor and the Hulk compete in the Grandmaster's Contest of Champions in Marvel Studios' *Thor: Ragnarok*.

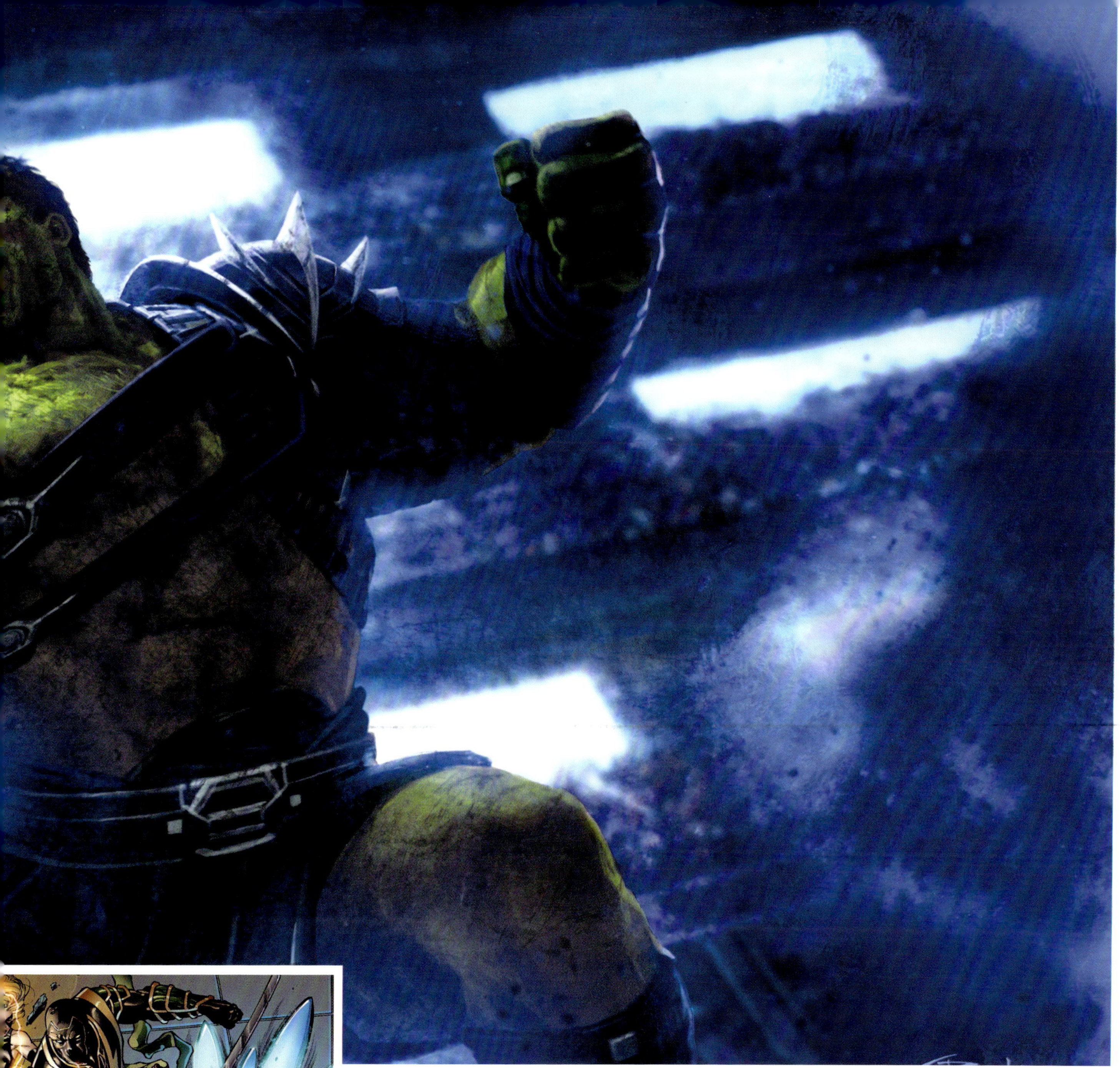

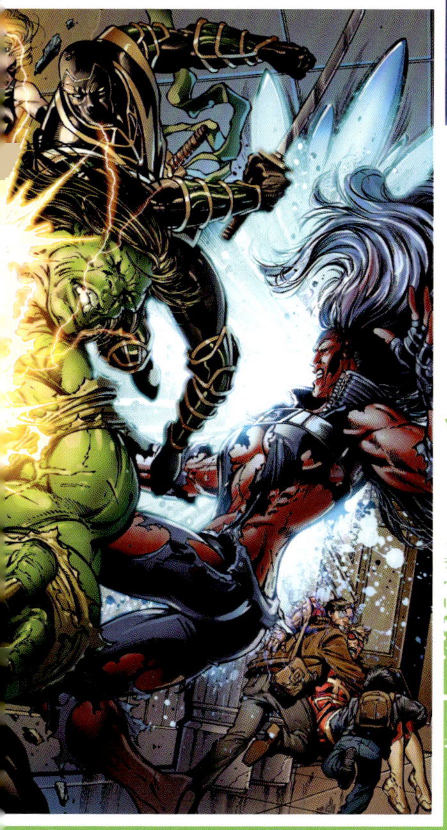

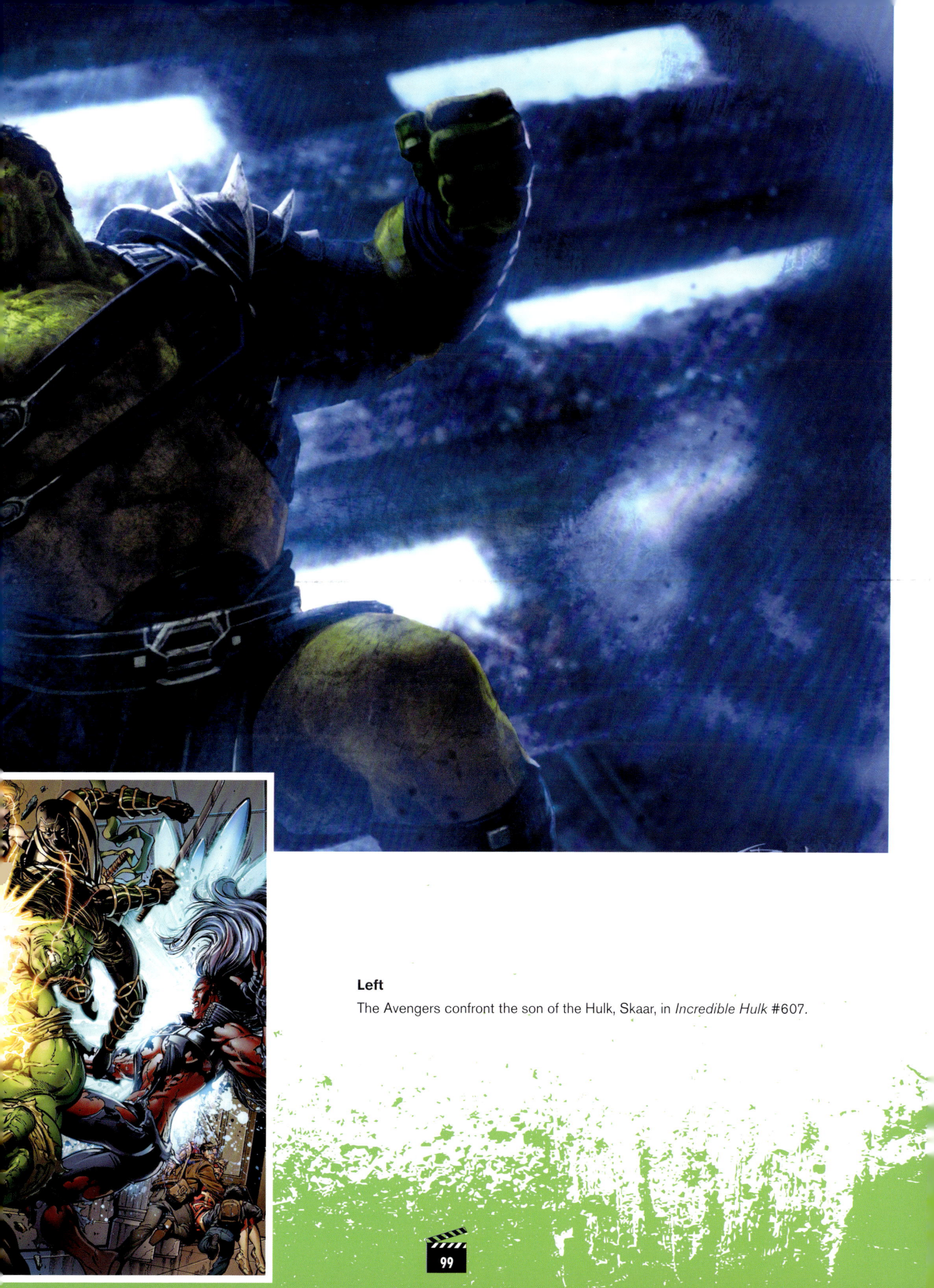

**Left**

The Avengers confront the son of the Hulk, Skaar, in *Incredible Hulk* #607.

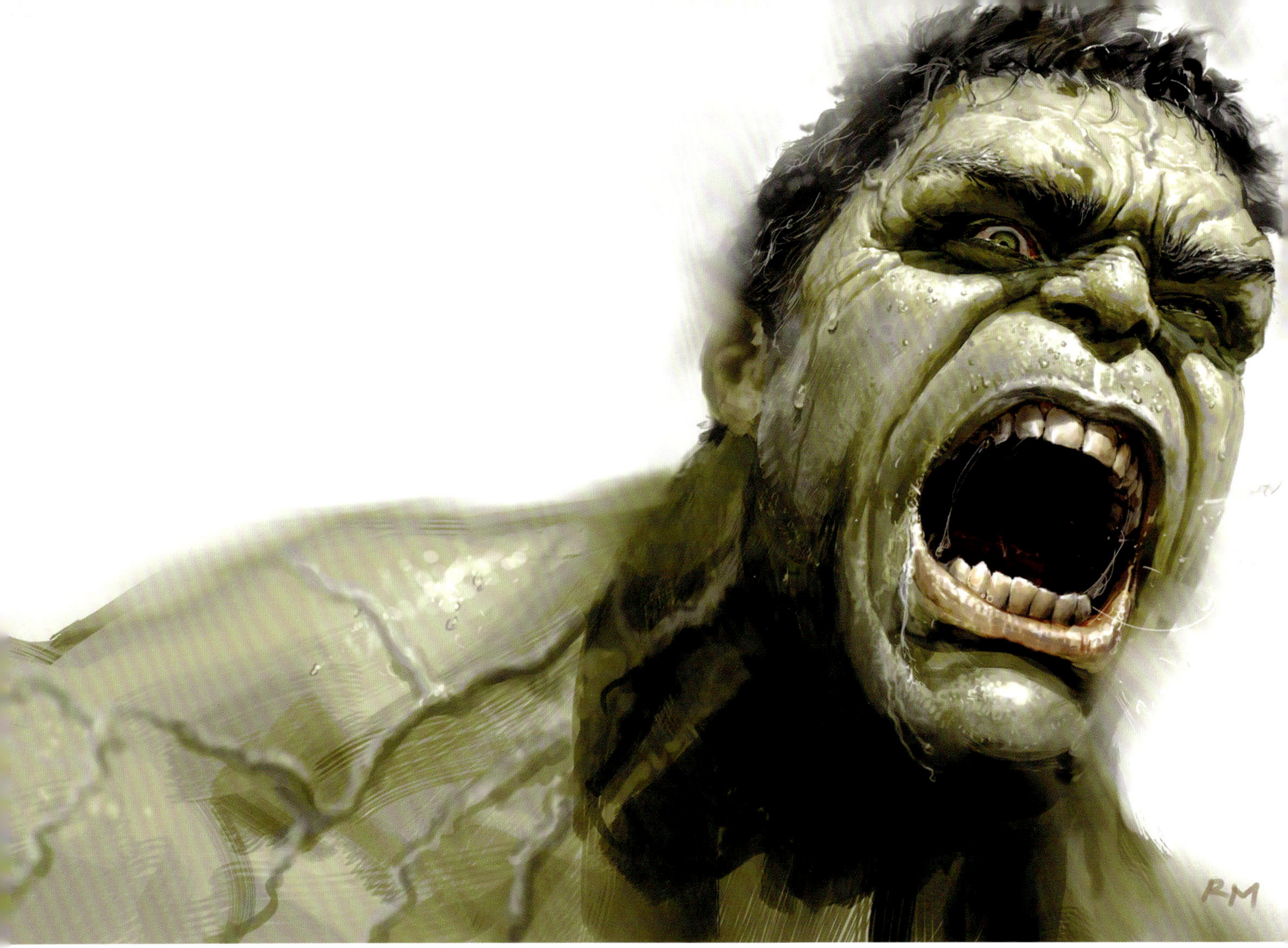

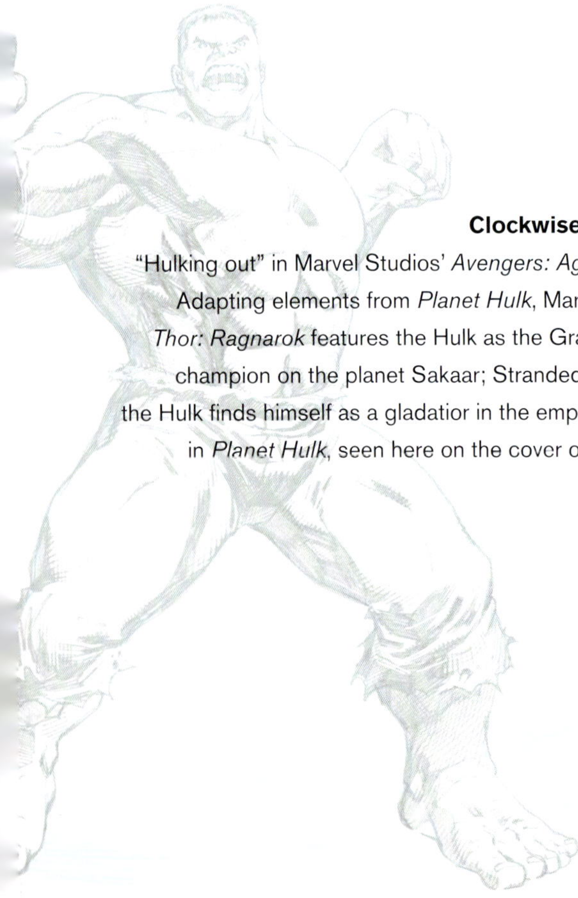

**Clockwise, from Top**

"Hulking out" in Marvel Studios' *Avengers: Age of Ultron*; Adapting elements from *Planet Hulk*, Marvel Studios' *Thor: Ragnarok* features the Hulk as the Grandmaster's champion on the planet Sakaar; Stranded on Sakaar, the Hulk finds himself as a gladatior in the emperor's arena in *Planet Hulk*, seen here on the cover of *Hulk* #94.

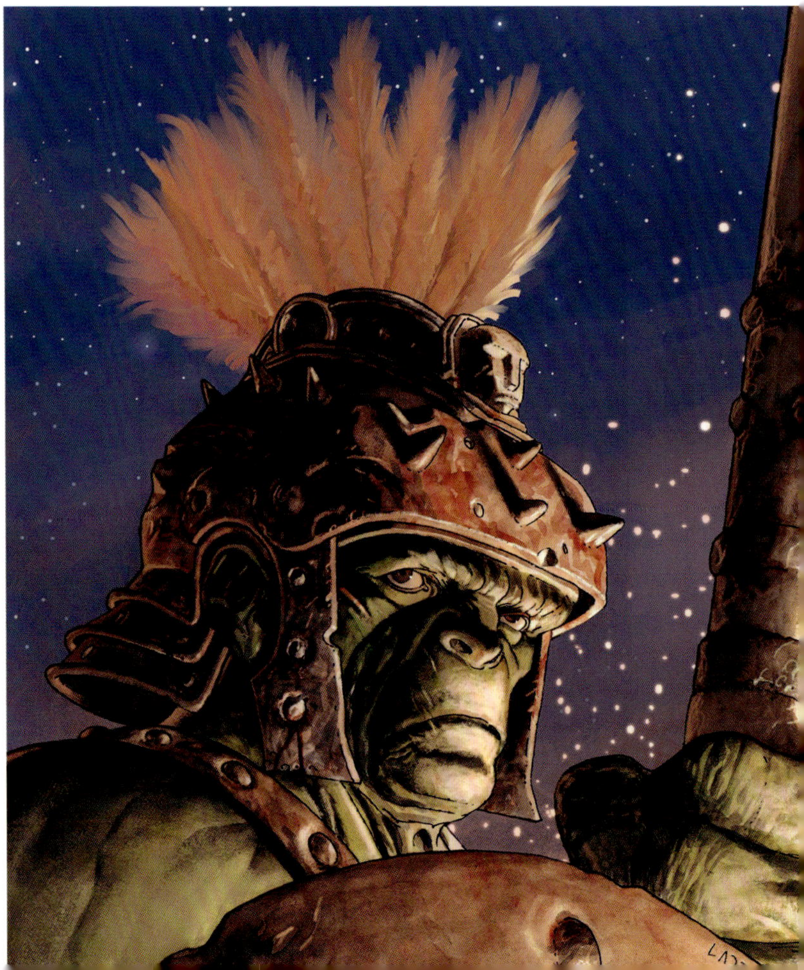

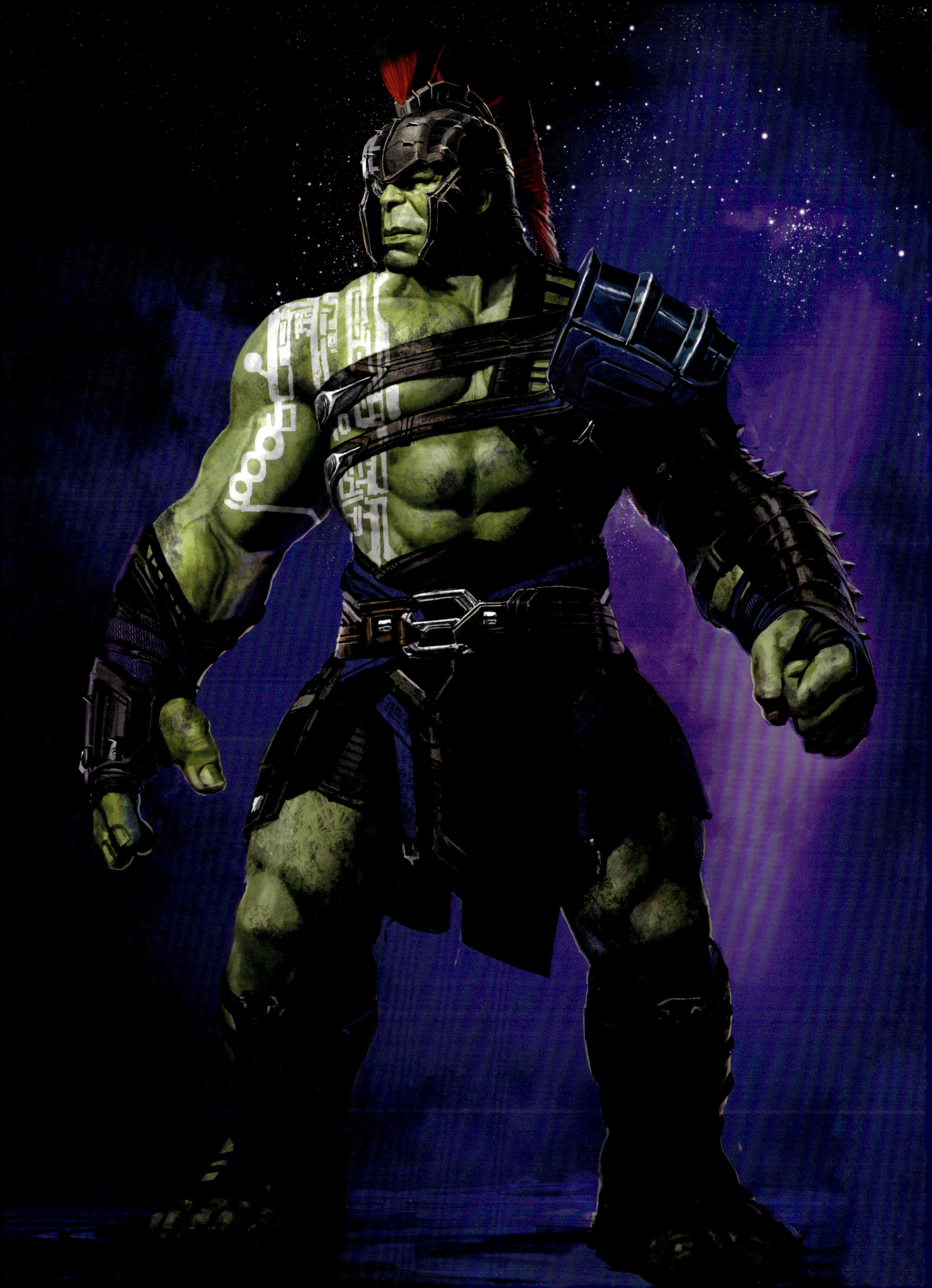

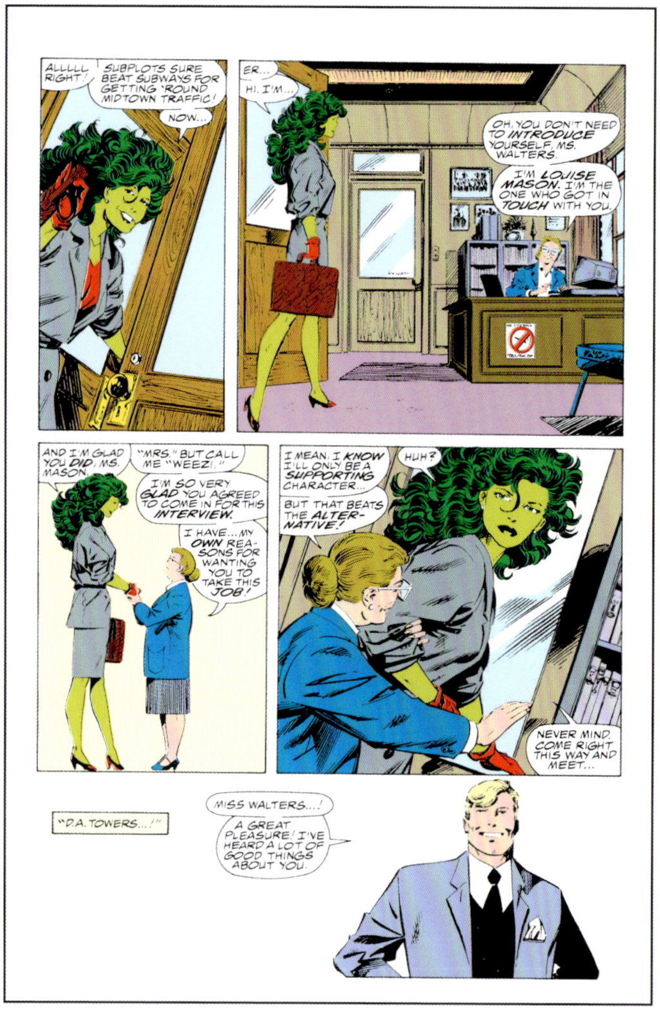
ALLLLL RIGHT!
SUBPLOTS SURE BEAT SUBWAYS FOR GETTING 'ROUND MIDTOWN TRAFFIC!
NOW...
ER...
HI, I'M...
OH, YOU DON'T NEED TO INTRODUCE YOURSELF, MS. WALTERS.
I'M LOUISE MASON. I'M THE ONE WHO GOT IN TOUCH WITH YOU.
AND I'M GLAD YOU DID, MS. MASON.
"MRS." BUT CALL ME "WEEZI."
I'M SO VERY GLAD YOU AGREED TO COME IN FOR THIS INTERVIEW.
I HAVE... MY OWN REASONS FOR WANTING YOU TO TAKE THIS JOB!
I MEAN, I KNOW I'LL ONLY BE A SUPPORTING CHARACTER...
HUH?
BUT THAT BEATS THE ALTERNATIVE!
NEVER MIND. COME RIGHT THIS WAY AND MEET...
"D.A. TOWERS...!"
MISS WALTERS...!
A GREAT PLEASURE! I'VE HEARD A LOT OF GOOD THINGS ABOUT YOU.

**Top Left, Bottom Right**

A talented attorney, Jennifer Walters works as a criminal defense lawyer in John Byrne's *The Sensational She-Hulk* #4.

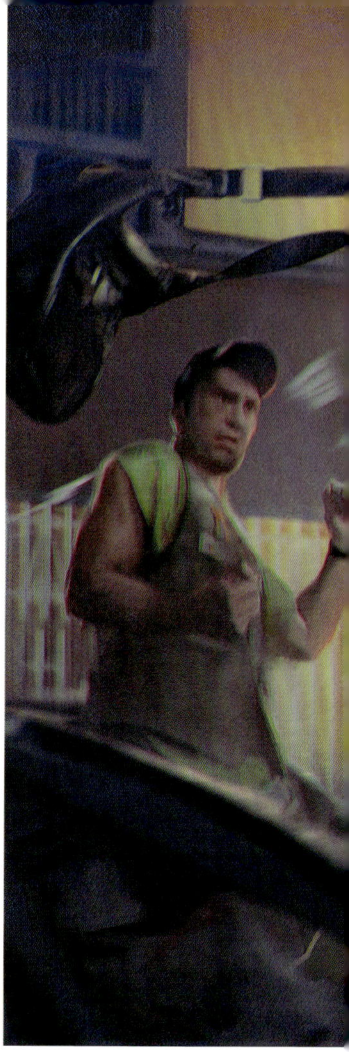

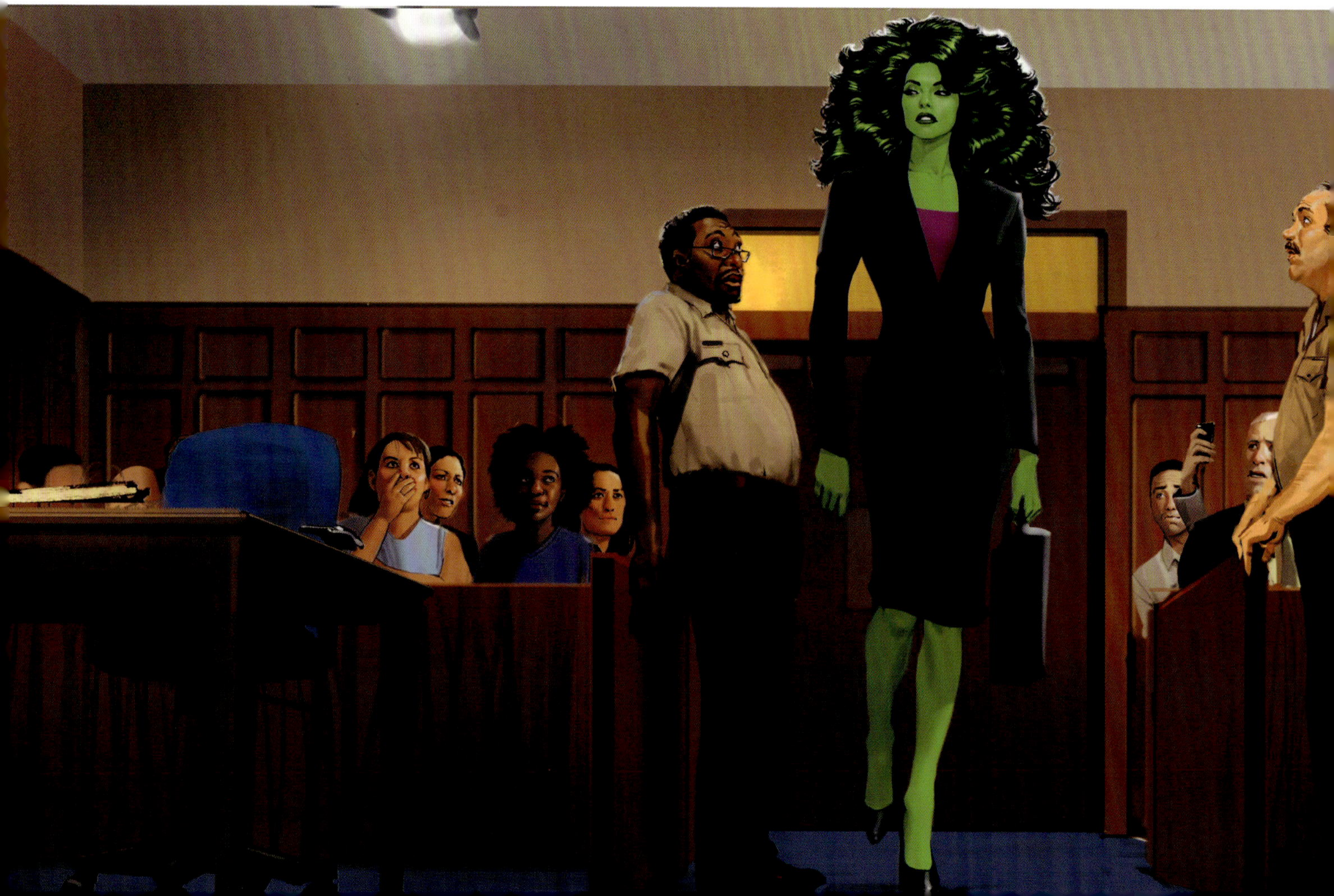

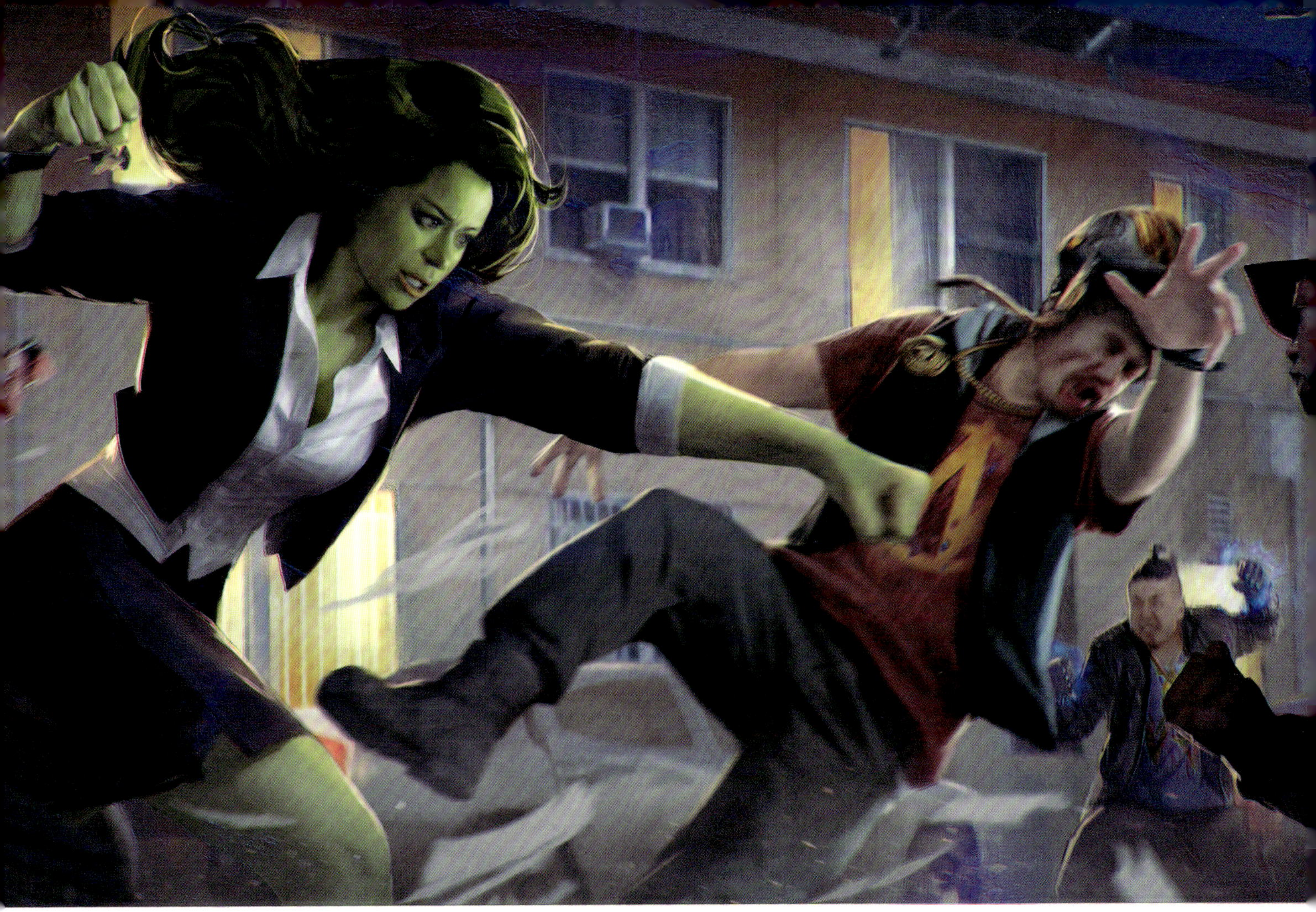

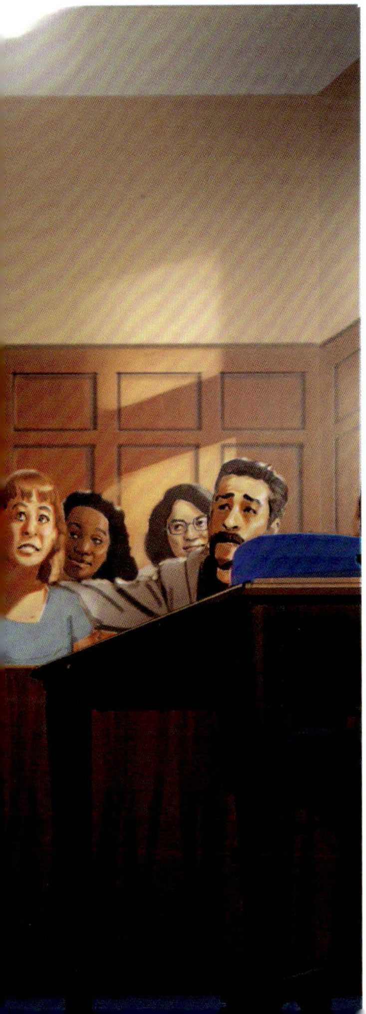

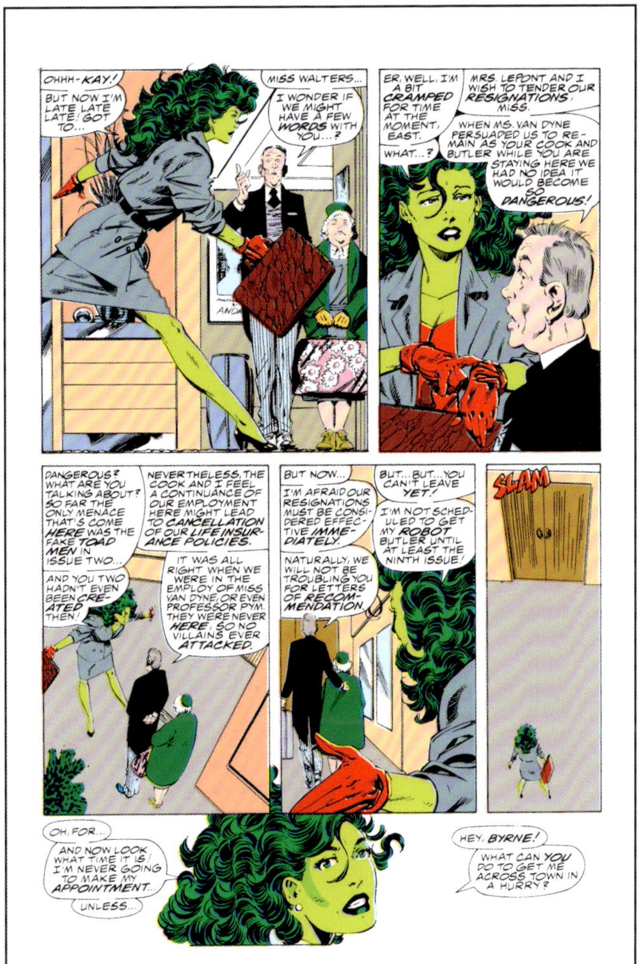
OHHH-KAY!
BUT NOW I'M LATE LATE LATE! GOT TO...
MISS WALTERS...
I WONDER IF WE MIGHT HAVE A FEW WORDS WITH YOU...?
ER, WELL, I'M A BIT CRAMPED FOR TIME AT THE MOMENT, EAST.
WHAT...?
MRS. LEPONT AND I WISH TO TENDER OUR RESIGNATIONS, MISS.
WHEN MS. VAN DYNE PERSUADED US TO RE-MAIN AS YOUR COOK AND BUTLER WHILE YOU ARE STAYING HERE WE HAD NO IDEA IT WOULD BECOME SO DANGEROUS!
DANGEROUS? WHAT ARE YOU TALKING ABOUT? SO FAR THE ONLY MENACE THAT'S COME HERE WAS THE FAKE TOAD MEN IN ISSUE TWO...
AND YOU TWO HADN'T EVEN BEEN CRE-ATED THEN!
NEVERTHELESS, THE COOK AND I FEEL A CONTINUANCE OF OUR EMPLOYMENT HERE MIGHT LEAD TO CANCELLATION OF OUR LIFE INSUR-ANCE POLICIES.
IT WAS ALL RIGHT WHEN WE WERE IN THE EMPLOY OF MISS VAN DYNE, OR EVEN PROFESSOR PYM. THEY WERE NEVER HERE, SO NO VILLAINS EVER ATTACKED.
BUT NOW...
I'M AFRAID OUR RESIGNATIONS MUST BE CONSI-DERED EFFEC-TIVE IMME-DIATELY.
NATURALLY, WE WILL NOT BE TROUBLING YOU FOR LETTERS OF RECOM-MENDATION.
BUT...BUT...YOU CAN'T LEAVE YET!
I'M NOT SCHED-ULED TO GET MY ROBOT BUTLER UNTIL AT LEAST THE NINTH ISSUE!
SLAM
OH, FOR...
AND NOW LOOK WHAT TIME IT IS! I'M NEVER GOING TO MAKE MY APPOINTMENT...
UNLESS...
HEY, BYRNE!
WHAT CAN YOU DO TO GET ME ACROSS TOWN IN A HURRY?

**Top Right, Bottom Left**
She-Hulk confronts her foes in and out of the courtroom in Marvel Studios' *She-Hulk: Attorney at Law.*

**Right**

She-Hulk has faced many antagonists throughout her comic career, including Toad Men conjured by Mysterio in *The Sensational She-Hulk* #2.

**Below**

Aided by the Sorcerer Supreme Wong, She-Hulk battles against magic demons in Marvel Studios' *She-Hulk: Attorney At Law*.

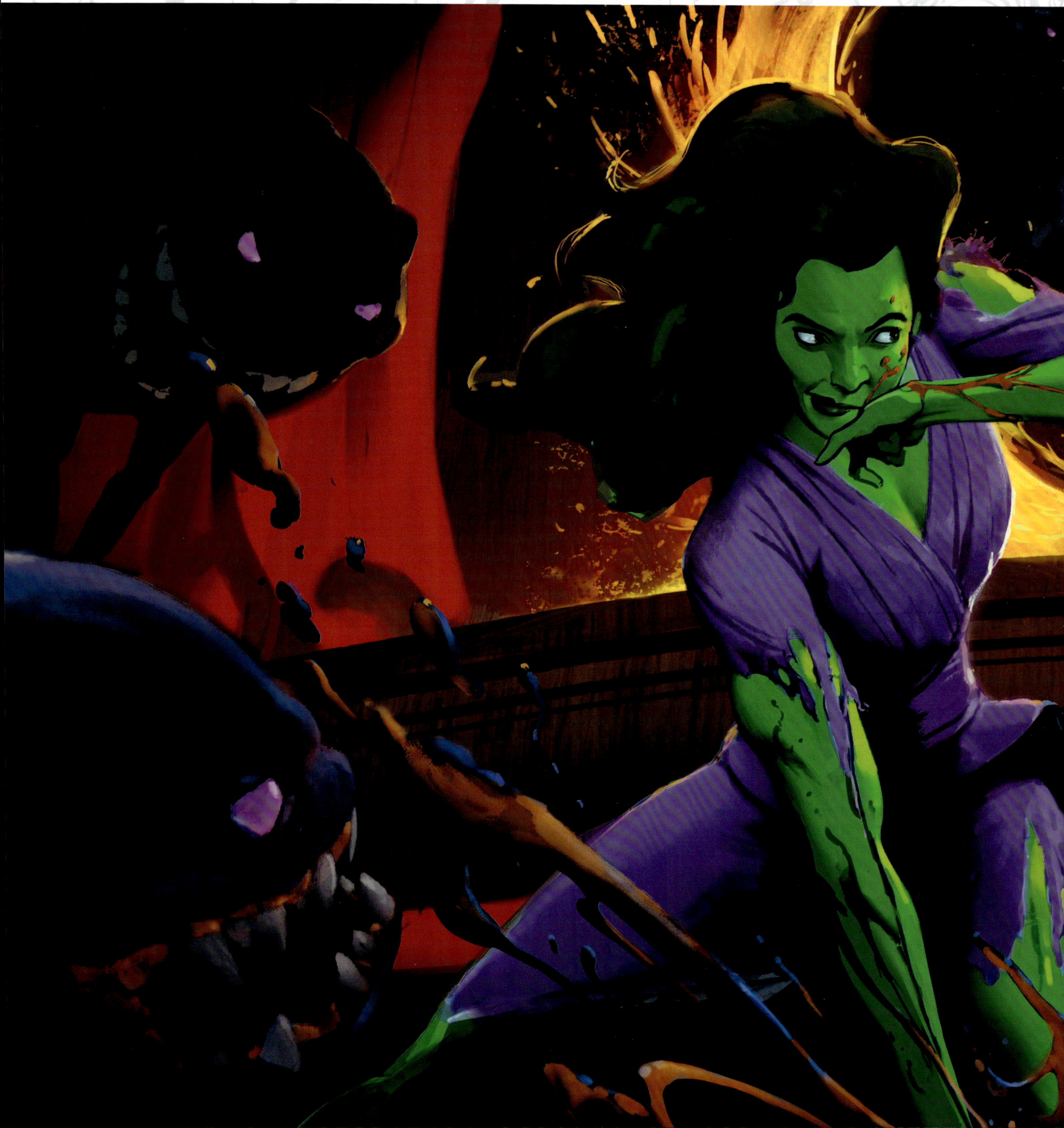

?!?
THEY'RE SHOOTING AT ME...???
EIGHT MILLION NEW YORKERS TO CHOOSE FROM, AND THEY'RE SHOOTING AT ME??
THUMP!
WHAT...??
TOAD MEN, BYRNE??
TOAD MEN?
I THOUGHT THE COVER WAS JUST A GAG!
I WAS ALL SET FOR THE KREE OR THE SKRULLS...
OR EVEN THE CRUMMY KRYLOREANS!
BUT YOU STICK ME WITH THE TOAD MEN??

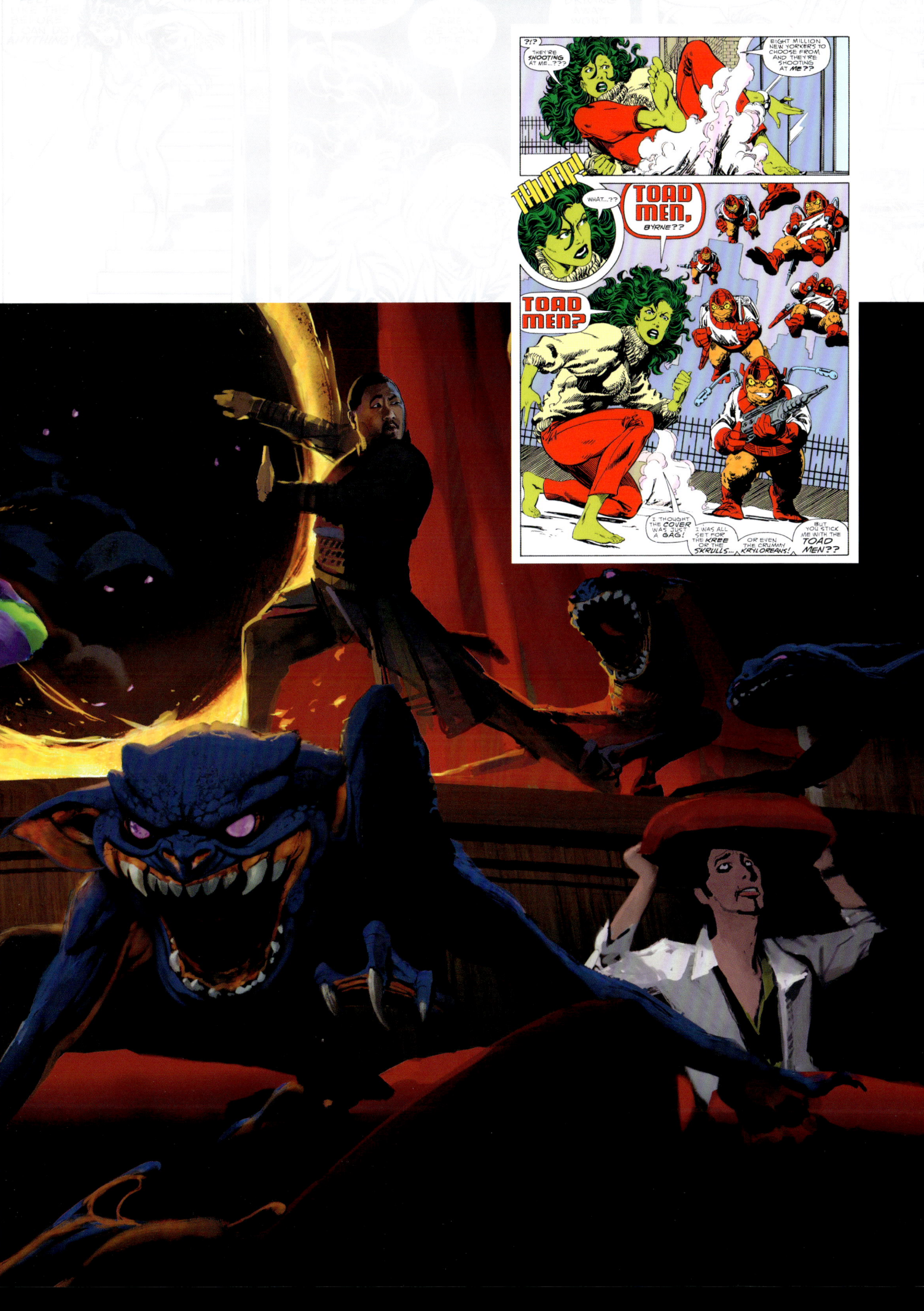

C3

## CHAPTER THREE:

# SAVAGE

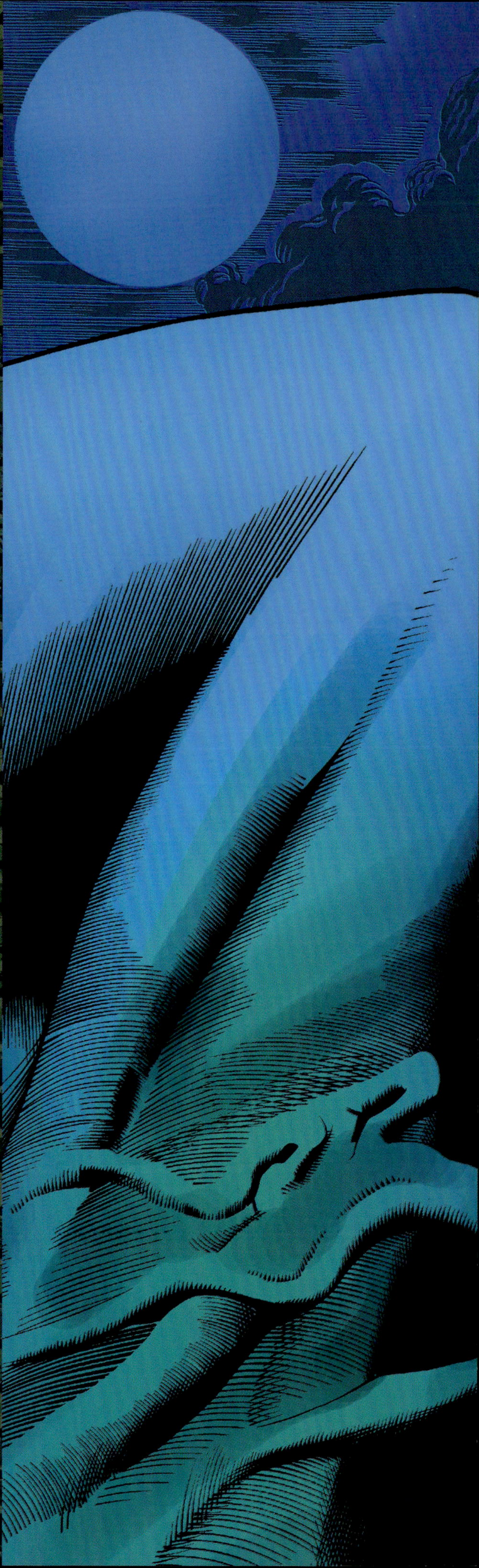

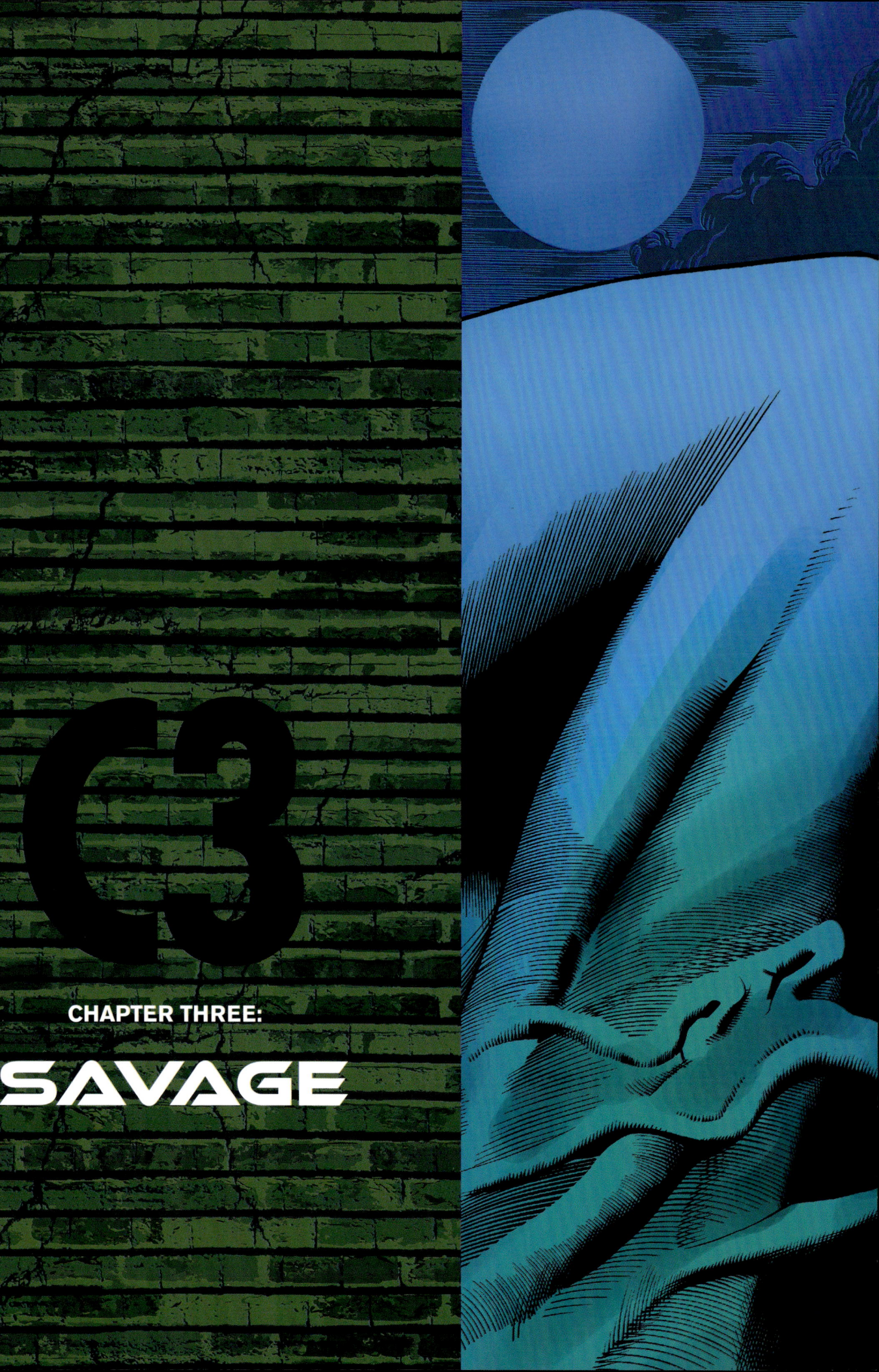

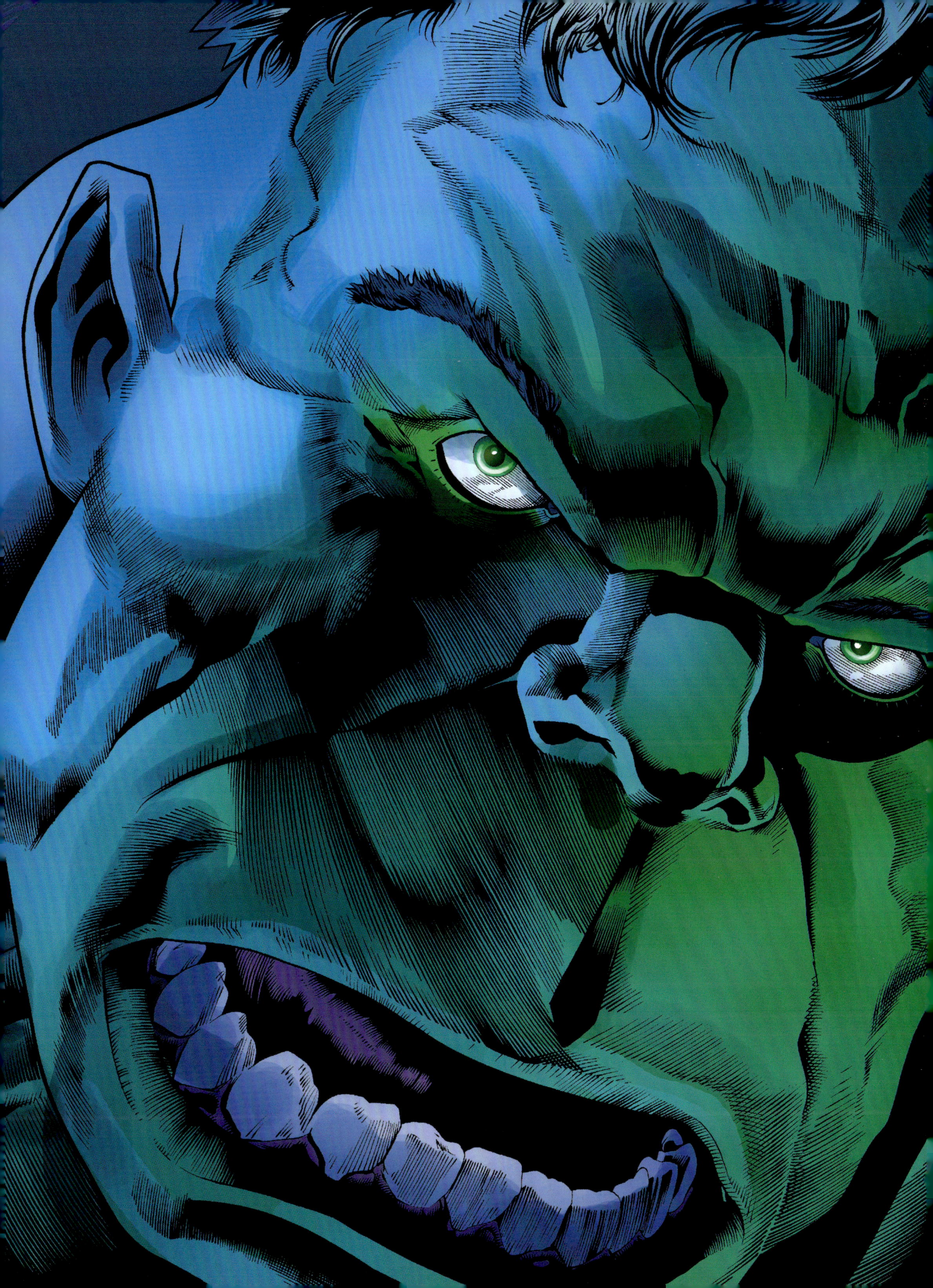

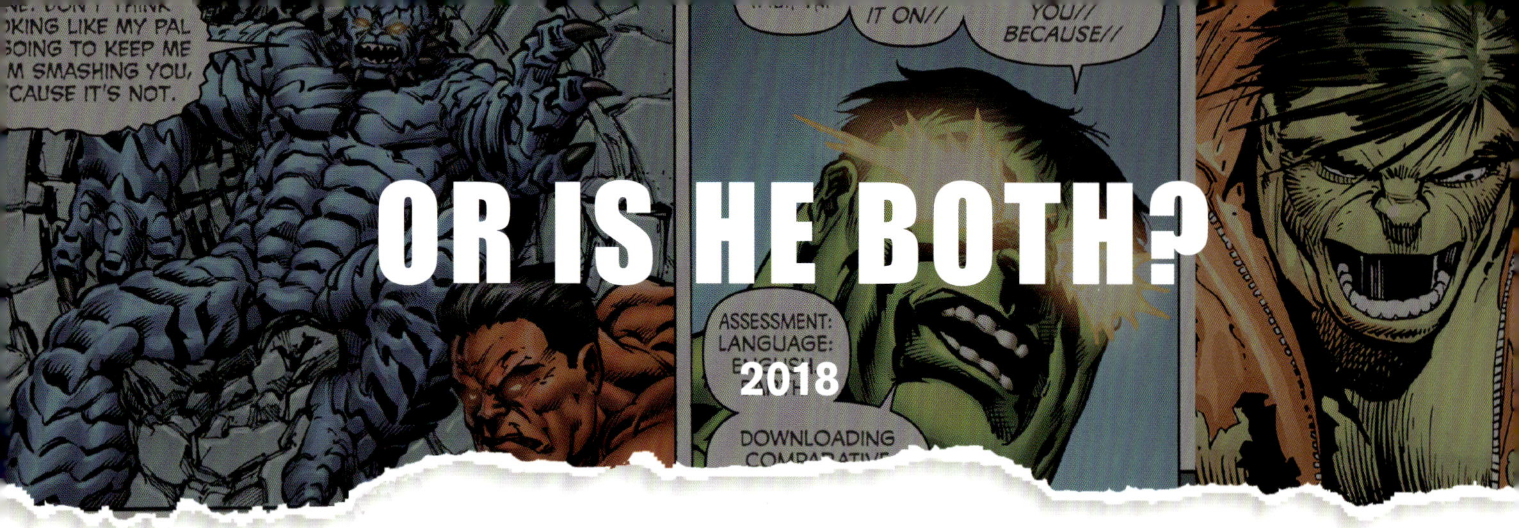

IT ON//
YOU// BECAUSE//
ASSESSMENT: LANGUAGE:
DOWNLOADING


# OR IS HE BOTH?

## 2018

Bruce Banner and the Hulk are dead. At least, this is what we were led to believe following the events of *Civil War II*. With the launch of the new series *The Immortal Hulk*, we first see a young man with a gun, driving to a gas station. He's not there to fill up his tank. There is a mom at a gas pump, shouting to her daughter heading into the convenience store to get something heathy for a snack. We sense that this isn't going to end well.

Inside the store, a man checks out a tabloid magazine announcing on its cover a fresh Hulk sighting. Simultaneously, the man with the gun, now hooded and wearing a cloth mask that covers the bottom half of his face, enters the store and demands the cashier open the register and hand over the money in the till. The young girl from earlier is startled by the man with the gun and drops her drink, which crashes to the floor. Startled in turn, the man spins and shoots, and the girl follows her drink and down to the floor. The man at the magazine rack reacts to the shot, his eyes start to glow green. But before anything else happens, the green-eyed man is met with a bullet to the middle of his forehead. In a panic, the shooter also takes care of the cashier, leaving three dead on the convenience store floor.

The bodies are taken to the morgue. A hand emerges from under one of the sheets, and turns green. Cut to a biker hangout, where the gas station shooter, whose name is Tommy, tearfully tells the head of the gang what happened. The leader is not interested in what happened; he just wants the money from the robbery. He tells Tommy that this is only the first installment of paying down his debt. Tommy pleads with the biker that he needs some of the money to keep the lights on in his house and to feed his family. The biker calls him weak and tells him to "toughen up." But his lecture is cut short by a loud noise—"THOMM!"

The room goes black. People panic, and suddenly two huge green hands break through the wall and grab the biker by the head. Outside, Tommy tries to escape, but he is stopped by the green monster. The Hulk towers over the terrified Tommy,

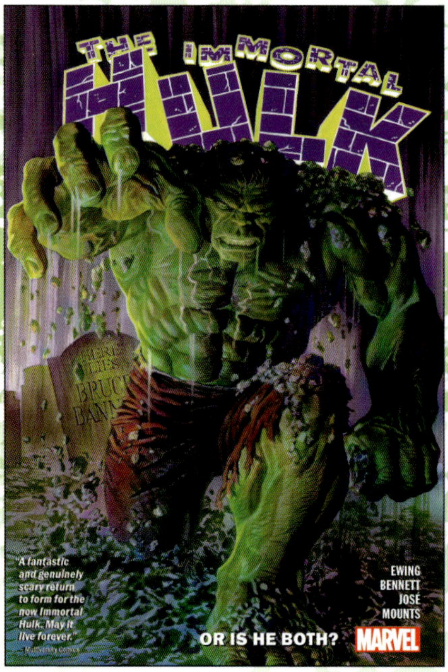

THE IMMORTAL HULK
A fantastic and genuinely scary return to form for the now Immortal Hulk. May it live forever.
EWING
BENNETT
JOSE
MOUNTS
OR IS HE BOTH?
MARVEL


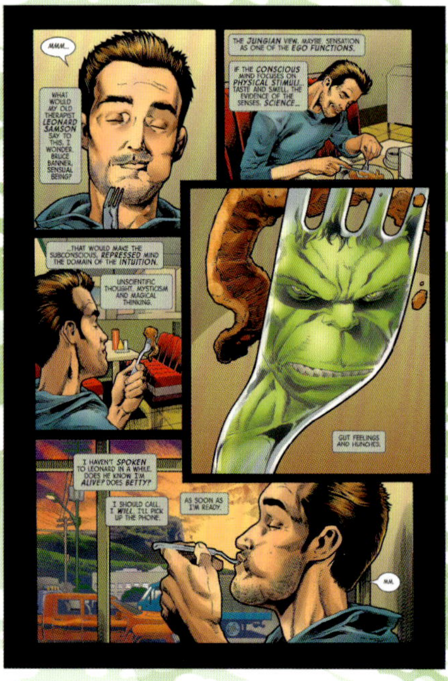

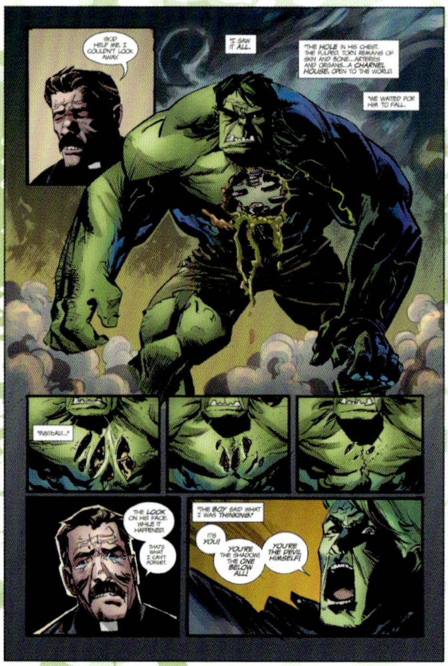

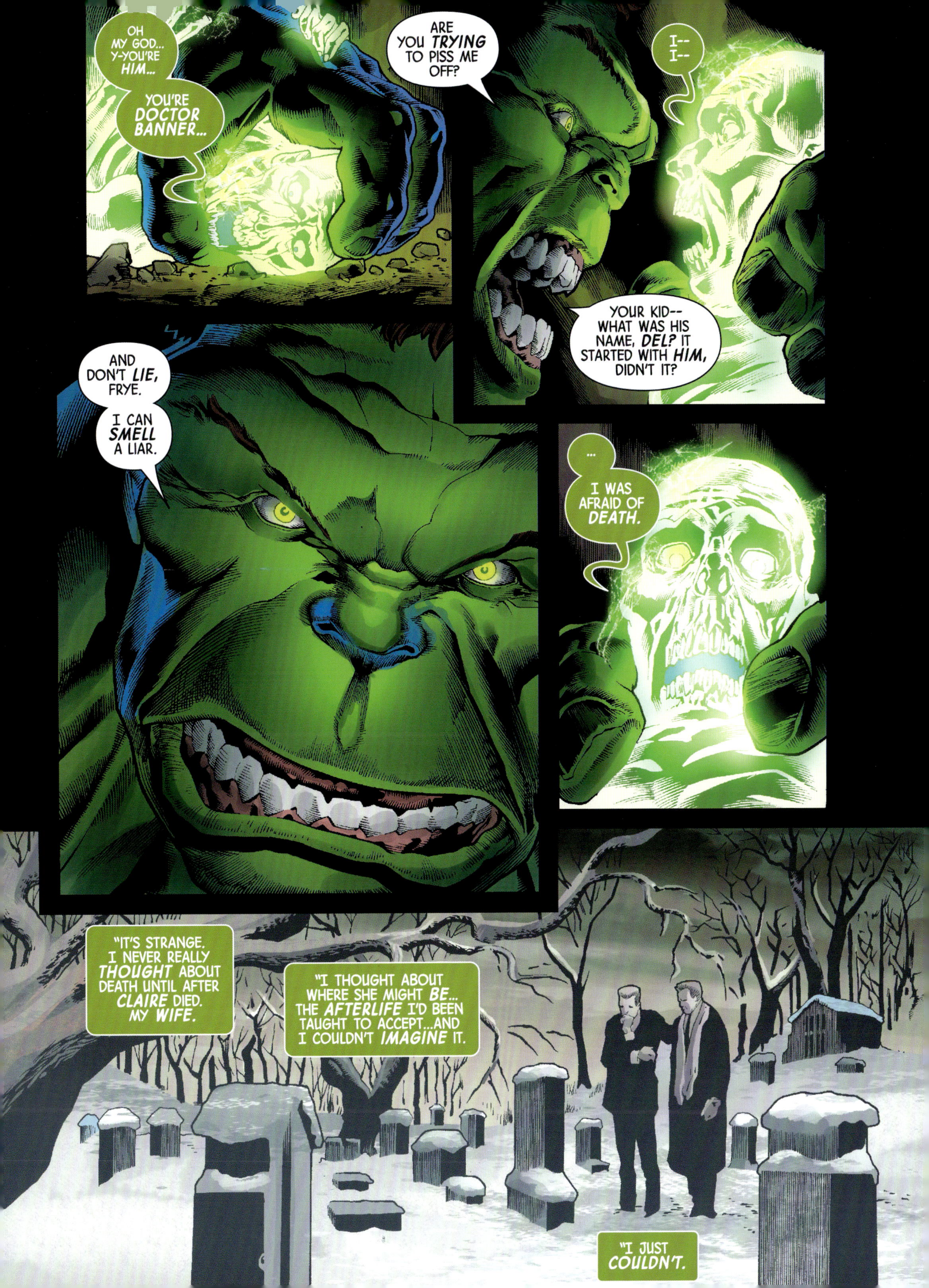
OH MY GOD... Y-YOU'RE HIM...
YOU'RE DOCTOR BANNER...
ARE YOU TRYING TO PISS ME OFF?
I-- I--
YOUR KID-- WHAT WAS HIS NAME, DEL? IT STARTED WITH HIM, DIDN'T IT?
AND DON'T LIE, FRYE.
I CAN SMELL A LIAR.
...
I WAS AFRAID OF DEATH.
"IT'S STRANGE. I NEVER REALLY THOUGHT ABOUT DEATH UNTIL AFTER CLAIRE DIED. MY WIFE.
"I THOUGHT ABOUT WHERE SHE MIGHT BE... THE AFTERLIFE I'D BEEN TAUGHT TO ACCEPT...AND I COULDN'T IMAGINE IT.
"I JUST COULDN'T.

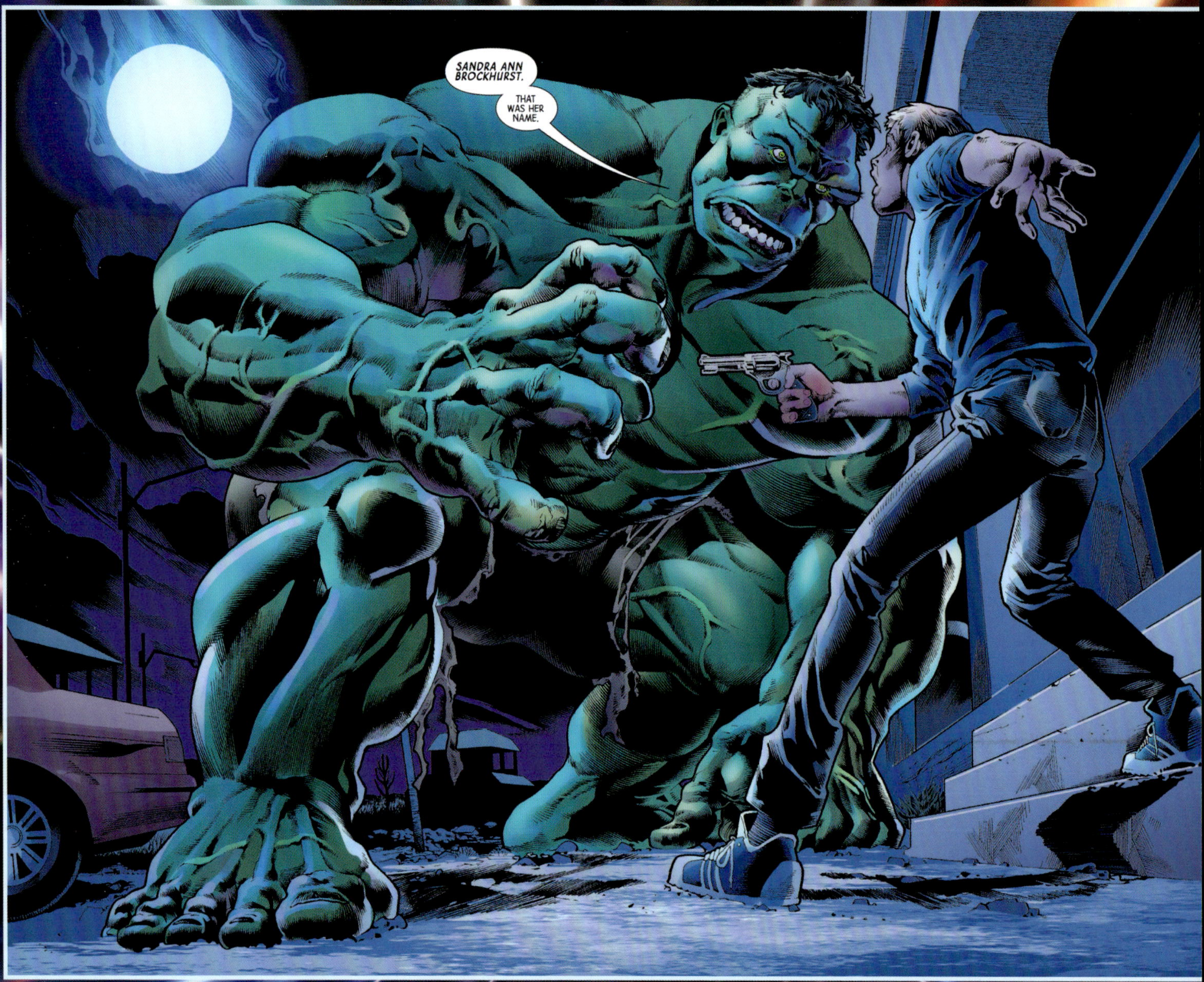
SANDRA ANN BROCKHURST.
THAT WAS HER NAME.

who waves his gun, clearly useless against the Hulk. The Hulk is not a store clerk or a young girl. Tommy shoots, and the bullets bounce off the Hulk's green skin. Before the Hulk acts further, he wants Tommy to know the name of the girl he killed with his gun. Her name is Sandra Ann Brockhurst, and she was twelve years old.

Tommy winds up in the hospital, unconscious, full of tubes, with pins holding his bones together, his neck in a brace, and most of his limbs in casts. He will never walk again. He may never even wake up again. Meanwhile, in a cheap motel, Bruce Banner remembers what the Hulk did. He looks into a mirror and wonders if he is a "bad guy" for what he did to Tommy.

Later, Banner roams the desert, making money where he can in various desert towns. He savors the little things life has to offer. A simple breakfast of eggs and bacon at a local diner transports him to a place where the world and the Hulk don't exist. A place where he feels normal before he is dragged back into the violent world of the Hulk.

As much as Banner tries to keep to himself, as much as he tries to avoid any situations that might change him into the Hulk, it's only a matter of time before he transforms again. He is haunted by his alter ego. Whenever he looks into a reflective surface, he sees the Hulk staring back at him.

Several of these single-issue comics, which make up this story, open with a quote. The most relevant one is from Vladimir Nabokov: "For I do not exist: There exist but the thousands of mirrors that reflect me." Does the mirror reflect who you truly are? Is Banner more than the green giant that lives inside him?

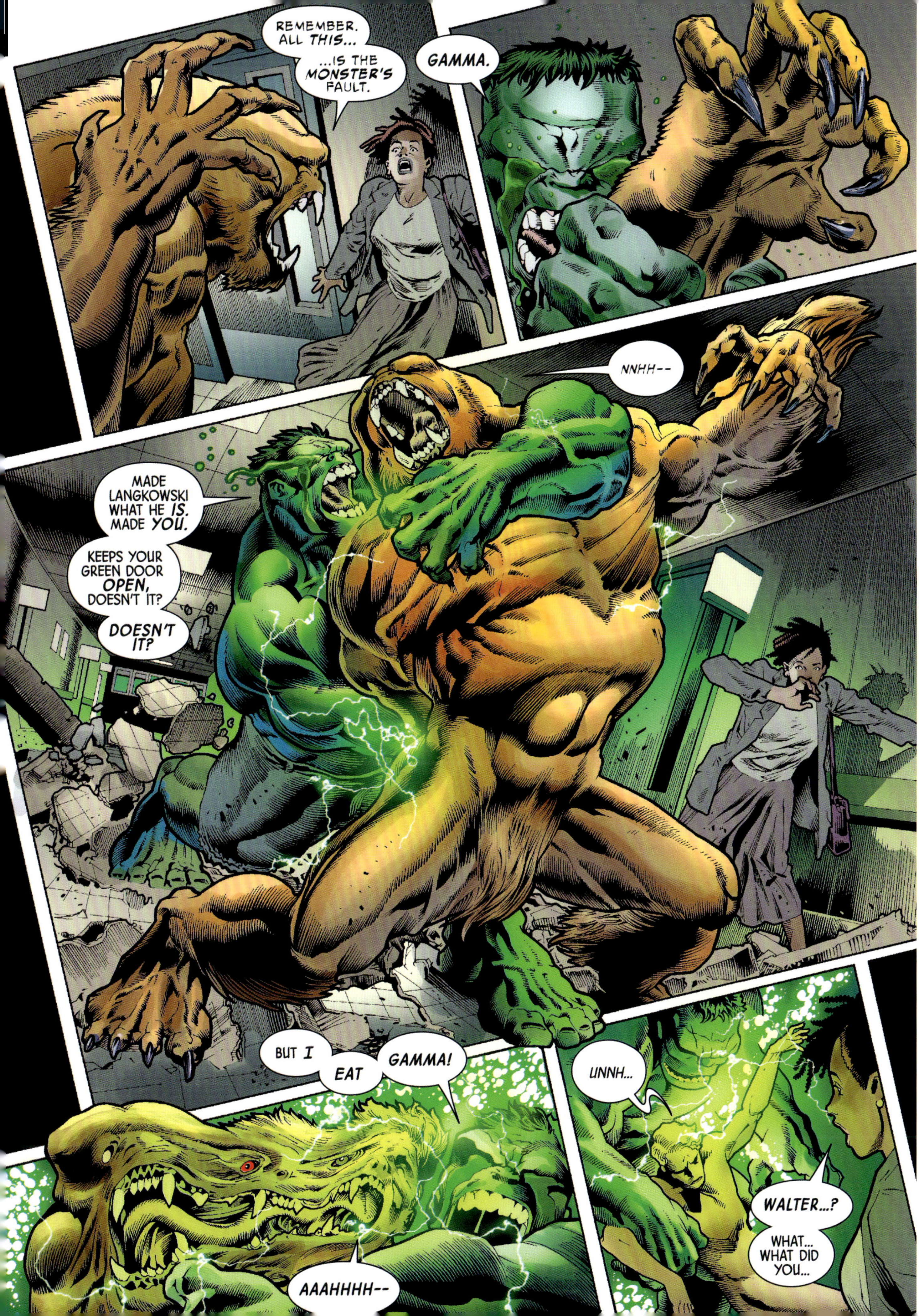
REMEMBER. ALL THIS...
...IS THE MONSTER'S FAULT.
GAMMA.
NNHH--
MADE LANGKOWSKI WHAT HE IS. MADE YOU.
KEEPS YOUR GREEN DOOR OPEN, DOESN'T IT?
DOESN'T IT?
BUT I
EAT
GAMMA!
AAAHHHH--
UNNH...
WALTER...?
WHAT... WHAT DID YOU...

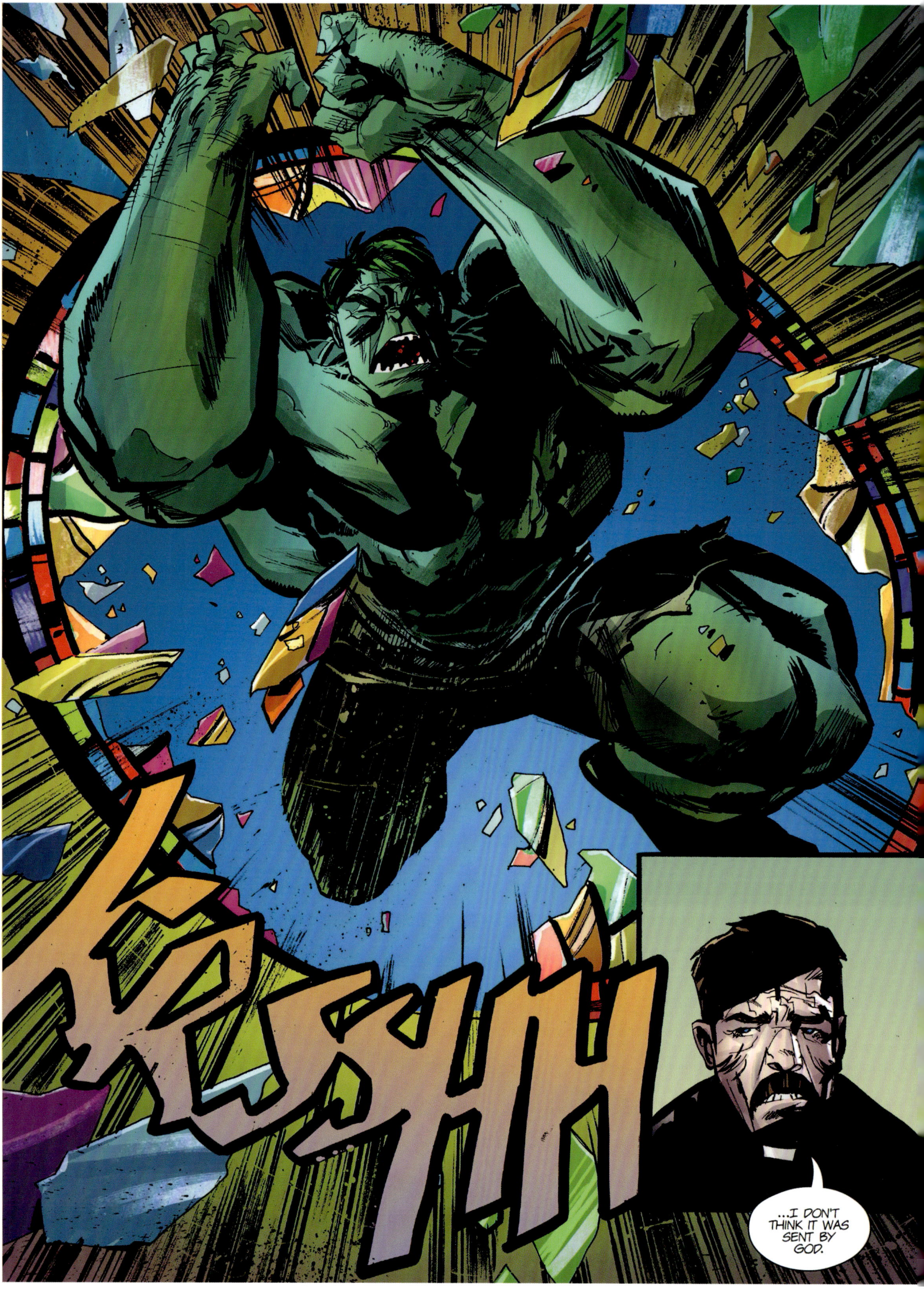
KRSHH
...I DON'T THINK IT WAS SENT BY GOD.

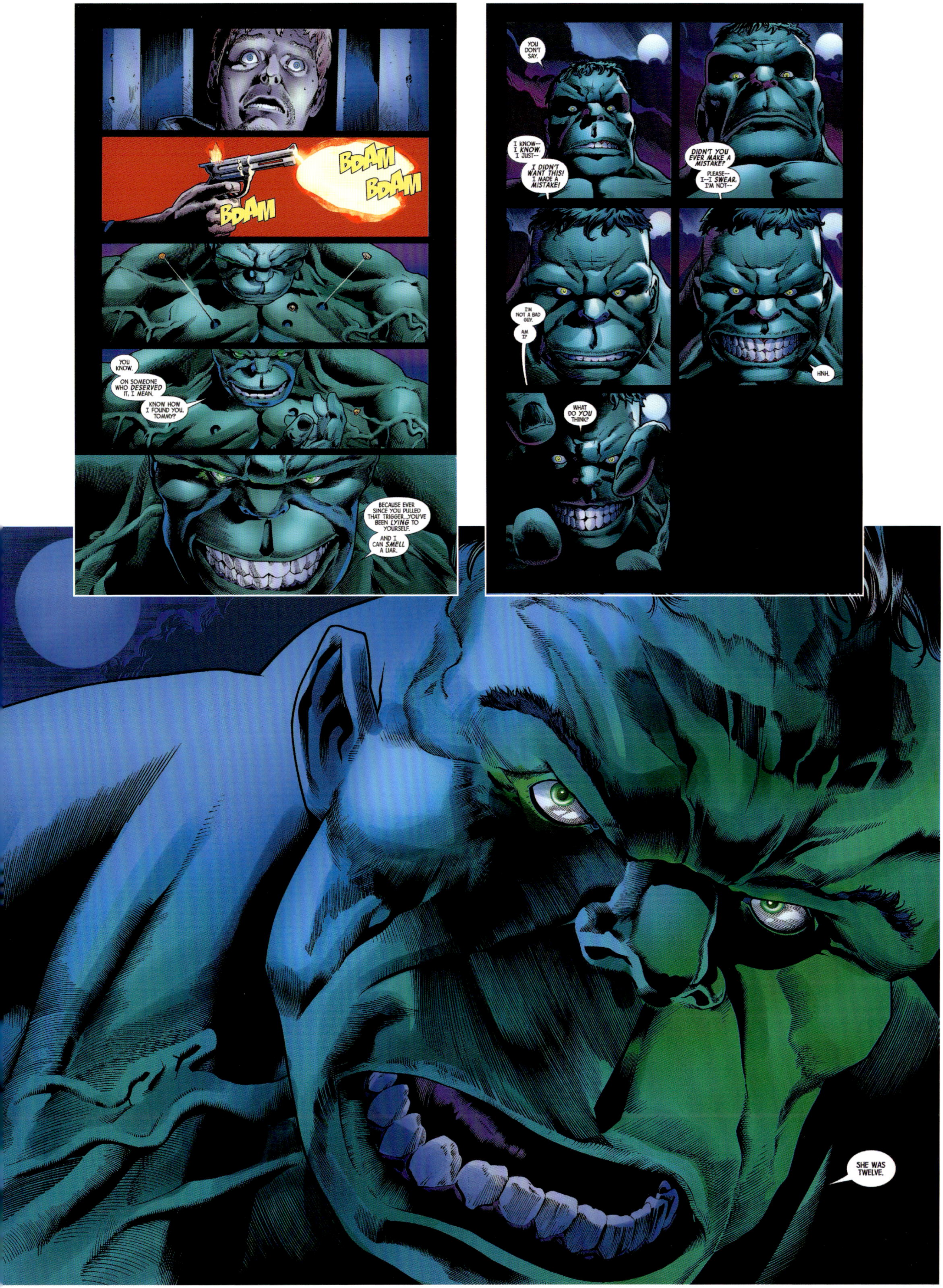
BDAM
BDAM
BDAM
YOU KNOW.
ON SOMEONE WHO DESERVED IT, I MEAN.
KNOW HOW I FOUND YOU, TOMMY?
BECAUSE EVER SINCE YOU PULLED THAT TRIGGER...YOU'VE BEEN LYING TO YOURSELF.
AND I CAN SMELL A LIAR.
YOU DON'T SAY.
I KNOW-- I KNOW. I JUST--
I DIDN'T WANT THIS! I MADE A MISTAKE!
DIDN'T YOU EVER MAKE A MISTAKE?
PLEASE-- I--I SWEAR, I'M NOT--
I'M NOT A BAD GUY.
AM I?
HNH.
WHAT DO YOU THINK?
SHE WAS TWELVE.

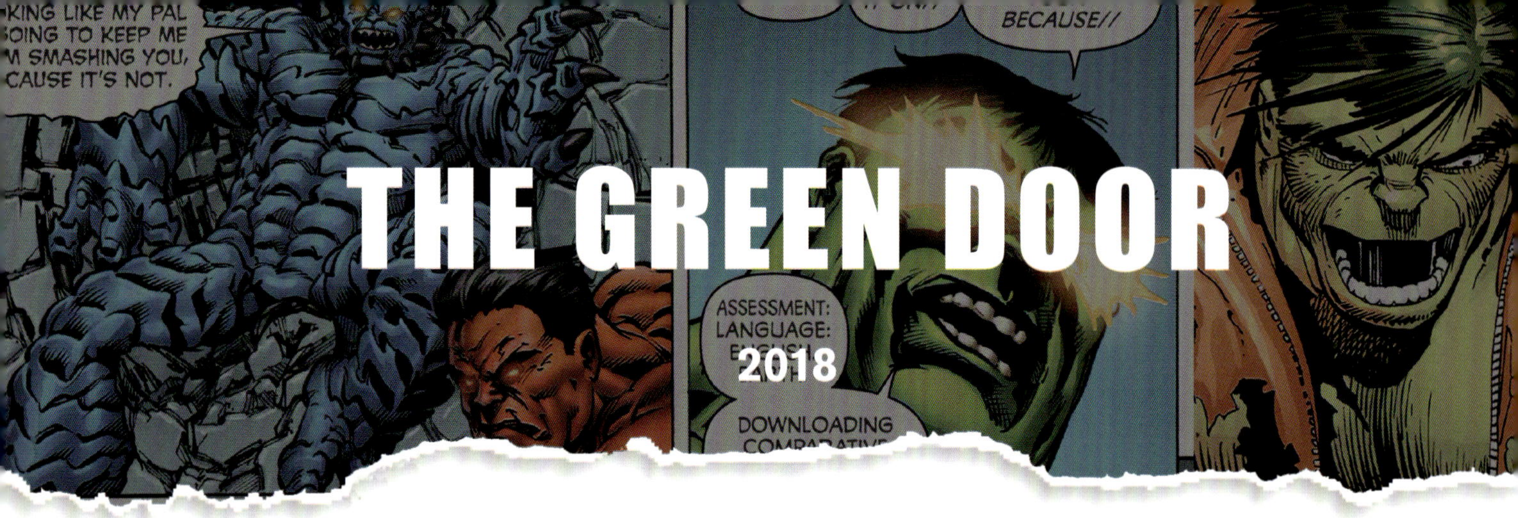
BECAUSE//
ASSESSMENT: LANGUAGE:
DOWNLOADING

# THE GREEN DOOR

## 2018

It seems that everyone is trying to track down the Hulk. He has a reporter for the *Arizona Herald*, Jackie McGee, on his trail. His old college roommate Walter Langkowski, aka Sasquatch, is also looking for the Hulk. (Langkowski became Sasquatch after his experimentations with gamma radiation in his attempt to become like the Hulk went awry.) Even the Avengers, led by Captain Marvel, want to bring him in.

The Avengers find and confront him. They are close to defeat when Iron Man launches something called the Helios Laser, which is laced with ultra-violet radiation and is, in effect, a beam of hard sunlight. It turns the Hulk into a skeleton. This Hulk is more like the Hulk from the first few issues of *The Incredible Hulk*, in that he changes based on the time of day. During the day he is Banner and at night he changes into the Hulk.

The Hulk's remains are taken to Shadow Base, which is run by a General Reginald Fortean, who is tasked with managing the Hulk situation. The skeleton of the Hulk begins to regenerate back to normal. In order to prevent the Hulk from becoming whole and conscious, the scientist in charge of examining the body, Dr. Jeffery Clive, uses a scalpel made of adamantium, the same rare metal that makes up Wolverine's claws, to slice the Hulk's body up like a Thanksgiving turkey.

Dr. Clive stores the pieces of the Hulk in jars, as if they are part of a freak show in a carnival. Clive sits in the lab staring at the jars, contemplating what to do with the pieces of the Hulk, when he notices that the Hulk is smiling from one of the jars. And are his fingers moving in another jar? Suddenly, all the Hulk parts burst from their glass containers and they gather and reassemble. As the Hulk re-forms, Dr. Clive is absorbed into the green monster. The Hulk then escapes Shadow Base and makes his way back to the research facility in nearby Los Alamos where he first became the Hulk. When the sun rises and the Hulk transforms back into Banner, the corpse of Dr. Clive falls to the ground.

A few days earlier at Shadow Base, Carl Creel, also known as Absorbing Man (whose powers are pretty self-explanatory),

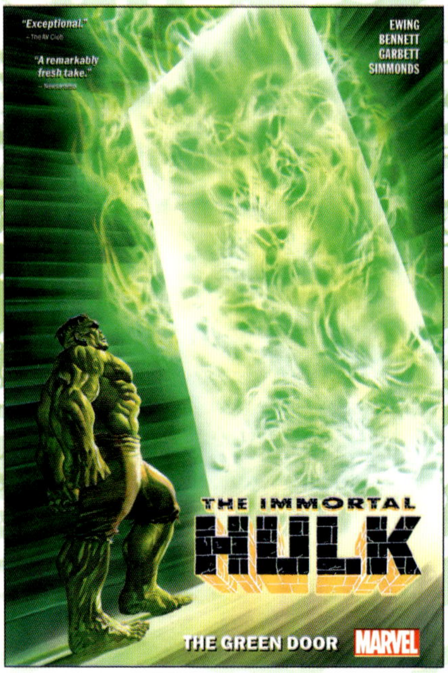
EWING
BENNETT
GARBETT
SIMMONDS
THE IMMORTAL HULK
THE GREEN DOOR
MARVEL

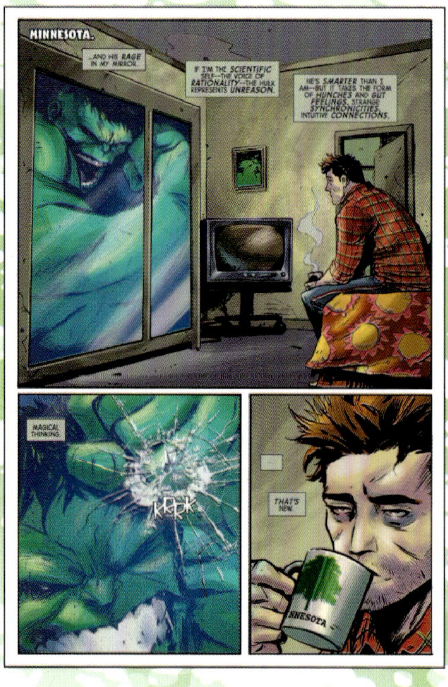
MINNESOTA.
...AND HIS RAGE IN MY MIRROR.
IF I'M THE SCIENTIFIC SELF--THE VOICE OF RATIONALITY--THE HULK REPRESENTS UNREASON.
HE'S SMARTER THAN I AM--BUT IT TAKES THE FORM OF HUNCHES AND GUT FEELINGS, STRANGE SYNCHRONICITIES, INTUITIVE CONNECTIONS.
MAGICAL THINKING.
KRRK
THAT'S NEW.

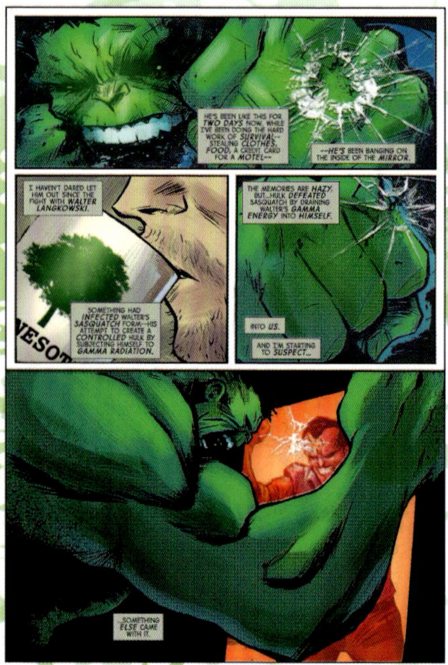
HE'S BEEN LIKE THIS FOR TWO DAYS NOW. WHILE I'VE BEEN DOING THE HARD WORK OF SURVIVAL-- STEALING CLOTHES, FOOD, A CREDIT CARD FOR A MOTEL--
--HE'S BEEN BANGING ON THE INSIDE OF THE MIRROR.
I HAVEN'T DARED LET HIM OUT SINCE THE FIGHT WITH WALTER LANGKOWSKI.
SOMETHING HAD INFECTED WALTER'S SASQUATCH FORM--HIS ATTEMPT TO CREATE A CONTROLLED HULK BY SUBJECTING HIMSELF TO GAMMA RADIATION.
THE MEMORIES ARE HAZY, BUT...HULK DEFEATED SASQUATCH BY DRAINING WALTER'S GAMMA ENERGY INTO HIMSELF.
INTO US.
AND I'M STARTING TO SUSPECT...
...SOMETHING ELSE CAME WITH IT.

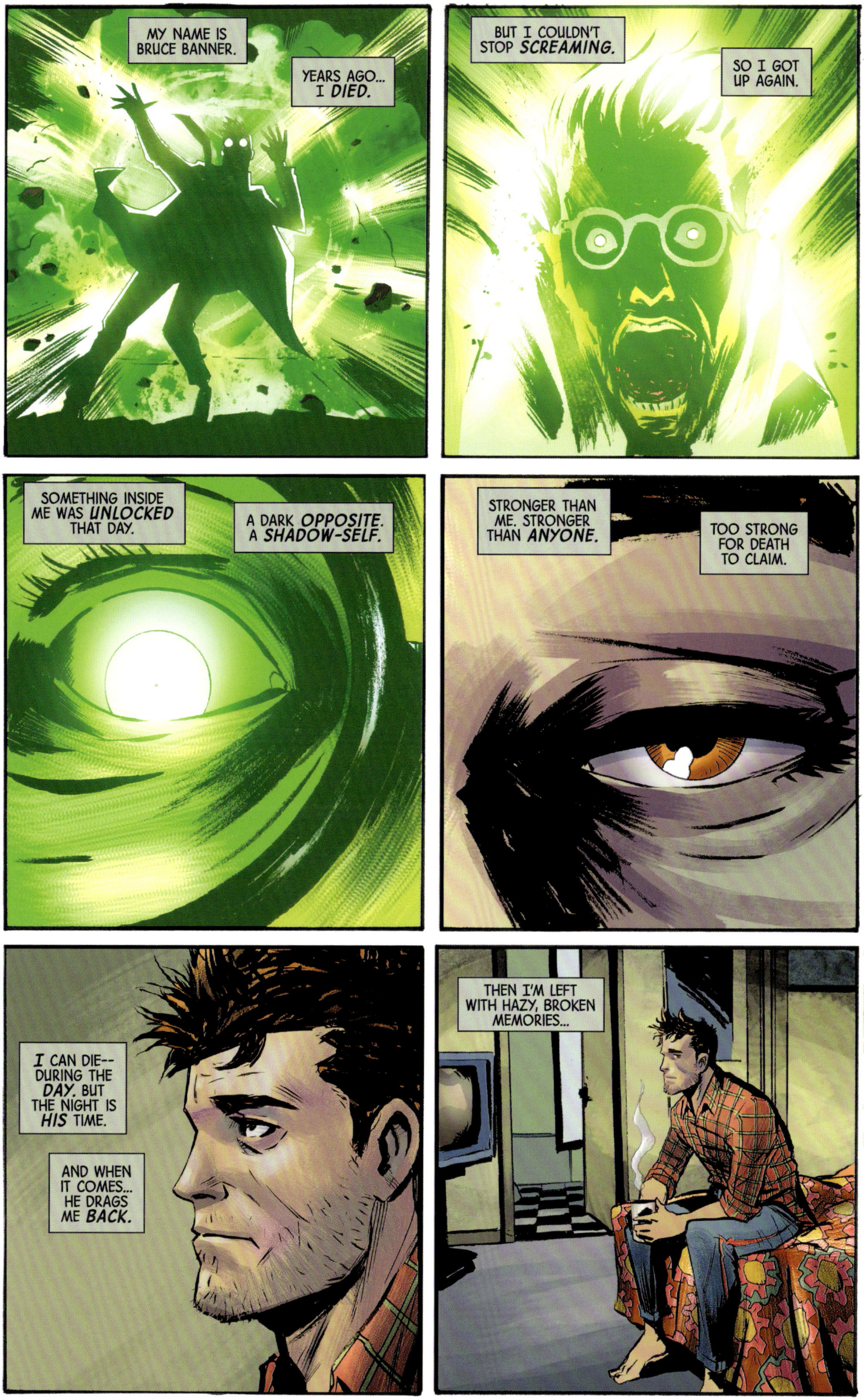
MY NAME IS BRUCE BANNER.
YEARS AGO... I DIED.
BUT I COULDN'T STOP SCREAMING.
SO I GOT UP AGAIN.
SOMETHING INSIDE ME WAS UNLOCKED THAT DAY.
A DARK OPPOSITE. A SHADOW-SELF.
STRONGER THAN ME. STRONGER THAN ANYONE.
TOO STRONG FOR DEATH TO CLAIM.
I CAN DIE-- DURING THE DAY. BUT THE NIGHT IS HIS TIME.
AND WHEN IT COMES... HE DRAGS ME BACK.
THEN I'M LEFT WITH HAZY, BROKEN MEMORIES...

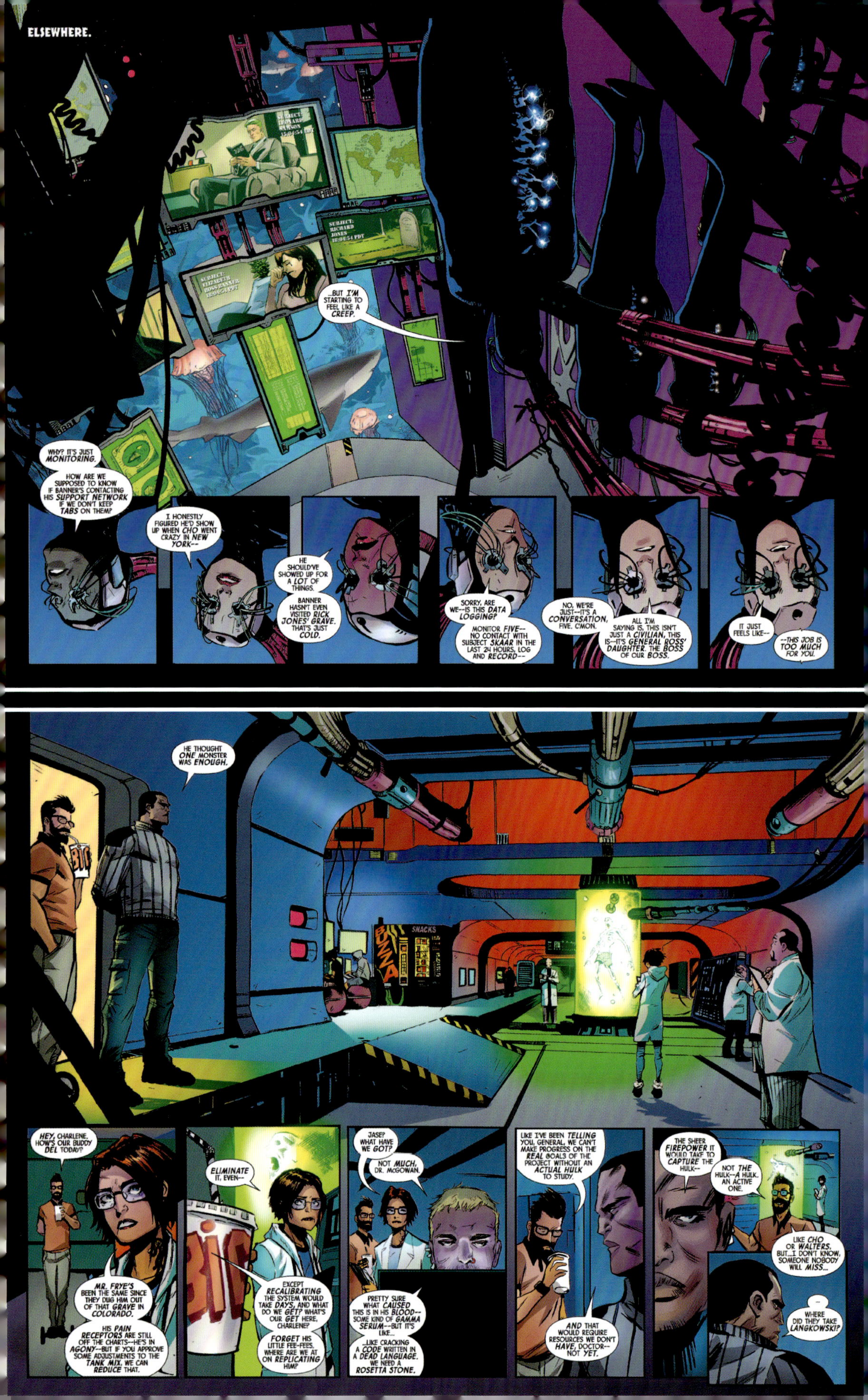

ELSEWHERE.
...BUT I'M STARTING TO FEEL LIKE A CREEP.
WHY? IT'S JUST MONITORING.
HOW ARE WE SUPPOSED TO KNOW IF BANNER'S CONTACTING HIS SUPPORT NETWORK IF WE DON'T KEEP TABS ON THEM?
I HONESTLY FIGURED HE'D SHOW UP WHEN CHO WENT CRAZY IN NEW YORK--
HE SHOULD'VE SHOWED UP FOR A LOT OF THINGS.
BANNER HASN'T EVEN VISITED RICK JONES' GRAVE. THAT'S JUST COLD.
SORRY, ARE WE--IS THIS DATA LOGGING?
MONITOR FIVE--NO CONTACT WITH SUBJECT SKAAR IN THE LAST 24 HOURS, LOG AND RECORD--
NO, WE'RE JUST--IT'S A CONVERSATION, FIVE. C'MON.
ALL I'M SAYING IS, THIS ISN'T JUST A CIVILIAN, THIS IS--IT'S GENERAL ROSS' DAUGHTER. THE BOSS OF OUR BOSS.
IT JUST FEELS LIKE--
--THIS JOB IS TOO MUCH FOR YOU.
HE THOUGHT ONE MONSTER WAS ENOUGH.
SNACKS
HEY, CHARLENE. HOW'S OUR BUDDY DEL TODAY?
MR. FRYE'S BEEN THE SAME SINCE THEY DUG HIM OUT OF THAT GRAVE IN COLORADO.
HIS PAIN RECEPTORS ARE STILL OFF THE CHARTS--HE'S IN AGONY--BUT IF YOU APPROVE SOME ADJUSTMENTS TO THE TANK MIX, WE CAN REDUCE THAT.
ELIMINATE IT, EVEN--
EXCEPT RECALIBRATING THE SYSTEM WOULD TAKE DAYS, AND WHAT DO WE GET? WHAT'S OUR GET HERE, CHARLENE?
FORGET HIS LITTLE FEE-FEES. WHERE ARE WE AT ON REPLICATING HIM?
JASE? WHAT HAVE WE GOT?
NOT MUCH, DR. McGOWAN.
PRETTY SURE WHAT CAUSED THIS IS IN HIS BLOOD--SOME KIND OF GAMMA SERUM--BUT IT'S LIKE...
...LIKE CRACKING A CODE WRITTEN IN A DEAD LANGUAGE. WE NEED A ROSETTA STONE.
LIKE I'VE BEEN TELLING YOU, GENERAL, WE CAN'T MAKE PROGRESS ON THE REAL GOALS OF THE PROJECT WITHOUT AN ACTUAL HULK TO STUDY.
AND THAT WOULD REQUIRE RESOURCES WE DON'T HAVE, DOCTOR--NOT YET.
THE SHEER FIREPOWER IT WOULD TAKE TO CAPTURE THE HULK--
NOT THE HULK--A HULK. AN ACTIVE ONE.
LIKE CHO OR WALTERS. BUT...I DON'T KNOW, SOMEONE NOBODY WILL MISS...
...
WHERE DID THEY TAKE LANGKOWSKI?

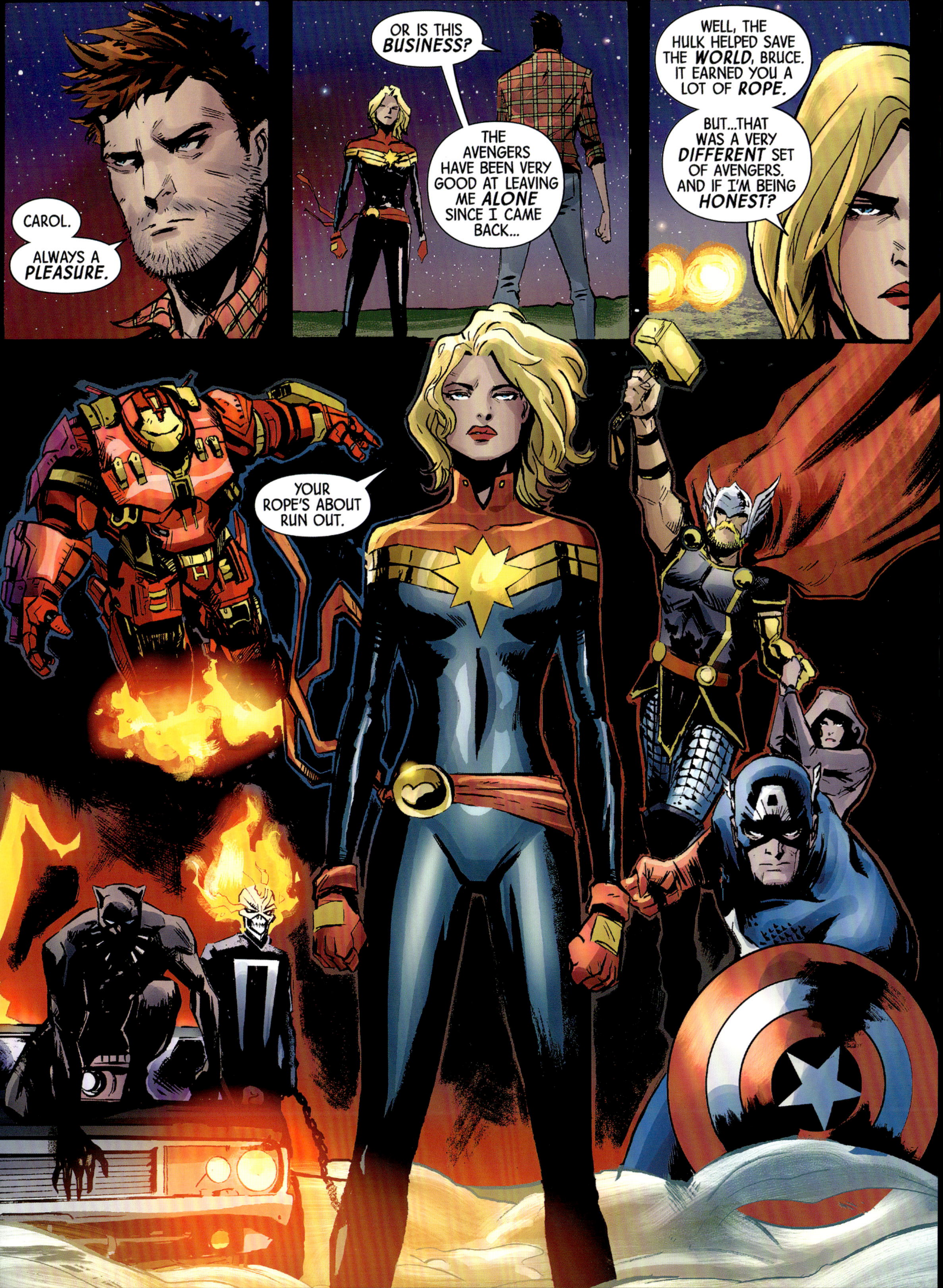
CAROL.
ALWAYS A PLEASURE.
OR IS THIS BUSINESS?
THE AVENGERS HAVE BEEN VERY GOOD AT LEAVING ME ALONE SINCE I CAME BACK...
WELL, THE HULK HELPED SAVE THE WORLD, BRUCE. IT EARNED YOU A LOT OF ROPE.
BUT...THAT WAS A VERY DIFFERENT SET OF AVENGERS. AND IF I'M BEING HONEST?
YOUR ROPE'S ABOUT RUN OUT.

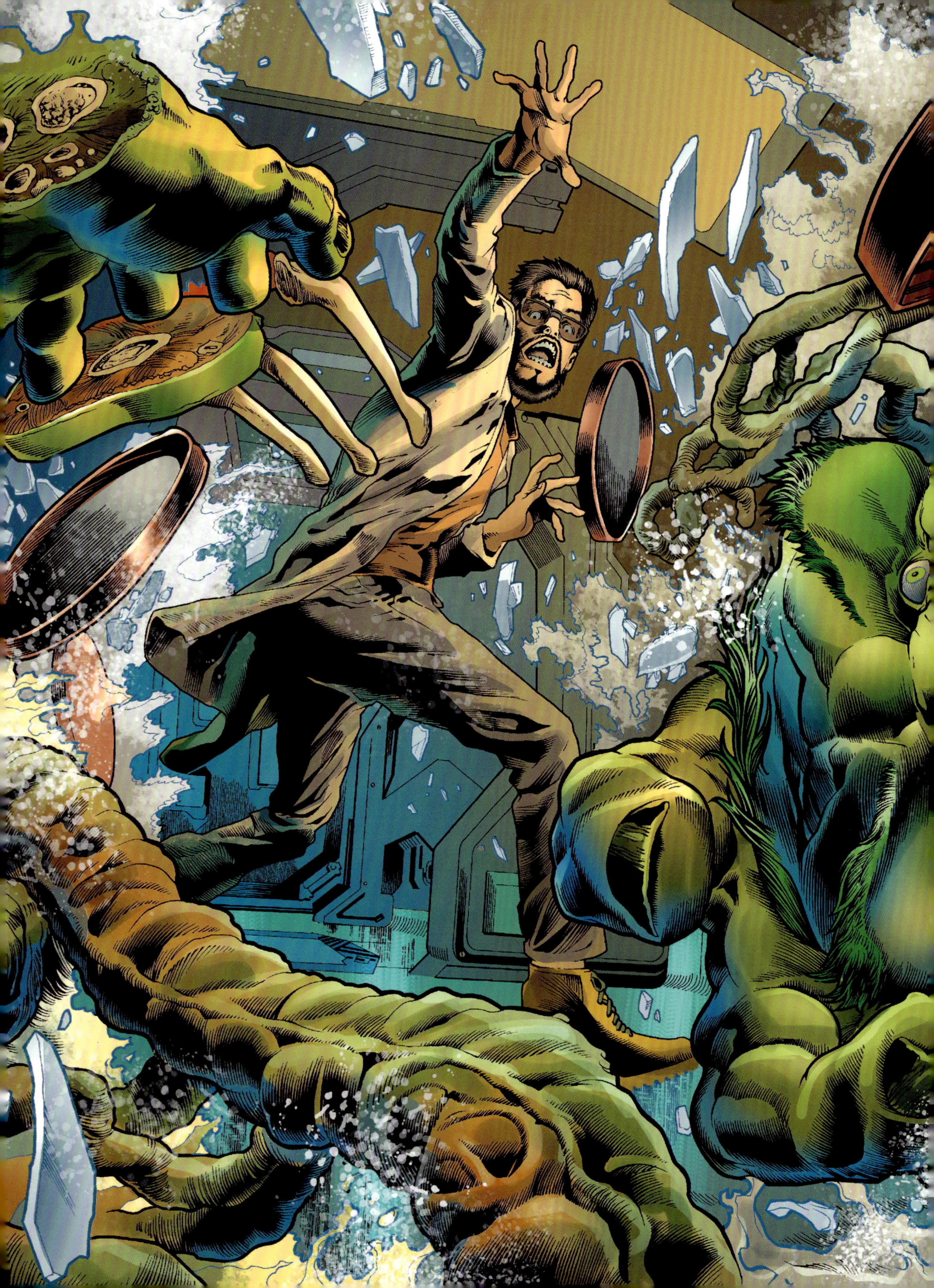

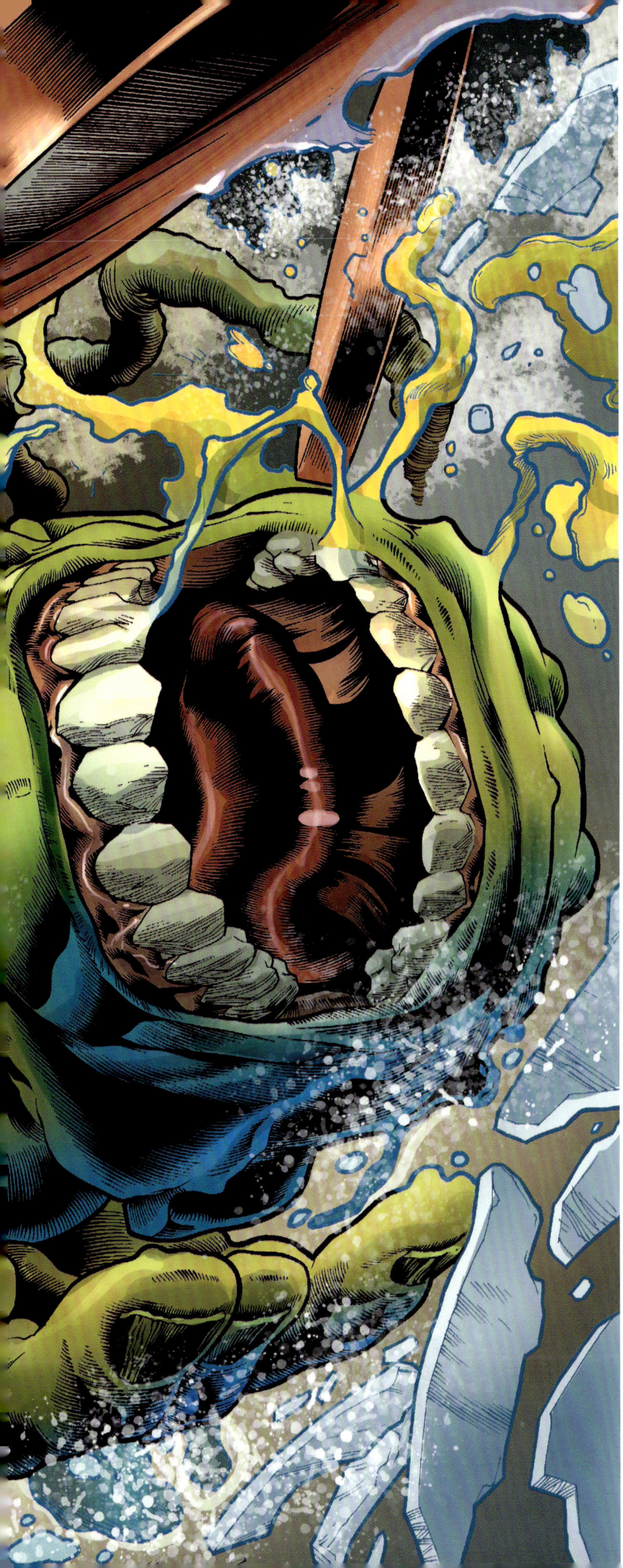

was being held prisoner. In order for him to secure his freedom he allowed himself to be injected with a red liquid by Dr. Clive. He absorbed what was in the syringe and as a result, he turned red. He was freed and told to go and bring in the Hulk.

Creel goes to Los Alamos to confront the Hulk. Creel wields a ball and chain, which he uses to attack the Hulk. It does its damage. Creel starts to absorb the gamma radiation from the Hulk who begins to look emaciated. But something goes wrong, and Creel starts to disintegrate.

Little do these two know that they are being watched by a sharpshooter from Shadow Base. Additionally, Langkowski and his crew called Gamma Flight are also there. Although he lost his powers in a battle with the Hulk, Langkowski is still a brilliant physicist and was recruited by Carol Danvers, aka Captain Marvel, to track down and capture the Hulk.

The Hulk has taken the ball and chain from Creel and begins to use it on whatever is left of Creel's body. Things escalate and Langkowski and his crew confront the Hulk. One of the Gamma Flight crew tries a weapon on the Hulk, who crushes the weapon as if it were a cardboard prop. Suddenly, the Hulk has a realization: the original gamma bomb that created him left a door open. The Hulk knows that if Creel/Absorbing Man absorbs enough gamma radiation from the site, he could tear the door open again.

A bright green light shines down and bathes all of them in its glow. The light changes from green to red. A door has been opened. The monster that was Creel is gone and what is left is again re-formed into a human shape. He kneels in the dirt saying, "I'm sorry. I'm so sorry." A door has been opened. The door to hell.

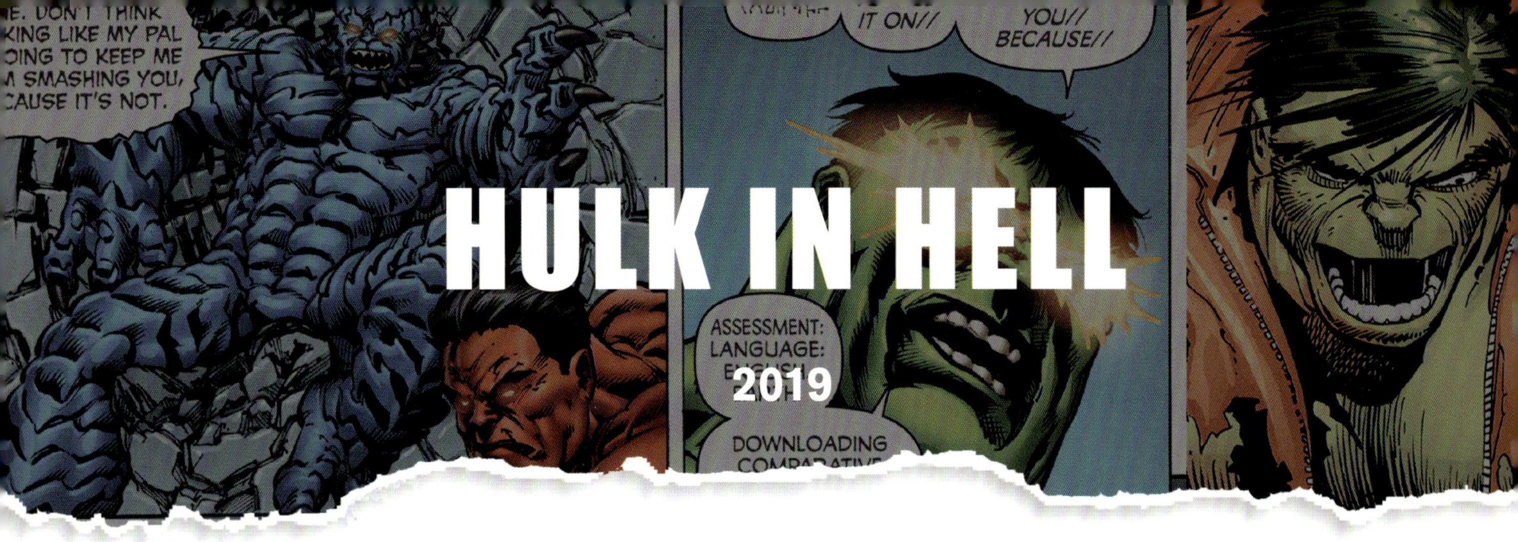
IT ON//
YOU// BECAUSE//
ASSESSMENT:
LANGUAGE:
DOWNLOADING

# HULK IN HELL

## 2019

In the follow-up to *Hulk: The Green Door*, we find our green giant standing at the entrance to hell. The fight between him and Creel/Absorbing Man opened the portal. The Hulk is with Jackie McGee, a reporter for the *Arizona Herald*. She has been reporting on the Hulk wandering across the western United States. They walk through the door, and as they make their way through hell, she discusses one of her motives for following the Hulk. Beyond being a good reporter, she wants to be like the Hulk. She tells the Hulk that she wants to be able to have and feel rage just like he does. She doesn't tell him why.

They are suddenly confronted by a walking, talking, decayed corpse with hollowed-out eyes. It's the Hulk's old friend Rick Jones, who died during the events of *Secret Empire*. Suddenly, an older man warns them not to look into Rick's eyes—that man is McGee's late father. Their heads turn: General Thaddeus "Thunderbolt" Ross, the father of Betty, the woman Banner loves, approaches them. General Ross hates the Hulk, and he is also the man who became Red Hulk.

Unlike McGee's dad and Rick Jones, General Ross is not dead. Ross quickly transforms into Red Hulk. They battle, and as the Hulk tears Red Hulk apart he screams "Kill you! Hulk kill everything!" At that moment a green light appears, and within that light is a person that Banner has feared since he was a child—his father.

The Hulk flashes back to when he was young. Young Bruce is playing with building blocks and is creating a city. Banner's father, drunk, enters the room. He picks up the box and sees that the instructions are still in the box—Bruce didn't even need them. Banner's father is a scientist, a smart man who is suddenly afraid that his son might be smarter than him. This angers his drunken father. His father needs to let his son know who rules, who's in control, so he berates his son, telling him that his mother was happier before he was born and that's he's ruined everything. He hurls his glass of whiskey at Bruce's block city, smashing it. His father tells Bruce to "break all this nonsense apart" and walks away. Bruce picks

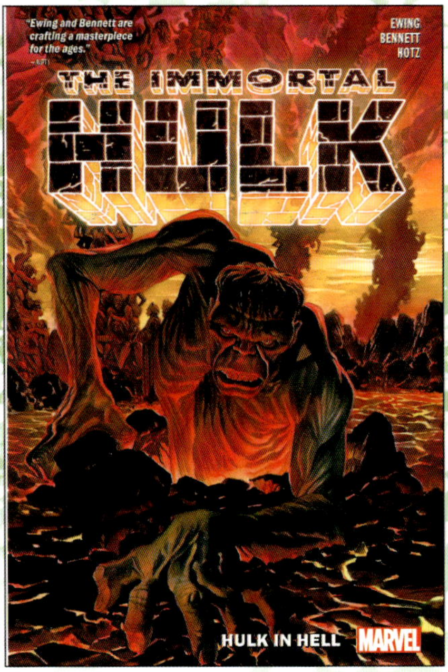
"Ewing and Bennett are crafting a masterpiece for the ages."
EWING
BENNETT
HOTZ
THE IMMORTAL
HULK
HULK IN HELL
MARVEL

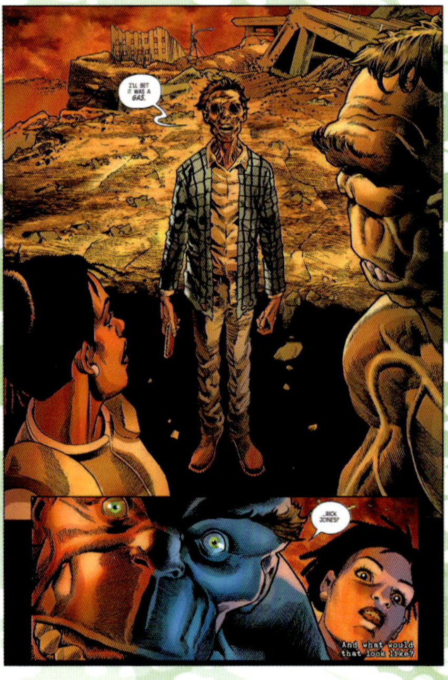
And what would that look like?

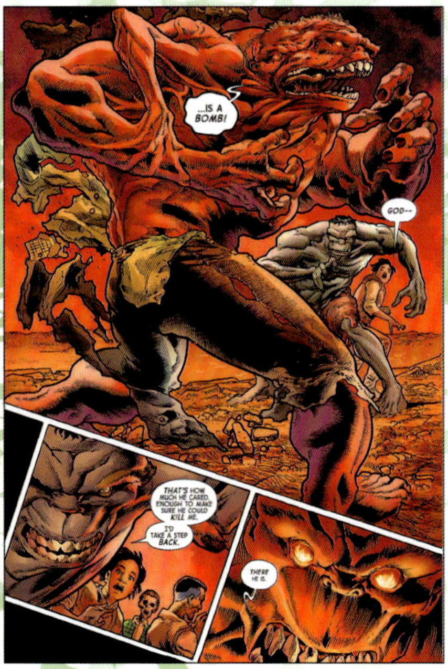
...IS A BOMB!
GOD--

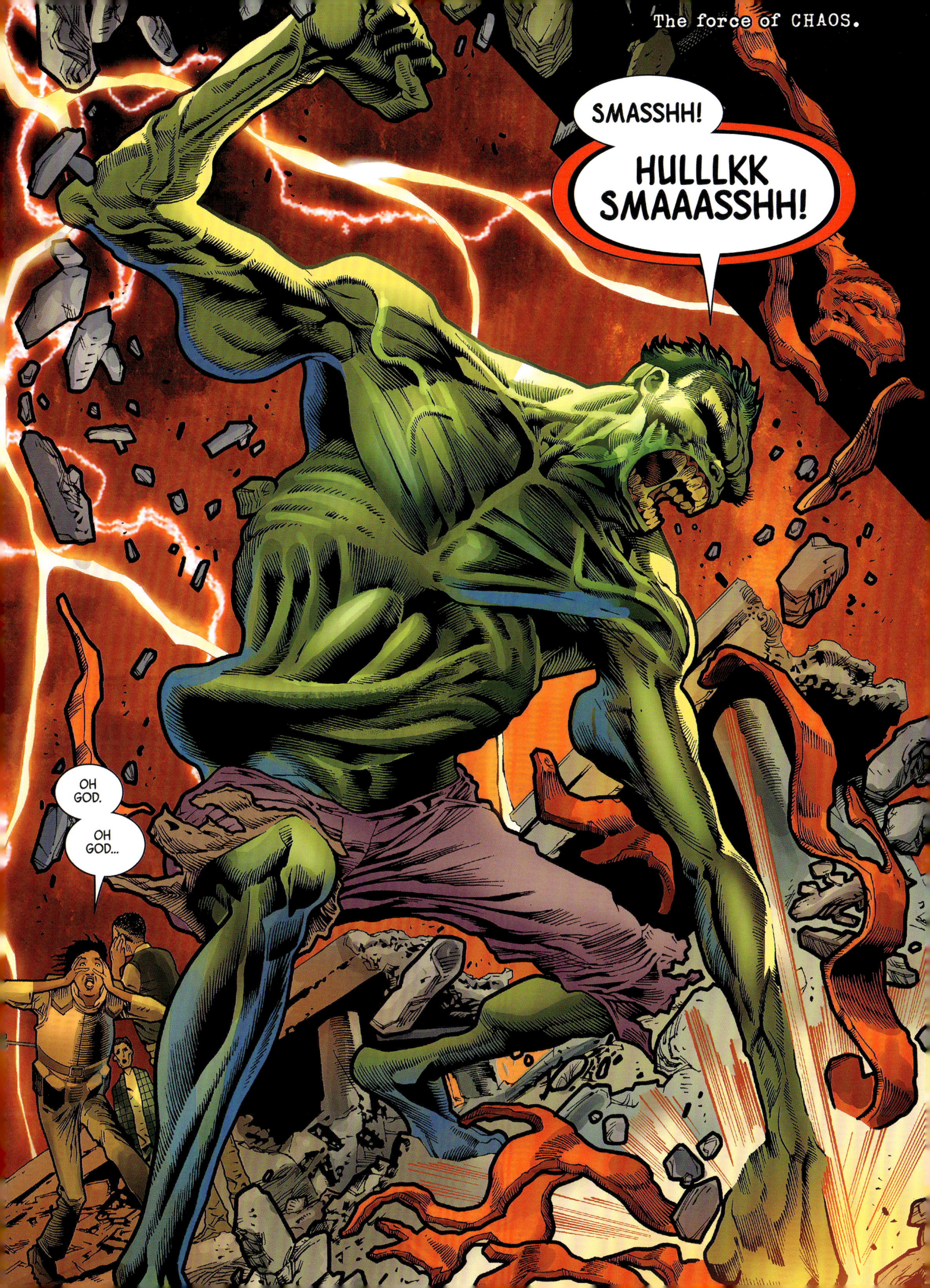
The force of CHAOS.
SMASSHH!
HULLLKK SMAAASSHH!
OH GOD.
OH GOD...

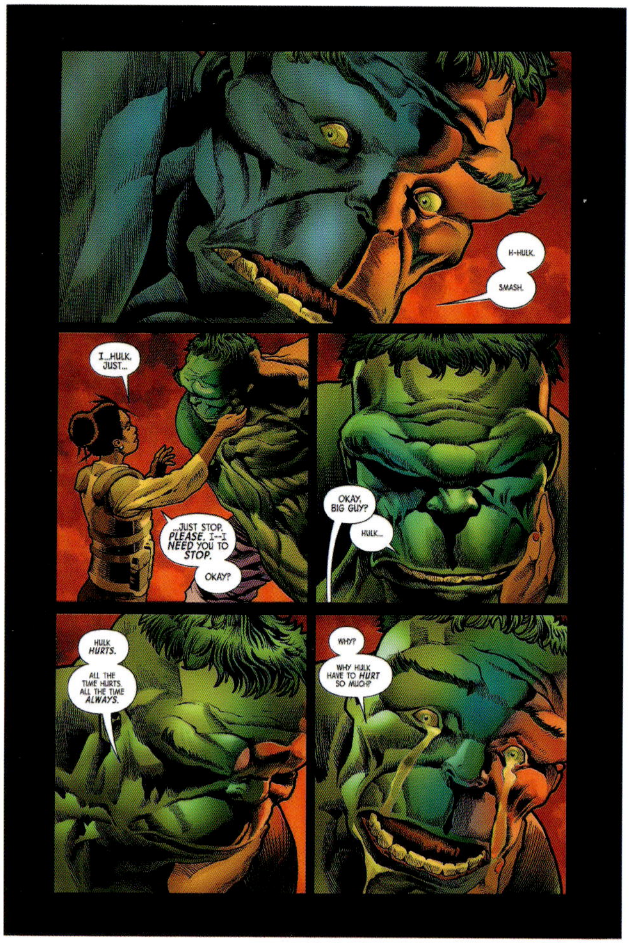
H--HULK.
SMASH.
I...HULK. JUST...
...JUST STOP, PLEASE. I--I NEED YOU TO STOP.
OKAY?
OKAY, BIG GUY?
HULK...
HULK HURTS.
ALL THE TIME HURTS. ALL THE TIME ALWAYS.
WHY?
WHY HULK HAVE TO HURT SO MUCH?

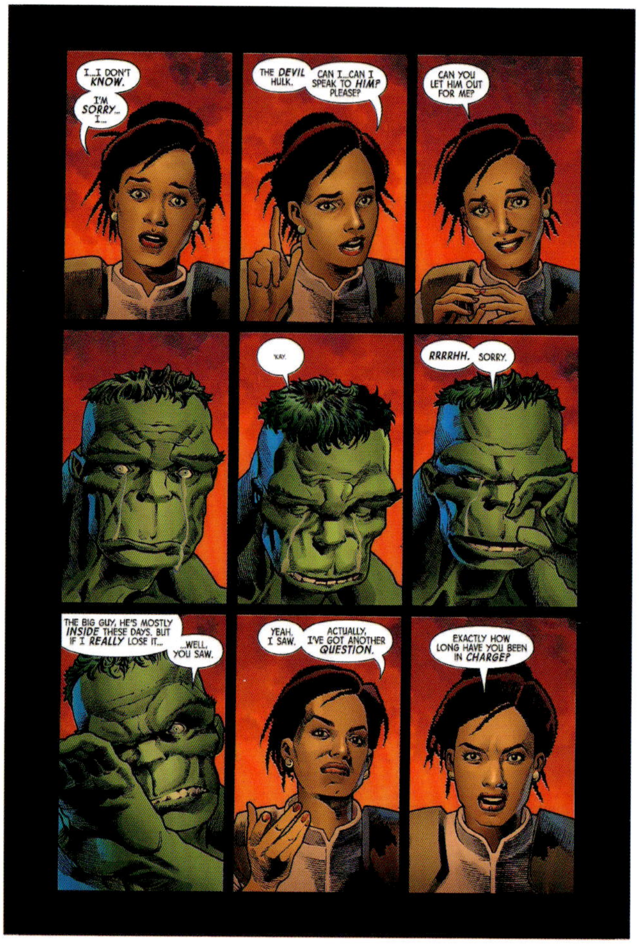
I...I DON'T KNOW.
I'M SORRY... I...
THE DEVIL HULK.
CAN I...CAN I SPEAK TO HIM? PLEASE?
CAN YOU LET HIM OUT FOR ME?
'KAY.
RRRRHH. SORRY.
THE BIG GUY, HE'S MOSTLY INSIDE THESE DAYS. BUT IF I REALLY LOSE IT...
...WELL, YOU SAW.
YEAH. I SAW.
ACTUALLY, I'VE GOT ANOTHER QUESTION.
EXACTLY HOW LONG HAVE YOU BEEN IN CHARGE?

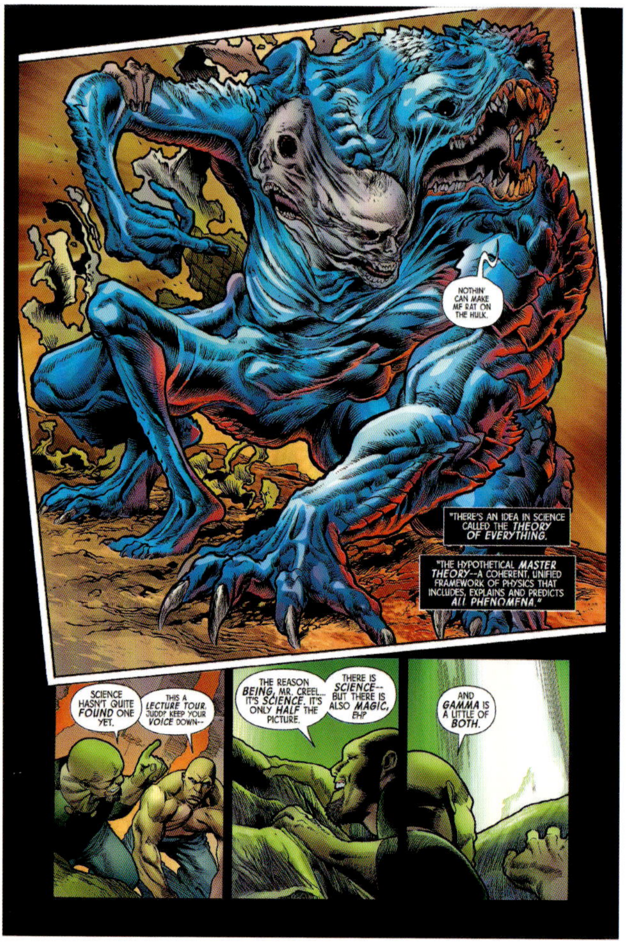
NOTHIN' CAN MAKE ME RAT ON THE HULK.
"THERE'S AN IDEA IN SCIENCE CALLED THE THEORY OF EVERYTHING.
"THE HYPOTHETICAL MASTER THEORY--A COHERENT, UNIFIED FRAMEWORK OF PHYSICS THAT INCLUDES, EXPLAINS AND PREDICTS ALL PHENOMENA."
SCIENCE HASN'T QUITE FOUND ONE YET.
THIS A LECTURE TOUR, JUDD? KEEP YOUR VOICE DOWN--
THE REASON BEING, MR. CREEL... IT'S SCIENCE. IT'S ONLY HALF THE PICTURE.
THERE IS SCIENCE--BUT THERE IS ALSO MAGIC, EH?
AND GAMMA IS A LITTLE OF BOTH.

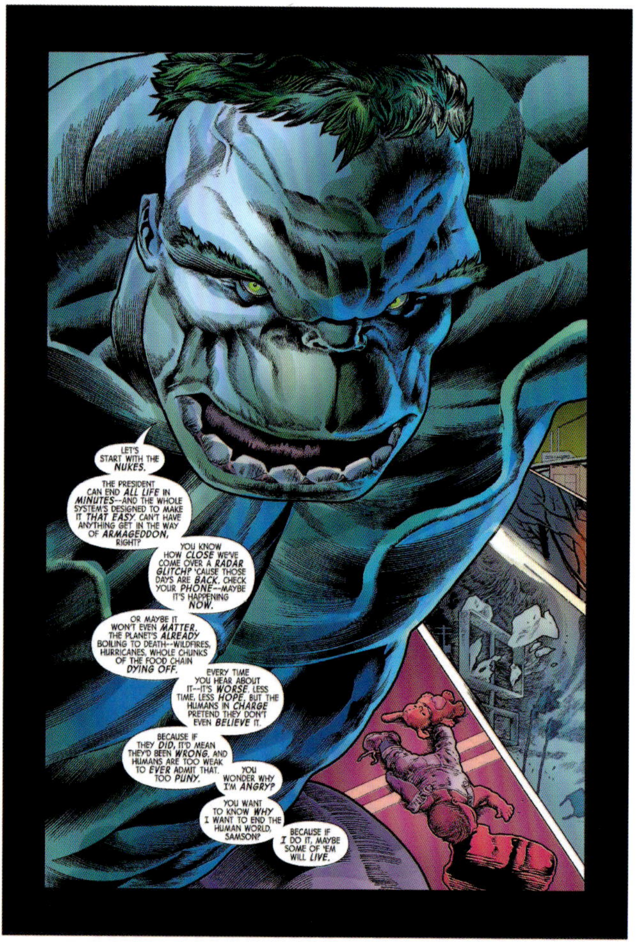
LET'S START WITH THE NUKES.
THE PRESIDENT CAN END ALL LIFE IN MINUTES--AND THE WHOLE SYSTEM'S DESIGNED TO MAKE IT THAT EASY. CAN'T HAVE ANYTHING GET IN THE WAY OF ARMAGEDDON, RIGHT?
YOU KNOW HOW CLOSE WE'VE COME OVER A RADAR GLITCH? 'CAUSE THOSE DAYS ARE BACK. CHECK YOUR PHONE--MAYBE IT'S HAPPENING NOW.
OR MAYBE IT WON'T EVEN MATTER. THE PLANET'S ALREADY BOILING TO DEATH--WILDFIRES, HURRICANES, WHOLE CHUNKS OF THE FOOD CHAIN DYING OFF.
EVERY TIME YOU HEAR ABOUT IT--IT'S WORSE. LESS TIME, LESS HOPE. BUT THE HUMANS IN CHARGE PRETEND THEY DON'T EVEN BELIEVE IT.
BECAUSE IF THEY DID, IT'D MEAN THEY'D BEEN WRONG. AND HUMANS ARE TOO WEAK TO EVER ADMIT THAT. TOO PUNY.
YOU WONDER WHY I'M ANGRY?
YOU WANT TO KNOW WHY I WANT TO END THE HUMAN WORLD, SAMSON?
BECAUSE IF I DO IT, MAYBE SOME OF 'EM WILL LIVE.

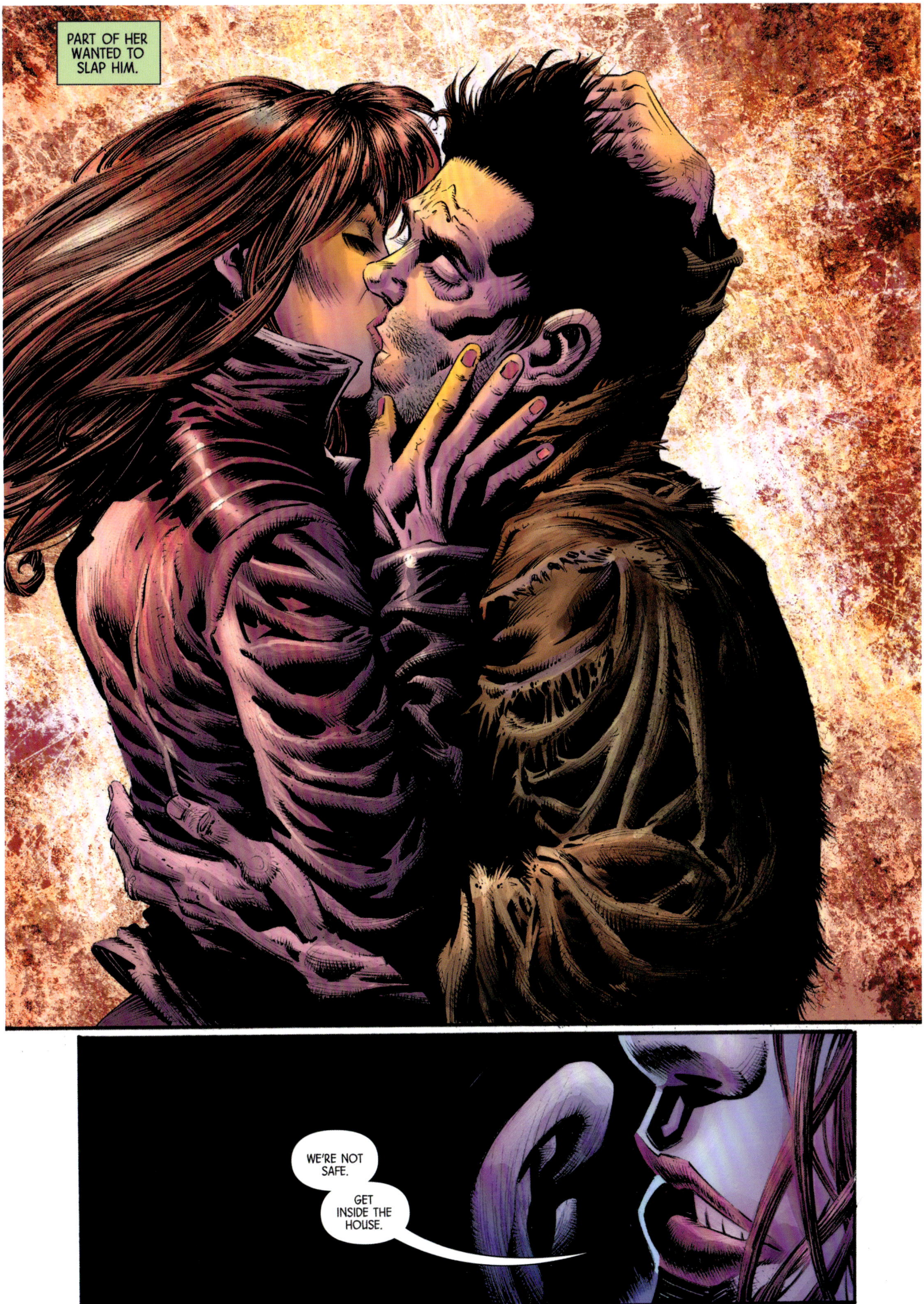
PART OF HER WANTED TO SLAP HIM.
WE'RE NOT SAFE.
GET INSIDE THE HOUSE.

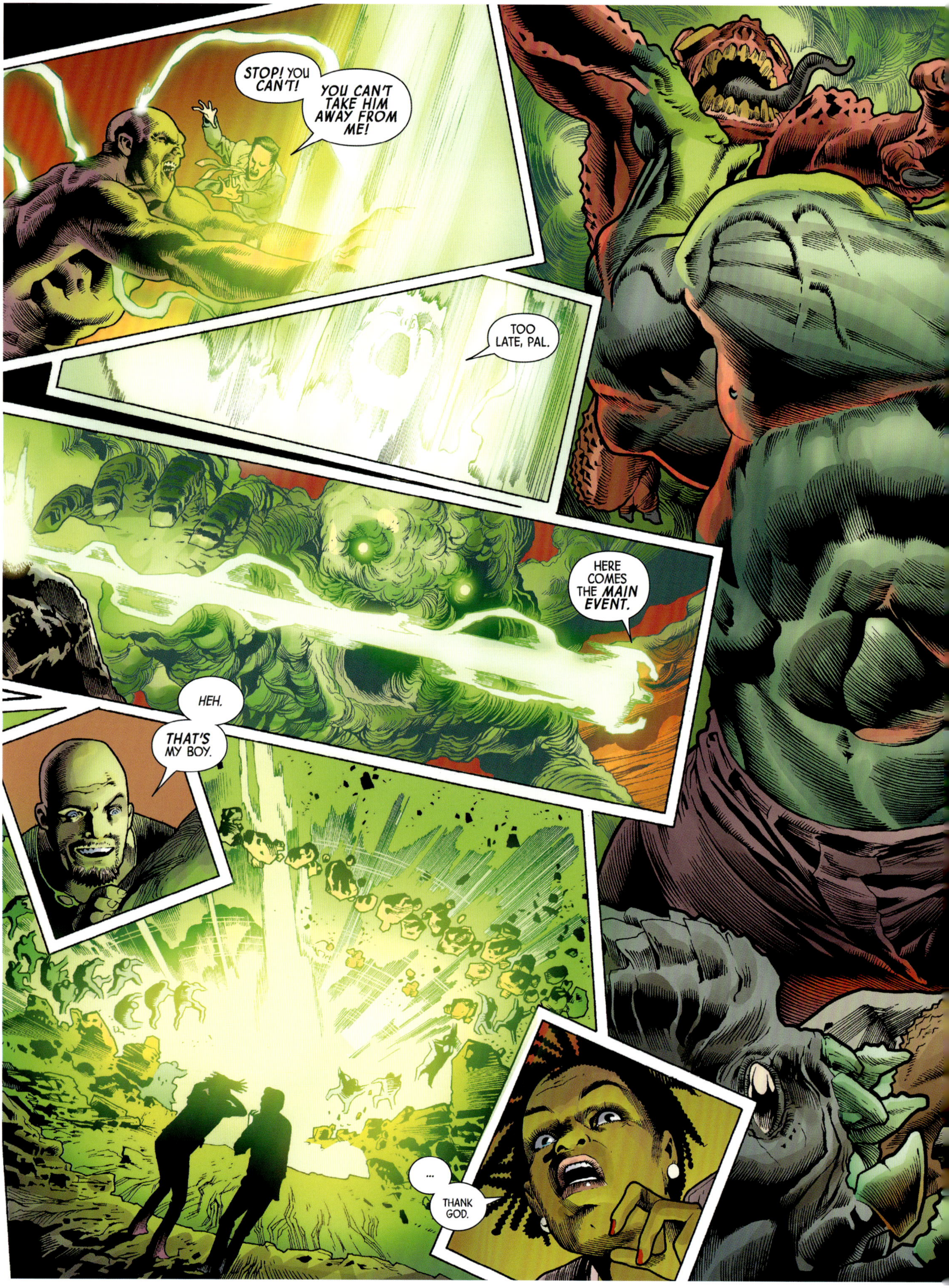
STOP! YOU CAN'T!
YOU CAN'T TAKE HIM AWAY FROM ME!
TOO LATE, PAL.
HERE COMES THE MAIN EVENT.
HEH.
THAT'S MY BOY.
...
THANK GOD.

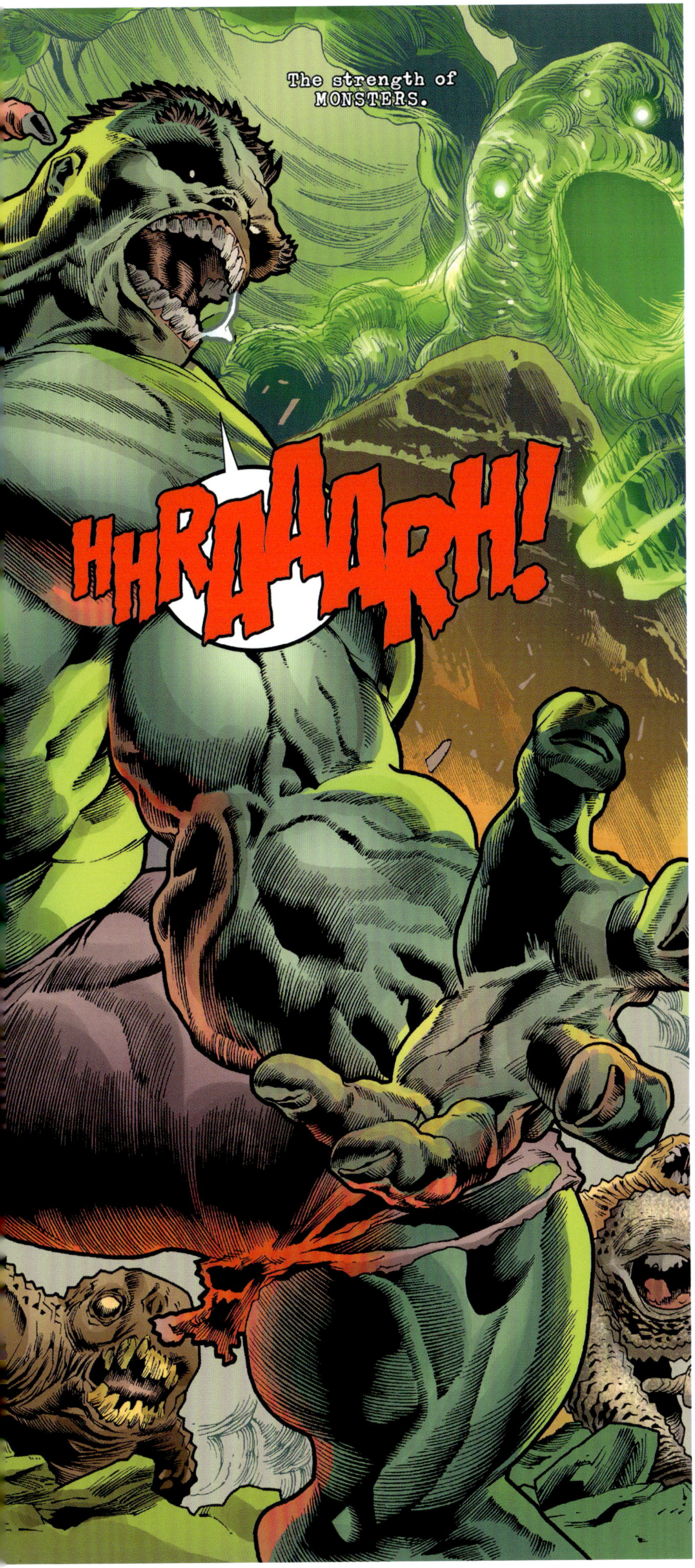
The strength of MONSTERS.
HHRAAARH!

up the empty glass and destroys what he'd built, chanting, "smash, smash, smash."

Back in hell, McGee sees the Hulk growing angry and she tries to calm him down. He tells her that he hurts, he hurts all the time. McGee realizes what is happening to the Hulk. She asks, "How long have you been in charge?" It's not the Hulk or Banner she's talking to—it's the Devil Hulk himself.

Rick Jones transforms into his alter ego A-Bomb to join the battle against the Devil Hulk. Creel gathers himself and joins Rick. Creel reverses his Absorption Man powers and gives the gamma radiation he absorbed back to the Hulk. The radiation restores his body and his mind. During the battle with the Devil, Banner is physically removed from the Hulk.

Once he defeats the Devil Hulk, the Hulk looks down at Banner lying on the ground and tells him that the Hulk can close the door to hell and bring them both home. The Hulk tells Banner that he knows he scares him, but that he loves him, and will always protect him. He tells him to "Come on home."

Meanwhile on Earth, a phone rings in a small house in California. Betty Ross picks up the phone and there is no sound from the other end. She tells the caller that if they don't say something she'll hang up. A voice says, "I need to come home." Bruce is back from hell.

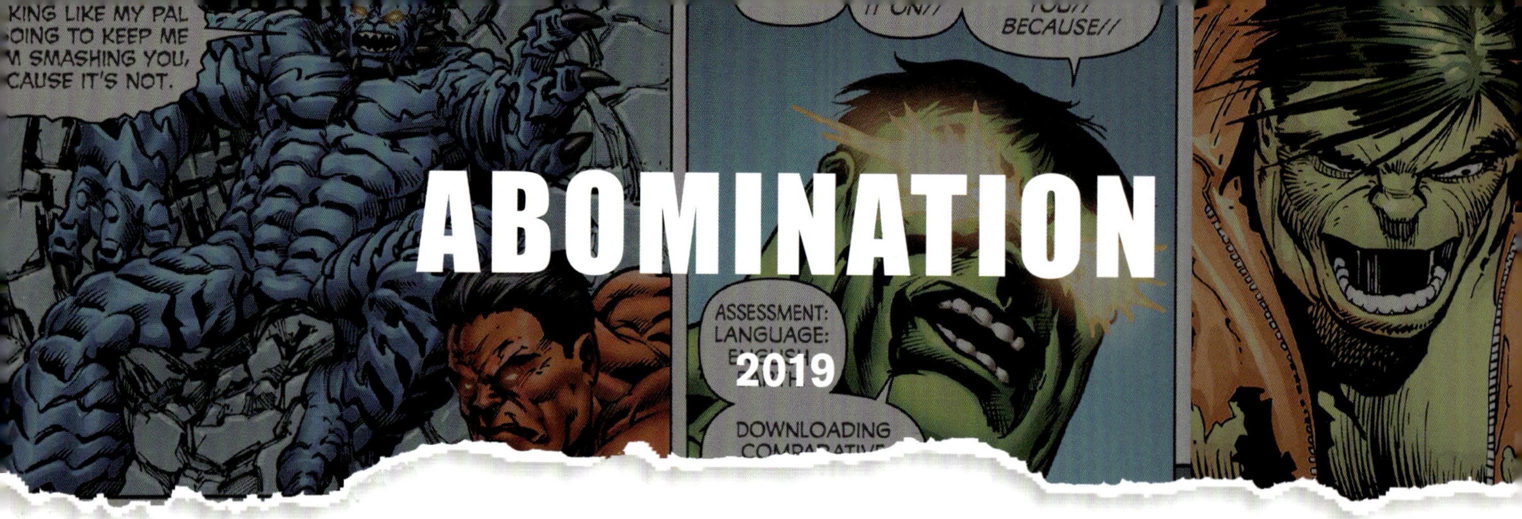
CAUSE IT'S NOT.
BECAUSE//
ASSESSMENT:
LANGUAGE:
DOWNLOADING

# ABOMINATION

## 2019

When last we saw the Hulk in *Hulk in Hell*, he was standing in the woods with a hole in his head after Agent Burbank shot him. (Burbank works for General Fortean, who runs the Hulk Operation from Shadow Base.) Burbank had targeted both Banner and Betty in her home in California. Burbank's thermal imaging was scrambled by a device in the house, and he was unable to tell the difference between the two. He shot Betty in the head. The Hulk gave chase, and Burbank shot him in the head too.

While the Hulk was running after Burbank, a man stepped out of the woods and put himself between them. That man was Doc Samson, the super hero and psychiatrist who is Bruce Banner's friend.

The Hulk is enraged about the attempt on Betty's life by Bushwacker (Agent Carl Burbank), in *Hulk in Hell*, and he takes it out on Samson. Samson calms the Hulk down. They return to the house to find Betty's body missing. But the Hulk doesn't seem too concerned, saying that "Betty can take care of herself." Samson, too, had been recently killed and rose from the dead. They head to a cemetery, but it's not to look for Betty. They go to a gravesite, and discover the body of Rick Jones is missing. The Hulk says that the four of them are part of a club; they can't stay dead.

In the *Arizona Herald* newsroom, reporter Jackie McGee is back on the beat after her trip with the Hulk to hell and back. Her boss tells her to investigate the disappearance of Betty Ross, whose house has a huge hole in it.

The Hulk and Samson head to Shadow Base where the Hulk was once held. The Hulk and Samson open a door and find several Hulk-like creatures. But it's a trap: they are being monitored by General Fortean, who knew they were coming. His operative Agent Burbank is there, who triggers intense UV lights that change the Hulk back into Banner. Burbank turns and shoots Samson in the head. Banner manages to

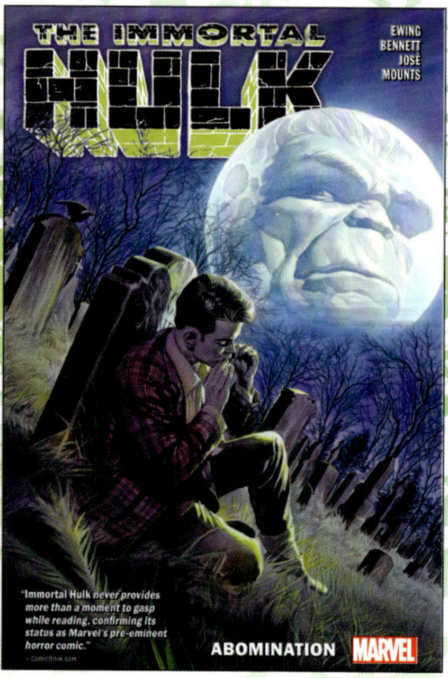
THE IMMORTAL HULK
EWING
BENNETT
JOSÉ
MOUNTS
"Immortal Hulk never provides more than a moment to gasp while reading, confirming its status as Marvel's pre-eminent horror comic."
ABOMINATION
MARVEL

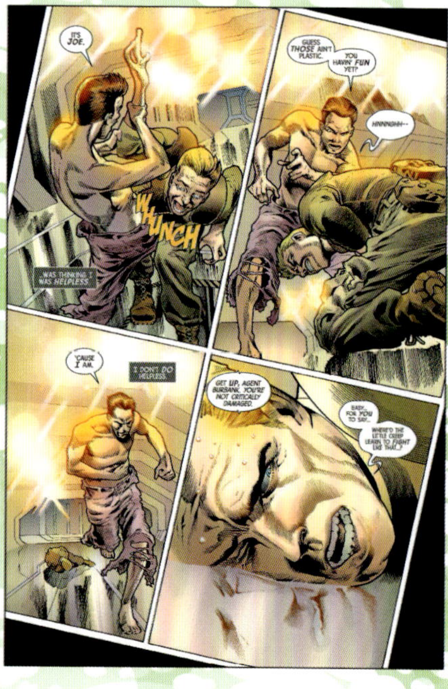
WHUNCH

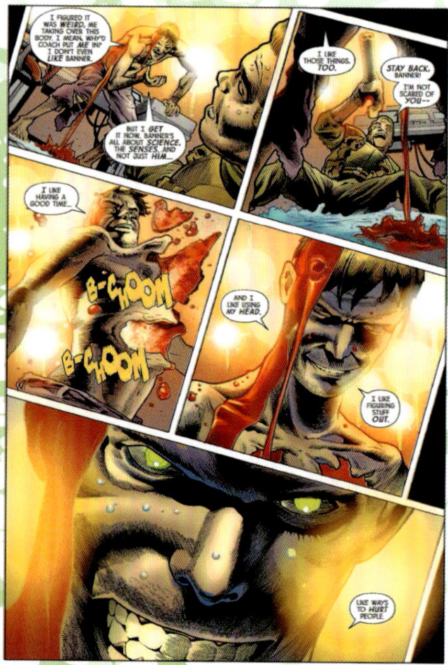
B-CHOOM
B-CHOOM

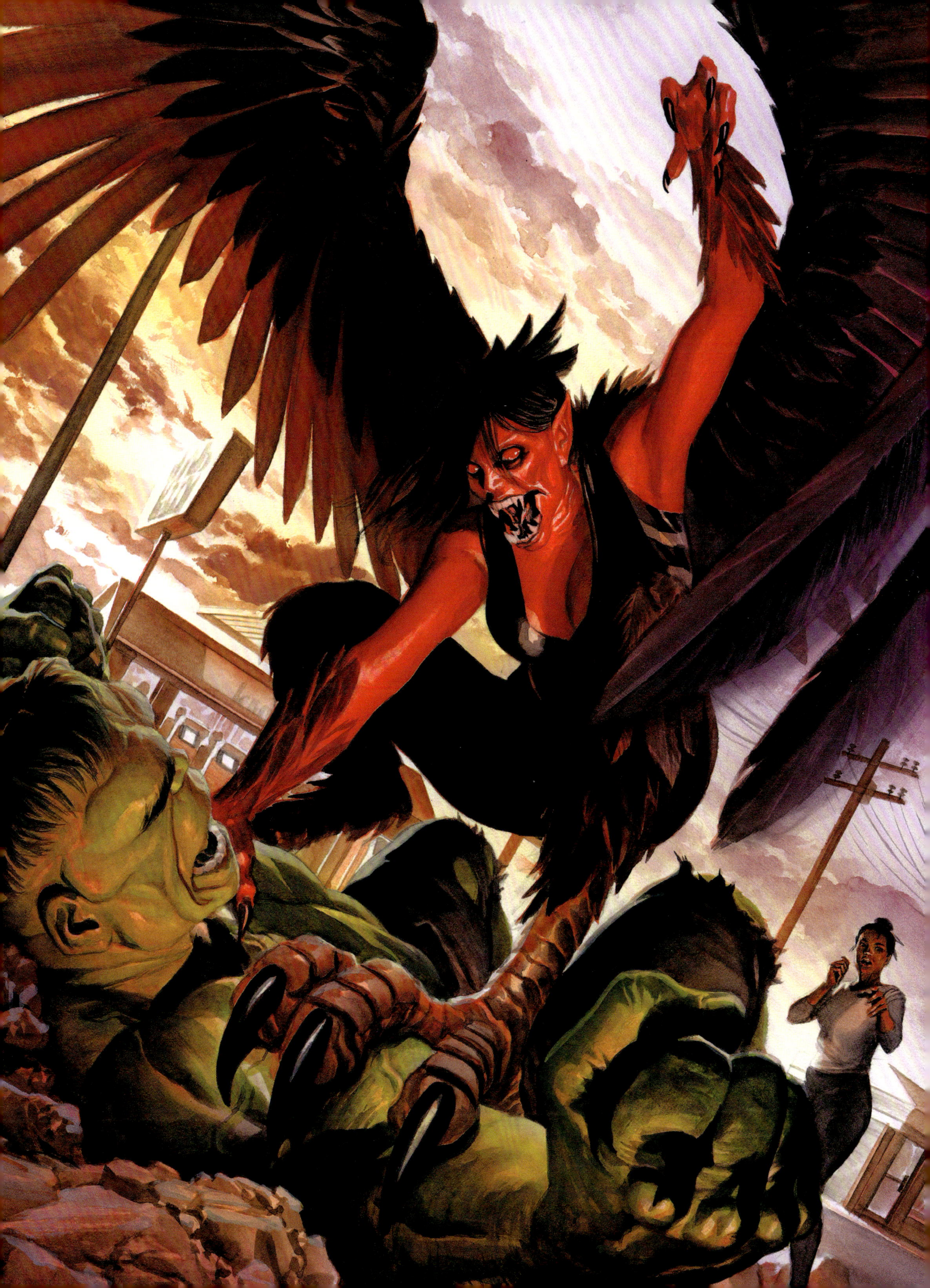

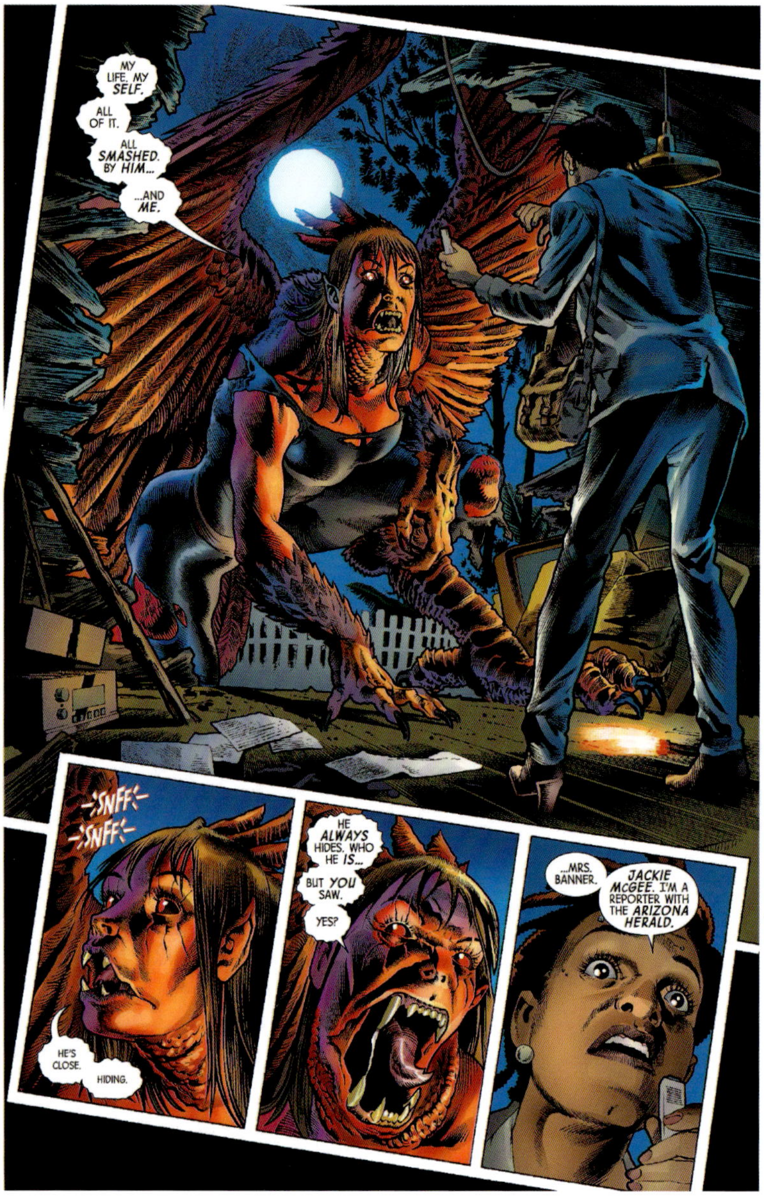

MY LIFE. MY SELF.
ALL OF IT.
ALL SMASHED. BY HIM...
...AND ME.
SNFF
SNFF
HE'S CLOSE.
HIDING.
HE ALWAYS HIDES. WHO HE IS...
BUT YOU SAW.
YES?
...MRS. BANNER.
JACKIE MCGEE. I'M A REPORTER WITH THE ARIZONA HERALD.


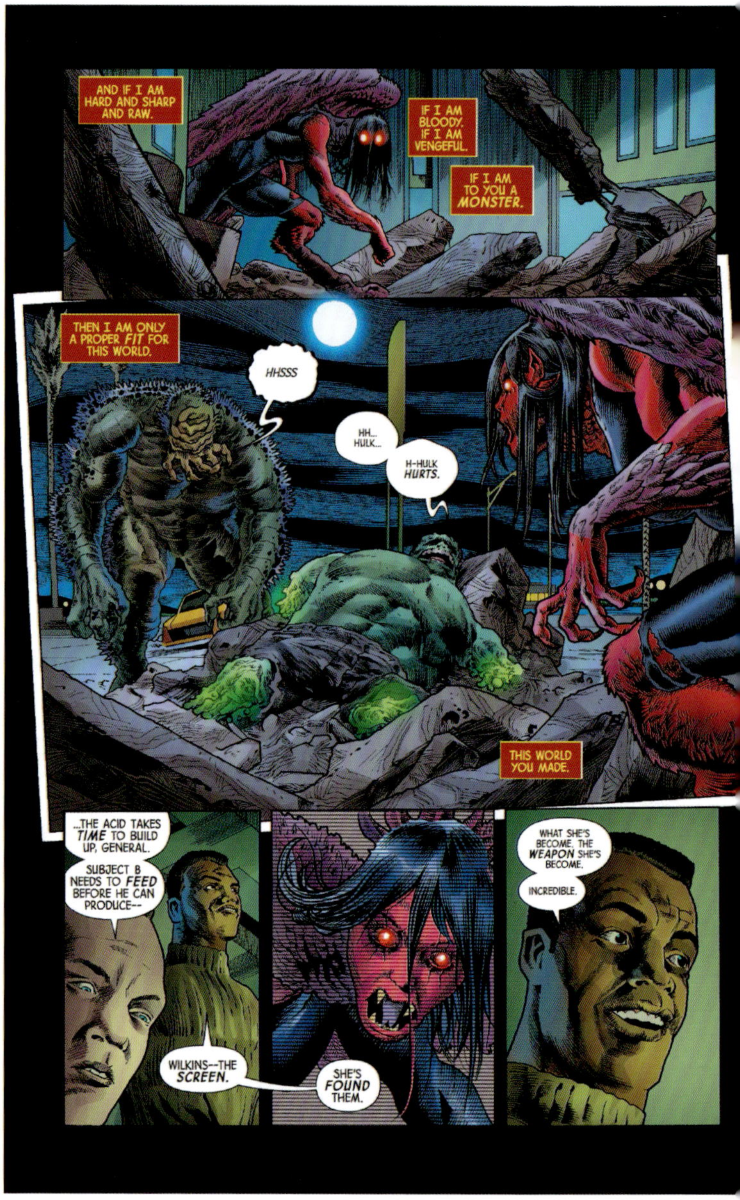

AND IF I AM HARD AND SHARP AND RAW.
IF I AM BLOODY. IF I AM VENGEFUL.
IF I AM TO YOU A MONSTER.
THEN I AM ONLY A PROPER FIT FOR THIS WORLD.
HHSSS
HH... HULK...
H-HULK HURTS.
THIS WORLD YOU MADE.
...THE ACID TAKES TIME TO BUILD UP, GENERAL.
SUBJECT B NEEDS TO FEED BEFORE HE CAN PRODUCE--
WILKINS--THE SCREEN.
SHE'S FOUND THEM.
WHAT SHE'S BECOME. THE WEAPON SHE'S BECOME.
INCREDIBLE.


incapacitate Burbank and escape. But it's not actually Banner who took down Burbank; Banner suffers from dissociative identity disorder (DID) and as a result has another identity. Banner calls this identity Joe Fixit, a Las Vegas tough guy and enforcer. When Fixit turns into the Hulk, it's the Hulk as he originally appeared in the sixties comics—he is gray.

Fixit is more confident and resourceful than Banner and is able to take on Burbank. Fixit finds and hacks into the central computer and has the base bombarded with gamma radiation. The Hulk overdoses on the radiation and mutates into a hideous deformed version of himself.

Meanwhile, McGee is at Betty's house investigating her disappearance. McGee finds a blood-soaked red feather. Suddenly a winged female creature appears: Betty Ross has transformed into one of her alter egos, the Harpy. Ross became the Harpy after M.O.D.O.K. kidnapped her and exposed her to gamma radiation. Her transformation into the Harpy saved her from being killed by Burbank's bullet to her head.

Days later, we find Fixit in his hotel in Las Vegas. He hears screams in the lobby. The Abomination has tracked him down. But this is not Emil Blonsky, the former KGB agent—it's Rick Jones! Rick's body was taken to Shadow Base and used for experimentation. He is the new Abomination.

Outside, Shadow Base operatives have surrounded the hotel. An employee of the hotel tries to escape, and she is shot in the head. Jackie McGee witnesses this and identifies herself as a reporter. She, too, would have been killed if not for her back-up—the Harpy.

The Hulk finds the Abomination and they begin to fight, but something is wrong with the Hulk. The effects of being sliced apart by Dr. Jeffery Clive in *The Green Door* are coming back to haunt the Hulk. The Hulk punches the Abomination in the mouth and the Hulk's hand dissolves, but he doesn't heal the way he used to. Soon the Hulk is missing his legs and arms. The Hulk lies helpless. The Harpy flies to him and slashes his body with her claws. The Hulk screams in pain. She removes his heart and eats it. With his heart gone, the Hulk dies, and goes back to hell. In hell, he is Banner. He confronts his abusive father, who taunts him. Suddenly, he is back on Earth, regenerated and ready to physically remove Rick Jones from the Abomination. He rips him open and finds Jones, pale and thin, but alive. He tells Betty that it hurt when she ripped his heart out and he asks that she never do that again. But it was Betty's actions as the Harpy that allowed him to regenerate.

The last scene is of General Ross's gravesite. The general's body is gone, just like Rick Jones's body was. What will become of Rick? Where is General Ross? Will Betty revert back from being the Harpy? And will McGee ever get her wish—to become like the Hulk?

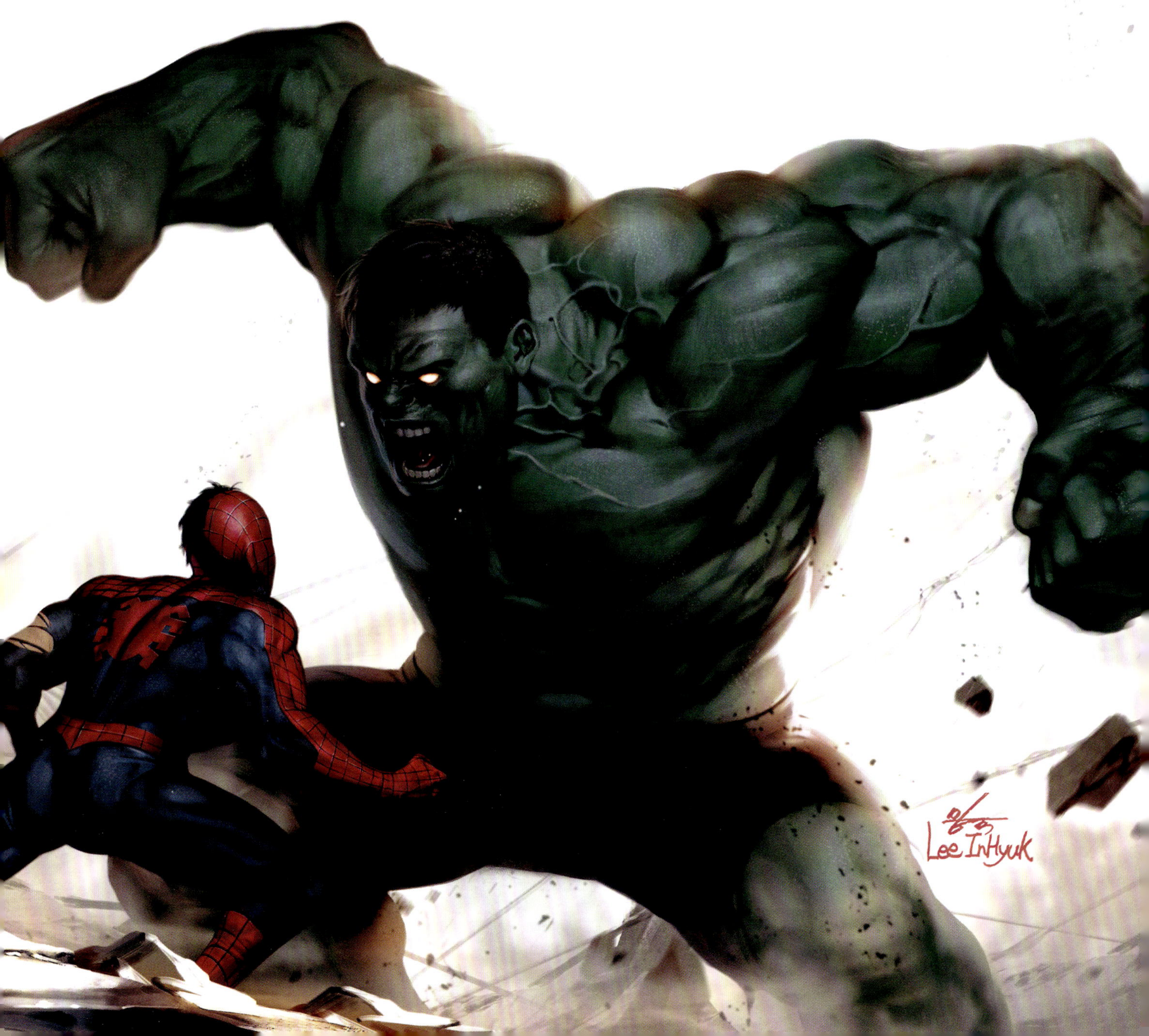
Lee InHyuk

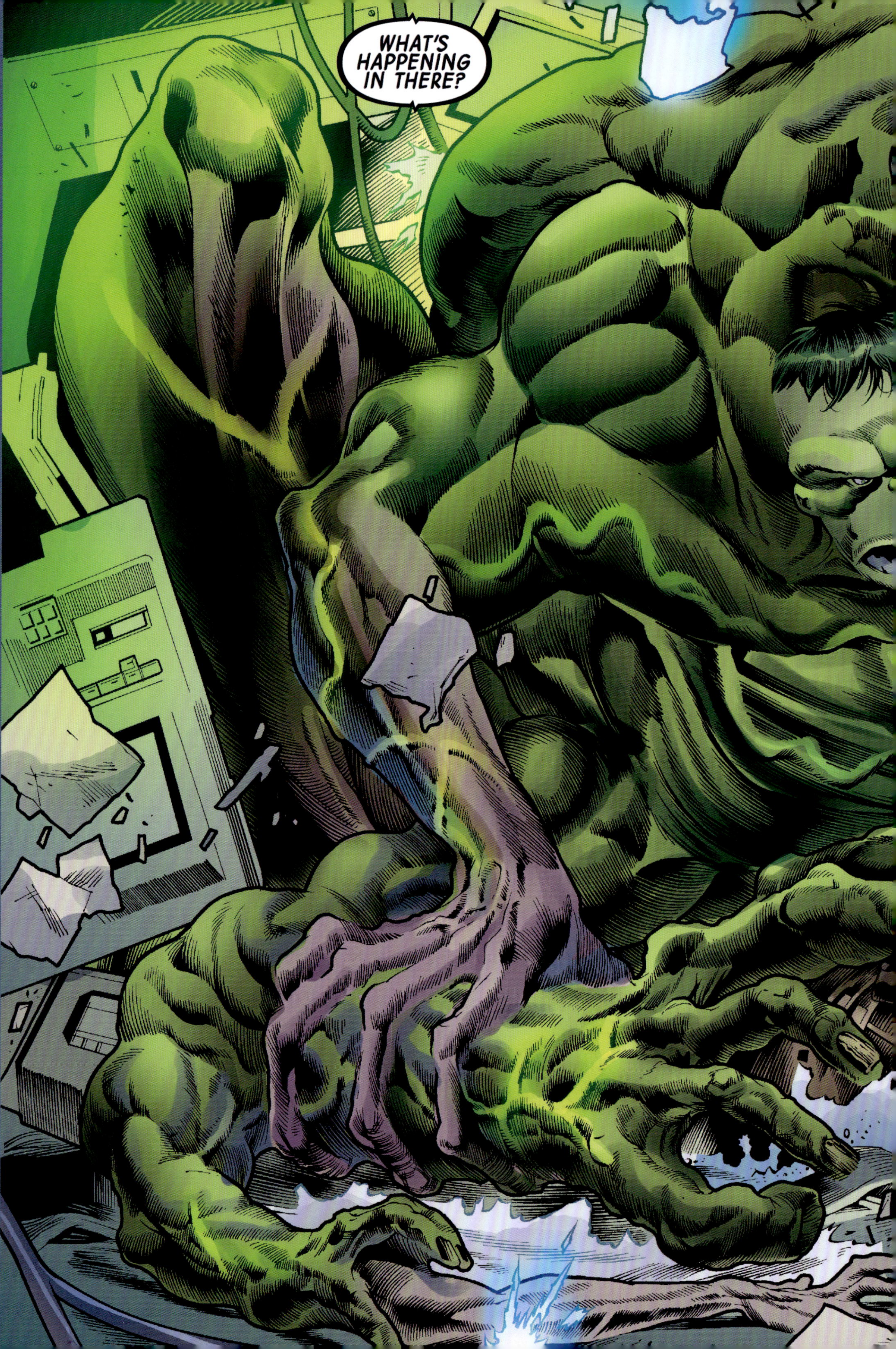
WHAT'S HAPPENING IN THERE?

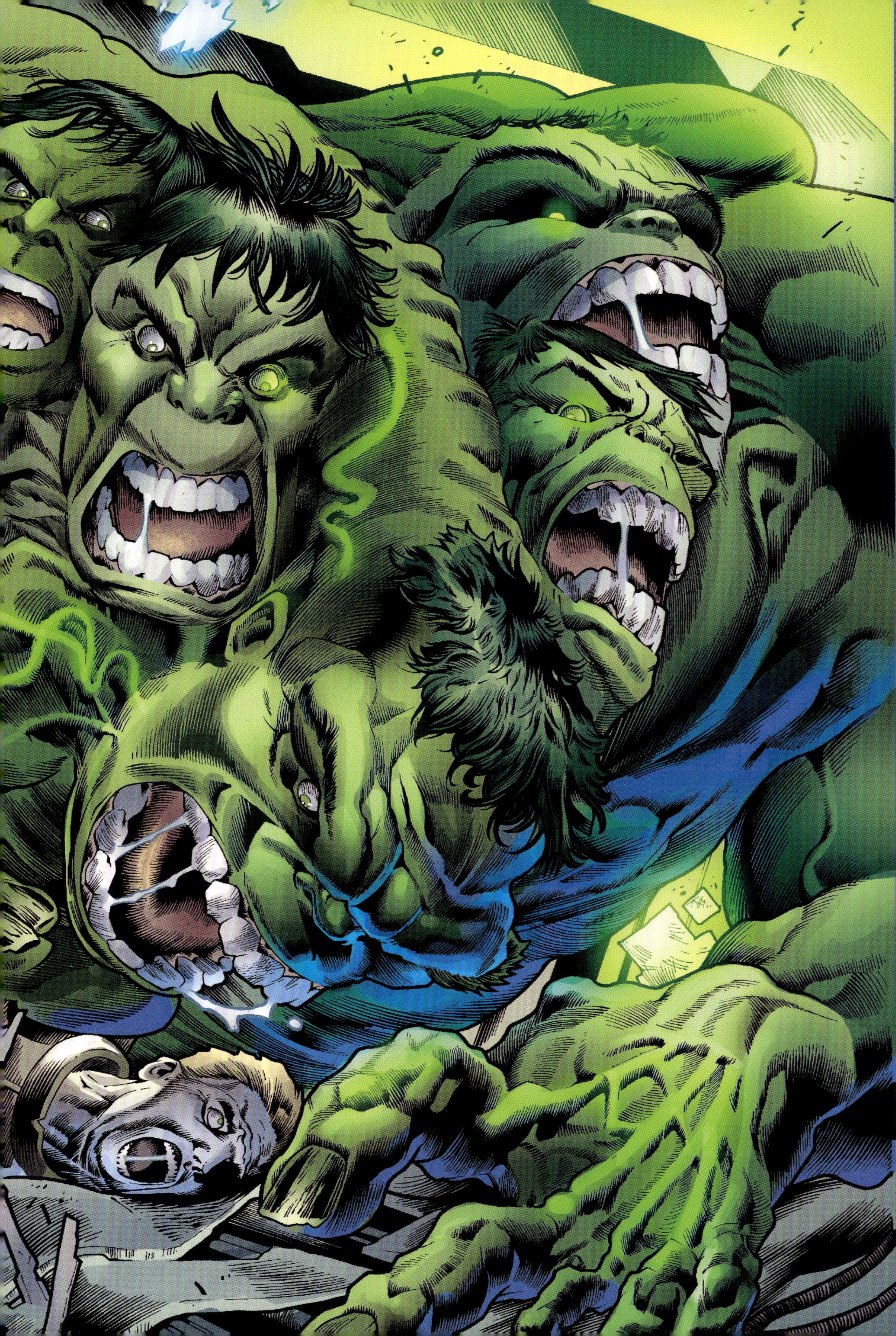

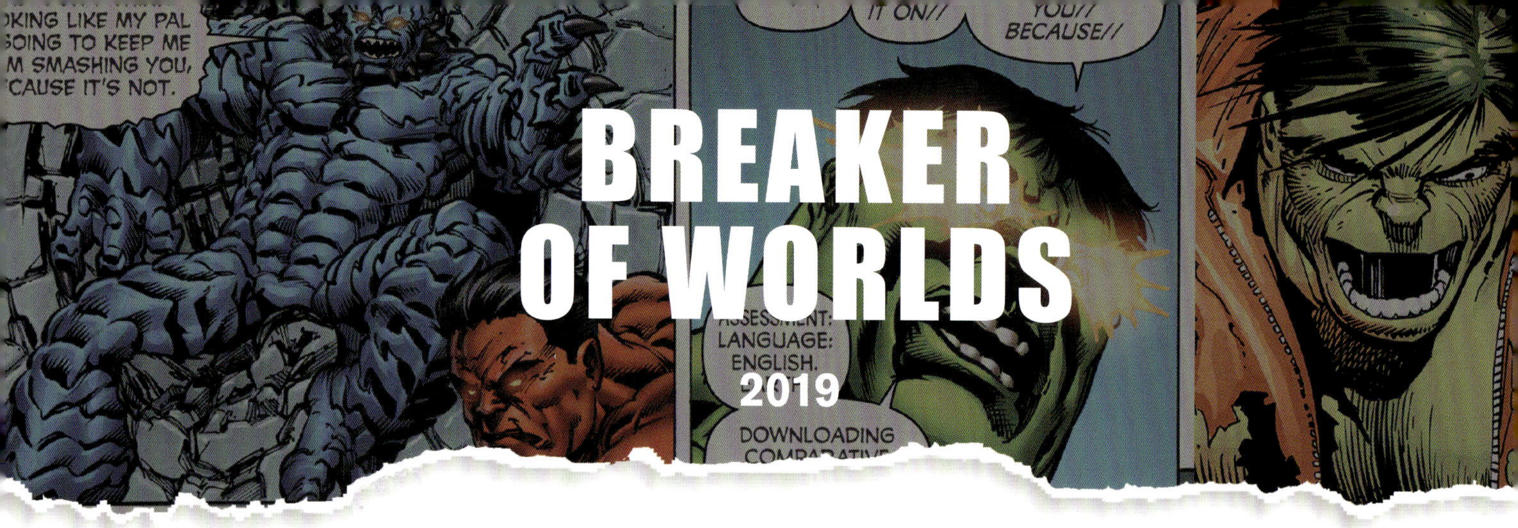
LANGUAGE:
ENGLISH.
DOWNLOADING

# BREAKER OF WORLDS

## 2019

In the final chapter of *Immortal Hulk*, we learn the background of General Reginald Fortean, head of Shadow Base. As a young man, Fortean watched with amazement the Hulk in action. His mentor was General Thaddeus "Thunderbolt" Ross, the Hulk's nemesis and father of the woman Bruce Banner loves. When Ross is killed (one of many times in the comic books), Fortean wants revenge against the Hulk, but his superiors tell him not to pursue it. So, Fortean turns to others in military high command and convinces them to divert some of their discretionary funds to him so he can create Shadow Base, an organization formed to monitor and bring down the Hulk.

The Shadow Base scientists have developed a translocation platform that can transport people to other places; and the place Fortean wants to go is Alpha Flight Space Station, home to Captain Marvel and the crew of super heroes she has assembled, called Alpha Flight. The station was created after Hydra took over the United States during *Secret Empire*. Fortean appears in the middle of the space station and takes them all out, neutralizing Carl Creel, Titania, and Puck while killing Leonard Samson and Walter Langkowski. He takes the carcass of the Abomination—formerly KGB spy Emil Blonsky, who exposed himself to gamma radiation—back to Shadow Base. Shadow Base also happens to hold Bruce Banner's friend Rick Jones, who was previously taken away from a site after a battle with the Hulk. Fortean reaches out to the Abomination's carcass lying on a gurney. He is quickly commanded not to touch it. But Fortean's arrogance wins out, and what is left of the Abomination grabs hold of him and wraps itself around Fortean. It seems it's still a living creature, even without a host.

Rick Jones now lies in a bathtub in a motel somewhere in California. Betty Ross—who was previously turned into a creature called the Harpy by M.O.D.O.K.—has changed back to her human form, sits, waits, and watches to monitor any changes. Bruce Banner knocks on the door to check

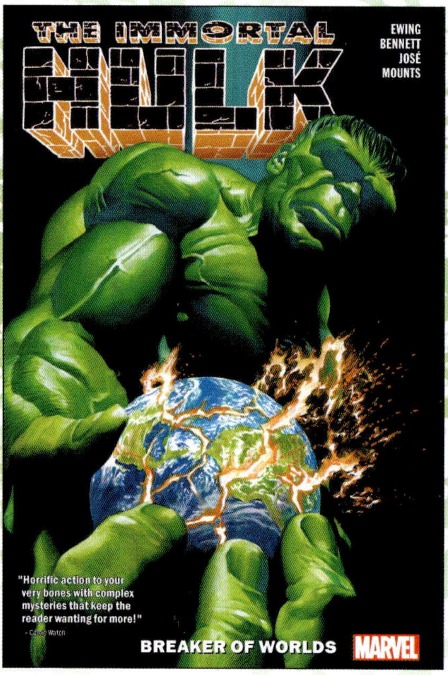
THE IMMORTAL HULK
EWING
BENNETT
JOSÉ
MOUNTS
BREAKER OF WORLDS
MARVEL

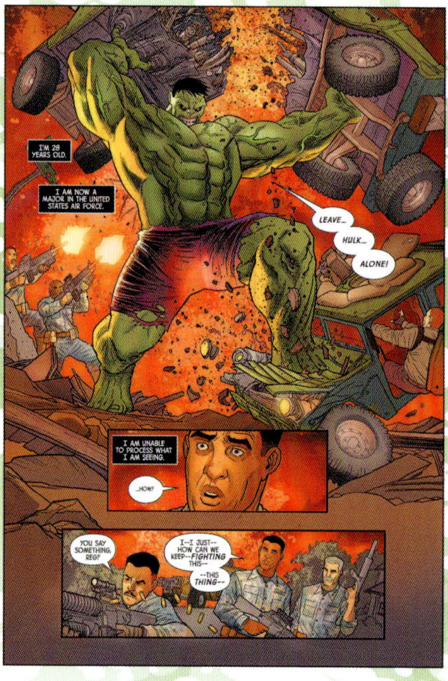
I'M 28 YEARS OLD.
I AM NOW A MAJOR IN THE UNITED STATES AIR FORCE.
LEAVE...
HULK...
ALONE!
I AM UNABLE TO PROCESS WHAT I AM SEEING.

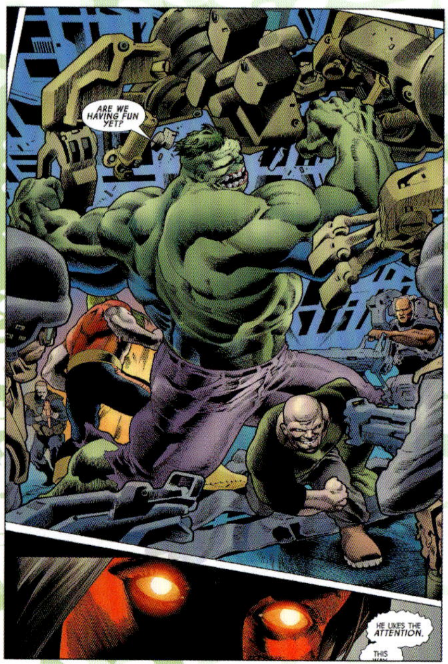
ARE WE HAVING FUN YET?
HE LIKES THE ATTENTION.

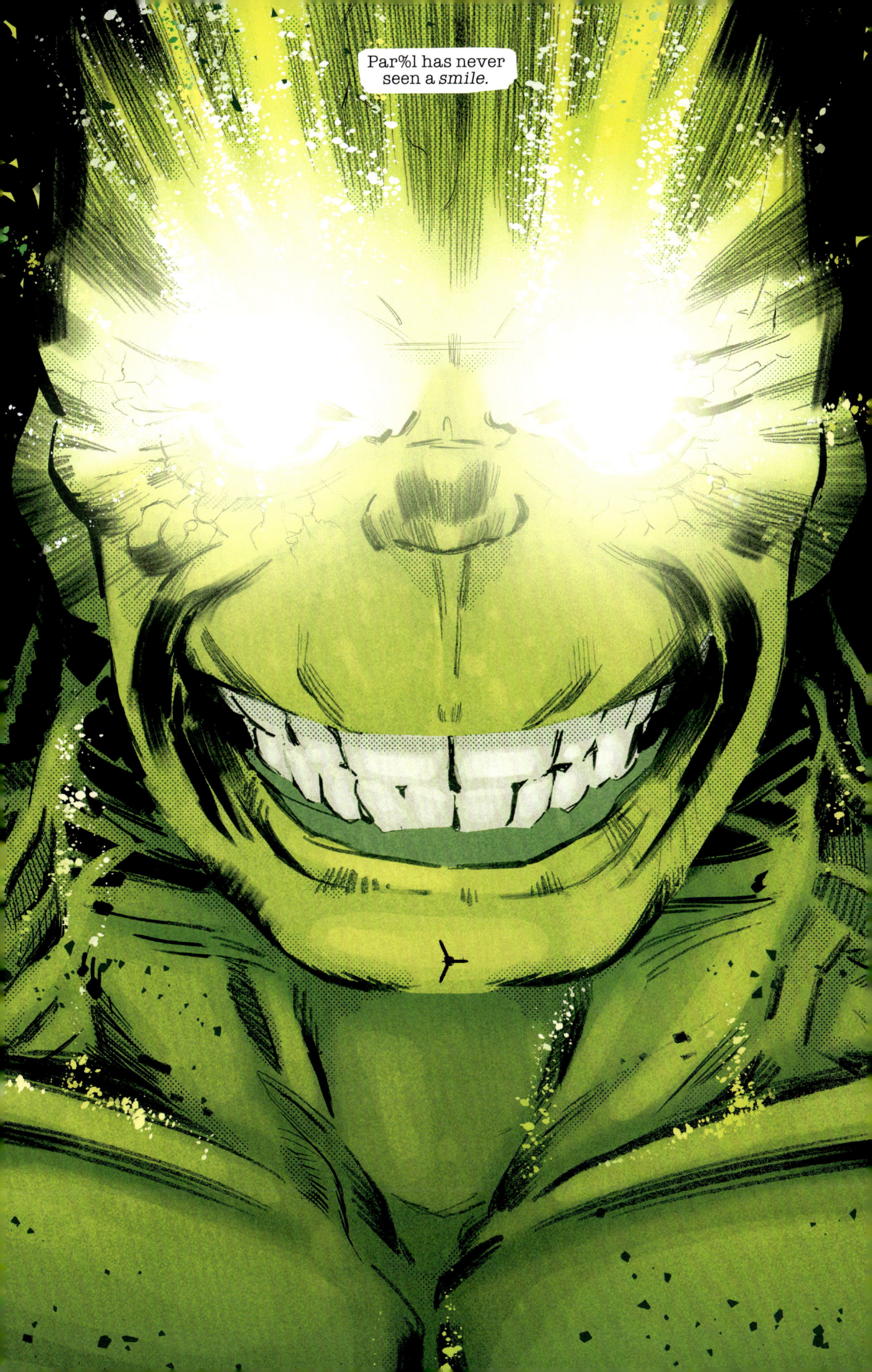
Par%l has never seen a *smile.*

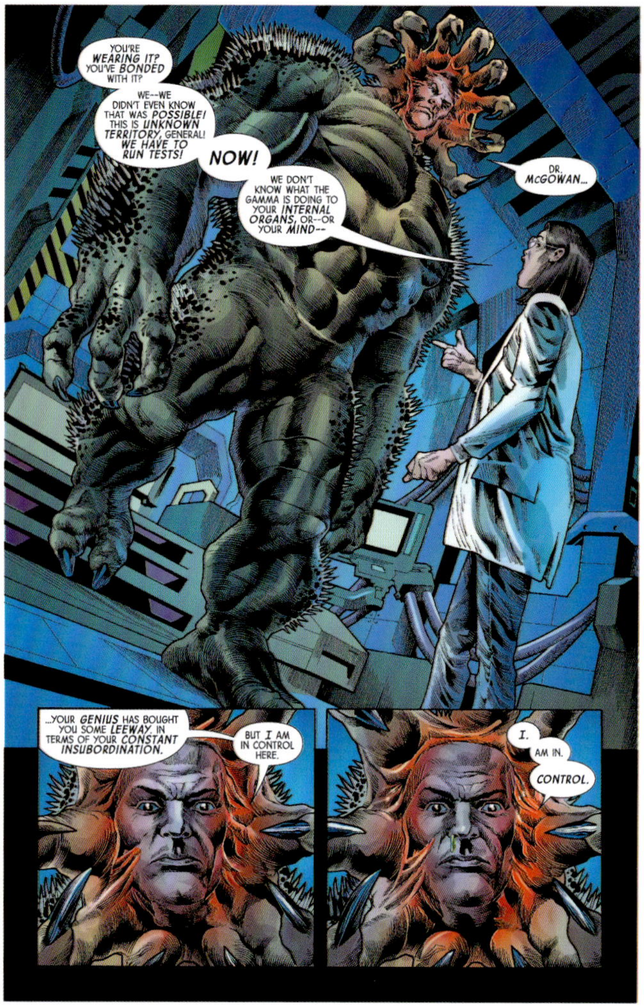
YOU'RE WEARING IT? YOU'VE BONDED WITH IT?
WE--WE DIDN'T EVEN KNOW THAT WAS POSSIBLE! THIS IS UNKNOWN TERRITORY, GENERAL! WE HAVE TO RUN TESTS!
NOW!
WE DON'T KNOW WHAT THE GAMMA IS DOING TO YOUR INTERNAL ORGANS, OR--OR YOUR MIND--
DR. McGOWAN...
...YOUR GENIUS HAS BOUGHT YOU SOME LEEWAY, IN TERMS OF YOUR CONSTANT INSUBORDINATION.
BUT I AM IN CONTROL HERE.
I.
AM IN.
CONTROL.

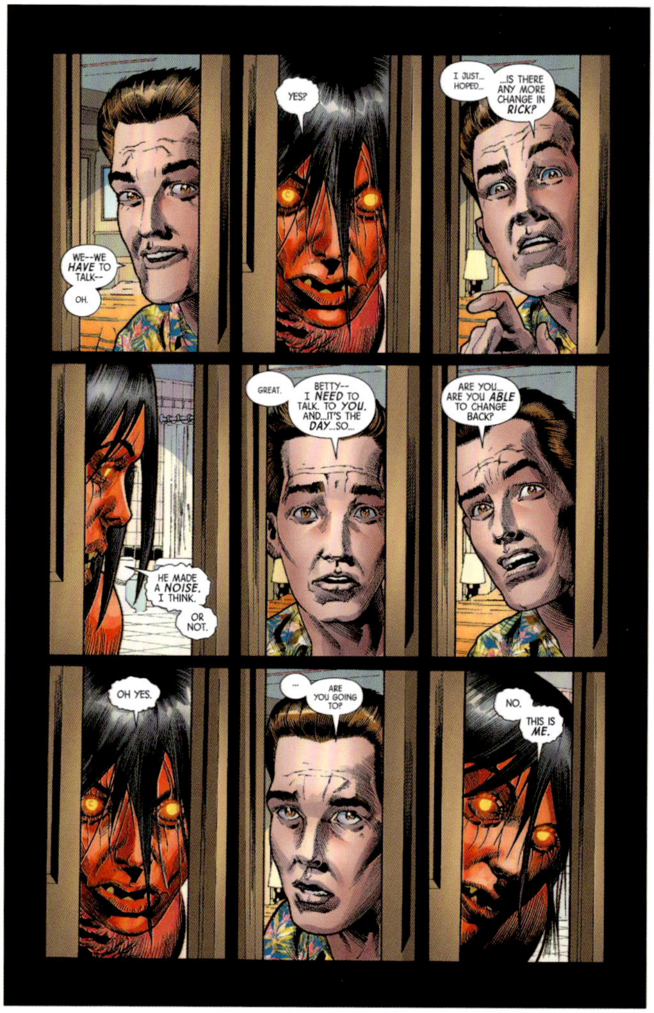
WE--WE HAVE TO TALK--
OH.
YES?
I JUST... HOPED...
...IS THERE ANY MORE CHANGE IN RICK?
HE MADE A NOISE. I THINK.
OR NOT.
GREAT.
BETTY-- I NEED TO TALK. TO YOU. AND...IT'S THE DAY...SO...
ARE YOU... ARE YOU ABLE TO CHANGE BACK?
OH YES.
...
ARE YOU GOING TO?
NO.
THIS IS ME.

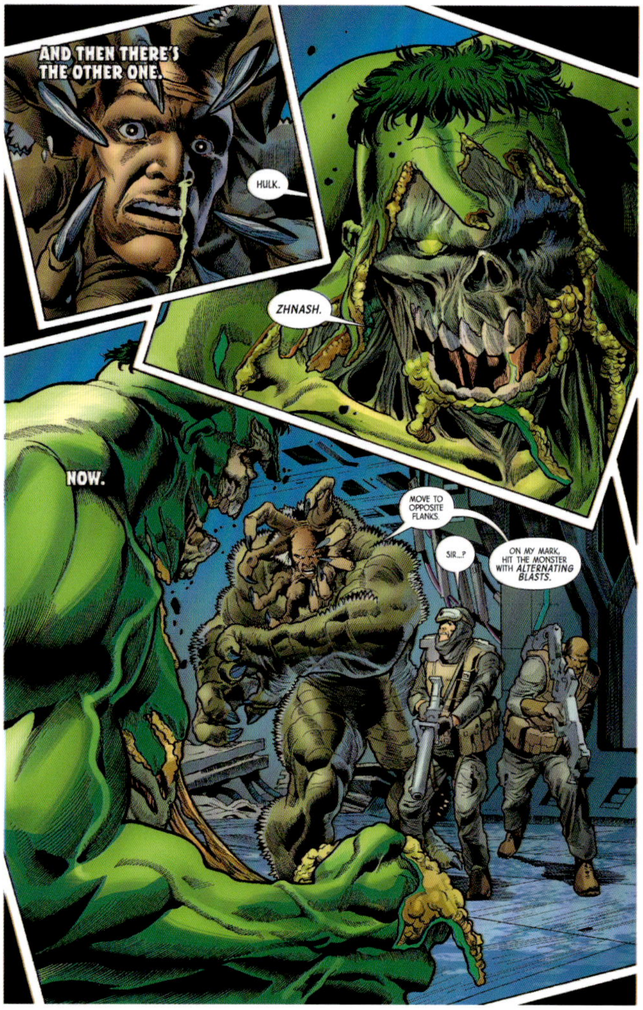
AND THEN THERE'S THE OTHER ONE.
HULK.
ZHNASH.
NOW.
MOVE TO OPPOSITE FLANKS.
SIR...?
ON MY MARK, HIT THE MONSTER WITH ALTERNATING BLASTS.

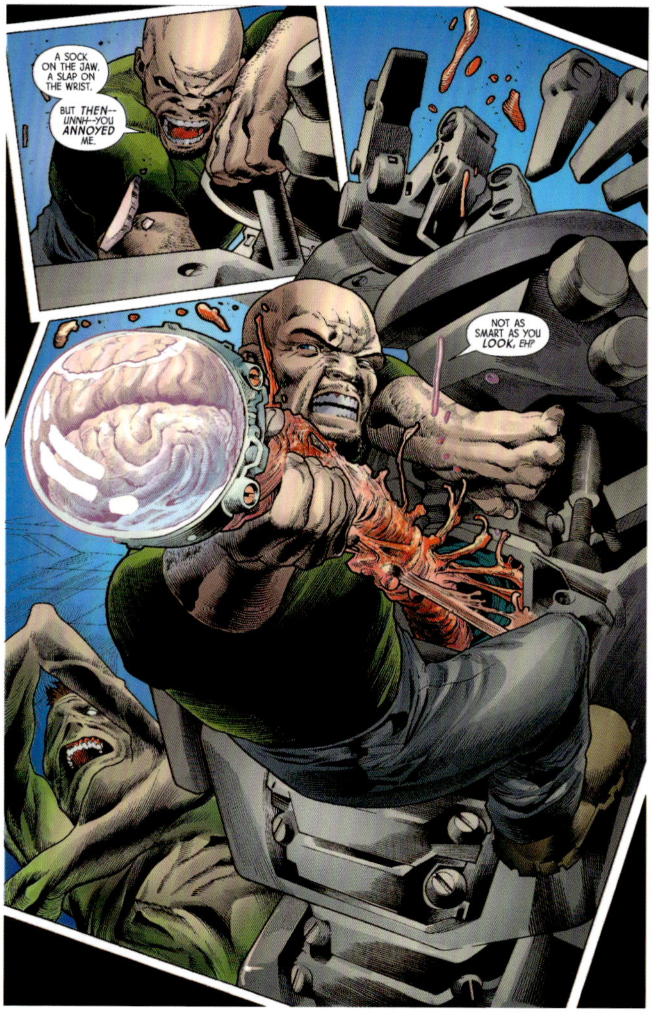
A SOCK ON THE JAW. A SLAP ON THE WRIST.
BUT THEN-- UNNH--YOU ANNOYED ME.
NOT AS SMART AS YOU LOOK, EH?

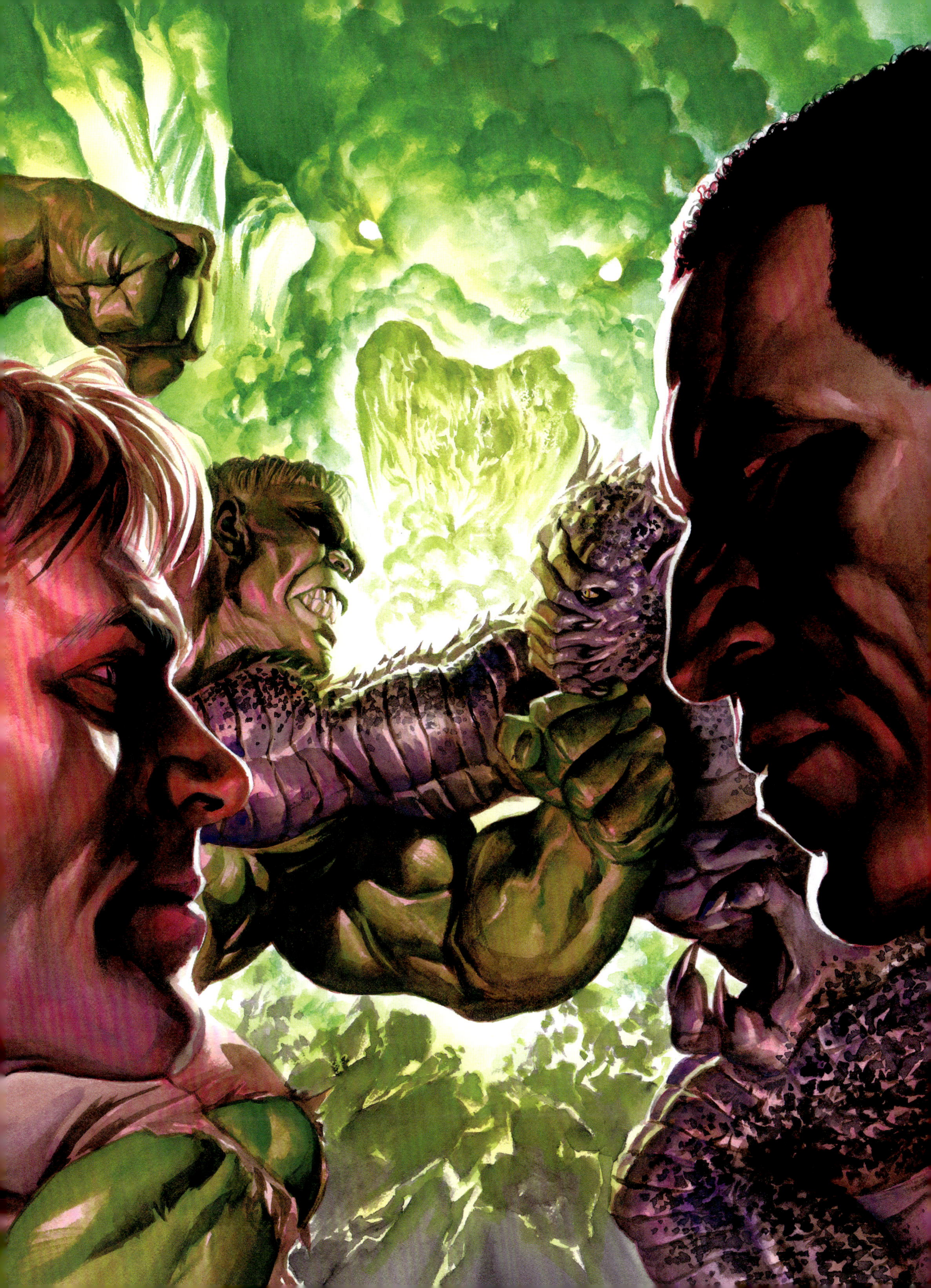

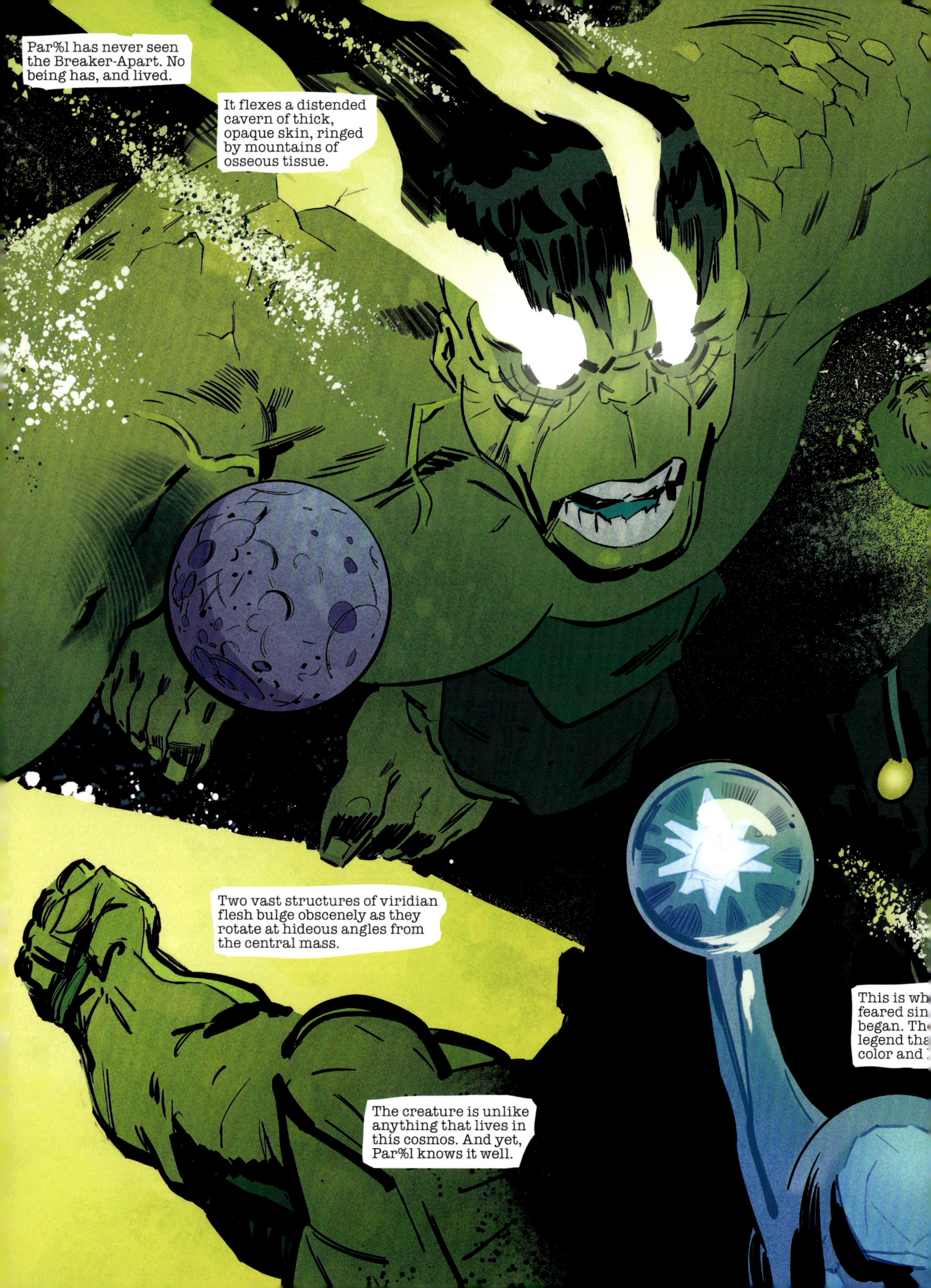
Par%l has never seen the Breaker-Apart. No being has, and lived.
It flexes a distended cavern of thick, opaque skin, ringed by mountains of osseous tissue.
Two vast structures of viridian flesh bulge obscenely as they rotate at hideous angles from the central mass.
The creature is unlike anything that lives in this cosmos. And yet, Par%l knows it well.
This is wh feared sin began. Th legend tha color and

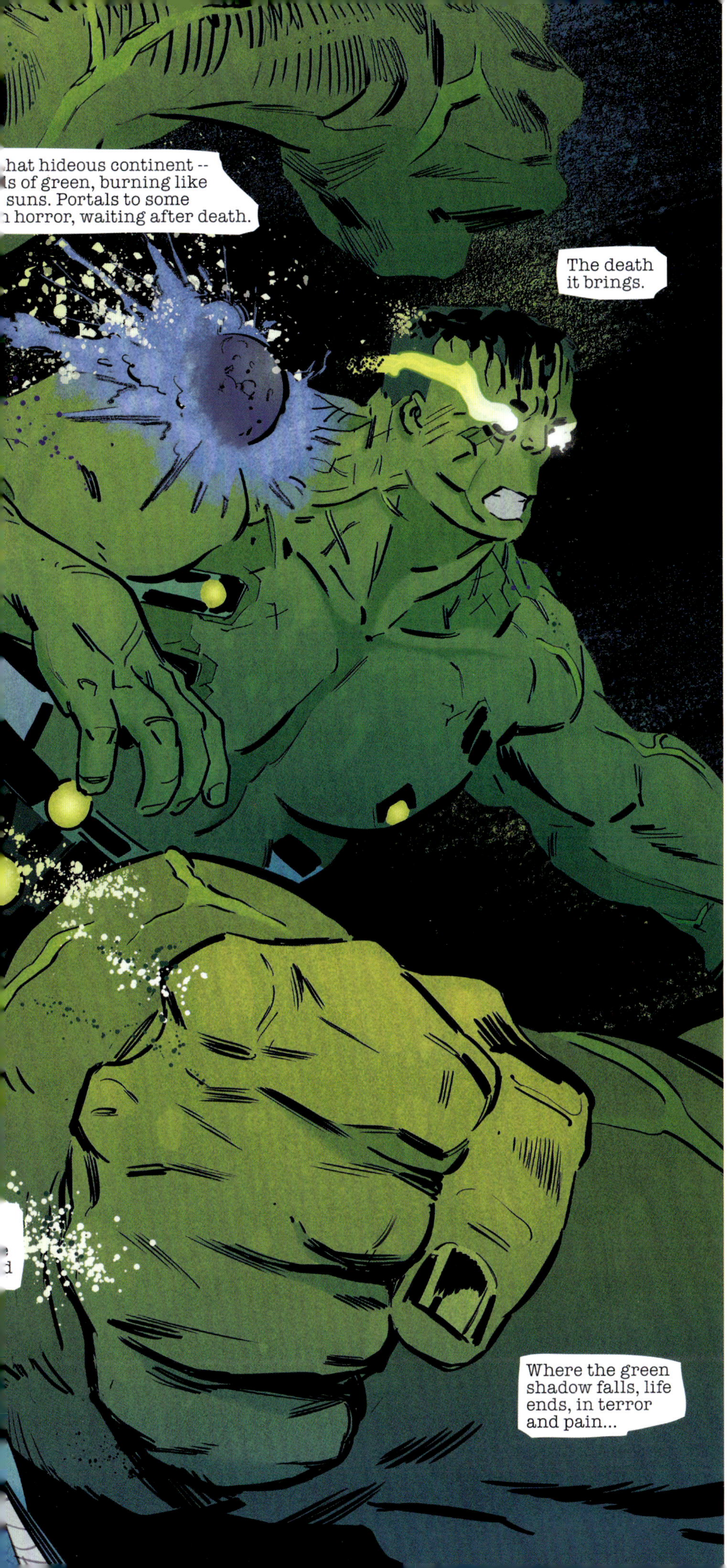
hat hideous continent --
s of green, burning like
suns. Portals to some
horror, waiting after death.
The death it brings.
Where the green shadow falls, life ends, in terror and pain...

on them both. When she opens the door, Betty again turns into the Harpy. She lies to Banner, telling him that she can't change back. This causes Banner to revert to one of his other alternate identities, Joe Fixit.

Fixit steps out on the balcony of the cheap motel and has a conversation with reporter Jackie McGee. We last saw McGee, who is fixated on the Hulk, with the Harpy while she helped the Hulk battle the Abomination. From inside we hear the Harpy call out Joe's name. Rick Jones is conscious, but floating and glowing green. He tells them that he remembers what they did to him at Shadow Base. How they forced him to be the Abomination.

Back on the Space Station, it appears Shadow Base isn't the only place that has a translocation machine. Soon members of Alpha Flight materialize in the middle of the Shadow Base, where they find themselves surrounded by the Abomination and his men. The Abomination brags about what he will do to each of them, and suddenly they hear a sound. A green fist breaks through the wall. It's the Hulk, joined by the Harpy, McGee, and Rick Jones (whose body has recovered), his eyes glowing green.

Alpha Flight quickly realizes that if they are to survive, they must fight alongside the Hulk instead of trying to capture him. The Abomination can still spit acid, which causes the Hulk to literally lose face, at least part of it. But things change when the Abomination spits acid on his own men. Something he refers to as "friendly fire." Fortean's crew at Shadow Base knows that this is not something the general would do. The Abomination has taken full control.

How will this end? What will happen to Shadow Base? Can the Hulk finally defeat the Abomination?

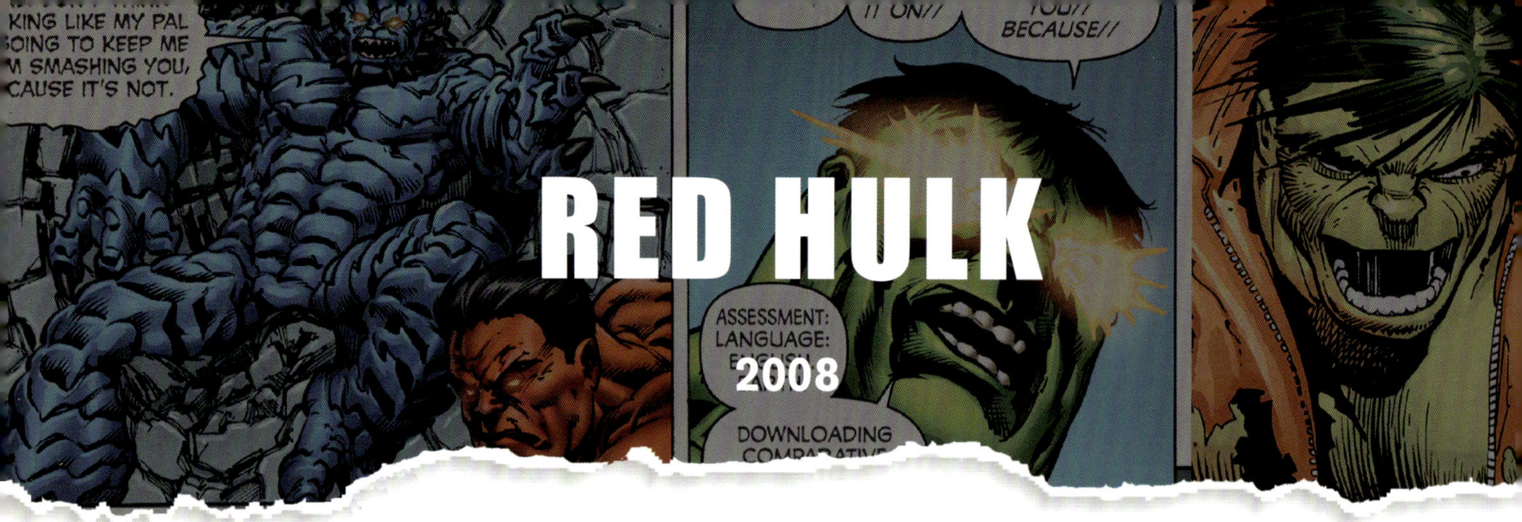
BECAUSE//
ASSESSMENT:
LANGUAGE:
DOWNLOADING

# RED HULK

## 2008

Dimitri, Russia: a village one hundred miles southwest of Odessa. The village is in ruins. A large green monster lies dead, his body riddled with bullets. The village was destroyed during a battle between the Hulk and a former KGB agent, Emil Blonsky. Blonsky is also known as the Abomination, a green-skinned giant who, like the Hulk, was created by gamma ray exposure. The Abomination was meant to be bigger and stronger than the Hulk, but he now lies on the ground with a bullet hole in his chest. Witnesses say it was the Hulk who killed him. But the Hulk with a gun? The Hulk doesn't use a gun, does he? And where would he find a gun big enough for his gigantic hands? And to add to the mystery, the man who transforms into the Hulk currently sits in an underground jail cell on a military base. There is no way he could have escaped and killed the Abomination.

Meanwhile, Iron Man, S.H.I.E.L.D. agent Maria Hill, and She-Hulk are on the new S.H.I.E.L.D. Helicarrier. Agent Hill revealsthat the giant gun that killed the Abomination was manufactured by S.H.I.E.L.D. Suddenly, a red creature breaks through the carrier's hull and drags She-Hulk out of the Helicarrier. There is a huge crash, and She-Hulk's unconscious body is thrown back into the compartment.

The Helicarrier's power supply is breached, and Iron Man goes to investigate. Whatever breached the hull and grabbed She-Hulk is giving off gamma rays. Suddenly Iron Man is confronted by the Hulk, but it's not the Hulk we know. This Hulk is red. Red Hulk destroys the Helicarrier, and it crashes down in a field in New Jersey.

Across the country a young man is hitchhiking outside the Gamma Base in Death Valley, Nevada. It's the Hulk's old friend, Rick Jones. Rick is suddenly confronted by the Red Hulk, when something triggers him, and he transforms into a blue-skinned creature with scalelike skin. Rick calls himself A-Bomb, and is roughly the same size as the Hulk, and, like the Hulk, he has super-strength. A-Bomb and Red Hulk fight.

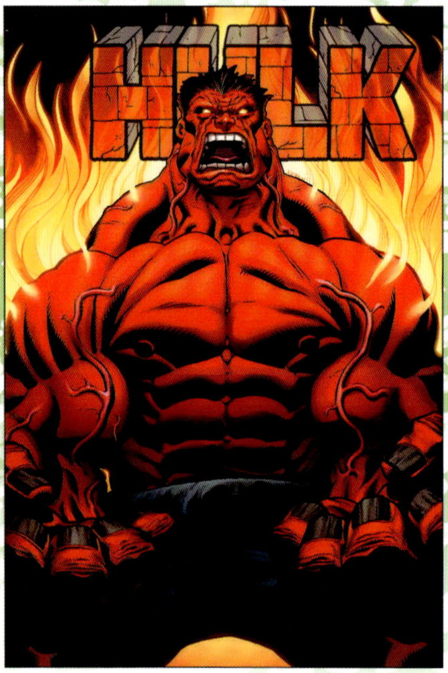
HULK

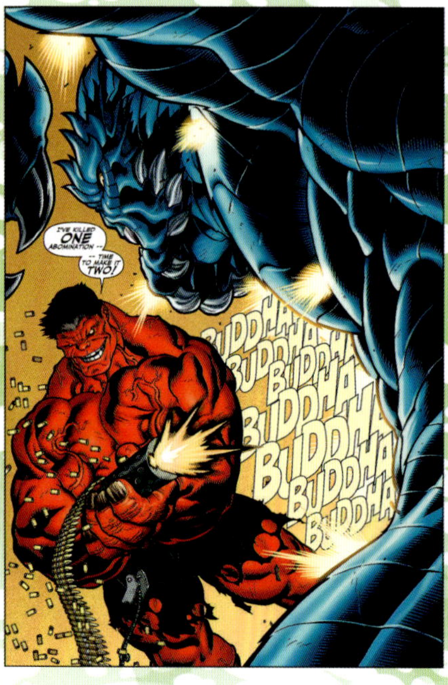
I'VE KILLED ONE ABOMINATION --
-- TIME TO MAKE IT TWO!
BUDDHA BUDDHA BUDDHA BUDDHA BUDDHA BUDDHA BUDDHA

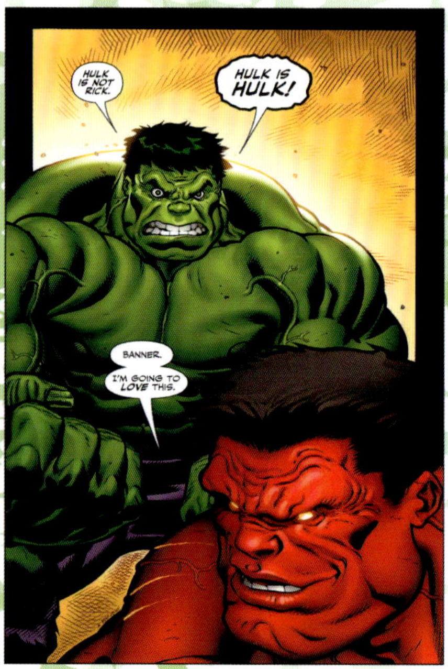
HULK IS NOT RICK.
HULK IS HULK!
BANNER.
I'M GOING TO LOVE THIS.

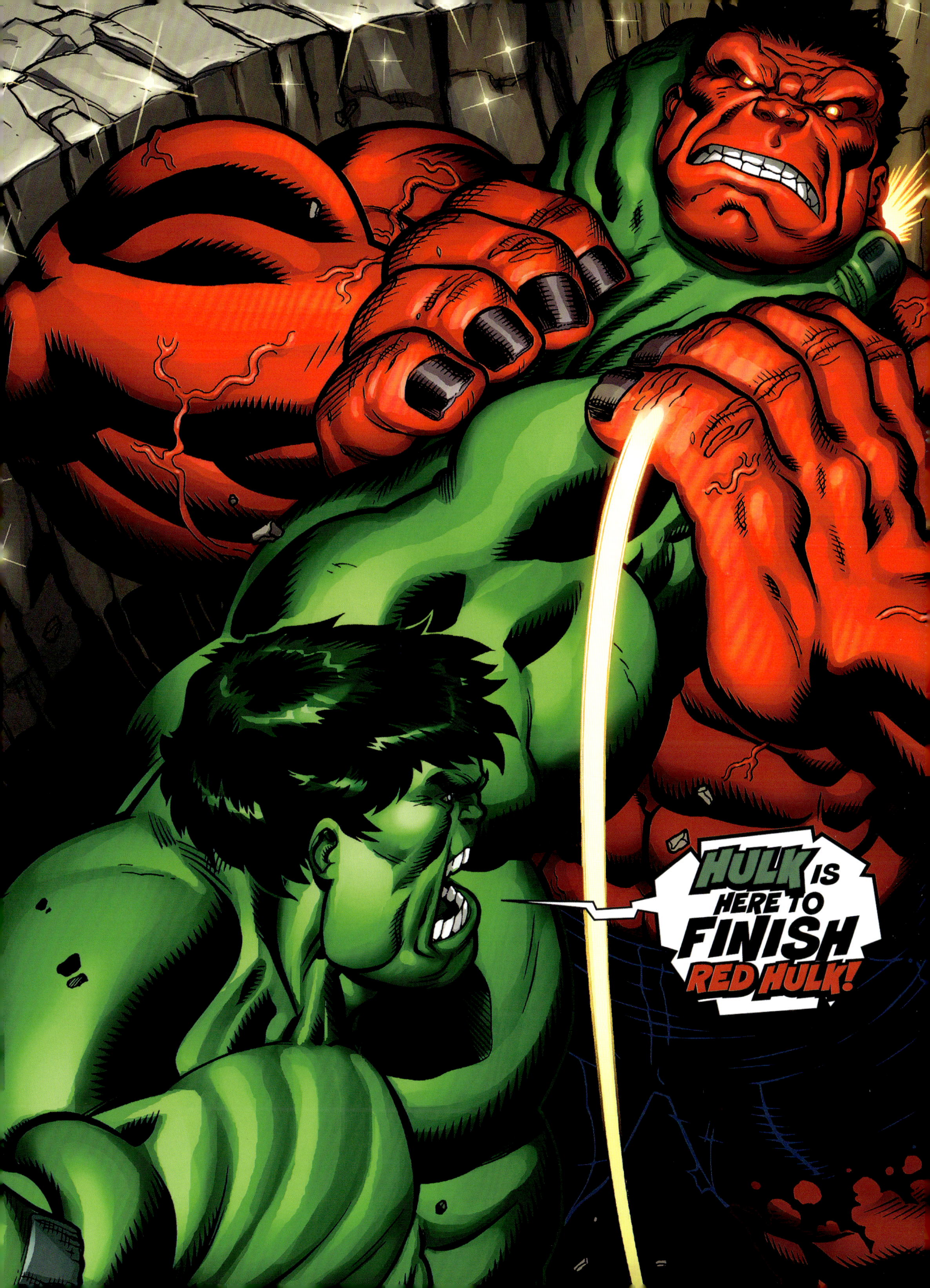
HULK IS HERE TO FINISH RED HULK!

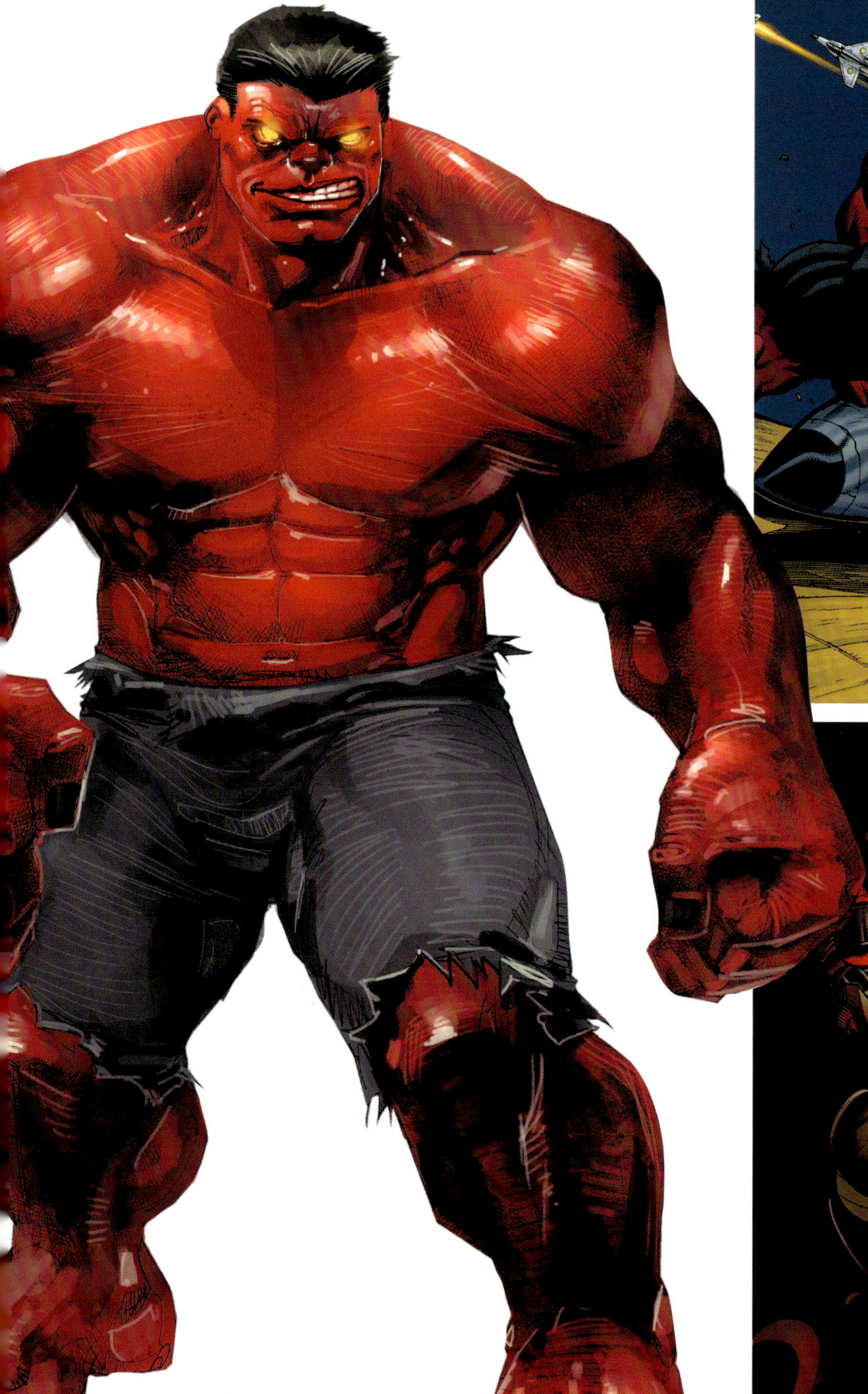

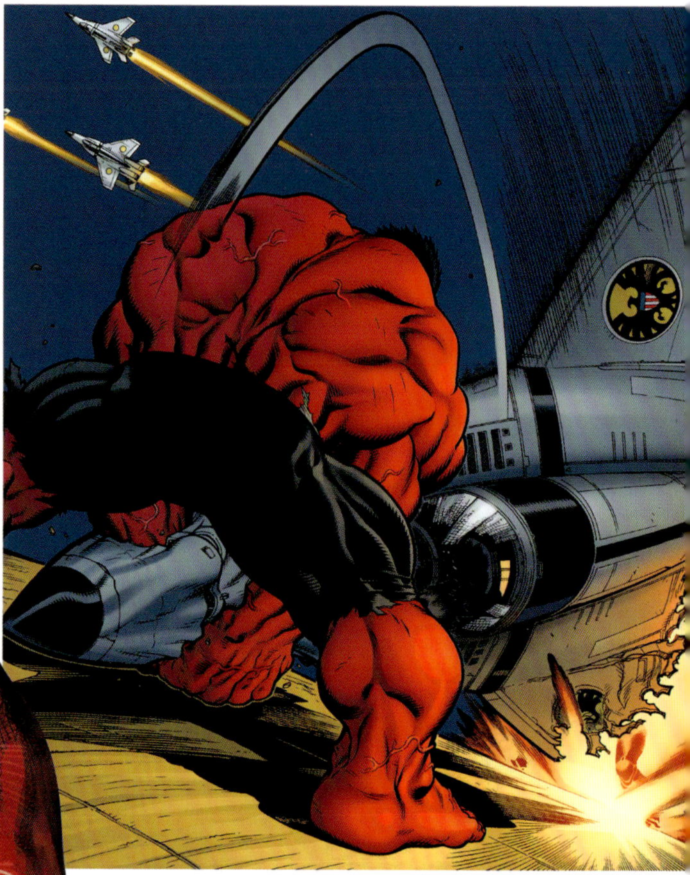

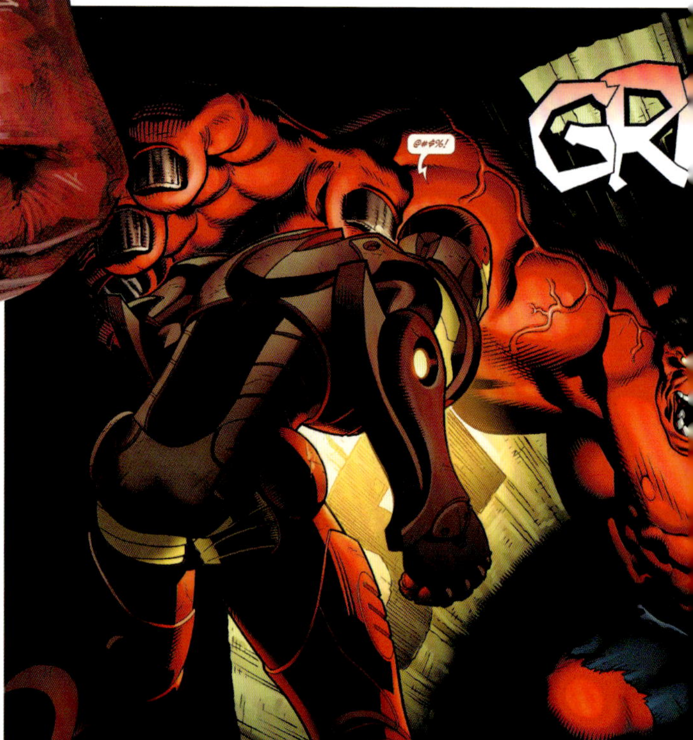
@#$%!
GR

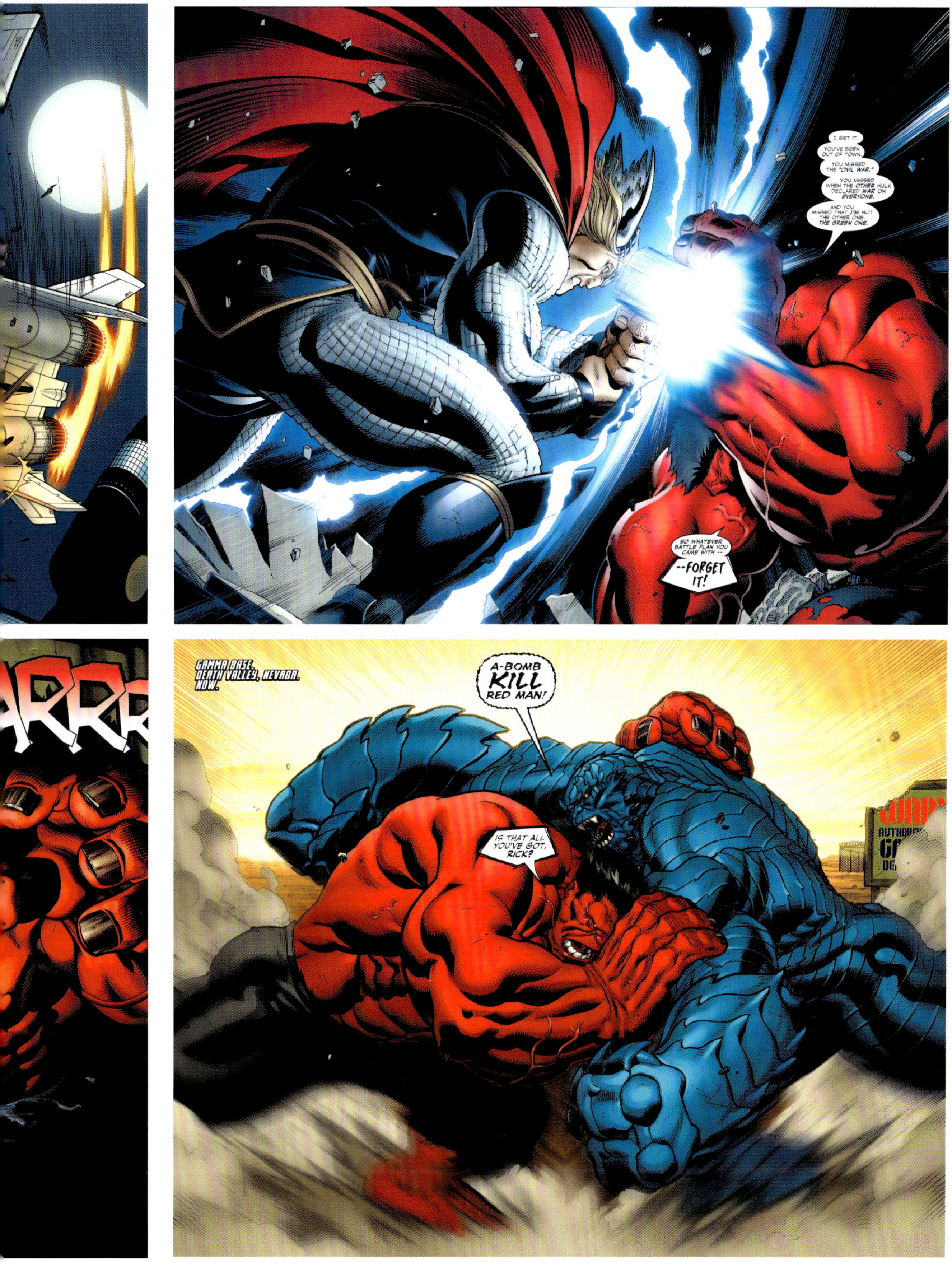
I GET IT.
YOU'VE BEEN OUT OF TOWN.
YOU MISSED THE "CIVIL WAR."
YOU MISSED WHEN THE OTHER HULK DECLARED WAR ON EVERYONE.
AND YOU MISSED THAT I'M NOT THE OTHER ONE. THE GREEN ONE.
SO WHATEVER BATTLE PLAN YOU CAME WITH --
--FORGET IT!
GAMMA BASE. DEATH VALLEY, NEVADA. NOW.
A-BOMB KILL RED MAN!
IS THAT ALL YOU'VE GOT, RICK?

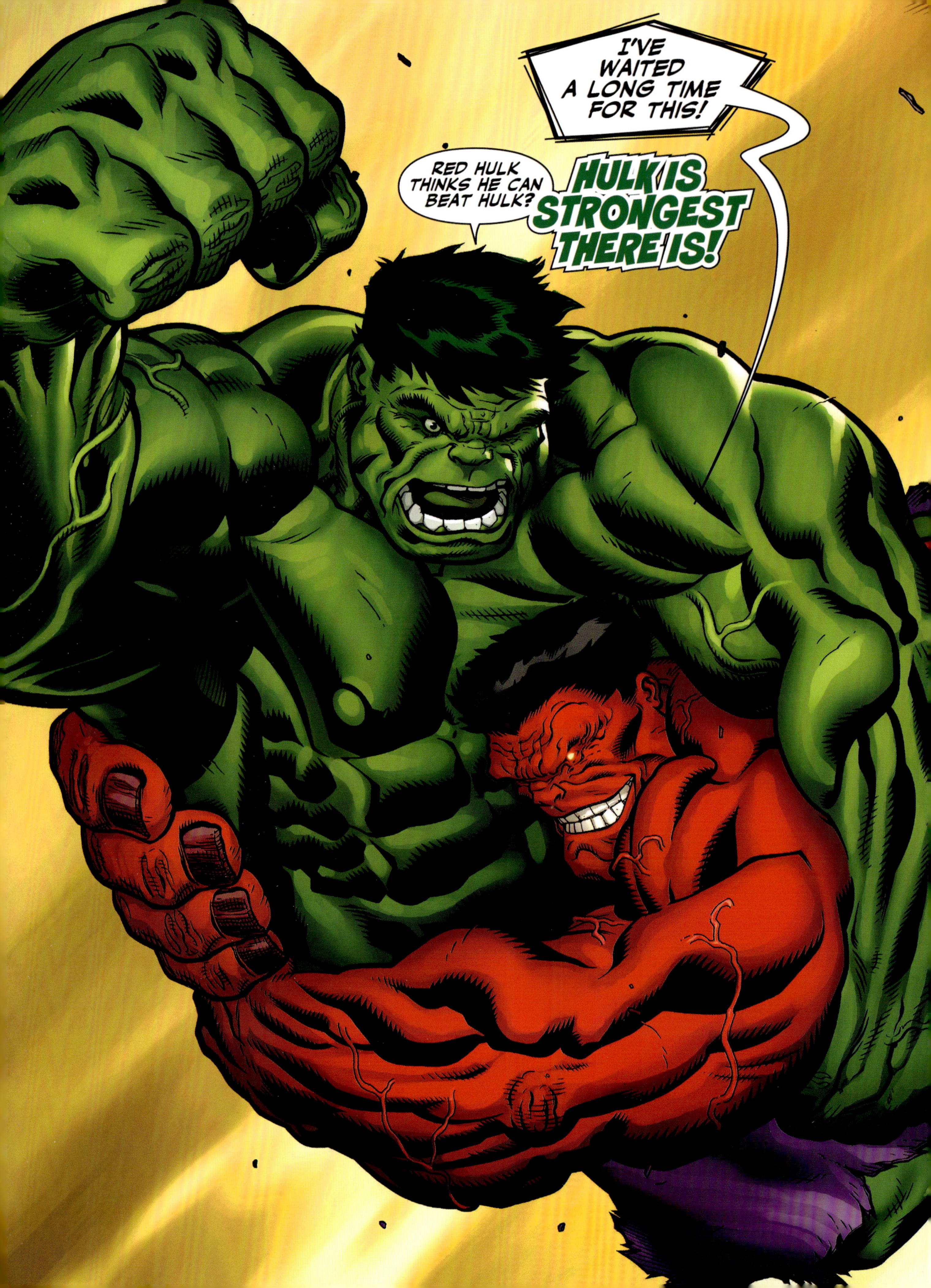
I'VE WAITED A LONG TIME FOR THIS!
RED HULK THINKS HE CAN BEAT HULK?
HULK IS STRONGEST THERE IS!

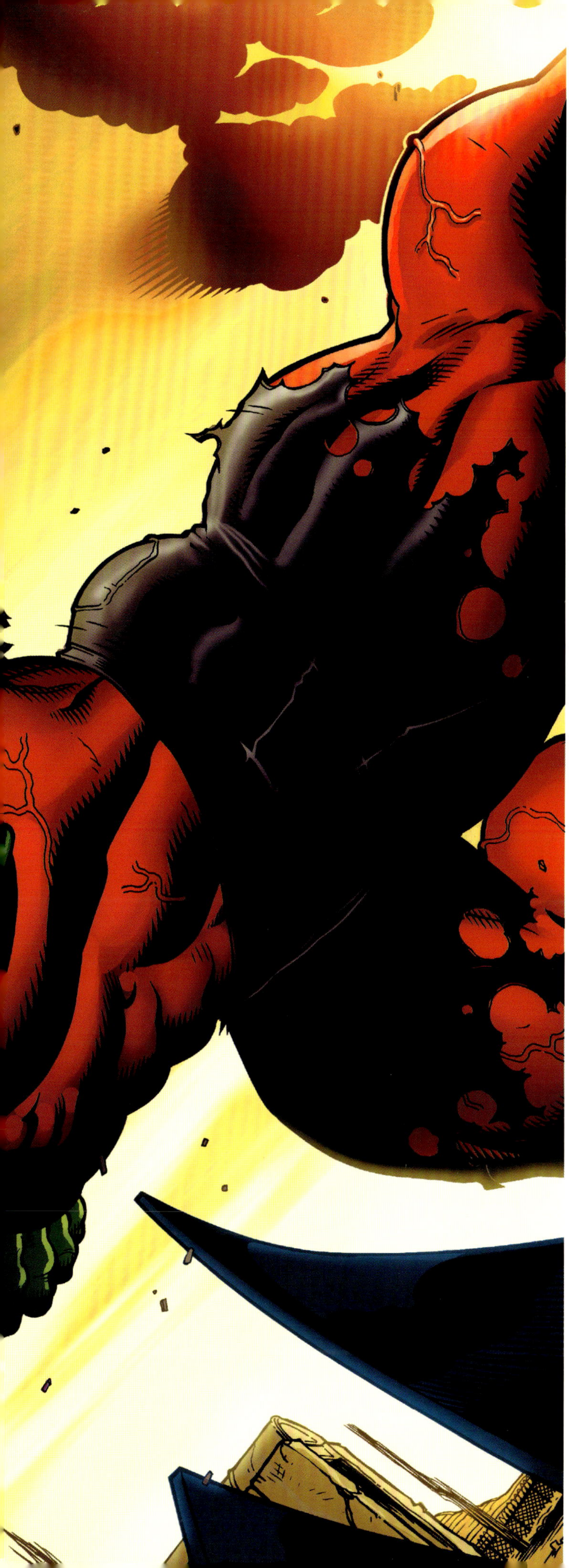

The battle escalates fiercely, and manages to disrupt a jail cell that lies hundreds of feet below the surface, which houses Bruce Banner, who quickly transforms into the Hulk. The original Hulk, the green Hulk.

The Red Hulk seems unstoppable. Not only is he strong, he's also smart, as if Banner and the Hulk had merged. Thor arrives and gets into the action, but Red Hulk figures out a clever way to take away his hammer. Their battle soon ends up on the moon, where the Red Hulk defeats Thor. Red Hulk leaves Thor lying in the lunar dust. Can anyone stop the Red Hulk?

Back on Earth, Iron Man has enlisted Reed Richards/Mr. Fantastic and the Fantastic Four to help solve the mystery of Red Hulk's identity. One clue they have is a surveillance video from the military base that was attacked. In the video, General "Thunderbolt" Ross is talking to Banner in a cell. At one point, General Ross's voice is garbled, and it's difficult to hear what he's saying. Richards deduces that the audio has been purposely altered. But why? What could Ross have said to Banner?

Thor returns from the moon, and he and the green Hulk team up with the other super heroes to take down the Red Hulk. Once Red Hulk is finally lying unconscious on the desert floor, Rick (who has transformed back from his other identity, A-Bomb) yells to the Hulk that he knows the Red Hulk's identity. But before Rick can tell the Hulk, Doc Samson, a psychiatrist who works with Ross and who has also been exposed to gamma rays, unexpectedly shoots Rick with a blaster. General Ross looks down on the unconscious Red Hulk and tells him that he "failed" and that from now on he is "on his own." Ross walks away.

Who is this mysterious Red Hulk and what is his connection to General Ross? Did Ross create the Red Hulk in order to defeat the original Hulk? The answers to these and other questions can be found in the series *Red Hulk*.

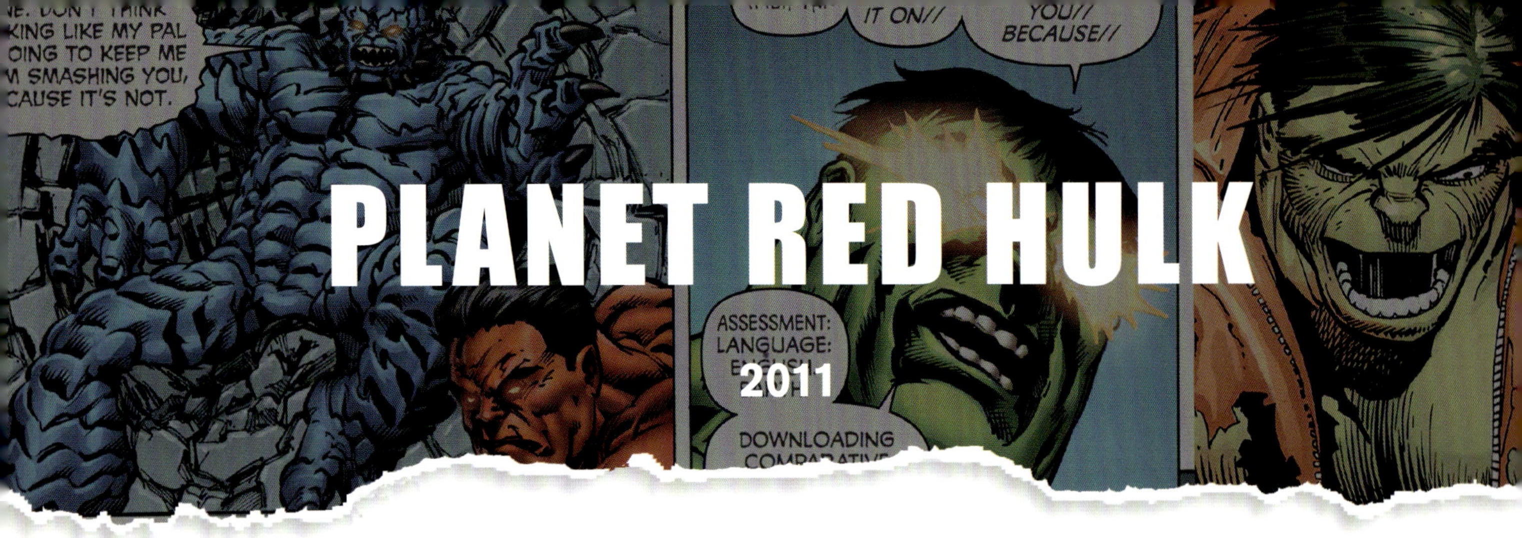
ASSESSMENT:
LANGUAGE:
DOWNLOADING

# PLANET RED HULK

## 2011

"Whoever fights monsters should see to it that in the process he does not become a monster." —Nietzsche

We find that this and other relevant quotes open up each issue of the *Planet Red Hulk* comics. Perhaps none is more relevant to what happens in the pages of *Planet Red Hulk* than this one.

General Thaddeus "Thunderbolt" Ross is dead and buried—at least that is what he wants everyone to think. Ross is the father of Betty Ross, who is in love with her father's nemesis, Bruce Banner, aka the Hulk. In his effort to bring the Hulk down, Ross partnered with the villain M.O.D.O.K., who had siphoned gamma radiation from the Hulk and used it on Ross. Ross became a monster in order to defeat a monster.

The man who replaced Ross at Shadow Base is General Reginald Fortean. Fortean had served under Ross and was devoted to him and his cause—tracking down and defeating the Hulk. But not everyone believed in Ross's mission. Many in the military thought that Ross was a dangerous zealot because of his mission to stop the Hulk at all costs. Well, the costs were too high, and Fortean found that, with Ross gone, his funding was cut. Fortean turned to other like-minded officers and talked them into diverting some of their discretionary funds to him to support his hunt for the Hulk.

General Fortean believes that Red Hulk was responsible for the death of General Ross, and Fortean has plans to take down Red Hulk. He and Red Hulk meet in the desert. Fortean wears an Iron Man-type suit called the Redeemer Armor. Red Hulk tries to talk to Fortean, to tell him that he is Ross, but he doesn't listen and attacks. Fortean fires micro-mines, which bring down Red Hulk.

After Red Hulk comes to, Fortean tells him that his brain is now full of micro-mines, and when he reverts back into human form, Fortean will be able to melt his brain with them. He tells Red Hulk that he'll never be able to rest, and because Red Hulk can't transform back to Ross, he can be easily tracked by Fortean's crew.

Elsewhere, a man named Jacob Feinman, who has burns all over his entire body, is wheeled into a hospital exam room. He will need multiple skin grafts. He is in pain. The window in the exam room stretches as if it were a shower curtain, a hand

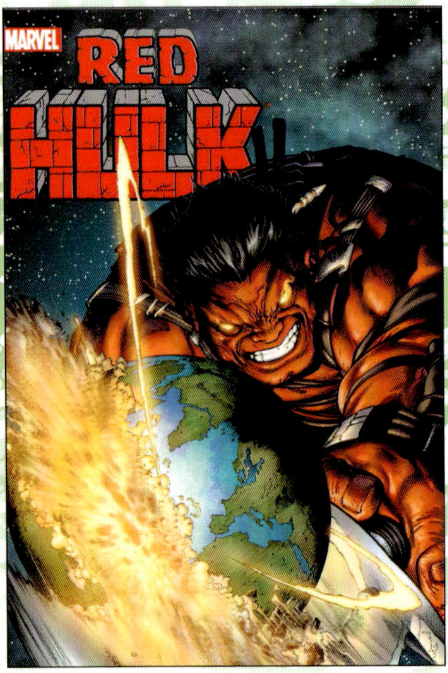
MARVEL
RED HULK

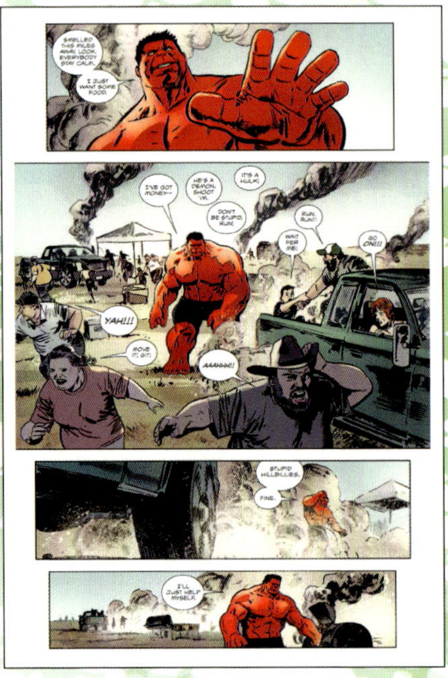

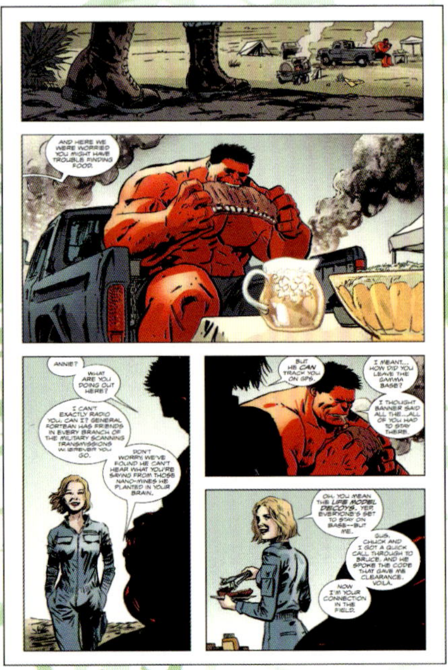

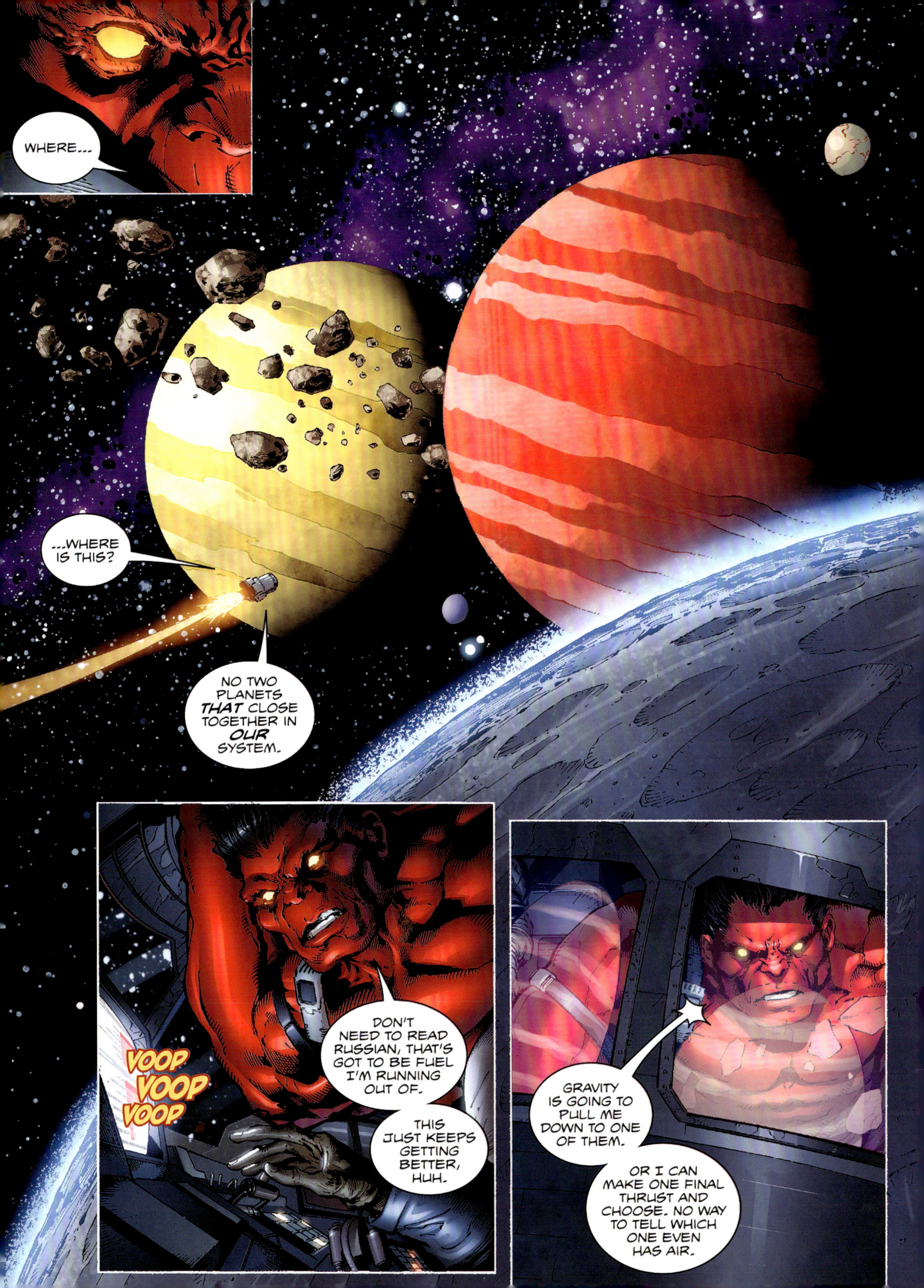
WHERE...
...WHERE IS THIS?
NO TWO PLANETS THAT CLOSE TOGETHER IN OUR SYSTEM.
DON'T NEED TO READ RUSSIAN, THAT'S GOT TO BE FUEL I'M RUNNING OUT OF.
VOOP VOOP VOOP
THIS JUST KEEPS GETTING BETTER, HUH.
GRAVITY IS GOING TO PULL ME DOWN TO ONE OF THEM.
OR I CAN MAKE ONE FINAL THRUST AND CHOOSE. NO WAY TO TELL WHICH ONE EVEN HAS AIR.

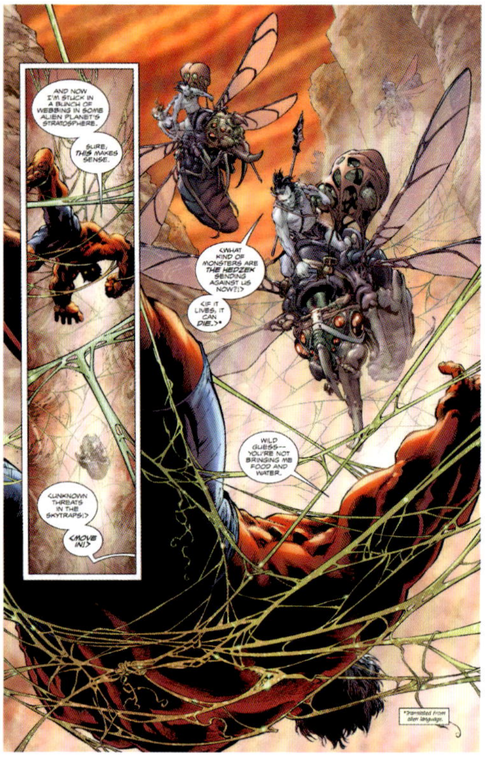
AND NOW I'M STUCK IN A BUNCH OF WEBBING IN SOME ALIEN PLANET'S STRATOSPHERE.
SURE, THIS MAKES SENSE.
<WHAT KIND OF MONSTERS ARE THE HEDZEK SENDING AGAINST US NOW?!>
<IF IT LIVES, IT CAN DIE.>*
WILD GUESS-- YOU'RE NOT BRINGING ME FOOD AND WATER.
<UNKNOWN THREATS IN THE SKYTRAPS!>
<MOVE IN!>

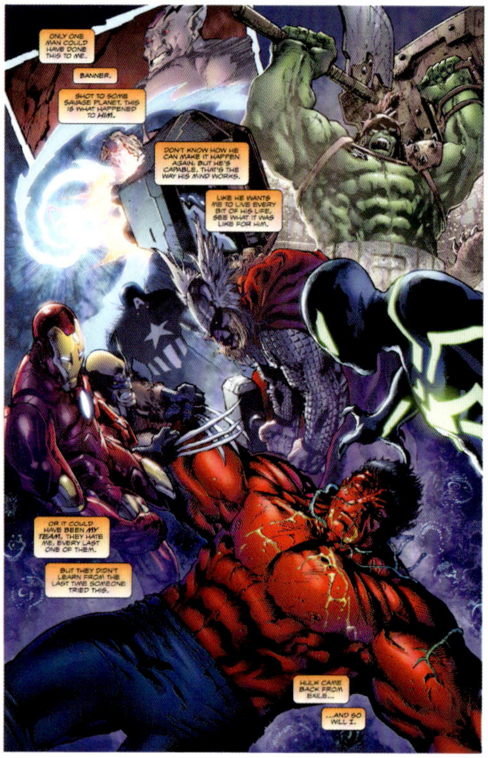
ONLY ONE MAN COULD HAVE DONE THIS TO ME.
BANNER.
SHOT TO SOME SAVAGE PLANET. THIS IS WHAT HAPPENED TO HIM.
DON'T KNOW HOW HE CAN MAKE IT HAPPEN AGAIN, BUT HE'S CAPABLE. THAT'S THE WAY HIS MIND WORKS.
LIKE HE WANTS ME TO LIVE EVERY BIT OF HIS LIFE, SEE WHAT IT WAS LIKE FOR HIM.
OR IT COULD HAVE BEEN MY TEAM. THEY HATE ME. EVERY LAST ONE OF THEM.
BUT THEY DIDN'T LEARN FROM THE LAST TIME SOMEONE TRIED THIS.
HULK CAME BACK FROM EXILE...
...AND SO WILL I.

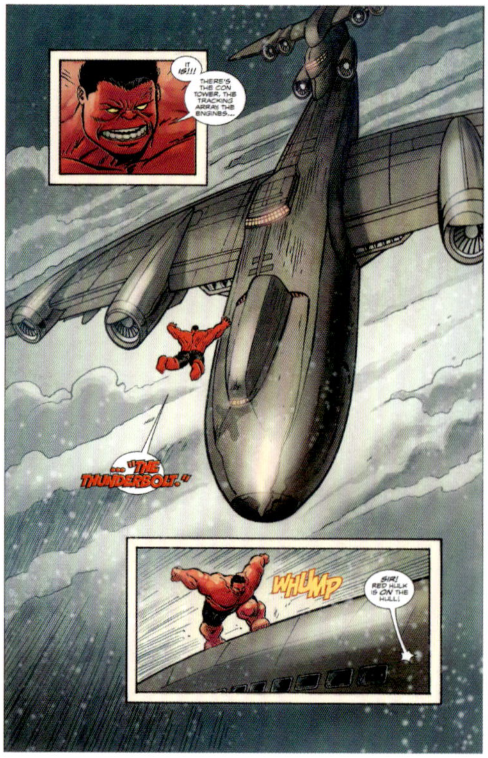
IT IS!!!
THERE'S THE CON TOWER, THE TRACKING ARRAY, THE ENGINES...
... "THE THUNDERBOLT."
WHUMP
SIR! RED HULK IS ON THE HULL!

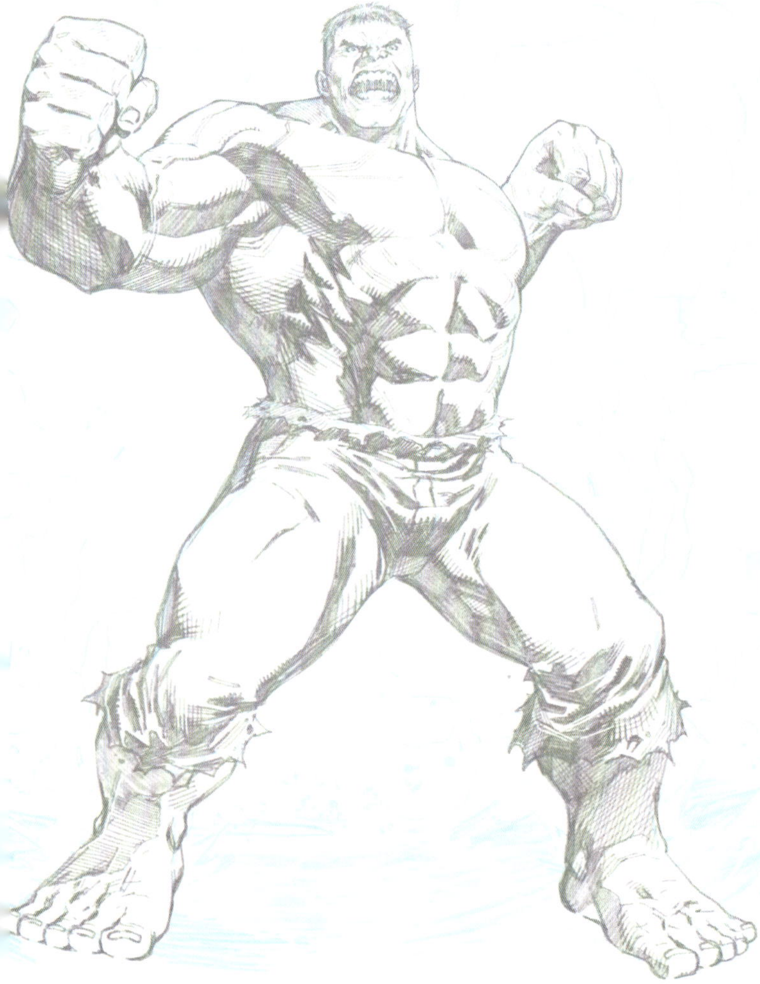

reaching into the room. A woman, glowing white, appears. She identifies herself as Zero/One. She tells Jacob that she has a gel that can ease his pain and heal his scarring skin. She tells him that they can "build the future!" and that together they can "create, innovate . . . eradicate." They leave together.

Jacob heals well enough to travel to India with Zero/One. In India, Zero/One is tracking down a man named Black Fog. She tracks him to a prison. He is a serial killer, and Zero/One wants Black Fog to help her kill Red Hulk. Black Fog is in bad shape, maimed and scarred, but she still breaks him out of the prison.

Meanwhile, the Red Hulk has been trying to stay awake. He knows that the micro-mines will detonate the minute he sleeps. He's been awake for an entire week. He lies on the forest floor in western Arkansas. The rain gently falls on him as he drifts off to sleep. While asleep, he transforms back into General Ross, and the micro-mines start to explode in his brain. The pain awakens him and transforms him back into the Red Hulk. He can't afford to sleep.

Fortean is relentless in his pursuit of Red Hulk. He has since partnered with Zero/One, who restores Black Fog with cybernetic elements and sends him out to destroy Red Hulk. Black Fog tracks down Red Hulk, and they battle. Red Hulk prevails, and Black Fog retreats.

Red Hulk is given an injection by a scientist named Gus who works at Gamma Base, one that prevents his transforming back into Ross, and he is finally able to get some rest. He gets a message from Steve Rogers/Captain America, who tells him that he's needed—aliens are attacking Earth. Red Hulk is shot into space where he goes to investigate. He boards a Russian spacecraft and, after finding the crew dead, he is suddenly blasted to another galaxy. To save himself, Red Hulk decides to land on a red planet.

What will the Red Hulk find on the planet? Can he get back to Earth? And if he does, will the general and a serial killer be there waiting for him?

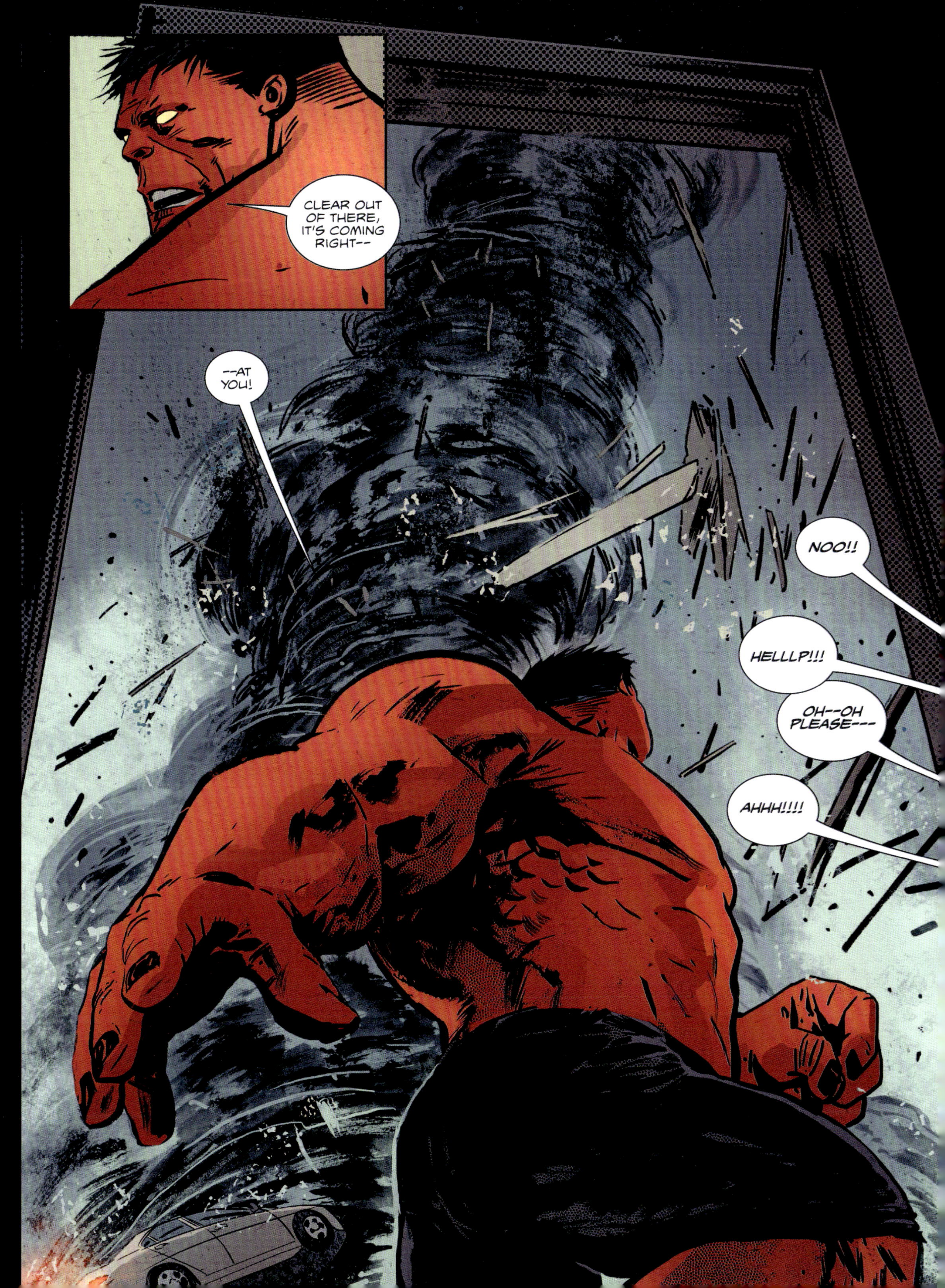
CLEAR OUT OF THERE, IT'S COMING RIGHT--
--AT YOU!
NOO!!
HELLLP!!!
OH--OH PLEASE---
AHHH!!!!

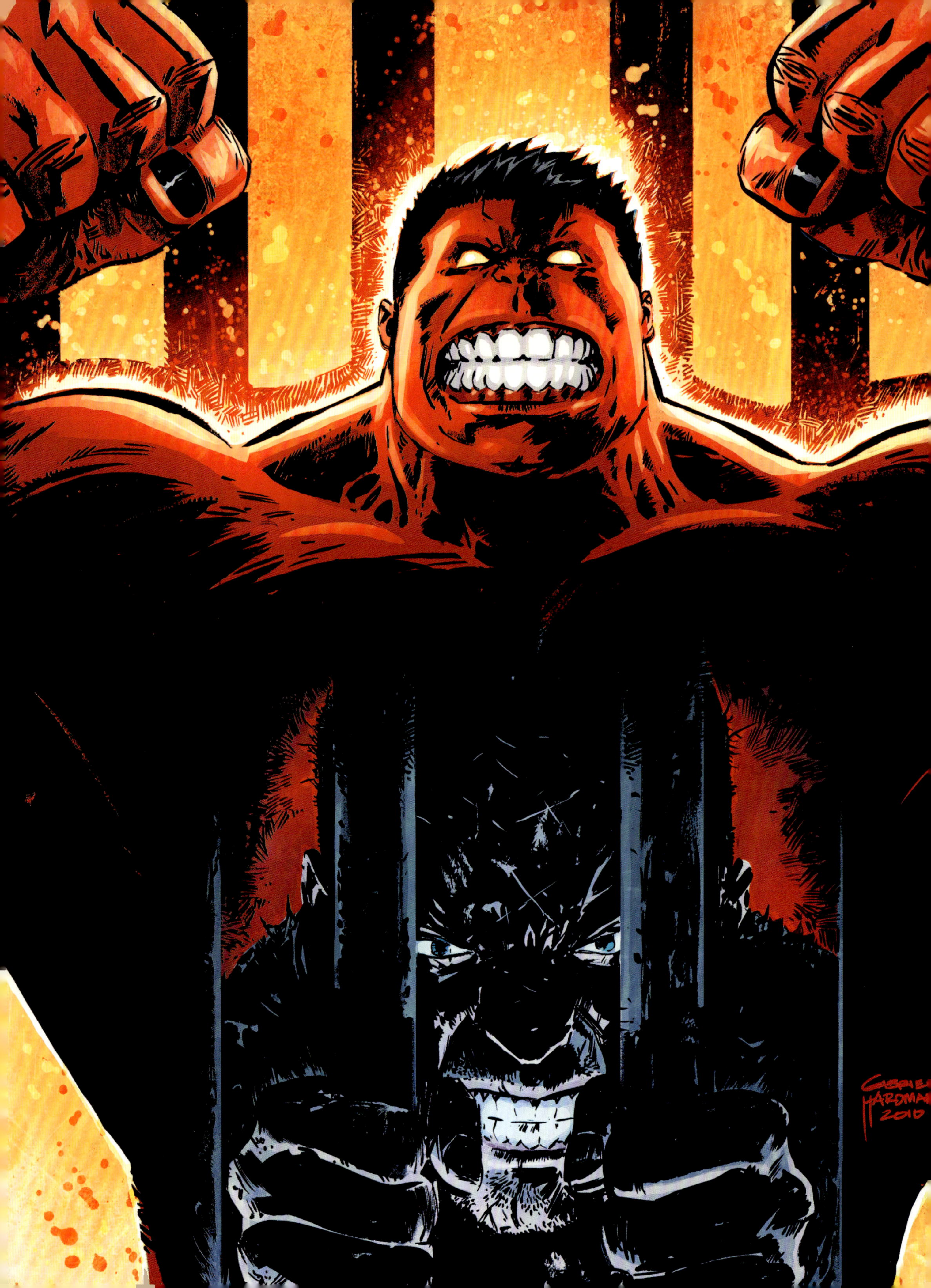
GABRIEL HARDMAN 2010

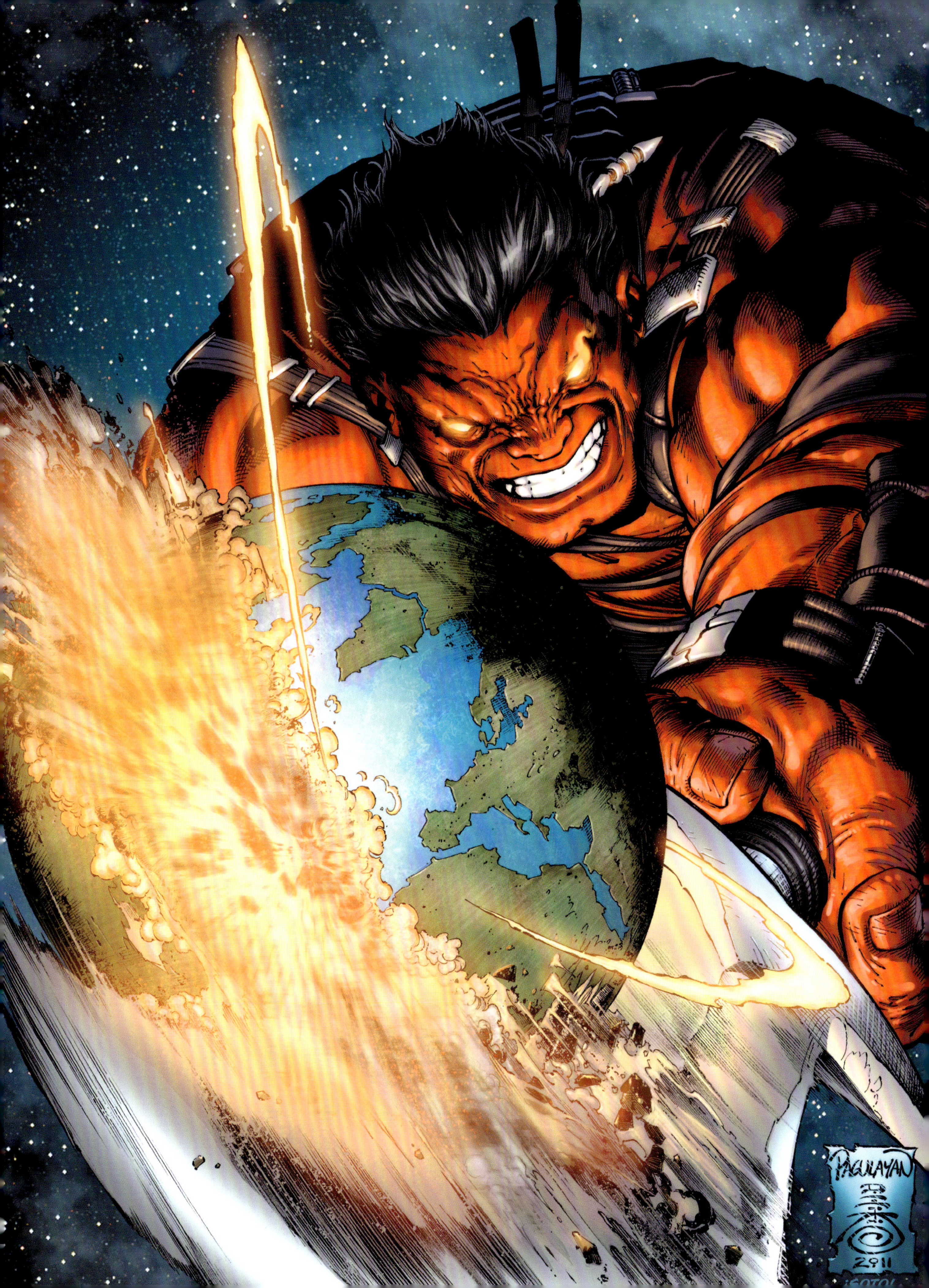
PAGULAYAN
2011

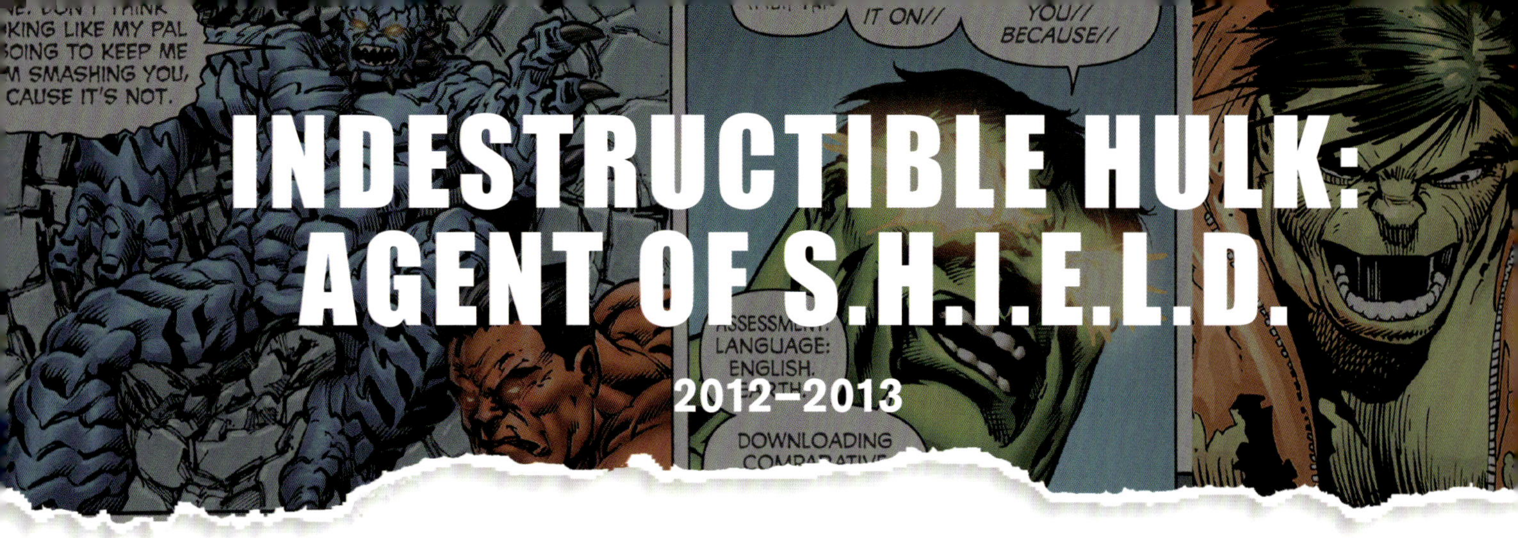
CAUSE IT'S NOT.
IT ON//
YOU// BECAUSE//
LANGUAGE: ENGLISH.
DOWNLOADING

# INDESTRUCTIBLE HULK: AGENT OF S.H.I.E.L.D.

## 2012–2013

The name's Banner, Bruce Banner, Agent of S.H.I.E.L.D. Or is that the Hulk, Agent of S.H.I.E.L.D.? That is what Banner is pitching to Maria Hill, the Director of S.H.I.E.L.D. Banner has arranged a meeting with Hill in a diner in Manchester, Alabama. They talk over lunch. There he pitches her the idea. It appears that Banner had an epiphany: Banner concludes that he can never be cured of being the Hulk. He has to find a way to live with the monster inside of him. In fact, he has devised technology that allows him to monitor his anger. He now wears contact lenses that show his vital signs, and they alert him to when he is about to transform into the Hulk. With this early warning signal, he is able to stop the transformation. He now believes that he can control the beast within.

Banner also describes to Hill a recent incident where he and other heroes battled the cosmic entity the Phoenix Force. The Hulk battled while other "smart people" like Tony Stark figured out a way to defeat her. Banner expresses his anger to Hill over the idea that Tony Stark is thought of as the smart one, and Banner is merely considered the hammer that breaks things.

Banner wants to prove his intelligence, but he also realizes the value of the Hulk as a weapon. His proposition is for S.H.I.E.L.D. to fund his research in exchange for offering up the Hulk as a WMD. They reach an agreement, and Banner begins to build his team.

One of his first research projects is an untapped natural gas deposit in the Himalayas. Tony Stark offers to join him to check on the gamma fracking project; none of the other S.H.I.E.L.D. agents are comfortable with Banner. When they arrive on site, Tony tinkers with Banner's technology in typical Stark fashion. Banner sees this as an arrogant move and tells Stark not to touch it. Stark ignores him and he asks Banner why he didn't come directly to him to help him set up his research. Stark's arrogance and actions make it clear why Banner didn't go to Stark Enterprises. Banner is getting

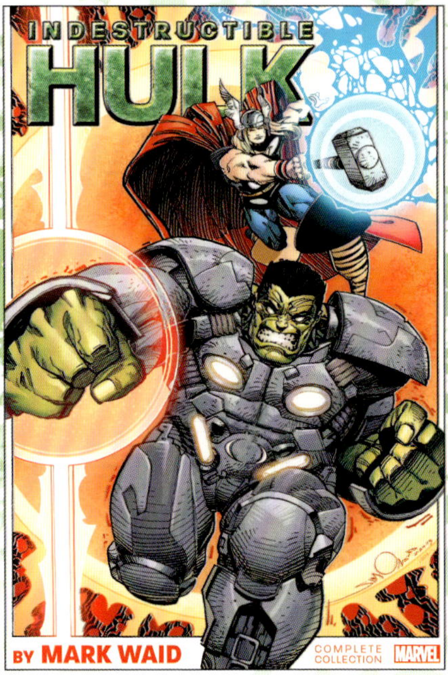
INDESTRUCTIBLE
HULK
BY MARK WAID
COMPLETE COLLECTION
MARVEL

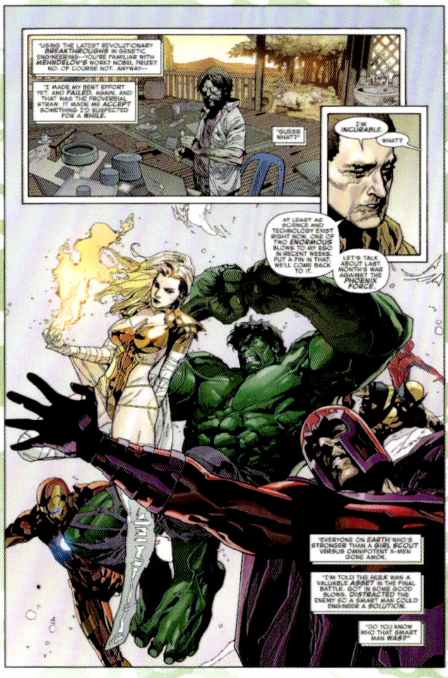
"USING THE LATEST REVOLUTIONARY BREAKTHROUGHS IN GENETIC ENGINEERING--YOU'RE FAMILIAR WITH MEHNDELOV'S WORK? NOBEL PRIZE? NO. OF COURSE NOT. ANYWAY--
"I MADE MY BEST EFFORT YET, AND FAILED. AGAIN. AND THAT WAS THE PROVERBIAL STRAW. IT MADE ME ACCEPT SOMETHING I'D SUSPECTED FOR A WHILE.
"GUESS WHAT?"
I'M INCURABLE.
WHAT?
AT LEAST AS SCIENCE AND TECHNOLOGY EXIST RIGHT NOW. ONE OF TWO ENORMOUS BLOWS TO MY EGO IN RECENT WEEKS. PUT A PIN IN THAT. WE'LL COME BACK TO IT.
LET'S TALK ABOUT LAST MONTH'S WAR AGAINST THE PHOENIX FORCE.
"EVERYONE ON EARTH WHO'S STRONGER THAN A GIRL SCOUT VERSUS OMNIPOTENT X-MEN GONE AMOK.
"I'M TOLD THE HULK WAS A VALUABLE ASSET IN THE FINAL BATTLE. GOT IN SOME GOOD BLOWS. DISTRACTED THE ENEMY SO A SMART MAN COULD ENGINEER A SOLUTION.
"DO YOU KNOW WHO THAT SMART MAN WAS?"

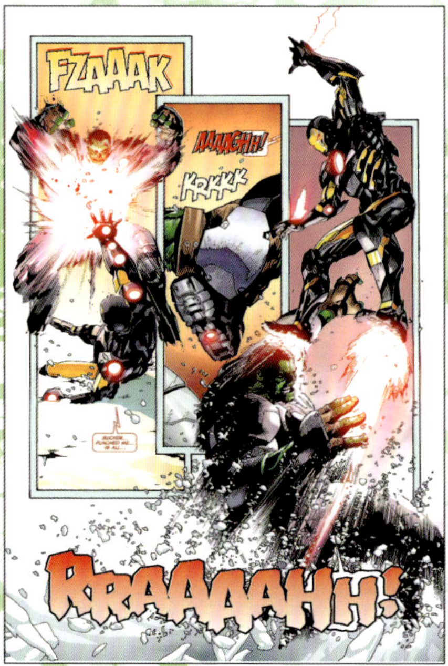
FZAAAK
AAAGHH!
KRKKK
RRAAAAAHH!

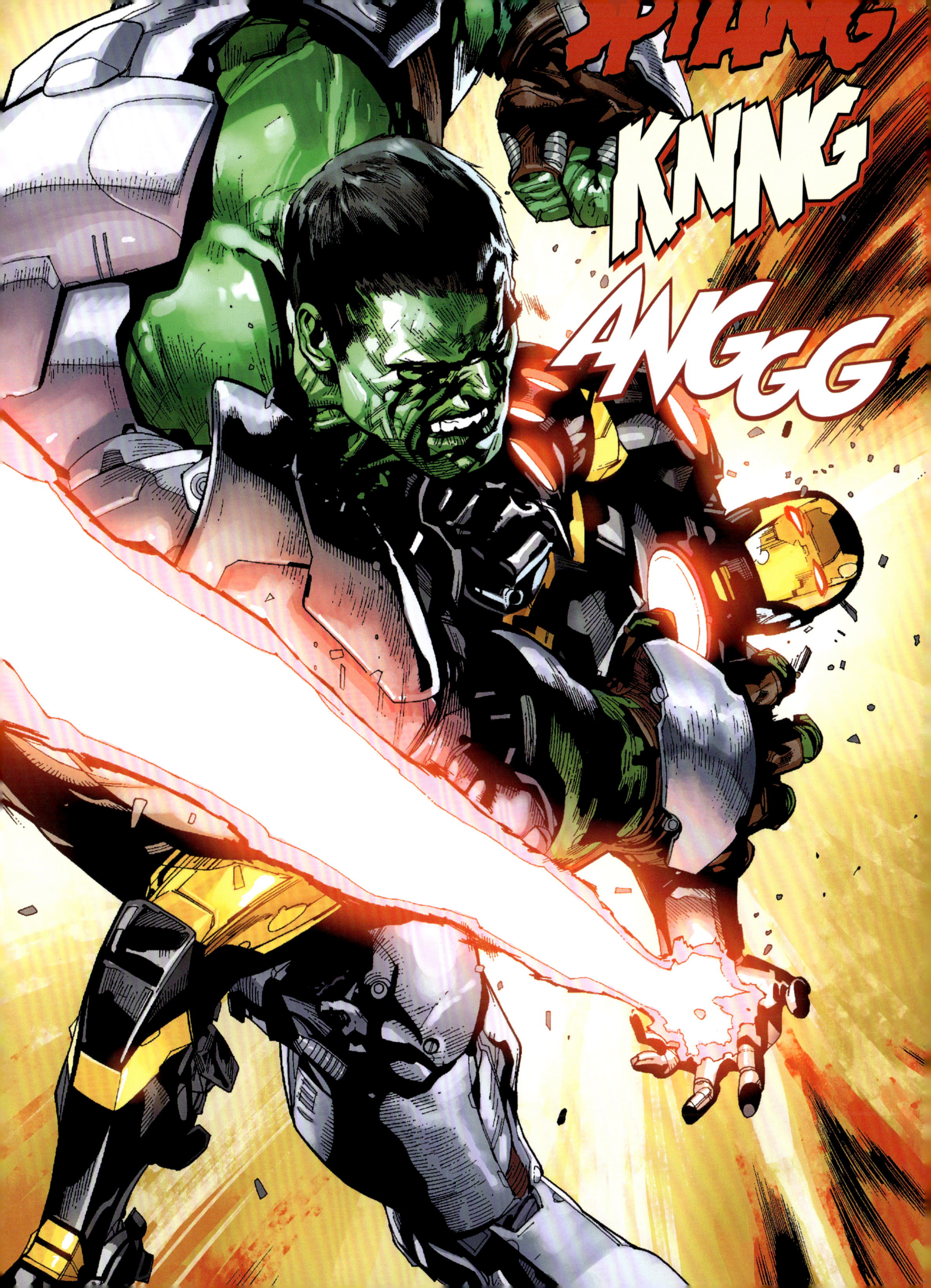
KNNG
ANGGG

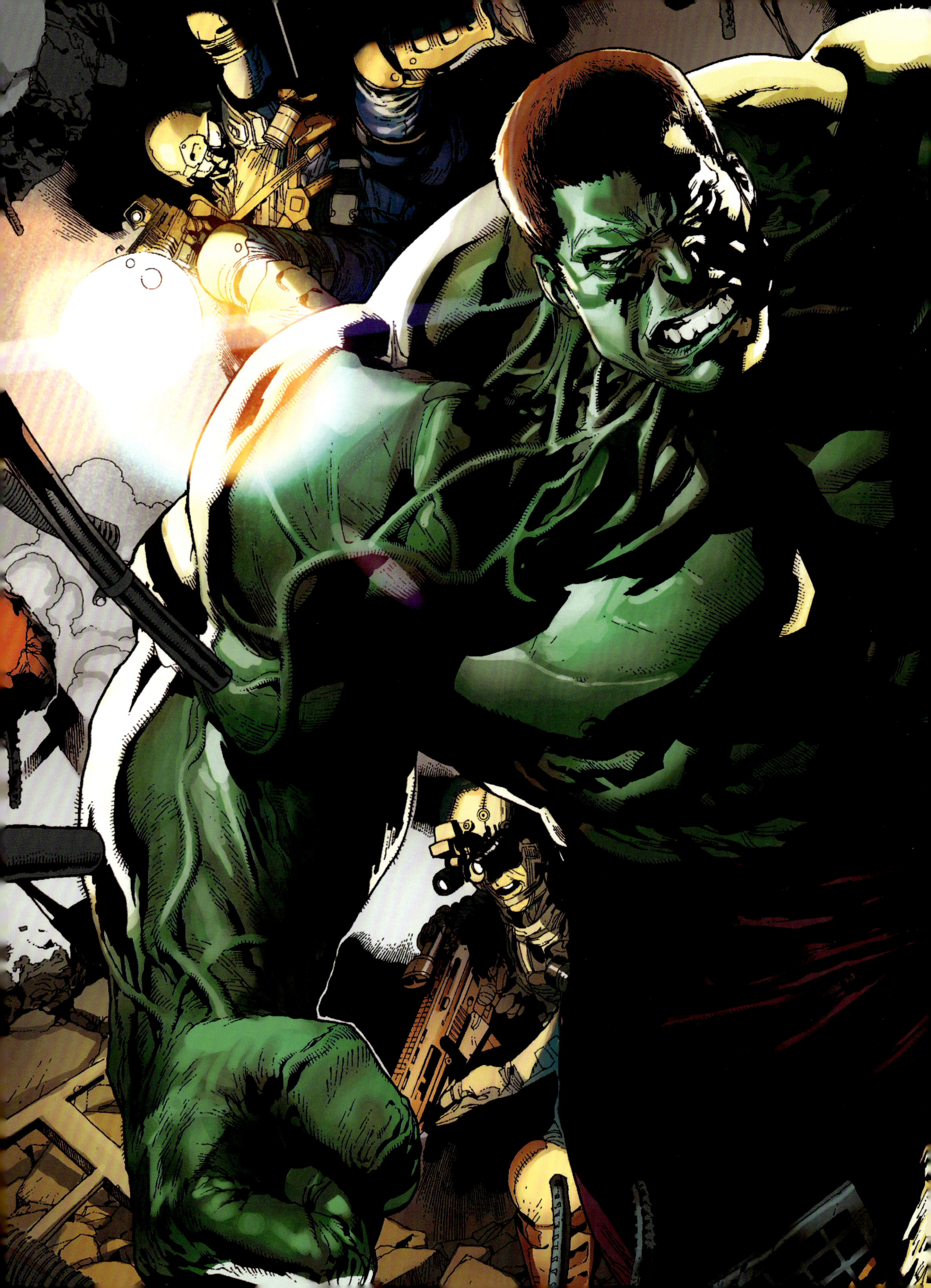

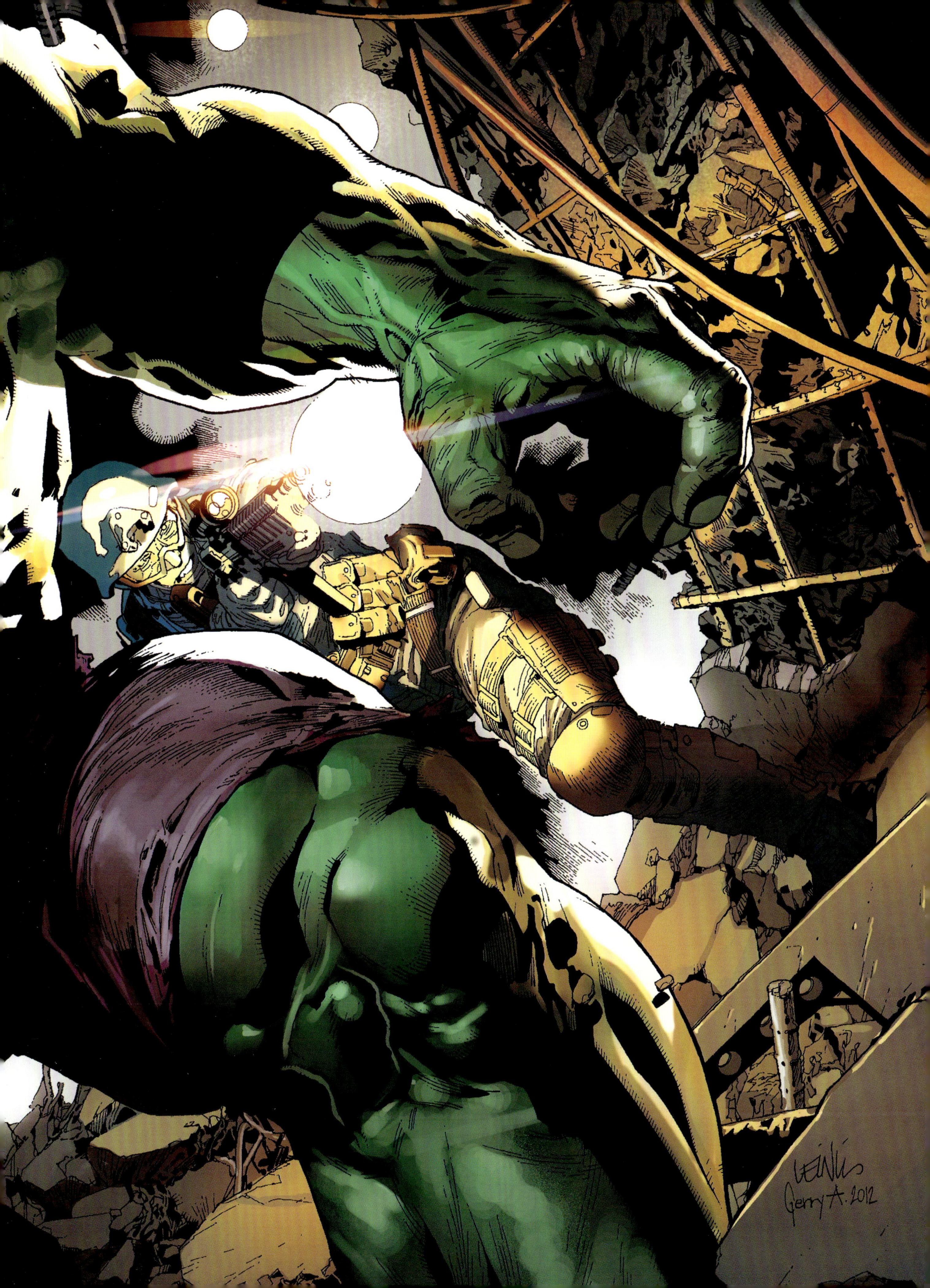
Gerry A. 2012

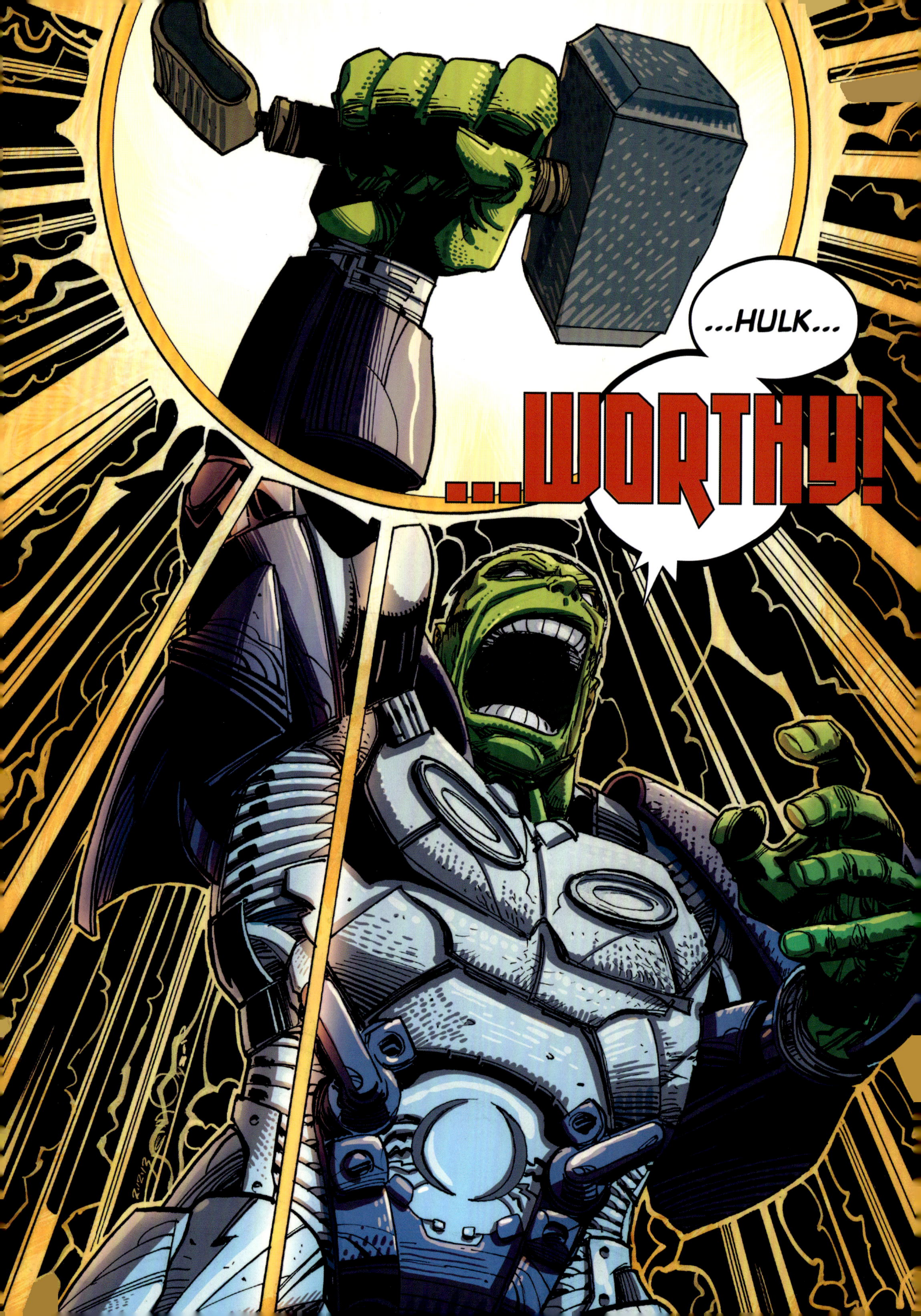
...HULK...
...WORTHY!

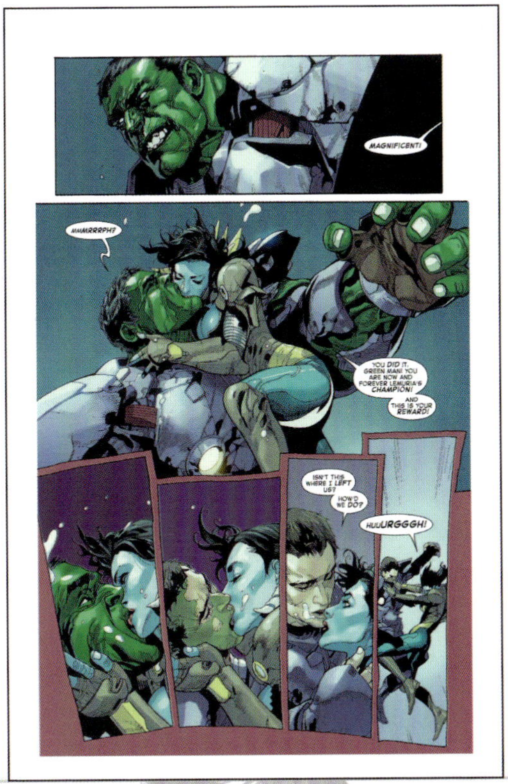
MAGNIFICENT!
MMMRRRPH?
YOU DID IT, GREEN MAN! YOU ARE NOW AND FOREVER LEMURIA'S CHAMPION!
AND THIS IS YOUR REWARD!
ISN'T THIS WHERE I LEFT US?
HOW'D WE DO?
HUUURGGGH!

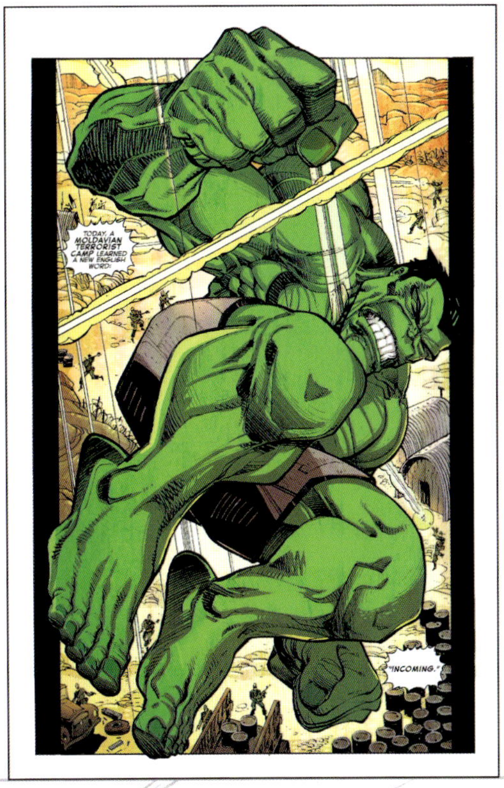
TODAY, A MOLDAVIAN TERRORIST CAMP LEARNED A NEW ENGLISH WORD:
"INCOMING."

mad, and there's an old saying: "You don't want to see me when you start to fiddle with my gamma fracking machine high up in the Himalayas." Wait—there's a shorter version: "You don't want to see me when I'm angry."

Banner gets mad and transforms into the Hulk, and he and Iron Man go at it. Maybe Bruce isn't monitoring his anger today. They are too busy fighting to realize that the fracking machine is overloading, and it explodes. Surviving the avalanche, they make their way to a lodge at the base of the mountain. Later, as they finish a meal and talk, the rivalry between Banner and Stark remains even after they fought it out as the Hulk and Iron Man. Each seems to be intimidated by the other, and neither will admit it. They are more similar than they think. But there are differences too: while Stark can simply remove his armor and revert from the super hero to the man, Banner can never leave the Hulk behind. And if his reaction to getting mad at Stark is to immediately change into the Hulk, how will Banner manage his new role at S.H.I.E.L.D.? Can he really keep the Hulk in check and become a weapon that can be used on command, or will his anger win out?

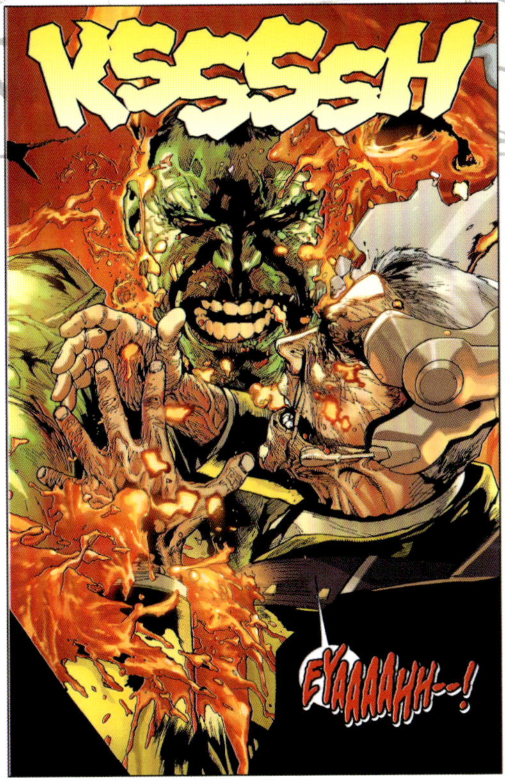
KSSSSH
EYAAAAHH--!

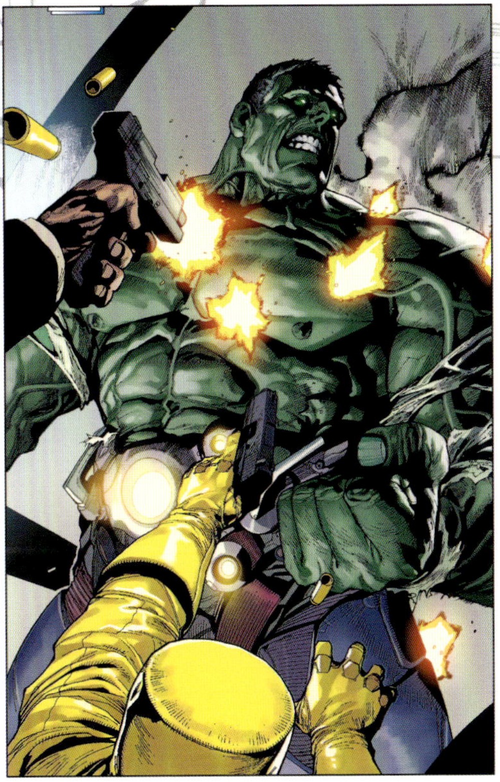

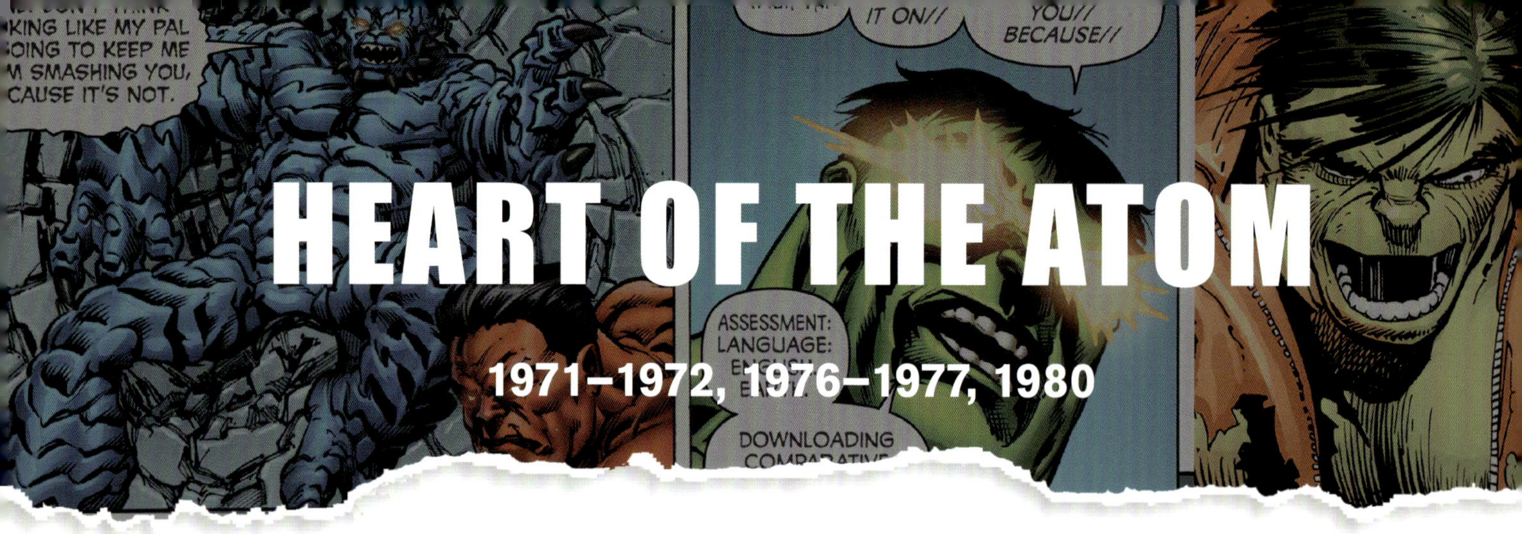
KING LIKE MY PAL
OING TO KEEP ME
M SMASHING YOU,
CAUSE IT'S NOT.
IT ON!!
YOU!!
BECAUSE!!
ASSESSMENT:
LANGUAGE:
DOWNLOADING

# HEART OF THE ATOM

## 1971–1972, 1976–1977, 1980

The Hulk lies unconscious, strapped to a table in a lab, and some kind of experiment is about to take place. Suddenly, the Avengers—Captain America, Iron Man, Thor, and others—burst into the lab to save the Hulk. The person who captured the Hulk is Psyklop, a semi-humanoid who has evolved from insects. But before the super heroes can release the Hulk, the machine above the table discharges and a ray rains down on him. The Hulk is transported to what looks like another galaxy, and eventually he finds himself on a different—and subatomic!—planet.

Suddenly, a giant boar attacks him, but it is no match for the Hulk, who quickly defeats it. The Hulk then makes his way to a type of citadel. More giant boars—called warthos—attack the Hulk, and as he fights off one after another, he hears the residents of the citadel celebrate his victories. The Hulk happily discovers that these people are green-skinned—just like he is. The aliens bring him into the city, where he is introduced to their leader, Princess Jarella of the planet K'ai. There is an instant attraction between them.

Jarella quickly asks one of her sorcerers Torla to use his magic to teach the Hulk their language. As he learns their language, Bruce Banner's mind wakes up in the Hulk's body. Instead of fighting Banner, the Hulk accepts having Banner in his head. He now has the Hulk's strength and Banner's brain.

In no time, the Hulk is set to marry Jarella, and it is quickly apparent that the Hulk will soon become king. Not everyone is happy with this outsider coming in and taking the role of king. Jarella's rival, Lord Visis, won't have it. He decrees that this stranger must die. He sends out his assassins to kill the Hulk, but they are no match for the green goliath. He not only defeats them, he gets them to reveal that it was Lord Visis behind the attempt on his life.

In the Great Hall of Assembly, the Hulk addresses the gathered group and tells them of the plot hatched by Lord Visis to kill him and Jarella. But before any action can be taken against the traitor Lord Visis, Psyklop appears from above and takes the Hulk back to Earth.

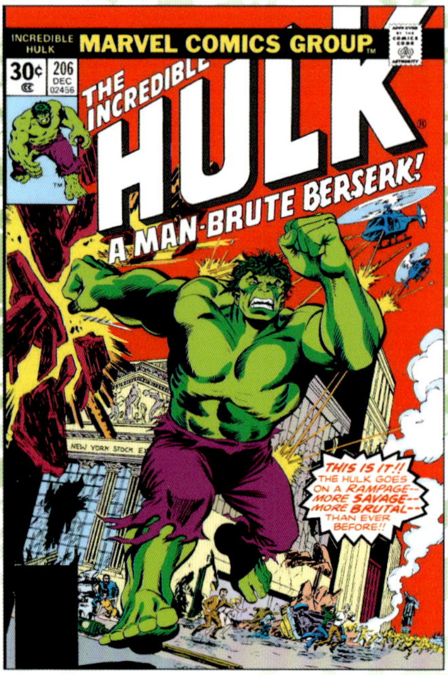
MARVEL COMICS GROUP
30¢ 206 DEC
THE INCREDIBLE HULK
A MAN-BRUTE BERSERK!
THIS IS IT!! THE HULK GOES ON A RAMPAGE-- MORE SAVAGE-- MORE BRUTAL-- THAN EVER BEFORE!!

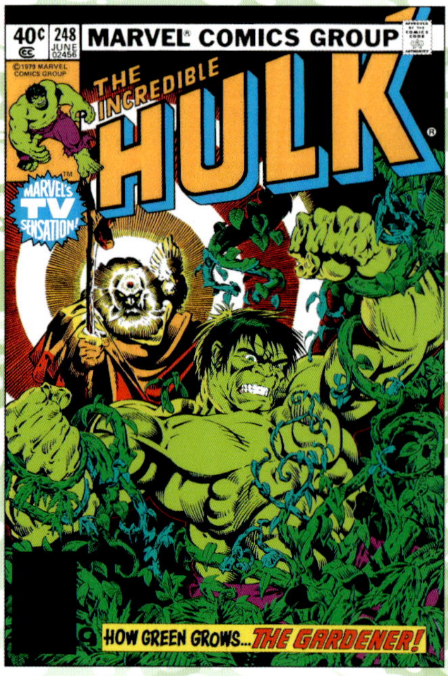
40¢ 248 JUNE
MARVEL COMICS GROUP
THE INCREDIBLE HULK
MARVEL'S TV SENSATION!
HOW GREEN GROWS... THE GARDENER!

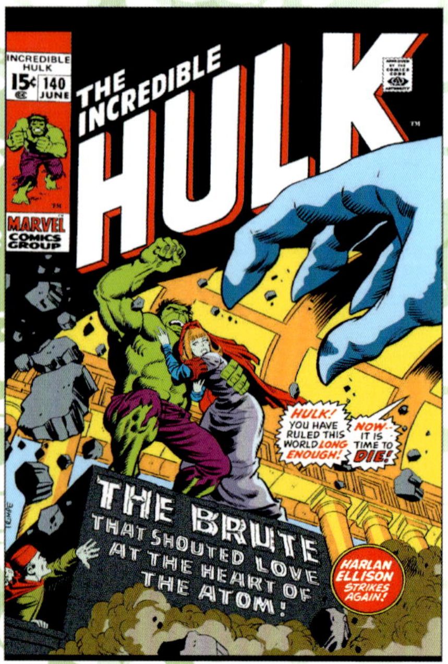
15¢ 140 JUNE
THE INCREDIBLE HULK
MARVEL COMICS GROUP
HULK! YOU HAVE RULED THIS WORLD LONG ENOUGH!
NOW-- IT IS TIME TO DIE!
THE BRUTE THAT SHOUTED LOVE AT THE HEART OF THE ATOM!
HARLAN ELLISON STRIKES AGAIN!

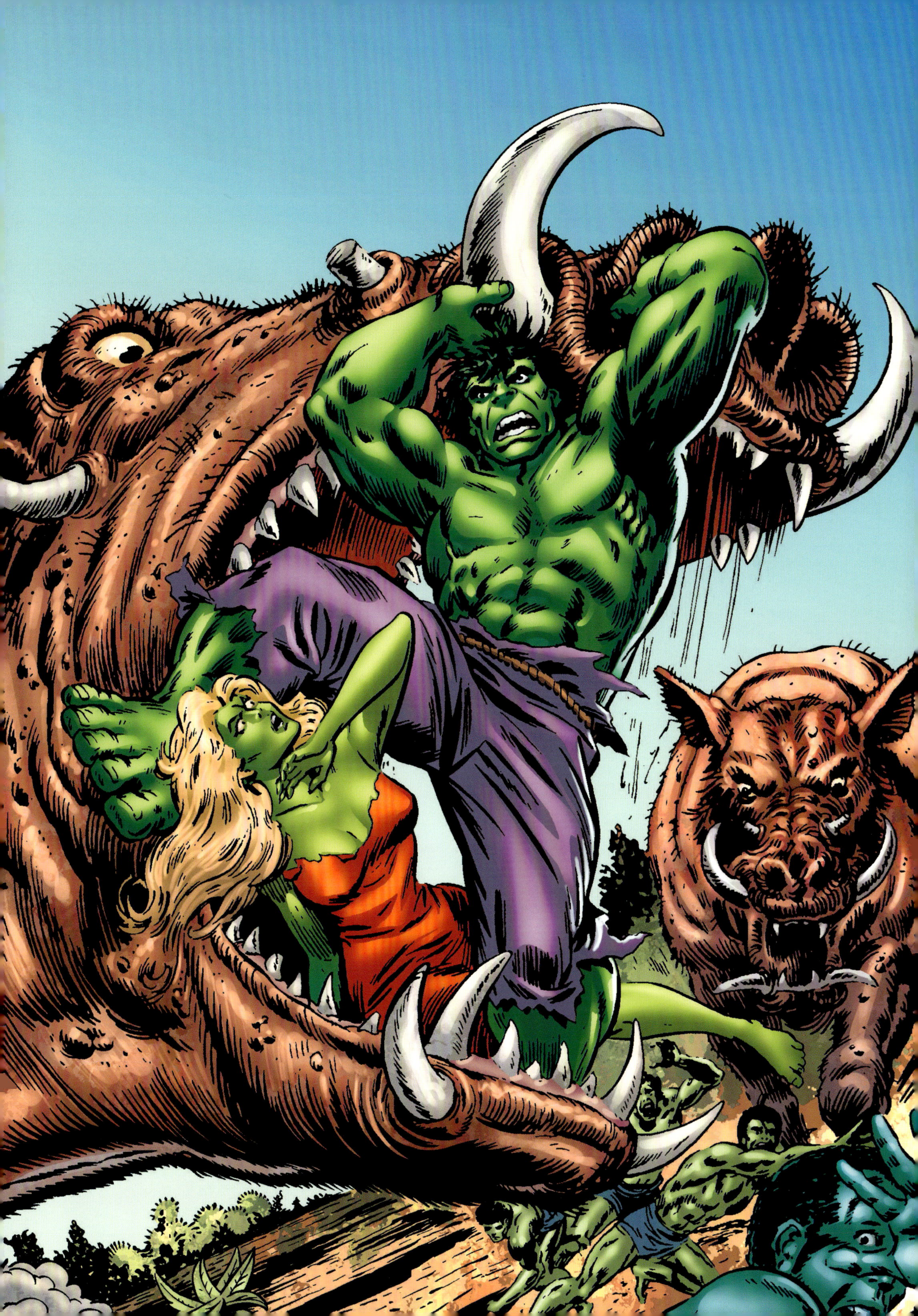

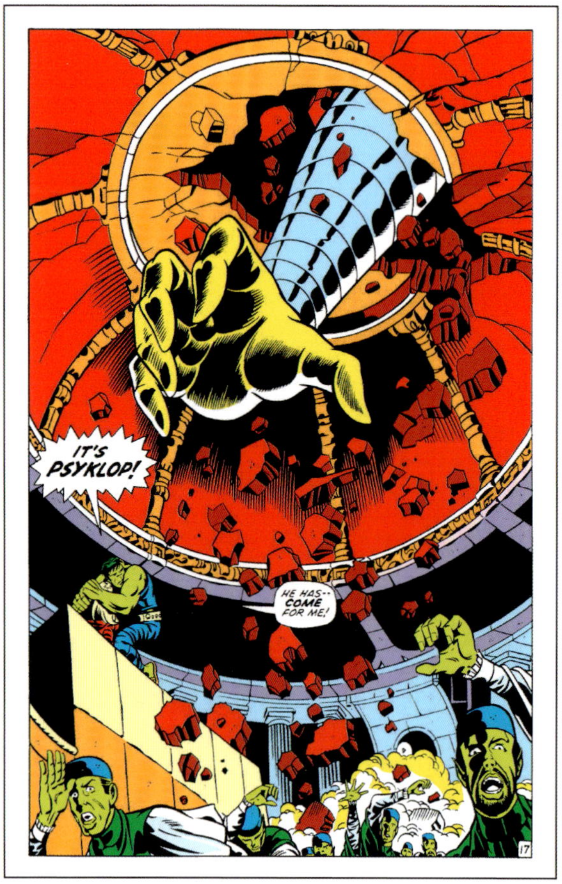
IT'S PSYKLOP!
HE HAS-- COME FOR ME!
17

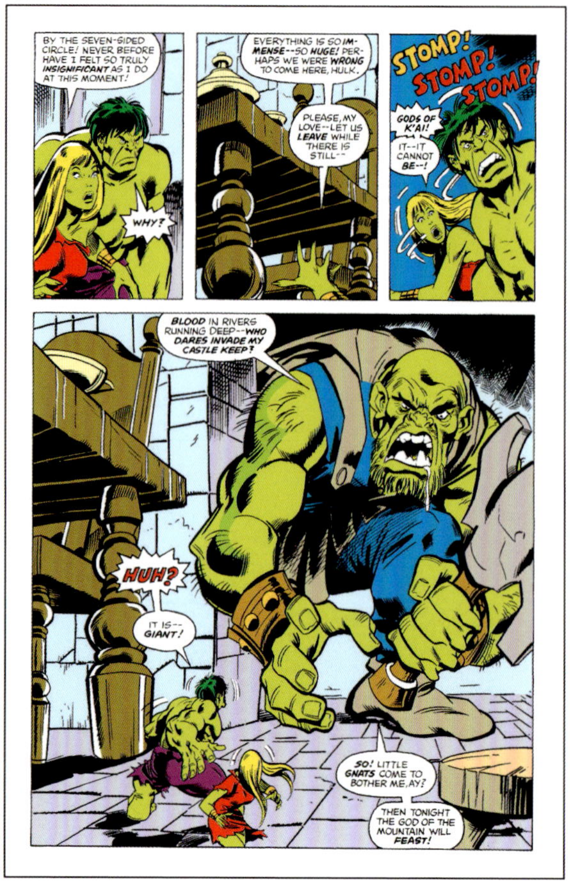
BY THE SEVEN-SIDED CIRCLE! NEVER BEFORE HAVE I FELT SO TRULY INSIGNIFICANT AS I DO AT THIS MOMENT!
WHY?
EVERYTHING IS SO IM-MENSE--SO HUGE! PER-HAPS WE WERE WRONG TO COME HERE, HULK.
PLEASE, MY LOVE--LET US LEAVE WHILE THERE IS STILL--
STOMP! STOMP! STOMP!
GODS OF K'AI!
IT--IT CANNOT BE--!
BLOOD IN RIVERS RUNNING DEEP--WHO DARES INVADE MY CASTLE KEEP?
HUH?
IT IS-- GIANT!
SO! LITTLE GNATS COME TO BOTHER ME, AY?
THEN TONIGHT THE GOD OF THE MOUNTAIN WILL FEAST!

With the Hulk back on Earth, Banner quickly disappears. The Hulk is angry that he was pulled away from his newfound love Jarella, and he fights and defeats Psyklop. With the Hulk back on Earth, Jarella must battle against Lord Visis on her own. After a fierce fight, Jarella goes to Torla and tells him that she needs to have the Hulk back. Can Torla find a way to return him to their world? The sorcerer tells her that he will try, but there might be consequences.

Back on Earth, General "Thunderbolt" Ross has tracked down and captured the Hulk. Ross brings in the famed physician Dr. Corbeau, who believes he can remove the Hulk from Banner. His plan is to use a satellite that beams a solar wave that will shower the Hulk in sheer solar energy. The solar wave works and the Hulk disappears, leaving behind only Banner.

Back on K'ai, Jarella is being subjected to a different sort of experiment. Her sorcerers have figured out a way to send her to Earth to reunite with Banner. After she arrives, what she doesn't know is that Lord Visis has followed her to Earth. In addition to the threat Visis poses, the sun has been acting up ever since the military used the sun's rays to rid Banner of the Hulk.

Additionally, an object from another dimension has ripped open the fabric of time and space. That object is Jarella. Will she have to go back to her world in order to save the Earth? Will the Hulk join her? Or will Lord Visis assassinate Princess Jarella and take over the planet K'ai?

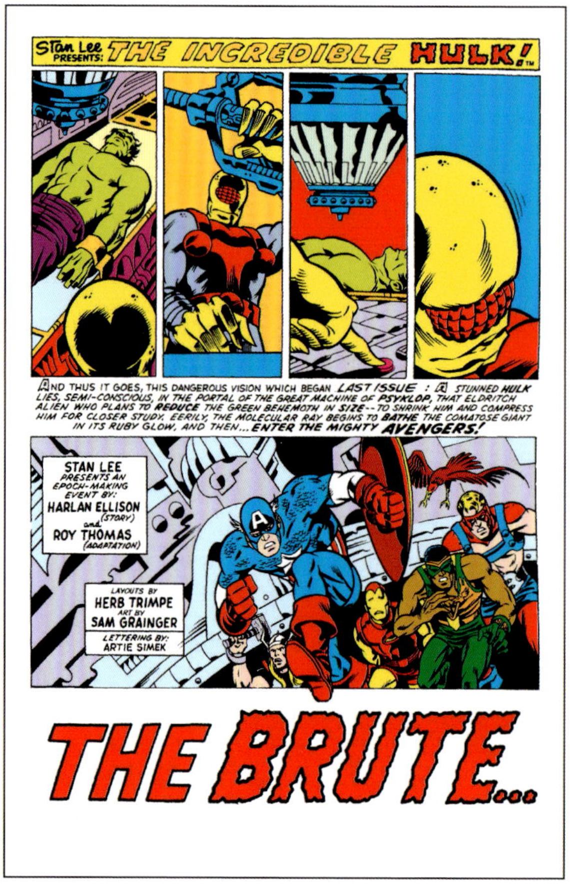
Stan Lee PRESENTS: THE INCREDIBLE HULK!
AND THUS IT GOES, THIS DANGEROUS VISION WHICH BEGAN LAST ISSUE : A STUNNED HULK LIES, SEMI-CONSCIOUS, IN THE PORTAL OF THE GREAT MACHINE OF PSYKLOP, THAT ELDRITCH ALIEN WHO PLANS TO REDUCE THE GREEN BEHEMOTH IN SIZE--TO SHRINK HIM AND COMPRESS HIM FOR CLOSER STUDY. EERILY, THE MOLECULAR RAY BEGINS TO BATHE THE COMATOSE GIANT IN ITS RUBY GLOW, AND THEN... ENTER THE MIGHTY AVENGERS!
STAN LEE PRESENTS AN EPOCH-MAKING EVENT BY: HARLAN ELLISON (STORY) and ROY THOMAS (ADAPTATION)
LAYOUTS BY HERB TRIMPE ART BY SAM GRAINGER
LETTERING BY: ARTIE SIMEK
THE BRUTE...

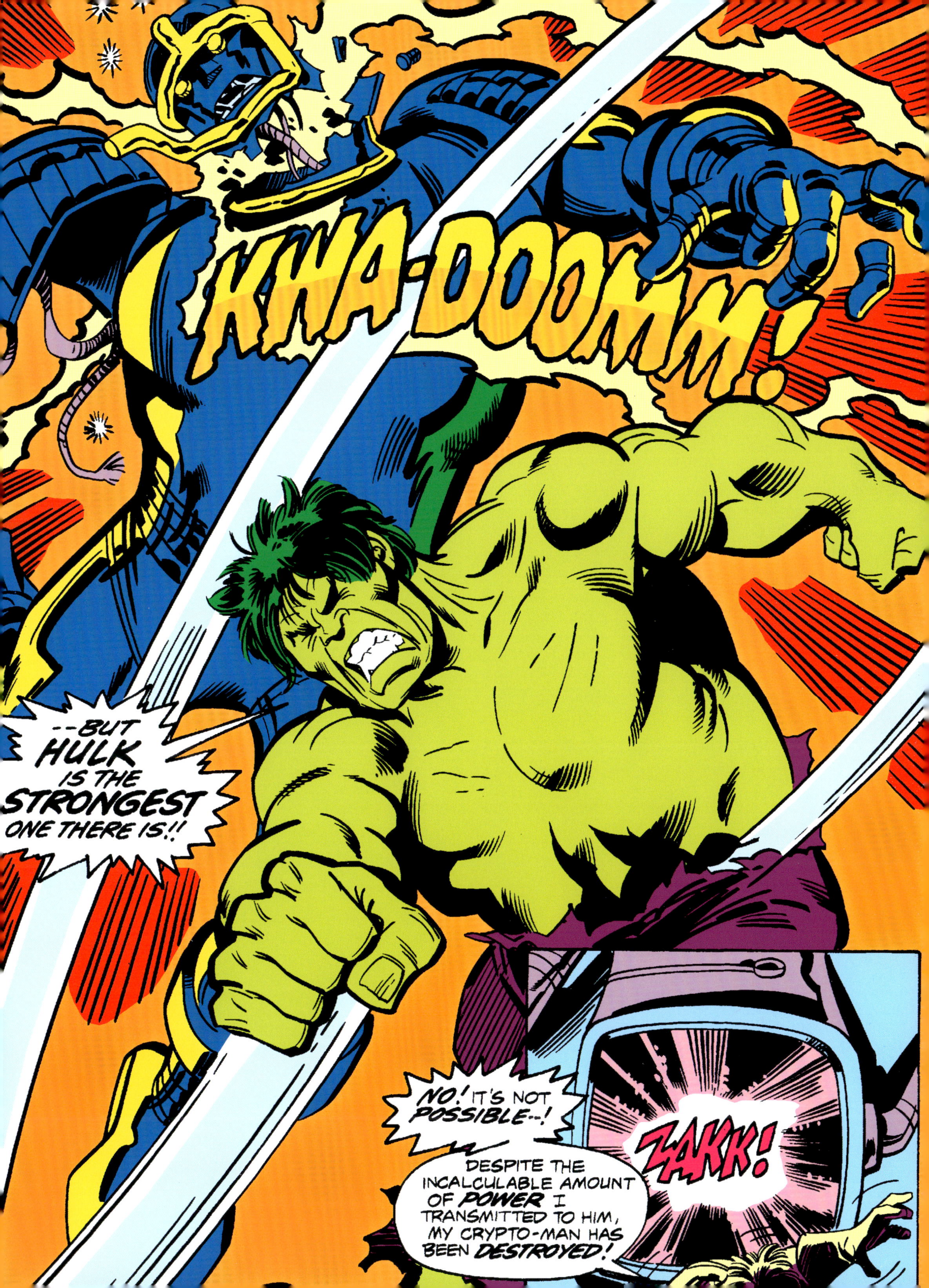
KHA-DOOMM!
--BUT HULK IS THE STRONGEST ONE THERE IS!!
NO! IT'S NOT POSSIBLE--!
DESPITE THE INCALCULABLE AMOUNT OF POWER I TRANSMITTED TO HIM, MY CRYPTO-MAN HAS BEEN DESTROYED!
ZAKK!

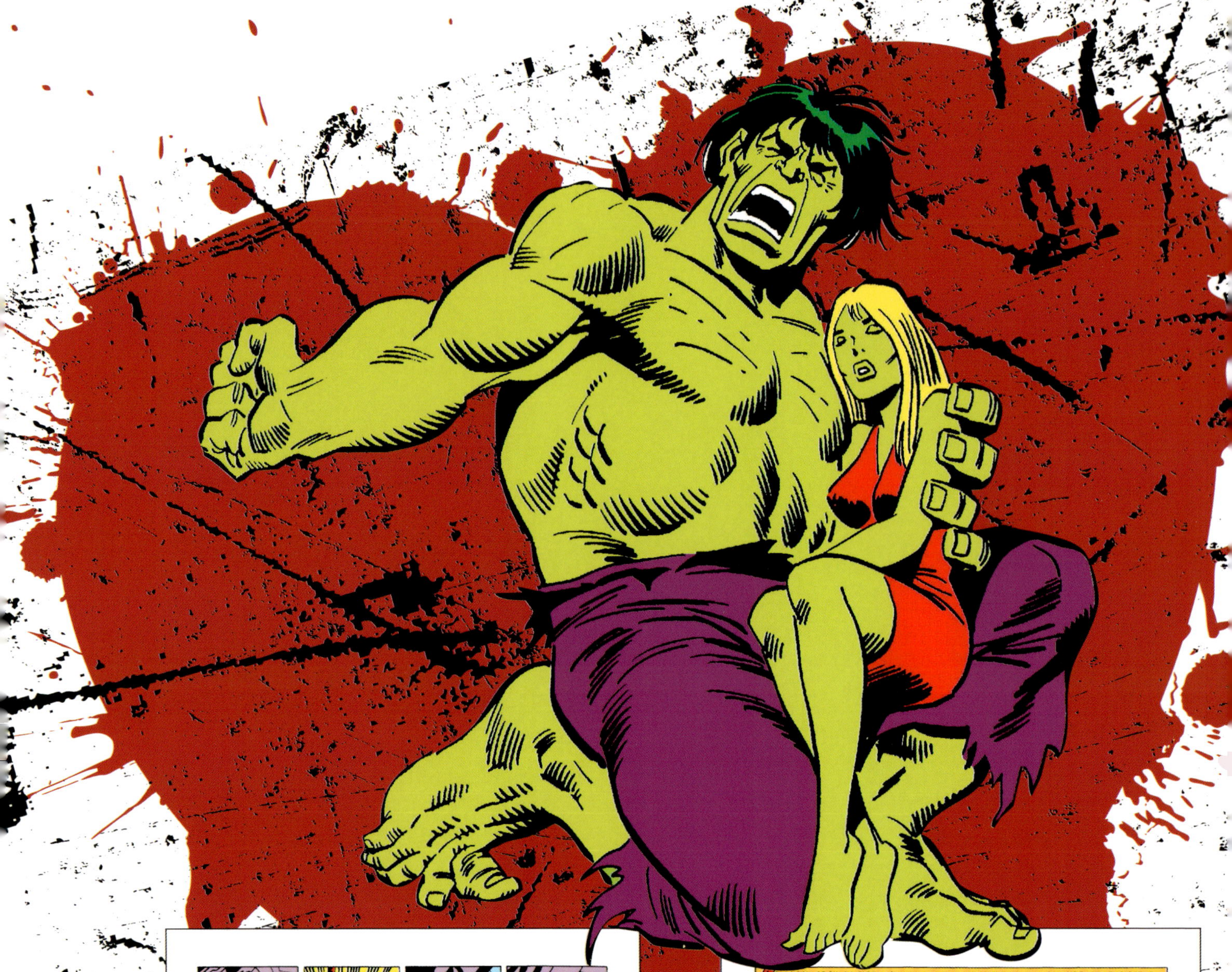

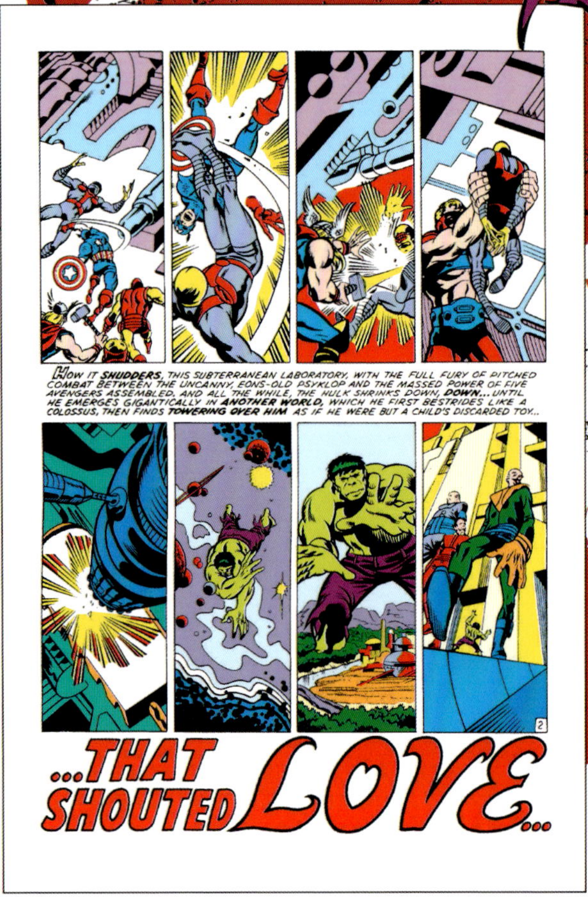

HOW IT SHUDDERS, THIS SUBTERRANEAN LABORATORY, WITH THE FULL FURY OF PITCHED COMBAT BETWEEN THE UNCANNY, EONS-OLD PSYKLOP AND THE MASSED POWER OF FIVE AVENGERS ASSEMBLED. AND ALL THE WHILE, THE HULK SHRINKS DOWN, DOWN... UNTIL HE EMERGES GIGANTICALLY IN ANOTHER WORLD, WHICH HE FIRST BESTRIDES LIKE A COLOSSUS, THEN FINDS TOWERING OVER HIM AS IF HE WERE BUT A CHILD'S DISCARDED TOY...
2
...THAT SHOUTED LOVE...


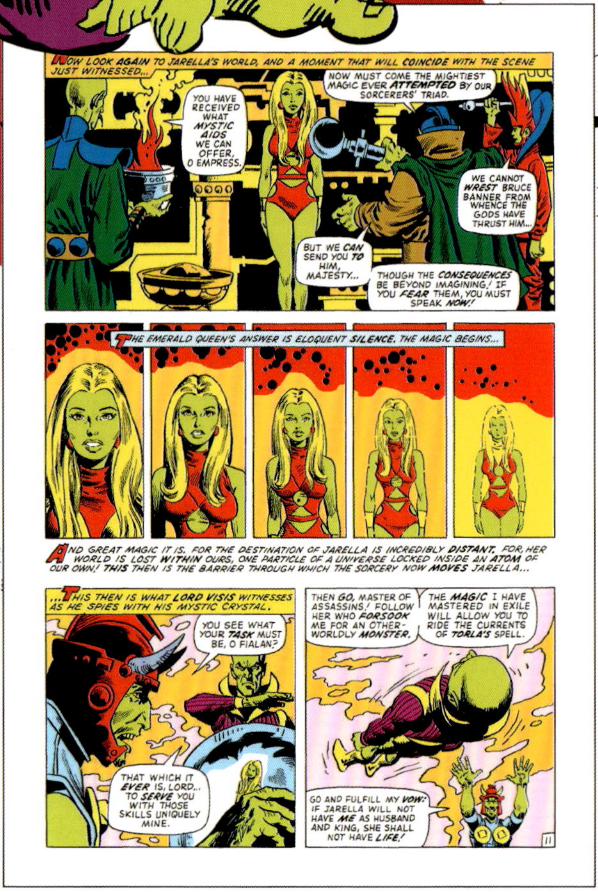

NOW LOOK AGAIN TO JARELLA'S WORLD, AND A MOMENT THAT WILL COINCIDE WITH THE SCENE JUST WITNESSED...
YOU HAVE RECEIVED WHAT MYSTIC AIDS WE CAN OFFER, O EMPRESS.
NOW MUST COME THE MIGHTIEST MAGIC EVER ATTEMPTED BY OUR SORCERERS' TRIAD.
WE CANNOT WREST BRUCE BANNER FROM WHENCE THE GODS HAVE THRUST HIM...
BUT WE CAN SEND YOU TO HIM, MAJESTY...
THOUGH THE CONSEQUENCES BE BEYOND IMAGINING! IF YOU FEAR THEM, YOU MUST SPEAK NOW!
THE EMERALD QUEEN'S ANSWER IS ELOQUENT SILENCE. THE MAGIC BEGINS...
AND GREAT MAGIC IT IS. FOR THE DESTINATION OF JARELLA IS INCREDIBLY DISTANT. FOR, HER WORLD IS LOST WITHIN OURS, ONE PARTICLE OF A UNIVERSE LOCKED INSIDE AN ATOM OF OUR OWN! THIS THEN IS THE BARRIER THROUGH WHICH THE SORCERY NOW MOVES JARELLA...
...THIS THEN IS WHAT LORD VISIS WITNESSES AS HE SPIES WITH HIS MYSTIC CRYSTAL.
YOU SEE WHAT YOUR TASK MUST BE, O FIALAN?
THAT WHICH IT EVER IS, LORD... TO SERVE YOU WITH THOSE SKILLS UNIQUELY MINE.
THEN GO, MASTER OF ASSASSINS! FOLLOW HER WHO FORSOOK ME FOR AN OTHER-WORLDLY MONSTER.
THE MAGIC I HAVE MASTERED IN EXILE WILL ALLOW YOU TO RIDE THE CURRENTS OF TORLA'S SPELL.
GO AND FULFILL MY VOW: IF JARELLA WILL NOT HAVE ME AS HUSBAND AND KING, SHE SHALL NOT HAVE LIFE!
11

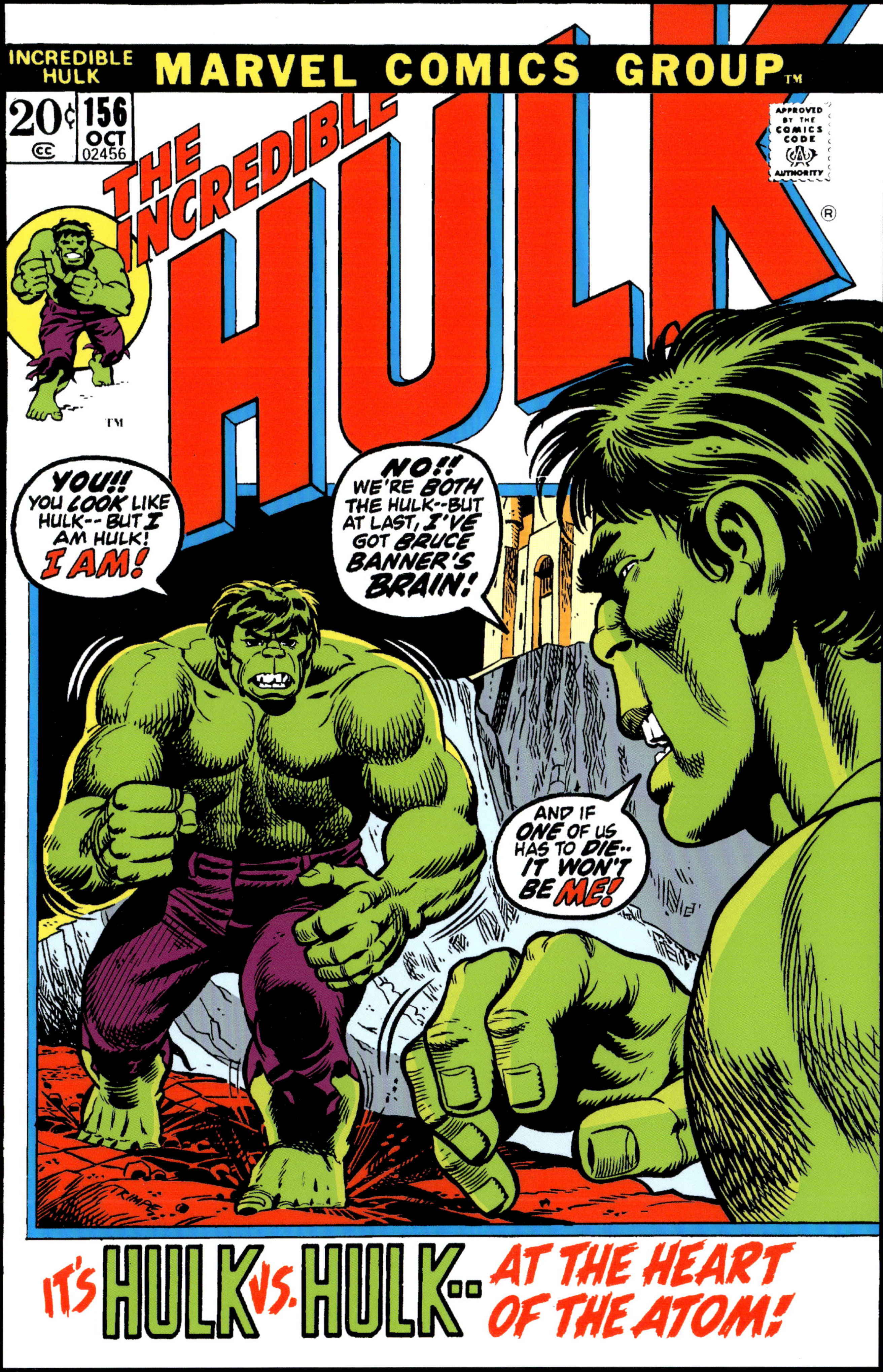
INCREDIBLE HULK
MARVEL COMICS GROUP
20¢ 156 OCT 02456
THE INCREDIBLE HULK
YOU!! YOU LOOK LIKE HULK-- BUT I AM HULK! I AM!
NO!! WE'RE BOTH THE HULK--BUT AT LAST, I'VE GOT BRUCE BANNER'S BRAIN!
AND IF ONE OF US HAS TO DIE.. IT WON'T BE ME!
IT'S HULK VS. HULK-- AT THE HEART OF THE ATOM!

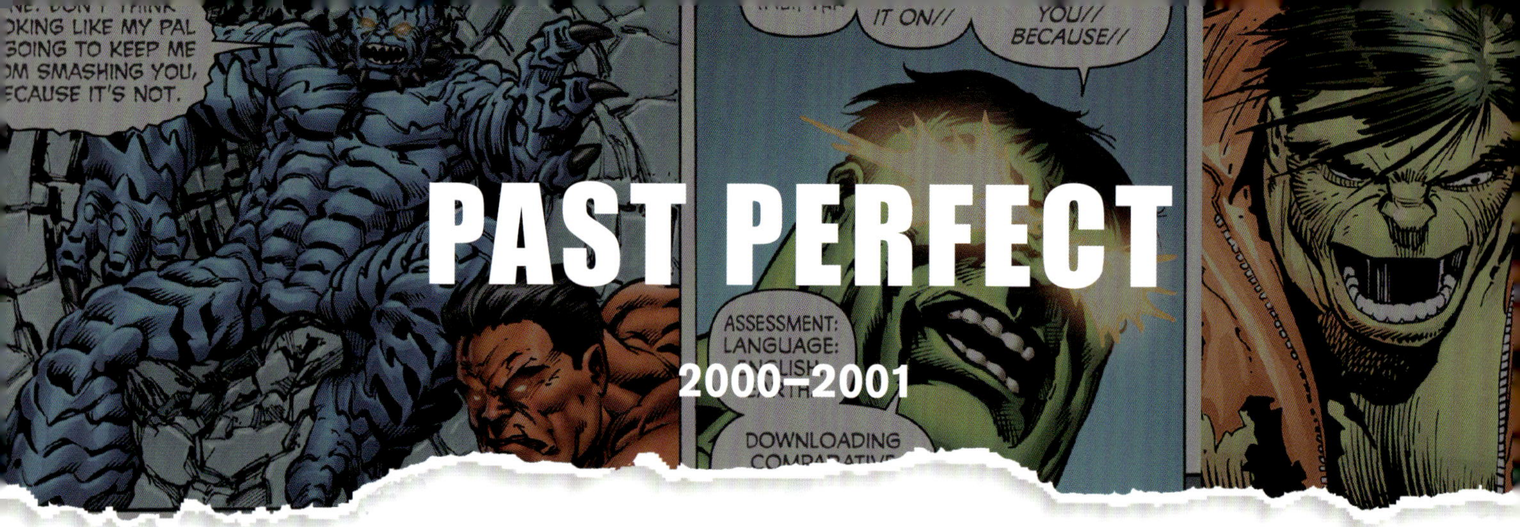
IT ON//
YOU// BECAUSE//
ASSESSMENT: LANGUAGE:
DOWNLOADING

# PAST PERFECT

## 2000–2001

Bruce Banner is in therapy. He is trying to learn how to cope with the loss of his beloved wife, Betty. After growing up with an abusive father, he never expected to find love. He never thought that Betty could go for someone like him, a nerdy scientist. And when he became the Hulk, well, it didn't help the situation. But Betty still loved Bruce. However, Betty's father did not love Bruce—and he hated the Hulk. Betty's father, General Thaddeus "Thunderbolt" Ross, has been trying to get rid of the Hulk ever since the green creature emerged out of that desert. Ross thinks Banner is responsible for the death of his daughter. He believes that Betty died from being around Banner and the Hulk too long. Her close contact exposed her to life-threatening levels of gamma radiation.

In fact, someone gave her a transfusion of gamma-irradiated blood, and it killed her. General Ross thought it was the Hulk, but it was the Abomination. Emil Blonsky was transformed into the Abomination in a program run by General Ross using gamma rays—the same method that created the Hulk. Ross wanted someone who rivaled the Hulk in strength and whom he could control. It hasn't quite worked out that way—no one controls the Abomination.

The reason the Abomination wanted Betty dead is because he believed that the Hulk was responsible for his own wife Nadia leaving him. Nadia believed her husband to be dead when he became the Abomination. But when she found out what Emil had become, she both loved and hated the man she once called her husband. If the Hulk had never existed, Blonsky never would have agreed to be exposed to the same gamma rays that turned Banner into the Hulk. So, if Blonsky can't have his wife, Banner can't have his wife Betty either.

The Abomination now wears a head-to-toe cloak to conceal his identity. He has been hiding out in New Hampshire, teaching a creative writing course at a library. But he knows someone will come for him. He tells his class that for their safety he can no longer teach them and that he needs to move on.

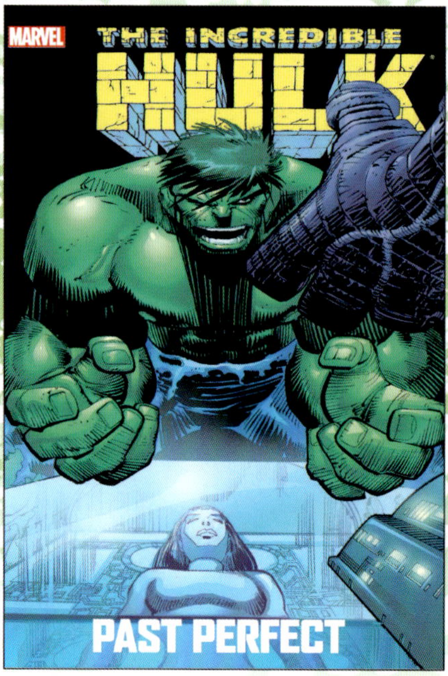
MARVEL
THE INCREDIBLE
HULK
PAST PERFECT

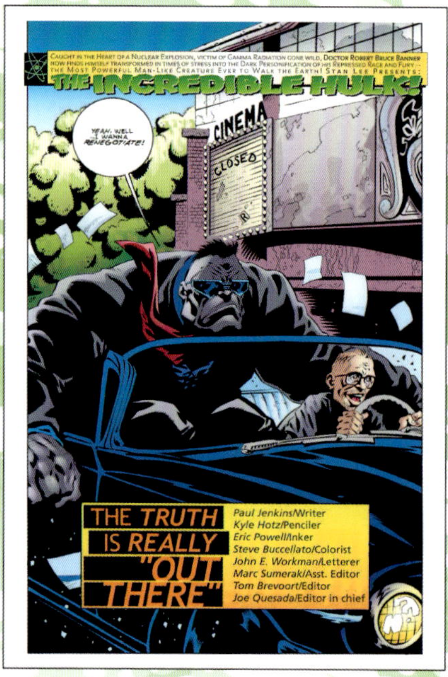
CAUGHT IN THE HEART OF A NUCLEAR EXPLOSION, VICTIM OF GAMMA RADIATION GONE WILD, DOCTOR ROBERT BRUCE BANNER NOW FINDS HIMSELF TRANSFORMED IN TIMES OF STRESS INTO THE DARK PERSONIFICATION OF HIS REPRESSED RAGE AND FURY — THE MOST POWERFUL MAN-LIKE CREATURE EVER TO WALK THE EARTH! STAN LEE PRESENTS:
THE INCREDIBLE HULK!
YEAH, WELL ...I WANNA RENEGOTIATE!
CINEMA
CLOSED
THE TRUTH IS REALLY "OUT THERE"
Paul Jenkins/Writer
Kyle Hotz/Penciler
Eric Powell/Inker
Steve Buccellato/Colorist
John E. Workman/Letterer
Marc Sumerak/Asst. Editor
Tom Brevoort/Editor
Joe Quesada/Editor in chief

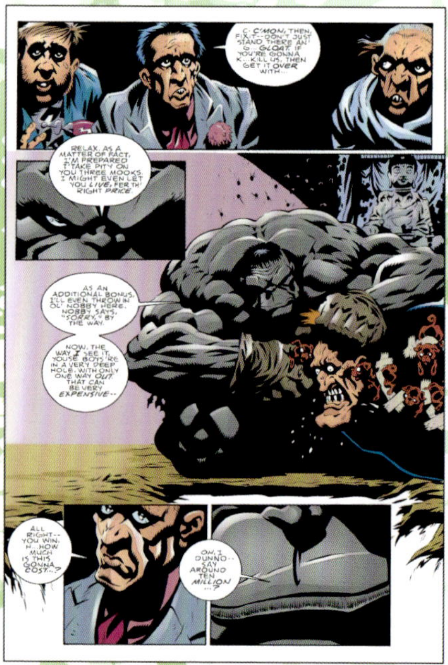
C-C'MON, THEN, FIX IT--DON'T JUST STAND THERE AN' G...GLOAT. IF YOU'RE GONNA K...KILL US, THEN GET IT OVER WITH...
RELAX. AS A MATTER OF FACT, I'M PREPARED T'TAKE PITY ON YOU THREE MOOKS. I MIGHT EVEN LET YOU LIVE, FER TH' RIGHT PRICE.
AS AN ADDITIONAL BONUS, I'LL EVEN THROW IN OL' NOBBY HERE. NOBBY SAYS, "SORRY," BY THE WAY.
NOW, THE WAY I SEE IT, YOUSE BOYS'RE IN A VERY DEEP HOLE. WITH ONLY ONE WAY OUT. THAT CAN BE VERY EXPENSIVE--
ALL RIGHT-- YOU WIN. H...HOW MUCH IS THIS GONNA COST...?
OH, I DUNNO-- SAY AROUND TEN MILLION ...?

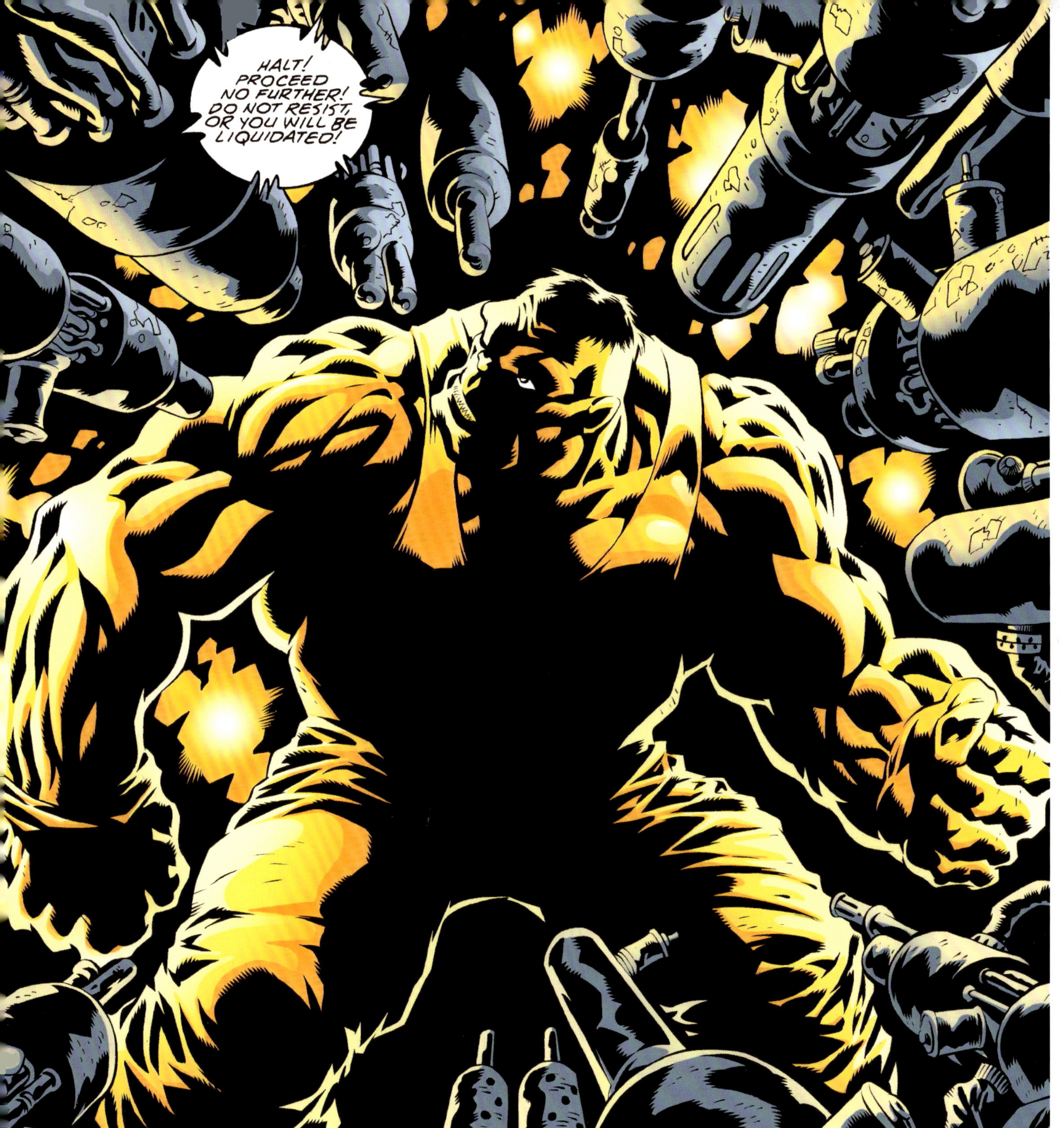
HALT! PROCEED NO FURTHER! DO NOT RESIST, OR YOU WILL BE LIQUIDATED!

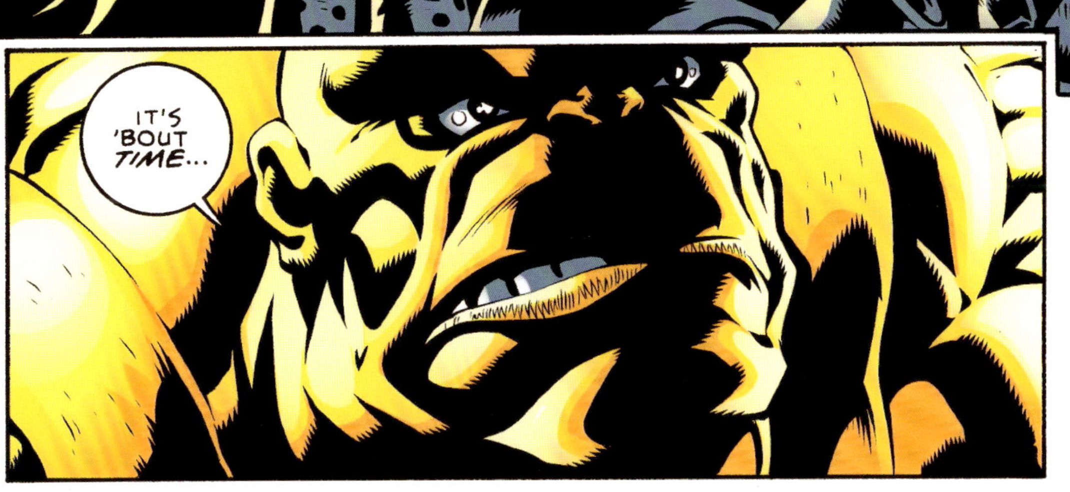
IT'S 'BOUT *TIME*...

YOU MUST TRY TO PUT THESE THINGS OUT OF YOUR MIND, BRUCE.
HULK WILL...
...HULK WILL...

OMIGOD...
...WHAT AM I DOING?

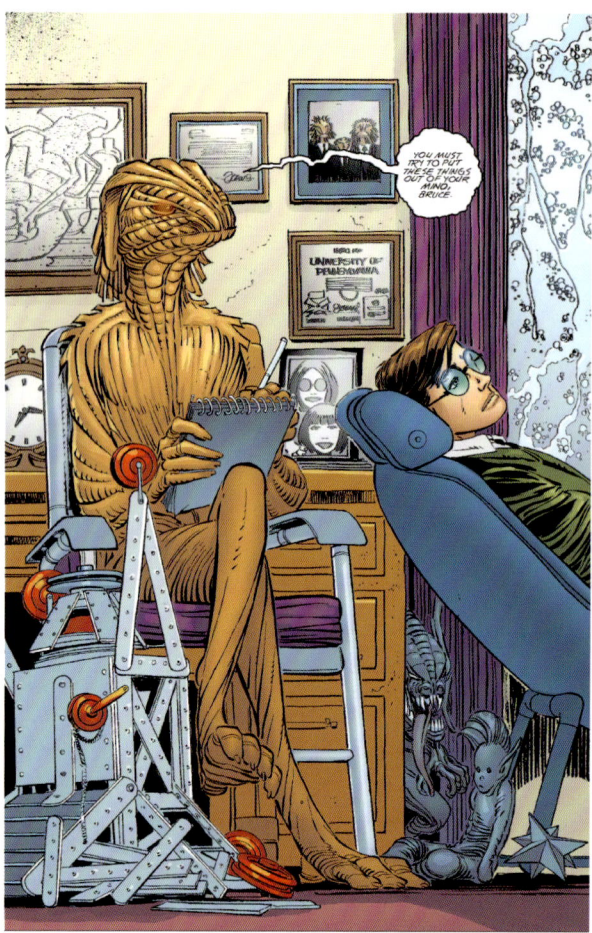

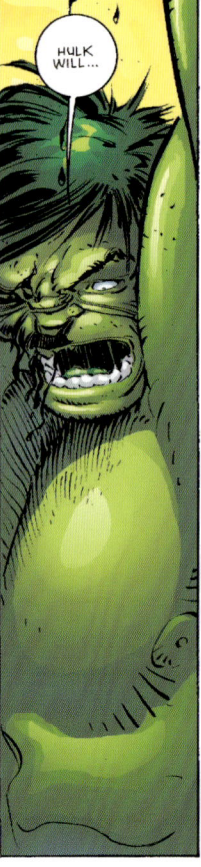

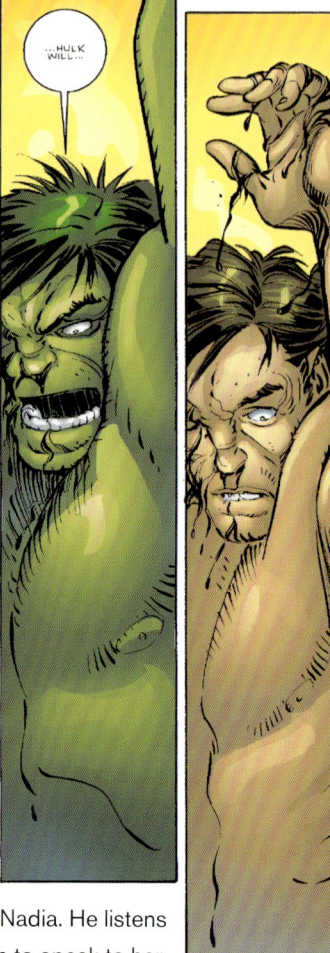

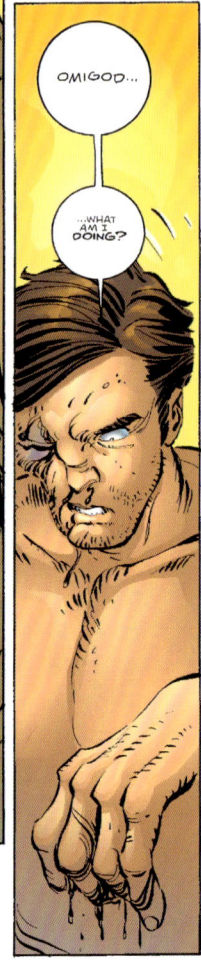

The Abomination stands in the rain at a phone booth and calls his former wife Nadia. He listens to her voice, and, for all the power he possesses, he doesn't have the strength to speak to her. Banner, too, is outside in the cold. He sits outside of Doc Samson's house, watching Samson and his girl Angela sitting on the couch together, Banner's heart aching for Betty.

General Ross suddenly appears. He tells Banner that he's not there to kill him. He confesses that blaming him for Betty's death was wrong. He suggests that they work together to bring the real killer to justice. But Banner isn't interested. He claims to have put it all behind him. Ross tells him that there is something he needs to see.

Ross takes Banner to a lab and there, lying in a stasis tube, is Betty. General Ross put her there while he searched for a way to bring her back to life. The sight of Betty is more than Banner can bear. He breaks down and cries, and then he gets angry. This is one time the General wants to see him angry. Banner transforms into a raging Hulk and sets out to bring the Abomination to justice.

General Ross just watches him go. He mutters under his breath, "Go gettim, killer."

Banner had finally put Betty to rest, but now . . . now there is a chance. A chance for her to return to him, as well as a chance to take vengeance on the one who killed her.

Will Betty come back to life? As for the Abomination, in the end, is he just another damaged soul, angry and vengeful, and blaming others for his choices?

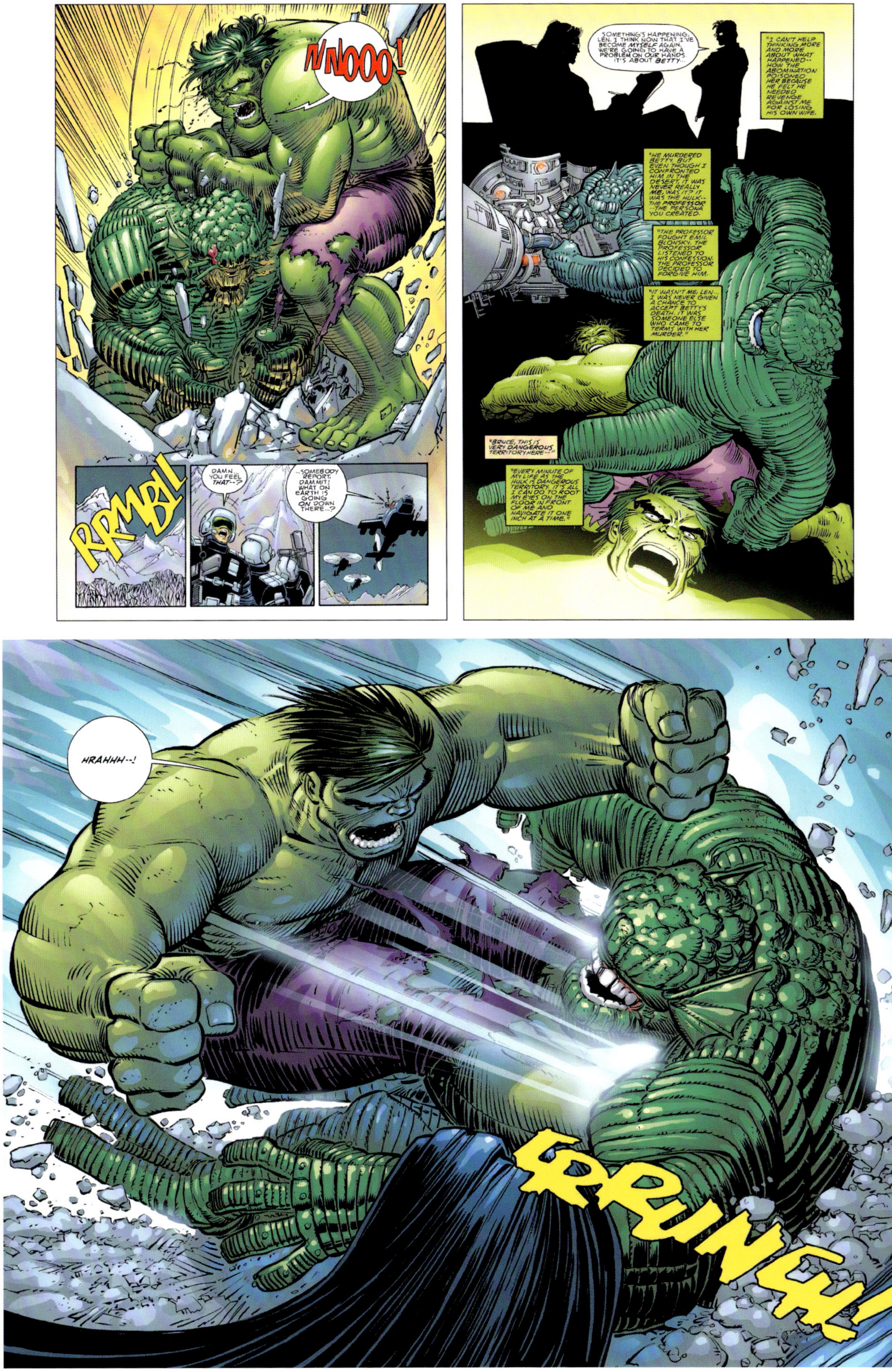
NNOOO!
RRMBL!
DAMN... YOU FEEL THAT--?
...SOMEBODY REPORT, DAMMIT! WHAT ON EARTH IS GOING ON DOWN THERE...?
SOMETHING'S HAPPENING, LEN. I THINK NOW THAT I'VE BECOME MYSELF AGAIN, WE'RE GOING TO HAVE A PROBLEM ON OUR HANDS. IT'S ABOUT BETTY...
"I CAN'T HELP THINKING MORE AND MORE ABOUT WHAT HAPPENED-- HOW THE ABOMINATION POISONED HER BECAUSE HE FELT HE NEEDED REVENGE AGAINST ME FOR LOSING HIS OWN WIFE.
"HE MURDERED BETTY. BUT EVEN THOUGH I CONFRONTED HIM IN THE DESERT, IT WAS NEVER REALLY ME, WAS IT? IT WAS THE HULK-- THE PROFESSOR --THE PERSONA YOU CREATED.
"THE PROFESSOR FOUGHT EMIL BLONSKY. THE PROFESSOR LISTENED TO HIS CONFESSION. THE PROFESSOR DECIDED TO FORGIVE HIM.
"IT WASN'T ME, LEN... I WAS NEVER GIVEN A CHANCE TO ACCEPT BETTY'S DEATH. IT WAS SOMEONE ELSE WHO CAME TO TERMS WITH HER MURDER."
"BRUCE, THIS IS VERY DANGEROUS TERRITORY HERE--"
"EVERY MINUTE OF MY LIFE AS THE HULK IS DANGEROUS TERRITORY. IT'S ALL I CAN DO TO ROOT MY EYES ON THE FLOOR IN FRONT OF ME AND NAVIGATE IT ONE INCH AT A TIME."
HRAHHH--!
GRUNCH!

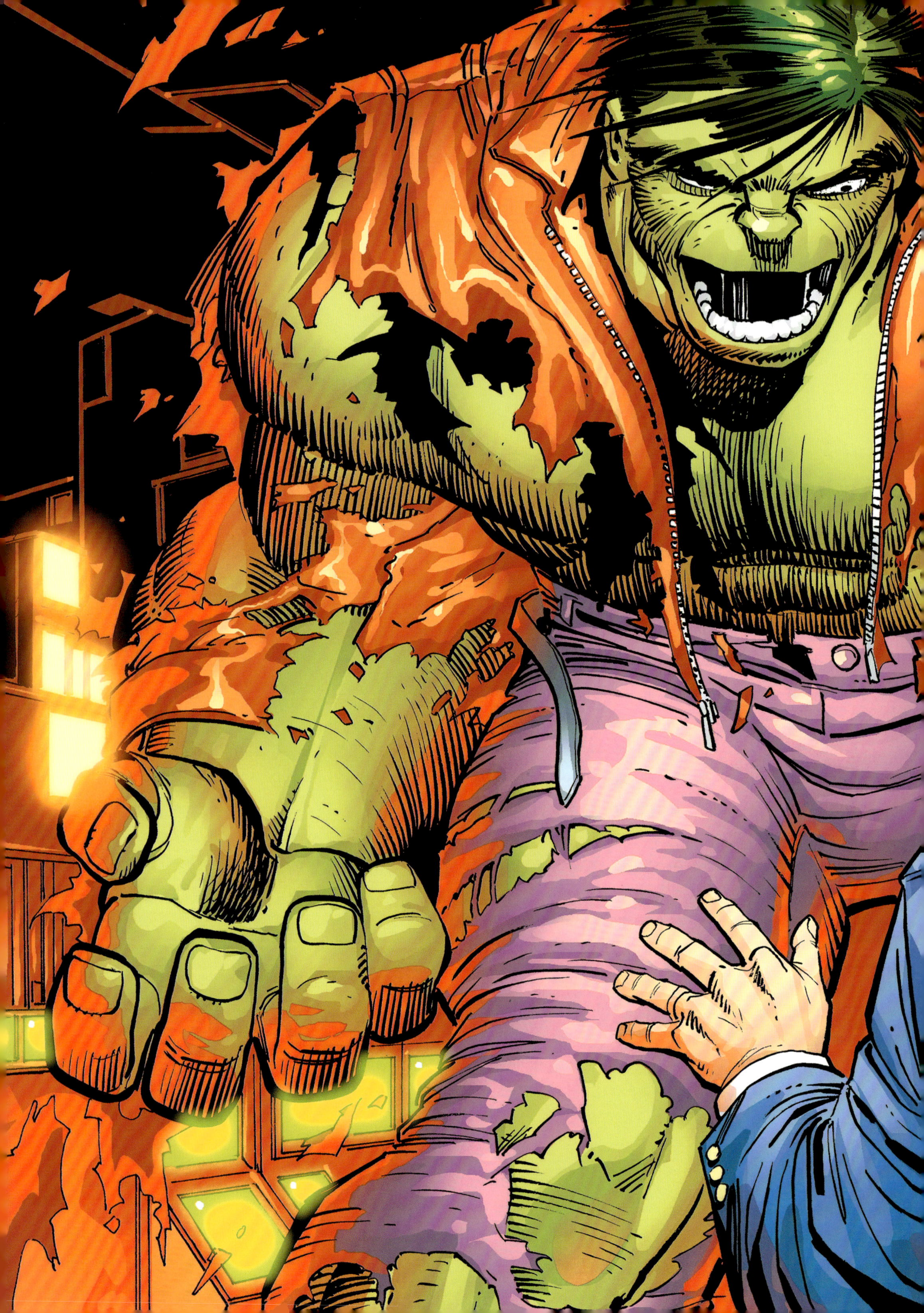

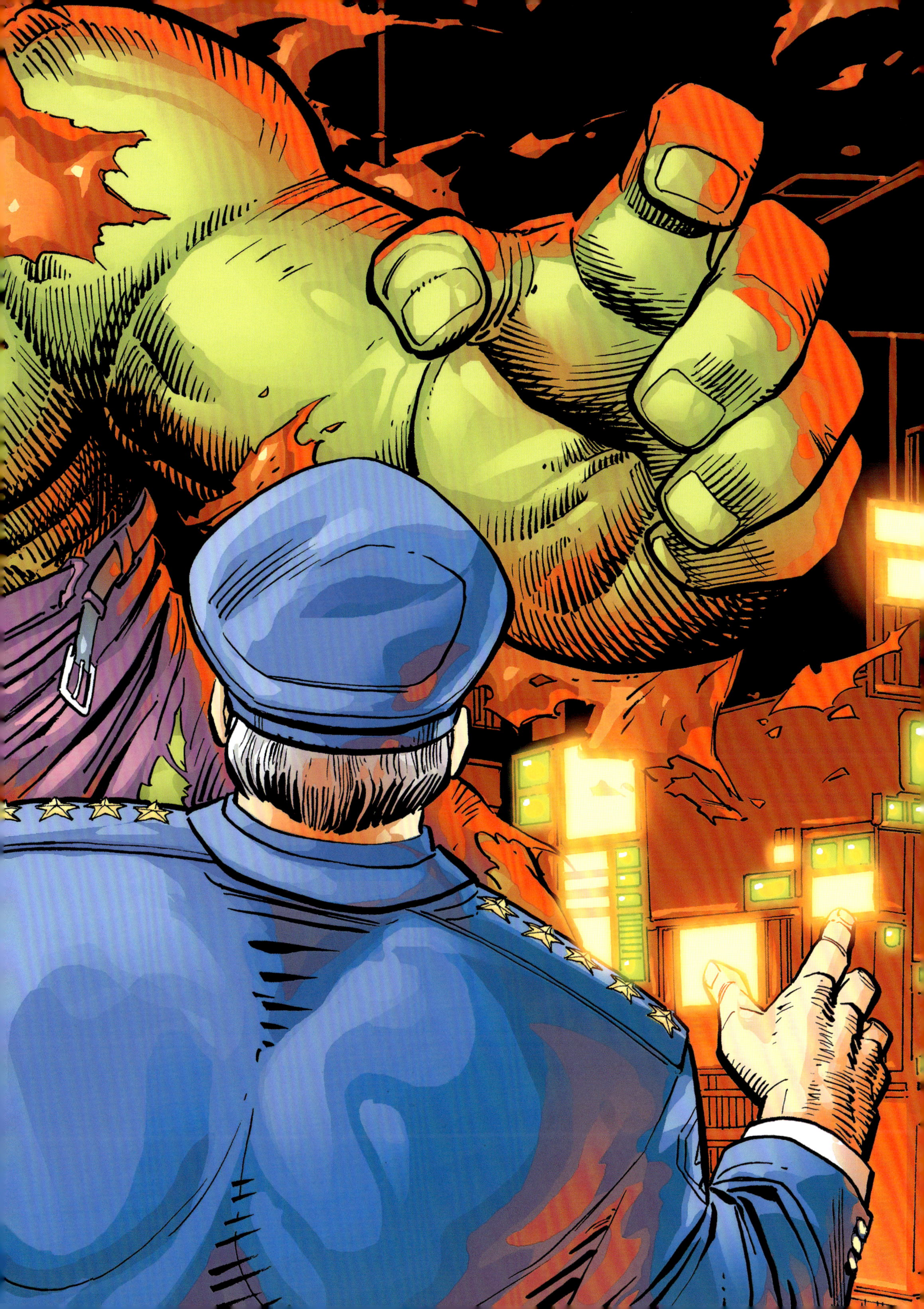

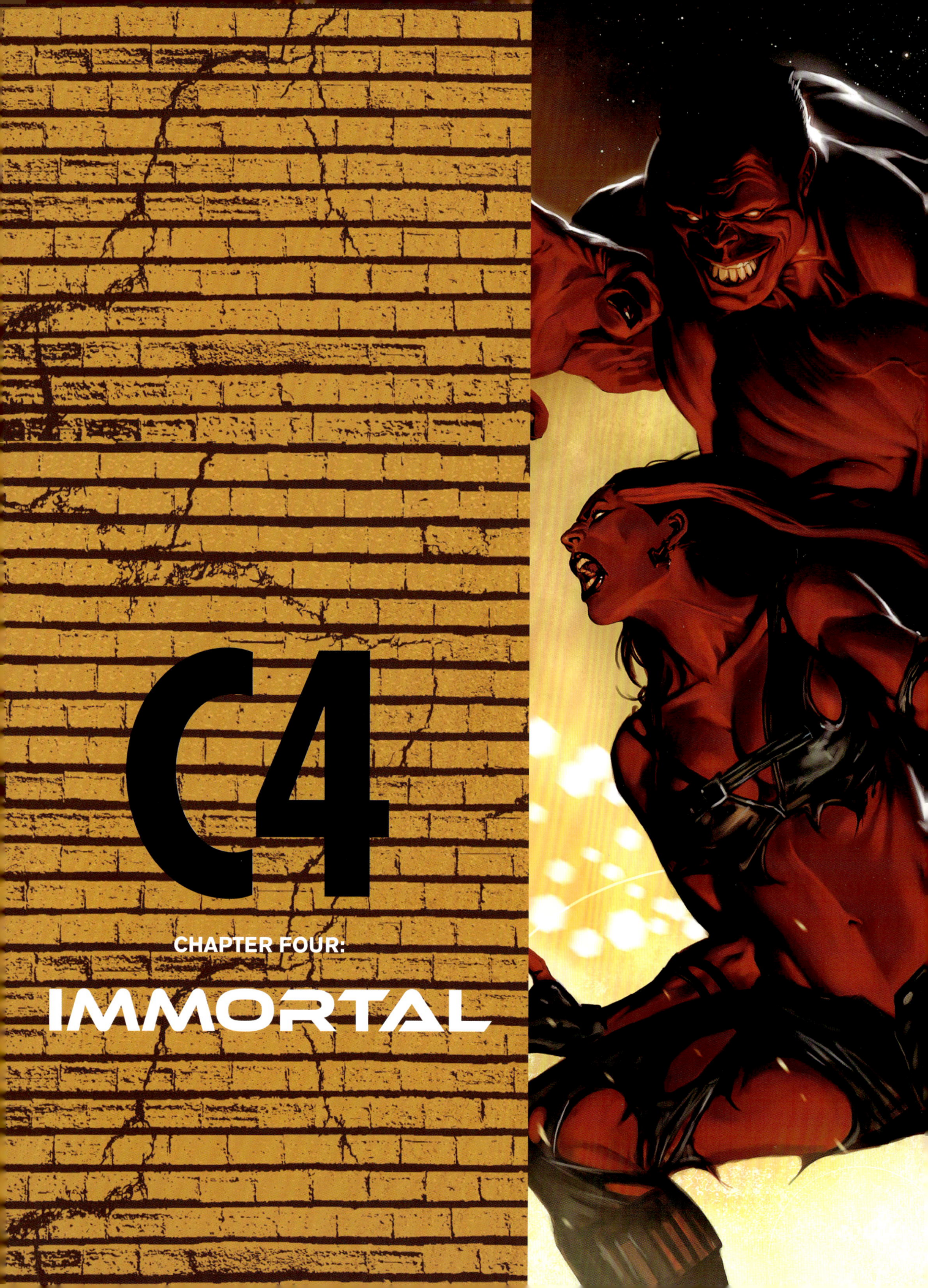

# C4

CHAPTER FOUR:

## IMMORTAL

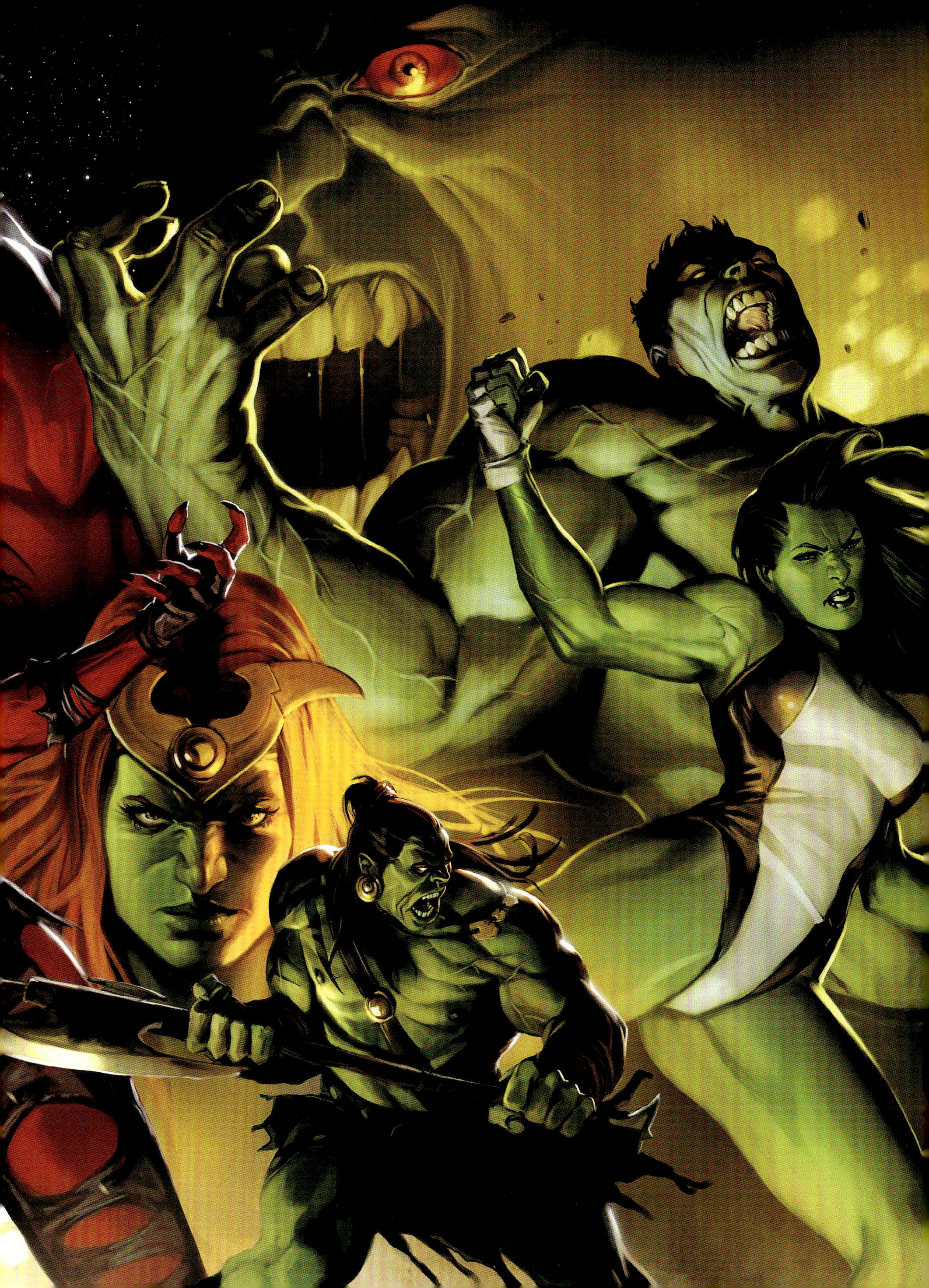

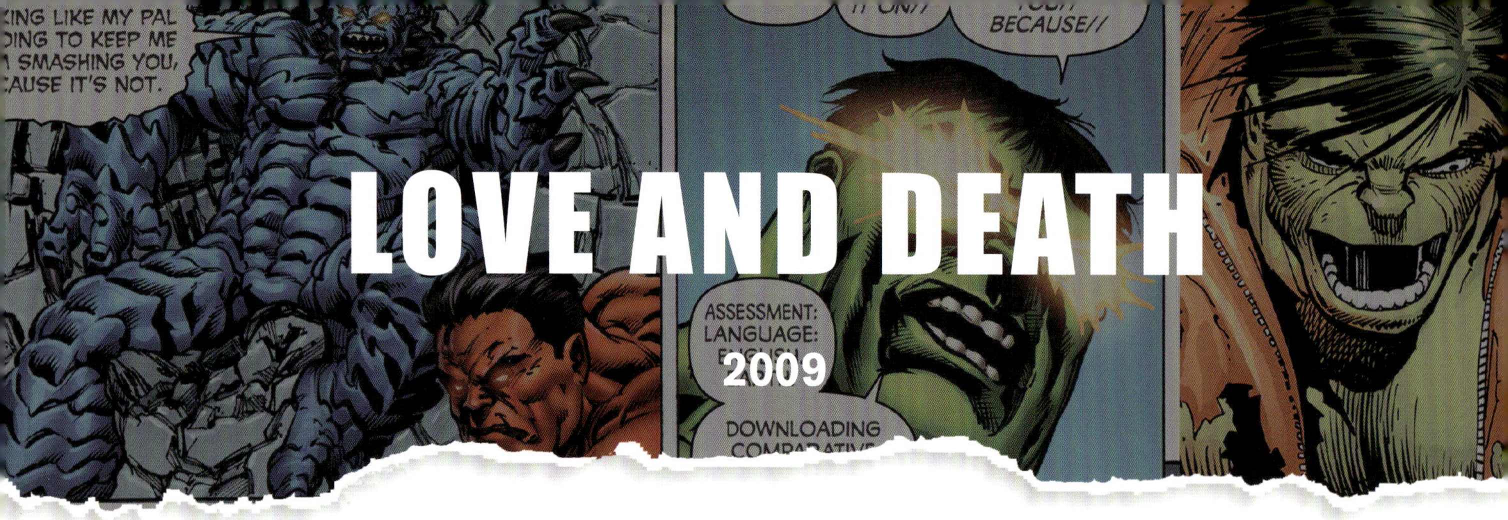
BECAUSE//
ASSESSMENT:
LANGUAGE:
DOWNLOADING

# LOVE AND DEATH

## 2009

It's what we all wish for, what we hope for, dream of . . . to be loved for who we are. Even if we're a giant green rage monster, a cosmic being riding a silver surfboard, the ruler of the seven seas, or a sorcerer supreme—we all want to be loved. But if that love that we never expected to find is taken from us, what would we do to get it back?

This is the question that the Hulk, the Silver Surfer, Doctor Strange, and Namor the Sub-Mariner now face. These men all have something in common: they are carrying the death of their loved ones on their shoulders. The Hulk has been thinking of Jarella, the woman he met and fell in love with on planet K'ai. Her tragic death was the result of her bravery: she prevented a boy from being crushed under the weight of a collapsed building, but died in the process. The Hulk was able to take her back to her home world to be buried.

The Hulk surfaces from his memories of Jarella to be greeted by the Grandmaster. He and his brother, the Collector, are Elders of the Universe. The Elders are some of the oldest living beings in the Universe. The Grandmaster is a master at games of skill and chance. He has an offer for the Hulk. He wants to set up a competition between two teams, and the Hulk can choose whom he wants to be on his team. The Hulk chooses Namor, the Silver Surfer, and Doctor Strange. The competition will be to the death, but if the Hulk's team succeeds, their loved ones will return to them.

The Hulk feels that the three he has chosen will be as motivated as he is to see their loved ones again. But they may take a bit of convincing; they are not thrilled to see the Hulk. The Hulk visits each of them at the exact moment in time when they lost their loved one. He tells a reluctant Silver Surfer that if he joins the team it could result in the return of his beloved Shalla-Bal. He approaches the Sub-Mariner moments after he lost his love Dorma, who had been murdered. And Doctor Strange wants to be reunited with his beloved Clea, who moments earlier had been sucked into

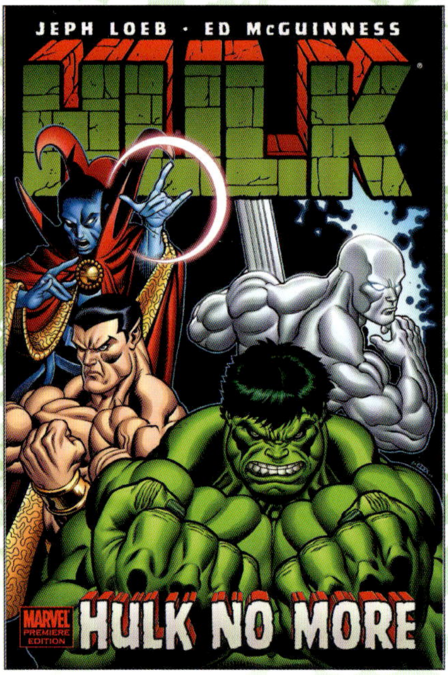
JEPH LOEB · ED McGUINNESS
HULK
MARVEL PREMIERE EDITION
HULK NO MORE

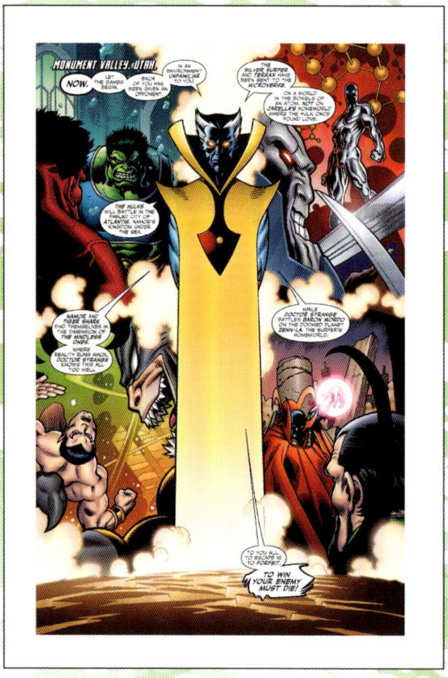
MONUMENT VALLEY, UTAH.
NOW.

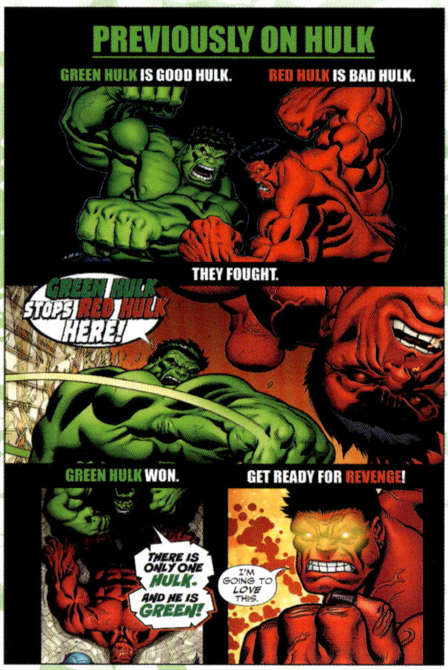
PREVIOUSLY ON HULK
GREEN HULK IS GOOD HULK.
RED HULK IS BAD HULK.
THEY FOUGHT.
GREEN HULK STOPS RED HULK HERE!
GREEN HULK WON.
GET READY FOR REVENGE!
THERE IS ONLY ONE HULK. AND HE IS GREEN!
I'M GOING TO LOVE THIS.

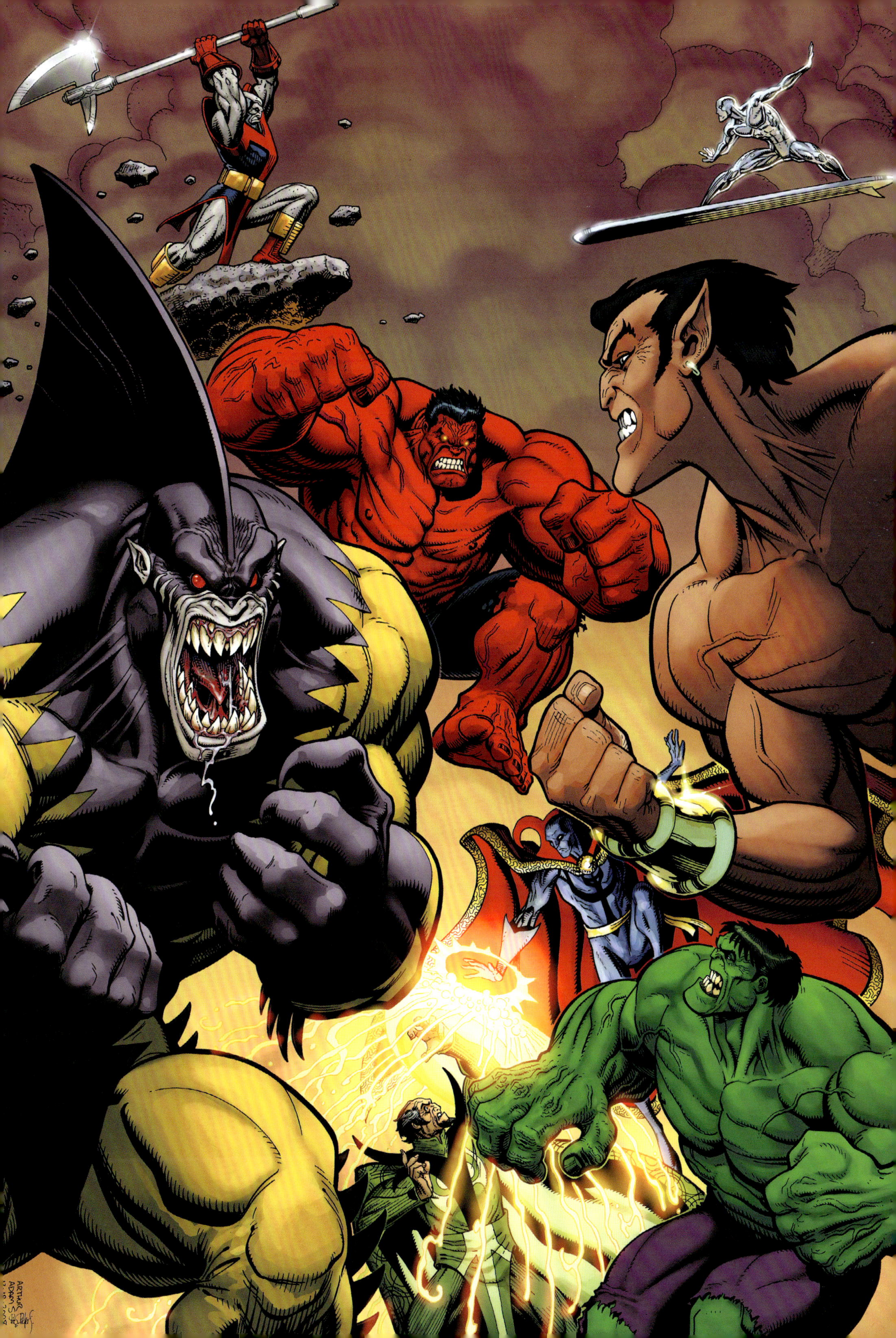

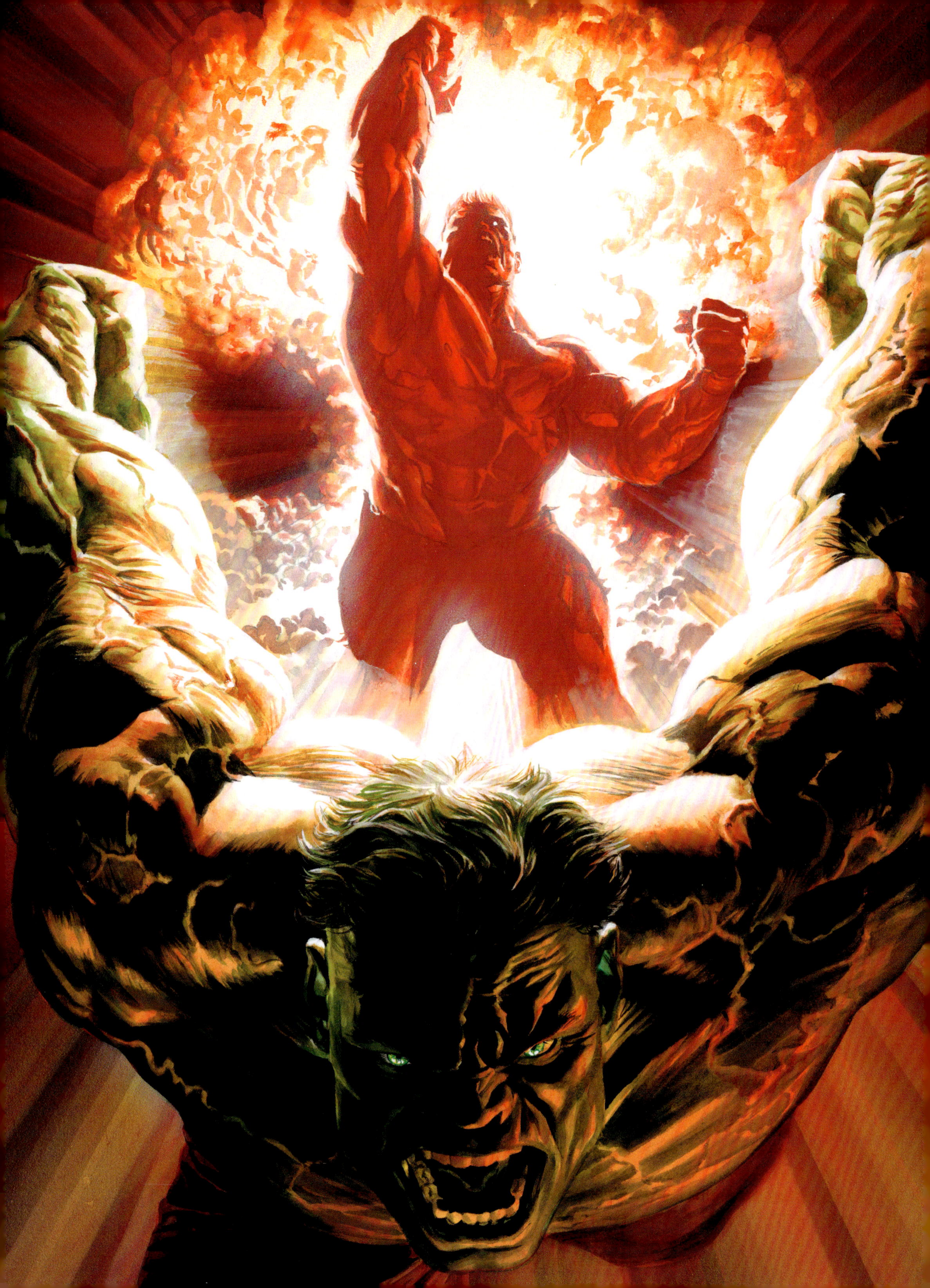

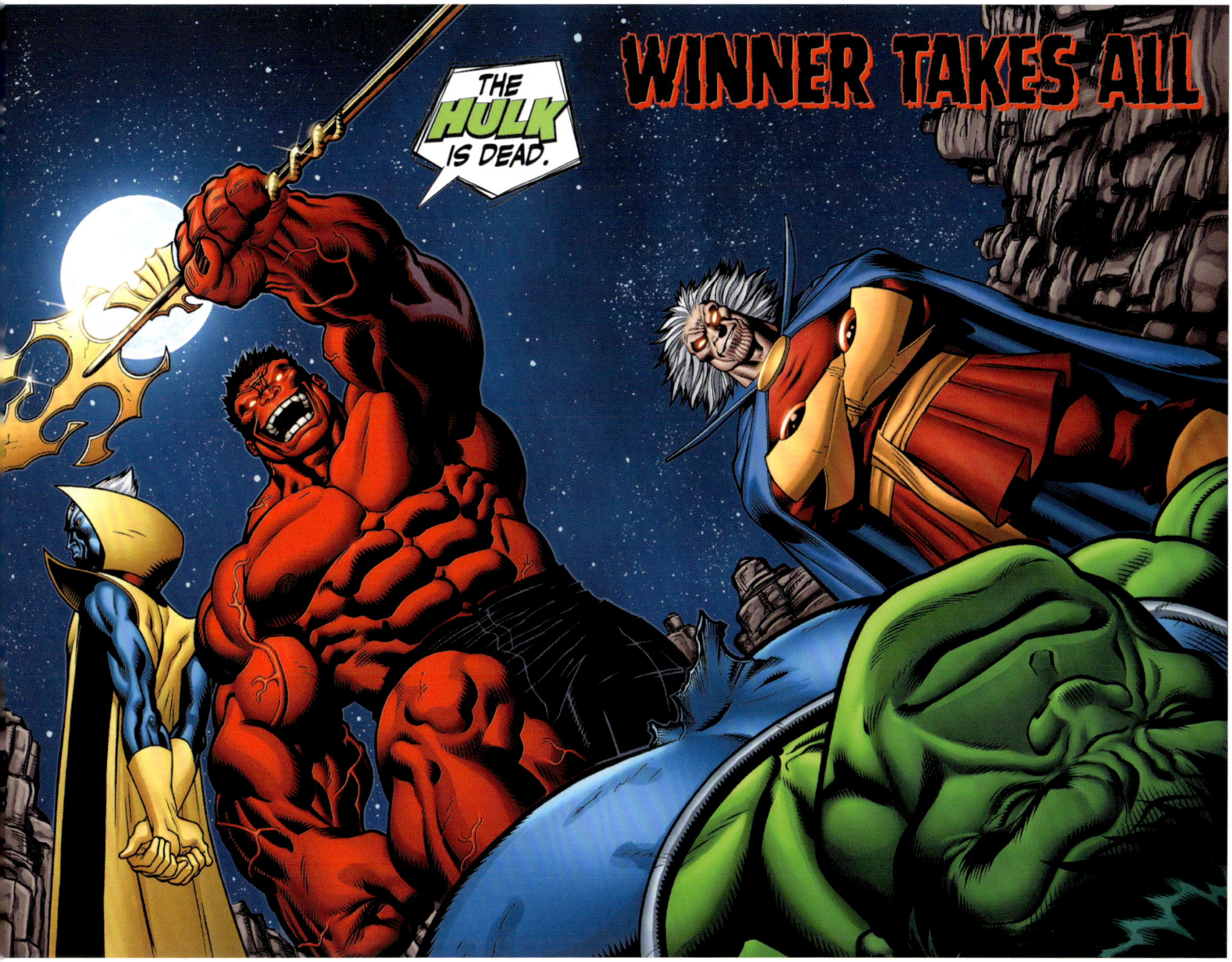
WINNER TAKES ALL
THE HULK IS DEAD.

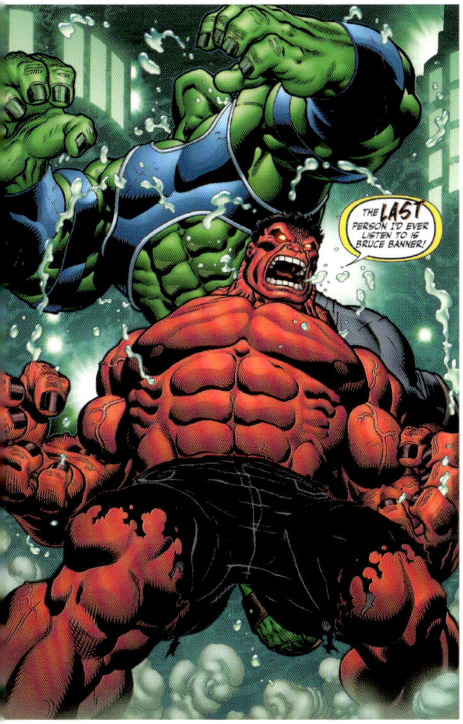
THE LAST PERSON I'D EVER LISTEN TO IS BRUCE BANNER!

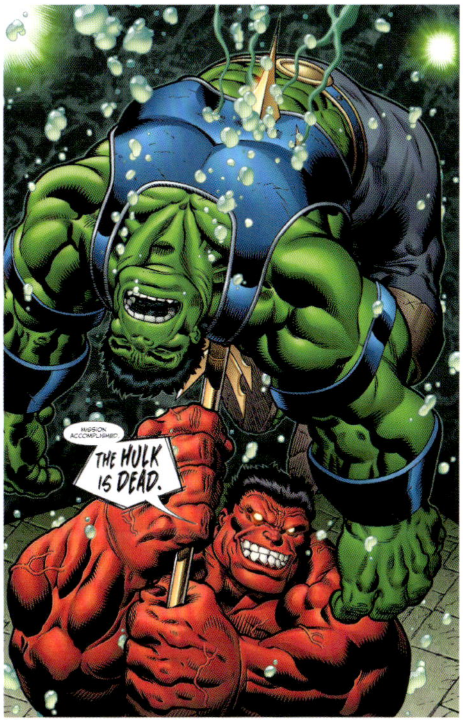
MISSION ACCOMPLISHED.
THE HULK IS DEAD.

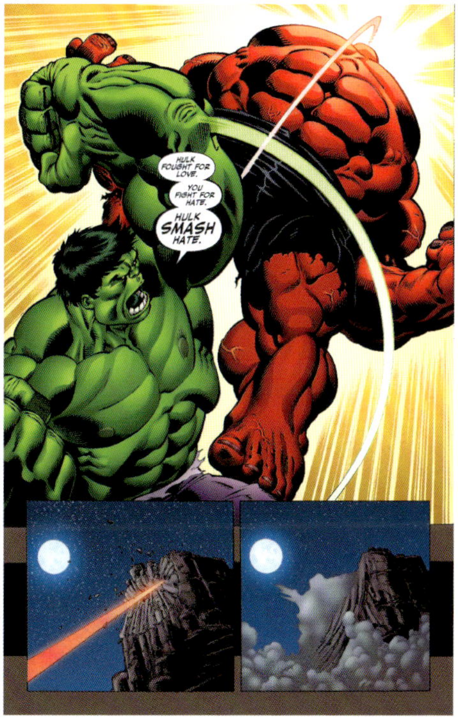
HULK FOUGHT FOR LOVE.
YOU FIGHT FOR HATE.
HULK SMASH HATE.

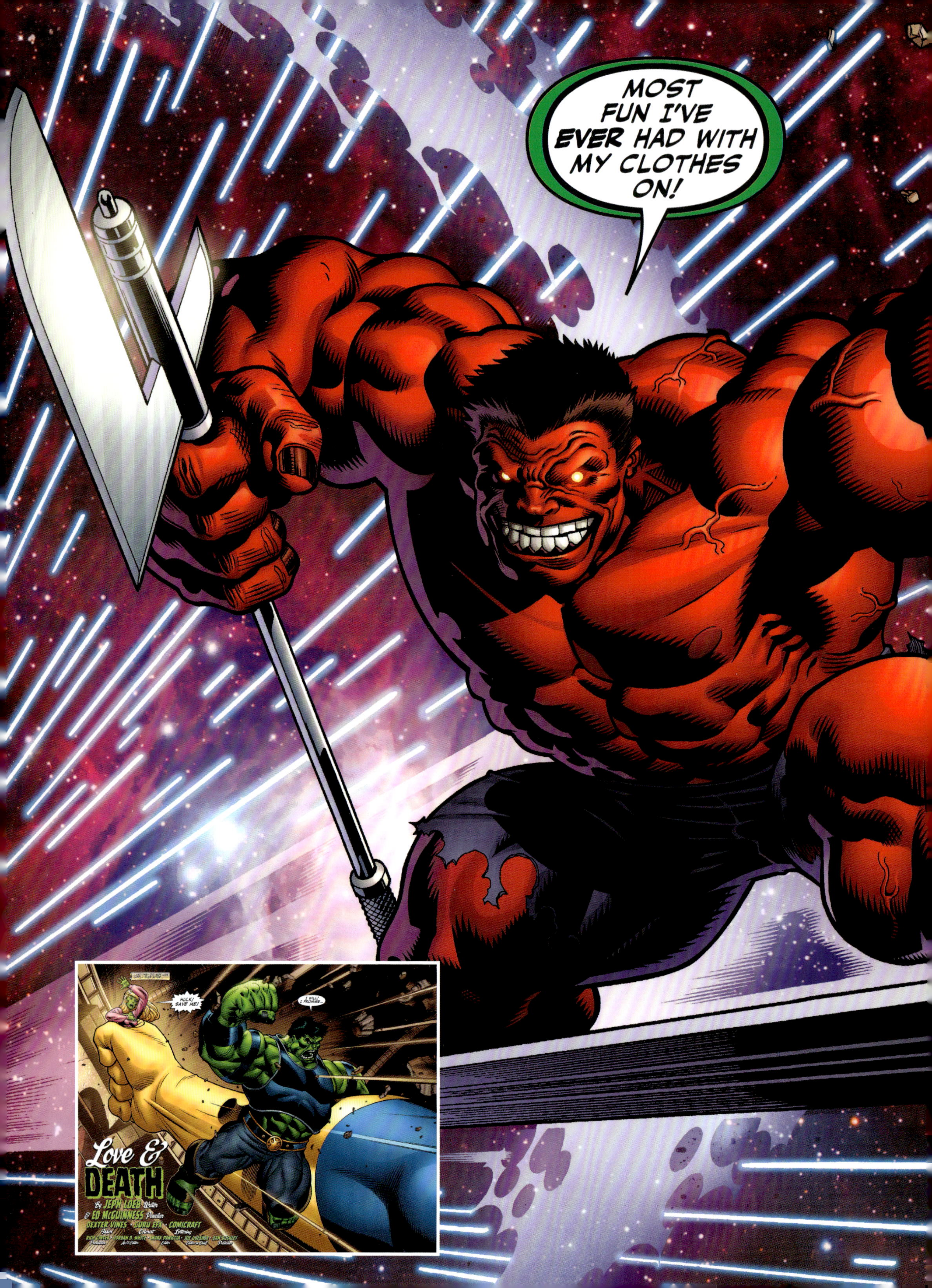
MOST FUN I'VE EVER HAD WITH MY CLOTHES ON!
HULK! SAVE ME!
I WILL! I PROMISE...
Love & DEATH
By JEPH LOEB Writer
& ED McGUINNESS Penciler
DEXTER VINES • GURU EFX • COMICRAFT
Inker Colorist Lettering
RICH GINTER • JORDAN D. WHITE • MARK PANICCIA • JOE QUESADA • DAN BUCKLEY

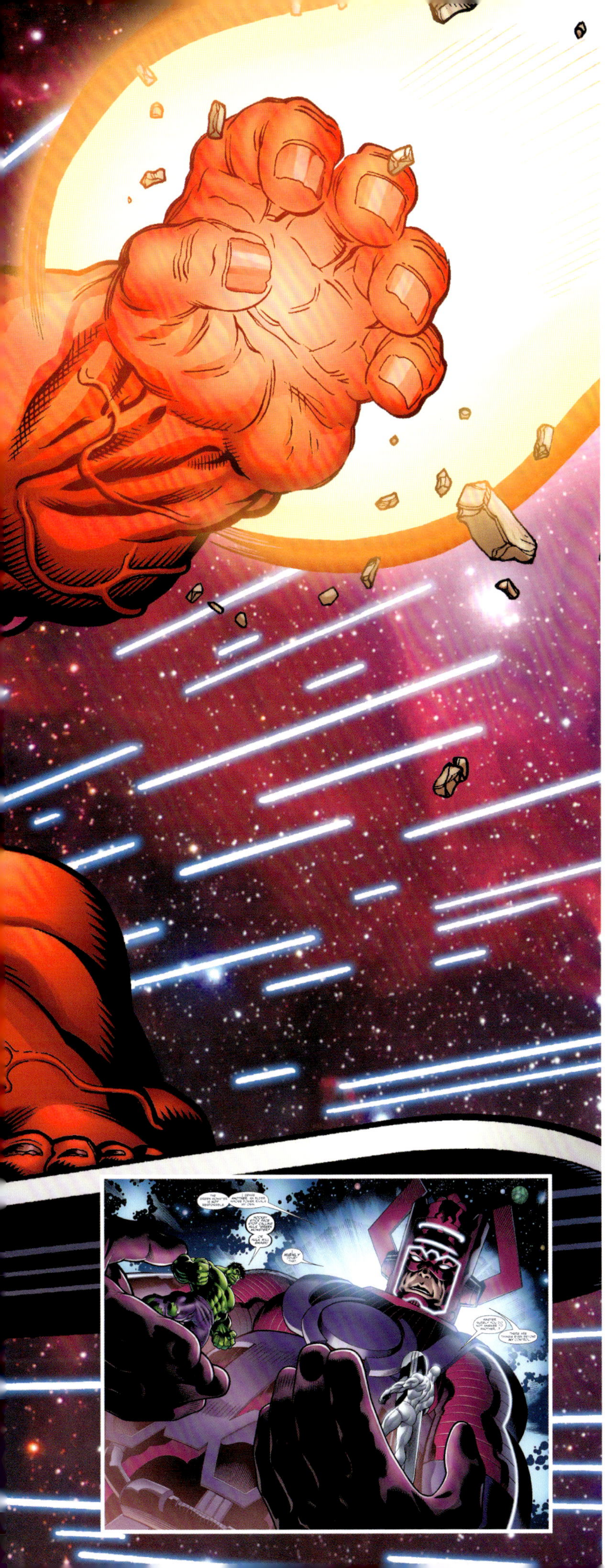

another dimension. They all agree to join the Hulk's team, which is called the Offenders. But Grandmaster and the Collector's promise that they will be reunited is not charitable. What will be the consequences for the team that loses? Will they become a part of the Collector's collection?

We soon learn that the other team consists of the Red Hulk, Baron Mordo, Terrax, and Tiger Shark. They call themselves the Defenders. Before the fight begins, Bruce Banner's brain gets dropped into the Hulk's mind. Will that be an advantage or disadvantage?

Terrax takes on the Silver Surfer, Tiger Shark confronts Namor, Baron Mordo challenges Doctor Strange, and the Red Hulk faces the green Hulk. The Hulks first are sent underwater to battle. The Hulk tries to reason with the Red Hulk, and he explains the situation they're in. But Red Hulk thinks what's needed right now isn't talk, but action—the Red Hulk isn't even listening to what his green doppelgänger has to say.

In fact, the Red Hulk doesn't even care about his fellow teammates—he quickly turns on them. Red Hulk attacks them. He thinks he doesn't need their help. He is more powerful than all of them combined.

Will our heroes defeat the Defenders? Will they get their loved ones back? And, if so, at what cost?

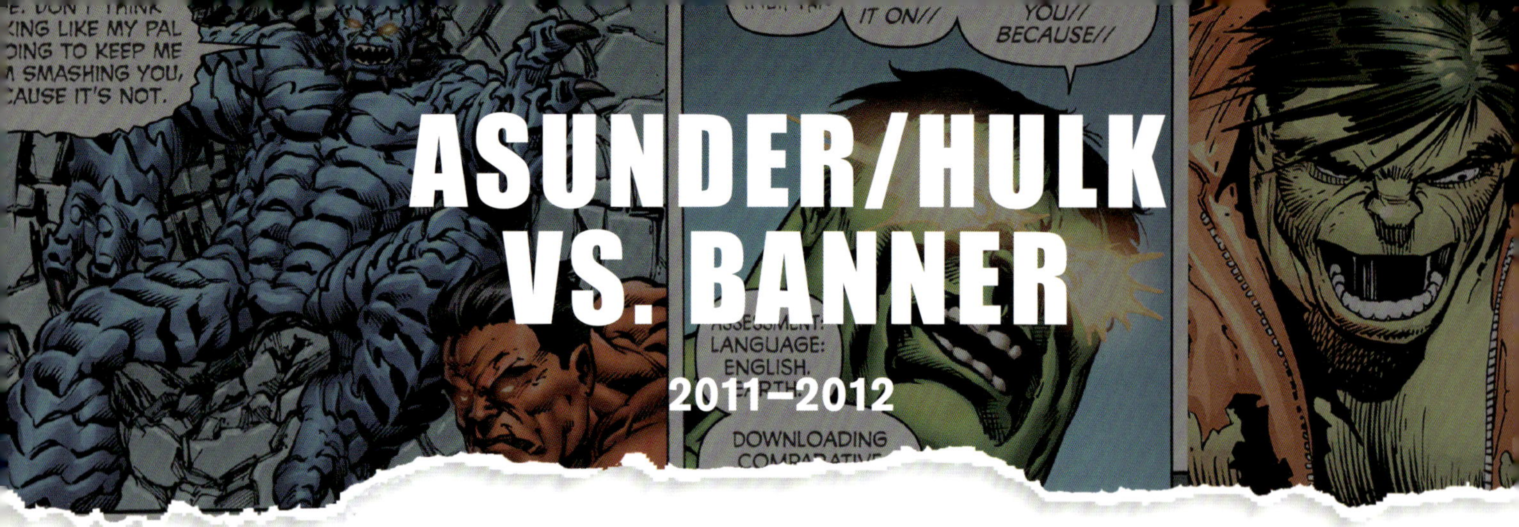

IT ON//
YOU// BECAUSE//
LANGUAGE: ENGLISH.
DOWNLOADING


# ASUNDER/HULK VS. BANNER

## 2011–2012

A creature with razor-like teeth rises from the bowels of the Earth, and the Hulk, also deep underground, is ready for it. Below the surface of the Earth this creature is normally without fear; it never had anyone challenge it, until now. The Hulk subdues it, but he does not kill it. He speaks to the creature and allows it to rest and to regain its breath. The Hulk is not attacked very often down here. This is where he lives now. On the surface it seemed like everyone was after him. Down here he is at peace.

There is a humanlike civilization in this place in addition to the creature the Hulk fought, known as the Moloids. These people who live below love and respect the Hulk, and the respect is mutual. The Hulk is content down here, but he knows that it won't last. It never lasts. It's only a matter of time before someone discovers his subterranean hideout and comes for him. Sure enough, someone in an armored costume appears, with robots, and the robots immediately attack the Hulk. They battle, and the Hulk easily defeats the robots. He then shreds the armor of the other attacker, and he discovers a woman who introduces herself as Amanda von Doom (no relation to Doctor Doom), who tells him that she is from the "deepest darkest corners of the US government."

Amanda von Doom tells the Hulk that the reason she attacked was to get his attention; he wouldn't "take them seriously" if they hadn't provided a show of force. The Hulk advises her to leave before it gets ugly. Von Doom makes no attempt to charm him, calling him a "pea-brained sack of radioactive lard." She tells him that "something has to be done about Banner."

The Hulk and Banner now live in separate bodies. While the Hulk has been laying low beneath the Earth's surface, Banner has been busy conducting experiments in a lab on an island. Now that the Hulk is not with him, Banner feels like a piece of him has been stolen. It was the Hulk who split them apart. After they were separated, Banner decided to create his own personal Island of Dr. Moreau (like the classic book

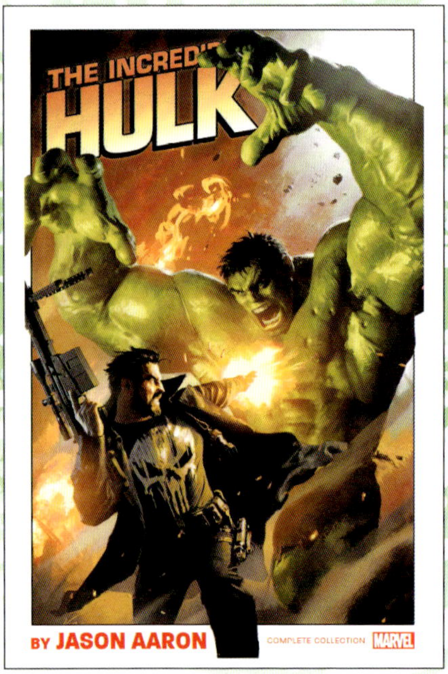

THE INCRED
HULK
BY JASON AARON
COMPLETE COLLECTION
MARVEL


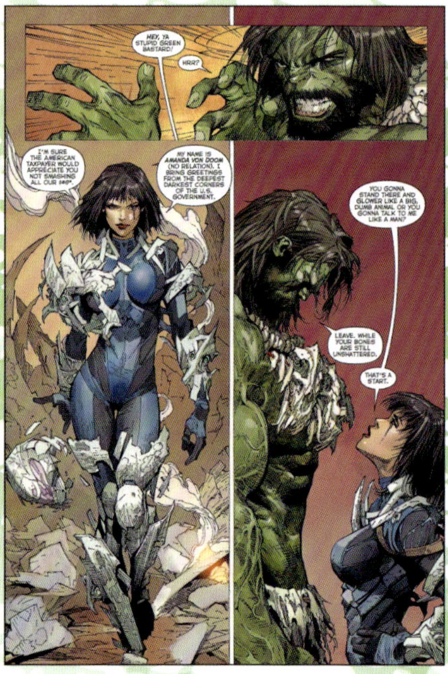

HEY, YA STUPID GREEN BASTARD!
HRR?
I'M SURE THE AMERICAN TAXPAYER WOULD APPRECIATE YOU NOT SMASHING ALL OUR #@*.
MY NAME IS AMANDA VON DOOM (NO RELATION). I BRING GREETINGS FROM THE DEEPEST DARKEST CORNERS OF THE U.S. GOVERNMENT.
YOU GONNA STAND THERE AND GLOWER LIKE A BIG, DUMB ANIMAL OR YOU GONNA TALK TO ME LIKE A MAN?
LEAVE. WHILE YOUR BONES ARE STILL UNSHATTERED.
THAT'S A START.


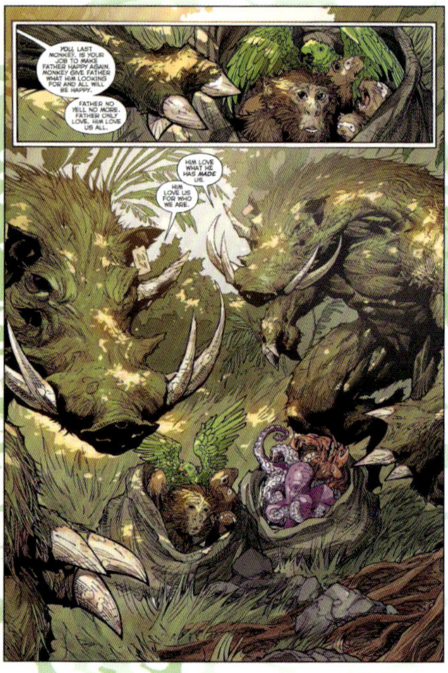

YOU, LAST MONKEY. IS YOUR JOB TO MAKE FATHER HAPPY AGAIN. MONKEY GIVE FATHER WHAT HIM LOOKING FOR AND ALL WILL BE HAPPY.
FATHER NO YELL NO MORE. FATHER ONLY LOVE. HIM LOVE US ALL.
HIM LOVE WHAT HE HAS MADE US.
HIM LOVE US FOR WHO WE ARE.

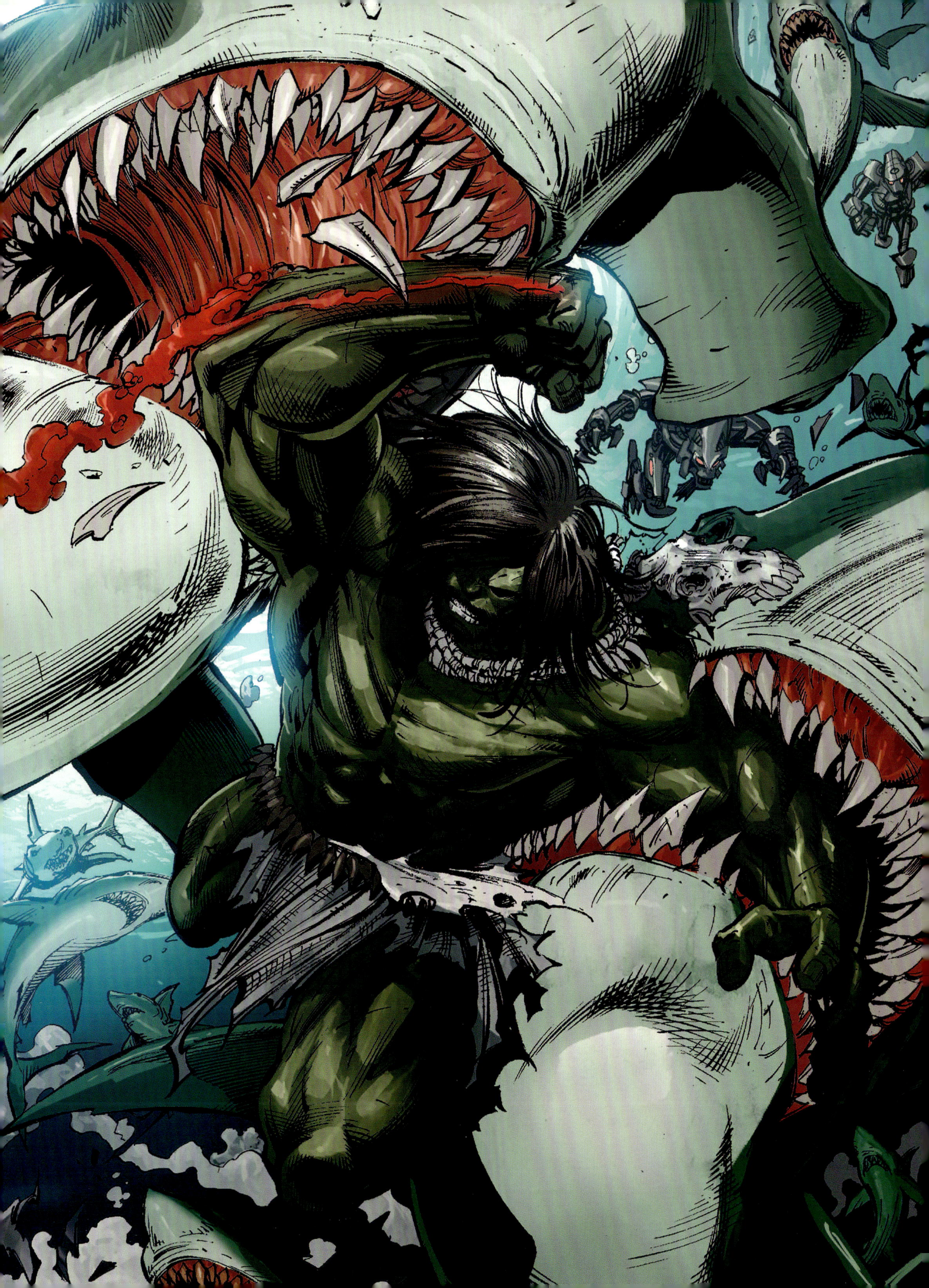

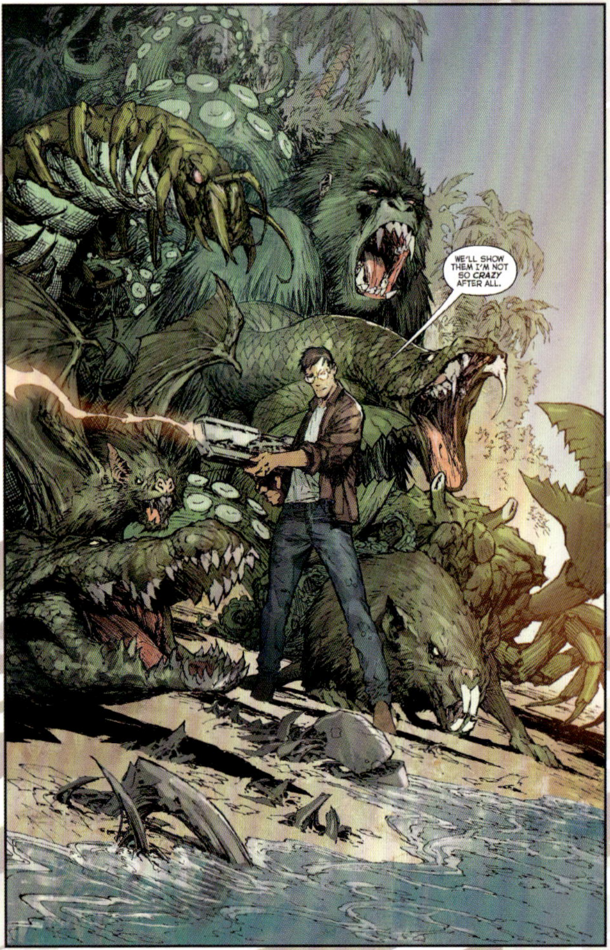
WE'LL SHOW THEM I'M NOT SO *CRAZY* AFTER ALL.

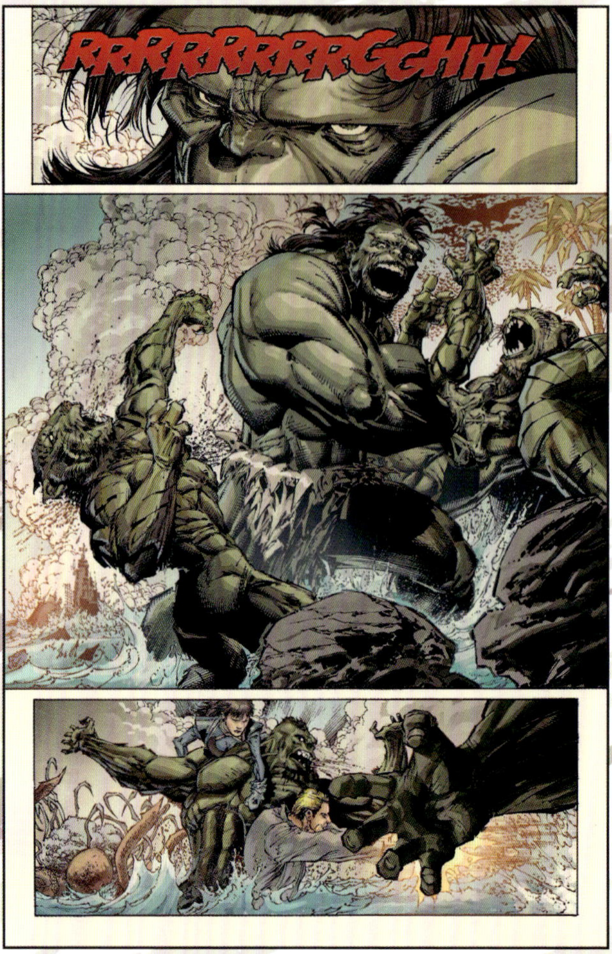
RRRRRRRRRGGHH!

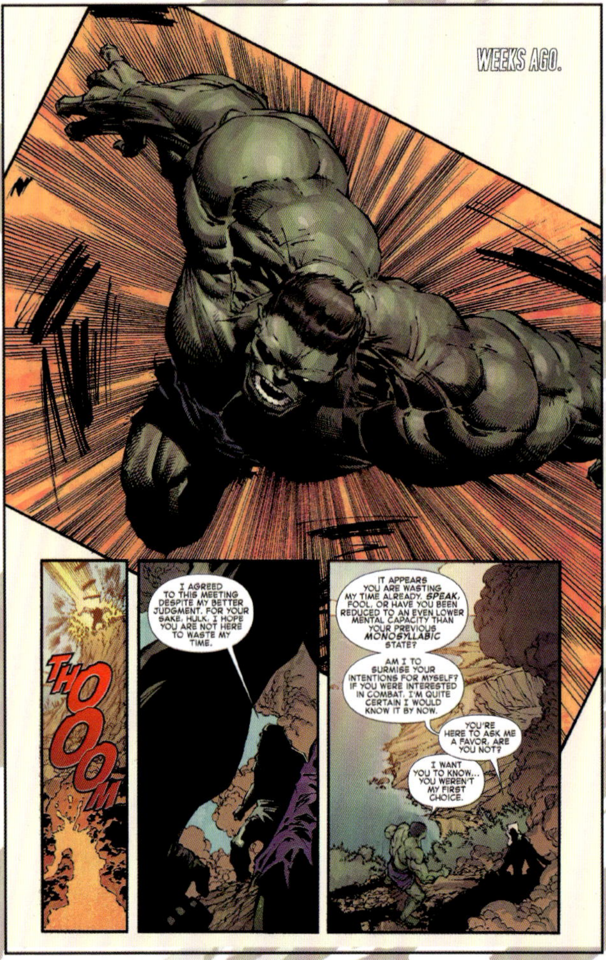
WEEKS AGO.
THOOOM
I AGREED TO THIS MEETING DESPITE MY BETTER JUDGMENT. FOR YOUR SAKE, HULK, I HOPE YOU ARE NOT HERE TO WASTE MY TIME.
IT APPEARS YOU ARE WASTING MY TIME ALREADY. *SPEAK,* FOOL, OR HAVE YOU BEEN REDUCED TO AN EVEN LOWER MENTAL CAPACITY THAN YOUR PREVIOUS *MONOSYLLABIC* STATE?
AM I TO SURMISE YOUR INTENTIONS FOR MYSELF? IF YOU WERE INTERESTED IN COMBAT, I'M QUITE CERTAIN I WOULD KNOW IT BY NOW.
YOU'RE HERE TO ASK ME A FAVOR, ARE YOU NOT?
I WANT YOU TO KNOW... YOU WEREN'T MY FIRST CHOICE.

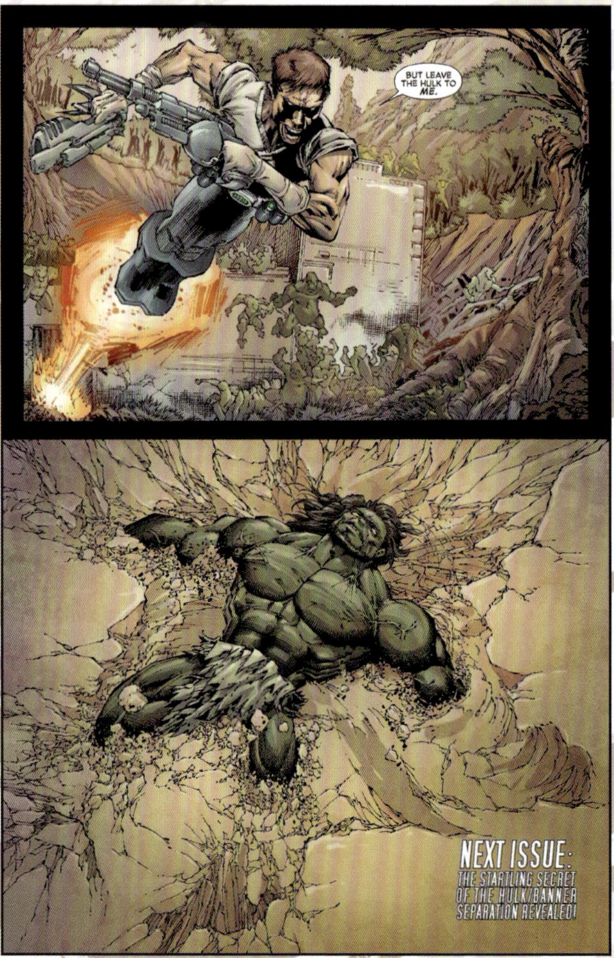
BUT LEAVE THE HULK TO *ME.*
NEXT ISSUE:
THE STARTLING SECRET OF THE HULK/BANNER SEPARATION REVEALED!

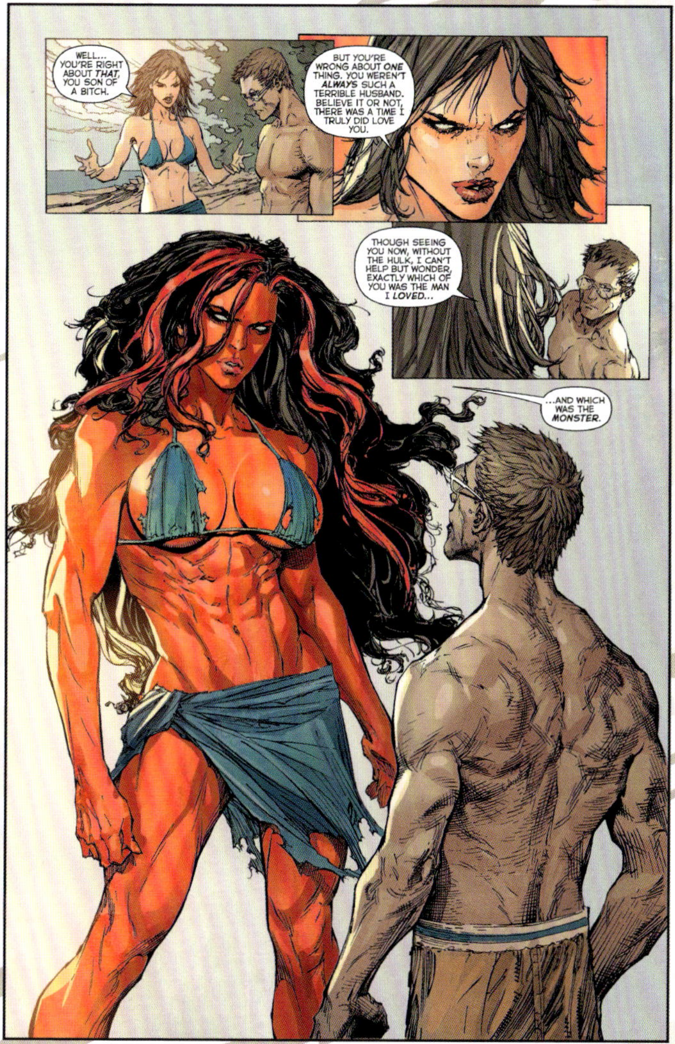
WELL... YOU'RE RIGHT ABOUT *THAT,* YOU SON OF A BITCH.
BUT YOU'RE WRONG ABOUT *ONE* THING. YOU WEREN'T *ALWAYS* SUCH A TERRIBLE HUSBAND. BELIEVE IT OR NOT, THERE WAS A TIME I TRULY DID LOVE YOU.
THOUGH SEEING YOU NOW, WITHOUT THE HULK, I CAN'T HELP BUT WONDER, EXACTLY WHICH OF YOU WAS THE MAN I *LOVED...*
...AND WHICH WAS THE *MONSTER.*

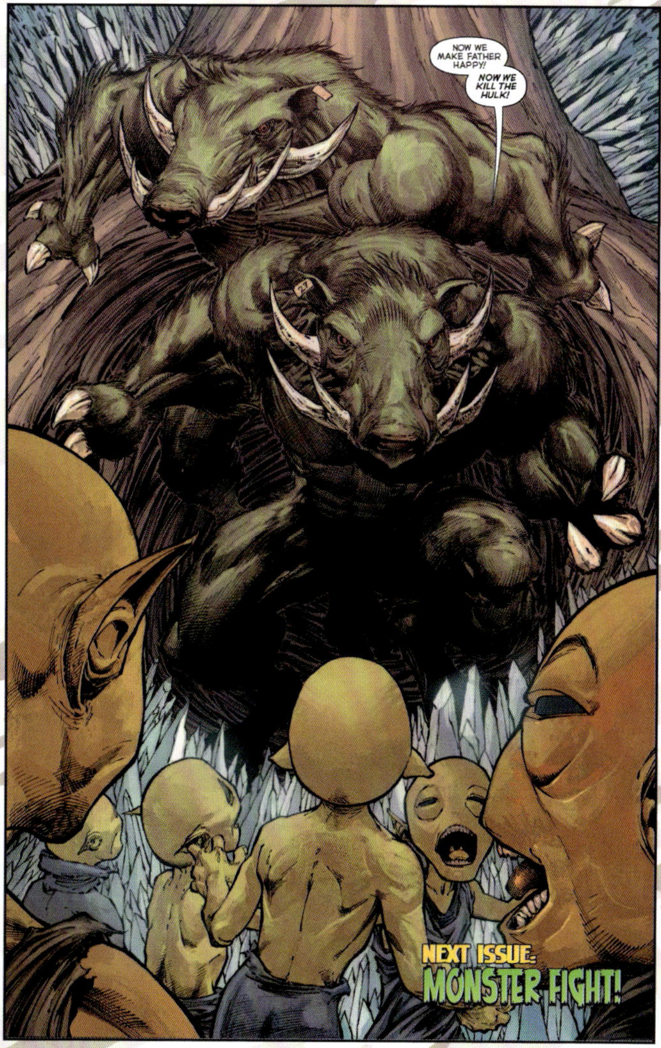
NOW WE MAKE FATHER HAPPY!
*NOW WE KILL THE HULK!*
NEXT ISSUE: MONSTER FIGHT!

about a mad scientist who experimented on animals). He is trying to create Hulk-like creatures who become oversized, green versions of themselves, and he experiments with hammerhead sharks, wild boars, monkeys, snakes, and lizards.

The Hulk and von Doom get a taste of these Hulked-out creatures when they travel to Banner's island and are attacked by giant green sharks. After they defeat the sharks, the Hulk lets von Doom know that he wants nothing to do with Banner and he leaves.

He changes his mind once he returns underground and discovers that Banner sent some of these freaks to hurt the Moloid. The Hulk takes down two green wild boars that were dispatched to do harm. He thought he was finally free but he realizes there is only one way to be truly free. The Hulk returns to the island and tells von Doom "Banner's mine."

Meanwhile, Banner attacks a military facility. There is something inside he wants—radioactive isotopes—and nothing will stop him. The scientists working there all wear protective suits that shield them from the radiation, but not Banner. We find out later that his constant exposure has given him a malignant brain tumor.

The Hulk rejoins von Doom on the island. He tells her that he knows she won't kill Banner, but he will. But first, the Hulk needs to fight some of the Hulked-out monsters: a couple of giant tigers and a bat.

The Hulk comes face-to-face with his other side. At this moment, the Hulk seems to be the calm logical one and Banner the out-of-control monster. How will this end? Can they ever live without each other? Or, do they need each other in the end?

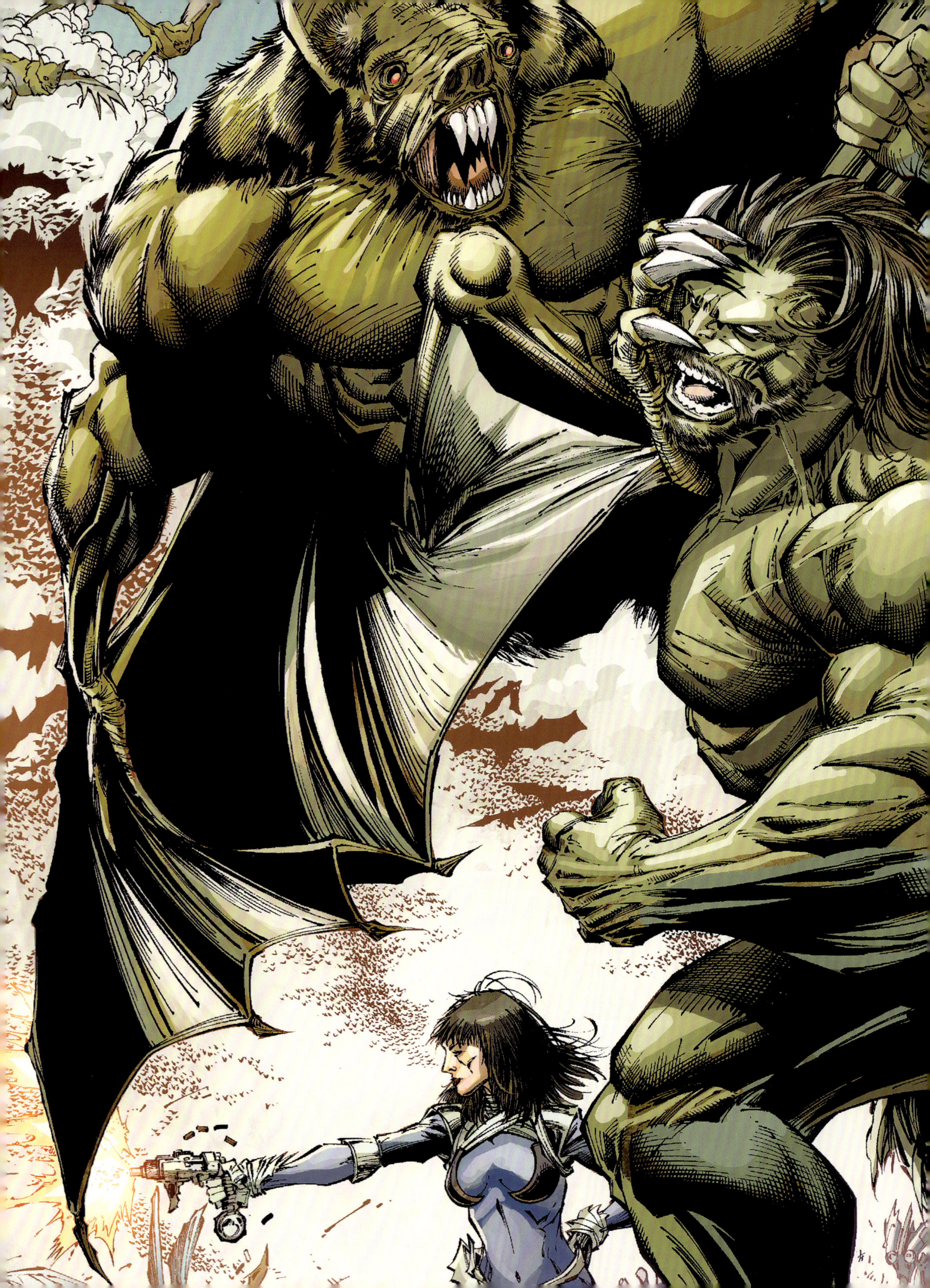

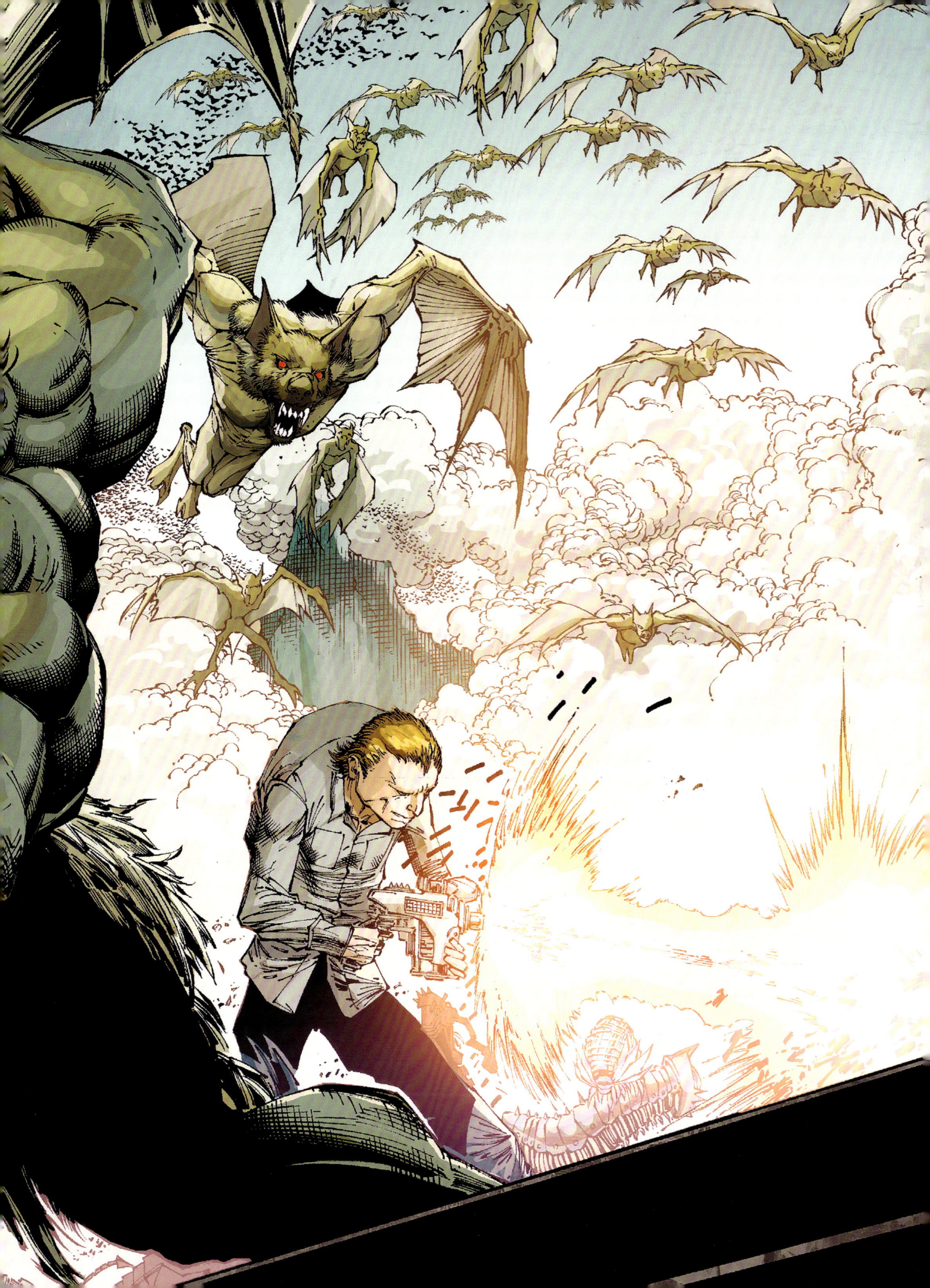

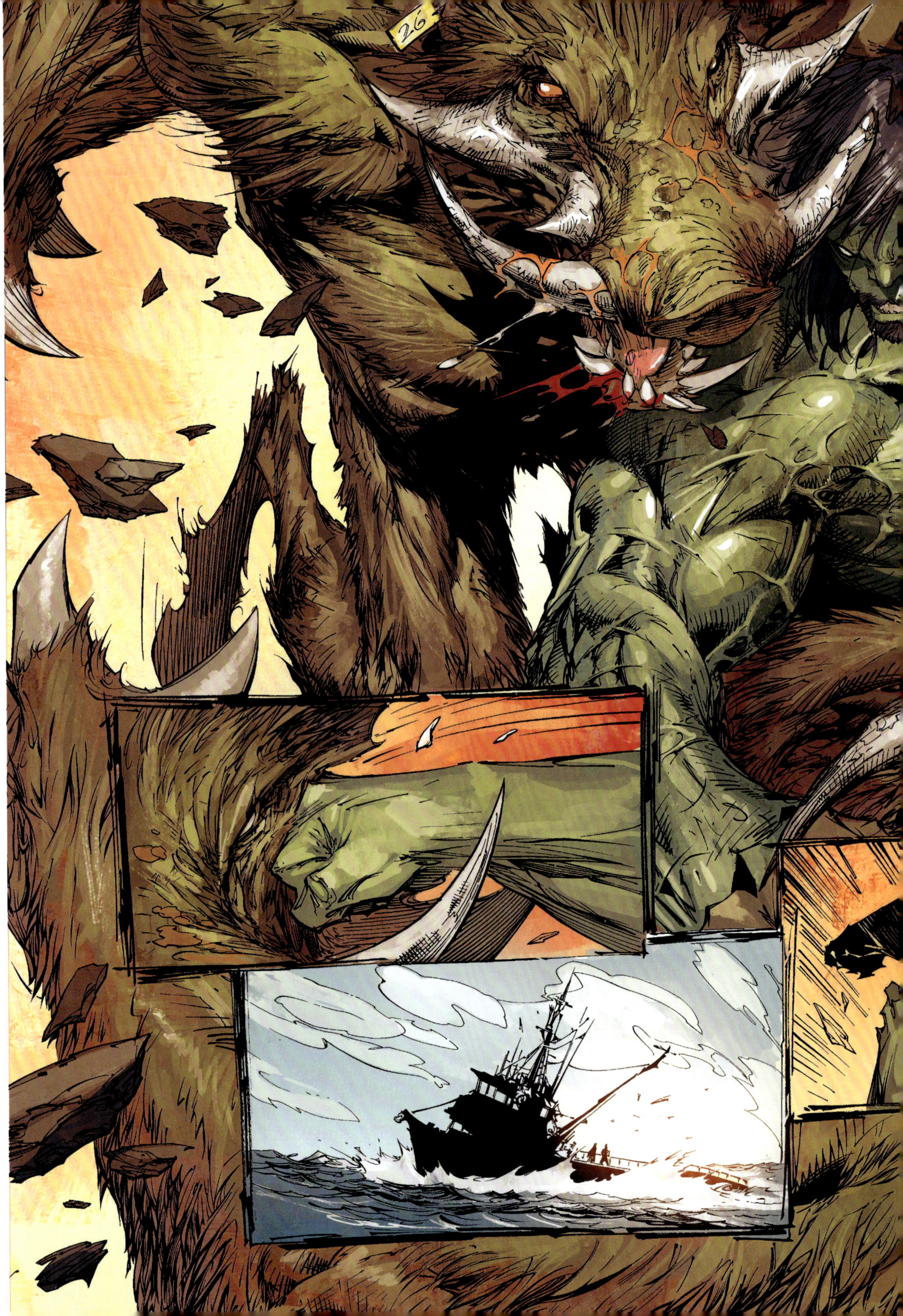

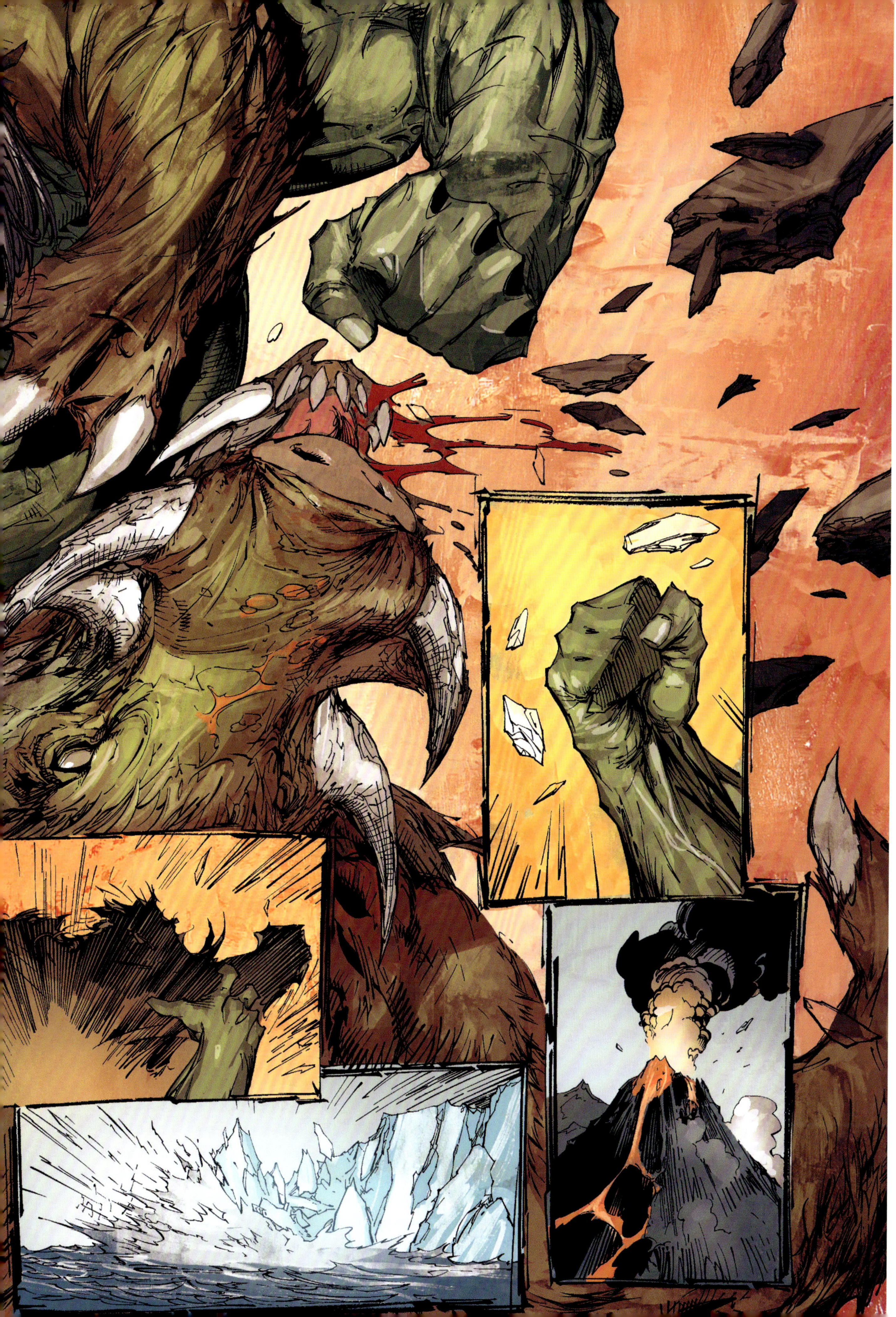

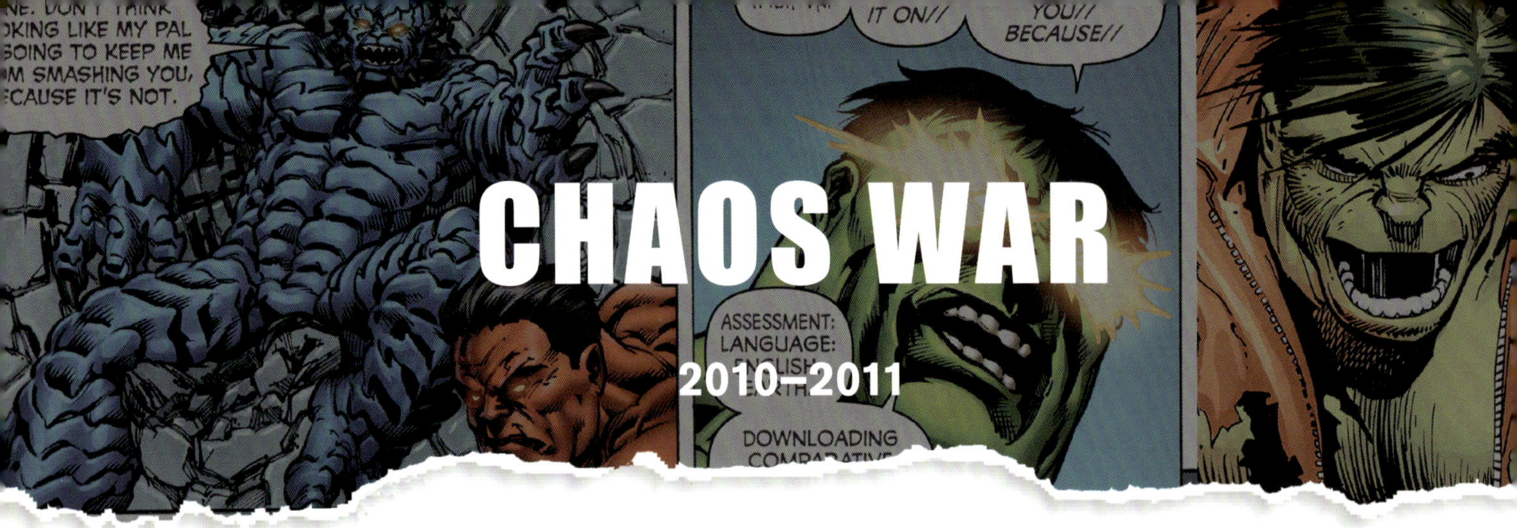
IT ON//
YOU// BECAUSE//
ASSESSMENT: LANGUAGE:
DOWNLOADING

# CHAOS WAR

## 2010–2011

Earth is in trouble. Cities are in chaos, oil spills are burning, and nuclear power plants are exploding. The Hulk and his crew—Red She-Hulk/Betty Ross Banner, A-Bomb/Rick Jones, She-Hulk/Jennifer Walters, Korg of Kronan, and the Hulk's son Skaar—are on a spaceship on their way back to Earth. Doctor Strange suddenly projects himself into the spaceship. He warns them about the Chaos King, who is the culprit behind the dire situation on Earth. When the Hulk and his crew return to Earth, they discover a world full of humans in a waking sleep. Death herself has fled from Earth, which means no one can die, and the Chaos King has released demons and the damned to roam his new domain.

The Hulks try to contact other super heroes but are met with silence. Where have they gone? It appears the Hulks are on their own. They land in Manhattan and head to Grand Central Terminal. There they see people lying unconscious in the train station. Suddenly, demons rise from underground, led by the Abomination, who grabs A-Bomb. He wants to know where Marlo is. Marlo is Rick Jones's wife, who, at one time, was possessed by the personification of Death herself.

As A-Bomb and the Abomination battle, Doctor Strange appears—this time in person—and he fights off the Abomination. He tells A-Bomb and the rest of the Hulk's crew that if the Abomination finds Marlo, he will extract the spark of Death still within her and use it to kill those who are now sleeping and send them to hell.

But things take a turn when Doctor Strange himself becomes possessed by the demon Zom, a longtime nemesis. Zom has teamed up with the Abomination to hunt down Marlo. The Hulk and his crew need to get to Marlo before Zom and the Abomination do. The Hulk transforms into Banner so he can deploy a transportation device called the Shadowtech Warp.

Meanwhile, Rick/A-Bomb locates his wife Marlo, who is being hunted down by the dead, recently released from the underworld and now chasing that spark of Death in Marlo. The Hulks arrive via the Shadowtech Warp just in time to save her.

While the Hulks battle the Abomination and Doctor Strange, Banner hides Marlo inside the Shadowtech Warp machine. A-Bomb is already injured, and Marlo doubts that their plan

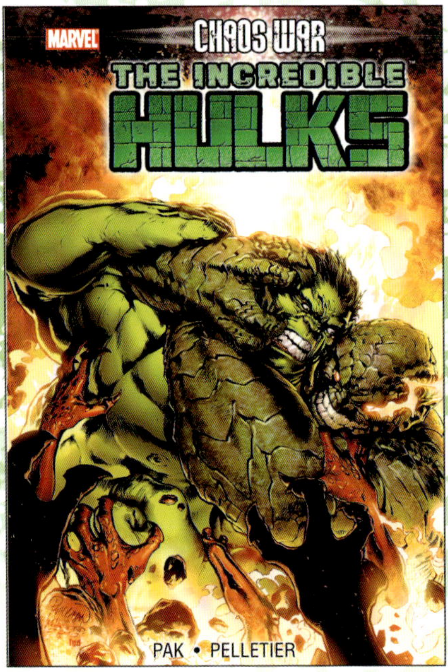
MARVEL
CHAOS WAR
THE INCREDIBLE HULKS
PAK • PELLETIER

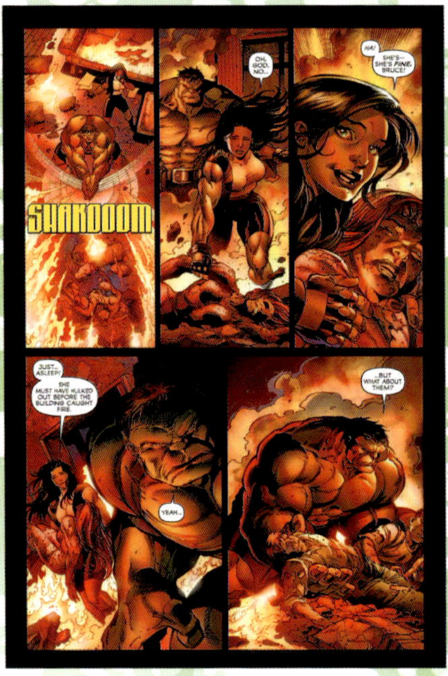

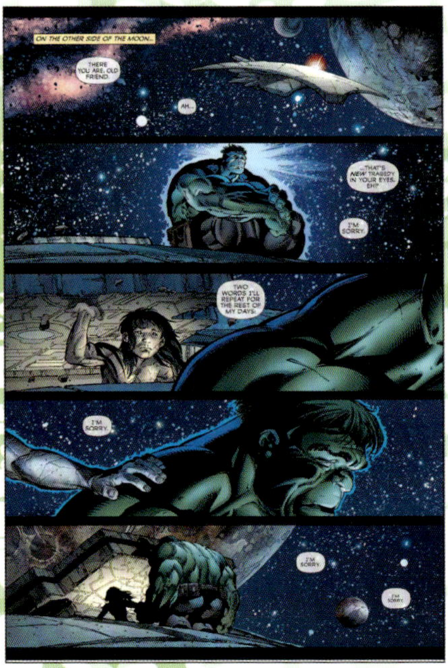

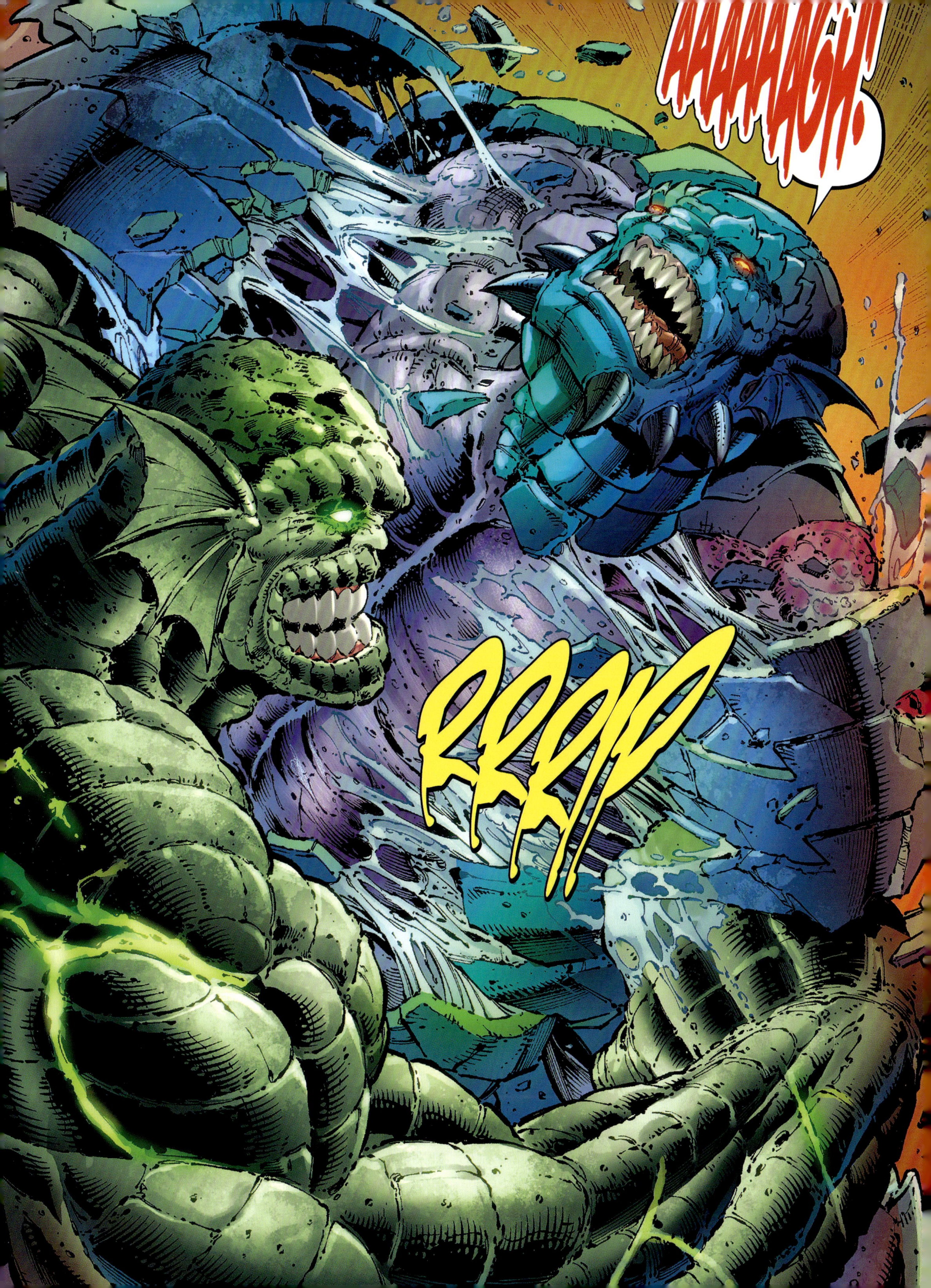
AAAAAAGH!!
RRRIP

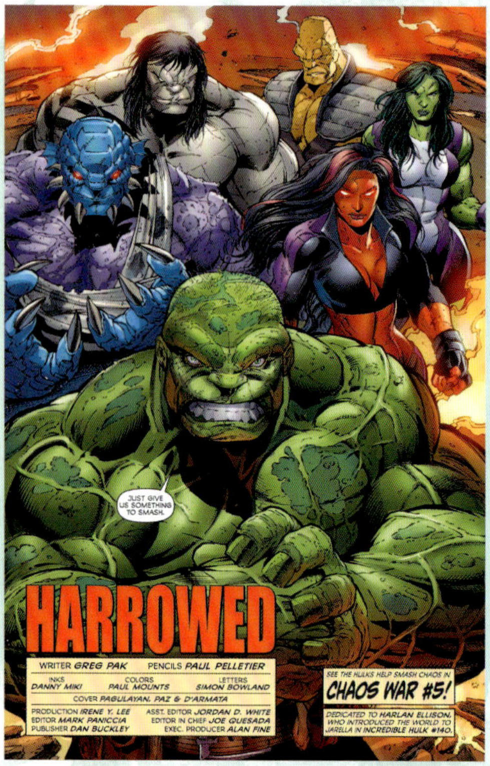
JUST GIVE US SOMETHING TO SMASH.
HARROWED
WRITER GREG PAK PENCILS PAUL PELLETIER
INKS DANNY MIKI COLORS PAUL MOUNTS LETTERS SIMON BOWLAND
COVER PAGULAYAN, PAZ & D'ARMATA
PRODUCTION IRENE Y. LEE ASST. EDITOR JORDAN D. WHITE
EDITOR MARK PANICCIA EDITOR IN CHIEF JOE QUESADA
PUBLISHER DAN BUCKLEY EXEC. PRODUCER ALAN FINE
SEE THE HULKS HELP SMASH CHAOS IN
CHAOS WAR #5!
DEDICATED TO HARLAN ELLISON, WHO INTRODUCED THE WORLD TO JARELLA IN INCREDIBLE HULK #140.

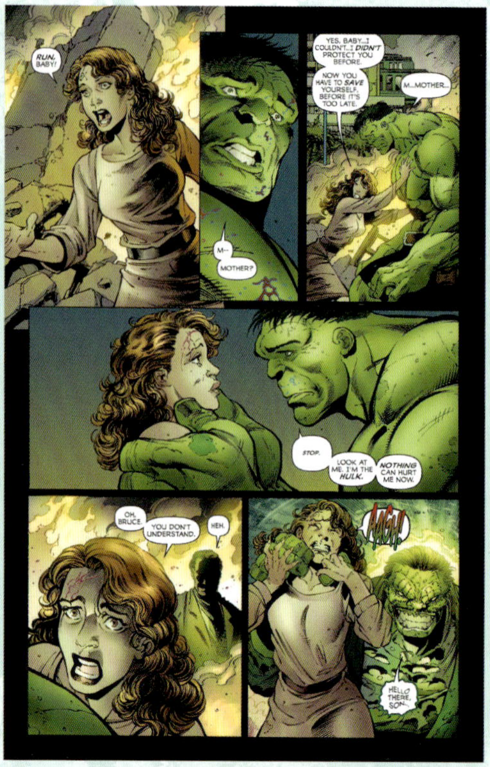
RUN, BABY!
M--
MOTHER?
YES, BABY...I COULDN'T...I DIDN'T PROTECT YOU BEFORE.
NOW YOU HAVE TO SAVE YOURSELF, BEFORE IT'S TOO LATE.
M...MOTHER...
STOP.
LOOK AT ME. I'M THE HULK.
NOTHING CAN HURT ME NOW.
OH, BRUCE.
YOU DON'T UNDERSTAND.
HEH.
AAGH!
HELLO THERE, SON...

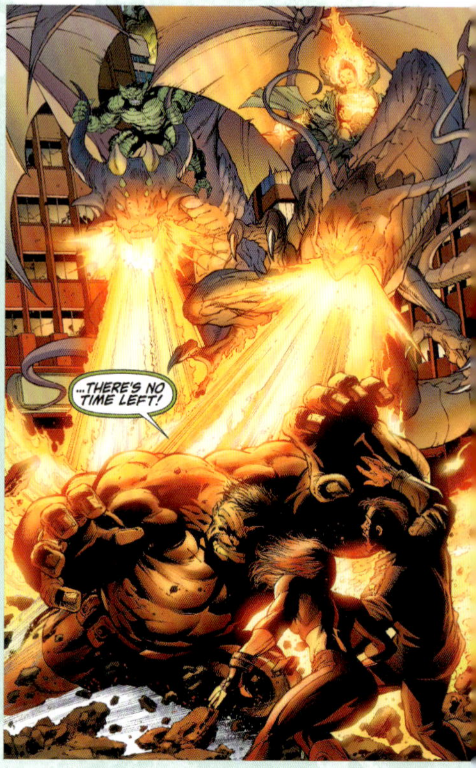
...THERE'S NO TIME LEFT!

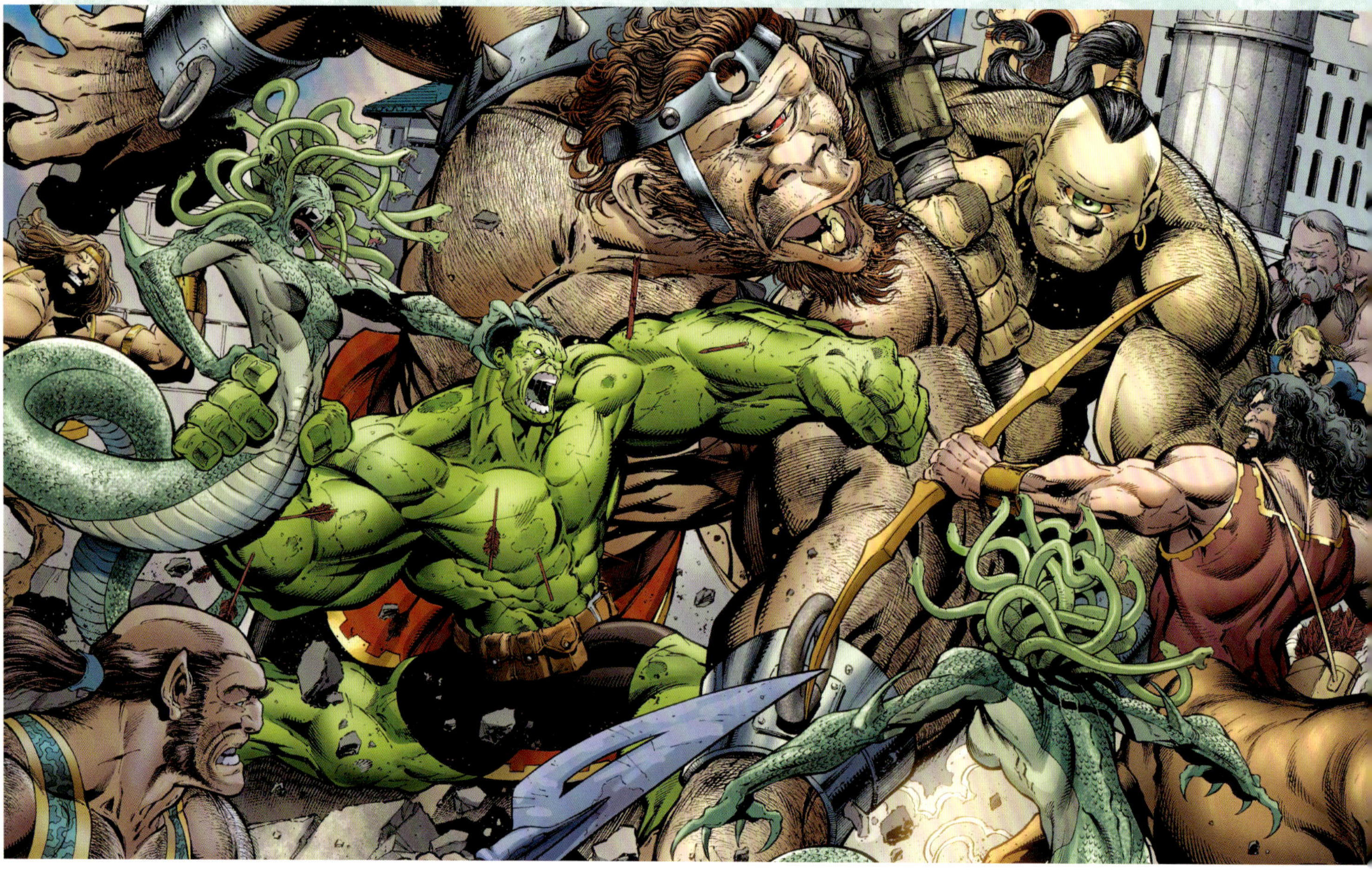

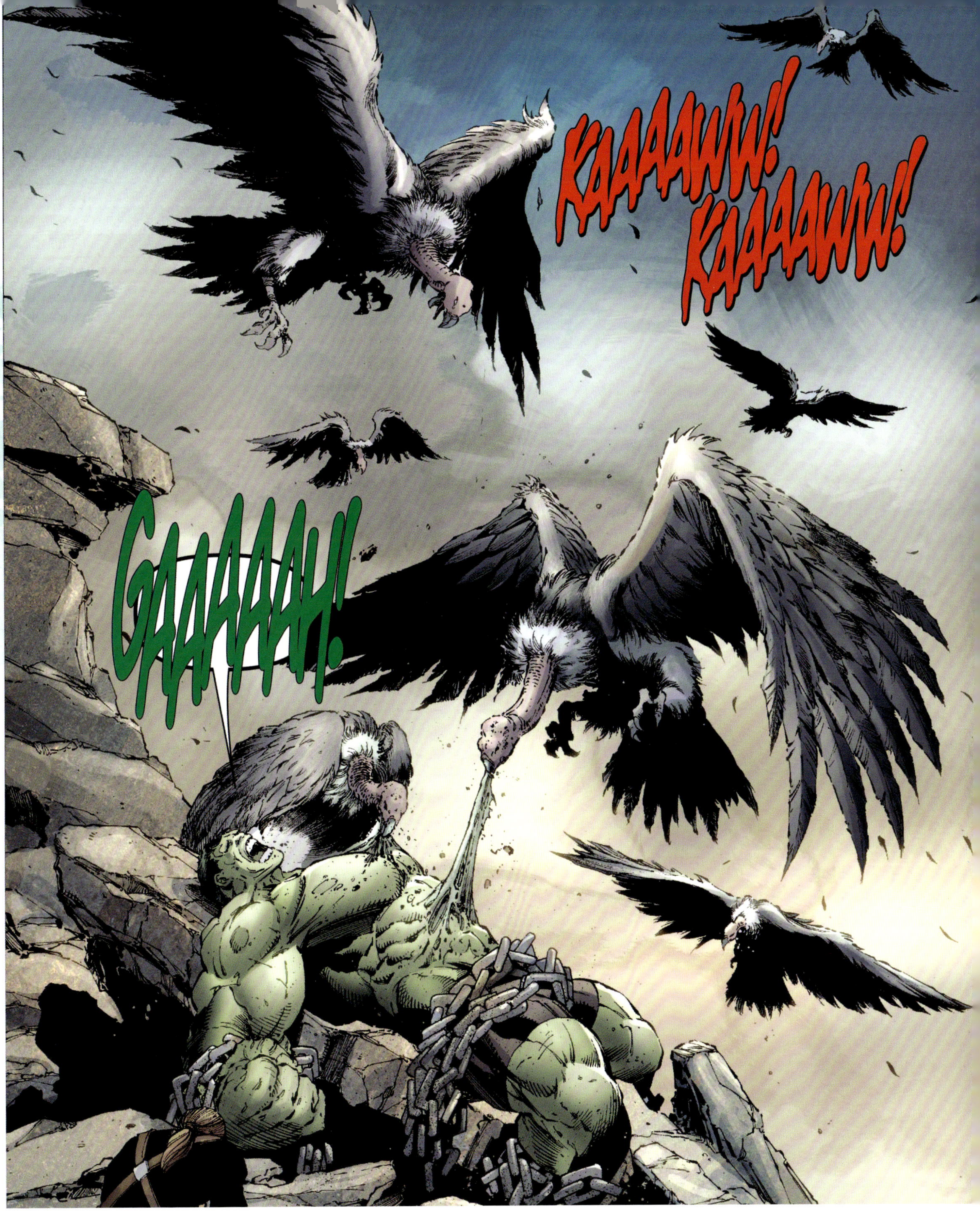
KAAAAWW! KAAAAWW!
GAAAAH!

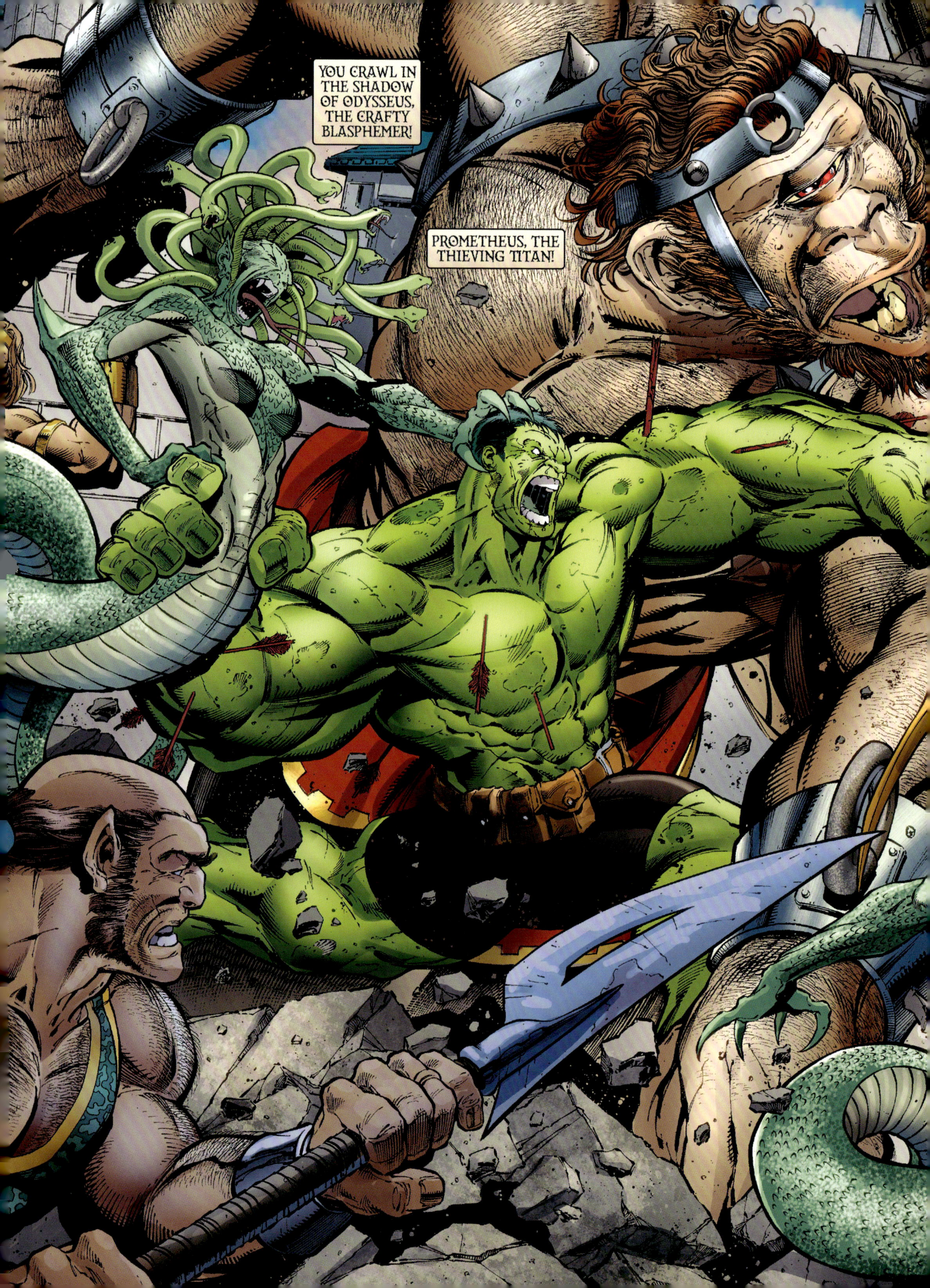
YOU CRAWL IN THE SHADOW OF ODYSSEUS, THE CRAFTY BLASPHEMER!
PROMETHEUS, THE THIEVING TITAN!

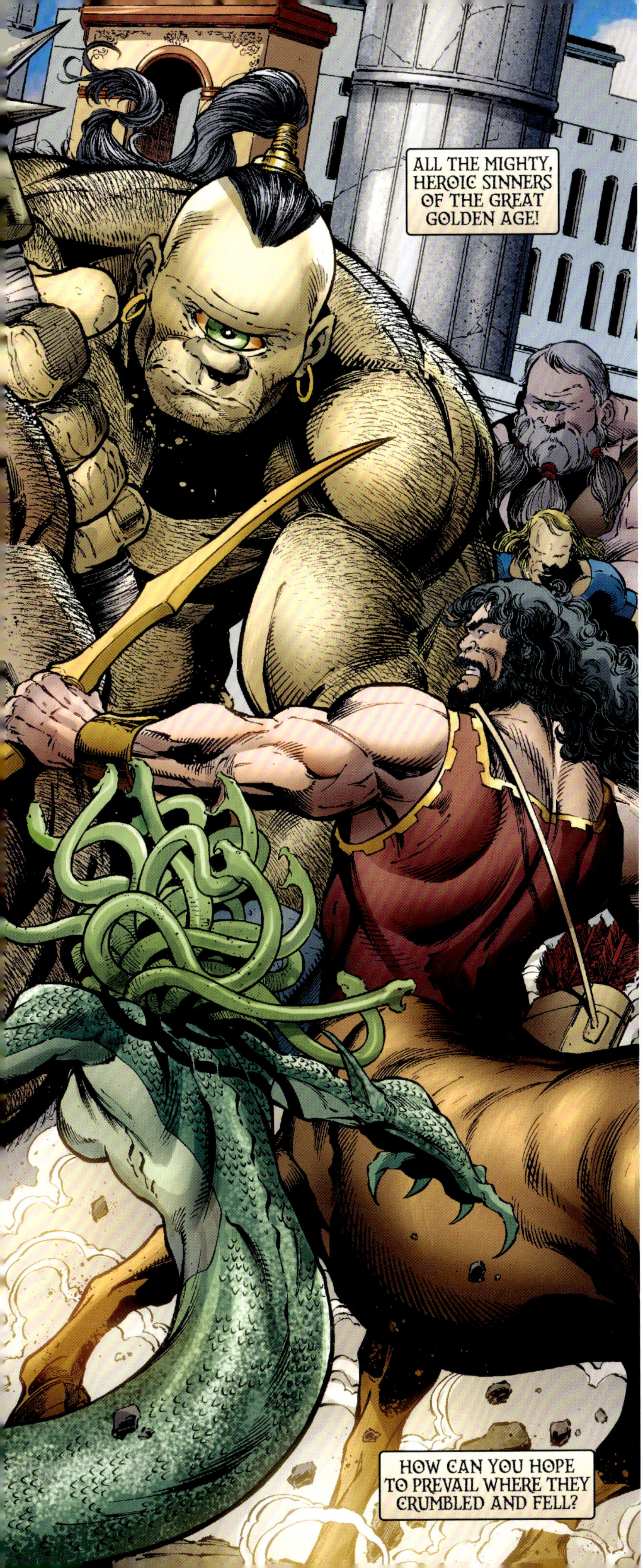
ALL THE MIGHTY, HEROIC SINNERS OF THE GREAT GOLDEN AGE!
HOW CAN YOU HOPE TO PREVAIL WHERE THEY CRUMBLED AND FELL?

to "hit harder" will work. Red She-Hulk, too, doubts their chances of success. She tells the Hulk that they had their butts kicked by the Chaos King, and asks, "What makes you think we can beat him now?" He tells her, "We're Hulks—we don't lose."

Marlo uses her powers as Death to marshal some reinforcements. She brings some old friends and loved ones back to life. They include Doc Samson; the Hulk's first wife Jarella, Queen of K'ai; Major Glenn Talbott, Betty Ross's first husband; and Hiroim the Oldstrong.

The crew seem happy to see their loved ones alive again, except for Red She-Hulk. She grabs her resuscitated husband, her arm cocked back, ready to punch his lights out. She says that he betrayed her to Samuel Sterns, aka the Leader, and to give her one good reason not to rip him in half. Samson intervenes and tells her that the man who betrayed her was not her husband, but a robot. Just as Red She-Hulk transforms back into Betty to greet her husband, all hell breaks loose.

The demons, alongside Doctor Strange, attack. When it appears that the Hulk and his newly resurrected team might be winning, the Abomination has an idea: if Marlo can raise an army of the dead, so can he. Banner's mother appears, and, right behind her appears Banner's abusive father. The monster that always existed inside Banner's drunken, abusive father transforms him into an actual demon. Father and son battle. But the more the Hulk hates, the stronger his father becomes.

Can the Hulk bury his demons? Will Zom release Doctor Strange? Can the sleeping awaken? And what will become of the dead who returned to help the living?

# HEART OF THE MONSTER

## 2011

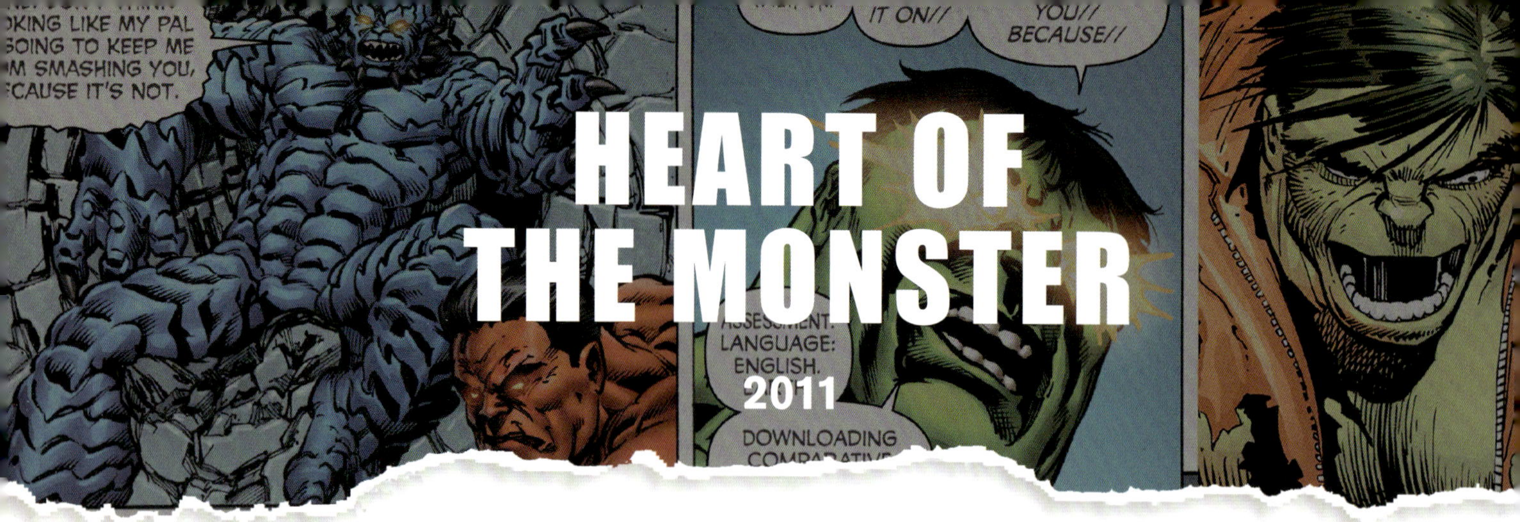

OKING LIKE MY PAL
GOING TO KEEP ME
M SMASHING YOU,
CAUSE IT'S NOT.
IT ON//
YOU// BECAUSE//
LANGUAGE: ENGLISH.
DOWNLOADING


How can you mend a big, green broken heart? The love of Bruce Banner's life, Betty Ross, is with someone else. Well, not actually Betty; it's her alter ego, Red She-Hulk, who is with someone named Tyrannus, Lord of Subterranean. Tyrannus rules over a kingdom three miles beneath Las Vegas. Tyrannus is also known as Romulus Augustulus, an immortal who was once a child emperor of the Western Roman Empire. In this kingdom underneath Las Vegas, there is a well that offers eternal youth.

The water is the reason why Monica Rappaccini—Scientist Supreme of Advanced Idea Mechanics (A.I.M.), a former branch of Hydra—has invaded Tyrannus's kingdom with A.I.M. agents. Once she gains control of the well, she kills the agents and explains to Tyrannus that it is actually a wishing well. Red She-Hulk appears, plunges her hand into the wishing well, and tells Monica that she's "gonna wish that she'd never been born." A huge rush of water heads up to the surface and explodes on the Vegas strip. Monica is able to call for an evacuation. A hang glider suddenly appears to pick her up and fly her away.

Hours later, the Hulk sits in the desert at the Gamma Base. He knows about Betty and is out there to think. His thoughts are interrupted by someone approaching behind him. A white-haired woman lands her glider and stumbles toward him. She is barely able to speak the word "Hulk" before she collapses. This old woman, now lying in the lab's medical bay, is Monica Rappaccini—and she has aged.

While lying in bed, Monica tells the Hulk that Red She-Hulk is in trouble. She tells him she invaded the underground kingdom because she wanted to use the wishing well to fix the world. Hulk transforms back to Banner, and he, Amadeus Cho, and Red She-Hulk, fly out to Las Vegas.

As they approach the city, a giant creature with long, sharp fangs comes out of the ground and attacks the plane Banner and his crew flew in on. The ship crashes, and they end

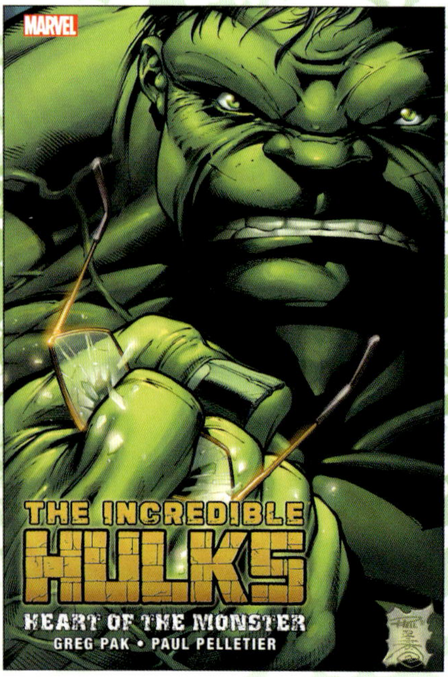

MARVEL
THE INCREDIBLE HULKS
HEART OF THE MONSTER
GREG PAK • PAUL PELLETIER


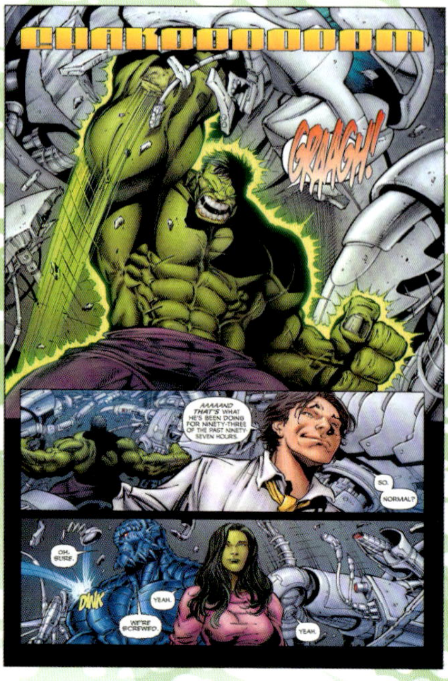

GRAAGH!
AAAAAND THAT'S WHAT HE'S BEEN DOING FOR NINETY-THREE OF THE PAST NINETY-SEVEN HOURS.
SO.
NORMAL?
OH. SURE.
DINK
YEAH.
WE'RE SCREWED.
YEAH.


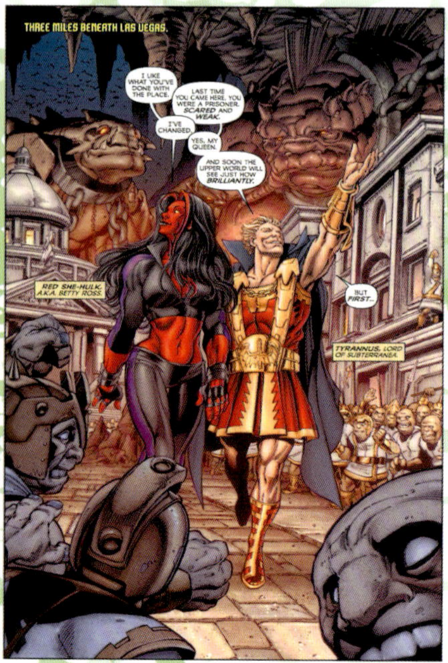

THREE MILES BENEATH LAS VEGAS.
I LIKE WHAT YOU'VE DONE WITH THE PLACE.
LAST TIME YOU CAME HERE, YOU WERE A PRISONER. SCARED AND WEAK.
I'VE CHANGED.
YES, MY QUEEN.
AND SOON THE UPPER WORLD WILL SEE JUST HOW BRILLIANTLY.
RED SHE-HULK, A.K.A. BETTY ROSS.
BUT FIRST...
TYRANNUS, LORD OF SUBTERRANEA.

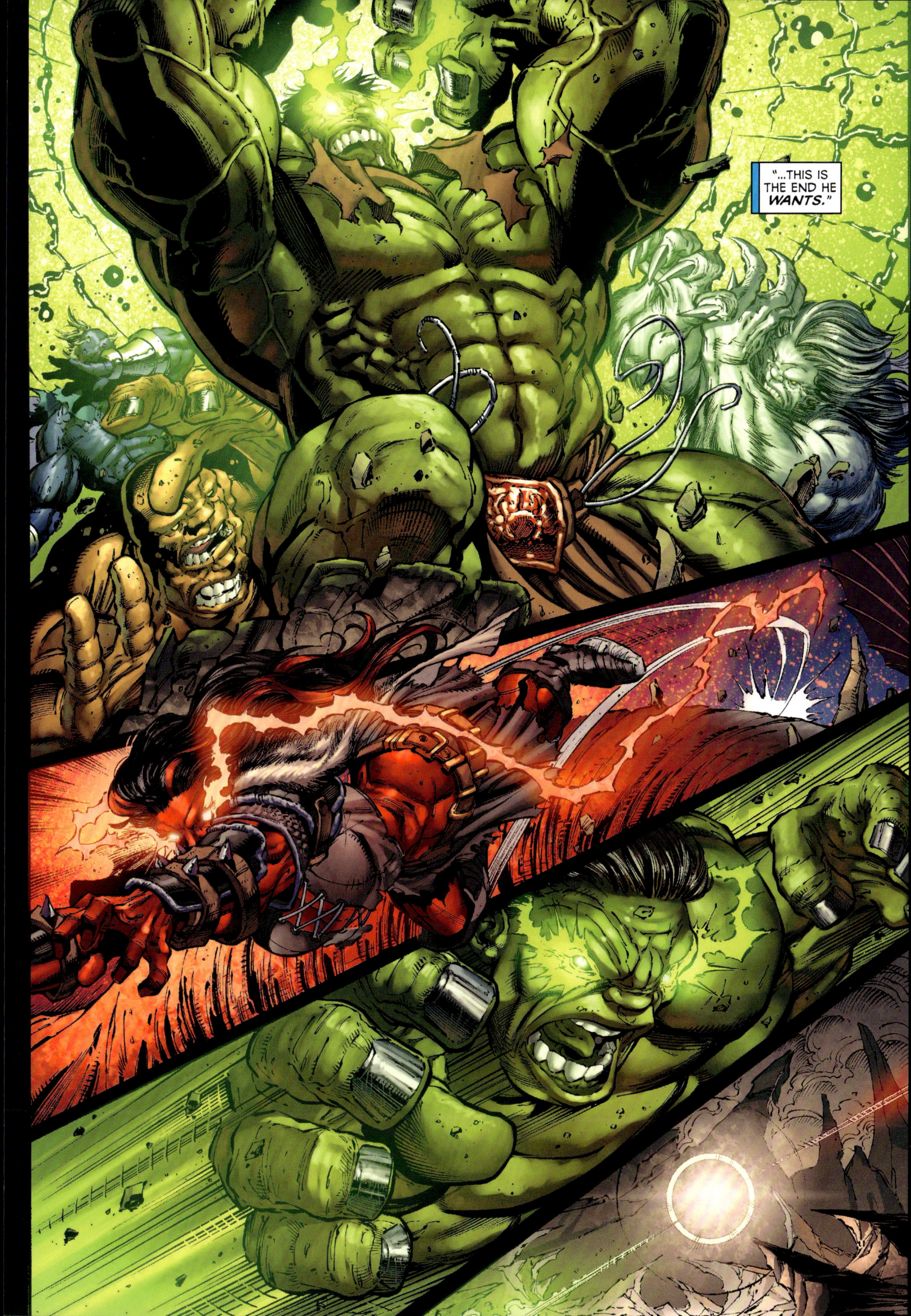
"...THIS IS THE END HE *WANTS.*"

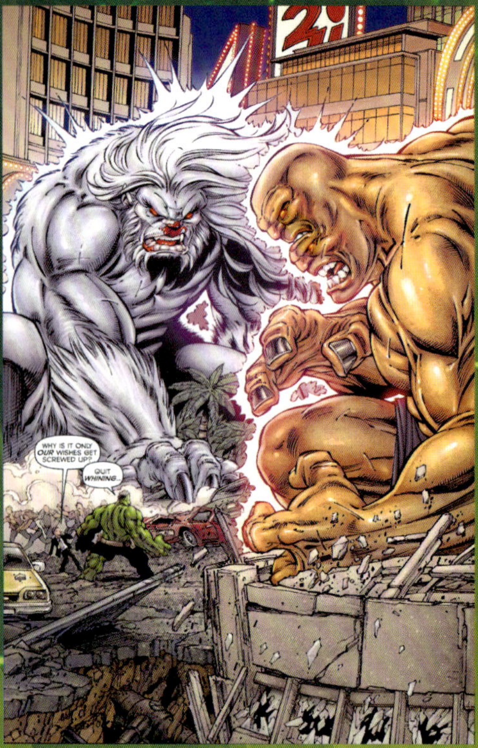
WHY IS IT ONLY OUR WISHES GET SCREWED UP?
QUIT WHINING...

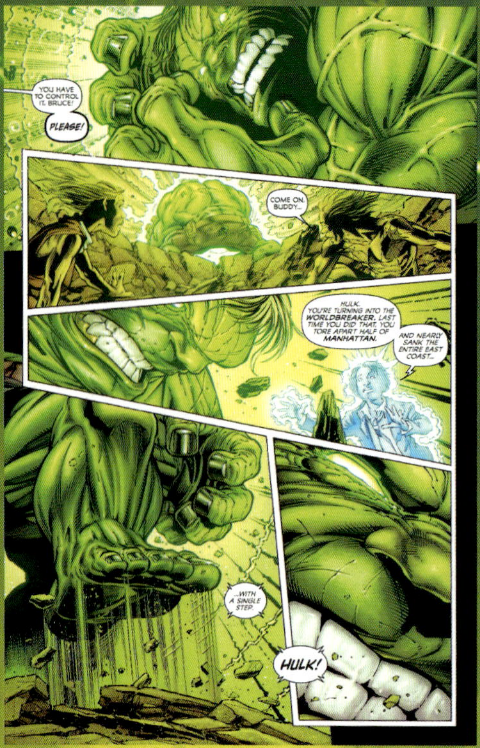
YOU HAVE TO CONTROL IT, BRUCE!
PLEASE!
COME ON, BUDDY...
HULK. YOU'RE TURNING INTO THE WORLDBREAKER. LAST TIME YOU DID THAT, YOU TORE APART HALF OF MANHATTAN.
AND NEARLY SANK THE ENTIRE EAST COAST...
...WITH A SINGLE STEP.
HULK!

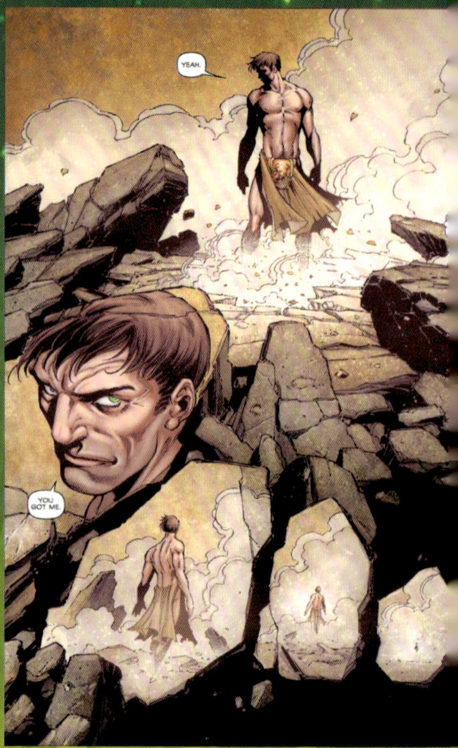
YEAH.
YOU GOT ME.

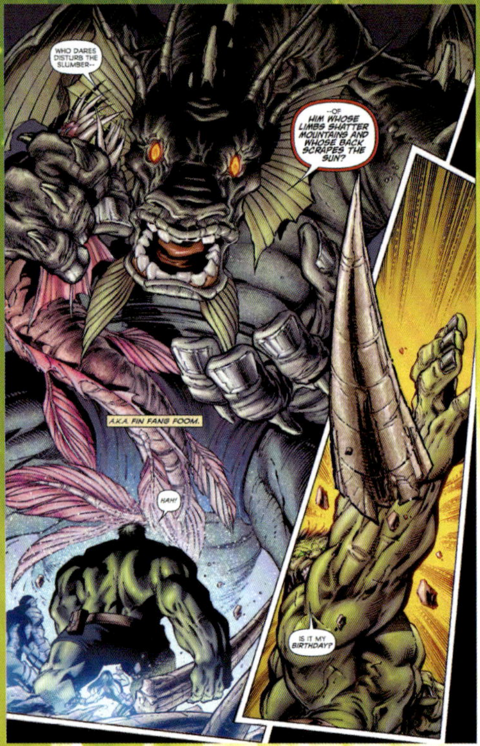
WHO DARES DISTURB THE SLUMBER--
--OF HIM WHOSE LIMBS SHATTER MOUNTAINS AND WHOSE BACK SCRAPES THE SUN?
A.K.A. FIN FANG FOOM.
HAH!
IS IT MY BIRTHDAY?

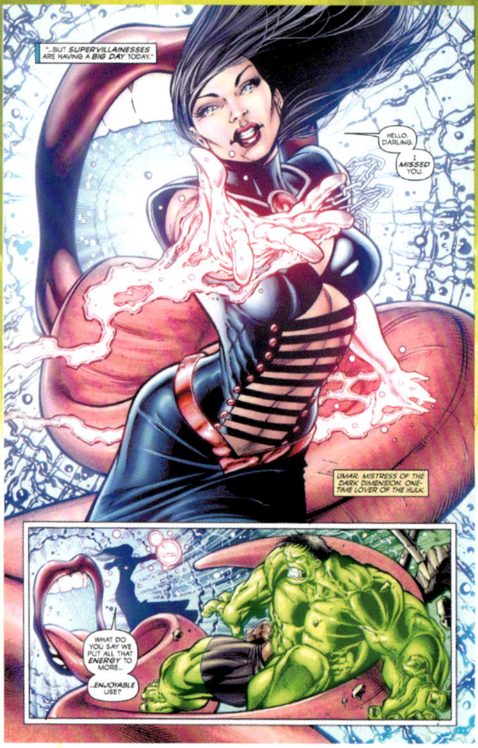
"...BUT SUPERVILLAINESSES ARE HAVING A BIG DAY TODAY."
HELLO, DARLING.
I MISSED YOU.
UMAR, MISTRESS OF THE DARK DIMENSION, ONE-TIME LOVER OF THE HULK.
WHAT DO YOU SAY WE PUT ALL THAT ENERGY TO MORE...
...ENJOYABLE USE?

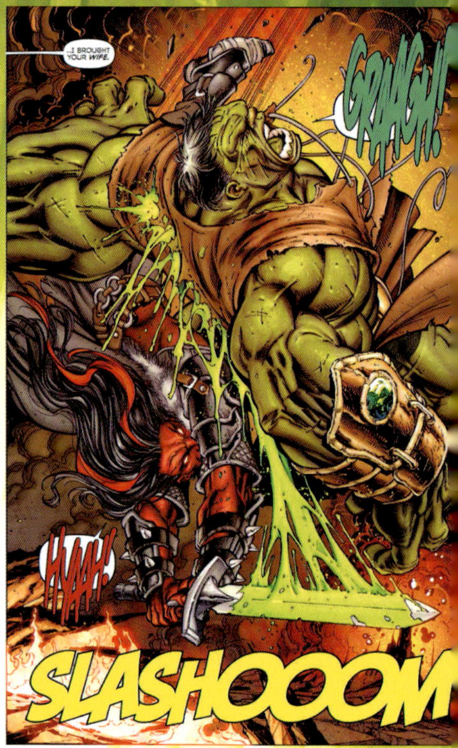
...I BROUGHT YOUR WIFE.
SLASHOOOM

up in Tyrannus's underground kingdom. Amadeus gets up, not realizing he is standing in the wishing well, and says, "We could use a little help down here." Suddenly, Bi-Beast, Armageddon, Fin Fang Foom, Umar, and Wendigo appear—not exactly the kind of help Amadeus was looking for. These are some of the Hulk's fiercest foes. There is a lesson here: be careful what you wish for.

His enemies come up from the underground, and now they are gigantic. It appears that Red She-Hulk is wishing up a storm. A fierce battle ensues, which ends up on the streets of Las Vegas, and the Hulk is victorious—for now.

Meanwhile, Amadeus Cho gets a hold of the President of the United States. Cho tells the president about the wishing well and wants the government's best scientist to research it. But the president needs to talk to Banner, and the Hulk won't let Banner out. He's mad. And when Banner's mad, the Hulk has control.

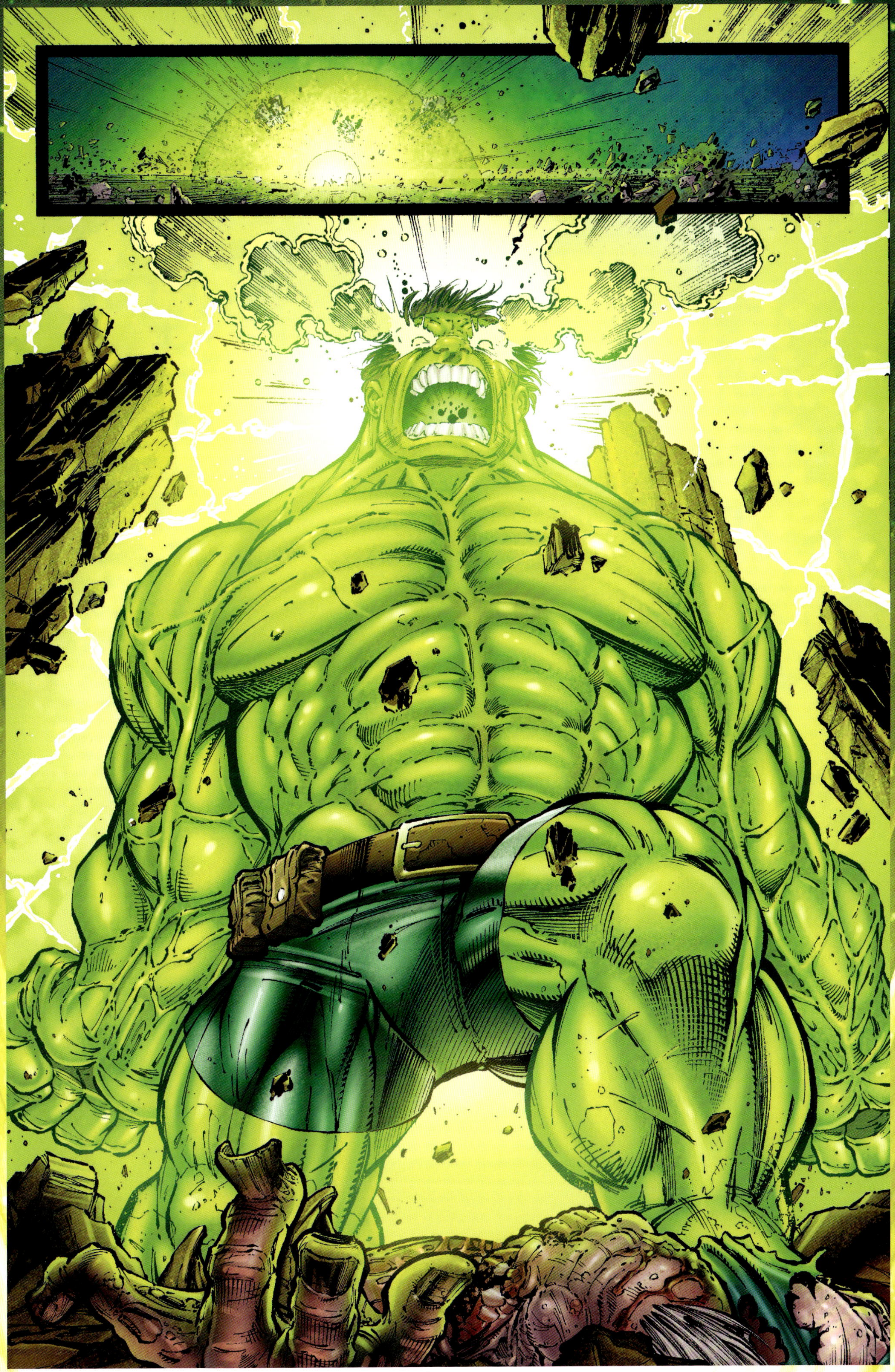

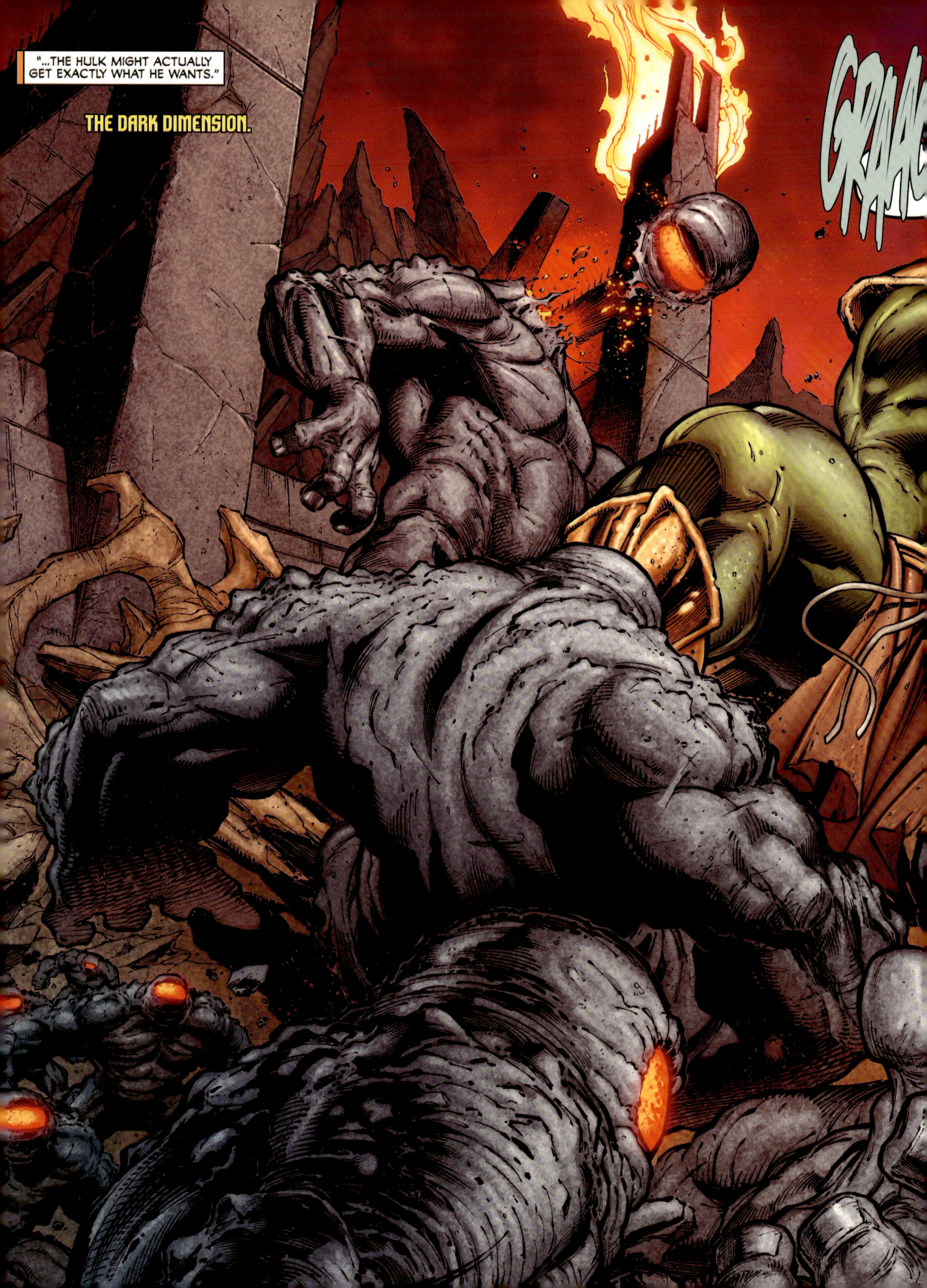
"...THE HULK MIGHT ACTUALLY GET EXACTLY WHAT HE WANTS."
THE DARK DIMENSION.

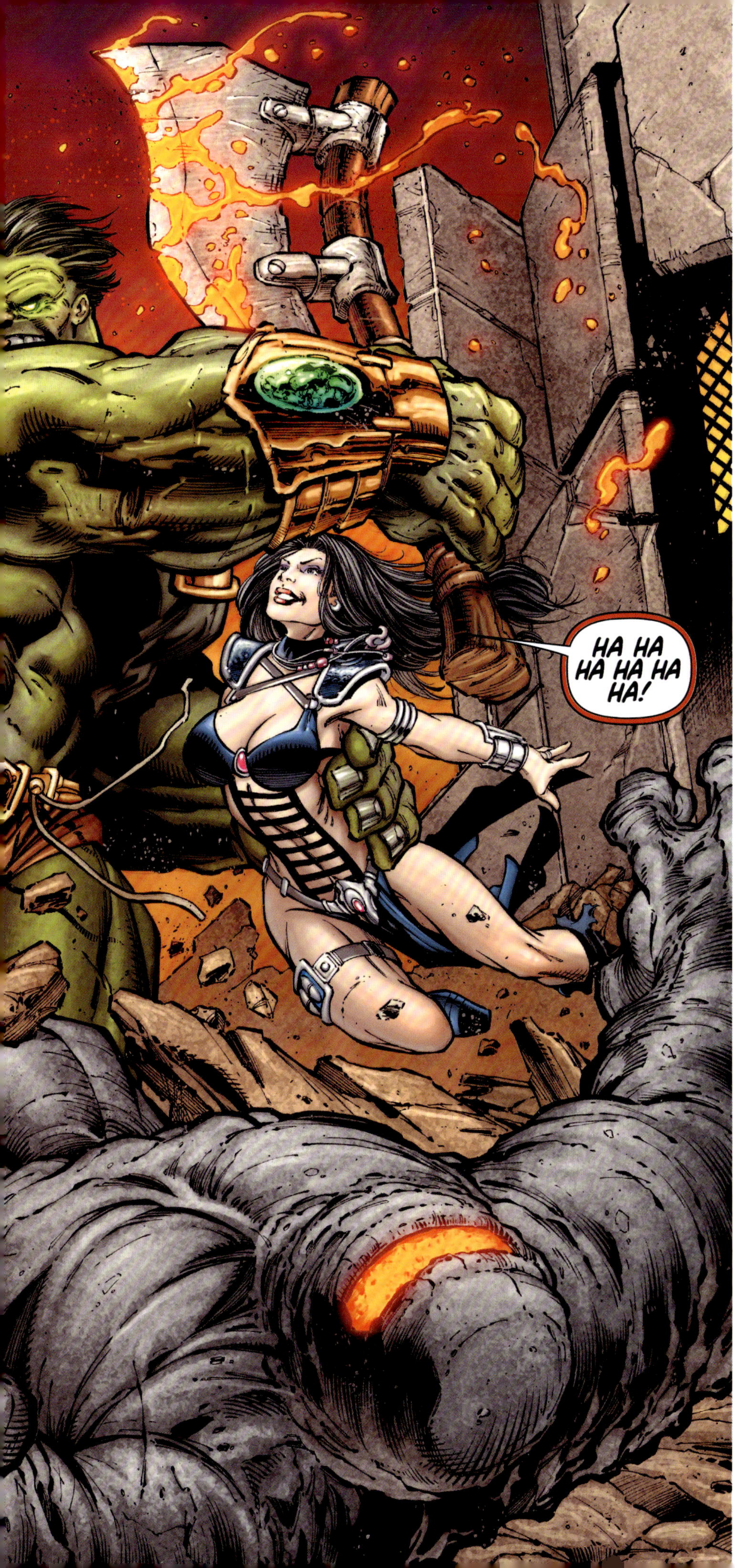
HA HA HA HA HA HA!

In space, another of the Hulk's enemies has appeared: Arm'Chedon, leader of the Trojan Empire. He now holds Red She-Hulk and A-Bomb hostage. Before Arm'Chedon tosses them back down like rag dolls to Earth, he injects something into their skulls. Arm'Chedon reminds the Hulk, "You killed my *son*, Hulk. *Twice. Laughing*." After Red She-Hulk and A-Bomb crash back to Earth, they change back to Jennifer Walters and Rick Jones—and they are dying.

The Hulk is enraged, and he starts transforming into Worldbreaker—a smarter, stronger, and more dangerous version of the Hulk. While he is Worldbreaker, he has no regard for others around him. This time, Amadeus Cho is able to stop the Hulk from transforming into Worldbreaker. He talks him down.

The Hulk's enemies are on the loose, his friends are dying, and the woman he loves is not only with another man, but she also seems to hate the Hulk. How can the Hulk and Bruce Banner come together and get what they both wish for?

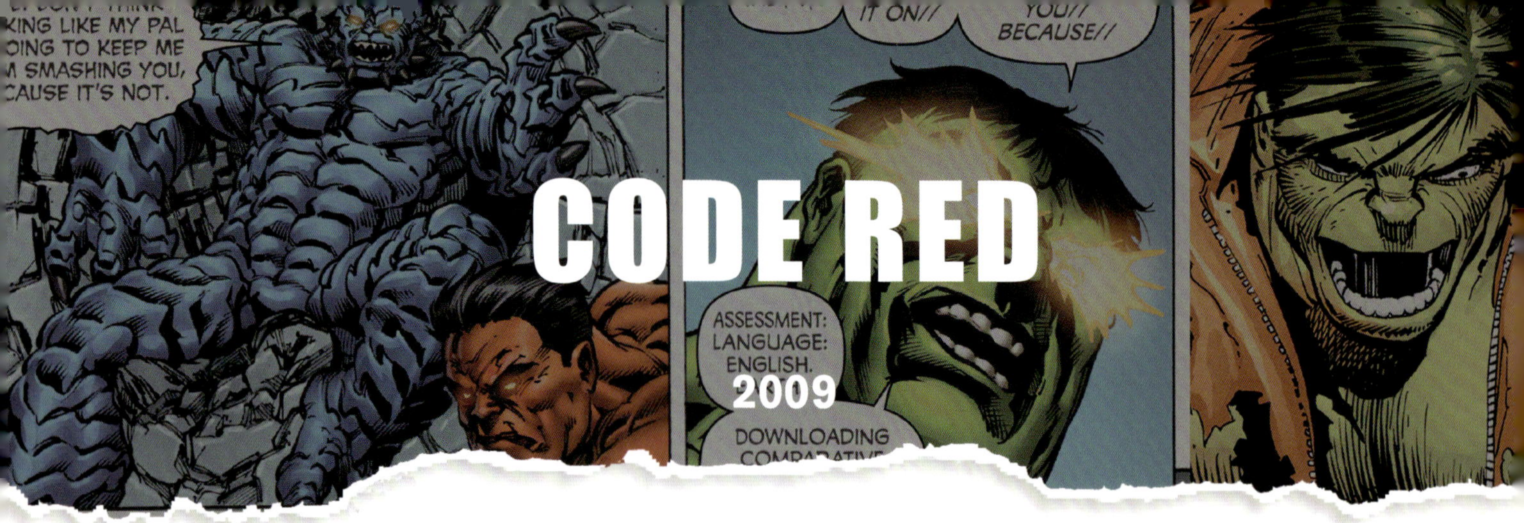
KING LIKE MY PAL
OING TO KEEP ME
A SMASHING YOU,
CAUSE IT'S NOT.
IT ON//
YOU// BECAUSE//
ASSESSMENT: LANGUAGE: ENGLISH.
DOWNLOADING

# CODE RED

## 2009

The group of scientists known as the Intelligencia lead by M.O.D.O.K. and made up of Leader, Doctor Doom, Mad Thinker, Wizard, Egghead, and the Red Ghost have devised a method to create a super powered creature that they can control. They create their own version of the Red Hulk.

Bruce Banner sits alone in a lab deep inside a cave in the New Mexico desert. The Hulk no longer lives inside of him: he was killed by Intelligencia's Red Hulk. But Norman Osborn believes that the Hulk is still alive. Osborn calls in Ares, God of War, to track down Banner. Where he finds Banner, he will find the Hulk.

Rick Jones now lives permanently as his alter-ego A-Bomb. Jones/A-Bomb knows where Banner is hiding. A-Bomb tells Bruce that he believes that because they both have been exposed to gamma radiation, the radiation acts as a sort of beacon. This beacon shows him where Banner is located.

A-Bomb's theory is immediately put to the test once Ares walks in. To be fair, you don't need a gut full of gamma rays to know that the first place to look for Bruce Banner is his own lab. It's either that or almost any diner anywhere in the Southwest.

Ares starts a fight with Banner in order to lure the Hulk to come out and fight. Hulk doesn't manifest, and Banner manages to lock Ares in a containment cell, set to open automatically in twenty-four hours. This gives Banner and A-Bomb a chance to escape.

After Ares is released from the cell, he immediately reports back to Osborn, who seems pleased about the account. Ares did what Osborn wanted—he confirmed that the Hulk is no longer in Banner.

Domino, the mercenary and member of X-Force (whose power is being lucky—extremely lucky), is sitting on a rooftop with a sniper rifle. Through her scope she sees a group of men that appears to be arguing. Domino follows one of the men. Domino's luck might have finally run out, because the man she is tracking is the Red Hulk. He confronts her, wanting to know why she is there and what she witnessed.

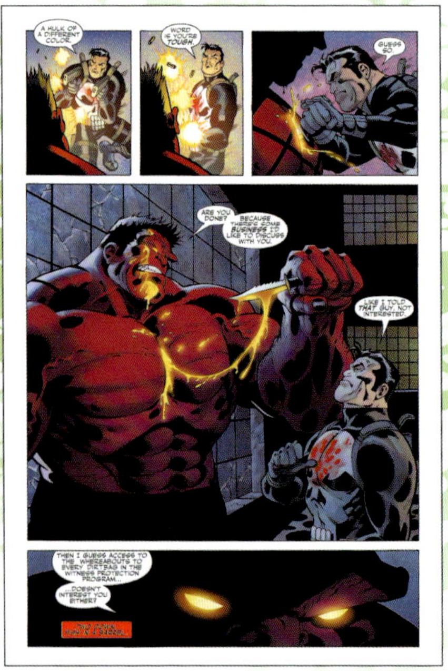

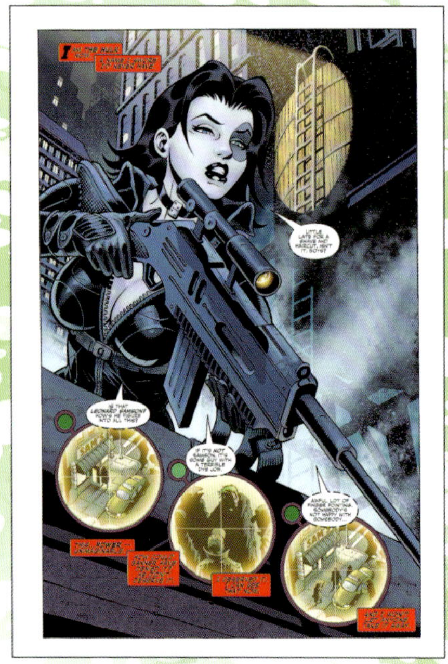

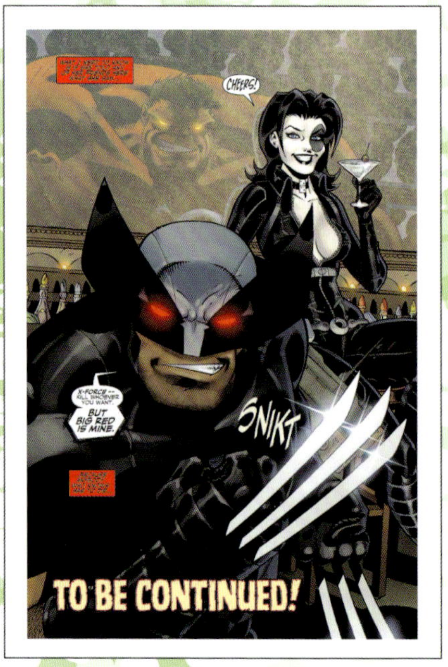
CHEERS!
SNIKT
TO BE CONTINUED!

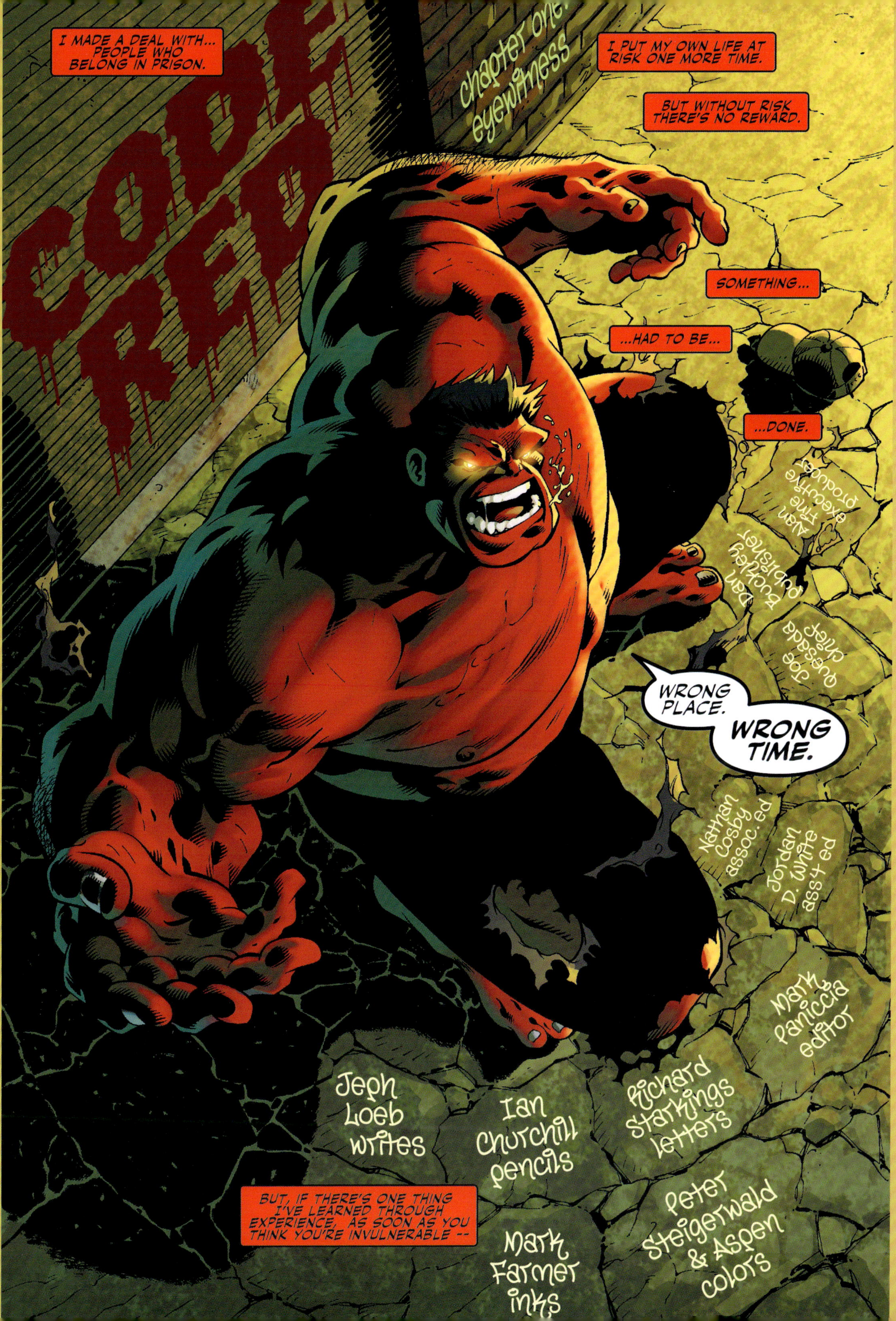
I MADE A DEAL WITH... PEOPLE WHO BELONG IN PRISON.
CODE RED
chapter one: eyewitness
I PUT MY OWN LIFE AT RISK ONE MORE TIME.
BUT WITHOUT RISK THERE'S NO REWARD.
SOMETHING...
...HAD TO BE...
...DONE.
WRONG PLACE.
WRONG TIME.
BUT, IF THERE'S ONE THING I'VE LEARNED THROUGH EXPERIENCE, AS SOON AS YOU THINK YOU'RE INVULNERABLE --
Jeph Loeb writes
Ian Churchill pencils
Mark Farmer inks
Richard Starkings letters
Peter Steigerwald & Aspen colors
Mark Paniccia editor
Nathan Cosby assoc. ed
Jordan D. White ass't ed
Joe Quesada chief
Dan Buckley publisher
Alan Fine executive producer

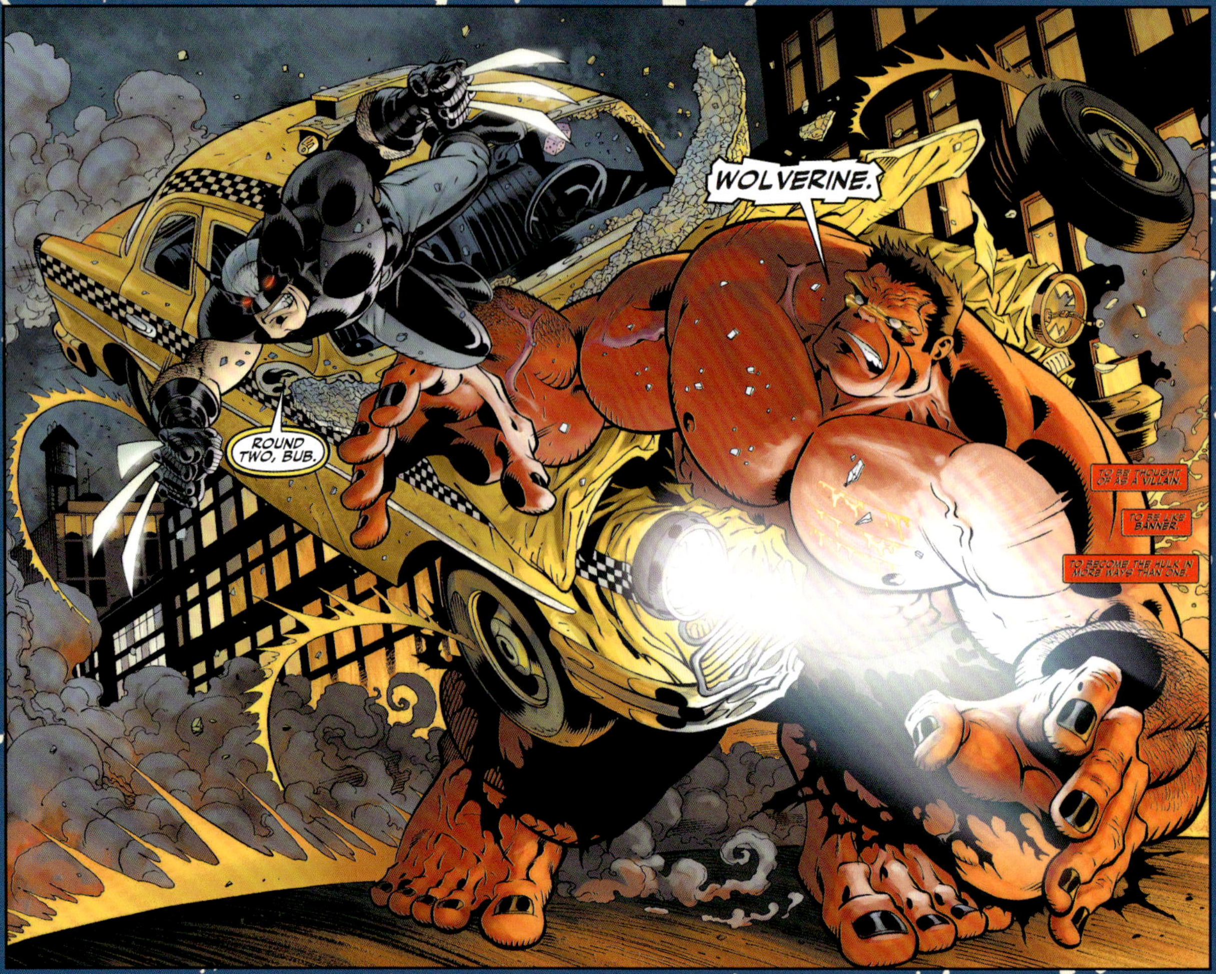
ROUND TWO, BUB.
WOLVERINE.
TO BE THOUGHT OF AS A VILLAIN.
TO BE LIKE BANNER.
TO BECOME THE HULK IN MORE WAYS THAN ONE.

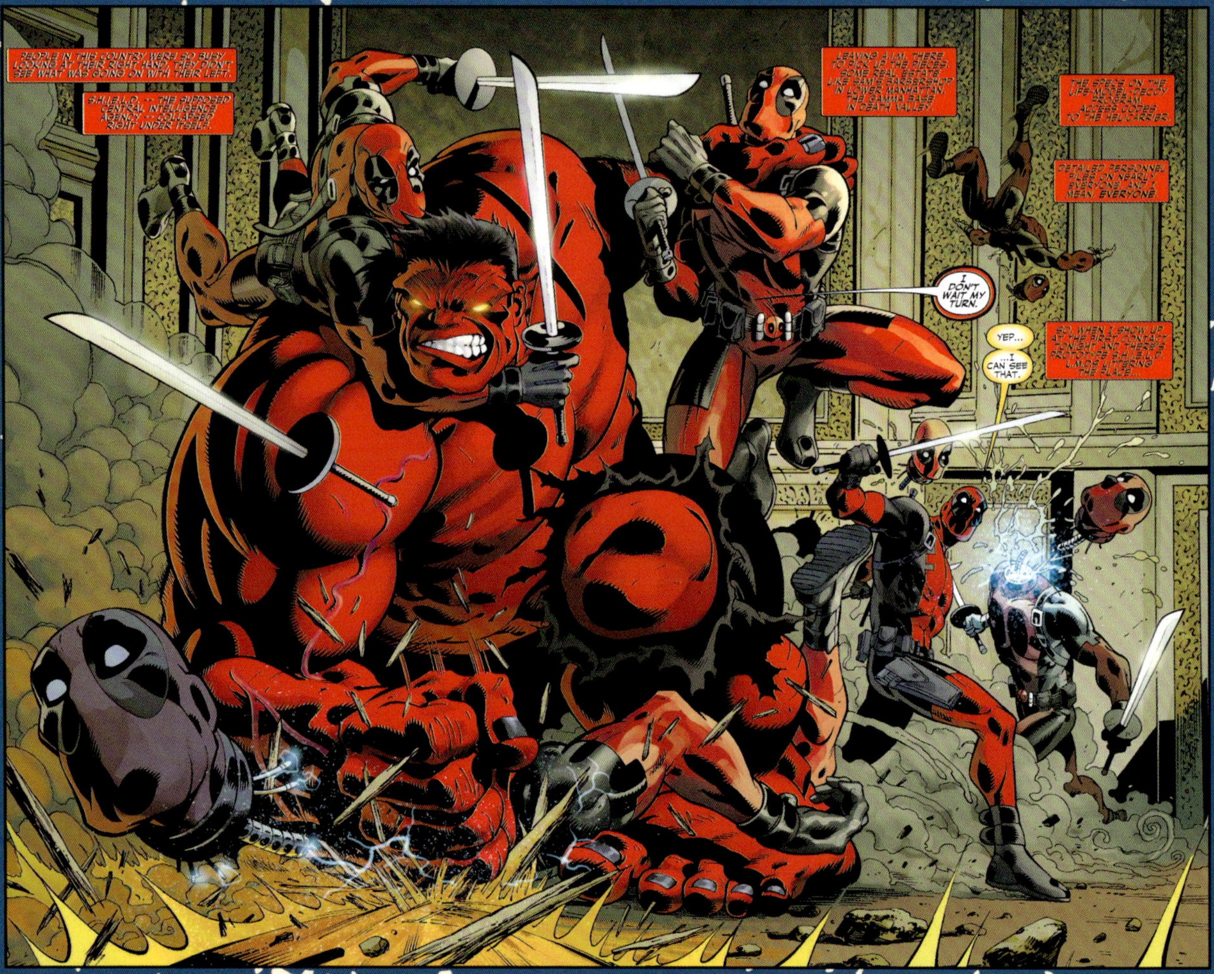
PEOPLE IN THIS COUNTRY WERE SO BUSY LOOKING AT THEIR RIGHT HAND, THEY DIDN'T SEE WHAT WAS GOING ON WITH THEIR LEFT.
S.H.I.E.L.D. -- THE SUPPOSED CENTRAL INTELLIGENCE AGENCY -- COLLAPSED RIGHT UNDER ITSELF.
LEAVING A.I.M. THERE TO PICK UP THE PIECES. SOME REAL ESTATE LIKE SAM'S BARBERSHOP IN LOWER MANHATTAN. THE GAMMA BASE IN DEATH VALLEY.
THE SPECS ON THE LIFE-MODEL-DECOY PROGRAM. ACCESS CODES TO THE HELICARRIER.
DETAILED PERSONNEL FILES ON NEARLY EVERYONE. AND I MEAN, EVERYONE.
I DON'T WAIT MY TURN.
YEP...
...I CAN SEE THAT.
SO, WHEN I SHOW UP AT THE FIRST CONTACT TONIGHT AND THERE'S PROTOTYPE S.H.I.E.L.D. L.M.DS LITTERING THE PLACE...

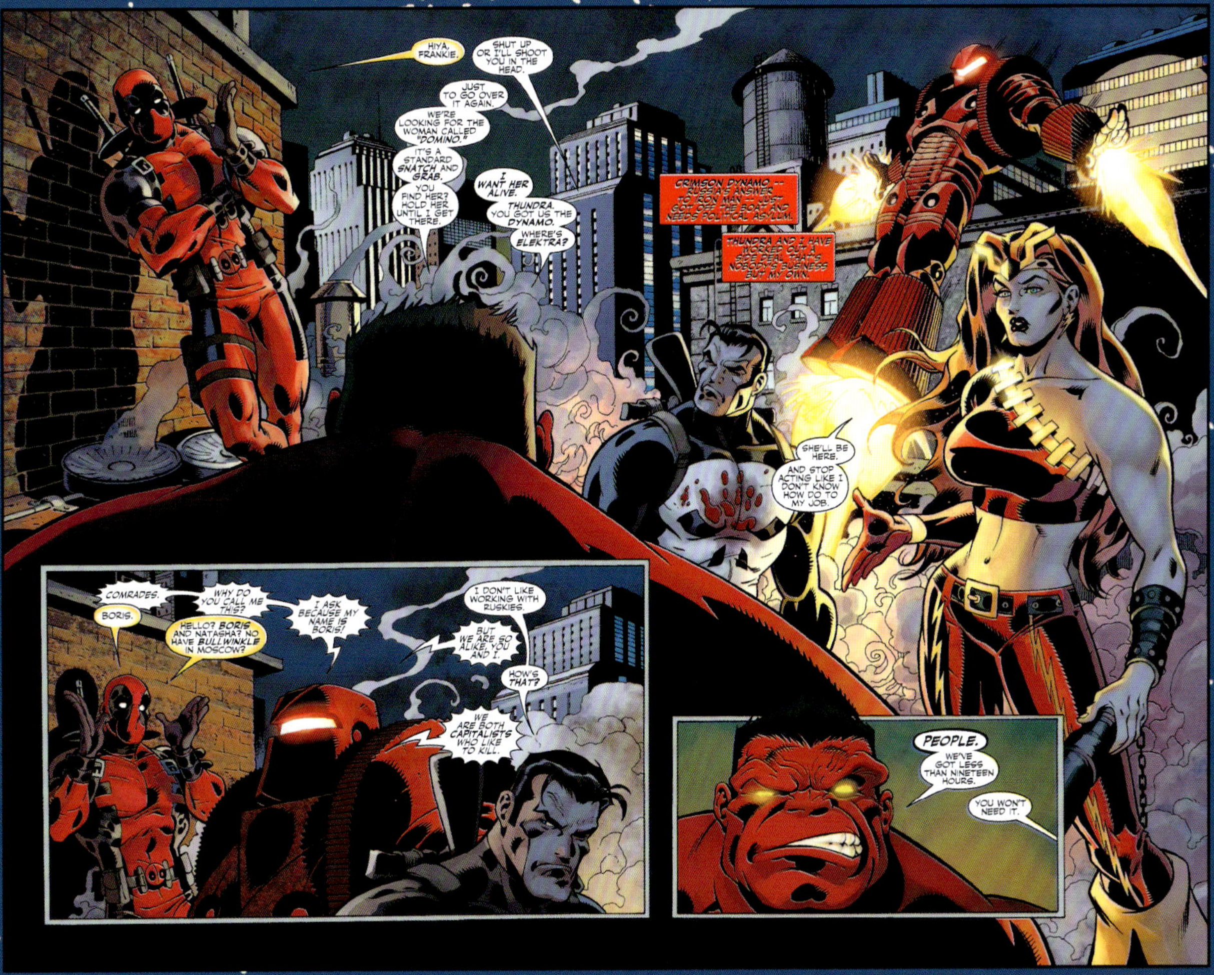
HIYA, FRANKIE.
SHUT UP OR I'LL SHOOT YOU IN THE HEAD.
JUST TO GO OVER IT AGAIN.
WE'RE LOOKING FOR THE WOMAN CALLED "DOMINO."
IT'S A STANDARD SNATCH AND GRAB.
YOU FIND HER? HOLD HER UNTIL I GET THERE.
I WANT HER ALIVE.
THUNDRA. YOU GOT US THE DYNAMO.
WHERE'S ELEKTRA?
CRIMSON DYNAMO -- RUSSIA'S ANSWER TO IRON MAN -- JUST GOT OFF THE BOAT AND NEEDS POLITICAL ASYLUM.
THUNDRA AND I HAVE WORKED OUT A SIDE DEAL THAT'S NOBODY'S BUSINESS BUT MY OWN.
SHE'LL BE HERE.
AND STOP ACTING LIKE I DON'T KNOW HOW DO TO MY JOB.
COMRADES.
BORIS.
WHY DO YOU CALL ME THIS?
HELLO? BORIS AND NATASHA? NO HAVE BULLWINKLE IN MOSCOW?
I ASK BECAUSE MY NAME IS BORIS!
I DON'T LIKE WORKING WITH RUSKIES.
BUT WE ARE SO ALIKE, YOU AND I.
HOW'S THAT?
WE ARE BOTH CAPITALISTS WHO LIKE TO KILL.
PEOPLE.
WE'VE GOT LESS THAN NINETEEN HOURS.
YOU WON'T NEED IT.

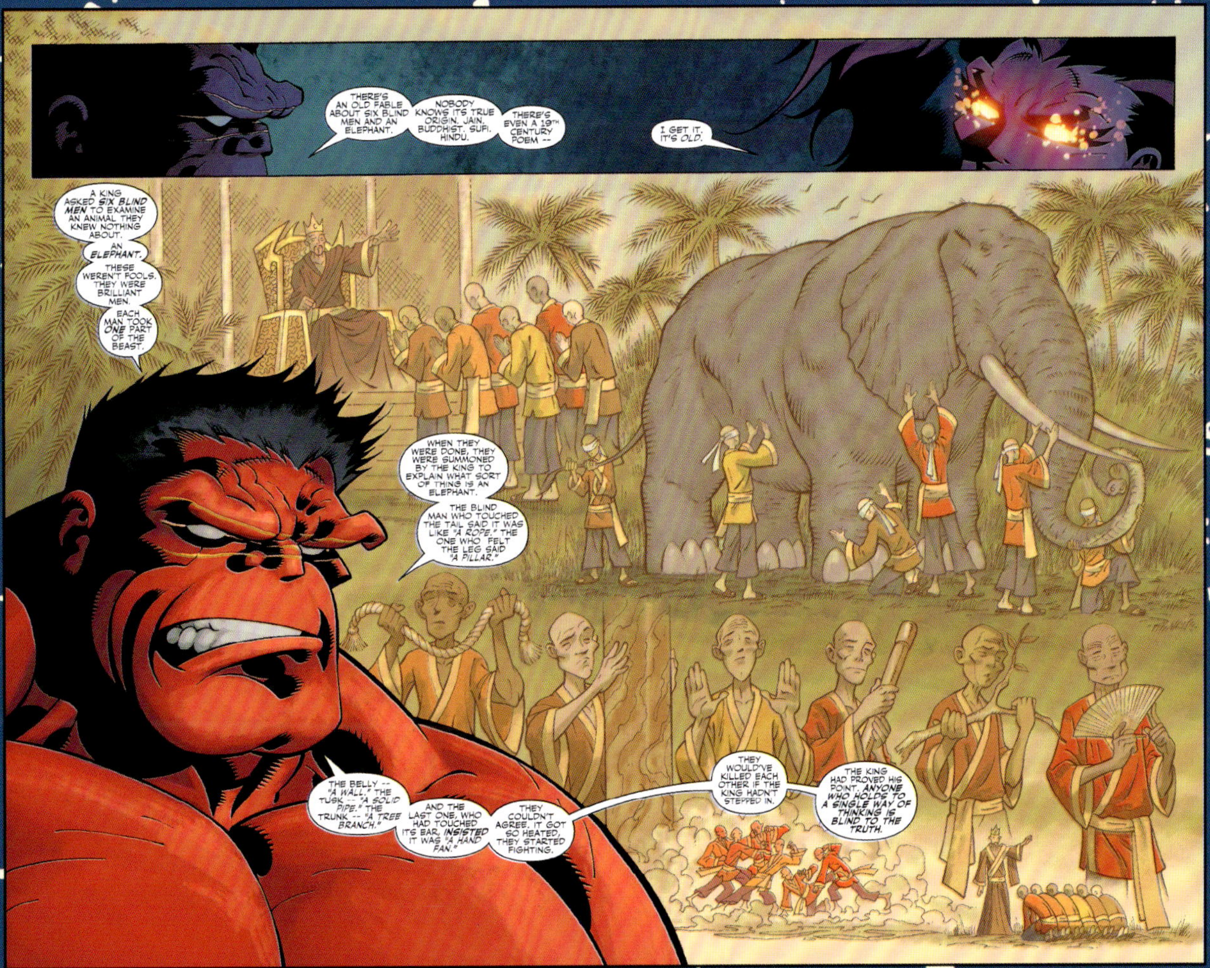
THERE'S AN OLD FABLE ABOUT SIX BLIND MEN AND AN ELEPHANT.
NOBODY KNOWS ITS TRUE ORIGIN. JAIN. BUDDHIST. SUFI. HINDU.
THERE'S EVEN A 19TH CENTURY POEM --
I GET IT. IT'S OLD.
A KING ASKED SIX BLIND MEN TO EXAMINE AN ANIMAL THEY KNEW NOTHING ABOUT.
AN ELEPHANT.
THESE WEREN'T FOOLS. THEY WERE BRILLIANT MEN.
EACH MAN TOOK ONE PART OF THE BEAST.
WHEN THEY WERE DONE, THEY WERE SUMMONED BY THE KING TO EXPLAIN WHAT SORT OF THING IS AN ELEPHANT.
THE BLIND MAN WHO TOUCHED THE TAIL SAID IT WAS LIKE "A ROPE." THE ONE WHO FELT THE LEG SAID "A PILLAR."
THE BELLY -- "A WALL." THE TUSK -- "A SOLID PIPE." THE TRUNK -- "A TREE BRANCH."
AND THE LAST ONE, WHO HAD TOUCHED ITS EAR, INSISTED IT WAS "A HAND FAN."
THEY COULDN'T AGREE. IT GOT SO HEATED, THEY STARTED FIGHTING.
THEY WOULD'VE KILLED EACH OTHER IF THE KING HADN'T STEPPED IN.
THE KING HAD PROVED HIS POINT. ANYONE WHO HOLDS TO A SINGLE WAY OF THINKING IS BLIND TO THE TRUTH.

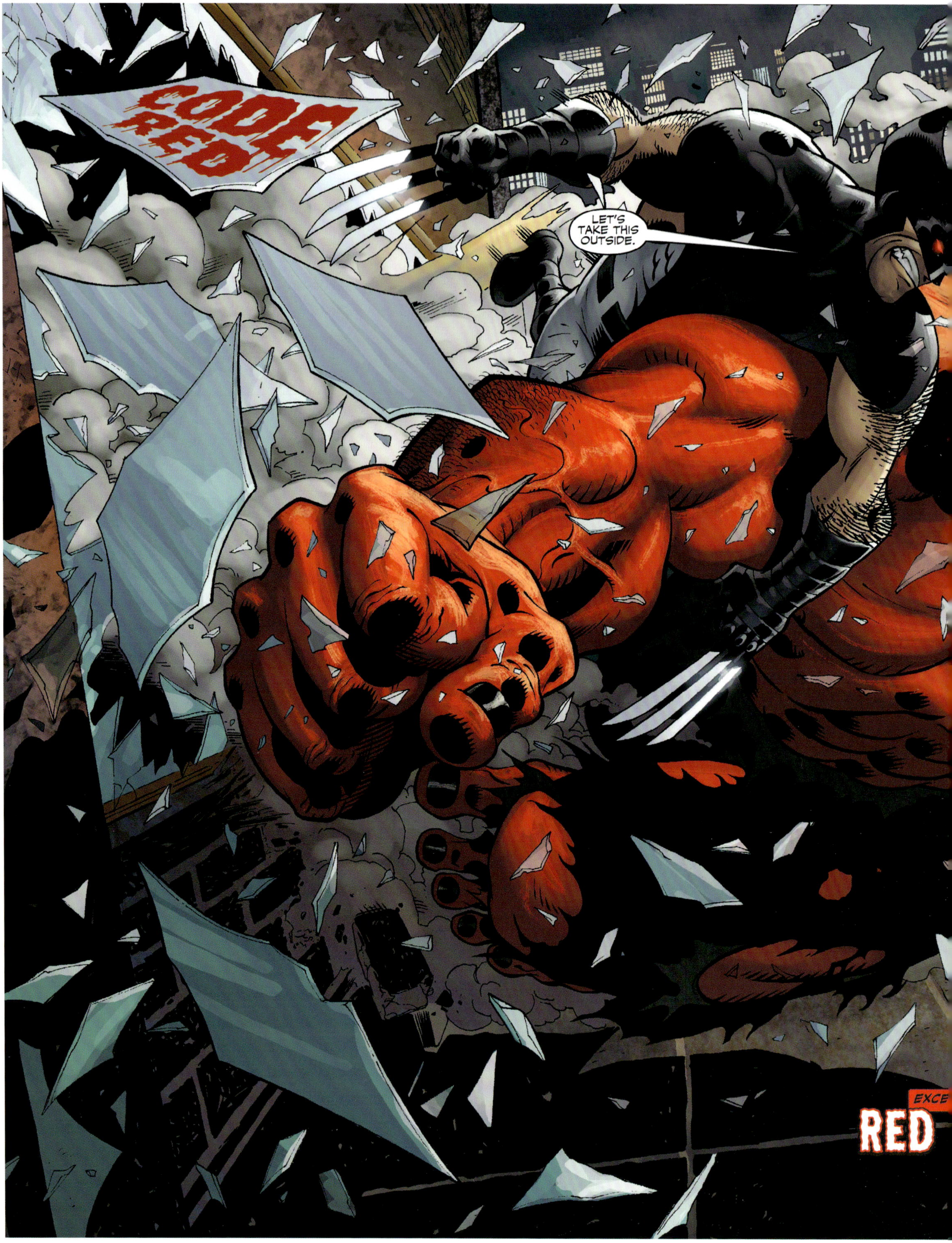
CODE RED
LET'S TAKE THIS OUTSIDE.
EXCE
RED

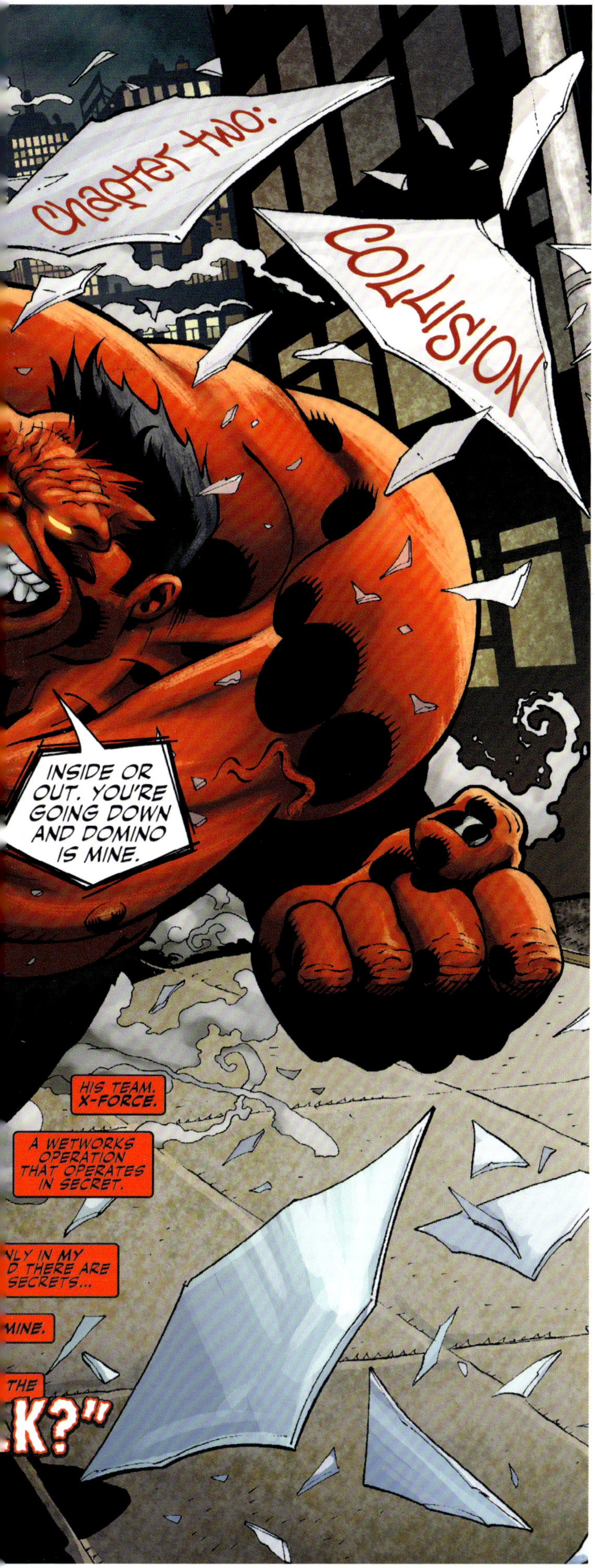
Chapter two:
COLLISION
INSIDE OR OUT. YOU'RE GOING DOWN AND DOMINO IS MINE.
HIS TEAM. X-FORCE.
A WETWORKS OPERATION THAT OPERATES IN SECRET.

She tries to explain, but Hulks tend to attack during questioning. She runs, and he pursues. Her luck comes flooding back when the Red Hulk smashes a water tank that spills onto a rooftop. The rooftop can't hold the weight of the water and it collapses. The Red Hulk goes down with it, allowing Domino time to escape.

Leonard Samson, Bruce Banner's former psychiatrist who exposed himself to gamma radiation, shows up to talk to Red Hulk. He is not alone: General Thaddeus "Thunderbolt" Ross is with him. Ross gives Red Hulk a list of people who can help him. Red Hulk doesn't want a team, but General Ross insists.

Ross's group consists of Deadpool, the Punisher, Thundra, Crimson Dynamo, and Elektra, who claims that she's already tracked down Domino. They head to a bar in Hell's Kitchen where Domino sits with her drink. But Domino is not alone; members of the X-Force are with her—Warpath, Archangel, X-23, and Wolverine. Of course, Wolverine strikes first, attacking Red Hulk, leaving glowing rivers of yellow blood.

Wolverine then strikes a bigger blow, slashing his claws across Red Hulk's eyes, blinding him. Red Hulk's eyes will heal, but it will take time. As the battle rages, Wolverine shows up driving a taxi and crashes it into Red Hulk, who doesn't see it coming. Someone shoots Wolverine in the back; a tall woman who looks like the female version of Red Hulk appears with a gun in her hand and her foot on Wolverine's head. She's certainly not the green She-Hulk. Is she Red She-Hulk?

While Red She-Hulk tries to pin Wolverine down, he escapes by jamming one of his claws into an electrical cable and another into Red She-Hulk's leg. The fighting continues, and Red She-Hulk uses this distraction to take Red Hulk away from it all. Without his sight, he is vulnerable.

A mysterious figure suddenly arrives, breaks up the fight, and tells Wolverine that he needs to focus on finding Domino and Elektra, who are now missing. This mystery man tells Red Hulk's allies that he will never make good on the deals that were made with the team. The man is Leonard Samson and he says that he is not like them—he's a man of his word.

The Red Hulks make their way through the subway tunnels. Red-Hulk is still unable to see. They walk and talk, and finally she reveals what's really on her mind. She turns on him, stabs him in the neck, and calls him sloppy and expendable.

Who is this Red She-Hulk, and whose side is she on? Will green Hulk come back? And why are General Ross and Samson involved? And, come to think of it—where are Domino and Elektra?

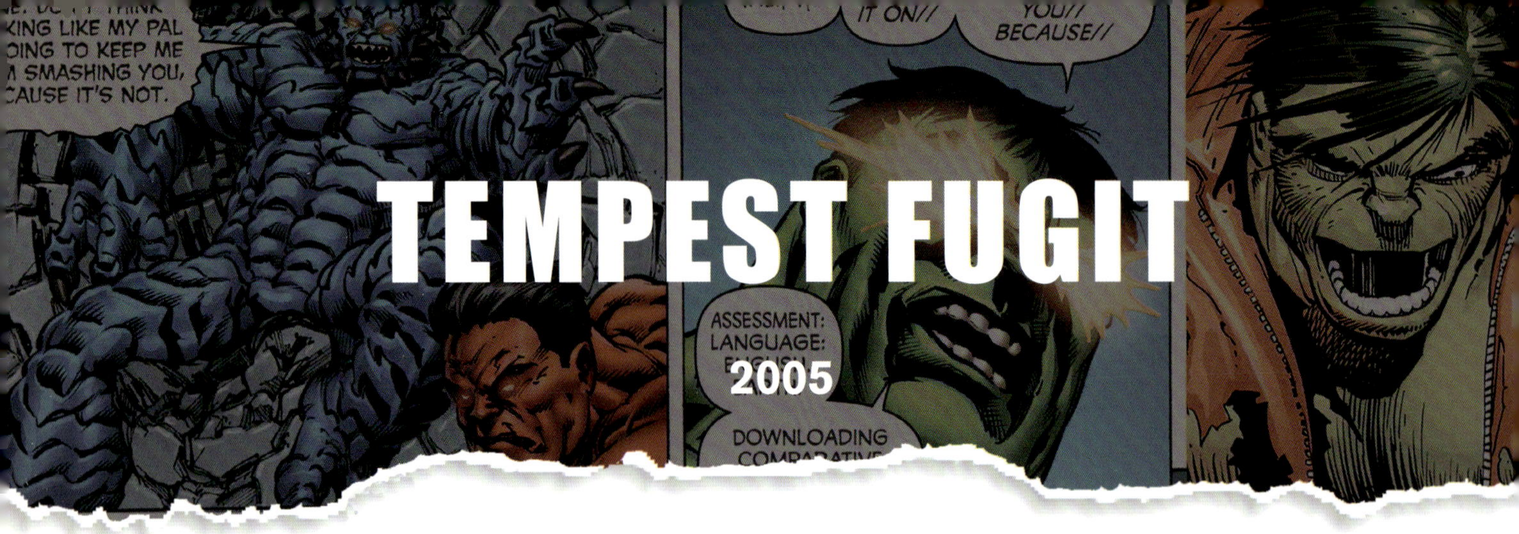
IT ON//
YOU//
BECAUSE//
ASSESSMENT:
LANGUAGE:
DOWNLOADING

# TEMPEST FUGIT

## 2005

Bruce Banner is a high school student, sitting in a classroom. The teacher calls him out for muttering to himself. Well, it looks like he's muttering to himself, but he's really talking to an old imaginary friend. Someone who is always there—the Hulk. At lunch a jerk named Ken is aggressively asking a girl named Carla how long she's going to be mad at him. Banner walks over and tells Ken to let her go. They start to argue. Banner pushes his glasses up his nose to show he means business. He tells Ken that it's his last chance, and that he won't like him when he's angry. It's the last thing Banner says before being taken down by a lunch tray. Banner mumbles for the Hulk to help him, but the Hulk ignores him. He's too busy at the lunch table playing solitaire. The Hulk mumbles "jerk." Does he mean Ken, or Banner?

Speed forward to today: we find the Hulk underwater fighting a giant squid who fends off the mighty Hulk by shooting black ink all over him. The Hulk ends up on shore throwing up—something he doesn't do. Banner pukes—not the Hulk! He suddenly transforms back into Banner. Out of the jungle a two-headed creature appears. Two people come to Banner's rescue; one is a man named Ripley who wields a flame-thrower. Ripley also has a cloth over his eyes, it appears that he can't see. With him is a girl is named Gwen and she is tending to the sick Banner.

Suddenly, standing in front of them is the Gray Hulk. He raises his arms, ready to attack. Something stops him, he recognizes Banner. The Gray Hulk tells Ripley and Gwen to, "Give him here." Ripley fires the flamethrower, engulfing Gray Hulk. Gwen starts dragging the weakened Banner out of the way. Banner mumbles something about being a hero. He asks where he is. Gwen tells him that he's on Monster Island.

With the Gray Hulk on fire, the three run into the jungle—but are stopped when they come to a ravine. A giant tree crashes down, creating a bridge across the ravine; the Green Hulk has come to their rescue.

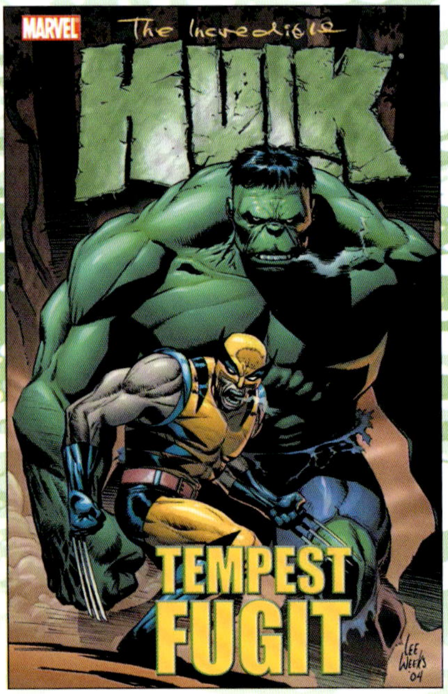
MARVEL
The Incredible
HULK
TEMPEST
FUGIT

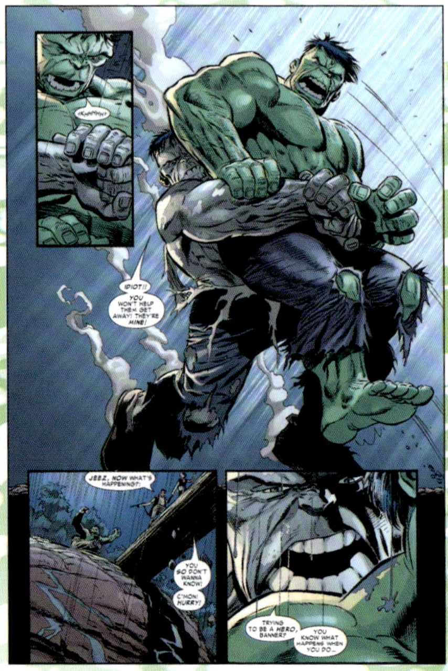

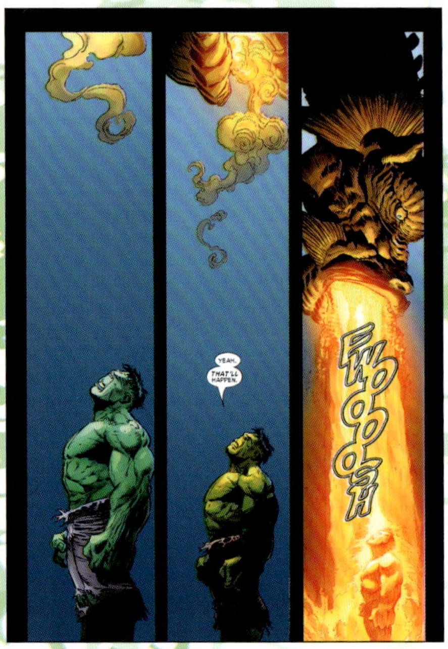

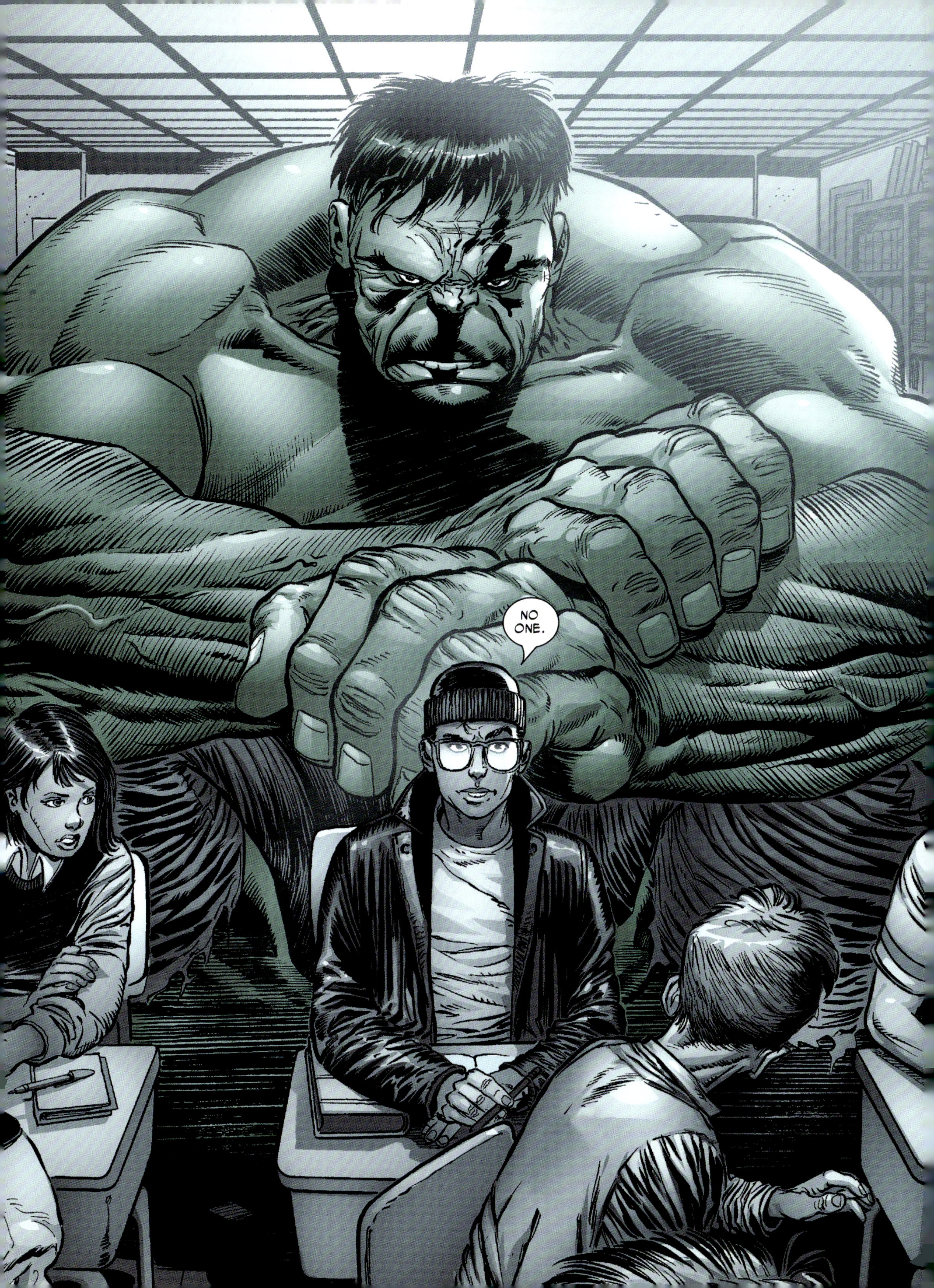
NO ONE.

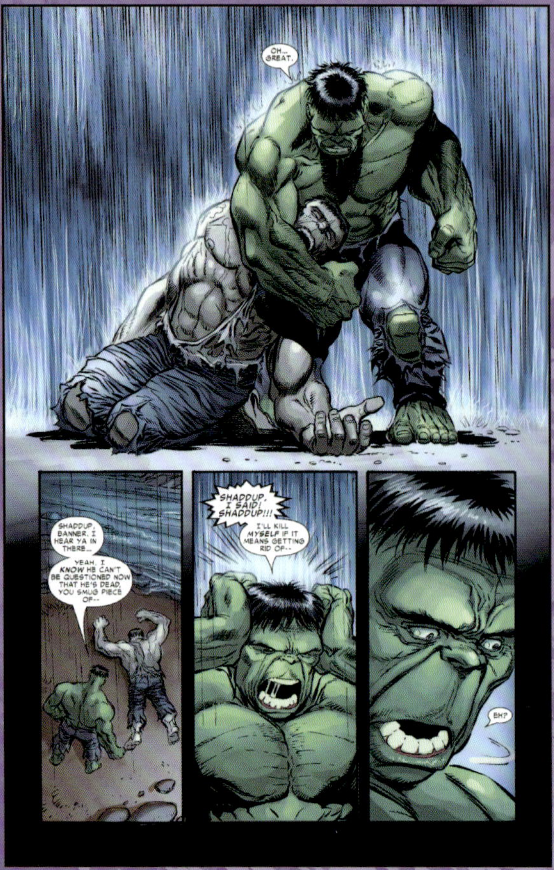
OH... GREAT.
SHADDUP, BANNER. I HEAR YA IN THERE...
YEAH. I KNOW HE CAN'T BE QUESTIONED NOW THAT HE'S DEAD, YOU SMUG PIECE OF--
SHADDUP, I SAID! SHADDUP!!!
I'LL KILL MYSELF IF IT MEANS GETTING RID OF--
EH?

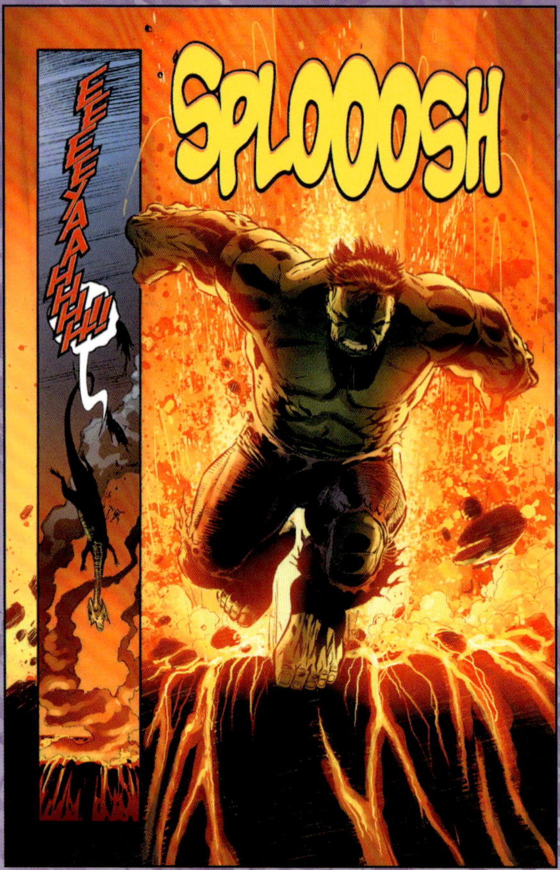
EEEEYAAHHH!!
SPLOOOSH

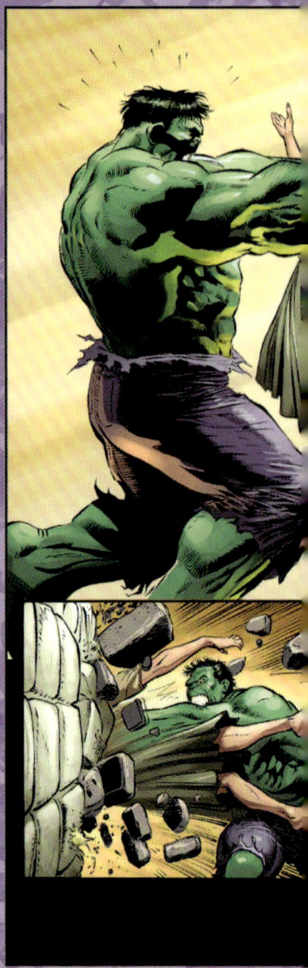

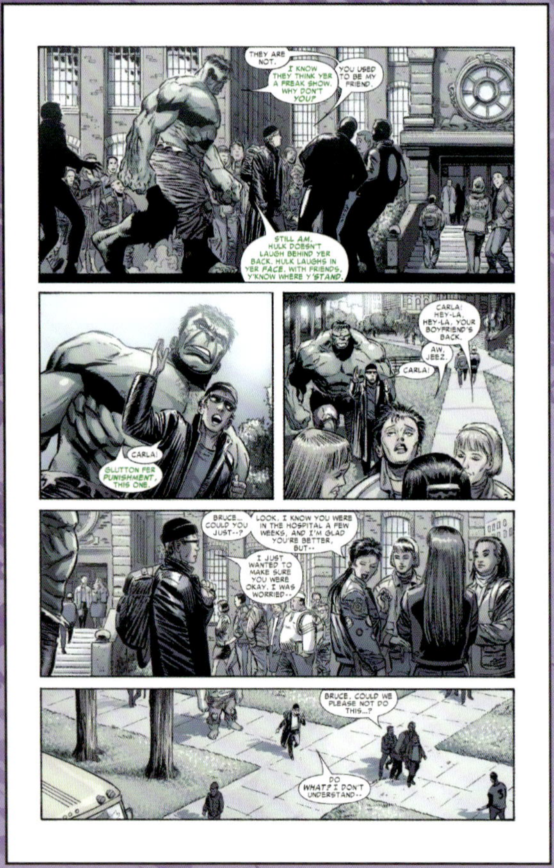
THEY ARE NOT.
I KNOW THEY THINK YER A FREAK SHOW. WHY DON'T YOU?
YOU USED TO BE MY FRIEND.
STILL AM. HULK DOESN'T LAUGH BEHIND YER BACK. HULK LAUGHS IN YER FACE. WITH FRIENDS, Y'KNOW WHERE Y'STAND.
CARLA!
GLUTTON FER PUNISHMENT, THIS ONE.
CARLA! HEY-LA, HEY-LA, YOUR BOYFRIEND'S BACK.
AW, JEEZ.
CARLA!
BRUCE... COULD YOU JUST--?
LOOK, I KNOW YOU WERE IN THE HOSPITAL A FEW WEEKS, AND I'M GLAD YOU'RE BETTER, BUT--
I JUST WANTED TO MAKE SURE YOU WERE OKAY. I WAS WORRIED--
BRUCE, COULD WE PLEASE NOT DO THIS...?
DO WHAT? I DON'T UNDERSTAND--

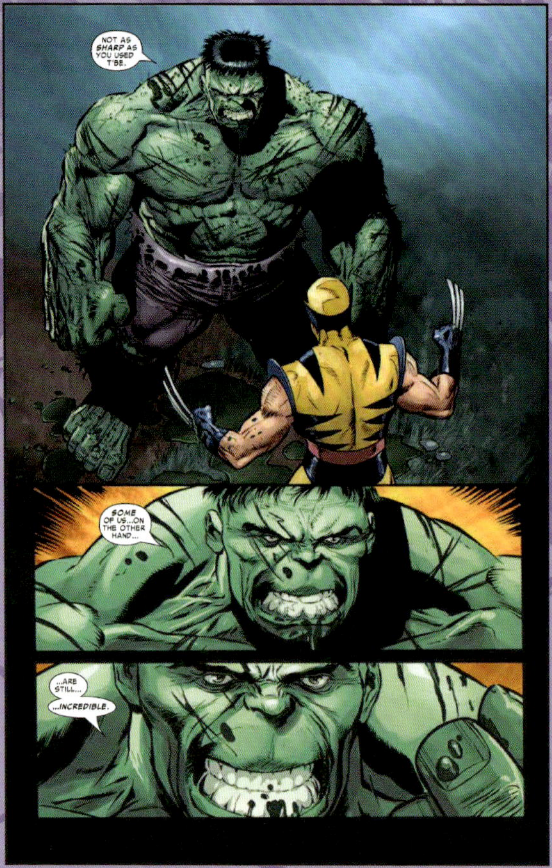
NOT AS SHARP AS YOU USED T'BE.
SOME OF US...ON THE OTHER HAND...
...ARE STILL...
...INCREDIBLE.

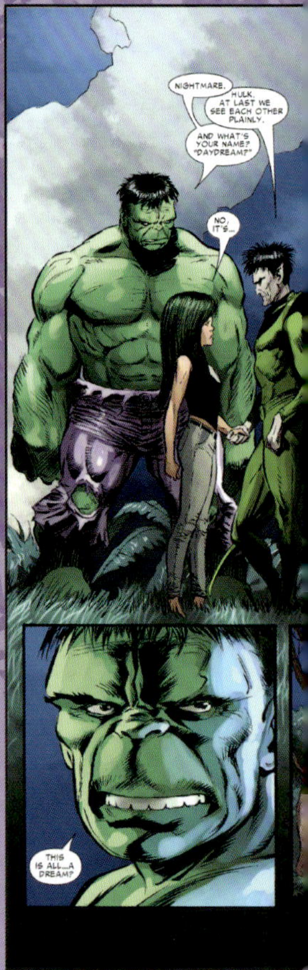
NIGHTMARE.
HULK. AT LAST WE SEE EACH OTHER PLAINLY.
AND WHAT'S YOUR NAME? "DAYDREAM?"
NO, IT'S...
THIS IS ALL...A DREAM?

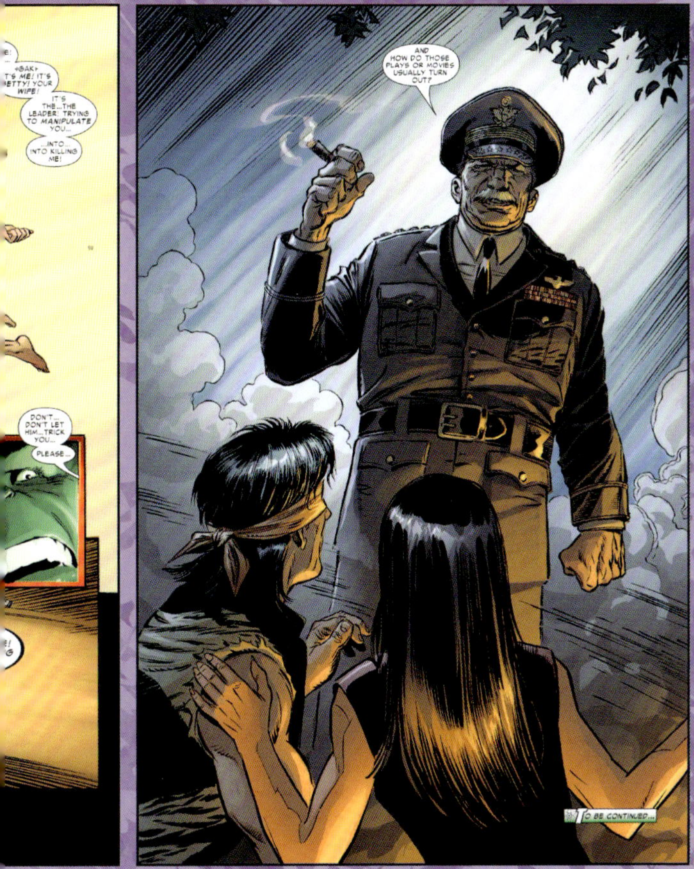
IT'S THE...THE LEADER! TRYING TO MANIPULATE YOU...
...INTO... INTO KILLING ME!
DON'T... DON'T LET HIM...TRICK YOU...
PLEASE...
AND HOW DO THOSE PLAYS OR MOVIES USUALLY TURN OUT?
TO BE CONTINUED...

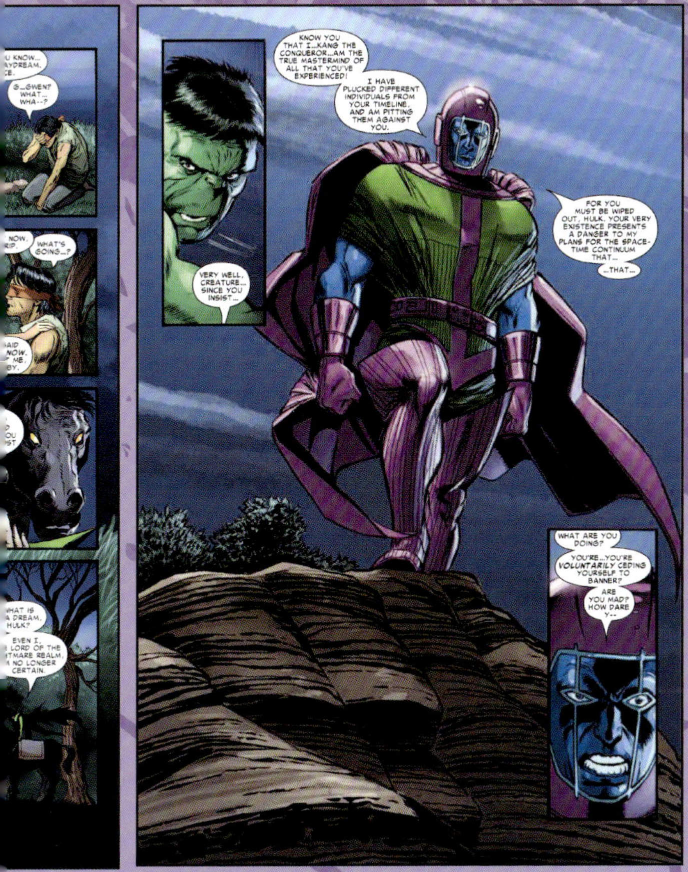
G...GWEN? WHAT... WHA--?
WHAT'S GOING...?
KNOW YOU THAT I...KANG THE CONQUEROR...AM THE TRUE MASTERMIND OF ALL THAT YOU'VE EXPERIENCED!
I HAVE PLUCKED DIFFERENT INDIVIDUALS FROM YOUR TIMELINE, AND AM PITTING THEM AGAINST YOU.
FOR YOU MUST BE WIPED OUT, HULK. YOUR VERY EXISTENCE PRESENTS A DANGER TO MY PLANS FOR THE SPACE-TIME CONTINUUM THAT...
...THAT...
VERY WELL, CREATURE... SINCE YOU INSIST...
WHAT ARE YOU DOING?
YOU'RE...YOU'RE VOLUNTARILY CEDING YOURSELF TO BANNER?
ARE YOU MAD? HOW DARE Y--

Back to student Banner, who is in a hospital bed, his face battered and bruised, his head wrapped in bandages. Banner's Aunt Sue is sitting in the principal's office demanding that the student who beat up her nephew be arrested. The principal tells her the boy that Bruce identified denied it. So, it's Bruce's word against the bully's. The principal suddenly changes the subject and asks Aunt Sue—"Who's the Hulk?"

Back on Monster Island, the Gray Hulk catches up with the Hulk, Gwen, and Ripley, and the two Hulks battle. The Green Hulk defeats the Gray Hulk. He stands over the defeated Gray Hulk, who suddenly transforms into a man wearing a silver suit and a helmet. As the Green Hulk looks down upon this person who looks like an astronaut, he says, "Wonder what other weirdness the stupid island's got." As he says this, someone looms behind the Hulk—Fin Fang Foom.

Meanwhile, General "Thunderbolt" Ross unexpectedly appearsn front of Ripley and Gwen. He tells them that he can help get them off the island.

What is up with this island? General Ross attacks Gwen. In addition to Fin Fang Foom, Wolverine and Kang the Conqueror show up on the island and confront the Hulk. And: what will happen to young Banner?

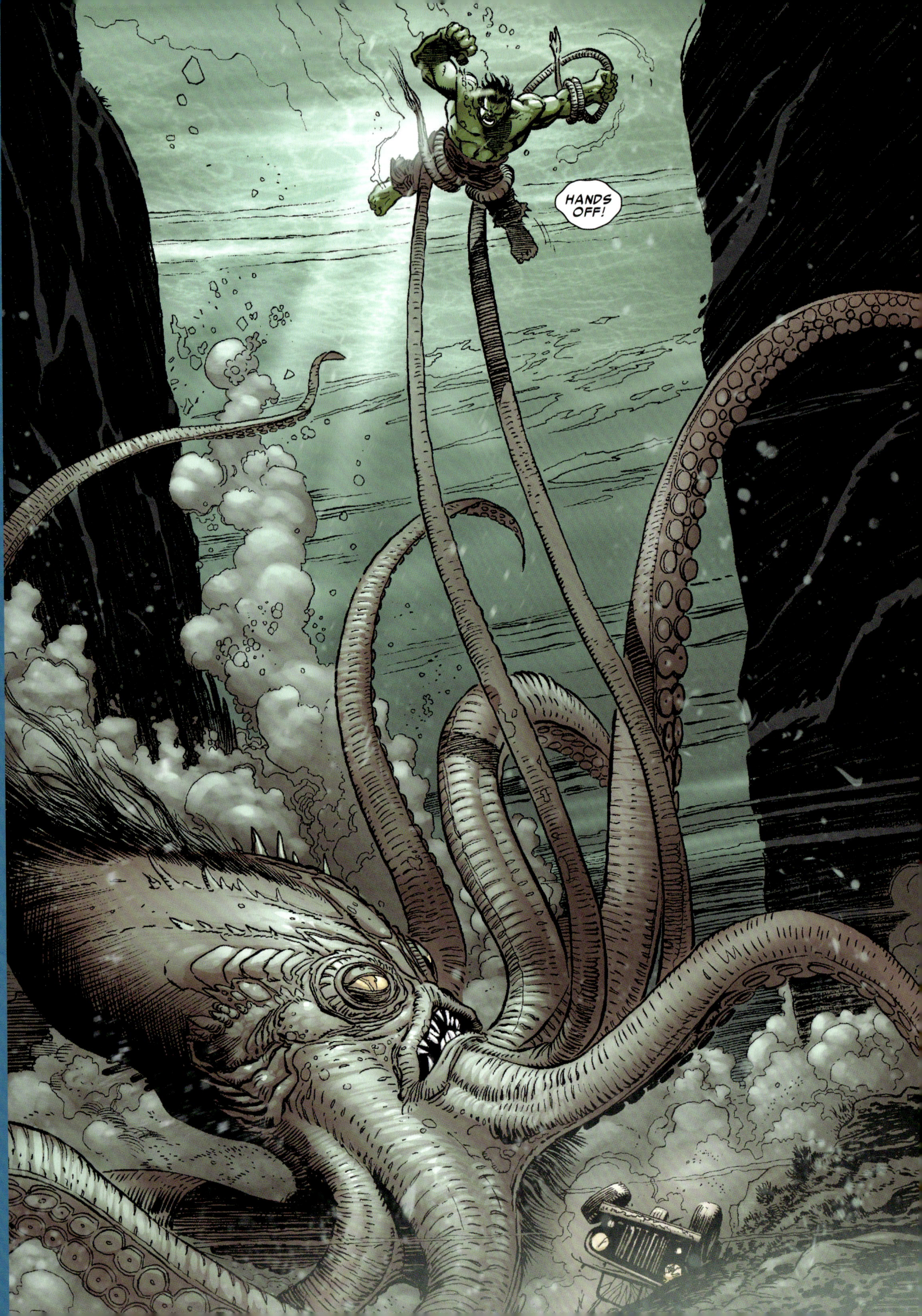
HANDS OFF!

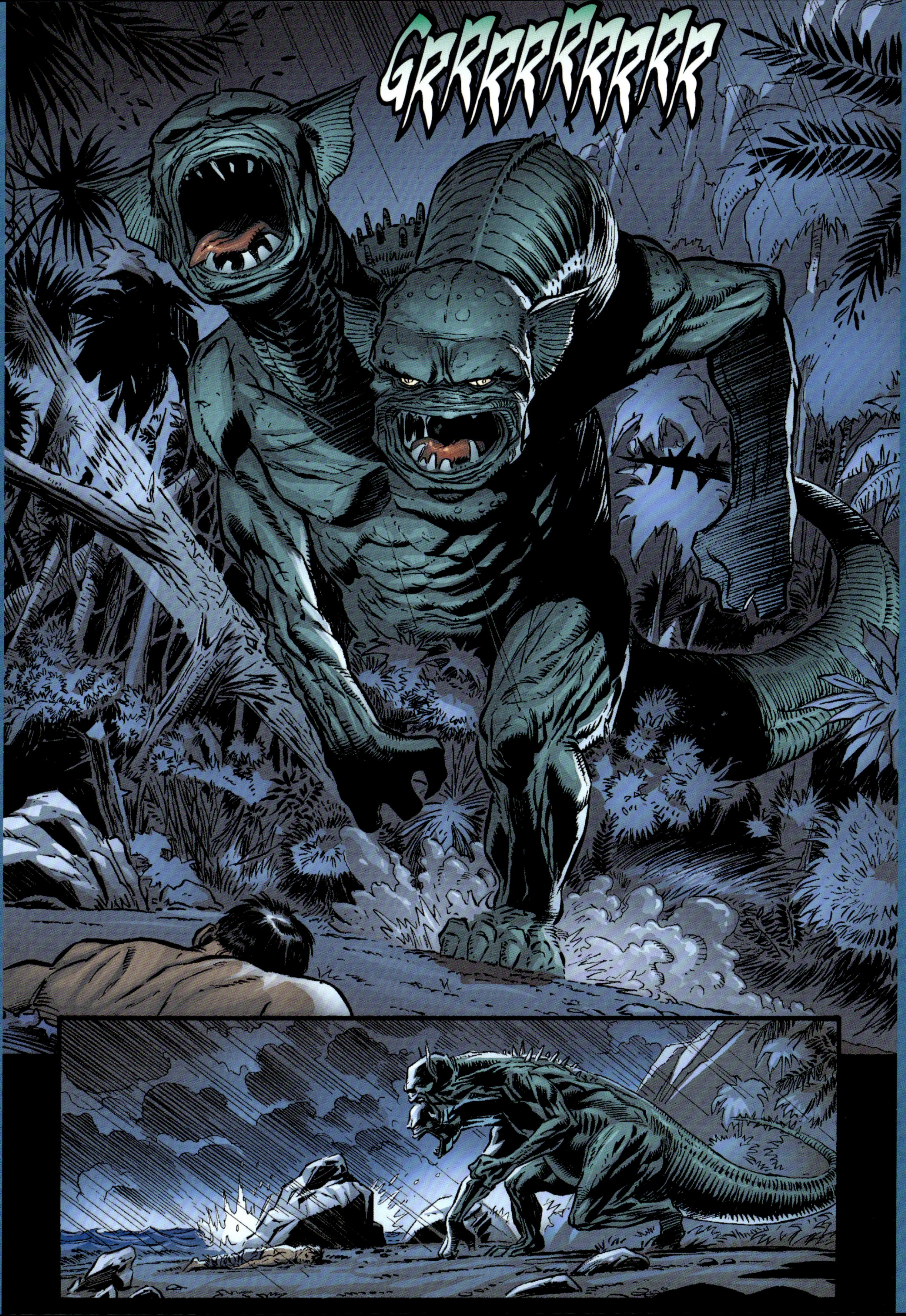
GRRRRRRRRR

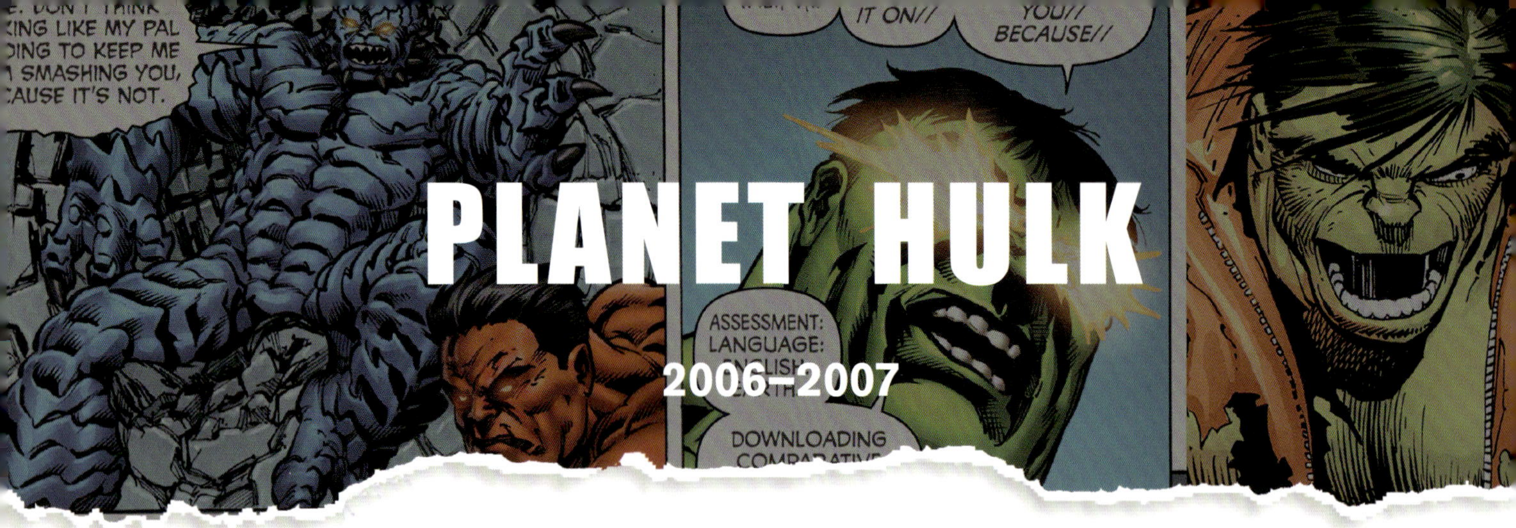
IT ON//
YOU//
BECAUSE//
ASSESSMENT:
LANGUAGE:
DOWNLOADING

# PLANET HULK

## 2006–2007

In this story, the Hulk we see has managed to retain Bruce Banner's brilliant mind while living in the body of the Hulk. A gamma bomb is found on the outskirts of Las Vegas, and the government thinks that this Hulk—with Bruce's brain and the Hulk's body—is the perfect choice to defuse the bomb. Unfortunately, he fails to defuse it, and the bomb explodes. The gamma bomb kills all the soldiers around the area. It also resets the Hulk to the original rage monster when he was first exposed to gamma rays. The brilliant mind of Bruce Banner is gone.

The Hulk goes on a rampage in nearby Las Vegas. The Human Torch and the Thing are recruited to bring him down. The Thing and the Hulk have battled before; it's almost an annual event. The Thing sees himself in the Hulk; he knows they are both monsters. But the Thing has always retained the mind of Ben Grimm. He still has his intelligence and personality, and, unlike the Hulk, he can't change back into his original human form. The effects of the cosmic rays that turned Ben Grimm into the Thing are permanent.

During the battle, the Hulk hits the Thing harder than he's ever hit him before. The Hulk is not holding back. The Thing's ribs are broken, and the Human Torch has to take over the fight. An intense blast of heat from the Human Torch finally stops the Hulk.

Some time goes by, and Nick Fury calls on the Hulk to help S.H.I.E.L.D. Fury tells the Hulk that back in the 1960s the Soviet government sent a satellite into orbit, and its mission was to use artificial intelligence to build itself into a weapon that can trigger nuclear bombs in the United States to launch. The satellite is programmed to find and use all available technology, and anything S.H.I.E.L.D. sends to destroy the satellite is instead absorbed into and "grows" the satellite. Fury brings in the Hulk because he is not a piece of technology, and therefore he can't be absorbed by the satellite. The Hulk can be sent into space to smash the satellite.

After a series of battles with various robots housed in the now-massive satellite, the Hulk is finally able to destroy it.

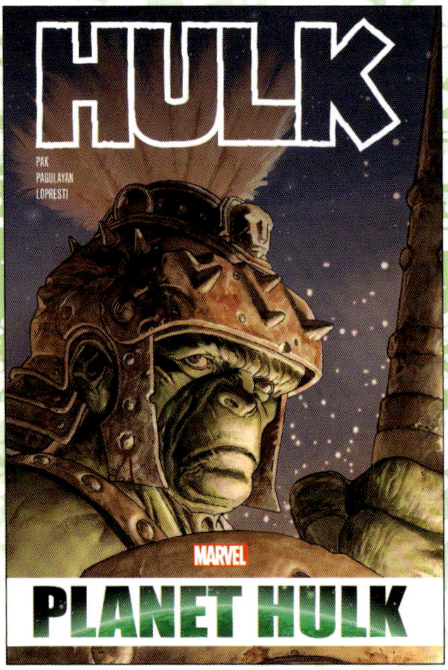
HULK
PAK
PAGULAYAN
LOPRESTI
MARVEL
PLANET HULK

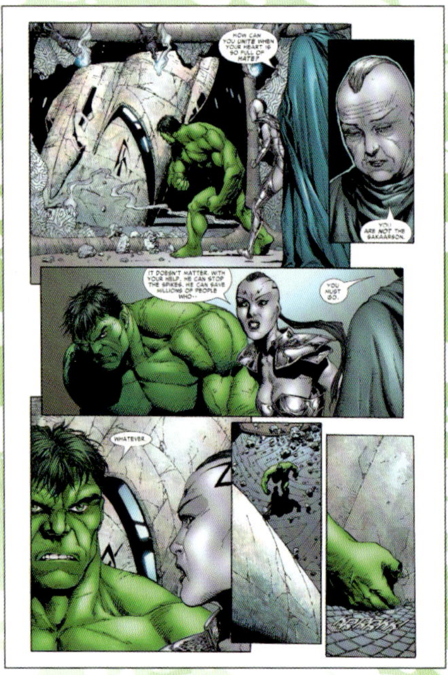

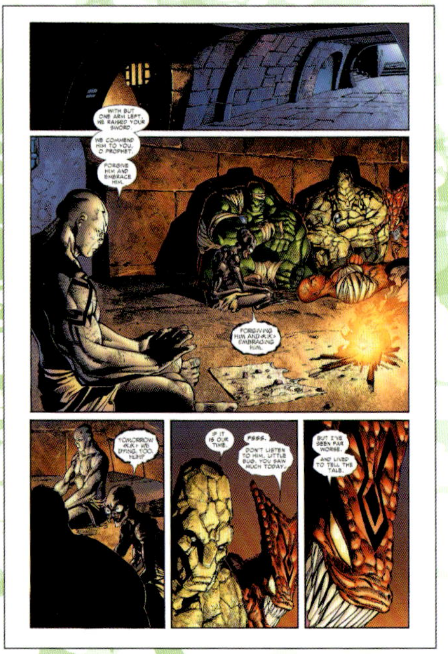

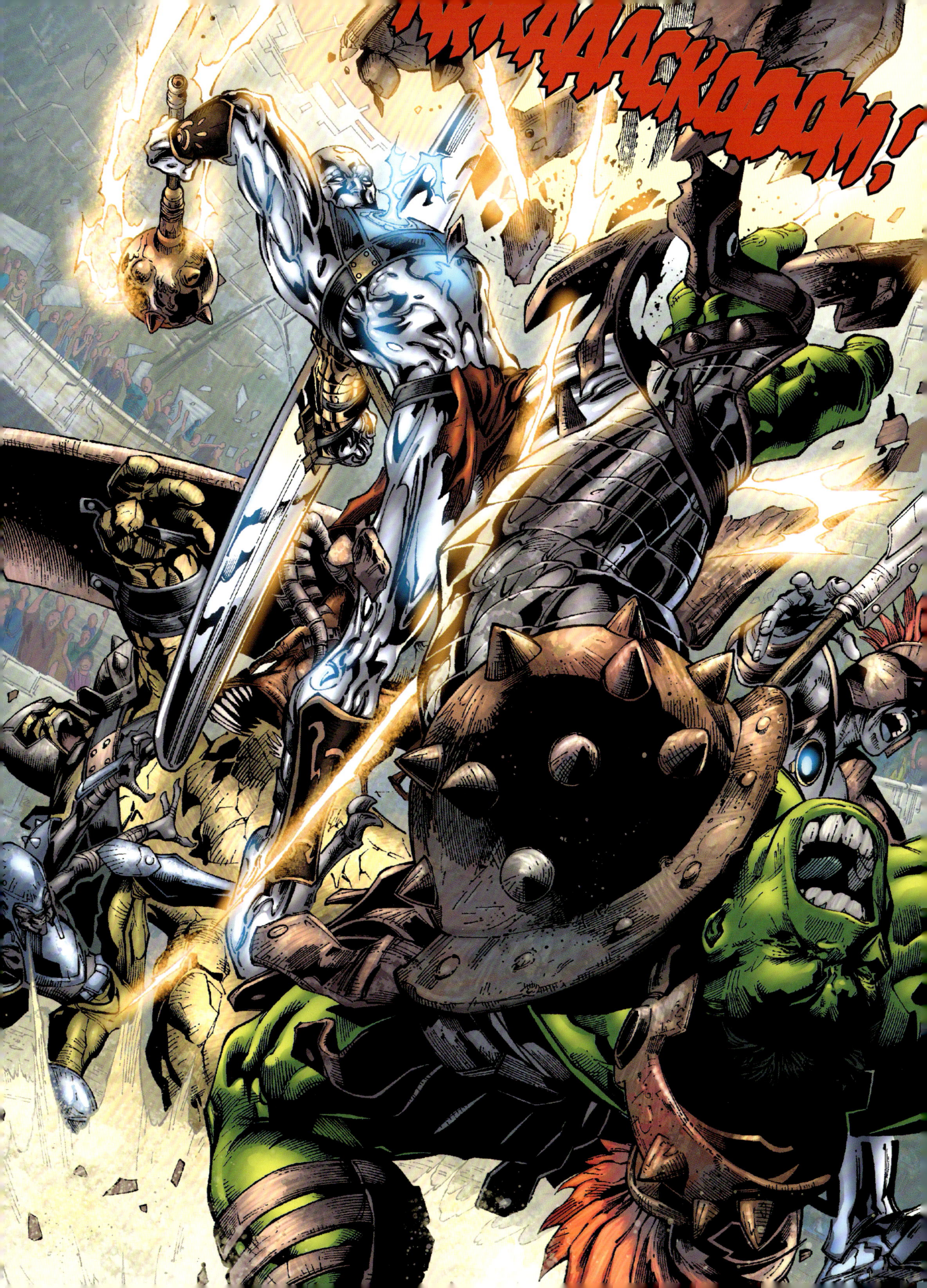
AAACKOOOM!

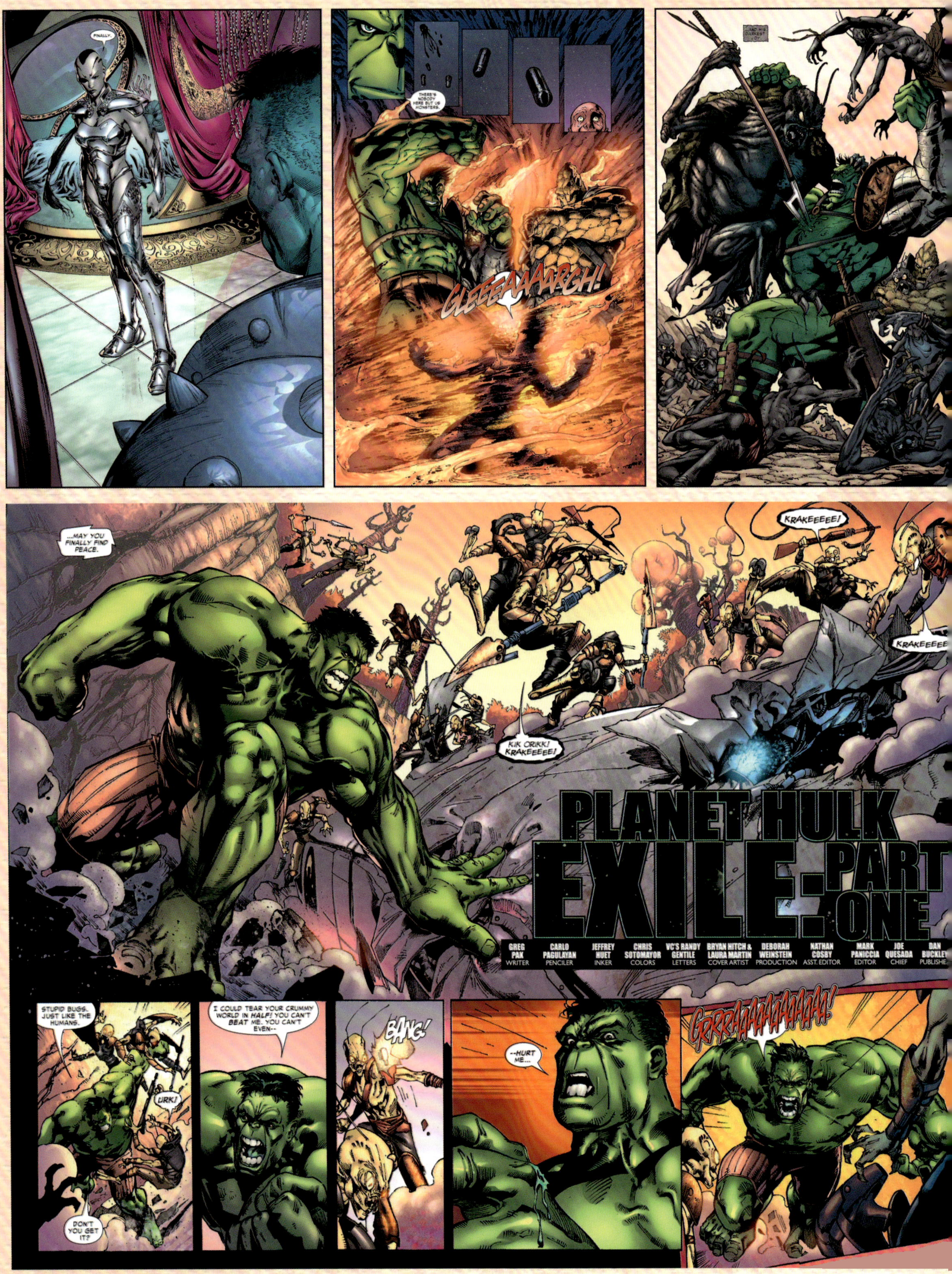
FINALLY.
THERE'S NOBODY HERE BUT US MONSTERS.
GLEEEAAAARGH!
...AND HIS DARKEST JOY.
...MAY YOU FINALLY FIND PEACE.
KRAKEEEEE!
KRAKEEEEE
KIK ORIKK! KRAKEEEEE!
PLANET HULK
EXILE: PART ONE
GREG PAK WRITER
CARLO PAGULAYAN PENCILER
JEFFREY HUET INKER
CHRIS SOTOMAYOR COLORS
VC'S RANDY GENTILE LETTERS
BRYAN HITCH & LAURA MARTIN COVER ARTIST
DEBORAH WEINSTEIN PRODUCTION
NATHAN COSBY ASST. EDITOR
MARK PANICCIA EDITOR
JOE QUESADA CHIEF
DAN BUCKLEY PUBLISHER
STUPID BUGS. JUST LIKE THE HUMANS.
URK!
DON'T YOU GET IT?
I COULD TEAR YOUR CRUMMY WORLD IN HALF! YOU CAN'T BEAT ME. YOU CAN'T EVEN--
BANG!
--HURT ME...
GRRRAAAAAAAAAAAAAA!

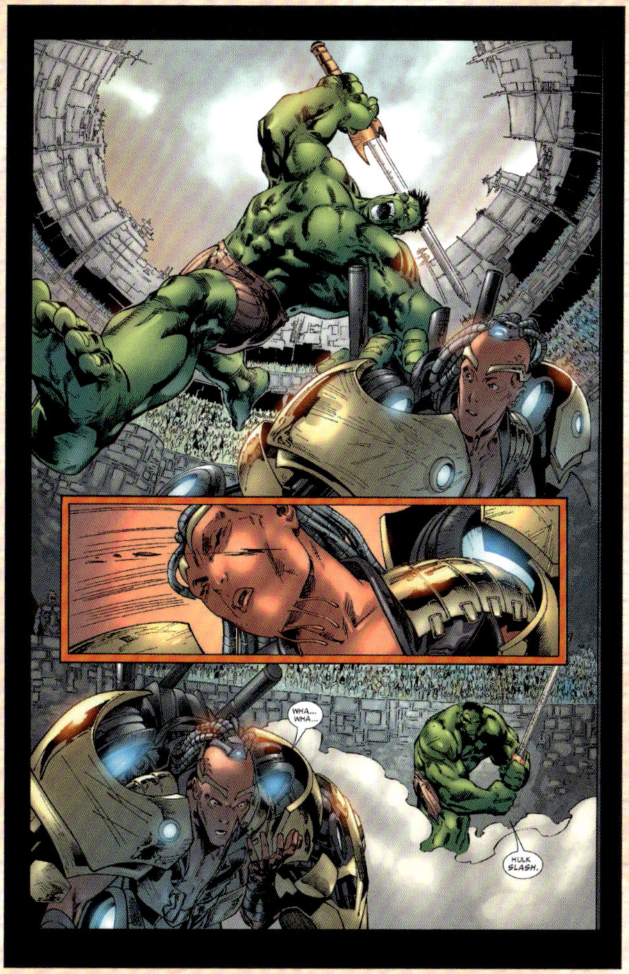
WHA... WHA...
HULK SLASH.

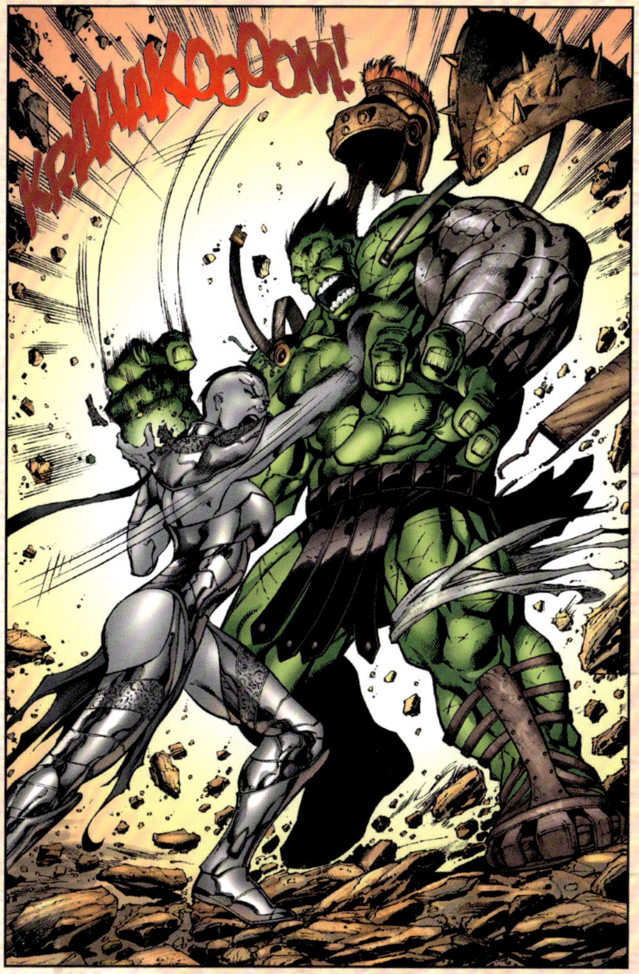
KRAAAKOOOOM!

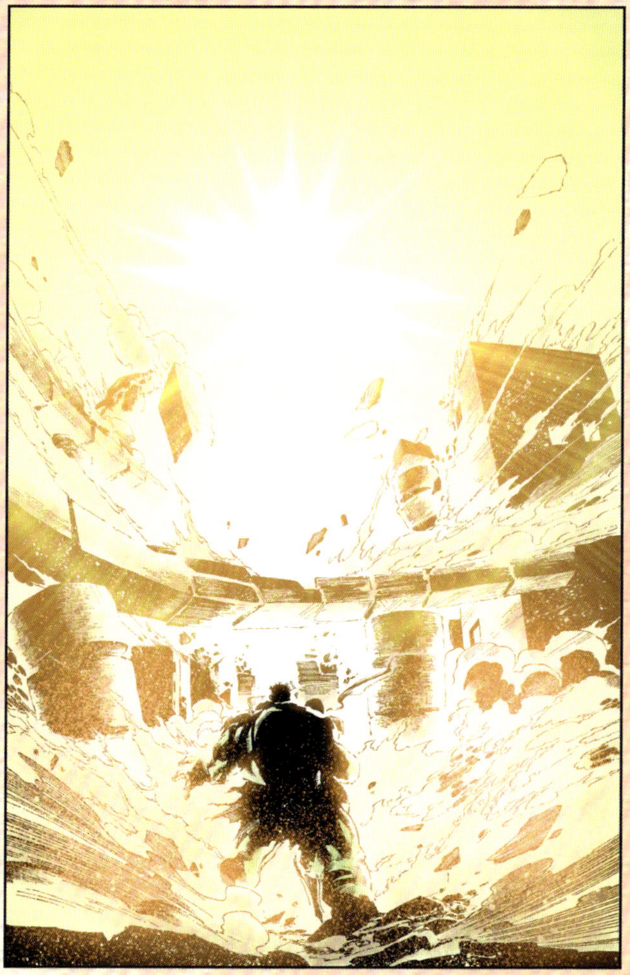

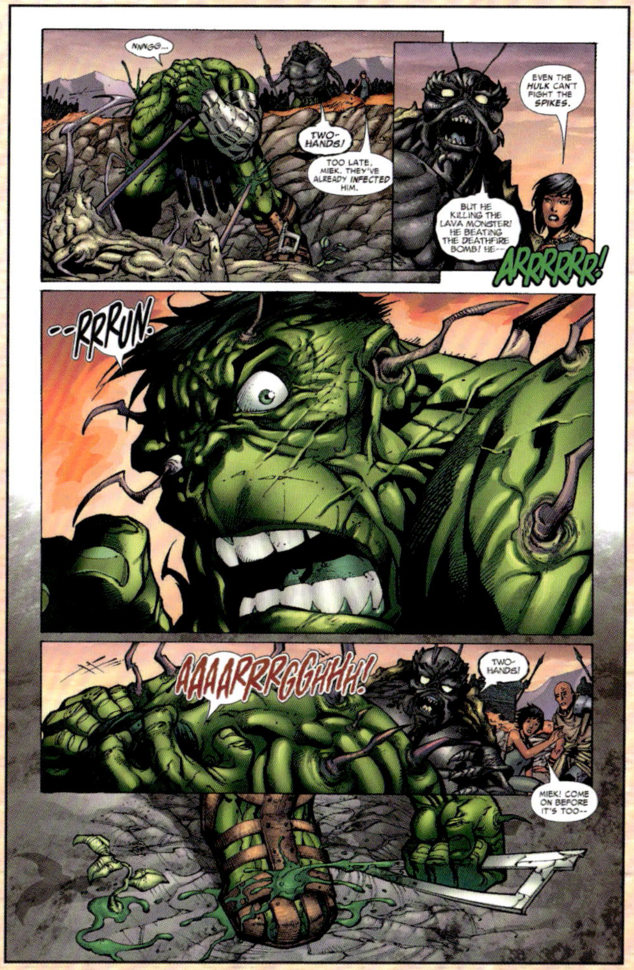
NNNGG...
TWO-HANDS!
TOO LATE, MIEK. THEY'VE ALREADY INFECTED HIM.
EVEN THE HULK CAN'T FIGHT THE SPIKES.
BUT HE KILLING THE LAVA MONSTER! HE BEATING THE DEATHFIRE BOMB! HE--
ARRRRRR!
--RRRUN.
AAAARRRGGHHH!
TWO-HANDS!
MIEK! COME ON BEFORE IT'S TOO--

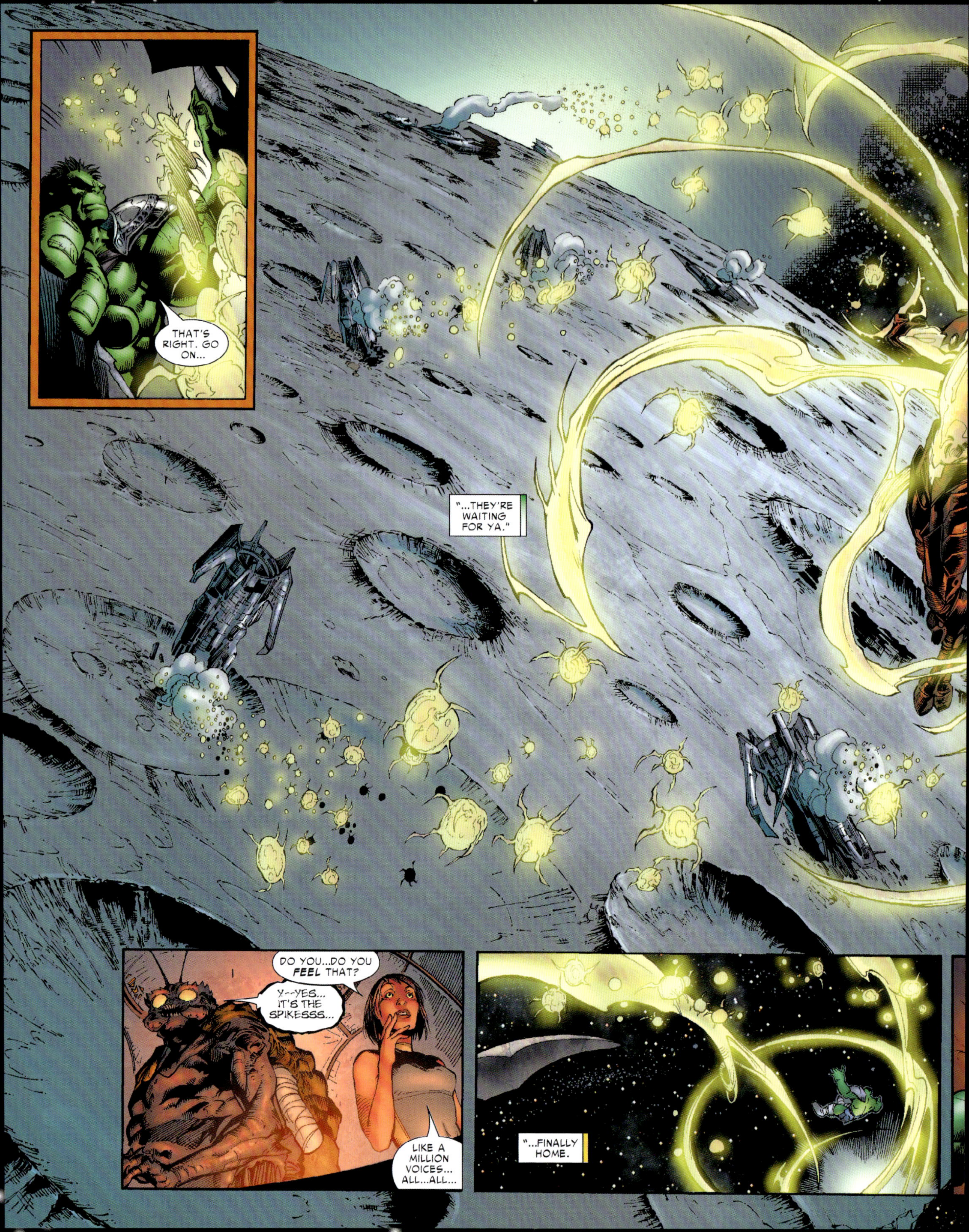
THAT'S RIGHT. GO ON...
"...THEY'RE WAITING FOR YA."
DO YOU...DO YOU FEEL THAT?
Y--YES... IT'S THE SPIKESSS...
LIKE A MILLION VOICES... ALL...ALL...
"...FINALLY HOME."

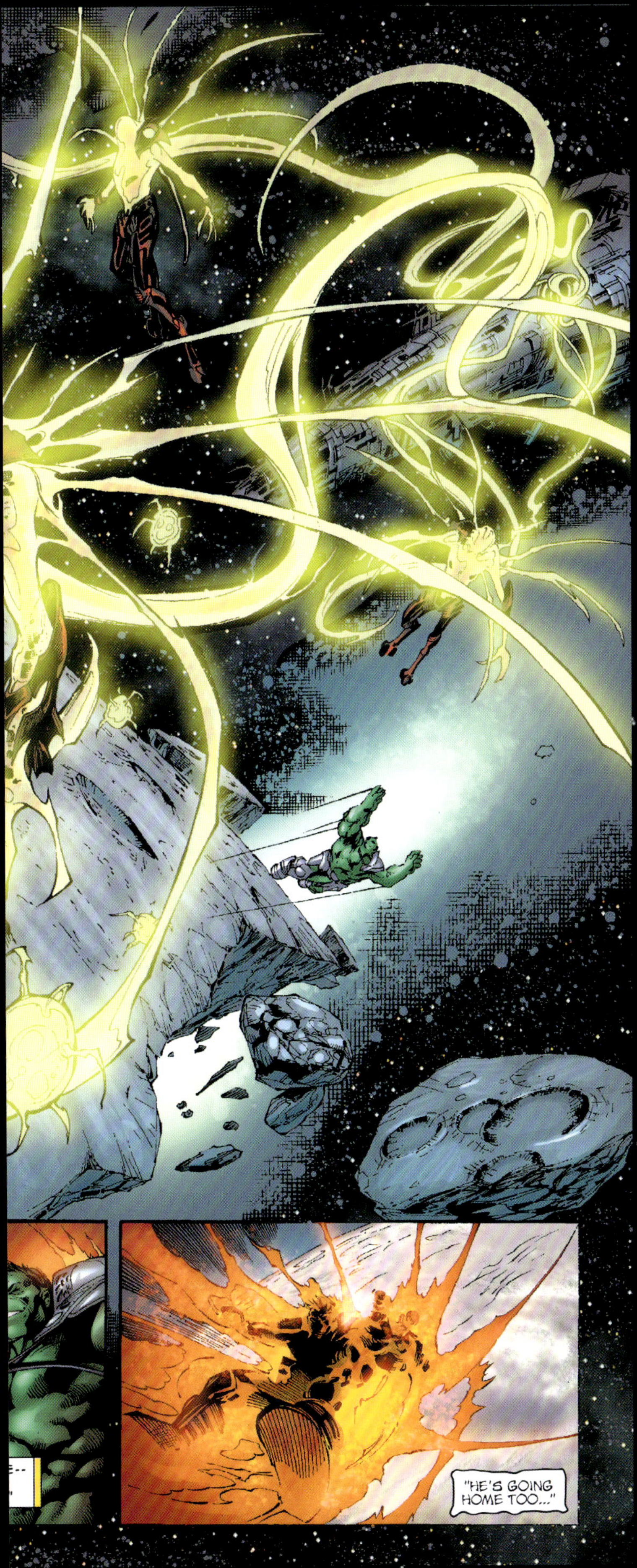
"HE'S GOING HOME TOO..."

The Hulk then gets into a shuttle sent by S.H.I.E.L.D., which is supposed to bring him back to Earth.

Unfortunately, there is still the matter of the destruction the Hulk caused in Las Vegas. Twenty-six people (including two children) and a dog were killed during the rampage. A group called the Illuminati, which includes Reed Richards/Mr. Fantastic, Iron Man, Black Bolt, Professor Xavier, Namor the Sub-Mariner, Doctor Strange, and others, decides to program this shuttle to send the Hulk to an uninhabited but livable planet to live out his days. This exile is his punishment for the death and destruction in Las Vegas. The Earth will be safe from the Hulk.

The group gives the Hulk this news while he's in flight. In fact, the Illuminati staged this whole scenario. The Illuminati had Nick Fury approach the Hulk to smash the satellite. It wasn't even a Soviet satellite; it was a Stark Industries satellite that was giving Tony Stark some trouble, and it needed to be destroyed. Because of this group, the Hulk is banished from Earth. The Hulk is not happy that he was lied to and that he is being exiled. The Hulk goes into a rage and he rips open the ship's hull, which sends the spaceship off course. It gets sucked into a black hole, and he ends up on a completely different planet.

The planet is named Sakaar. The Hulk is immediately captured and put into slavery by the Red King. Sakaar is populated by nonhumans and in many ways it's perfect for the Hulk. But he is forced into an arena similar to ancient Roman times, when gladiators battled to the death. While he loves fighting, the Hulk does not want to be a slave. He fights, wins, then fights some more, and eventually ends up defeating the Red King and becoming emperor. The Hulk finds love with Caiera, a native of planet Sakaar. They marry, and she becomes pregnant with his child. The shuttle that brought him to Sakaar is turned into a monument. But a self-destruct feature was built into the shuttle, and it destroys the city and kills his wife.

In an effort to banish the Hulk, the Illuminati accidently gave the Hulk something he couldn't find on Earth—happiness. After he loses his family and community, the Hulk makes his way back to Earth in a rage to wreak vengeance on those who sent him there. The Illuminati don't know it yet, but they have just started *World War Hulk*.

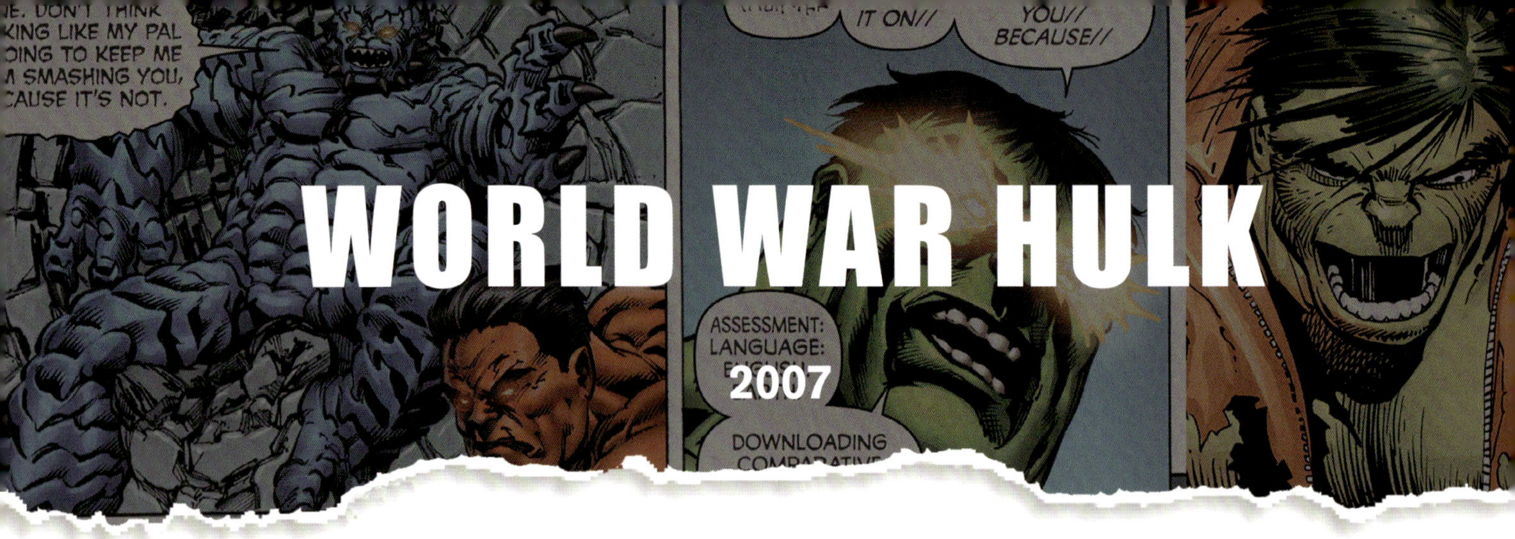
IT ON//
YOU// BECAUSE//
ASSESSMENT: LANGUAGE:
DOWNLOADING

# WORLD WAR HULK

## 2007

The Hulk wants revenge. He was banished to planet Sakaar, where slaves fight gladiator-style in an arena for entertainment. While there, the Hulk defeated an evil king and even found love and married the Sakaarian Caiera. But his new life disappeared in an instant when an explosion killed millions of the planet's citizens, including his beloved wife Caiera. The explosion originated from a monument that was created from the warp core of the spaceship the Hulk arrived in. Tragically, his wife was at the epicenter of the blast.

The focus of the Hulk's rage is those who built the spaceship that exiled him to Sakaar: Tony Stark/Iron Man and the Illuminati. The Illuminati is a group that includes Iron Man, Doctor Strange, Namor, and Reed Richards/Mr. Fantastic, who wanted to exile the Hulk to an uninhabited planet. Instead, he ended up in a place where he was happy, a place he could have made home. That is, until his wife dies in that horrific explosion.

The Hulk and some of his allies from planet Sakaar head to Earth to avenge the mass Sakaarian deaths and to punish the Illuminati and anyone else who stands in the Hulk's way. His allies are known as the Warbound, those who also fought in the gladiator arena on Sakaar. They include Korg, No-Name of the Brood, Hiroim, Elloe Kaifi, Miek, Mung, and Arch-E-5912. They are ostensibly the Hulk's army, and they are a force to be reckoned with.

The Hulk first lands on Earth's moon, where he is greeted by Black Bolt. Black Bolt was sent to the moon to stop the Hulk before he could reach Earth, but it's futile. In a matter of minutes, the Hulk broadcasts to the world that he is coming for the Illuminati. As proof of his intent, the Hulk holds up a beaten, unconscious Black Bolt for all the world to see.

The Hulk famously has never been one whose actions are precise; there is usually a lot of collateral damage once the

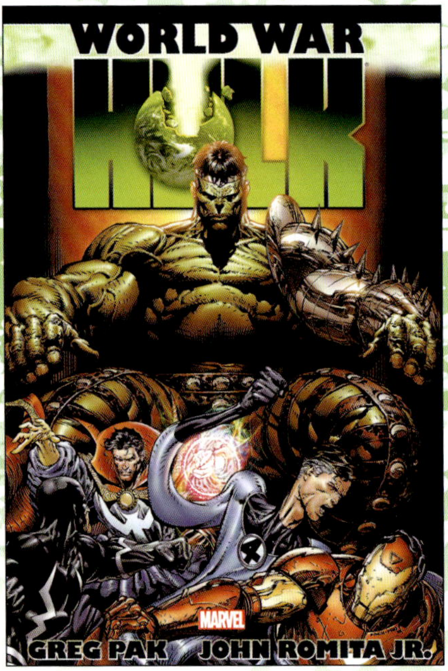
WORLD WAR HULK
MARVEL
GREG PAK
JOHN ROMITA JR.

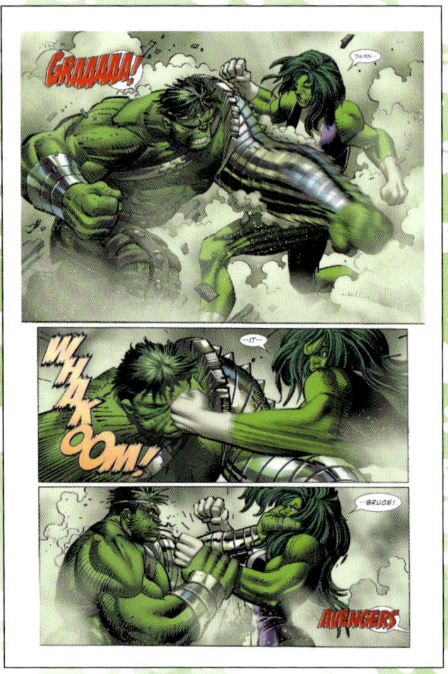
GRAAAAA!
WHAKOOM!
AVENGERS

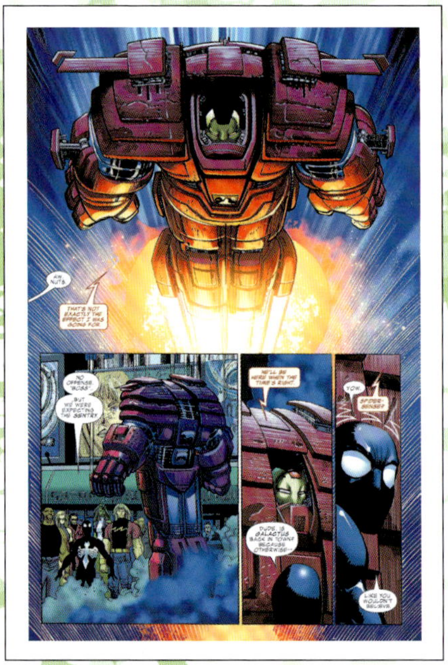

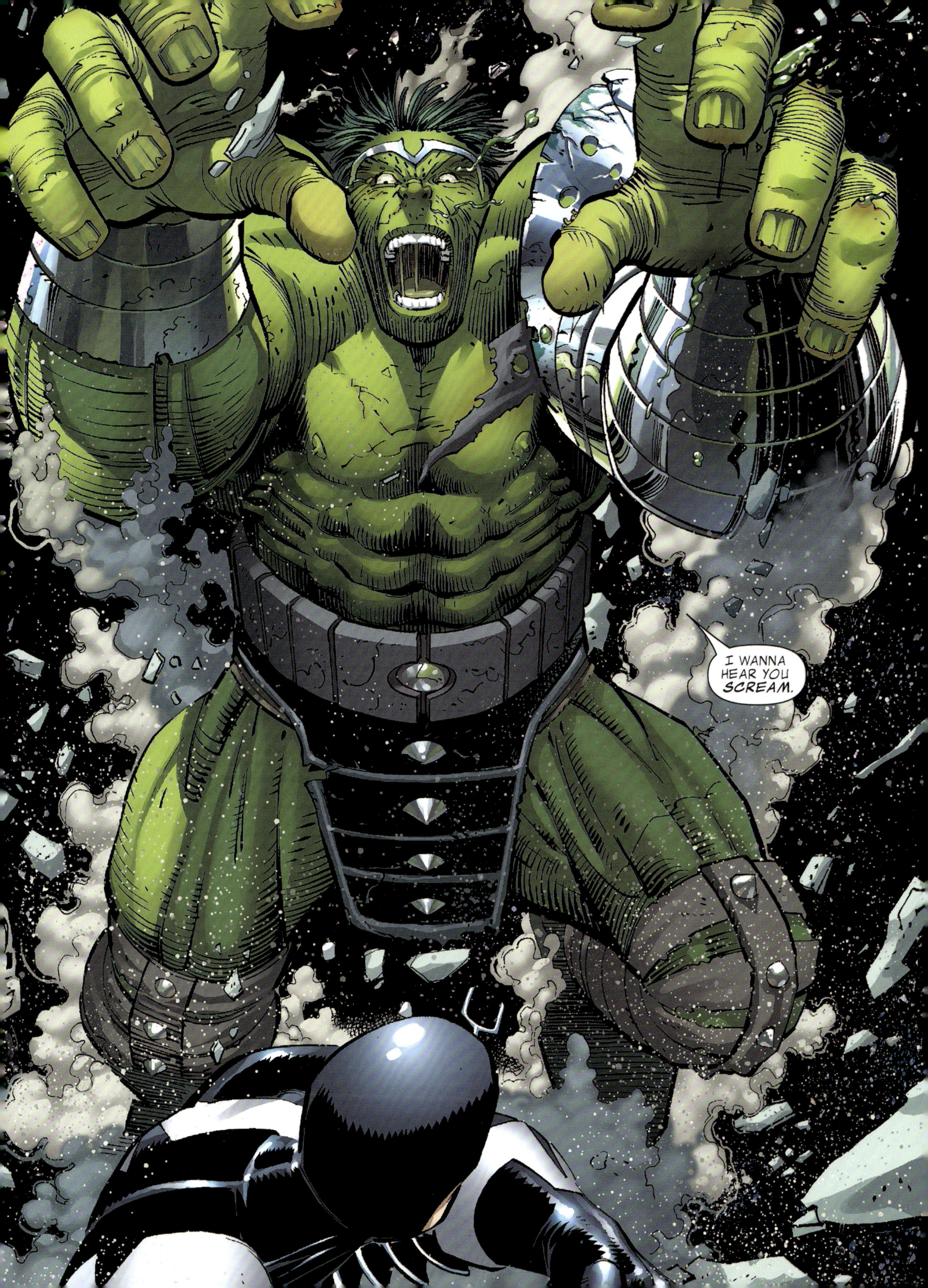
I WANNA HEAR YOU SCREAM.

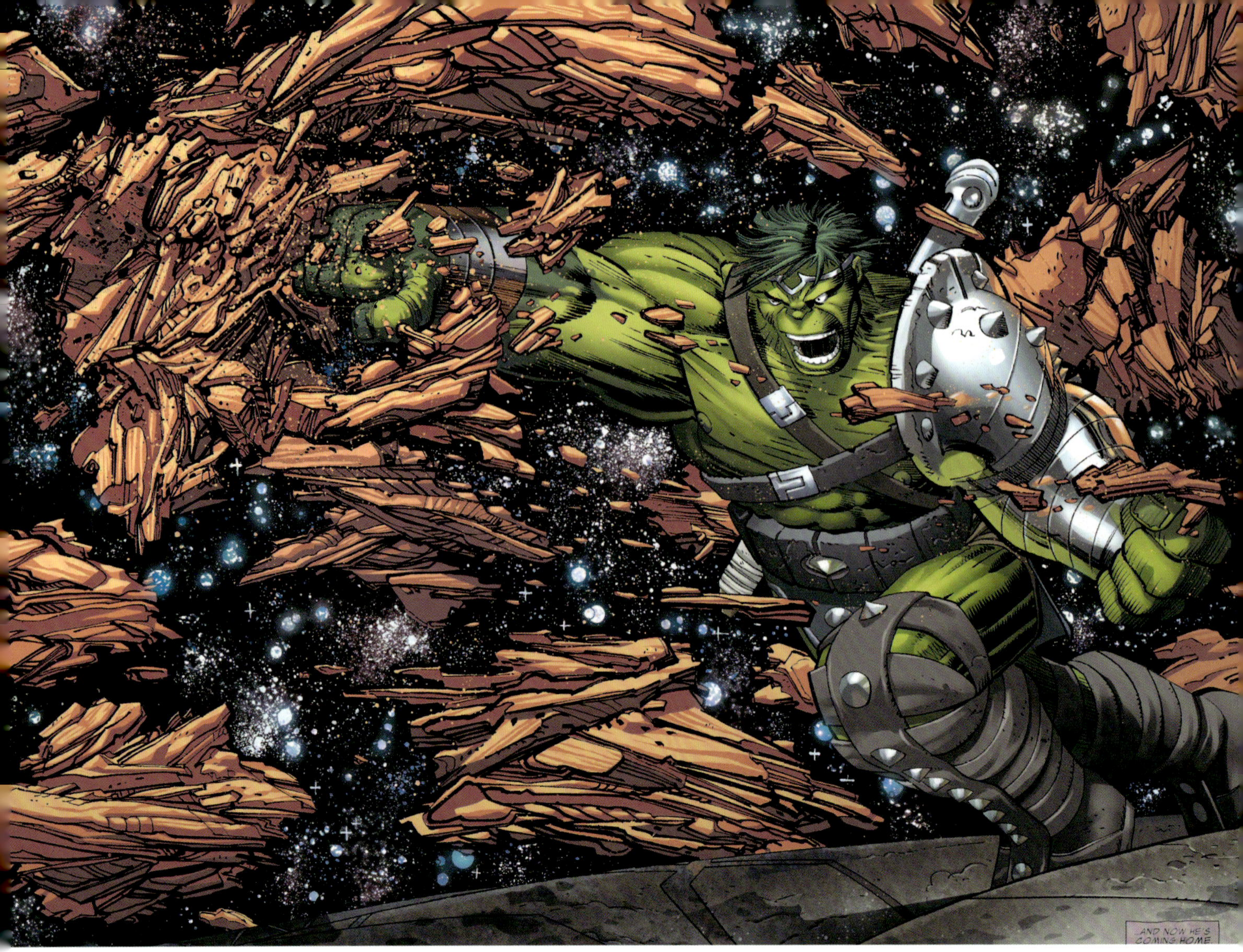
...AND NOW HE'S COMING HOME

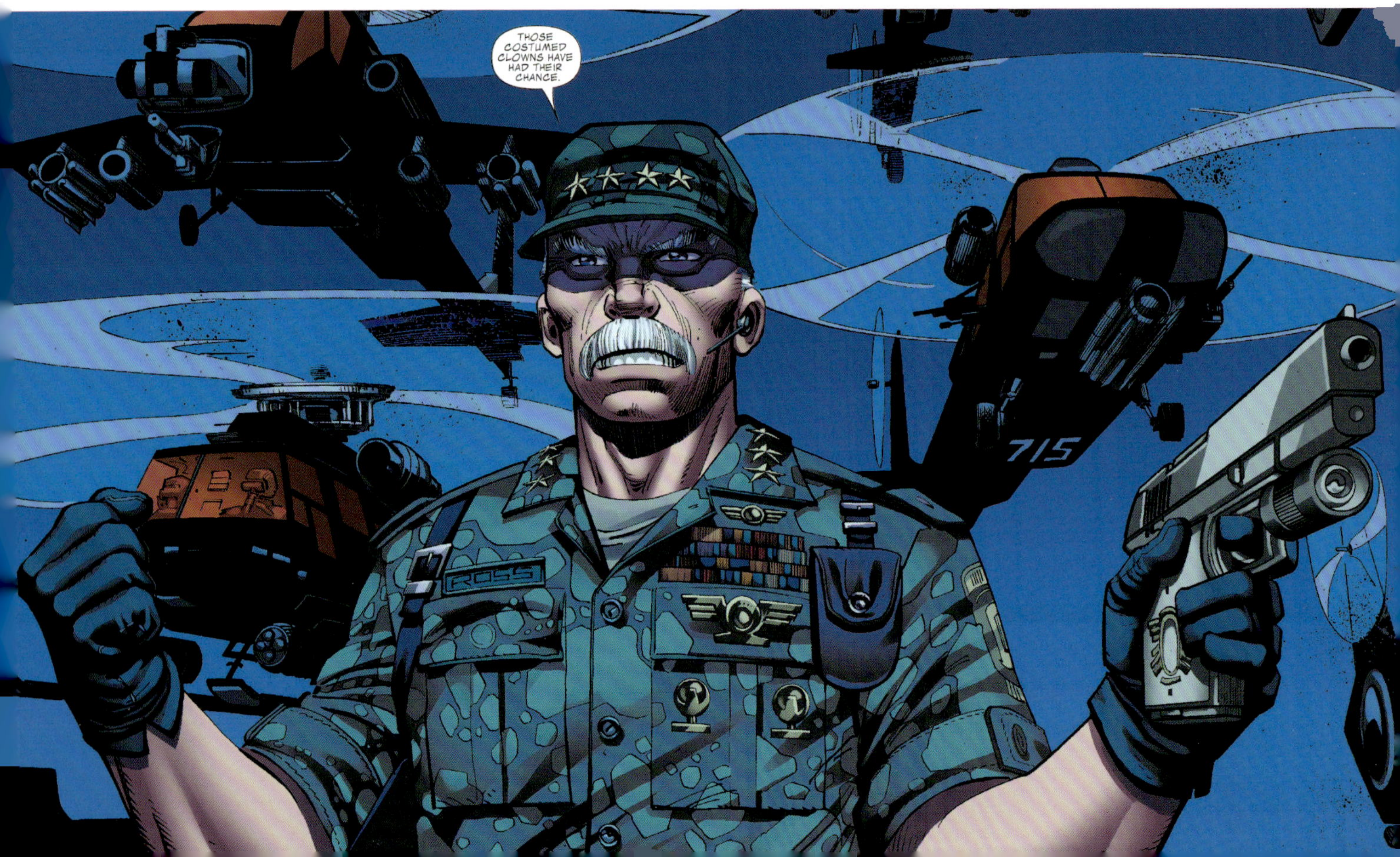
THOSE COSTUMED CLOWNS HAVE HAD THEIR CHANCE.
ROSS
715

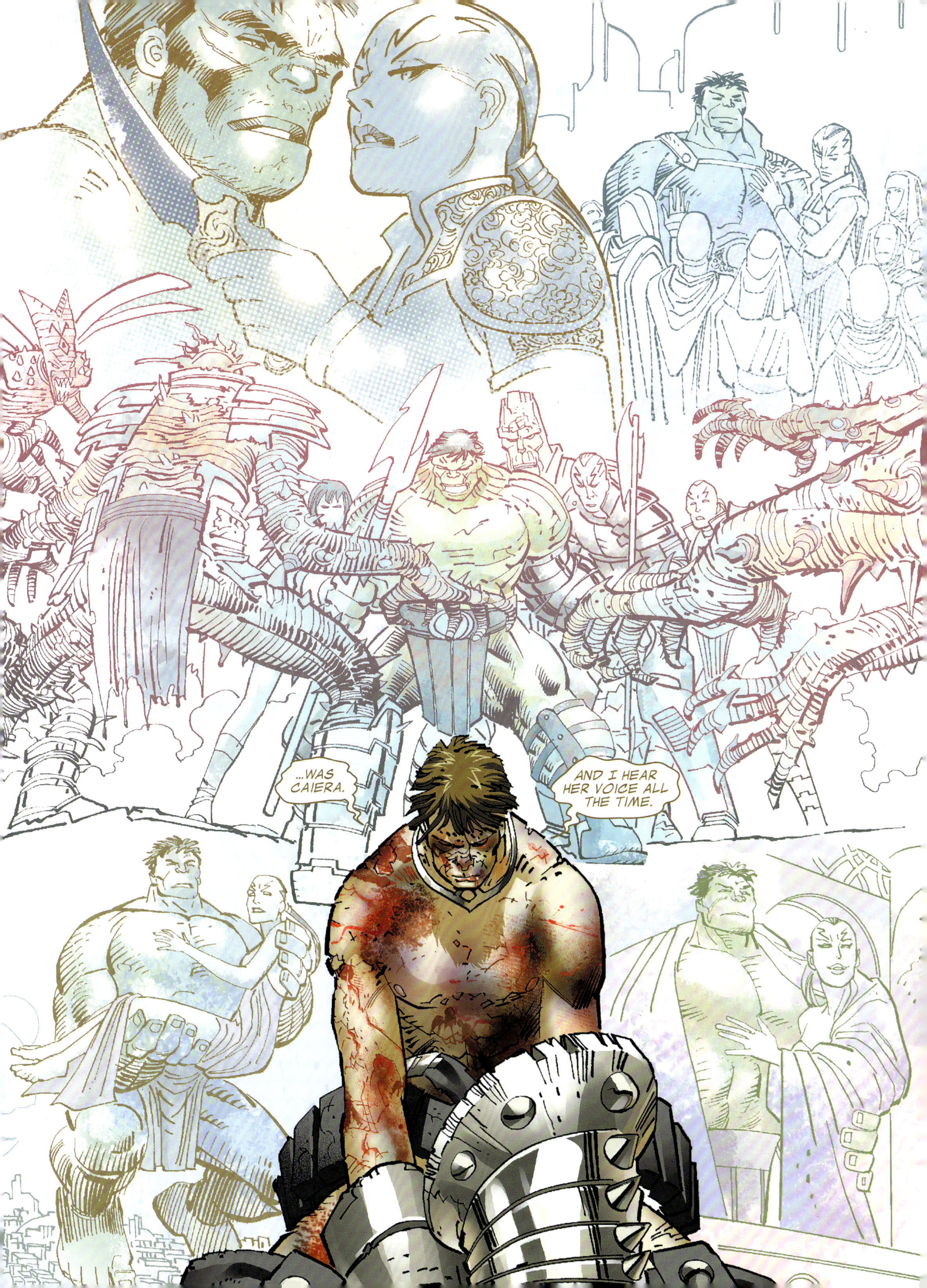
...WAS CAIERA.
AND I HEAR HER VOICE ALL THE TIME.

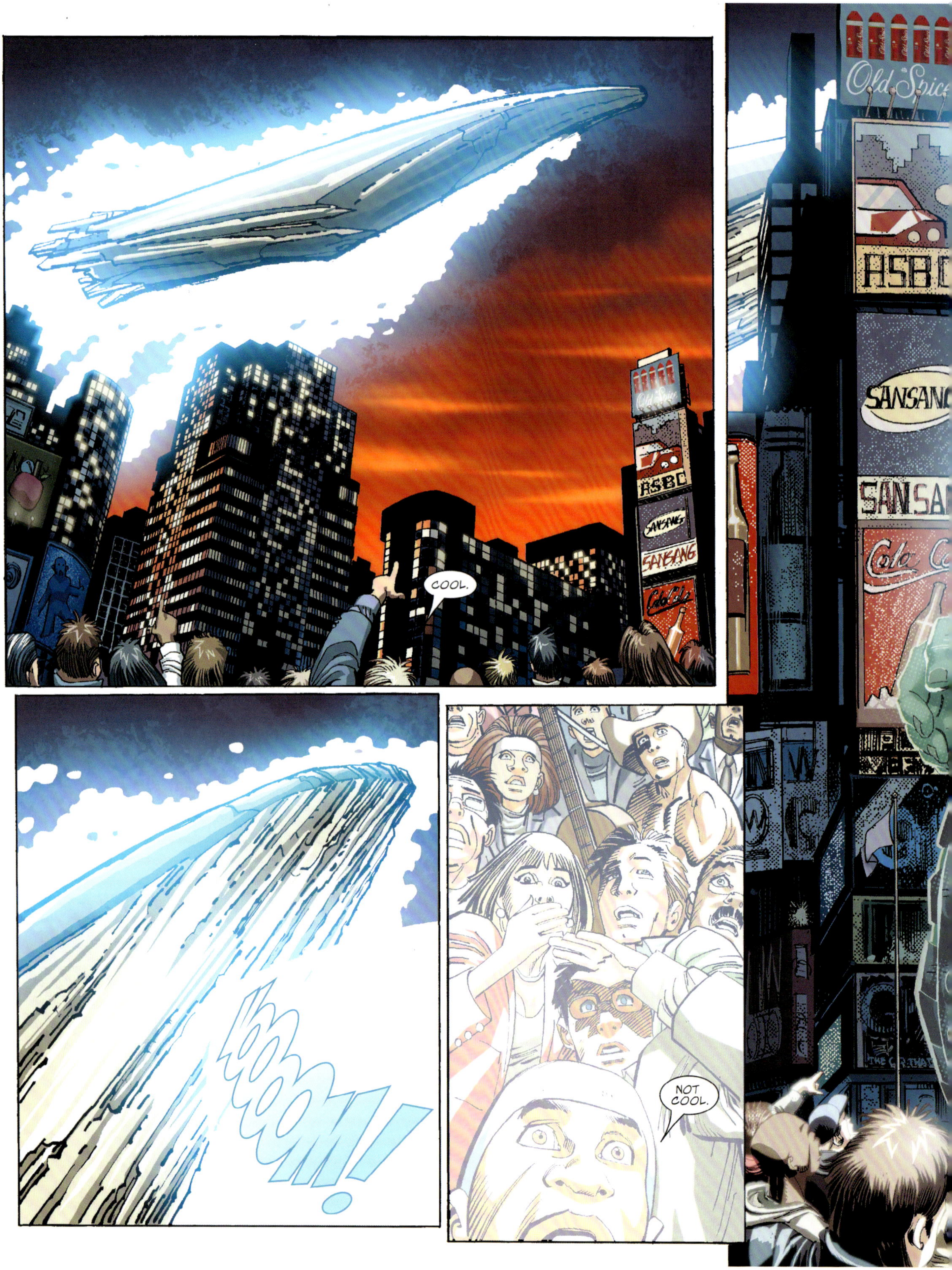
Old Spice
ASBC
SANSANG
SANSANG
COOL.
VOOOOM!
NOT COOL.

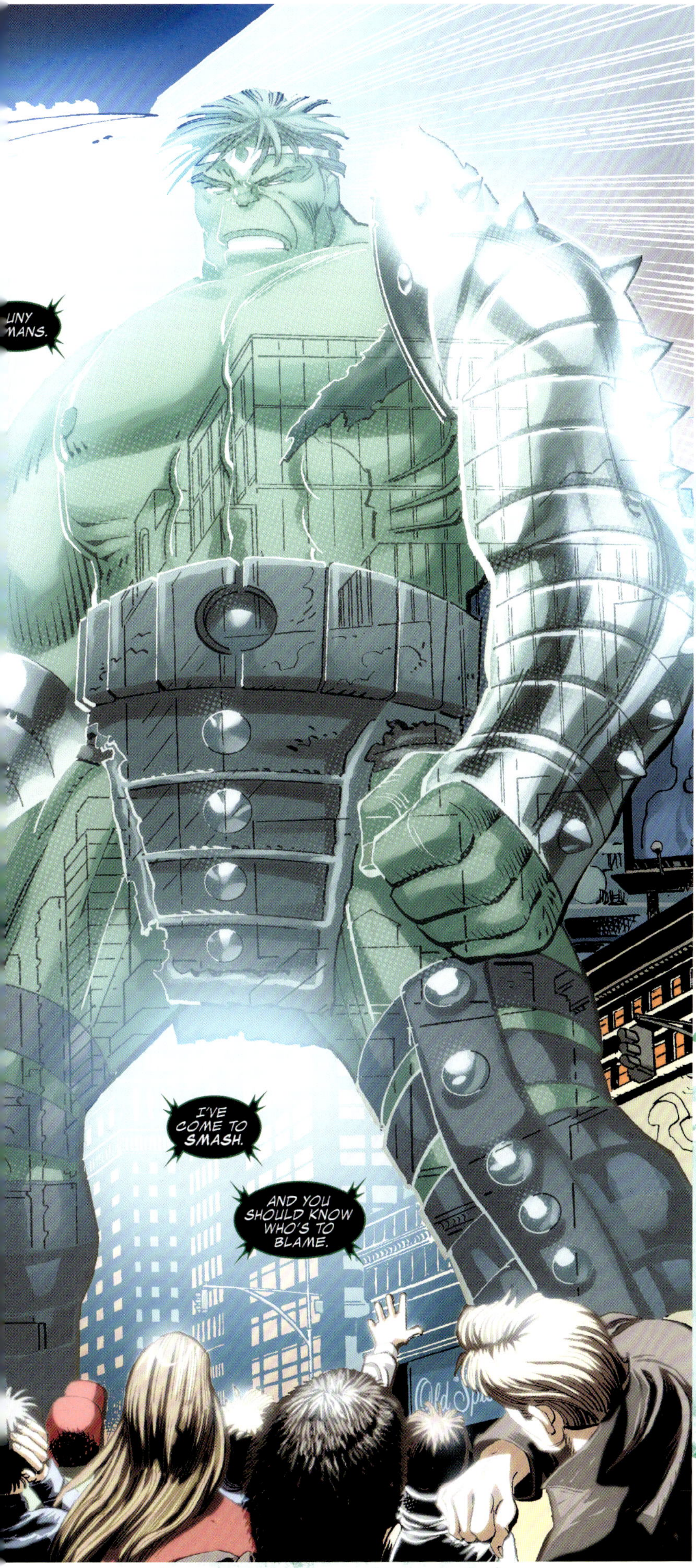
UNY
MANS.
I'VE COME TO SMASH.
AND YOU SHOULD KNOW WHO'S TO BLAME.

Hulk is on a rampage. As a result, there is a call to evacuate New York City, because the city will likely be the Hulk's battleground. Iron Man steps up first in his Hulkbuster suit to confront the Hulk. Imagine a giant version of the Iron Man armor tricked-out with more firepower—that is the Hulkbuster suit. Unfortunately, Iron Man and his new armor are no match for the raging Hulk. Eventually, the super heroes fall, one after the next: the Fantastic Four, She-Hulk, Doctor Strange, and even the Hulk's old friend Rick Jones. Rick, who has no powers (he lost them in the Marvel six-issue story arc titled *Extremis*, where a version of the Hulk called Doc Green creates a cure for the gamma mutations and uses it on Rick), bravely stands up to the Hulk, but the Hulk refuses to stand down.

The Hulk wants the other heroes to know what he experienced on planet Sakaar. He takes over Madison Square Garden and hosts a gladiator match between the heroes. The Hulk wants them to defeat each other in a battle to the death—just as he was forced to do on the other planet.

There is one last hope to defeat the Hulk, which lies in the most powerful super hero on Earth: the Sentry. The problem: the Sentry is agoraphobic. Yes, this super hero is afraid to leave his house. It will be difficult for Sentry to defeat the Hulk from his living room. Despite the Sentry's disorder, the other super heroes plead with him to take on the Hulk.

Some wars are started because of a random event, some are planned, and some are the result of the actions of only a few people. The Hulk started a war on Earth because he believed the Illuminati were responsible for the explosion that killed so many on his adopted planet. But things might not be what they seem. There is a truth that will be revealed, and once the Hulk is enlightened about those circumstances, will he be able to have the control to stand down and end the war?

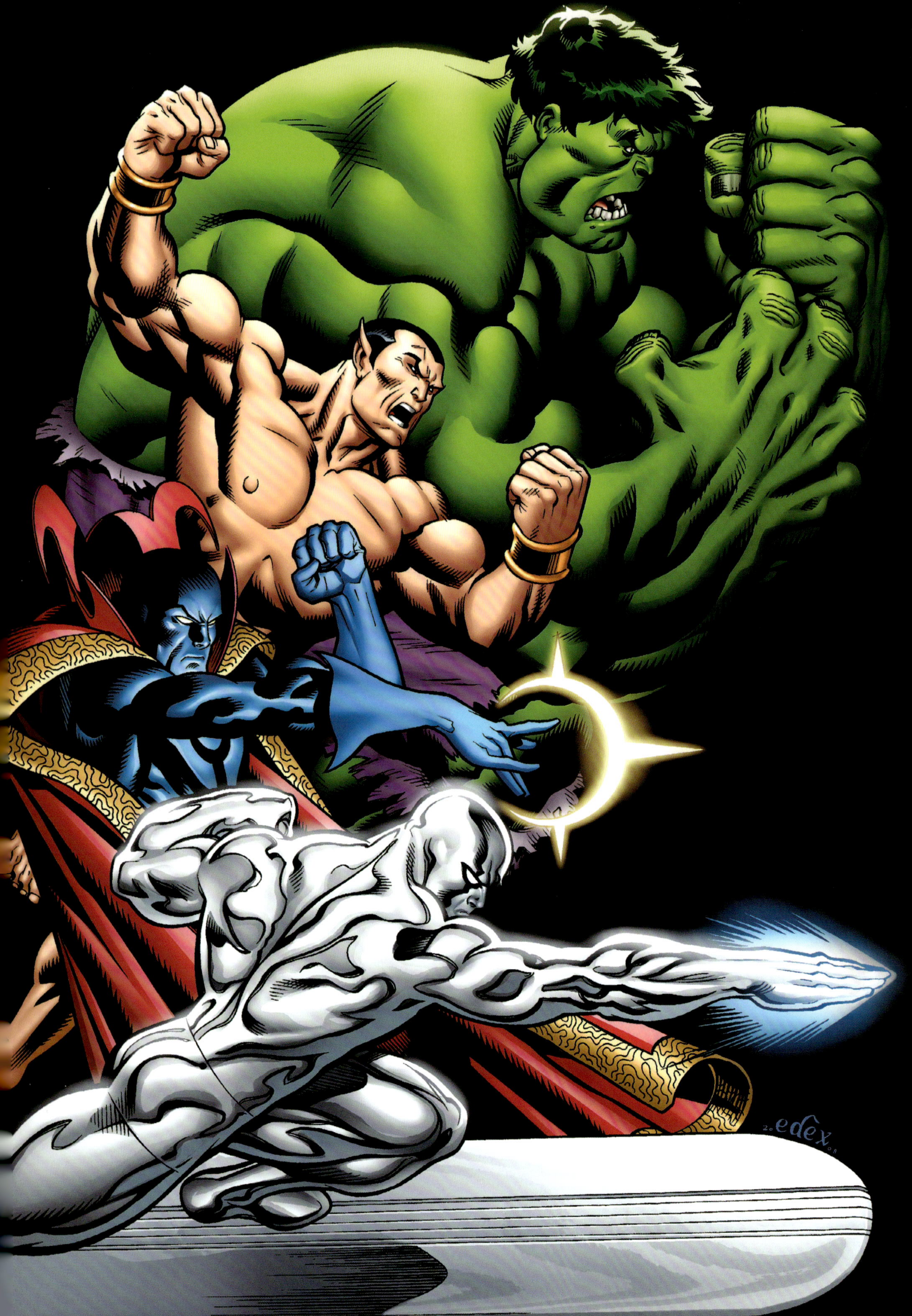
edex

# CREDITS

## INCREDIBLE

### FIRST APPEARANCE
Issues: *Incredible Hulk* #1–6
Writer: Stan Lee
Artist: Jack Kirby

### HULK: GRAY
Issues: *Hulk: Gray* #1–6
Writer: Jeph Loeb
Artist: Tim Sale

### THE SENSATIONAL SHE-HULK
Issues: *Sensational She-Hulk* #1–8, 31–46, 48–50
Writers: John Byrne, Howard Mackie, Michael Eury
Artists: John Byrne, Dave Gibbons, Frank Miller, Wendy Pini, Walt Simonson, Terry Austin, Howard Chaykin, Adam Hughes, Howard Mackie, Todd Britton

### INCREDIBLE HULK & THE THING: HARD KNOCKS
Issues: *Incredible Hulk & The Thing: Hard Knocks* #1–4
Writer: Bruce Jones
Artist: Jae Lee

### THE SAVAGE SHE-HULK
Issues: *Savage She-Hulk* #1–14
Writers: Stan Lee, David Anthony Kraft
Artists: John Buscema, Mike Vosburg

## RAMPAGING

### CROSSROADS
Issues: *Incredible Hulk* #301–313, *Incredible Hulk Annual* #13
Writer: Bill Mantlo
Artists: Sal Buscema, Bret Blevins, Mike Mignola

### PARDONED
Issues: *Incredible Hulk* #269–285
Writer: Bill Mantlo
Artists: Sal Buscema, Mark Gruenwald

### ULTIMATE WOLVERINE VS. HULK
Issues: *Ultimate Wolverine vs. Hulk* #1–6
Writer: Damon Lindelof
Artist: Leinil Francis Yu

### FUTURE IMPERFECT/THE END
Issues: *Hulk: Future Imperfect* #1–2, *Incredible Hulk: The End* #1
Writer: Peter David
Artists: George Perez, Dale Keown

### RETURN OF THE MONSTER
Issues: *Incredible Hulk* #34–38
Writer: Bruce Jones
Artist: John Romita Jr.

### GOING GRAY
Issues: *Incredible Hulk* #314–330
Writers: John Byrne, Al Milgrom, Peter David
Artists: John Byrne, Al Milgrom, Steve Geiger, Dwayne Turner, Todd McFarlane

### TOTALLY AWESOME HULK
Issues: *The Totally Awesome Hulk* #1–6
Writer: Greg Pak
Artists: Frank Cho, Mike Choi

## GAMMA BASE

Production and VizDev Artists: Aaron McBride (92–93), Bryan Andrews, Jim Mitchell, and Charlie Wen (94–95), Ryan Meinerding (96–97, 100–101, 102), Andy Park (98–99), Mushk Rizvi (103), Joshua James Shaw (104–105)

## SAVAGE

### OR IS HE BOTH?
Issues: *Immortal Hulk* #1–5
Writer: Al Ewing
Artists: Joe Bennett, Leonardo Romero, Garry Brown, Paul Hornschemeier, Marguerite Sauvage

### THE GREEN DOOR
Issues: *Immortal Hulk* #6–10
Writer: Al Ewing
Artists: Lee Garbett, Joe Bennett, Martin Simmonds

### HULK IN HELL
Issues: *Immortal Hulk* #11–15
Writer: Al Ewing
Artists: Joe Bennett, Eric Nguyen, Kyle Hotz

### ABOMINATION
Issues: *Immortal Hulk* #16–20
Writer: Al Ewing
Artists: Joe Bennett, Brian Level

### BREAKER OF WORLDS
Issues: *Immortal Hulk* #21–25
Writer: Al Ewing
Artists: Ryan Bodenheim, Joe Bennett, German Garcia

### RED HULK
Issues: *Hulk* #1–6
Writer: Jeph Loeb
Artist: Ed McGuinness

### PLANET RED HULK
Issues: *Hulk* #30.1, 31–36
Writer: Jeff Parker
Artists: Gabriel Hardman, Carlo Pagulayan, Patch Zircher

### INDESTRUCTIBLE HULK: AGENT OF S.H.I.E.L.D.
Issues: *Indestructible Hulk* #1–8
Writer: Mark Waid
Artists: Leinil Francis Yu, Walter Simonson

### HEART OF THE ATOM
Issues: *Incredible Hulk* #140, 148, 156, 202–203, 205–207, 246–248
Writers: Roy Thomas, Harlan Ellison, Archie Goodwin, Chris Claremont, Len Wein, Bill Mantlo
Artists: Sam Grainger, Herb Trimpe, Sal Buscema

### PAST PERFECT
Issues: *Incredible Hulk* #21–33
Writers: Paul Jenkins, Sean McKeever, Christopher Priest
Artists: Kyle Hotz, John Romita Jr., Joe Bennett, Jon Bogdanove

## IMMORTAL

### LOVE AND DEATH
Issues: *Hulk* #10–12, *Incredible Hulk* #600
Writer: Jeph Loeb
Artist: Ed McGuinness

### ASUNDER/HULK VS. BANNER
Issues: *Incredible Hulk* #1–7, 7.1, 8–15
Writers: Jason Aaron, Cullen Bunn
Artists: Michael Broussard, Eric Basaldua, Billy Tan, Pasqual Ferry, Tom Raney, Dalibor Talajić, Carlos Pacheco, Jefté Palo, Marc Silvestri, Whilce Portacio, Steve Dillon

### CHAOS WAR
Issues: *Incredible Hulks* #618–622
Writers: Greg Pak, Joshua Williamson
Artist: Paul Pelletier

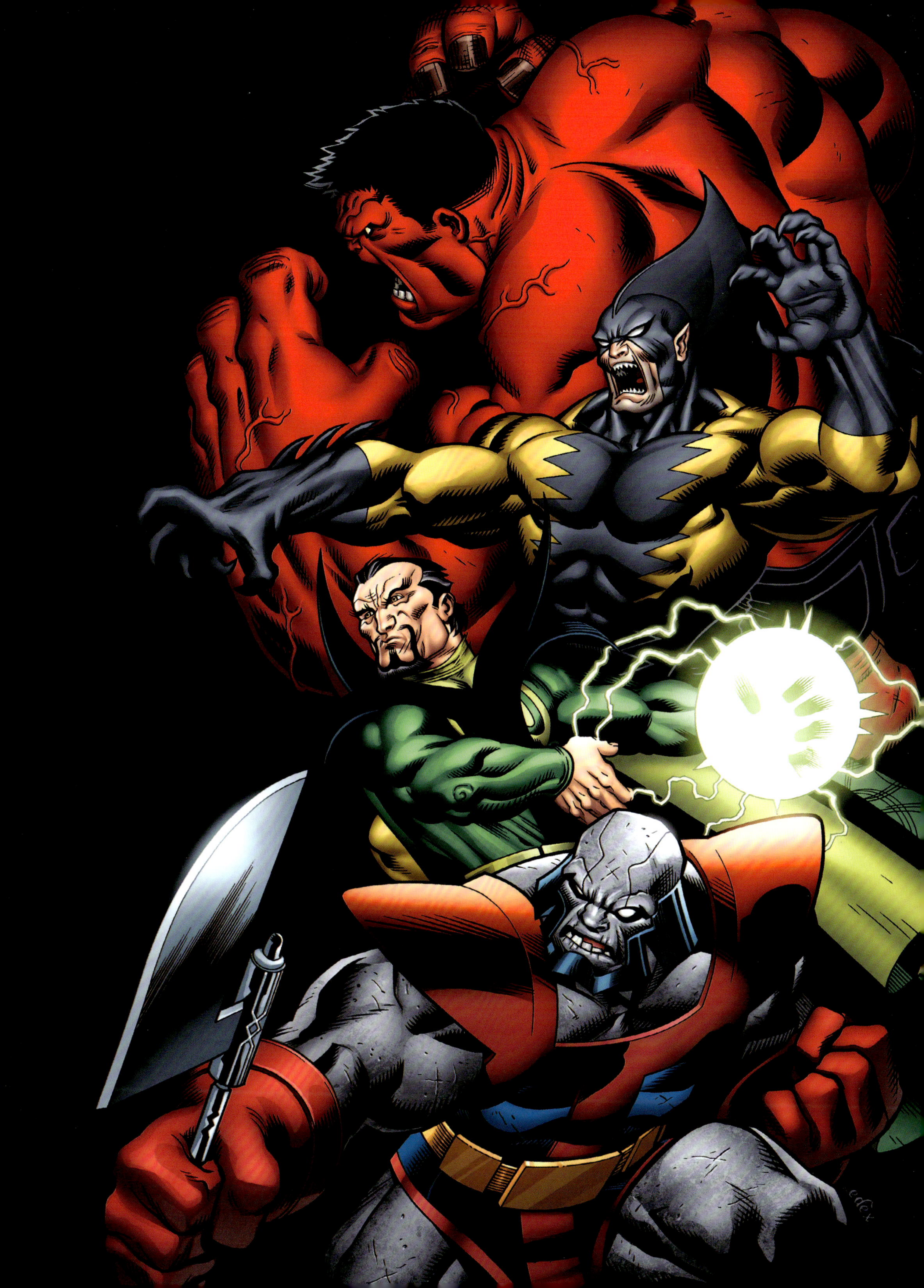

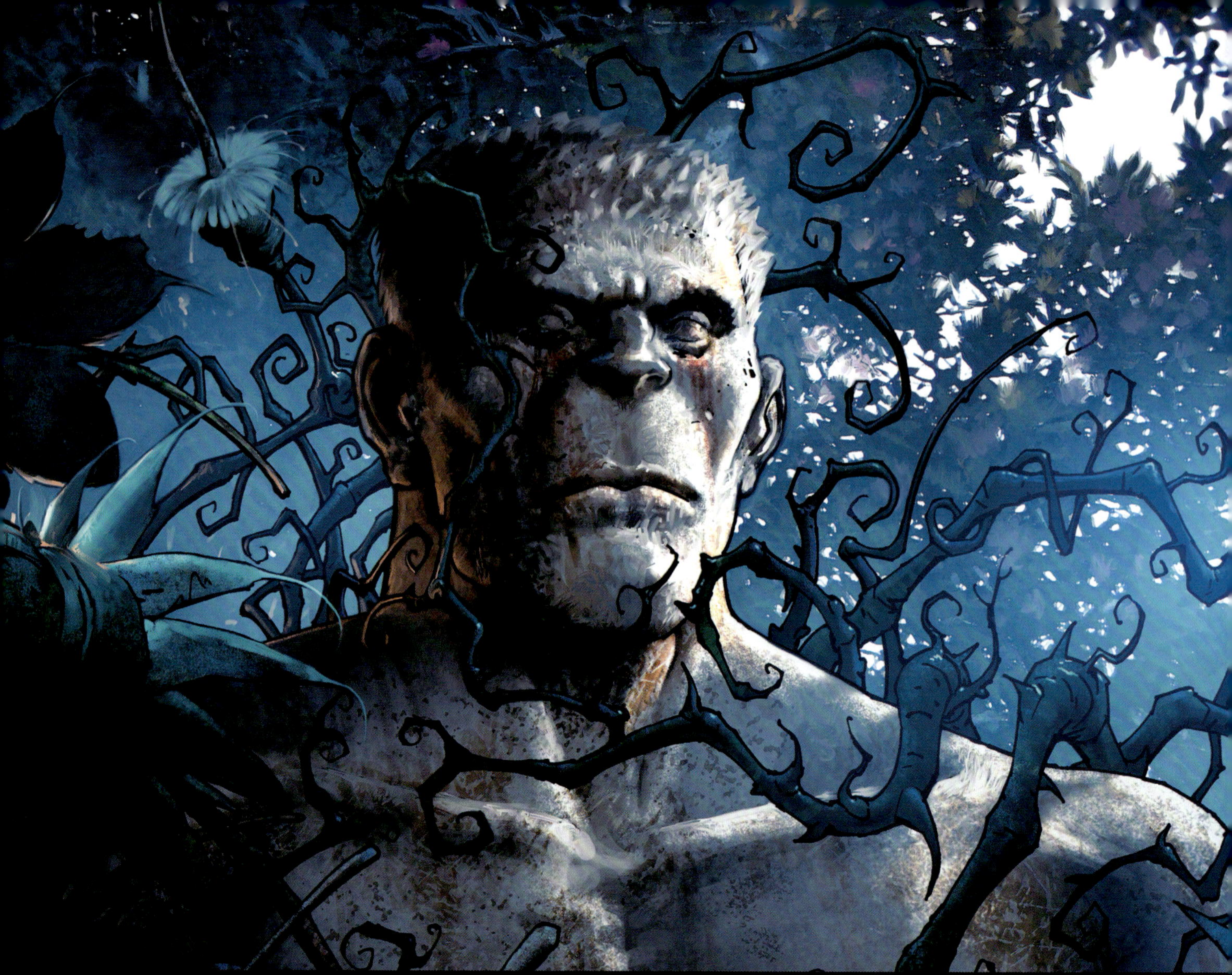

**HEART OF THE MONSTER**
Issues: *Incredible Hulks* #630–635
Writer: Greg Pak
Artists: Paul Pelletier, Tom Grummett

**CODE RED**
Issues: *Hulk* #14–17
Writer: Jeph Loeb
Artists: Ed McGuinness, Ian Churchill

**TEMPEST FUGIT**
Issues: *Incredible Hulk* #77–82
Writer: Peter David
Artists: Jae Lee, Lee Weeks

**PLANET HULK**
Issues: *The Incredible Hulk* #92–105
Writer: Greg Pak
Artists: Carlo Pagulayan, Aaron Lopresti, Alex Niño, Michael Avon Oeming, Marshall Rogers, Gary Frank

**WORLD WAR HULK**
Issues: *World War Hulk* #1–5
Writer: Greg Pak
Artist: John Romita Jr.